Media, Migrants and Human Rights

Gevisa La Rocca, Roberto Di Maria, Gino Frezza (eds.)

Media, Migrants and Human Rights

In the Evolution of the European Scenario of Refugees' and Asylum Seekers' Instances

PETER LANG

Bibliographic Information published by the Deutsche Nationalbibliothek
The Deutsche Nationalbibliothek lists this publication in the Deutsche Nationalbibliografie; detailed bibliographic data is available online at http://dnb.d-nb.de.

Library of Congress Cataloging-in-Publication Data
A CIP catalog record for this book has been applied for at the Library of Congress.

Printed with financial support from the research fund of the Kore University of Enna

Cover Image: *Elefanti* by Jari Di Giampietro/yaridg.net

Printed by CPI books GmbH, Leck

ISBN 978-3-631-82253-1 (Print)
E-ISBN 978-3-631-82684-3 (E-PDF)
E-ISBN 978-3-631-82685-0 (EPUB)
E-ISBN 978-3-631-82686-7 (MOBI)
DOI 10.3726/b17162

Peter Lang – Berlin · Bern · Bruxelles · New York · Oxford · Warszawa · Wien

This publication has been peer reviewed.

www.peterlang.com

Contents

Preface

In 2019 the Kore University of Enna hosted the multiplier event of the Paris project, *Teaching Partnership Addressed to Refugee's Instances Strengthening*, financed by the European Union under the European Program ERASMUS + – KEY ACTION 2 *Strategic Partnership for Higher Education* (*Development of Innovation*) Round 1 – Agreement number: 2016–1–T02–KA203–024406.

An international conference was organized within the multiplier event. This international conference from the beginning has enjoyed the support of many Italian and foreign institutions.

On that occasion, numerous scholars gathered to discuss new migrations and the condition of refugees and asylum seekers.

A community of interests was born spontaneously: a community of good feelings.

To the Organizing and Scientific Committee, it seemed appropriate to continue the intellectual friendship born in those days, trying to expand the group to include also other scholars interested in working on the topic of migration.

Before long, numerous other scholars accepted the invitation.

Thus this volume was born, which collects the reflections of those who work on new migrations.

The goal is to give voice to reasonable thoughts about the processes of globalization of migration, refugees, asylum seekers, and the "bloody" Mediterranean.

Reflections on human rights and their state of application, reflections on migrants and the media-system. Reflections guided by the will to understand and not to generate fear. Studies far from slogans, research based on data collected through scientific methods, in short, human glances.

The chapters of this volume discuss research projects, observations, and studies on phenomena that are not, then, so far from us.

The picture obtained from reading this volume is of a Europe that is committed, a Europe that welcomes, and a Europe that has no intention of closing harbors.

The Editors

Gevisa La Rocca
Roberto Di Maria
Gino Frezza

Part One Media, Migrants, and Human Rights

Gevisa La Rocca

Chapter One Academics' Sense of Migration

Abstract: How are scholars dealing with migration? And how should they do it? What are the objectives of their analyses? The title of this chapter is provocative, so as to underline what is the role of "those who know," or rather "of those who have studied the past." In these few pages, the reader finds indications of the content of the volume.

1 Introduction

The academic sense of migration is, of course, a provocative title, which – simply – wants to make us reflect on the role of today's "intellectuals" in the fight against cultural hegemony. It aims to provide us with the sense and direction on how to deal with reading the pages of this volume.

The year 2019 saw a wave of obscurantism coming; of course, those who had eyes and interest in looking at it saw it. We can summarize what happened in Italy with the very popular slogan: "first the Italians."

We already live in a multiethnic society; Italians are people of emigration, and they should understand by themselves the reasons why people leave their land. We should work for integration, not for separation. How can migration be stopped? How can you tell those who run away that he must go home?

The current situation of reception migrants and the difficulties in accepting the "others" and, therefore: resistances, fears, silences, delays, clashes, suppression suffered, that arise from them, for its *banality*, can be remembered for what Hannah Arendt wrote in the *Eichmann in Jerusalem: A Report on the Banality of Evil* (1963).

The banality of evil is basically the diary of Hannah, who, as a correspondent for the *New Yorker*, attended the process of Adolf Eichmann – the Nazi hierarch who was tried for genocide in 1961 in Jerusalem and sentenced to death by hanging. The sentence was carried out on May 31, 1962. In the courtroom debate, in fact, Arendt found the idea of banality of evil.

She said that the evil done by Eichmann – like many people who became co-responsible for the Holocaust – is not due to malignant nature, rather it is due to the unawareness of the meaning of those actions and their consequences.

Probably today, someone does not understand what the effects of closure harbor, or what is happening in Africa.

In Italy, the turning point can be represented by the case of the Palermitan teacher Rosa Maria Dell'Aria. The pupils of the Palermitan teacher compare the Italian security decree with the fascist racial laws, during a task assigned to them; because of this parallelism (La Rocca, 2019) and because of tweets posted on social media that denounce what happened during the lesson and that ask for intervention by the competent authorities, the teacher was suspended from her role. Thus, the reminiscence of a recent past finally finds its place in the public debate. It is undeniable that memory is always and only of the individual (Halbwachs, 1952), but it is nevertheless influenced by the community, that is, by how events are communicated and by the processes of interaction that are generated starting from them within the social group. Unaware makers, these students, of having introduced a parallelism on the media – on which perhaps some had already reflected – but which until then had remained dormant, engulfed in a spiral of silence, preventing people who had found no trace of it in the media from expressing their opinion diverging from that of the majority. As Noelle Neumann (1980) argues, opinions diverging from the majority and of which there is no response in the media end up being swallowed up by the spiral of silence, given that the media create culture, the symbolic universe within which the individual lives and uses social interactions to attribute a socially shared meaning to his or her actions. The media therefore maintain social control but, at the same time and with the same force, when they convey new demands, they can favor social change.

There is a close link between the faculty of thinking and acting, the ability to distinguish and understand what is right and what is not, the autonomy of judgment, the choices and their moral implications, and not least the strength, the courage to demonstrate for something you believe in realizing that there is a right that is being violated and that needs to be reaffirmed. There is a close link between all this and the sense of academia, with the figure of the *magister*, the greatest, that is, the most expert, the most competent with regard to a subject, an art, a skill, such as to be the point of reference for those who want to learn such knowledge, or the one who is deputy – in a designated place – to sow the seed so that virtue and knowledge are followed. So around a question, that of new migrations, which for more than twenty years has been characterized by the trait of crisis and emergency, a new perspective is grafted that allows the acquisition of a different point of view, enlarging that of the inhumanity, of the unstoppable search of the #remainhuman and crafting – in consonance with Appadurai's thesis (1996) – a new group landscape.

It is a lever, a point where the banality of evil in a tweet allows, who knows, to trace a new human action.

Morin (1976) argues that the crisis implies a decision, a process of discernment whose consequence is represented by the evolution that opens the way to a different type of human action. So, if on the one hand the action, which is based on predictability and determinism, is almost suffocated, on the other hand, the crisis creates new conditions for action, following a pattern of multiplication of alternatives, creating favorable conditions for the deployment of bold and inventive strategies that invalidate the possibility of the persistence of a banality of evil.

2 The Migration-Scape in This Volume

This volume's content can be considered as a group landscape. It is for this reason that this chapter is titled "Academics' Sense of Migration."

In these first pages, we try to reconstruct the main themes addressed in the volume. The goal is therefore to reconstruct the interpretative dimensions developed by the several authors in this volume. To extract this information from the text, we use a lexicon extraction, a procedure developed by Reinert (1986, 1990, 1995). It is a technique that allows us to group together and then analyze the context of units typical of one kind of word or another found in texts. "Choosing a place from where to talk, who speaks chooses with this fact itself a new way of seeing. This is therefore also the place of a new identity" (Reinert, 1995, 222). Following this vision, Reinert explores lexical worlds and identifies a technique to extract them. It is with this premise that we choose to apply this procedure to the *corpus*. The aim is to identify the general system of reference, the semantics of the narration expressed by the authors of these contributions.

It is possible to discern information[1] about the migration that is explored by its four-dimensional interpretation: 1) the role of culture, 2) refugees and asylum seekers, 3) economy and sustainability of migration, and 4) media representation.

Not wanting to take anything away from the pleasure of reading the book, here we simply identify the prevailing thematic lines, which are represented in Fig. 1.1. Although the title of the volume does not contain any word related to "culture", it is culture that is most often written about in this volume.

Cultivation of culture seems to be the way against *banality*. It seems to be the way to reiterate the importance of *historia vero testis temporum, lux veritatis, vita memoriae, magistra vitae, nuntia vetustatis*, a statement, a concept, something in which Cicero believed and which we all must remember.

---

1 The text analyzed has got several token words (occurrences) equal to 107.457; of type words equal to 8.162. *Hapax*, that occur only once, are 3.713.

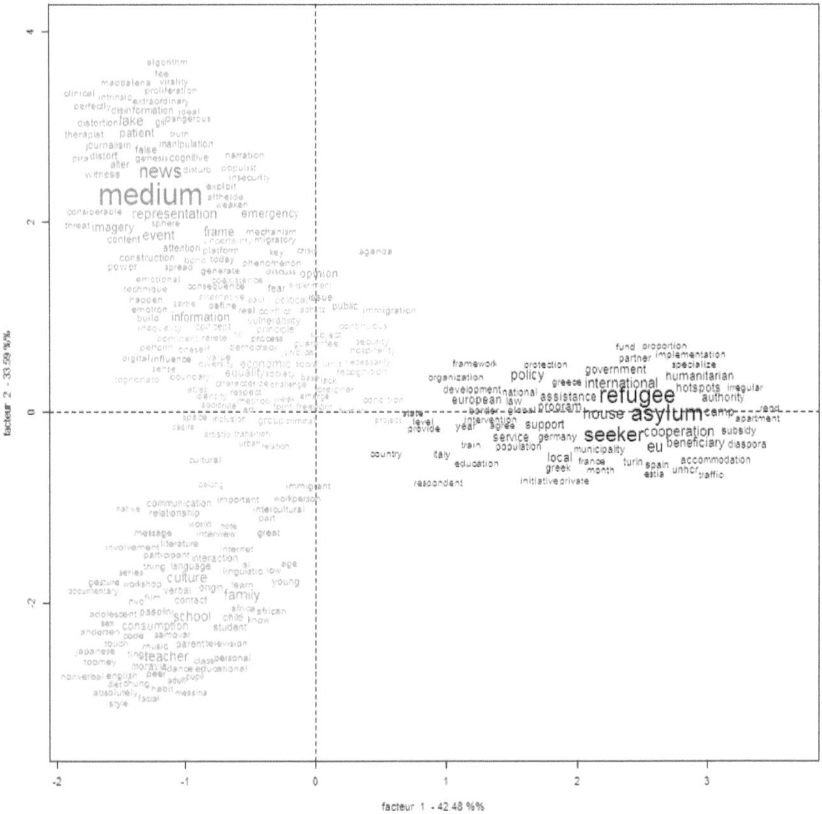

Fig. 1.1: Our migration-scape

The importance of culture is underlined in its multiple aspects: "confrontation between people of different cultures"; the imposition of culture in the history of colonization: "the phenomenon of colonization when the culture of a people is imposed by force on another people"; and as a tool to analyze our communication guidelines: "in our culture the terms prejudice and stereotype are characterized by a strong negative value." It is about understanding, on the one hand, the possibility that each social group has its own culture and, on the other, the need to integrate the foreigner, acquiring: "the study of asylum seekers legislation and integration as well as that of human right"; developing specific knowledge for: "humanitarian aid to refugees and asylum seekers"; without underestimating that: "the right to asylum since 2015 has dominated the public debate."

Within the volume, the debate around refugees and asylum seekers is also addressed through the economic dimension, in fact: "the first link between the foreigner and society is the competition that affects the economic balance and the division of labor"; the reasons for migration can be: "economic or political motives", and considering this opens up a new perspective in the way of looking at who lands along our shores.

It is about: "extraordinary situation amplified by the media";since: "in fact traditional media play a central role in the process of the symbolic and social construction of reality" and "both traditional and new media have referred to the three prevailing frames" on how to read this migration. For these reasons, we need to get back in touch with the sense of what is the study of migration processes, linking them to the representation that the media – old, new, and social – give of it.

The academic sense, rather than being a specific characteristic, is a warning. It is a warning with which this volume opens and at the same time, all those who write these pages undertake to apply it.

References

Appadurai, A. (1996). *Modernity at Large: Cultural Dimensions of Globalization.* Minneapolis: University of Minnesota Press.

Arendt, H. (1963). *Eichmann in Jerusalem: A Report on the Banality of Evil.* New York: Viking Press.

Halbwachs, M. (1952). *Les cadres sociaux de la mémoire*. Paris: Presses Universitaires de Fran.

La Rocca, G. (2019). La banalità del mate in un tweet. Rosa Maria Dell'Aria e un'Italia che sta cambiando. *Comunicazionepuntodoc, 21*, 93–104.

Morin, E. (1976). Pour une crisiologie. *Communications, 25*, 149–163.

Noelle Neumann, E. (1980). *Die Schweigespirale.* München: Piper.

Reinert, M. (1986). Un logiciel d'analyse lexicale: Alceste. *Cahiers de l'Analyse des Données, 4*, 471–484.

Reinert, M. (1990). Alceste: une méthodologie d'analyse des donne textuelles et une application: Aurélia de G. de Nerval. *Bulletin de Méthodologie Sociologique, 26*, 24–54.

Reinert, M. (1995). I mondi lessicali di un corpus di 304 racconti di incubi attraverso il metodo "Alceste". In R. Cipriani & S. Bolasco (a cura di). *Ricerca qualitativa e computer. Teorie, metodi e applicazioni* (pp. 203–223). Milano: Franco Angeli.

Graziella Di Marco, Zira Hichy, and Valentina Giuffrida

Chapter Two Secularism, Community Boundaries Loss, and Prejudice

Abstract: This research study aims to verify the interaction between secularism and the perception of community boundaries loss and how it affects prejudice towards immigrants. A questionnaire containing the Blatant and Subtle Prejudice Scale, Perception of Community Boundaries Loss Scale, and Secularism of State Scale was completed by 102 Italian participants. The analysis of the data indicated that secularism moderates the relationship between the perception of community boundaries loss and prejudice. When people strive for a secular state, the higher the community boundaries loss, the higher is prejudice, both latent and manifest. The implications of these results are discussed herein.

1 Introduction

The theme of migration and its related implications is among the most investigated in the social sciences. Human mobility is not only due to the desire to seek new opportunities, experiences, and lifestyles but also to numerous additional push and pull factors, such as poverty in the origin countries, wars, lack of democracy, and ethnic or religious discrimination (Castelli, 2018; EASO, 2016). The constant migration flow in Europe strongly affects the social and economic environment of the host communities. The migration phenomenon has transformed states of old emigration, such as Italy, into states of immigration. Indeed, the political and social instability in many regions of Africa and the Middle East has imposed a large migration crisis on Italy.

Since 2012, the Italian government has closed regular channels for economic migrants, granting only short-term visas for seasonal workers to citizens of non-EU countries. As a result, immigrants in search of work arrive illegally in Italy in the same way as refugees; and once in Italy, they apply for asylum, even though they are not eligible for international protection (IOM, 2018). However, forced repatriations affect only a minority of the illegal immigrants, as the police are able to detect less than 10 % of migrants fleeing the reception centers (Eurostat, 2017). Adequately controlling the sea borders is impossible, and a large number of immigrants live illegally in the country. These factors, as well as the lack of support from other European countries in managing the migration phenomenon, have largely contributed to the public opinion that Italy is paying too high a social and economic cost and that it has been left alone (Hermanin, 2017) to manage what is perceived as an invasion.

Non-EU citizens living in Italy comprise 6.15 % of the population, to which must be added about 600,000 (1 %) irregular immigrants (Istat, 2019). Due to the controversial agreement (Osservatorio Diritti, 2019) signed in February 2017 between the Italian and Libyan governments, the number of immigrant landings decreased by 86 % during the summer of 2018 compared to the previous year. However, the perception of immigration in Italy is distorted; this leads to a publicly estimated immigrant population of around 25 % of the total population. This estimate is even higher in Italians with a low level of education (28 %) and is highest in people with a right-wing political orientation (32.4 %; Istituto Cattaneo, 2018). Although incorrect perceptions of the presence of immigrants are widespread all over the world, Italian respondents have shown the greatest gap between real and perceived percentages, and their negative evaluation of the consequences of immigration is based on this distortion. In this way, Italians (74 %), more than other Europeans (57 %), believe that immigrants are responsible for the increase of criminal actions (Istituto Cattaneo, 2018).

Various studies have shown that, compared to other western European countries, Italy has the highest levels of ethnic prejudice (Zick, Pettigrew, & Wagner, 2008) and hostility toward immigration and religious minorities (Diamant & Starr, 2018). However, other research studies have described a less negative scenario. Although public opinion is mostly opposed to immigration (because of the large number of irregular arrivals with false asylum requests, the market crisis of work, and the distrust toward the ability of institutions to manage immigration), these studies showed that the majority of Italians are in favor of welcoming those seeking protection from war and discrimination (Dixon, Hawkins, Heijbroek, Juan-Torres, & Demoures, 2018). Therefore, this study analyzed Italian prejudice against immigrants and tested the effect of the interaction between secularism and the perception of community boundaries loss on prejudice.

1.1 Prejudice

Prejudice is an attitude or tendency to respond promptly, whether positively or negatively, to a particular social object (Brown, 1995). As a psychosocial construct, however, prejudice indicates the negative evaluation (Voci & Pagotto, 2010) of a social group or an individual as a member of that group (Allport, 1954). Originally, the phenomenon was interpreted and analyzed in terms of individual differences – that is, as a distinctive attitude of psychopathological personalities (see Gault, 1923; Adorno, Frenkel-Brunswick, LeVinson &

Stanford,1950; Rokeach, 1960). Subsequently, studies have shown that, on a cognitive level, prejudice is the result of normal categorization processes (Fiske, 2000); generalization is the natural basis for ordering reality (Allport, 1954). However, on the social level, prejudice emerged as a multidimensional phenomenon (Taguieff, 2011) stimulated whenever socioeconomic, historical, and cultural circumstances (Kinder & Sears, 1981; Lepore & Brown, 1997; Crandall & Schaller, 2004) caused the groups to be compared (Runciman, 1966) or to compete with each other (Sherif, 1966). Finally, prejudice has been investigated as the outcome of the link between individual processes (motivational, emotional, and cognitive) and relationships between groups, and the social identity theory was developed based on the possible articulations of this link (Tajfel & Turner, 1979). According to the social identity theory, categorization in groups is sufficient to stimulate outgroup devaluation (Tajfel, Billing, Bundy, & Flament, 1971) and to reinforce prejudice (Brewer, 1999).

Over time, the diffusion of "politically correct" behaviors has made manifesting negative attitudes toward minorities socially undesirable. Therefore, the expression of prejudice has evolved into less explicit forms that are more difficult to detect. To address this issue, Pettigrew and Meertens (1995) proposed a two-dimensional model that distinguishes blatant and subtle prejudice. Blatant prejudice, which corresponds to "classic" (old-fashioned) prejudice, has two components: the perceived threat from the outgroup and the rejection of intimacy with its members. This form is emotionally heated because aversion to and discrimination of the outgroup are openly declared. On the other hand, subtle prejudice is emotionally cold and distant and is typical of individuals who consider themselves liberal, democratic, and favorable to equality and equal opportunities. The subtle form has three components: the defense of the values and traditions of the ingroup, the exasperation of differences to justify the separation between the groups, and the lack of positive emotions toward members of the outgroup. Using cultural motivations, these components allow insidious and socially acceptable expressions of the outgroup's inferiority. The present study measured the two dimensions of prejudice using the Italian version (see Arcuri & Boca, 1996; Manganelli Rattazzi, & Volpato, 2001; Villano, 1999) of the Blatant and Subtle Prejudice Scale proposed by Pettigrew and Meertens (1995).

1.2 Secularism of State

Secularism affirms the principle of separation between the state and church (Feldman, 2005); this means that political institutions must not interfere in the religious sphere and that religious institutions must not influence governmental issues. Secular countries can promote hard secularism (e.g., the People's Republic of China, which is officially atheist) or soft secularism (e.g., the United Kingdom, where the relationship between the church and state is purely formal). Other countries fall somewhere in the middle of this continuum; examples of these countries include the United States, France, and Italy, whose constitutions affirm the independence of the church and state and allow religious freedom (Kosmin, 2007).

Some studies have shown that attitudes toward state secularism are associated with attitudes toward private (e.g., religion and political orientation) and social (e.g., same-sex marriage and pre-implantation genetic diagnosis) values (see Hichy & Di Marco, 2014; Hichy, Falvo, Santisi, & Dazzi, 2014; Hichy, Gerges, Platania, & Santisi, 2015a; Hichy, Coen, & Di Marco, 2015b). Regarding the relationship between secularism and attitudes toward immigrants, studies have shown that people who claim to be secular have more favorable attitudes toward immigrants than people who claim to be Christian (Smith, 2006; Storm, 2011). Therefore, this study hypothesized that positive attitudes toward secularism may be correlated with a lower degree of prejudice toward immigrants. Moreover, it hypothesized that the secularism of the state should moderate the relationship between the perception of community boundaries loss and both kinds of prejudice.

1.3 Perception of Community Boundaries Loss

The perception of community boundaries loss is a dynamic and situational variable associated with specific social and environmental conditions (Talò, 2010), such as the co-presence of immigrants and natives in a certain territorial context. Indeed, as a result of phenomena such as globalization and immigration, feelings of fear may emerge due to the loss of distinctiveness of a certain community (ingroup) in respect to the others (outgroups), as well as the perception that the traditions and culture of belonging are in danger (Talò, 2010).

Although migratory flows to Italy are now a historical and structural phenomenon, the presence of immigrants creates a collective perception of social and cultural instability, which is also due to the high number of illegal arrivals (IOM, 2018). Recent studies have shown that, in municipalities where many immigrants live, the cost for the local police increases even if the crimes do not increase (Bove, Elia & Ferraresi, 2019). Studies have also shown that the attitude of Italians toward immigrants arriving in the country is increasingly wary and hostile (Mannheimer, 2016). In a study conducted by Dixon et al. (2018), 59 % of Italians stated that national identity was disappearing due to migrants, and 50 %

said they sometimes felt foreign in their own country. Overall, the majority of Italians believe that immigration hurts society, are concerned about security, and fear that the country no longer has control over its borders (Dixon et al., 2018). Therefore, the negative feelings toward immigrants are caused by the fear that the immigrants' presence is endangering not only territorial but also symbolic boundaries (i.e., identity, traditions, and culture). Following this evidence, this study hypothesized a negative association between the perception of community boundaries loss and prejudice toward immigrants.

2 Methods

2.1 Participants and Procedure

The study's participants included 102 university students (67 % female, 32 % male, and 1 % missing). All participants were born and lived in Italy, and they were aged from 19 to 33 years (mean = 22.76, SD = 2.54). The participants were selected from an opportunity sample of university students who were approached and then volunteered to take part in the study. All participants were informed that their responses would remain confidential. Ethical approval for the study was granted by the principal investigator's institution.

2.2 Measurements

The Blatant and Subtle Prejudice Scale. To measure prejudice, the Italian version of the Blatant and Subtle Prejudice Scale was used (Arcuri & Boca, 1996; Manganelli Rattazzi, & Volpato, 2001). Before answering the scale's questions, the participants were asked an open question: "When you think about immigrants from outside the EU, what is the first ethnic or racial group that comes to mind?" The participants then had to refer to this group during the compilation of the scale. Of the participants, 72.6 % indicated African groups ("African," 50 %; "Moroccan," 10.8 %, etc.). The scale is articulated in 20 items: 10 for blatant prejudice (alpha = .73) and 10 for subtle prejudice (alpha = .66). Examples of items (and relative kind of prejudice) are as follows: "(Target group) have a job that Italians should have" (blatant prejudice) and "(Target group) living here teach their children values and skills different from those required to be successful in Italy" (subtle prejudice). The participants answered on a 6-point scale, ranging from 1 ("absolutely disagree") to 6 ("absolutely agree").

The Secularism of State Scale. Attitudes toward secularism were measured using the Secularism of State Scale (Hichy et al., 2012), which consists of eight items, including the following: "The Church should remain in its place and avoid getting involved in political affairs," and "I think it is appropriate that the Church gives its opinion on State laws" (reverse coded). For each item, participants expressed their opinion on a 7-point scale ranging from 1 ("strongly disagree") to 7 ("strongly agree"), with 4 meaning neither agree nor disagree (alpha= .91).

Perception of Community Boundaries Loss Scale. The Perception of Community Boundaries Loss Scale (Talò, 2010) was used to measure opinions related to the distinctiveness of Italian culture and traditions. The scale consists of 16 items with a 4-point response scale, ranging from 1 ("strongly disagree") to 4 ("strongly agree"). Examples of items are as follows: "It is not clear where the Italian culture ends and where other cultures begin," and "I think that there are no longer any differences between peoples coming from different countries" (alpha= .75).

3 Results

3.1 Preliminary Analyses

The means, standard deviations, and intercorrelation of investigated constructs are reported in Tab. 2.1. The results showed that the participants had positive attitudes toward state secularism, while their prejudice (both blatant and subtle) toward the immigrants was low. As for the perception of community boundaries loss, the results indicated that participants perceived a medium threat to national identity and culture. The correlations among measurements showed a positive correlation between blatant and subtle prejudice and between the perception of community boundaries loss and both kinds of prejudice. State secularism negatively correlated with both kinds of prejudice and with the perception of community boundaries loss.

Tab. 2.1: Means, standard deviations, and correlations

	Mean	SD	1	2	3	4
1 Blatant prejudice	2.77	0.72	1			
2 Subtle prejudice	2.16	0.68	0.690***	1		
3 Secularism of state	5.43	1.23	-0.291**	-0.360***	1	
4 Perception of community boundaries loss	2.01	0.37	0.366***	0.430***	-0.197*	1

* $p < .05$, *** $p < .01$, *** $p < .001$

3.2 Moderating Effects of Secularism of State on the Relationship Between the Perception of Community Boundaries Loss and Prejudice

To test the moderating effect of secularism of state on the relationship between the perception of community boundaries loss and prejudice, PROCESS macro for SPSS (Hayes, 2013) was employed. Two moderation analyses (one for blatant and one for subtle prejudice) were conducted using Model 1 with 5,000 bootstrap samples. Regarding subtle prejudice (Tab. 2.2), the results showed that the perception of community boundaries loss positively influenced this kind of prejudice, while state secularism negatively influenced it. Moreover, the interaction between the perception of community boundaries loss and secularism was significant.

Decomposing the moderation, the perception of community boundaries loss positively influenced subtle prejudice only when secularism was high, while no significant relationship was found between the perception of community boundaries loss and subtle prejudice when secularism was low (Tab. 2.3).

Concerning blatant prejudice (Tab. 2.4), the results showed that the perception of community boundaries loss positively influenced this kind of prejudice,

Tab. 2.2: Moderating effects of secularism of state on the relationship between perception of community boundaries loss and subtle prejudice

	Subtle prejudice		
	B (*SE*)	LLCI	ULCI
Perception of community boundaries loss	0.7271*** (0.1775)	0.3748	1.0794
Secularism of state	-0.1277* (0.0521)	-0.2312	-0.0242
Interaction	0.4829** (0.1627)	0.1601	0.8057
R^2	0.25		
F	10.99***		
df	3,98		
R^2_{ch}	0.0673		
F	8.8136**		
df	1,99		

* $p < .05$, *** $p < .01$, *** $p < .001$

Tab. 2.3: Effects of the perception of community boundaries loss on subtle prejudice for high and low levels of secularism of state

	Subtle prejudice		
	B ***(SE)***	**LLCI**	**ULCI**
Low secularism of state	0.0365 (0.2651)	-0.4897	0.5626
High secularism of state	10.4249*** (0.3198)	0.7903	2.0594

*** $p < .001$

Tab. 2.4: Moderation effects of secularism of state on the relationship between the perception of community boundaries loss and blatant prejudice

	Blatant prejudice		
	B **(SE)**	**LLCI**	**ULCI**
Perception of community boundaries loss	0.7558*** (0.1619)	0.4345	1.0771
Secularism of state	-0.1538** (0.0476)	-0.2482	-0.0594
Interaction	0.3314* (0.1484)	0.0370	0.6258
R^2	0.2991		
F	13.9377***		
df	3,98		
R^2_{ch}	0.0357		
F	4.9911*		
df	1,98		

* $p < .05$, *** $p < .01$, *** $p < .001$

while state secularism negatively influenced it. Moreover, the interaction between the perception of community boundaries loss and secularism was significant.

Decomposing the moderation, the perception of community boundaries loss positively influenced blatant prejudice only when secularism was high, while there was no significant relationship between the perception of community boundaries loss and blatant prejudice when secularism was low (Tab. 2.5).

Tab. 2.5: Effects of the perception of community boundaries loss on blatant prejudice for high and low levels of secularism of state

	Blatant prejudice		
	B* *(SE)	**LLCI**	**ULCI**
Low secularism of state	0.2818 (0.2418)	-0.1981	0.7616
Hight secularism of state	10.2346*** (0.2916)	0.6559	1.8134

*** $p < .001$

4 Discussion

This study aimed to investigate the relationships between attitudes toward state secularism, the perception of community boundaries loss, and subtle and blatant prejudice toward immigrants. It hypothesized that the orientation toward secularism should moderate the effects of the perception of community boundaries loss on prejudice. The results showed that both subtle and blatant prejudice were low, while the perception of threat to the culture was medium. Additionally, the attitudes toward secularism of state were favorable. Contrary to what was expected, the relationship between the perception of community boundaries loss and prejudice was significant only when secularism was high. This was an unexpected result since the desire to have a secular state is associated with progressive ideas and cultural openness (Hichy et al., 2014). A posteriori explanation can be formulated by referring to the target group indicated by the participants. Since the majority of the participants who answered the questionnaire had an African group in mind (usually identified as Muslims), the strong religious connotation of immigrants following the Islamic faith may have induced people who desire a secular state to fear that such immigrants might threaten the principle of secularism. This fear is widely present throughout Europe (Ansari & Hafez, 2012; Foner, 2015), and Islamophobia is often the central element in the anti-immigrant political rhetoric of countries that have built their identity on the principle of secularism (Doebler, 2014).

The correlational nature of this study did not allow for establishing the causal relationship between the variables considered. Furthermore, the use of university students as participants may have reduced the generalizability of the results. Further studies should be conducted on a more general sample to better understand the causal relationships between secularism, the perception of community boundaries loss, and prejudice against Muslim immigrants.

References

Adorno T.W., Frenkel-Brunswick E., LeVinson D.J., Stanford R.N. (1950). *The Authoritarian Personality.* New York: Harper.

Allport G.W. (1954). *The Nature of Prejudice.* Cambridge: Addison-Wesley.

Ansari H., Hafez F. (Eds.). (2012). *From the Far Right to the Mainstream: Islamophobia in Party Politics and the Media.* Frankfurt: Campus Verlag.

Arcuri L., Boca S. (1996). Pregiudizio e affiliazione politica: destra e sinistra di fronte all'immigrazione dal Terzo Mondo. In P. Legrenzi, V. Giotto (Eds.), *Psicologia e politica* (pp. 241–274). Milano: Raffaello Cortina Editore.

Bove V., Elia L., Ferraresi M. (2019). Immigration, fear of crime and public spending on security. *Working Paper Series* (434). Worwick: The University of Worwick. Retrieved October 5, 2019 from: https://warwick.ac.uk/fac/soc/economics/research/centres/vage/manage/publications/434-2019_bove.pdf

Brewer M.B. (1999). The psychology of prejudice: Ingroup love or outgroup hate? *Journal of Social Issues, 55*, 429–444.

Brown R. (1995). *Prejudice. Its Social Psychology.* Oxford: Blackwell.

Castelli F. (2018). Drivers of migration: Why do people move? *Journal of Travel Medicine, 25*, 1, Retrieved September 1, 2019, from: https://doi.org/10.1093/jtm/tay040

Crandall C.S., Schaller M. (2004). *Social Psychology of Prejudice: Historical and Contemporary Issues.* Lawrence, Kansas: Lewinian Press.

Diamant J., Starr K.J. (2018). *Western Europeans vary in their nationalist, anti-immigrant and anti-religious minority attitudes.* Pew Research Center. Retrieved August 20, 2019, from: https://www.pewresearch.org/fact-tank/2018/06/19/western-europeans-vary-in-their-nationalist-anti-immigrant-and-anti-religious-minority-attitudes/

Dixon T., Hawkins S., Heijbroek L., Juan-Torres M., Demoures F.X. (2018). *Attitudes towards National Identity, Immigration and Refugees in Italy. More in Common.* Retrieved March 25, 2019, from: https://www.thesocialchangeinitiative.org/wp-content/uploads/2018/07/Italy-EN-Final_Digital.compressed.pdf

Doebler S. (2014). Relationships between religion and intolerance towards Muslims and immigrants in Europe: A multilevel analysis. *Review of Religious Research, 56*(1), 61–68.

EASO – European Asylum Support Office – (2016). *The Push and Pull Factors of Asylum-Related Migration. A Literature Review.* Retrieved September 3, 2019, from: https://www.easo.europa.eu/sites/default/files/publications/

The%20Push%20and%20Pull%20Factors%20of%20Asylum%20-%20Related%2

Eurostat. (2017). *Third-Country Nationals Who Have Left the Territory by Type of Return and Citizenship*. Retrieved September 8, 2019, from: http://appsso.eurostat.ec.europa.eu/nui/show.do?dataset=migr_eirt_vol&lang=en

Feldman N. (2005). *Divided by God: America's Church-State Problem- and What We Should Do About It.* Farrar, Straus and Giroux. Retrieved January 9, 2018, from: https://books.google.it/books/about/Divided_by_God.html?id=5xZ-ajvJpXIC&redir_esc=y.

Fiske S.T. (2000). Stereotyping, prejudice, and discrimination at the seam between the centuries: Evolution, culture, mind, and brain. *European Journal of Social Psychology, 30*(3), 299–322.

Foner N. (2015). Is Islam in Western Europe Like Race in the United States? *Sociological Forum, 30*(4), 885–899.

Gault R.H. (1923). *Social Psychology. The Bases of Behavior Called Social.* New York: Holt.

Hayes A.F. (2013). *Introduction to Mediation, Moderation, and Conditional Process Analysis: A Regression-Based Approach*. New York: Guilford Press.

Hermanin C. (2017). Immigration Policy in Italy: Problems and Perspectives. *Istituto Affari Internazionali*. Retrieved March 25, 2019, from: http://www.iai.it/sites/default/files/iaiwp1735.pdf

Hichy Z., Rodriguez Espartal N., Trifiletti E., Di Bernardo G.A. (2012). The secularism of state scale. *TPM—Testing, Psychometrics, Methodology in Applied Psychology, 19*, 151–63.

Hichy Z., Di Marco G. (2014). Effects of state secularism, Catholic identity, and political orientation on issues related to technologies involving embryos. *TPM—Testing, Psychometrics, Methodology in Applied Psychology, 21*, 37–50.

Hichy Z., Falvo R., Santisi G., Dazzi C. (2014). Effects of political orientation, religious identification and religious orientations on attitude toward a secular state. *Archive for the Psychology of Religion, 36*, 70–85.

Hichy Z., Gerges M.H., Platania S., Santisi G. (2015a). The role of secularism of state on the relationship between Catholic identity, political orientation, and gay rights issues. *Journal of Homosexuality, 62*, 1359–73.

Hichy Z., Coen S., Di Marco G. (2015b). The Interplay Between Religious Orientations, State Secularism, and Gay Rights Issues. *Journal of GLBT Family Studies, 11*, 82–101.

IOM – the International Organization for Migration – (2018). *Mixed Migration Flows in the Mediterranean. Compilation of Available Data and Information July 2018.* Retrieved April 5, 2019, from: https://migration.iom.

int/sites/default/files/public/reports/Flows%20Compilation%20Report_December_2018_0.pdf

Istat. (2019). *Istat*. Retrieved April 10, 2019 from: http://demo.istat.it/

Istituto Cattaneo. (2018). *Immigrazione in Italia: tra realtà e percezione*. Retrieved April 20, 2019, from: https://www.cattaneo.org

Kinder D.R., Sears D.O. (1981). Prejudice and politics: Symbolic racism versus racial threats to the good life. *Journal of Personality and Social Psychology*, *75*, 1155–1178.

Kosmin B.A. (2007). Contemporary secularity and secularism. In B.A. Kosmin & A.Keysar (Eds.), *Secularism and Secularity* (pp. 1–13). Hartford: Institute for the Study of Secularism in Society and Culture.

Lepore L., Brown R. (1997). Category and stereotype activation: Is prejudice inevitable? *Journal of Personality and Social Psychology*, *72*, 275–287.

Manganelli Rattazzi A.M., Volpato C. (2001). Forme sottili e manifeste di pregiudizio verso gli immigrati. *Giornale Italiano di Psicologia*, *28*, 351–375.

Mannheimer R. (2016). *L'opinione degli italiani sull'arrivo degli immigrati*. EUMETRA MR. Retrieved June 2, 2019, from: https://www.eumetramr.com/it/lopinione-degli-italiani-sullarrivo-degli-immigrati

Osservatorio Diritti. (2019). *Accordo Italia-Libia: ecco come vengono violati i diritti dei migranti*. Retrieved August18, 2019, from: https://www.osservatoriodiritti.it/2019/02/08/accordo-italia-libia-migranti/

Pettigrew T.F., Meertens R.W. (1995). Subtle and blatant prejudice in Western Europe. *European Journal of Social Psicology*, *25*, 57–75.

Rokeach M. (1960). *The Open and Closed Mind*. New York: Basic Books.

Runciman W.G. (1966). *Relative Deprivation and Social Justice*. London: Routledge and Keagan Paul.

Sherif M. (1966). *Group Conflict and Cooperation*. London: Routledge.

Smith G.A. (2006). *Attitudes Toward Immigration: In the Pulpit and the Pew*. Pew Research Center. Retrieved May 10, 2019, from: https://www.pewresearch.org/2006/04/25/attitudes-toward-immigration-in-the-pulpit-and-the-pew/#most-religiously-committed-are-less-negative-toward-immigrants

Storm I. (2011). «Christian Nations»? Ethnic Christianity and anti-immigration attitudes in four Western European Countries Nordic. *Journal of Religion and Society*, *24* (1), 75–96.

Tajfel H., Billing M.G., Bundy R.P., Flament C. (1971). Social categorisation and intergroup behaviour. *European Journal of Social Psychology*, *1*, 149–178.

Tajfel H., Turner J.C. (1979). An integrative theory of intergroup conflict. In W.G. Austin & S. Worchel (Eds.), *The Social Psychology of Intergroup Relations* (pp. 33–47). Monterey, CA: Brooks/Cole.

Talò C. (2010). L'autoritarismo come difesa della percezione di perdita dei confini della propria comunità. *Psychofenia, XIII, 23*, 51–88.

Villano P. (1999). Anti-semitic prejudice in adolescence: An italian study on shared beliefs. *Psychological Reports, 84*, 1372–1378.

Voci A., Pagotto L. (2010). *Il pregiudizio. Che cosa è, come si riduce.* Editori Laterza.

Zick A., Pettigrew T.F., Wagner U. (2008). Ethnic prejudice and discrimination in Europe. *Journal of Social Issues, 64*(2), 233–251.

Roberto-Luciano Barbeito

Chapter Three Facing Xenophobic Populism through Democratic Innovation

Abstract: This chapter examines the rise of far-right xenophobic populism and interprets it as a response to the institutional distress generated by neoliberal globalization. The text exposes the ways in which economic, cultural and political institutions have abandoned large sectors of the population and proposes several measures through which to regain confidence in those institutions. Finally, the text suggests that the success of the fight against xenophobic populism depends on a profound reform of the political system through democratic innovation. Specifically, it defends the desirability of developing new stochastic political institutions that favour a more representative participation of citizens, a better-founded debate and that prevents political corruption.

1 Introduction

1.1 Immigration at the Core of Global Agenda Setting

During the second decade of the current millennium, international migrations have strongly and generally become subject of global political and media attention. An eloquent example of this unusual interest was the UN high-level meeting held in September 2016, to analyse the displacement of refugees and migrants. The triggers had been, on the one hand, the Syrian refugees crisis in the European Union (EU) in 2015 and, on the other, the increase of African irregular immigration through the sea towards the same destination around the same dates, turning the Mediterranean Sea into the deadliest migration route (International Organization for Migrations, 2018). As a result of this meeting, the UN issued the New York Declaration for Refugees and Migrants, which expressed "the political will of the world leaders to save lives, protect rights and share global responsibility" (UN, 2016). Coherently with that purpose, the following year the UN created the role of Special Representative for International Migration, and in 2018 the Global Compact for Safe, Orderly and Regular Migration was passed, as a result of the Intergovernmental Conference on International Migration held in Morocco (UN, 2018). Consequently, along with the extensive media coverage put into the humanitarian crises that took place within European borders, in 2015, public concern on immigration grew into a common problem for the EU population, as well as the negative appraisal of the effects of immigration (European Commission [EC], 2019a). Three years later, in 2018, immigration was perceived, for the first time, as the main common problem for European people, above terrorism and unemployment (EC, 2018), and it still is, according to other sources, such as El País (2019), based on a survey conducted by YouGov among the European countries with the highest Gross Domestic Product. As a political response to that concern, the European Commission created, in 2019, a new and surprising post to protect European way of life regarding immigration, which coordinates competences in security, employment and education (EC, 2019b). Regarding this last century, this moment of greatest focus on the migration phenomenon is nothing but the zenith of a long journey that dates back to the late 1950s in the case of western Europe and United Kingdom in particular (Winder, 2013). Concerns on immigration in the countries that make up the current EU began then linked to the arrival of immigrants from the former colonies or other European countries, either because of the destruction derived from war or economic reasons. This wave would promote the debate on multiculturalism, which still remains. Further on, during the 1980s, illegal immigration became a pressing issue from the point of view of border control, due to the creation of the Schengen area, which allowed free flow of people within European countries who signed the Schengen Agreement. During the 1990s, after the fall of the Soviet Union, and German reunification, there were large flows of immigration from the old communist Europe. During that same decade, Huntington (1996) argued that migrations would represent the new largest source of global risk to capitalist liberal democracy and world order, once the communist enemy had disappeared. The sticking point would be the cultural clash, especially due to the ways of life typical of Islamic world, which were perceived as incompatible with the prevailing norms and values of the Western world, derived from its Christian roots. The terrorist attacks on the World Trade Center, in New York, on 9/11/2001, and its progressive spread throughout important European cities (London, Madrid, Paris and Barcelona), seemed to prove Huntington right, since war on terror became a common leitmotif of both domestic and foreign policies around the world, accounting for the limitation of citizens' rights and freedoms (especially regarding movement and telecommunications), and also justifying wars and invasions such as Afghanistan and Iraq. At the same time, in a deeply globalised context, of apparent economic upswing in the early 2000s, rich countries increased their attractiveness for international migrants, very clearly in the case of the EU. As a result of the political and media attention put on Islamic terrorism, after the arrival of broad quotas of immigrants, in combination with several humanitarian crises with less media impact in the past, far from Europe (Agier, 2011), the truth is that over the past decades, public opinion concerns for immigration has risen to historically high levels. The object of these concerns, entwined with the theses on the controversy of cultural clashes and the multicultural model, has been anticipated by a number of intellectuals for over a quarter century, with examples as conspicuous as Sartori (2000), Todd (2002, 2015), Todorov (2010), Bauman (2011), Courbage and Todd (2011), Zizeck (2016) and Eco (2019).

In contrast to the source of restlessness shown by national and international political and economic institutions, mass media, intellectuals and, eventually, public opinion, at a global level, international migrations constitute a relatively modest phenomenon from a statistical point of view: around 270 million international immigrants in 2019 (people who live in a country other than their country of birth), which represents less than 4 % of the world population that year, most of them economic migrants, followed at a long distance by refugees and, even further, students. As regards the time element, over the past 40 years there has been a tendency towards an increase of migrations in the world, although quite soft, showing the highest increase at the turn of the millennium, coinciding with the Great Recession: 2.3 % of the world population in 1980, 2.9 % in 1990, 2.8 % in 2000, 2.3 % in 2010 and 3.5 % in 2019 (Migrations Data Portal, 2019). Certainly, the distribution of migrations happens to be extremely unequal, regarding both origin and destination, and it depends much on the nature and situation of the migration. Both in terms of absolute flux of migrant inflows and quota of resident foreign population, there are three destinations that stand out as the world's largest recipients of migrants, especially in the case of economic migration and students abroad: the United States, the EU countries and the ones in the Arabian Peninsula. African countries also present large flows and quotas of migrants mostly related to ecological and armed conflicts.

Within the EU, the distribution of immigrant population is also quite unequal. According Eurostat (2019), and understandably, it concentrates in a handful of countries with larger demographic and economic congregations: Germany, the United Kingdom, France, Italy, and Spain. In relative terms, these five countries accommodate between 10 % (Italy) and 17 % (Germany) of total immigrant population. However, considering exclusively immigrant population from outside the EU, that proportion will never exceed 10 % in either country. Conspicuously, Poland, the sixth country on the list in terms of population, hosts a minuscule amount of immigrant population. Furthermore, there are small countries where the relative presence of immigrants (EU nationals and non-nationals) is way higher than the figures show (as in Austria, Sweden, Ireland, Belgium and Estonia). Other small countries, however, present a minimal proportion of immigrants (e.g. Bulgaria, Romania, Czech Republic and Hungary).

1.2 Rejection of Immigration and the Rise of Far-Right Populism

Against every expectation, the attitudes towards immigrants do not necessarily correspond with the size of the quotas nor the flow of immigrants. As a matter of fact, with data referring to about 20 European countries, Messing and Ságváry (2019) warned that xenophobic positions tend to be significantly higher in countries with a lower concentration of immigrant population. These authors established that attitudes against immigration have not become more judgemental after the refugee crisis in 2015. On the contrary, the rejection elicited by immigration is quite stable and has even decreased throughout the EU, even in countries with a higher absolute or relative number of immigrant population. According to these authors, this paradox is justified by the association of xenophobia with the degree of political empowerment, the sense of financial security and the social capital that can be gathered by native population, rather than simply the presence of immigrants. That is the reason why, at least in Europe, the determined rejection of immigration better defines people with less satisfactory social relationships, a higher sense of losing control over their lives, a higher sense of being exposed to economic difficulties and a bigger mistrust towards institutions in charge of protecting social welfare. This sociocultural profile best defines people who self-identify with the right side of the political scale, and who can be found across Europe in relevant proportions, especially in countries like Hungary and Poland. It so happens that in both countries, most of the population shows attitudes of open rejection towards immigrants, and far-right authoritarian populist parties are in office in the respective central governments. Considering this data, the conclusion is self-evident: people with the indicated sociocultural profile are more vulnerable to the discourse of far-right populist parties in terms of immigration, since they perceive them as the cause of their insecurity.

The previous conclusion is consistent with what is suggested by specialised literature: the greater part of the global *populist explosion* that took place over the past decade, especially over the past four years, involves the shocking rise of *far-right populism*, or *radical right*, and that is due to their ability to put problems related to immigration and social minorities in the media and political spotlight (Judis, 2016, 2018; Muddle & Rovira, 2017). This sort of populism, also referred to as *national populism* (Taguieff, 2004; Eatwell & Goodwin, 2018), started out in France in the 1970s, after the foundation of Jean-Marie Le Pen's National

Front, and has softly and steadily gathered electoral support since the 1980s, throughout Europe and around the world. For four decades, national populism has been the catalyst of an identity based on defensive, authoritarian and anti-elitist nationalism, thus luring a growing range of the electorate, even though its core is formed by a sector of the working class who had voted left-wing parties in the past (Betz, 1994; Casals, 2015). In recent years, however, national populist electorate seems to be expanding, at least in Europe, into population sectors who fit quite a different profile: women and LGTBI community members who fear the effects of Islamic religion on social rights and ways of life (Lancaster, 2019). One way or another, the truth is that after 40 years of almost continuous growth, coinciding with the end of the Great Recession and after the Syrian refugee crisis, nuanced versions of this populism have achieved electoral victories all over the world, frequently unexpectedly and overwhelmingly, but especially steep in America and Europe, resulting in the *populist explosion* (Judis, 2016) or the *Great Regression* (Geiselberger, 2017). So much so that, around mid-2019, radical right populism had achieved the U.S. Presidency, won the Brexit referendum in the United Kingdom and had a presence in 11 European governments –either independently or in a coalition – also gathering one out of four votes in the European Parliament elections (Timbro, 2019; European Parliament, 2019).

As every other type of populism, the one of the radical right feeds on a *host ideology* (Mudde & Rovira, 2017), weak and instrumental, which always implies electorate polarisation through basic contraposition that pits *people* against *elites*, or *us* against *them*. In the xenophobic and anti-immigration discourse, *people* and *us* equal the *natives*, who are considered the legitimate law-abiding citizens (locals); while *them* are immigrants and minorities, to whom they accuse of impoverishing the work market, abusing services and benefits, and impose their strange ways of life, taking advantage of the generosity of the law. In the same discourse, *elites* refer to power groups – including corporations, but above all, politicians and journalists from major political parties and large media players – who, unconcerned about the well-being of the natives, favour immigrants and social minorities instead – even because they want to take advantage of their workforce – pushing through measures of positive discrimination and political correctness, resulting in a preferential treatment unbearable for the natives.

Electoral success of xenophobic discourse shows the capability of populist political parties to attract disenfranchised voters from major traditional political parties, especially left-winged. Part of that capability resides in the strategy of moderation they have developed in their manners, arguments and proposals, along with their proven organisational capacity (Mudde & Rovira, 2017; Berman, 2019). Far from the violent and authoritarian image of the old neo-fascism, they have learnt how to present themselves as reasonable and trustworthy defenders of the legitimate interests of the good people who have been forsaken by the elites, since these would have left the true citizens unprotected from immigrants' and minorities' economic and cultural ambitions. By doing so, the xenophobic discourse is becoming highly effective to exploit the fear and insecurity – economic, identity – of many voters: it identifies the feeling of abandonment of these social groups, it fuels their sense of grievance and channels their anger against definable social groups under a promise of a return to a glorious past or, at least, a yearned past of protection and justice (Mishra, 2017). That way, radical right populism is an anti-elites proposal, although not an anti-system one, for instead of seeking the destruction of the system, it intends to retrieve it regarding anything they consider desirable, and shut it down, locking it away from the immigration and minorities menace, which is fostered by the elites for their own benefit. As a matter of fact, its success consists in turning immigration and problems related to minorities and political correctness of language a mainstream topic of discussion, building a new common sense (Mudde & Rovira, 2017; Mudde, 2019). Last conclusion is coherent with the findings of Denison and Geddes (2018), who observed that is the salience of immigration which explain the rise of anti-immigration political parties, not the increase of anti-immigrant sentiments – in fact, these sentiments decrease.

Deterioration of life conditions and collective identities related to neoliberal globalisation is the common factor usually indicated to explain the situation of fear and insecurity that the radical right sagaciously exploits to its own advantage (Bonelli, 2008; Mudde, 2019), understanding that the targets of this sort of populist messages – nationalist, xenophobic – are not strictly the losers of globalisation, but those who fear losing their status or see their expectations of social advancement frustrated (Casals, 2015). This general effect of globalisation may have been compounded in recent years because of the Great Recession and, lastly, the media impact of recent refugee crises, resulting in the current populist explosion (Judis, 2018). The fear of international Islamic terrorism, however, is barely mentioned as a relevant trigger of xenophobia and therefore populism.

In addition to the economic and sociocultural explanations related to neoliberal globalisation, it has been argued that the march of radical right and their attention to the immigration issue also depend on political factors that interact with the previously mentioned, and they should not be underestimated (Kriesi et. al, 2006; Bonelli, 2008; Oesch, 2008; Berman, 2019). The most common explanation refers to the neglect of left-wing parties on the working class (Casals, 2015), although other analyses expand responsibility also to conservative parties, for they consider that the rise of populism responds to the unsatisfactory response that traditional parties have given to the immigration and social minorities problem, as well as the ability of populism to utilise these issues to its own advantage (Berman, 2019). All of this may be taking place, furthermore, in a general context of systemic crisis aroused by neoliberal capitalism, which may also be undermining representative liberal democracy (Wallerstein, 2009; Wallerstein, Collins, Mann, Derluguian, & Calhoun, 2013; Streeck, 2016; Chomsky, 2017; Fontana, 2017; Castells, 2018, Milanovic, 2019), fostering among other effects an optimal *populist momentum*, profitable not only by the far right, but also by a new kind of left, as Laclau (2007), Fernández de Liria (2016) and Mouffe (2019) have noticed and defended.

1.3 Hypothesis, Objectives and Methodology

Once analysed the state of play, this text assumes that radical right xenophobic populism is thriving nowadays all over the world, and especially in Europe, as a result of a triple *institutional distress* (economic, cultural and political) in which broad sectors of population dwell, directly or indirectly due to the institutional decay inflicted by the stride of neoliberal globalisation. In accordance with this hypothesis, the immediate objective of the following pages is to briefly describe the key aspects of the different sorts of institutional distress, drawing from some relevant contributions in specialised literature. Secondly, this chapter suggests a number of measures which could be implemented to protect the clusters of population who feel helpless and, consequently, reduce the risk of populist allure. The proposals are made briefly and assertively as mere general operational guidelines, presuming that they need to be implemented in concert, through international agreements, for they should be enforced in the destination countries as much as in the immigrants' origin countries, migratory movements being a global issue. Lastly, this chapter states that any measure designed to reduce institutional distress needs profound changes in the political system, favouring more inclusive and more committed forms of participation, which foster more representative, clarifying and binding collective decisions. As of the display of debates and experiences regarding democratic innovation held all over the world in the last quarter of a century, this text argues that it might be convenient to create new democratic institutions of a stochastic nature, taking into consideration that they could prevent the gap between voters and representatives, political corruption, and they could also make better founded decisions. New institutions, indeed, better coinciding with the concept of democracy as a tool serve three higher purposes: development of the self, development of individual self-determination and promotion of common interests (Dahl, 1989).

2 Institutional Distress as a Trigger for Xenophobic Populism

Institutional distress is consistent with the belief that major institutions (economic, cultural and political) do not stand up for the majority of the population's interests, but their leaders', as well as that of specific minorities privileged by them. Although there is a complex landscape, it is an idea that has rooted globally, as is inferred from the high levels of distrust and disaffection the public opinion is showing all over the world towards institutions in general, and especially representative institutions, may be with the Chinese and Indian exceptions (Dimock, 2019; Gallup, 2019; Ipsos, 2019; Skinner, 2019). The wave of citizen protests at the start of the century, the largest since the end of World War II, was a clear collective expression – although from fundamentally progressive positions at the time – of the anger and hunger for change caused by the state of abandonment and helplessness in which the institutions engulf large groups of society (Ortiz, Burke, Berrada, & Cortés, 2013).

Seen in this way, institutional distress was noticed early and overcome by Bourdieu (2003), to whom it is an unbearable by-product of neoliberal globalisation, which leaves individuals defenceless against the law of the strongest. For Sennett (2006), this sort of distress represents, in fact, a defining feature of the new global capitalism, which is characterised by the advent of *flexible institutions*. These institutions, which emerged in the field of economy, and are barely bound to the state, stimulate a dissolving individualism that requires the greatest preparation and efficiency from people, however without committing to their well-being or their long-term future. In addition, they shape a fierce and indolent capitalism that creates new collective risks whose costs lie on the individuals, forcing them to take them as if they were personal responsibilities (Beck, 1998). Their economy-focused, individualistic and individualising logic colonises all spheres of life (political, communicative and cultural), isolating and unprotecting many people, forcing them to live in a continuous state of uncertainty and material or emotional precariousness (Bauman, 2000). In a context of growing social inequality, the feeling of abandonment by the institutions who provided with rues and protection translates into vulnerability, and it increases the likelihood of social confrontation and collective violence outbursts (Kirby, 2005).

Once social capitalism has been weakened due to the emergence of individualist capitalism of flexible and de-committed corporations, radical right xenophobic populism is out to take advantage of the general institutional distress, for it addresses the concerns of the groups who are most exposed to a lack of regulation and social integration. However, as opposed to left-wing populism, radical right populism does not advance a transforming revolution, but a systemic shutdown, a vow of protection of those who fear the most for economic, cultural and political effects of globalisation: loss of employment, well-being and collective identity (Bonelli, 2008; Oesch, 2008; Casals, 2015; Halikiopoulou & Vasilopoulou, 2015; Mudde & Rovira, 2017; Judis 2016). Its greatest success so far has precisely been to be able to put these concerns in the spotlight of public agenda, which makes it lightly that in the foreseeable future the strength of this sort of populism is not going to disappear, but more likely, it will root and grow (Mudde, 2019).

2.1 Economic Distress

The most evident form of institutional distress is the economic one, which comes from the impression that the institutions in charge of providing with employment and well-being have stopped guaranteeing it, without foreseeable substitutes. This group is composed of companies, although also unions and governments, for they are supposed to supervise economic activity and redistribution of wealth through the provision of public services. An extensive bibliography links this sort of economic distress with the rise of populism, in general, and particularly xenophobic populism (i.e., Pastor & Vernesi, 2016; Frey, Berger, & Chen, 2016; Rodrik, 2017; Gerber, Huber, & Biggers, 2017; Melin & Enarsson, 2018). The arguments usually coincide in the advance of inequality and the consequent disruption of living conditions for the majority of the population: deindustrialisation, stagnation, automatization, labour market impoverishment – unemployment, unstable employment, low salaries, illegal employment, disruption of public services, grovelling of rural areas and small cities in the interest of major global cities, which are overcrowding, and boosting the cost of living.

Both inequality and disruption of living conditions come together in a context that is especially prone to feed the xenophobic and anti-elite discourse, characterised by productive decentralisation, international competition, exports-oriented production and the arrival of immigrants willing to work under worse working conditions. These circumstances are usually marked as unintended effects of the deepening of the exchange of capital, goods and people at a global scale, favoured by the technological advancement of transportation and telecommunications (globalisation), as well as the growing automatisation of all sectors of productive activity. Other approaches, however, stress that inequality and forfeiture of well-being is consistent with the implementation of neoliberal economic policies of reforms and structural cuts: funding, market deregulation, privatisation of state-owned companies and public services and, of course, regressive taxes. The Great Recession may have pushed the limits of this sort of policies, aggravating the problems stemming from it and thus favouring social protests and populist responses, especially from the radical right (Funke, Schularick, & Trebesch, 2015; Blyth, 2016; Raghuram, 2019; Stiglitz, 2019).

2.2 Cultural Distress

Closely linked with the economic distress, specialised literature argues that radical right populism also thrives because of its ability to take advantage on another effect of globalisation: the cultural reaction against post-materialist values and multiculturalism (Norris & Inglehart, 2019), demand for recognition of one's identity (Fukuyama, 2018; Sides, J., Tesler, M., Vavreck, L. (2018). This reaction features those who fear losing their collective national identity, for they assume that it is undergoing an attack from minorities (immigrants and other formerly marginalised social groups) who now intend to impose their customs on others. This is a type of institutional distress, a cultural and identity fear, that is consistent with the diatribes of radical right populism against political correctness, promoting a sense of boredom and careless disregard, and encouraging the notion that such correctness is a form of unfair hegemonic authoritarianism exerted by minorities with the approval of the elites, inhibiting individual liberties and the normal course of the good native citizens' own customs.

Cultural distress is an expression of the undermining of the old identity references, which provided with meaning and cohesion within the nation state, although it can also be an expression of the fear of losing references of quite a different signature, collective achievements such as human rights regarding gender and sexual identity (Lancaster). This text posits that cultural distress is, in the end, caused by cognitive confusion that many people present with regards to common problems, helping establish cultural gaps between social groups, depending on their level of exposure to media and their experience throughout the education system. This results from the fact that media, social media and digital platforms provide low-quality information, which rather than clarifying creates confusion and turmoil regarding the reasons for common and personal problems, a circumstance xenophobic populism is using to throw in simple, but feasible, explanations.

With regards to media and social media, deterioration of information comes, firstly, from its commercial purpose, since the ratings war and the profit-and-loss account come before the democratic need to provide with relevant, proven and truthful information (Bourdieu, 1999; Sartori, 1997). This logic is strengthened in a context of concentration of wealth and digital format which erodes the profession of journalists and fosters the sensationalist treatment of news, resulting in *infotainment* (Thussu, 2007).

Digital platforms (web search, web browsers and social networking sites) take part in a similar commercial dynamic: they serve information, utilities and entertainment in exchange for access, management and sale of data produced by users of interconnected devices. Through the automated analysis of use of devices and browsing habits, these platforms choose the contents that reach each user, enticing them to make ill-considered decisions, depriving them of the control over the information they produce and, mostly, creating newsletter loops, as in personal bubbles that place each individual in hardly permeable social spheres that intensify ways of thinking and hamper rapprochement of individuals from different spheres. The effects of such processes on inequality and democracy can be devastating (O'Neil, 2016; Stephens-Davidowitz, 2017), as proven by the Cambridge Analytica scandal.

This chapter suggests that the education system could also be damaging the quality of information and feeding the cultural gap xenophobic populism benefits from. Such a hypothesis is sustained as a number of education systems seem to be more concerned about classifying students through a grading system rather than stimulating the development of their own personality, the understanding of common problems or mutual tolerance. By doing so, education, far from reducing social background differences, reinforces and perpetuates them, alienating social groups, raising incomprehension and even aversion between them (Bourdieu & Passeron, 1964). On the other hand, formal education is presented with an organisational inertia that resists adapting to the available technology, and drifts itself away from the vital expectations, experiences and needs of youth, even from those who abide and achieve the best marks (Fernández-Enguita, 2017). By providing with personally negligible knowledge, rather than creating discernment, the school system elaborates on clichés transmitted through rigid teaching programmes. Outdated and mandatory, education may be seen as an arbitrary and even repressive institution by youth, and that may become an unexpected breeding ground for simple answers to complex phenomena that populist alternatives offer, whichever their political orientation.

2.3 Political Distress

Political distress is the third type of institutional distress that justifies the rise of radical right xenophobic populism. Basically, it implies the perception that representative institutions of liberal democracy do not stand for the interests of the represented, but that of the representatives – politicians – complicit with the economic and cultural elites. It is an opinion that is broadly informed by studies (OCDE, 2019), and it also urged social protests at the turn of the century (Ortiz, Burke, Berrada, & Cortés, 2013; Mason, 2013; Pellizzetti, 2019). And it is well known that, beyond economic or cultural structural trends, the electoral behaviour depends strongly on the strategies developed by the parties (Meguid, 2008). So, according to specialised bibliography, there are three political arguments that justify the rise of radical right xenophobic populism. The first one is the strategy of moderation adopted by these populist parties that, far from the violent image of neo-fascism, allow them to even present themselves as genuine defenders of democracy against spurious interests of major traditional parties (Mudde & Rovira, 2017; Berman, 2019; Mudde, 2019). Simultaneously, they have strengthened their internal organisation, establishing solid activist groundwork and capitalising the media coverage of their leaders. Such strategy is complemented by sophisticated electoral persuasion techniques, which include an extensive – and doubtfully ethical – use of social media targeting extremely segmented public, in a similar way to Cambridge Analytica during Donald Trump's presidential campaign in the United States, or the supporters of Brexit in the United Kingdom.

The second argument sustains that radical right populism has been fed by erratic strategic decisions from the major traditional parties, both left and right-wing, regarding immigration management, understanding that it is a specially delicate subject, for the attitudes towards immigration have been forging for decades, they unevenly depict different social groups and root the *habitus*. For that reason, any strategy implemented by major parties (ignoring, adapting or rejecting immigration issues brought up by xenophobic parties) pose unpredictable, paradoxical and difficult-to-measure risks (Abou-Chadi, 2016; Abou-Chadi & Krause, 2018; Meguid, 2008). Certainly, these difficulties have not prevented, for decades, the immigration issue to be a recurring issue in political confrontation among major traditional parties, thus facilitating the extreme use far-right populism is making of it.

Lastly, the third argument – probably the most repeated one – suggests that xenophobic populism has thrived among constituents who feel forsaken by social democrat parties, after they refrained from applying redistributive economic policies which had protected working and middle classes in the past, and adopting instead the neoliberal theses on growth, market and efficiency (Casals, 2015; Judis, 2016; Mudde, 2019). Unable to differentiate themselves from conservative or liberal parties on the economic front, social democrat parties focused their electoral strategies on cultural problems, polarising identity policies (gender, LGTBI and ethnicity) and arrogating the protection of minorities. Ironically enough, this strategy may have provided an opportunity for new left-wing parties and populisms – especially amongst young university students – although more so for radical right populisms, for it allowed them to focus on identity issues – with immigration in mind – from the point of view of those who fear its economic and cultural effects, and feel grievance for the alleged preferential treatment to minorities, or simply those who feel overwhelmed by the hegemony of political correctness, since they consider it an unjust and smothering imposition. Moreover, social democrat parties' economic vagueness, and even the surging of government coalitions between them and traditional right-winged or centre-right-winged parties, allowed populism to spread the idea that all major parties are the same, and they remain indifferent to regular people's concerns, since they only respond to their own interests and those of the elites. Whatever the strategy adopted by major parties, once the far-right populist parties reach relevant quotas of electoral, the dynamics of the whole political competition change profoundly (Abou-Chadi & Krause, 2018).

Beyond the aforementioned arguments, political distress and its populist xenophobic corollary can be also interpreted as symptoms of a greater problem: the exhaustion of liberal democracy, in other words, the current representative institutions, as has been stated for a decade by a number of theorists and specialists, among them: Tilly (2007), Todd (2010), Mair (2013), Chomsky 2017, Castells (2018), Eatwell and Goodwin (2018), Levitsky and Ziblatt (2018) and Mounk (2018). In general, democratic exhaustion can be ascribed to the major transformations caused by neoliberal globalisation, which may have been exacerbated by the Great Recession (Posner, 2011; Kuttner, 2018; Iversen & Soskice, 2019). More broadly, the deterioration of democracy might be nothing but an especially visible part of a systemic crisis that affects all spheres of collective life, as it is said.

Even though they have been exacerbated lately, symptoms of democratic exhaustion have been observed since the end of the twentieth century, before and after the collapse of the Soviet Union, as denote, among many others, Dahl (1989), Held (1996), Pharr and Putnam (2000), Sartori (2007), Tilly (2007) and Norris (2011, 2015). The most visible part of this deterioration of democratic institutions is the enormous gap between the represented and representatives, with regards to their uneven interests as well as the uneven capacity of both to influence the collective decision-making process. Presumably, this gap may affect both the legitimacy and the efficacy of democratic institutions, for it hampers the accountability of government responsibility, bolsters corruption and does not improve government responsiveness.

In summary, the gap between representatives and the represented may have widened as a product of two general processes: on the one hand, the enormous complexity and scale of current societies, which implies a huge amount of subject-matter expertise whose follow-up is unaffordable to most citizens through means of current democratic institutions (Dahl, 1989) and on the other hand, the establishment of a new *public sphere* starred by media and political parties. With the sole purpose of controlling electoral preferences and social definitions of constituents, media and political parties compete to define the agenda setting through the management of visibility (Gil-Calvo, 2018). Therefore, forcing constituents to take a stand as sheer *political-spectacle* and *storytelling* consumers, so that the degree of freedom of citizens is confined to passively choosing among the different options (electoral options, policies) provided by the media and political parties. This type of political competition sparks the surge of a new kind of democracy: the *audience democracy* (Manin, 1997) or the *market democracy* (Gil-Calvo, 2018), characterised by the use and abuse of a wide variety of political lobbying tools, such as polarisation and anger (Ansolabehere & Iyengar, 1995; Tolchin, 1996; Mishra, 2017), personalisation (Poguntke & Webb, 2005) and fake news (D'Ancona, 2017). Just the same lobbying techniques and procedures now used by far-right populist parties with particular effectiveness, also assisted by the use of digital social networks. In the end, as warned by Weber and Schumpeter a long time ago, the logic of electoral competition in a system of plebiscite chieftaincy (liberal democracy) leads to the use and abuse of lobbying techniques (Barbeito, 2017). It is also true that we may have never witnessed before such an extreme use of such procedures, nor has it had such an eroding potential to legitimacy and efficacy of democratic institutions (Salmon, 2010).

Faced with such situation of democratic decay – and political distress – a type of completely new tools is proposed to be introduced in the political process: the implementation of big data techniques, robotisation and artificial intelligence. While it is premature to know how these utilities will affect the democratic process, it is easy to guess the great opportunities they offer for a non-democratic political control, such as technocratic control (Moreno & Jiménez, 2018; O'Neil, 2016; Bartlett, 2019), with the peculiarity that, nowadays, this enormous potential for control is in the hands of large corporations, as much or more as in the hands of states.

3 Facing Institutional Distress: A Few Action Proposals

Should radical right populism be caused by a triple institutional distress, which also causes a number of other fractures in life in society, corrodes coexistence and challenges democracy? It is necessary to think how to stem its advancement as well as its diatribe about immigration. The answer is obvious: to offer institutional shelter – economic, cultural and political – in countries of both origin and destination, an arduous and yet impetuous pursuit that demands the earnest determination of national governments and international institutions to work concertedly.

From an economic point of view, to shelter means to give all the residents of a country access to social welfare, ensuring identical rights and obligations, without any sort of discrimination – including positive discrimination. Of course, this protection will only be feasible should there be a brand-new economic policy, one that places social welfare before business benefit, redistributing wealth through progressive taxes, the same way it was carried out after World War II. In order to discourage immigration, economic protection should entail, in the countries of origin, endogenous sustainable growth, focused on decreasing inequality and increasing social welfare, along with the promotion of more balanced international commercial relations, responsibility for former metropolises to compensate for dependence derived from the process of decolonisation and financial development aids. Naturally, there is an urgent need for a concerted migration policy between countries that includes a determined aim to fight human trafficking. However, both in countries of destination and transit countries, control of migration flows should always imply humane treatment, under the Kantian principle of hospitality.

At the cultural level, protection equals fostering mutual knowledge of different social groups and classes, but also of the dynamics and the reasons for common problems, which requires a substantial improvement of information quality. Among other measures, media and the education system must be required to prioritise the right to a broad, detailed, proven and truthful information as a base of the media business and a fundamental principle of education. It is safe to assume that, should the education system give up competition over grades as an objective, and replace it with meaningful learning for the development of free personality, it will improve mutual recognition and more new cooperative attitudes will emerge among different social groups, reducing identity cleavages. Among the numerous effects of these measures, one can foresee that symbolic violence exerted through the use of language will decrease, especially the oppressing force of political correctness perceived by social groups who feel aggrieved. In the countries of origin, sheltering culturally also compels to remove heroic myths created regarding immigration, providing on one side truthful information through media and the education system, and on the other side, promoting spaces for the exchange of personal experiences related to emigration.

At the political level, to protect implies more and a better democracy: listening, discussing and taking action (Iglesias & Barbeito, 2014). That is to say, citizens must participate in more equal conditions in the decisions that affect them personally, implementing processes that are more representative of the diversity of interests and circumstances at stake, as well as informational resources to establish more competent deliberations (Dahl, 1989). This entails, in the immediate term, improving the running of current political institutions, meanwhile also the implementation of *democratic innovation*, this is, to imagine and try out new representative institutions that allow a more partaken decision-making process, with heterogeneous interests and viewpoints, well-informed deliberation and thus more legitimate and probably efficient results.

The improvement of current institutions should be oriented to shrink the gap between representatives and the represented; therefore, it must affect, at least, the funding of political parties, the duration of terms, concentration and rotation of offices, salaries and pensions constraint, perks control and a regime of incompatible activities after leaving office – *revolving doors*. The purpose is to avoid representatives to think they own the position they have taken, discourage bribery, prevarication and, lastly, force them to accept the consequences of their decisions the way citizens have to accept theirs. There is no doubt this institutional improvement should imply a more refined separation of powers, through weights and counterweights that preserve mutual independence, foster institutional cooperation and strengthen popular sovereignty. Finally, there should be an extension of direct participation mechanisms, especially referendums, although they should offer unambiguous assurances regarding the right of the initiative, whether it is consultive or binding, the wording of the question for the matter being consulted, the quality of information and a public debate respecting equality among the options in dispute.

4 The Role of the Political System and the Need for Democratic Innovation

Certainly, the implementation of these reforms in order to improve political representation and defeat the ghost of xenophobic populism is quite unlikely to happen, as shown by an eloquent fact: a decade after the greatest wave of global social protests after World War II, whose common content was the demand for improvement in democratic processes, and a Europe that had been hit by austerity policies and, more recently, by xenophobic populism, there have barely been worth-mentioning reforms in European countries – nor the European Union – to improve representative institutions. In the end, representation is quite a particular way of democracy, for it is based on aristocratic principles (Dahl, 1989; Manin, 1997). Indeed, liberal democracy was conceived as a peaceful competition process among the elites for political direction through elections (Schumpeter, 2015). Once universal suffrage was implemented, which implied large and heterogeneous constituencies, elections would rely on media; and they bolstered the development of all sorts of propaganda and persuasion techniques, more emotional even than rational, and with little or no compunction towards the truthfulness of the spread information (Schumpeter, 2015; Weber, 2019). Because of this logic of elite competition, elections foster the surge of charismatic leaderships that favours the centralisation of political parties, who see how their function is limited to being the machinery for the election, promotion and replacement of leaders, in exchange for perks in case of victory. This scheme – as described by Schumpeter almost 80 years ago – is precisely the one that has been followed by European political parties over the past few decades (Mair, 2013), in the context of audience democracy (Manin, 1997), also referred to as market democracy (Gil-Calvo, 2018). Such scheme of functioning was only qualified, after World War II and over scarcely a third of a century, by the implementation of *party democracy* (Manin, 1997), resulting from the rise of social democracy in junction with the labour movement, which was highly organised, as Weber noted (Barbeito, 2017).

Even though global social protests have not forced significant improvements of the mechanisms of (liberal) representative democracy, they have indeed caused an astonishing emergence of quite varied experiences in democratic innovation, both from participatory and deliberative approaches, resulting in the second wave of democratic innovation (Sintomer, 2019). Many of these experiences imply the use of random selection procedures of policymakers that had already been used at the end of the twentieth century, during the first wave of democratic innovation. Inspired by the influence of Dahl (1970, 1989), the first wave was based on the belief that there was a need for implementing procedures that would allow making better-informed decisions through the creation of *mini-publics*, or *actively aware publics*, selected through random procedures. Embedded by a deliberative logic, rather than a logic of self-governance and radical democracy, these first contemporary experiences were driven top-down, usually parting from collaborations between academics and political authorities, and resulted in thousands of patented and carefully designed experiments, such as citizen juries, consensus conferences and deliberative polls, whose objective was to make better-informed decisions, although not necessarily more participated, and of an advisory rather than binding nature. Despite its prolixity, most of these experiences did not intend to be pursued any further, but to prove the feasibility of the deliberative hypothesis. Neither did they have an impact in social change nor a major impact on public opinion. As a matter of fact, the experiences of the first wave were urged by a strong elitism, for they strived for *mini-publics* to take the place of public opinion in the political decision-making process, since they considered it ill-informed and highly susceptible to manipulation (Sintomer, 2019).

The second wave of democratic innovation basically coincides with the inception of the Great Recession and global social protests, and it implies the implementation of a large, diverse and inventive number of experiences which, sometimes applied on a large scale, try to reconcile deliberation and participative or direct democracy, by integrating in many cases random-selection procedures (Sintomer, 2019). This new wave of experiences expanded rapidly all over the world, frequently bolstered by social movements, unions, companies, foundations or other citizen organisations, sometimes with the support of media. Random selection has been a regular factor in some of the most notable experiences, such as the process of constitutional reform in Iceland in 2009, which started out as an assembly selected by draw to set the agenda of that reform, although in the end it was stalled by the new governing parties. A greater success and better acceptance by political parties took place in Ireland, where they established a constitutional convention from 2012 to 2014, with a hybrid House of Representatives, consisting of a majority of members chosen by draw amongst civil servants, along with a minority of representatives from political parties (Arnold, Farrel, Suiter, 2019). A number of recommendations resulted from this gathering, most of which were implemented by the government, as well as another which was later on passed via referendum on quite a controversial matter from a moral point of view, such as equal marriage. Later on – from 2016 to 2018 – there was a new house – only this time the selection of its members was completely random – to make proposals on equally controversial matters, such as abortion, climate change, legal age and the duration of parliamentary terms. During those years, a number of other innovations were carried out in other countries, which included processes of random selection, many of which intended to establish advisory councils within organisations and public institutions, especially within the fold of new left-wing organisations (as in Mexico, Spain and France). Precisely, in the capital of Spain, a new political party emerged from the agreement between social movements and new left-wing parties, and initiated from 2015 to 2019 one of the most ambitious projects of citizen direct participation (Decide Madrid), although it was only at the end of the process that they included a stochastic advisory council. A distinctive feature of this project was its digital nature, in the context of their own, freely licensed website, which has later been used by hundreds of organisations around the world. Through digital participation, the project intended to break down the barrier imposed by long commuting distances within big cities. However, digital participation happened to be marginal when compared to the one obtained through other traditional procedures – ballot boxes and postal votes – and global participation was also quite low when compared to electoral participation. This experience shows two things: the first one is that when there is a will, it is possible to implement very interesting innovations; secondly, participation depends mainly on factors different from the existence or non-existence of digital tools, even if these can be of great help (Iglesias & Barbeito, 2016). Being a well-argued and contrasted deliberation, with broad and heterogeneous participation, the aforementioned procedures could favour more sensible decisions regarding such controversial and emotional issues as immigration and multiculturalism, the core of xenophobic populism diatribes.

5 Conclusion: Democracy by Lot as an Antidote for Xenophobic Populism

The experiences that have taken place over the past decade have brought hope in the possibilities of democratic innovation, and especially in procedures of selection by draw as a tool for better-informed collective decision-making, in order to shrink concentration of power, political corruption and even to increase participation, whilst this objective has proven quite unequal so far. Either through legislative chambers, citizen councils or selection of political staff, drawing of lots has proved its great potential to refound democratic political systems, as illustrated by Gastil and Wright (2019) by launching an international call for academics and practitioners to jointly debate the feasibility of legislative systems consisting of two chambers, one of elected seats and another of selection by lottery, both focused on legislating on all sorts of matters, yet at the same time, compatible with an elected executive power.

While being quite a controversial and troubled proposal, this debate has encouraged the materialisation of other proposals, such as Bouricius' (2019), who urged to initiate the transition into an exclusively driven-by-draw democracy, whose final scenario would be an interconnected network of *mini-publics*, each one of them with a specific legislative function, and one only subject to decide on, as well as other mini-publics focused on selecting and holding the executive power accountable. This would entail the creation of, at least, five types of citizen bodies, specialised in the different legislative functions, and selected for the most part randomly on a rotational basis with different degrees of compulsion – in any case, never through competitive elections. In particular, an *agenda council*, in charge of establishing the issues that are to be subject to legislative attention during a certain period of time; *interest panels*, in charge of drafting the proposals subject to debate; *review panels*, consisting of large thematic areas with the objective of studying the different proposals related to the area in full – effects and feasibility – and bringing a final proposal; *policy jury*, brief in duration, whose task would be to decide – to pass or reject – the final proposal of a law; *meta-legislative bodies*, for example a *rules council* to oversee and improve the system performance or an *oversight council*, to ensure the impartiality of bureaucracy, and protect the citizens from the surge of a technocratic elite. In this scheme, at least another two types of dedicated mini-publics would be needed. The first one focused on choosing the people who are to exert executive power and the other focused on assessing their performance and, when appropriate, veto them or replace them.

All of the process sketched by Bouricius involves the participation of experts, civil servants and concerned parties, and it presents the convenience of combining physical and digital means for the tasks of information, discussion and meetings. Although Bouricius suggests a specialised supervisory board for the oversight of civil servants and experts, it is expected that this measure will be insufficient. Random procedures, along with rotation in service, could be an added control instrument, perfectly compatible with the need to have highly capable and specialised personnel available. Maybe the weakest point of Bouricius' project, like others that include random selection, is to establish the incentives to encourage participation, for a genuine democratic system requires a high and continued participation from all its citizens, even if, as presented here, they have to rotate among different institutions, matters and levels of decision, in order to avoid concentration of power and corruption, while taking advantage of the knowledge and the competences gathered through the very same participative processes. It is often a presumption that participation will increase as a consequence of personal satisfaction from knowing that individual contribution has a relevant weight in the final result. However, such presumption is an overestimation: it is well known that deeply aware and committed people do not participate as they would like to for a reason as simple as the lack of time. In this respect, it would be necessary to subsidise the time invested in political participation, so that working hours are reduced, and the deduced time – paid for – is put into political participation, whichever the institution, level or matter to be considered. Those unwilling to participate would stop being paid for the corresponding time, and they would not be able to compensate with any other type of paid work in any other activity. Surely, these regulations would be subject to a great number of personal situations that would have to be accounted for and considered. However, the general standard is clear: all citizens must always be taking part in any type of political body – including the most local action levels, neighbourhood included – under penalty of not being remunerated on the share of time they should be devoting to political participation.

Any democratic innovation, especially as radical as the one suggested here, faces the difficulties of implementation. Even in those places where other successful experiences –although limited – of democracy by draw have been carried out, the truth is that public opinion does not claim for its continuity, even if they acknowledge its usefulness (Arnold, Farrell, & Suiter, 2019). It is self-evident that democratic innovations as radical as the ones postulated here can only be accepted as a response to systemic crises, where other options have been proven wrong – predictably, authoritarian or plebiscitary options, such as populism or technocracy. Without being so extreme, it would be possible to implement a process of change and transition. Bouricius (2019) suggests starting by innovating on such controversial issues, or issues that entail conflicts of interests, highly unlikely to be solved since the parties are quite even, or rather encased in their individual positions. Starting by these issues would be especially easy should they also have little impact on the budget. It is predictable that immigration and multiculturalism are this kind of hot potatoes: they discomfort traditional political parties because they have political costs with unpredictable effects in the long term.

Even if there are issues that are especially appropriate to be subject to profound stochastic democratic innovation and could eventually remove elections, institutional resistance would predictably be many. It is futile to expect political parties to stand for them as if they were their own, unless they faced critical situations, of great delegitimacy, and prompted by other social agents, as it happened in Ireland (Arnold, Farrell, & Suiter, 2019). Just as the logic of electoral competition keeps politicians out from promoting democratic innovations which go against such logic – unless there is nothing left to lose – neither does competition over audience, with commercial or political purposes, favour media – including digital platforms – to bolster or claim for democratic innovation. Least could it be expected from major companies, except when they observe the imminence of a catastrophic crisis.

In all cases, it is imperative to start sensitising political parties, politicians, media, business corporations and other power groups about the necessity of undergoing a profound political reform to end elections and the establishment of multiple stochastic institutions with paid and rotational terms. The initiative of citizen non-profit movements and groups, networked and jointly working towards that end, could prove the feasibility of such proposals and lobby conventional representative institutions into implementing democracy by draw. Doubtlessly, the support of unions could prove itself quite useful to favour the work of citizen movements and groups, although it could also be valuable to gather support from University as an institution – professors and students together. Indeed, even though University has been colonised by commercial and representative logics, both of these have caused a severe deterioration of working conditions and the professional expectations of professors as well students,, its special field logic (the knowledge production and transmission) is still more favourable than that of any other institution to foster common interests, the development of free personality and individual autonomy. Even with professors and students being in precarious conditions and absorbed by exhausting and never-ending evaluation processes, University could play a fundamental role in disseminating democratic innovations.

Should populism be the result of institutional gaps discussed in this text, putting a stop to it requires an urgent and profound democratic innovation, for only with a new kind of democracy would it be possible to foster economic welfare, proven and truthful information, and the making of highly participated decisions, representative of social diversity. Stochastic democracy, as asserted here – extremely alien to our traditional schemes of political participation –, is postulated as a proportional response to face the magnitude of the great challenges that humanity is up against in this critical moment, of which xenophobic populism is a clear symptom.

References

Abou-Chadi T. (2016). Niche party success and mainstream party policy shifts – how green and radical right parties differ in their impact. *British Journal of Political Science*, *46*(2), 417–436.

Abou-Chadi T., Krause W. (2018). The causal effect of radical right success on mainstream parties' policy positions: A regression discontinuity approach. *British Journal of Political Science*, 1–19.

Agier M. (2011). *Managing the indesirables. Refugees camps and humanitarian government*. London: Polity Press.

Ansolabehere S., Iyengar Sh. (1995). *Going negative: How political advertisements shrink and polarize the electorate*. New York: The Free Press.

Arnold T., Farrell D.M., Suiter J. (2019). Lessons form a hybrid sortition chamber: The 2012-14 Irish Constitutional Convention. In J. Gastil, E.O. Wright (Eds.), *Legislature by Lot. Transformative designs for deliberative governance* (pp. 101–121). London: Verso.

doi:10.1111/j.1540-5907.2009.00369.x.

Barbeito R.L. (2017). ¿Qué hay de nuevo, viejo? Democracia de audiencia y personalización de la política. Pasos a la Izquierda, *10*. http://pasosalaizquierda.com/?p=3181

Bartlett J. (2019). *The people vs tech. How the internet is killing democracy (and how we save it)*. London: Ebury Publishing.

Bauman Z. (2000). *Liquid modernity*. Cambridge: Polity.

Bauman Z. (2011). Migration and identities in the globalized world. *Philosophy & Social Criticism*, *37*(4), 425–435.

Beck U. (1998). *World risk society*. Cambridge: Polity.

Berman Sh. (2019). *Democracy and dictatorship in Europe. From the Ancien Régime to the present day*. Oxford: Oxford University Press.

Betz H.G. (1994). *Radical right-wing populism in Western Europe*. London: Palgrave.

Blyth M. (2016). Global Trumpism. Why Trump's victory was 30 years in the making and why it won't stop here, *Foreign Affairs* (online). Retrieved December 5, 2019 from https://www.foreignaffairs.com/articles/2016-11-15/global-trumpism

Bonelli L. (2008). *La France a peur. Una histoire sociale d l''insecurité"*. Paris: La Découverte.

Bourdieu P. (1999). *On TV*. New York: The New Press.

Bourdieu P. (2003). *Counterfire: Against the tyranny of the market*. London: Verso.

Bourdieu P., Passeron J.C. (1964). *Les Héritiers. Les étudiants et la culture*. Paris: Les Éditions de Minuit.

Bouricius T. (2019). Why hybrid bicameralism is not right for sortition. In J. Gastil, E.O. Wright (Eds.), *Legislature by lot. Transformative designs for deliberative governance* (pp. 313–332). London: Verso.

Casals X. (2015). ¿Por qué los partidos obreros apoyan a la ultraderecha? Diez reflexiones para elaborar una respuesta. *Working Papers*, 341. Barcelona: Institut de Ciènces Politiques i Socials, Universitat Barcelona.

Castells M. (2017). *Rupture: The crisis of liberal democracy*. Hoboken, NJ: Wiley John & Sons.

Chomsky N. (2017). *Global discontents: Conversations on the rising threats to democracy*. New York: Metropolitan Books.

Courbage Y., Todd E. (2011). *A convergence of civilizations: The transformation of muslim societies around the world*. New York: Columbia University Press.

Dahl R. (1970). *After the revolution? Authority in a good society*. New Heaven: Yale University Press.

Dahl R. (1989). *Democracy and its critics*. New Haven: Yale University Press.

D´Ancona M. (2017). *Post-truth: The new war on truth and how to fight back*. London: Ebury Digital.

Denison, J., & Geddes, A.(2018). A rising tide? The salience of immigration and the rise of anti-immigration political parties in Western Europe. *The Political Quarterly*, 90(1), 107–116. https://doi.org/10.1111/1467-923X.12620

Dimock M. (2019). An update on our research into trust, facts and democracy. *Pew Research Centre*. Retrieve December 6, 2019 from https://www.pewresearch.org/2019/06/05/an-update-on-our-research-into-trust-facts-and-democracy/

Eatwell R., Goodwin M. (2018). *National populism. The revolt against liberal democracy*. Pelican Books.

Eco U. (2019). *Migrazioni e intolleranza*. Milano: La nave di Teseo.

El País (2019). Inmigración y medio ambiente centran la inquietud de los europeos. *El País* (2019 May 13). Retrieved November 11 2019, from https://elpais.com/internacional/2019/05/10/actualidad/1557507327_934513.html

European Commission. (2018). *Standard Eurobarometer 89 "European Citizenship"*. European Union. doi:10.2775/133636. Retrieved November 11, 2019, from http://ec.europa.eu/commfrontoffice/publicopinion/index.cfm/ResultDoc/download/DocumentKy/83538

European Commission. (2019a). *Public opinion data base*. Retrieved November 11, 2019, from https://ec.europa.eu/commfrontoffice/publicopinion/index.cfm/Chart/getChart/themeKy/59/groupKy/279

European Commission. (2019b). *Mission letter from Ursula von der Leyen to Maragritis Schinas*. Retrieved November 11, 2019 from https://ec.europa.eu/commission/sites/beta-political/files/mission-letter-margaritis-schinas-2019_en.pdf

European Parliament. (2019). *2019 European election results*. Retrieved December 6, 2019 from https://europarl.europa.eu/election-results-2019/en

Eurostat. (2019). *Migration and migrant population statistics*. Retrieved December 6, 2019 from https://ec.europa.eu/eurostat/statistics-explained/index.php?title=Migration_and_migrant_population_statistics/es#Poblaci.C3.B3n_migrante:_en_la_UE_viv.C3.ADan_22.2C3.C2.A0millones_de_ciudadanos_de_terceros_pa.C3.ADses_a_fecha_de_1_de_enero_de_2018

Fernández-Enguita M. (2017). *Menos escuela y más aula. La innovación en la perspectiva de un cambio de época*. Madrid: Morata.

Fernández de Liria C. (2016). *En defensa del populismo*. Madrid: Catarata.

Fontana J. (2017). *El siglo de la revolución: Una historia del mundo desde 1914*. Barcelona: Crítica.

Frey C.B., Berger Th., Chen Ch. (2016). Political machinery: Did robots swing the 2016 US presidential election. *Oxford Review of Economics Policy*, *34*(3), 2018, 418–442.

Funke M., Schularick M., Trebesch Ch. (2015). The political aftermath of financial crises: Going to extremes. *VOX CEPR Policy Portal*. Retrieve November 3, 2019, from https://voxeu.org/article/political-aftermath-financial-crises-going-extremes

Fukuyama F. (2018). *Identity: The demand for dignity and the politics of resentment*. New York: Farrar, Straus and Giroux.

Gallup. (2019). Confidence in institutions. Retrieved December 6, 2019 from https://news.gallup.com/poll/1597/confidence-institutions.aspx

Gastil J., Wright E.O. (Eds.) (2019). *Legislature by lot. Transformative designs for deliberative governance*. London: Verso.

Geiselberger H. (Ed.) (2017). *The great regression*. Cambridge: Polity.

Gerber A., Huber G., Biggers D. (2017). Self-interest, beliefs, and policy opinions: Understanding how economic beliefs affect immigration policy preferences. *Political Research Quaterly*, *70*(1), 155–171.

Gil-Calvo E. (2018). *Comunicación política*. Madrid: Catarata.

Halikiopoulou D., Vasilopoulou S. (2015). *The golden dawn's 'Nationalist Solution': Explaining the rise of the far right in Greece*. New York: Palgrave Mcmillan.

Held D. (1996). *Models of democracy*. London: Polity.

Huntington S. (1996). *The clash of civilizations*. New York: Simon & Schuster.

Iglesias A., Barbeito R. (2016). Does e-participation influence and improve political decision making processes? Evidence from a local government", *Lex-Localis – Journal of Local Self-Government*, *14*(4), 873–891.

Iglesias A., Barbeito R.L. (2014). Es posible más y mejor democracia? Democracia como empoderamiento político del ciudadano. *Barataria. Revista Castellano-Manchega de Ciencias Sociales*, *2014*(18), 215–242.

International Organization for Migrations. (2018). *Missing Migrants Project*. Global Migration Data Analysis Centre. Retrieved December 6, 2019 from https://gmdac.iom.int/missing-migrants-project

Ipsos. (2019). *Trust. The facts*. Retrieved December 6, 2019, from https://thinks.ipsos-mori.com/trust-the-facts/

Iversen T., Soskice D. (2019). *Democracy and prosperity: Reinventing capitalism through a turbulent century*. Princeton: Princeton University Press.

Judis J. (2016). *The Populist explosion. How the Great Recession transformed American and European politics*. New York: Columbia Global Report.

Judis J. (2018). *The Nationalist revival. Trade, immigration, and the revolt against globalization*. New York: Columbia Global Report.

Kirby P. (2005). *Vulnerability and violence: The impact of globalization.* London: Pluto.

Kriesi H., Grande E., Lachat R., Dolezal M., Bornschier S., Frey Th. (2006). Globalization and the transformation of the national political space: Six European countries compared. *European Journal of Political Research*, *45*, 921–956. Retrieved December 5, 2019, from doi:10.1111/j.1475-6765.2006.00644.x.

Kuttner R. (2018). *Can democracy survive global capitalism?* London: Norton.

Laclau E. (2007). *On populist reason*. London: Verso.

Lancaster C.M. (2019). Not so radical after all: Ideological diversity among radical right supporters and its implications. *Political Studies*, *64* (online first). doi:10.1177%2F0032321719870468.

Laval Ch., Dardot P. (2009). *La nouvelle raison du monde.* Paris: La Découverte.

Levitsky S., Ziblatt D. (2018). *How democracies die*. New York: Crown/ Archetype.

Mair P. (2013). *Ruling the void: The hollowing of Western democracy.* London: Verso.

Manin B. (1997). *The principles of representative government*. Cambridge: Cambridge University Press.

Mason P. (2013). *Why it's still kicking off everywhere: The new global revolutions.* London: Verso.

Meguid B. (2008). *Party competition between unequals. Strategies and electoral fortunes in Western Europe*. Cambridge: Cambridge University Press.

Melin C., Enarsson A.Th. (2018). The labour market basis for populism, *Social Europe* (online). https://www.socialeurope.eu/the-labour-market-basis-for-populism

Messing V., Ságvári B. (2019). *Still divided but more open: Mapping European attitudes towards migration before and after the migration crisis*. Budapest: Friedrich-Ebert-Stiftung.

Migrations Data Portal. (2019). *A global perspective*. Retrieved December 6, 2019 from https://migrationdataportal.org/es?i=stock_abs_&t=2019

Milanovic B. (2019). *Capitalism, alone. The future of the system that rules the world.* Cambridge: Harvard University Press.

Mishra P. (2017). *Age of anger: A history of the present.* London: Penguin.

Moreno L., Jiménez R. (2018). *Democracias robotizadas. Escenarios futuros en Estados Unidos y la Unión Europea.* Madrid: Catarata.

Mouffe Ch. (2019). *For a left-populism.* London: Verso.

Mounk Y. (2018). *The people vs. democracy: Why our freedom is in danger and how to save it.* Cambridge: Harvard University Press.

Mudde C. (2019). *The far right today.* London: Polity.

Mudde C., Rovira C. (2017). *Populism. A very short introduction.* Oxford: Oxford University Press.

Norris P. (2011). *Democratic deficit: Critical citizens revisited.* Cambridge: Cambridge University Press.

Norris P. (2015) *Why election fail?* Cambridge: Cambridge University Press.

Norris P., Inglehart R. (2019). *Cultural backlash. Trump, Brexit and authoritarian populism.* New York: Cambridge University Press.

OCDE. (2019). *Government at a glance 2019.* Paris: OECD Publishing. doi:10.1787/8ccf5c38-en.

Oesch D. (2008). Explaining workers 'support for right-wing populist parties in Western Europe: Evidence from Austria, Belgium, France, Norway and Switzerland. *International Political Science Review, 29*(3), 349–373.

O'Neil C. (2016). *Weapons of math destruction: How big data increases inequality and threatens democracy.* New York: Random House.

Ortiz I., Burke S., Berrada M., Cortés H. (2013). *World protest 2006–2013.* New York: Friedrich Ebert Stiftung. Retrieved December 5, 2019 from http://policydialogue.org/files/publications/papers/World_Protests_2006-2013-Complete_and_Final_4282014.pdf

Pastor L., Veronesi P. (2016). A rational backlash against globalisation. *VOX CEPR Policy Portal.* Retrieved December 5, 2019 from https://voxeu.org/article/rational-backlash-against-globalisation

Pastorella G. (4, 2016). Technocratic governments in Europe: Getting the critique right. Retrieved December 6, 2019 from http://eprints.lse.ac.uk/64023/7/Technocratic%20governments_2015.pdf

Pellizzetti P. (2019). *El fracaso de la indignación: Del malestar al conflicto.* Madrid: Alianza.

Pharr S.J., Putnam R. (Eds.). (2000). *Disaffected democracies: What's troubling the Trilateral countries?* Princeton: Princeton University Press.

Poguntke Th., Webb P. (Eds.). (2005). *The presidentialization of politics. A comparative study of modern democracies*. Oxford: Oxford University Press.

Posner R. (2011). *The crisis of capitalist democracy*. Cambridge: Harvard University Press.

Raghuram R. (2019). *The third pillar: How markets and the state leave the community behind*. Noida Uttar Pradesh: HarperCollins India.

Rodrik D. (2017). Economics of the populist backlash, *VOX CEPR Policy Portal* (online). Retrieved December 5, 2019 from https://voxeu.org/article/economics-populist-backlash

Salmon Ch. (2010). *Storytelling: Bewitching the modern mind*. London: Verso.

Sartori G. (1997). *Homo videns. Televisione e post-pensiero*. Roma-Bari: Laterza.

Sartori G. (2000). *Pluralismo, multiculturalismo e estranei. Saggio sulla società multietnica*. Segrate (Milano): Rizzoli.

Sartori G. (2007). *¿Qué es la democracia?* Barcelona: Taurus.

Schumpeter J. (2015). *Capitalism, socialism and democracy*. London: Routledge.

Sennett R. (2006). *The culture of the new capitalism*. New Haven: Yale University Press.

Sides J., Tesler M., Vavreck L. (2018). *Identity crisis: The 2016 presidential campaign and the battle for the meaning of America*. Princeton: Princeton University Press.

Sintomer Y. (2019). From deliberative to radical democracy: Sortition and politics in the twenty-first century. In J. Gastil & E.O. Wright (Eds.), *Legislature by lot. Transformative designs for deliberative governance* (pp. 47–73). London: Verso.

Skinner G. (2019). Is trust in crisis, or is it just complicated? *Ipsos Mori Thinks*. Retrieved December 6, 2019 from https://thinks.ipsos-mori.com/introduction-3/

Stephens-Davidowitz S. (2017). *Everybody lies: Big data, new data, and what the internet reveals about who we really are*. New York: Harper Collins.

Stiglitz J. (2019). *People power and profits. Progressive capitalism for an age of discontent*. London: Penguin.

Streeck W. (2016). *How will capitalism end? Essays on a failing system*. London: Verso.

Taguieff P. (2004). *Le retour du populisme*. Paris: Universalis.

Thussu D. (2007). *News as entertainment: The rise of global infotainment*. London: Sage.

Tilly Ch. (2007). *Democracy*. Cambridge: Cambridge University Press.

Timbro (2019). *Timbro Authoritarian Populism Index (TAP)*. Retrieved December 6, 2019 from https://populismindex.com/report/

Todd E. (2002). *El Destino de los inmigrantes. Asimilación y segregación en las democracias occidentales*. Barcelona: Tusquets.

Todd E. (2010). *Después de la democracia*. Madrid: Akal.

Todd E. (2015). *Who is Charlie? Xenophobia and the new middle class*. London: Polity.

Todorov T. (2010). *The fear of barbarians: Beyond the clash of civilizations*. Chicago: University of Chicago Press.

Tolchin S. (1996). *The angry american. How voter rage is changing the nation*. Oxford: Westview Press.

United Nations. (2016). *New York Declaration*. Retrieved November 11, 2019, from https://refugeesmigrants.un.org/declaration

Wallerstein I. (2009). *El futuro de la civilización capitalista*. Madrid: Icaria.

Wallerstein I., Collins R., Mann M., Derluguian B., Calhoun C. (2013). *Does capitalism have a future?* Oxford: Oxford University Press.

Weber M. (2019). *Economy and society: A new translation*. Cambridge: Harvard University Press.

Winder R. (2013). *Bloody foreigners: The story of immigration to Britain*. London: Abacus.

Zizeck S. (2016). *Refugees terror and other troubles with the neighbours*. New York: Random House.

Lucia Corso

Chapter Four Migration and Philosophy of Law

Abstract: After discussing the main arguments for open borders and closed borders, the chapter argues in favor of the three following ideas: a) that there is a presumption in favor of the right of human beings to move freely around the globe both within and outside national borders; b) that any regulation aimed at limiting such a right shall be grounded on sound reasons and therefore there is not an unrestricted right of states to denying entry; and c) that among the sound reasons, a special consideration shall be given to the interest of the hosting country population not to have their social model, acquired as a result of a collective responsibility and common history, threatened by the massive arrival of newcomers.

1 Introduction

Migration raises several issues to be addressed by the philosopher of law. Whether there is a right to freely move around the globe, whether settled populations have the right to exclude newcomers, whether migrants' rights can be trumped by policies' considerations, whether governments may prohibit their citizens to expatriate are all questions which cannot be simply left to lawyers and politicians. Ronald Dworkin once argued that 'studying our most heated political controversies at a more philosophical level [can] help to begin a process that might later reinvigorate the argumentative dimension of our politics'(Dworkin 2006, 8).

Immigration may be approached by three angles depending on the perspective we assume: Are we looking at the interests of the migrants, at the interests of the people of the host country (Waldron 2017), or at the interest of the people of the country which has been left? (Collier 2013). The chapter will address all three points of view.

I will start with the migrants' perspective and list a set of arguments for open borders. Then I discuss the interests of the host population and the theories making a case for closed borders. The fourth paragraph will briefly review possible arguments in the interest of the population left at home and the related normative claims. In the end, a normative proposal will be made, concerning not so much the content of immigration policies, but mostly the minimum requirements that any regulation of borders shall meet.

My aim is to argue in favor of the three following ideas: a) that there is a presumption in favor of the right of human beings to move freely around the globe both within and outside national borders; b) that any regulation aimed at limiting such a right shall be grounded on sound reasons and therefore there is not a unrestricted right of states to denying entry; and c) that among the sound reasons, a special consideration shall be given to the interest of the hosting country population not to have their social model, acquired as a result of a collective responsibility and common history, threatened by the massive arrival of newcomers. My arguments will be developed based on a main assumption: that migration does not concern few individuals but has become a mass phenomenon.

The chapter will not touch on some common topics. I leave out discussions concerning asylum rights and humanitarian protections, because I believe that, at least at a normative (although often formal) level, human rights provisions already compel governments around the globe to respect some principles such as the right to expatriate,[1] the right to seeking asylum from persecution[2] and to being offered protection for humanitarian reasons,[3] the right to a nationality,[4] and the right to be temporarily hosted in another country. Similarly, I will not consider economic arguments, which are mainly based on empirical data and are only indirectly related to moral considerations.

I can anticipate my conclusion. Immigration policies cannot be laid down at will, at full discretion. Governments not solely shall comply with human rights and international provisions (usually internalized by domestic laws), but shall as well fulfill the additional requirement to justify policies of closed borders with compelling normative arguments and considerations based on empirical accuracy.

People have a right to freely move around the globe. An issue arises solely because of the width of migration's fluxes. Where no issues of massive migration arise probably discussion on immigrants' rights would lead to different conclusions.

1 See, for example, Article 13 of the Universal Declaration of Human Rights (hereinafter 'UDHR'); Article 1, 2 of the Additional Protocol of the European Convention on Human Rights, hereinafter 'ECHR').

2 Article 14 of UDHR; Geneva Convention 1951.

3 Article 10, 3 of the Italian Constitution; Art. 5, 6 Legislative Decree n. 286/2998; see also decision n. 29460/2019 of the Italian Court of Cassation.

4 Article 15 of UDHR.

2 The Interest of the Migrants

Humans have been moving from one place to another from the remote past to the present (McNeill and Adams 1978). There is a widespread opinion among a great variety of theorists that the roving instinct is intrinsic to human nature and that it includes the need to search for food, pasture, and resources; the desire to travel and explore; but also to conquer and possess (Harari 2015; Castles and Miller 2009).

Humans move for a variety of reasons: because they love to move, in search of adventure, in pursuit of education or experience unavailable at home, or to make an adequate life into a better life (Macklin 2009, 4). However, most of the people migrate 'because of the wear and tear of anxiety' (Martel 2001, 87), 'because of the impression that the future is blocked up, that they might do all right but not their children. Because of the feeling that nothing will change, that happiness and prosperity are possible only somewhere else' (*Ibidem,* 87–88).

The interests of the migrants may therefore vary: people migrate to escape persecution and political oppression, to provide a decent life for family left behind, to make possible a decent life for their children and for them, or simply to improve life conditions and explore the globe. Once assessed that humans have qualified interests in moving from one place to another, could it be inferred that the migration drives ground a legitimate claim to be accepted into by any country?

2.1 The Right to Migrate as an Expression of the Right to Movement: Libertarianism

A first answer is given by the libertarian theory, whereby the right to migrate is simply an expression of the universally acknowledged right to move and travel. Thomas Jefferson situated the issue of immigration within an individual rights context, writing of the 'right which nature has given to all men of departing from the country in which chance, not choice has placed them' (Benhabib 2004, 136). More recently, Joseph Carens has argued that state's exclusive immigration policy is doubly disrespectful of individual rights, because it interferes with both an outsider's freedom of movement and an insider's property right to unilaterally invite foreigners onto her land (Carens 1987, 253).

According to this view, immigrants' rights are the natural extension of the principle of free movement. Within national borders, people cannot be prohibited to move their residency from one neighborhood to another, from towns to rural areas and vice versa. Internal passports, excessively burdensome bureaucratic requirements to change residency, and even forced relocation, although once widely in place in a variety of countries of the globe (including the European countries under the Soviet influence), are today, at least in Europe, a memory of the past. Similarly, as a result of the Schengen Treaty, the freedom of movement and settlement within the territory of the European Union (EU) can be greeted as a sign of progress in civilization. Following this line of reasoning, rules impinging on the freedom of movement are the result of an arbitrary conventional power, most often lacking any sound justification. State borders have been themselves artificially established in recent times. For libertarians, there is nothing natural in closing borders; on the contrary, migration's restrictions interfere with a natural *nomadic* inclination of human beings (Waldron 2015).

The libertarian argument is reinforced by the widely accepted right to expatriate. The idea of emigrants as defectors, deserving to being punished just on the basis of their attempt to leave their country (the images of DDR citizens killed while trying to climb over the Berlin Wall do not need to be commented), cannot be easily sustained. Thus, if individuals have the right to leave their country, a specular duty of other countries to accept them within their borders shall be acknowledged.

According to the libertarian defense of immigrants' rights, the motives which drive migration are not relevant for determining the appropriate policy to be put in place. Any distinction between asylum seekers and economic migrants is overcome by the general argument that any restriction to the right to entry is per se prima facie illegitimate and a violation of the fundamental right to move around the globe.

2.2 Egalitarianism

A different strategy to make a case for open borders is less about liberty than about some version of equality. This argument is based on the opinion that the accident of birth into citizenship of a prosperous, functioning, democratic state is a morally arbitrary event that confers enormous and undeserved advantages (Macklin 2009, 4). The normative claim for giving entry to immigrants is based on the necessity to remedy the 'birthright lottery' (Shachar 2009). As Joseph Carens puts it, 'Citizenship in Western liberal democracies is the modern equivalent to feudal privilege—an inherited status that greatly enhances one's life chances. Like feudal birthrights privileges, restrictive citizenship is hard to justify when one thinks about it closely' (Carens 1987, 252).

In other words, egalitarians regard open borders as a proper response to the enormous economic inequalities that currently exist between countries.

According to this view, reasons that drive migrants are of outmost importance for justifying their acceptance within the host community. Since immigration is seen as a way to deal with global unequal distribution, egalitarians can admit the possibility that wealthy immigrants not be granted entrance in the arrival country.

Michael Walzer is one of the strongest opponents of this view. The author claims that distributive justice shall be limited to the distribution within a political community, arguing that it would be impossible to conceive of global distribution (Walzer 1983, 31–63). Walzer's argument is shared by a great variety of authors (Trujillo 2007; Miller 2007), who from different points of view deny that global justice includes a generalized duty to redistribute scarce resources around the world population.

2.3 Civility and Equal Moral Value: Soft Cosmopolitanism

A third argument in favor of open borders can be traced back to the German philosopher Immanuel Kant. Kant argued in favor of a general right of 'an alien not to be treated as an enemy upon his arrival in another country' (Kant 1983, 118) and addressed the necessity for establishing the universal conditions of hospitality. Kant did not acknowledge a general right to reside permanently (or for a long period of time) in another country and limited his Articles for a perpetual peace to the right to *visit.* However, Kant did suggest that the limited nature of the globe compelling proximity creates the conditions for a moral community.

A general duty to respect the guest upon his arrival seems to be rooted into a long-standing tradition, especially when the stranger finds himself under difficult conditions. Giving hospitality before even acquiring information of the stranger, Homer seems to suggest, is the strongest form of civility. The Phaeacians provide Odysseys with food, entertainment, and lodging, before knowing his name. Their generous welcoming is contrasted with the Cyclops' incivility, exemplified by his aggressive request of his Greek visitors' identities, upon their landing: 'Strangers!' thundered the Cyclops, 'now, who are you? Where did you sail from?'

The duty to respect the stranger arises from the general principle of not doing to others what you would not want to be done to yourself and therefore is related to the core moral insight that all human beings, whether they are compatriots or foreigners, are equally deserving of moral consideration. This is why the bond between the host and the foreign guest is strengthened where the host had himself experienced the sorrow of being forced to leave his country. The *Bible* warns Israel 'not to oppress a foreign resident, for you yourselves were foreigners in the land of Egypt' (Exodus, 23: 9) and even commands to 'treat the foreigner living among you as native born and love him as yourself, for you were foreigners in the land of Egypt' (Leviticus, 19:34). Similarly, the Latin poet Virgil explains Dido's generous hospitality of the Trojan exiles with the circumstance that Dido herself had escaped tyranny in her own country and was forced to settle somewhere else. The poet even suggests that the glorious Roman civilization had its roots on the audacity of a Trojan refugee, Aeneas, and on the generosity of the hosting Italian shores.

2.4 Migrants' Perspective Is Where to Start from

Migrants' interests shall be taken seriously. Even assuming that some arguments for closed borders can be made, the interests of migrants are the starting point of any discussion on immigration policies. The classification of migrants on the basis of the reasons they had decided to migrate (economic, political, personal, and so forth) is a further evidence of the salience of migrants' interests in assessing immigration-appropriate policies.

The thousand years old tendency of humans in moving around the globe grounds a, prima facie, right to be accepted into a foreign country. The globe's limited nature creates the condition for a moral community (Flikshuh 2000, 179) where the land is not fully owned by any people but it is given in custody to all human beings (Waldron 2015) and thus has to be shared.

Although immigrants' claims may, under certain circumstances, be trumped by domestic policy's considerations, governments do not have a moral unrestricted right to deny entry to aliens within their own borders. Migration rules shall be supported by reasonable arguments which can justify the defeasibility of the general right to move from one place to another. The interests of the host population are where to start with to argue the case for restrictions upon immigrants' entry's rights.

3 The Interest of the People of the Hosting Country

What interest of the host population may justify such restrictions?

Is it the interest of a given group of people not to have newcomers among them or new neighbors with whom to share scarce resources? Is it the interest of the political community, intended as an entity, to preserve its own identity? Or is it the interest of the state – as the institutional highest expression of a set of people – to protect its own borders and its main functions, including that of providing its citizens with basic needs and services?

3.1 Protecting State Borders as the Quintessential Character of the State

Michael Walzer has argued that the very concept of state border implies the possibility of regulation of the borders on the part of the state. More in particular, Walzer alleges that a country's right to close its borders is merely one component of a state's more general right to political self-determination (Walzer 1983; Pevnick 2011). Walzer replicates the very common opinion that state sovereignty implies the right to decide whether to accept any immigrants at all, as well as the right to decide on the terms of admission (Sidwick 2012).

This argument may be associated to two related claims. The first rests on the link between self-determination and freedom of association. A legitimate state's right to freedom of association entitles it to choose whether or not to admit any given immigrants (Wellman 2008). According to this line of argument, then, there is nothing mysterious or complicated about a country's right to screen applicants for admission: it is merely a standard component of a state's more general right to self-determination (Wellman 2019). The second claim implies a link between self-determination and the obligation of the state to *protect* the rights of only those within their territory. Under this second claim, state borders define the limits of distributive justice among a given political community.

3.2 Welfare State, Limited Public Resources, and Trust Among Citizens

Another set of arguments for closed borders focus on the distribution of state benefits like welfare payments and health insurance. The basic idea is that open borders may allow masses of poor people from around the world to flock to countries providing strong health and welfare benefits to take advantage of their provisions and likely disrupt the welfare system.

Such an argument may take a more sophisticated form, as that introduced by David Miller (2016). Miller claims that redistributive welfare states rely upon trust among citizens that each will behave fairly under the terms of the scheme, paying taxes honestly and not drawing benefits to which they are not entitled. Miller points out, however, that there is evidence that as societies become more diverse, levels of trust tend to decline. The consequence is that open borders may have a negative impact on welfare states and even threaten their survival (*Ibidem*, 9). On the contrary, welfare states require that the political community shares a distinct national character, traditions, and so forth. Miller notes that national identities play a valuable role by providing reassurance that the national community of which one now forms part is solidly based in history, and that it embodies a real continuity between generations. He adds that national identity performs a moralizing role, by holding up before us the virtues of our ancestors and encouraging us to live up to them (2008).

The argument of scarce state resources, however, loses force where the host country decides not to grant welfare benefits to immigrants upon entry and condition the access to basic goods and services, such as health services, public housing or universal income, to a certain length of stay (typically five years, under EU provisions).

3.3 Cultural Identity

One of the most common arguments against open borders is grounded on the necessity to preserve a certain cultural homogeneity in the host country. Such an argument can take different forms, depending on the *thickness* attached to the concept of cultural homogeneity. National identity can be identified with ethnic, religious, and cultural uniformity and therefore with a form of *ethnic nationalism*. Ethnic nationalism is used to justify denial of immigrants' entry with the risk of contamination. The politics carried out by president Viktor Orbàn in Hungary and by the leader of Law and Justice party, Jarosław Aleksander Kaczyński, in Poland are examples of a contemporary version of ethnic nationalism, where ethnicity and religious uniformity are used as grounds to reject even relocation of asylum seekers. For ethnic nationalists the protection of national borders is not solely a right but also a duty of the states and a political responsibility to preserve the ethnic homogeneity of their own population. On this basis, razor wire fencing, water cannons, and paramilitary groups are presented as appropriate measures to contrast immigration.

National identity, however, can be attached a very different meaning. For example, David Miller and Sundas Ali argue in favor of what they define as liberal nationalism where 'national identities can escape from their ethnic origins, and in the process become more accessible to minority groups, especially immigrant groups who do not initially share in the culture of their host community' (Miller and Ali 2014, 239). On the other hand, liberal nationalists believe that it is not sufficient for citizens merely to share an identity as citizens, an identity focused entirely on the political institutions and constitution of the state. So, the authors argue, people trying to belong to the same nation have to perform a balancing act: they must try to foster identities that are 'thin' enough to avoid being ethnically exclusive, but 'thick' enough to bind people together and motivate then to support social justice (*Ibidem*, 239).

Miller and Ali's central claim is social justice not nationalism per se. It is related to the contention that in culturally diverse, market-driven societies, people will only be willing to support socially just institutions and policies – particularly those that together make up the welfare state – if they share a common identity with those who are likely to be net beneficiaries. However, liberal nationalism can work as an independent argument to justify protection of borders.

3.4 Social Model of Advanced Democracies

The argument of the social model achieved by the host country is a thinner version of Miller and Ali's case for liberal nationalism. Paul Collier endorses such an approach. With 'social model' that characterizes any stable community, Collier means its institutions, norms, and expectations, and in general a way of interacting – a way in which one person's getting on or one family's getting on relates to thousands or millions of others' getting on in the same society (Collier 2013, 33). Collier adds that a good social model conductive to security and prosperity is a long-term achievement and it is social capital built over centuries. Although Collier concedes that outsiders may not pose a security threat (they do not come as marauders), he argues that they often come from communities with dysfunctional social models. Following this reasoning, regulation of borders is justified to the extent that immigrants come in a significant number and where they carry with themselves social models (e.g., polygamy, unequal men-women relationships, and acceptance of honor killings) which may jeopardize the way of living acquired by the host country population.

4 The Interest of the People Left Behind

The impact that emigration has on the people of the country which has been left is uncertain. Emigration of educated people does not necessarily deplete the stock of the educated. On the contrary, at moderate levels, emigration can lead to a brain gain (Collier 2013, 252). Similarly, remittances benefit those left behind. However, at some point the relationships between the rate of migration change from being positive to negative. Since governments of the countries of origin do not control either the emigration rate or the rate of return, they are dependent upon controls set by the government of the host countries (*Ibidem*, 253).

5 Conclusion

Migration is one of the most dramatic phenomena of our times. If migration did not involve enormous masses of people, immigration could be simply solved by resorting to two specular rights: the right to expatriate and the right to freely move around the globe. Regulation of state borders amounting to a generalized denial of entry to immigrants would hardly pass the test of reasonableness which the liberal tradition of rights demands to ground the legitimacy of state power.

However, immigrants arrive at a fast rate and in conspicuous groups. While arguments based on the need to preserve ethnic and cultural homogeneity in the host population seem inappropriate when we are dealing with modern and plural democratic societies, the interest of the host country in preserving an achieved social model may ground the legitimacy of some restrictions on immigration.

Such a conclusion, however, shall be further tailored down by some additional considerations. First, governments cannot violate fundamental rights universally acknowledged by international treaties. No policy consideration may justify the refoulement of asylum seekers or the refusal to accept relocation of individuals entitled some kind of humanitarian protection. Second, the interest taken into account to justify restriction on entry cannot be forgotten. So, when no real threat is posed to the social model of the hosting population – for example, because of the limited number of individuals seeking to be admitted, or the substantial similarity between the social model of the immigrants and that of the host population – then, restrictions of entry may lose their force and legitimacy. Third, since one of the main reason of borders' regulation is to preserve the social model of the host country, immigrants accepted in the country shall have the opportunity to fully integrate.

References

Benhabib S. (2004). *The Rights of Others: Aliens, Residents, and Citizens.* Cambridge: Cambridge University Press.

Carens J. (1987). Aliens and citizens: The case for open borders. *Review of Politics*, 49: 251–273.

Castles S., de Haas H. and Miller M.J. (eds.) (2009) The Age of Migration International Population Movements in the Modern World. Fifth Edition, New York: Palgrave Macmillan.

Collier P. (2013). *Exodus. Immigration and Multiculturalism in the 21st Century.* Oxford: Oxford University Press.

Dworkin R. (2006). *Is Democracy Possible Here? Principles for a New Political Debate.* Princeton: Princeton University Press.

Flikshuh K. (2000). *Kant and Modern Political Philosophy.* Cambridge: Cambridge University Press.

Harari Y. N. (2015). *Sapiens. A Brief History of Humankind.* London: Random UK.

Kant I. [1795] (1983). To Perpetual Peace: A Philosophical Sketch. In: *Perpetual Peace and Other Essays* (Ted Humprey, transl.). Indianapolis: Hacket Publishing Company.

Macklin A. (2009). *A Theory About Theories of Migration, and a Comment About Michael Trebilcock's Theoly*. available at http://www.law.utoronto.ca/documents/conferences2/Trebilcock09 Macklin. pdf.

Martel Y. (2001). Life of Pi. New York: Penguin Random House.

McNeill W. and Adams R.S. (eds.) (1978) Human Migration: Patterns and Policies. Bloomington: Indiana University Press

Miller D. (2007). National Responsibility and Global Justice. Oxford: Oxford University Press.

Miller D. (2008). Immigrants, nations, and citizenship. *The Journal of Political Philosophy*, 16: 371–390.

Miller D. (2016). *Strangers in Our Midst: The Political Philosophy of Immigration*. Cambridge: Harvard University Press.

Miller D., Ali S. (2014). Testing the national identity argument. *European Political Science Review*, 6: 237–259.

Pevnick R. (2011). *Immigration, and the Constraints of Justice*. Cambridge: Cambridge University Press.

Shachar A. (2009). *The Birthright Lottery. Citizenship and Global Inequality*. Cambridge, MA: Harvard University Press.

Sidwick H. [1891] (2012). *The Elements of Politics*. Cambridge: Cambridge University Press.

Trujillo I. (2007). *Giustizia globale. Le nuove frontiere dell'eguaglianza*. Bologna: Il Mulino.

Waldron J. (2015). Immigration: A Lockean approach. *New York University Public Law and Legal Theory Working Papers*. 531. https://lsr.nellco.org/nyu_plltwp/531

Waldron J. (2017). The Philosophical Foundations of Immigration Law, Speech at the Library of Congress (Vth biannual lecture). 2017; at https://www.youtube.com/watch?v=pDnwQ-YIAoQ.

Walzer M. (1983). *Spheres of Justice. A Defense of Pluralism and Equality*. Oxford: Blackwell Publishers.

Wellman C. (2008). Immigration and freedom of association. *Ethics*, 119: 109–141.

Wellman C. (2019). Immigration. *The Stanford Encyclopedia of Philosophy*, at https://plato.stanford.edu/cgi-bin/encyclopedia/archinfo.cgi?entry=immigration

Fabio Aiello

Chapter Five Refugees and Asylum Seekers: An Assessment Survey

Abstract: In the last decade, thousands of migrants have reached European shores. Many countries affected by these flows have approved new laws to manage them and setting up efficient reception and social integration systems. The consistency of these flows has pushed many organizations of the Third Sector to get involved with the reception of migrants, refugees, and asylum seekers, having to face new problematic and multifaceted situations. This has led to an ever-increasing demand for skills and specializations, posed by operators regarding the skills needed to deal with these changes that redefine the skills of social workers. The analyses presented here are related to research on training needs (Training Needs Analysis – TNA) claimed by some operators employed in the reception system for refugees and asylum seekers, conducted within the PARIS project. The goal is to identify groups of homogeneous skills, by considering the operators' opinion.

1 Introduction

In the last decade, hundreds of thousands of refugees, asylum seekers, and migrants have put their lives at risk to reach European shores. The Internal Displacement Monitoring Centre states that what is happening in Europe is just the tip of an iceberg (IDMC, 2016) that results in a crisis (Dines et al., 2018; McMahon & Sigona, 2018). Indeed, according to the latest available data, over 65.6 million people worldwide are in need of protection and humanitarian assistance as a result of forced migration. They include refugees, internally displaced persons (IDPs), and asylum seekers.

A good number of countries affected by these migratory flows have approved new laws to contain and manage them while at the same time setting up efficient reception and social integration systems to deal with the phenomenon (Pasian & Toffanin, 2018). A need to pay particular attention to those professional figures and operators directly and concretely involved in the assistance system that is dedicated to refugees and asylum seekers has emerged. These professionals represent the core of any national reception, assistance, and social integration system. The consistency of incoming migration flows has pushed many organizations of the Third Sector, previously operating in other areas, to get involved with the reception of migrants, and having to face and solve new problematic and multifaceted situations, never faced before. This has led to an ever-increasing demand for skills and specializations, which in turn questions the evolutionary path to be followed by social science professions, the way to make use of previous and different professional experiences and what should be strengthened with specific training initiatives.

In this chapter, we deal with the demands posed by operators regarding the skills needed to deal with the changes that affect the European scenario, changes that redefine the skills of social workers (Reamer, 2000; Potocky-Tripodi, 2002), and demands that translate into educational opportunities. The analyses presented here are related to research on training needs (Training Needs Analysis – TNA, Leat & Lovell, 1997; Fleck, 2014; Davies & Isakjee, 2015) claimed by some operators employed in the reception system for refugees and asylum seekers, conducted within the PARIS project (Teaching Partnership Addressed to Refugees' Instances Strengthening, funded by Erasmus+, Programme – KEY ACTION 2, http://www.parisproject.eu/), which involves three European countries: Italy, Spain, and Romania.

The goal of this work is to identify groups of homogeneous skills, by considering the operators' opinion, that is, their perceptions, shortcomings, and training needs related to concrete experience gained from working in the field with refugees and asylum seekers. Given the objective and the nature of the data used here, the aim was pursued by Factor Analysis, using a matrix of polychoric correlations, instead of a Pearson's linear correlation.

The second section of this work contains a brief data summary of some of the relevant operators' information collected. The third section describes the factor analysis and, finally, the last section presents a number of concluding remarks.

2 The Data

The survey was carried out within the PARIS project and was preceded by an exploratory analysis, aimed at listening – by means of focus groups and interviews – to five groups of privileged witnesses: social workers, school teachers, psychologists, cultural mediators, mentors, and volunteers involved in refugee reception; refugees and/or asylum seekers; university teachers; community leaders and coordinators, service directors; and, finally, university students. The information collected was used to construct a multidimensional questionnaire to be administered to professionals working in the refugee reception sector.

In this section, the data will be described from three different perspectives. The first one is more general and offers a summary of the main characteristics of the operators to whom the questionnaire was administered (Fig. 5.1). The second one offers a summary of the degree of relevance attributed by the operators to the skills (Fig. 5.2). Finally, the third one concerns the investigation of the existence of relationships between some characteristics of the operators and the degree of relevance assigned by them to the skills. Only the noteworthy results are presented here (Fig. 5.3).

The questionnaire was administered online, from April to July 2017, in the three partner countries, reaching 413 professionals currently employed in the sector. In this work, we present the analysis and the results, for the data obtained from the Italian survey only (279 questionnaires).

The aim is to investigate the perceptions, shortcomings, and training needs related to the concrete experience of working in the field with refugees and asylum seekers, with respect to which respondents have a privileged and internal vision.

Before illustrating the analysis and the results, we present a brief description of the operators to which the questionnaire was administered, with respect to some relevant information on the respondents. As mentioned above, the data used here refer to the assessment made by 279 operators of the importance of a set of skills in their field. The operators' mean age was 36.8 ($sd = \pm 8.1$) years and included 202 women (36 ± 7.8 y.o.) and 77 men (38.8 ± 8.5 y.o.).

Figure 5.1 presents the distributions of the operators with respect to four variables, namely, grade level, professional role, education field, and seniority. As shown, for grade level, 81.7 % of the operators stated that they have at least a graduation, and only 1.5 % went no further than middle school. The main declared professional role is operational (47.7 %), followed by coordination (33 %). The education field mainly declared was Political and Social Sciences (37.6 %) followed by Psychological and Philosophical Sciences (26.9 %). Finally, most operators declared that they have a seniority of 1–3 years (35.1 %) (1 year and 9 months on average). It should be noted that the percentage of almost all other declared seniorities is identical (about 19 %).

As already mentioned, the core of this work is related to the operators' opinion about the relevance of each expertise/skill of a set of nine skills, in their working context: linguistics, legal, cultural, intercultural communication, mediation, cooperation, problem-solving, advocacy, and equal opportunity. Each operator assigned the relevance, using a single value from 1 (*not relevant at all*) to 7 (*absolutely relevant*), so that the higher the score the greater the relevance of the skill.

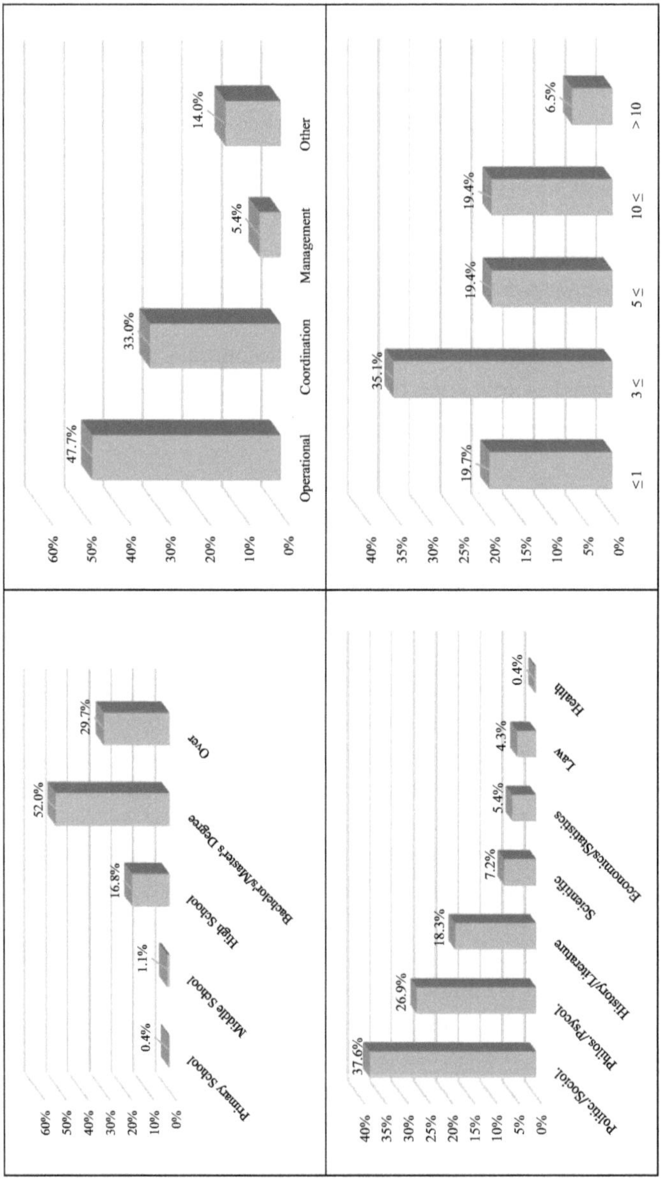

Fig. 5.1: From up to the bottom, from the left to the right: Operators' distributions by grade level, professional role, education field, and seniority

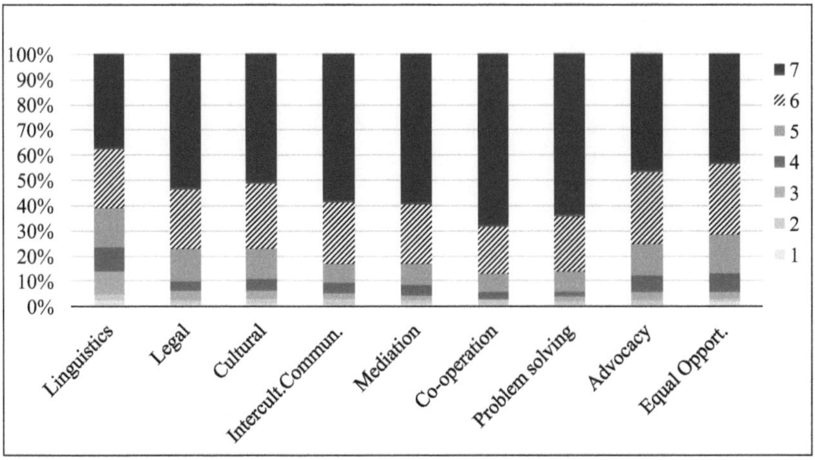

Fig. 5.2: Distributions of the degree of relevance assigned by the operators to the skills

Therefore, the data used here are ordinal (7-point Likert scale) and measure the relevance of a given competence in the operators' working context.

Figure 5.2 presents the distributions of the degrees of relevance assigned by the operators to the skills. The skills judged most relevant, for working in the field with refugees and asylum seekers and considering the percentages of the highest scores (6 and 7), are cooperation (19 % and 68.1 %), problem-solving (22.2 % and 64.2 %), and mediation (23.7 % and 59.5 %). On the contrary, using the same criterion, the skills judged less relevant are linguistics (23.3 % and 37.6 %), equal opportunities (27.9 % and 43.7 %), and advocacy (28.3 % and 46.9 %).

Finally, the possible relationships between operator characteristics, such as gender and education level, and the assigned degree of relevance were investigated, using the non-parametric X^2 Pearson's test to study the association. Due to the small number of responses collected ($n = 279$) and the high number of degrees of relevance attributable (from 1 to 7) to each skill, the response categories were reduced from 7 to 2, aggregating scores from 1 to 4 in a new "Not Relevant" category, and scores from 5 to 7 to the "Relevant" category. Among the characteristics of the operators, gender and education level were those that provided the most interesting and significant results. Table 5.1 shows the statistically significant relationships ($p < 0.05$) between gender and education level (column) and the nine skills (rows), represented by a tick. Clearly, males and females attribute the degree of relevance to skills, such as intercultural communication,

Skills	Sex	Education Level
Linguistics	-	-
Legal	-	✓
Cultural	-	✓
Intercultural Communication	✓	✓
Mediation	-	✓
Co-operation	✓	✓
Problem solving	✓	✓
Advocacy	-	-
Equal Opportunity	✓	✓

Tab. 5.1: Statistically significant ($p < 0.05$) associations

cooperation, problem-solving, and equal opportunities, differently. On the other hand, operators of different education levels assign the relevance to almost all skills, except for linguistics and advocacy, differently.

Figure 5.3 shows the conditional distributions of intercultural communication (1st column) and problem-solving (2nd column) by gender (1st row) and education level (2nd row). As evident, the two pairs of distributions are different with respect to both the gender and the education level. This means that, generally, the percentage of operators who consider a given competence relevant is higher among women than men and increases as the level of education increases.

3 Factor Analysis

This section is devoted to the data analysis that was carried out by means of Factor Analysis (FA), taking into account the ordinal nature of the answers (posed on a 7-point Likert scale) given by the operators to the items of the questionnaire, and assigning the degree of relevance of the skills. Starting from the overall set of skills, the aim of the FA was to allocate them to an appropriate number of groups (named factors) defined according to the strength of the relationships between the degrees of relevance of the skills included in them. As mentioned above, the relevance was measured by means of nine items posed on a Likert scale. There is a lot of debate about how to treat Likert scale data. Often, they are treated as if it were not really categorical but as they were on a continuum, and as if they were discrete normally distributed measurements about an underlying continuum. This allows the use of a Pearson's linear correlation matrix, in a FA framework. Actually, the data are technically ordered categories, that is, the categories do not really have quantitative distances (no unit of measurements). To use Likert data as is, yet providing information about the underlying continuum, the alternative

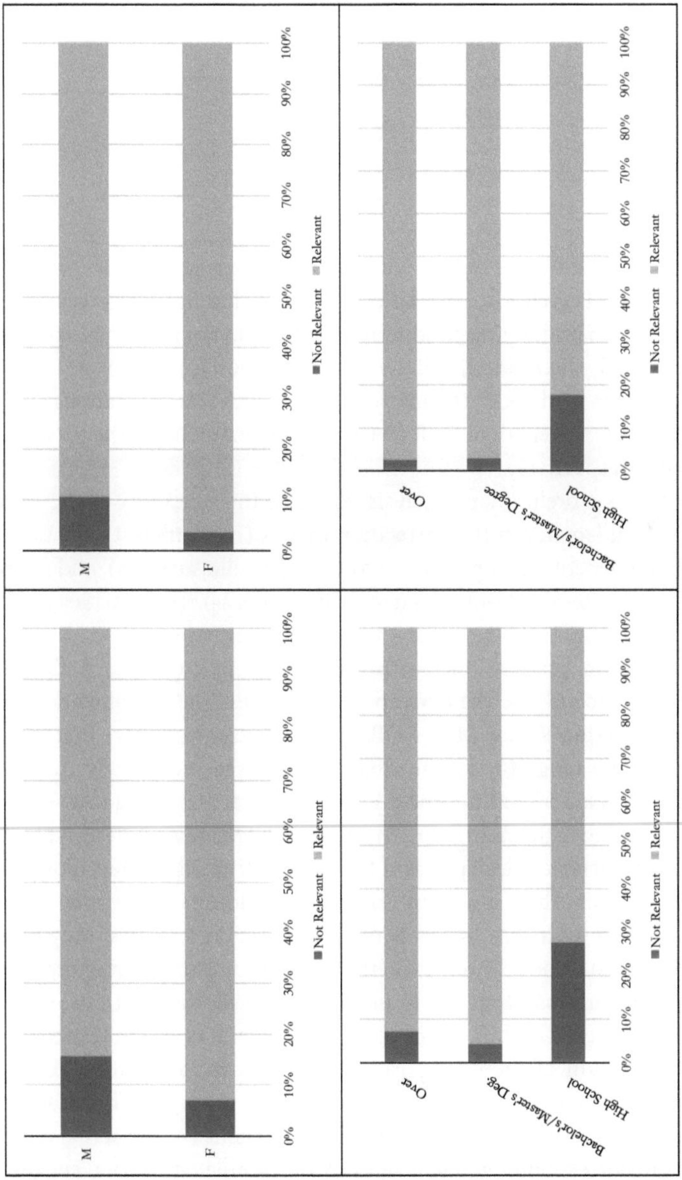

Fig. 5.3: Conditional distributions of intercultural communication (1st column) and problem-solving (2nd column) by sex (1st row) and education level (2nd row)

Statistics	*values*
KMO	0.91
Bartlett's test	$p < 0.0001$
N. of Factors	3
Cronbach's α	0.96
Guttaman's λ_6	0.97

Tab. 5.2: Statistics of preliminary analysis

is to base the FA on different type of correlations such as polychoric ones (Flora & Curran, 2004). Polychoric correlations assume that variables are ordered measurements of an underlying continuum and thus do not need to be truly continuous or normally distributed, and their interpretation is the same as Pearson's correlations. In this work, both the matrix of the Polychoric correlations and the FA (Field et al., 2013) were done in R (R Core Team 2019), using the *polycor* and *psych* packages, respectively.

The first step is a preliminary analysis, to assess the suitability of the dataset (KMO test), the adequacy of the correlation matrix (Bartlett's test), the number of factors (homogeneous groups) to be extracted (parallel analysis), and the reliability of the set of items (Cronbach's α and Guttman's λ_6). The statistics used for this step are shown in Tab. 5.2, where a summary is displayed.

The first column presents the statistics used to perform the preliminary analysis and the second one the corresponding values. The sampling adequacy was confirmed by the Kaiser-Meyer-Olkin (KMO) test (1st row) that can assume values in the range (0, 1); the closer to zero the more likely that FA is inappropriate. A value of 0.91 is almost superb. Bartlett's test (2nd row) of sphericity assesses whether the matrix of polychorich correlations is factorable, that is, whether each variable is independent from each other; its p value allows us to reject this hypothesis. There are many criteria for deciding on how many factors should be retained in an FA, but as is often the case in statistics, they mostly provide different solutions. In our case, the criteria suggested extracting one to three factors. The final solution was found by comparing the solutions provided by the different criteria, both in terms of number of factors and in terms of substantial interpretation of the configuration of the extracted factors. Here, the suitable number of factors (3rd row) was identified through parallel analysis, which suggests extracting the factors until the eigenvalues of the actual data are lower than the corresponding eigenvalues of the simulated factors, suggesting that three factors should be kept. In the last two rows, there are two indices of reliability, Cronbach's α and Guttman's λ_6 , which measure the quality of a questionnaire; the closer to one, the higher its capability to reproduce stable and consistent results in successive measurements and/or applications. Both the values are very good.

Given the adequacy of our data for FA, we can extract the factors by comparing two configurations: the first one with two factors and the second one with three factors. In any case, the set of factors will be ordered according to their ability to explain the total variability observed. The amount of explained variability could be used to choose between two alternative factor configurations. The later will be discussed further. The factors were extracted using the matrix of polychoric correlations, the "principal factor" as the factoring method (the maximum likelihood method gave the same results) and imposing an oblique rotation of the solution ("promax" and "oblimin" gave the same results). The choice to rotate (between orthogonal and oblique rotation) factors depends on whether there is a good theoretical reason to assume that the underlying factors must be related (oblique rotation) or independent (orthogonal rotation), and how the variables (i.e., the skills) cluster on the factors before rotation. Our FA was done using both types of rotation. Pedhazur and Schmelkin (1991) suggest that if an oblique rotation demonstrates a remarkable correlation between the extracted factors, then the oblique rotation solution should be chosen. In our case, the oblique rotation highlights a high correlation between the factors. Moreover, rotation of the factors improves their interpretability because it shows more clearly which variables relate to which factors.

Figure 5.4 displays the two compared configurations, with two and three factors. Moreover, both the skills are inside each factor as well as the coefficients of correlation between each couple of skills and each couple of factors.

All factors saturate their skills very well, for both the configurations, with factor lodging never below 0.7, very good values, given that $n > 200$ (Stevens, 2002, p. 293). Comparing the two configurations in Fig. 5.4, it is immediately observed that the skills of the first factor (PA1) of the two-factor configuration (on the left) are distributed between two different factors (PA1 and PA3) in the three-factor configuration (on the right), while the second factor (PA2) remains unchanged. Furthermore, it seems that the three-factor configuration increases internal coherence, especially for the second factor (PA3), since the correlations between its skills and the factor are higher than those with the first factor (PA1) of the two-factor configuration. In fact, the two factors (the 1st and 3rd) of the three-factor configuration have a higher average correlation with the skills than the first factor of the two-factor configuration (0.78 and 0.77 vs. 0.73, respectively). For this reason, we think that the three-factor configuration is more

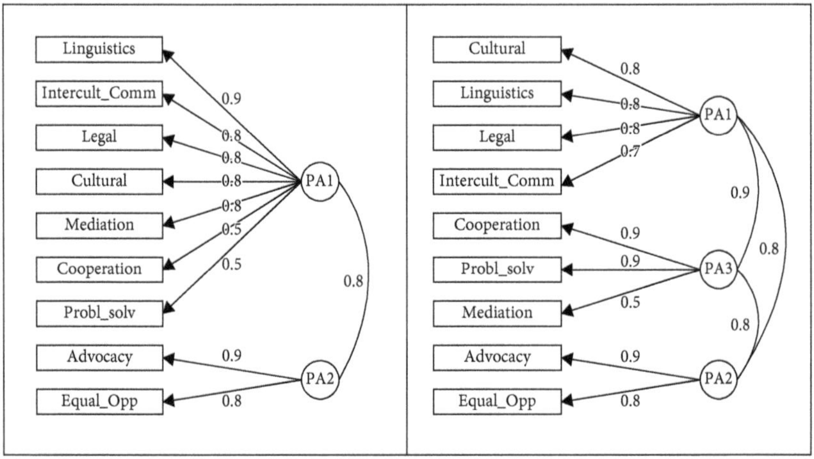

Fig. 5.4: Comparison between two configurations: two factors, on the left, and three factors, on the right

suitable than the two-factor one. The proportions of the variance explained (82 % vs. 78 %) and the BIC values (45.9 vs. 84.5) of the two configurations, always in favour of the three-factor configuration, further support our belief.

4 Conclusions

In the last decade, the flows of migrants towards the European shores, in general, and towards the Italian shores, more specifically, have increased almost regularly every year. Many of these migrants are refugees and asylum seekers. Many countries affected by these migratory flows have passed new laws to contain and manage the flows, and set up efficient reception, assistance, and social integration systems, to deal with this demographic phenomenon.

In this work, we considered the demand for skills as expressed by the operators in the reception sector who are active and privileged witnesses of the phenomenon. In fact, a need has been created to pay attention to those professional figures and operators directly and concretely involved in the assistance system and dedicated to refugees and asylum seekers. This need translates into a demand for theoretical skills required for working with ethnic groups and different cultures of migrants arriving at the reception centers, skills that are necessary for designing specific forms of accompaniment. To do this, we analyzed the answers given by 279 operators who assigned a degree of relevance to a set of previously tested skills, through focus groups and interviews. The skills related to the most requested educational (training) areas are: linguistics, legal-legislative, cultural, intercultural communication, mediation (and conflict resolution), cooperation, problem-solving, advocacy, and (gender) equal opportunity.

Firstly, it should be noted that all the competences in question were considered highly relevant. Among them, however, some were considered more relevant than others, namely, cooperation, problem-solving, and mediation. However, less relevance was attributed to language skills, equal opportunities, and advocacy.

Secondly, by investigating the existence of possible relationships between some characteristics of the operators and the degree of relevance assigned by them to the skills, it has emerged that operators of different gender and different education levels assessed the skills in different ways. For example, it was noted that the percentage of those who consider problem-solving and intercultural communication relevant is higher among women than among men, and that it increases as the level of education increases. Moreover, the education level also influences the relevance assigned to almost all skills, except for linguistics and advocacy.

Finally, starting from the overall set of skills, they were allocated to an appropriate number of groups by means of FA, according to the strength of the relationships between the degrees of relevance of the skills within each group.

A first step of the analysis was dedicated to the identification of the most suitable configuration to represent the data, both in terms of number of groups (factors) to be considered and in terms of group composition according to the skills included in them. Then, after considering the two possible alternative configurations, two-factor or three-factor, the second one was chosen, because it organizes the skills into groups that seem to be more consistent, both from a statistical and a substantial point of view. This configuration, in fact, distributes the skills previously included in a single factor (the first) to two distinct factors, whose internal coherence seems higher, considering the average correlations between the skills and their own factor. Therefore, the three-factor configuration produces groups of competences whose common features are more easily identifiable, from a substantial point of view. Moreover, it has a greater (if only slightly) explanatory capacity and better indexes of fit to our data.

In each factor, the skills are grouped according to the strength of the associations of relevance assigned to them. In other words, skills belonging to the same group are considered by operators to be relevant for carrying out their tasks, in a very similar way. The extracted factors (groups) are sorted according to the strength of the associations between the skills. Therefore, the first group includes the most closely associated skills, that is, cultural, linguistic, legal, and intercultural communication. The second group of skills includes cooperation, problem-solving, and mediation. The last one groups the skills whose association is weaker, that is, advocacy and equal opportunities, which are probably considered by operators to be less important than the previous ones, for carrying out their tasks.

Finally, regardless of any skill ranking with respect to the perception of their relevance in the opinion of specialized operators in the sector, the operators expressed a strong demand for training in view of improving their skills in the areas in question. This demand should be acknowledged and satisfied by the Higher Education sector, for example, universities.

References

Davies T., Isakjee A. (2015). Geography, Migration and Abandonment in the Calais Refugee Camp. *Political Geography, 49*, 93–95.

Dines N., Montagna N., Vacchelli E. (2018). Beyond Crisis Talk: Interrogating Migration and Crises in Europe. *Sociology, 52*(3), 439 – 447. DOI: 10.1177/0038038518767372.

Field A., Miles J., Field Z. (2013). *Discovering Statistics Using R*. Los Angeles, CA: Sage.

Fleck D. (2014). The Protection of the Environment in Armed Conflict: Legal Obligations in the Absence of Specific Rules. In *The Protection of the Environment in Armed Conflict: Legal Obligations in the Absence of Specific Rules* (pp. 45 – 57). Leiden, The Netherlands: Brill/Nijhoff.

Flora D.B., Curran P.J. (2004). An Empirical Evaluation of Alternative Methods of Estimation for Confirmatory Factor Analysis with Ordinal Data. *Psychological Methods, 9*(4), 466–491.

"Global Report on INTERNAL DISPACEMENT" (2016). Editor: Jeremy Lennard. Publisher: Norwegian Refugee Council/Internal Displacement Monitoring Centre (NRC/IDMC). Annual Reports https://www.internal-displacement.org/globalreport2016/

Leat M.J., Lovell M.J. (1997). Training Needs Analysis: Weaknesses in the Conventional Approach. *Journal of European Industrial Training, 21*(4), 143–153.

McMahon S., Sigona N. (2018). Navigating the Central Mediterranean in a Time of 'Crisis': Disentangling Migration Governance and Migrant Journeys. *Sociology, 52*(3), 497 – 514. DOI: 10.1177/0038038518762082.

Pasian P., Toffanin A.M. (2018). Richiedenti asilo e rifugiate nello SPRAR. *Mondi Migranti, 1*, 127 – 145.

Pedhazur E., Schmelkin L. (1991). *Measurement, Design and Analysis: An Integrated Approach*. Hillsdale, NJ: Erlbaum.

Potocky-Tripodi M. (2002). *Best Practices for Social Work with Refugees and Immigrants*. New York: Columbia University Press.

R Core Team. (2019). R: A language and environment for statistical computing. R Foundation for Statistical Computing, Vienna, Austria. https://www.R-project.org/.

Reamer FG. (2000). Social Work Practice with Immigrants and Refugees. Edited by Balgopal Pallassana R. Columbia University Press. DOI: 10.7312/balg10856.

Stevens J.P. (2002). *Applied Multivariate Statistics for the Social Sciences* (4th ed.). Hillsdale, NJ: Erlbaum.

Part Two Vulnerability and Human Rights

Liborialinda Ardizzone and Roberto Di Maria

Chapter Six Brief Reflections on "Vulnerability"

Abstract: This chapter introduces the concept of vulnerability, between human dignity and the principle of equality. Equality is a fundamental right of the person, and it is never "too much."

1 Introduction

The explosion, only apparently sudden, of the s.c. "migratory phenomenon" risks producing an altered and distorted representation of the same figure of the "migrant," as well as of the other subjects gravitating around the aforesaid phenomenon and its various social manifestations (i.e., the countries and the families of origin and their political and social conditions, the traffickers and criminal associations, the NGOs, etc.); in particular, public opinion has been diverted towards a (potentially) aggressive and, therefore, dangerous perception of the "migrant" – or better, of "migrants" – and so influencing the political choices regarding the management of flows (ordinary and extraordinary) of immigration[1].

It is precisely in the context of the migration phenomenon instead – as well as in the condition of each individual migrant – that it is indeed possible to identify the paradigm of the s.c. "vulnerability" according to the current juridical and social diction, concretely interfering with the effective protection of fundamental rights generally recognized by the modern social-democratic and pluralist State, in respect of a model that is also widely shared in Europe: in respect of the massive growth of such phenomenon, in fact, the condition of vulnerability emerges – just as strongly – in both the physical and legal subjectivity of the migrant, related to the different conditions that qualify him (i.e. refugee, asylum seeker, and irregular immigrant), besides as a subject on which different vulnerable conditions often converge and stratify: woman, sick, elderly (less often), and

1 Just think of the troubled procedure of discussion and approval of the legislative decrees 113/2018 and 53/2019 (s.c. "security decree" and "security decree-bis") as well as their equally troubled and problematic application (on this point, for example, see the recent Constitutional Court, sentence n. 194/2019).

the paradigmatic condition of minor, above all, "unaccompanied" (for a general overview of the topic and for a definition of "vulnerability" see: Casadei, 2012; Mackenzie, Rogers, & Dodds, 2014; Springhart & Thomas, 2017).

Paraphrasing a well-known nineteenth-century writing, there is a "ghost" floating through the European Union and – in particular – in the ganglia of the contemporary democracies: the "vulnerability" or, better, the ways for its protection (i.e., the protection of the s.c. "social fragility" or the "weak subjects")[2].

The "explosion" of rights – and of the related "Charters" – which has characterized the evolution of the modern State of pluralist democracy, especially in the last 20 years, has in fact highlighted the need to safeguard those who – for the most varied reasons – are not in a position to take advantage of these rights, in the ways and forms in which they are recognized and provided – as "performances" – by the public administrative and governmental apparatus.

In Italy, in particular, is the link-comparison between the Legislator and the judge that has been outlined and implemented a model of "dynamic" protection of rights – as expression of the responsibility, assumed by the republican order, to guarantee individual and social freedoms in respect of the principle of proportionality (articles 2 and 3 of the Constitution) – calibrating the form and content of the same rights on the specific living conditions in which the weak subjects pay. And yet, the aforesaid synthesis is the outcome of a "continuous dialectic" that cannot be "entirely absorbed within the juridical-jurisdictional circuit [. . .] unsuitable for permitting stable and systematic compositions"; if anything, they are the actual "processes of *political mediation*" that allow both the periodic redefinition of the notion of vulnerability and the deduction of the appropriate tools to ensure their "concrete" protection (Della Morte, 2016, pp. 1–8).

2 The Concept of "Vulnerability" Between Human Dignity and the Principle of Equality

As a "social subject" relating to other human beings, man is vulnerable due to the loss of a loved one, abuse, lack of care, and humiliation; as a "socio-political being," instead, he is vulnerable due to manipulation, oppression, violence, and abuse of rights (Mackenzie, Rogers, & Dodds, 2014); and it is in this perspective,

2 The paraphrase is taken from the well-known "Manifesto of the Communist Party", written by Karl Marx and Friedrich Engels between 1847 and 1848, published in London on 21 February 1848.

then, that the concept of "human dignity" comes into play, indeed always proclaimed in international declarations and constitutions.

This is how a vision of "vulnerability" emerges as a general human condition that materializes in society in different forms and that, however, must be universally opposed; so it is possible to speak of "universalism of vulnerability": phenomena such as pain, humiliation, and suffering, in fact, represent different ways of manifesting the vulnerability; and this is precisely the sense of this universalism: historically recognizable values and principles, in a given cultural context, can recur also in other contexts or in other cultures (Casadei, 2012, pp. 90–108).

Within this reflection, the issue of vulnerability is inextricably related to that of human dignity in the sense that "people have ensured the conditions so that their *life can be considered and felt as a life well-worth living* (as well as guaranteed as such) by eliminating forms of vulnerability and eliminating socially generated suffering, which erodes the bases of dignity, equal respect and mutual recognition" (Pastore, 2003, p. 44). It is, therefore, evident that, from a strictly normative point of view, "the (juridical) notion of *weak subject* is related to that of *equality*: a subject is (legally) weak as (juridically) not equal" (Di Maria, 2010, p. 99).

The condition of weakness is therefore strongly influenced by the principle of equality: a subject is weak to the extent that he does not take advantage of any rights or of the same rights as all the other subjects of the same socio-juridical order, so that it is possible to distinguish between "natural" or "de facto" conditions of weakness (i.e., women, minors, the elderly, etc.) and "positive" conditions of weakness regulated, instead, within the legal system (i.e., linguistic minorities or religious, workers, prisoners, bankruptcy, etc.); as well as between weakness "stricto sensu," resulting from a discrimination reasonably set by the Legislator with respect to the guarantee of the fundamental rights, and weakness "lato sensu," as effect instead of an unreasonable discrimination made between subjects potentially having the same rights.

The Italian legal system has opened up to the positive recognition of the concept of "weakness," above all, due to the supranational sources, noting that the protection guaranteed to certain subjects finds its *ratio* in the particular "conditions of life" in which they pay and on the basis of which, therefore, the need for specific protection concretely emerges; so that not only the human person, but also the aforesaid conditions reside on the back of the concept of "vulnerability," conditions which he or she experiences over the course of life and which involve an equally specific protection to the events that the juridical system considers worthy of attention.

For this reason, the reference to concepts such as age, gender, health conditions, disabilities (even mental), etc., is recurrent in Euro-unitary and international sources. A precise definition of "vulnerability" is instead absent, probably in order to achieve the maximum flexibility of the rules aimed at protecting vulnerable subjects: in an increasingly guaranteed perspective is the judge who – from time to time – plays a particularly important role in identifying the protective measures that can effectively safeguard the vulnerable subject; and the wide spectrum of discretion that governs the choices of the Legislator appears evident as well, at most limited by the need to prepare measures capable of providing adequate protection of the interests involved[3].

3 Equality as a Fundamental Right of the Person

The evoked legal instruments designed to protect vulnerable situations are defined as "positive actions" and are grouped within what – in a controversial manner – is defined as "unequal law". These actions are nothing more than procedures, ordered by the Legislator, aimed at achieving substantial equality in favor of categories of weak or disadvantaged subjects in a strictly "anti-discrimination" perspective, that is, within the limits outlined by article 3, paragraph 1, of the Constitution.

In particular, the principle of formal equality – contemplated in the aforesaid provision – is commonly understood as a criterion which imposes a tendential universality of the rule of law, in the sense that the norm is addressed to all the associates and cannot, in any way, differentiate on the basis of subjective categories; it could – if anything – differentiate itself on the basis of objective categories (i.e., the nature of the act, of the activity, of the goods, etc.) but this distinction – in a heterogeneous society, in which each individual is closely linked to a specific reality (of work, category, and class) – immediately translates into a

---

3 For instance, consider the tenor of the article 8 of the ECHR – entitled "Right to respect for private and family life" – which is not limited to a perspective of static coverage of a right but looks at the positive obligation that each State has to safeguard personal and family freedom and integrity, even in the compliance with the principle of proportionality ("Every person has the right to respect for his private and family life, his home and his correspondence. There can be no interference by a public authority in the exercise of this right unless such interference is required by law and constitutes a measure which, in a democratic society, is necessary for national security, public security, the economic well-being of the country, the defense of order and the prevention of crimes, the protection of health or morals, or to the protection of the rights and freedoms of others").

differentiation of a subjective nature that must therefore link equal consequences to similar cases and different consequences to different cases[4].

Understood in such way, the principle of equality then performs the function of expressing a right in the strict sense: on the one hand, in the prohibition of distinguishing on the basis of merely subjective categories and on the other hand, in the appreciation of the justification basis of a (possible) discrimination. On the interpretative level, therefore, the principle of nondiscrimination translates the principle of equality (Borelli, 2007, pp. 13–53).

The principle of substantial equality instead – mentioned in the paragraph 2 of the same article 3 of the Constitution – provides the jurist with the means to focus on the elements of differentiation and disadvantage that characterize certain categories of human beings: through the identification of diversity, it is in fact possible to operate the "logical leap" from the physical person, to which rights and duties are traced, to the person observed at different stages of existence (the s.c. "homme situé"); so, the article 3, paragraph 2 of the Constitution has become an instrument by which endorsing social reform policies (apparently) in contrast with the principle of formal equality expressed by the paragraph 1.

Thus, therefore, that "the principle of equality becomes [...] a meta-rule, a rule over rules, that is, the rule that prescribes the boundaries that the legislator cannot exceed in regulating any subject. This explains why article 3 of the Constitution, and above all its first part, is the parameter of constitutionality on which the vast majority of Constitutional Court rulings are based" (Curreri, 2015, p. 274). Equality represents a general principle that limits other rights and that is able to condition the juridical order in its objective structure; and it is only by respecting the canon of coherence at the base of the juridical order itself that we can prevent the law from operating an unreasonable disparity between juridical situations, independently of the consideration of the nature and qualification of the subjects to whom they are imputed[5].

And that's how legislation s.c. "positive" is addressed to the individual categories of individuals who are in disadvantageous positions compared to others: if the principle of formal equality seems to want to reach laws that are more general and abstract, the principle of substantial equality seems instead to be opposed

4 As pointed out in the well-known assumption "treat equal situations differently and different situations differently". For a brief summary on the subject, see Bin, R., Pitruzzella, G. (2017) (pp. 517–523).

5 See – for example – the arguments already used in the old Constitutional Court, sentence n. 25/1966, in particular n. 4 of the *aforementioned law*.

to the first, aiming at laws that protect the individual disadvantaged categories (Bin & Pitruzzella, 2017, pp. 518–520). Thus, from the jurisprudence of the Constitutional Court a concept of weakness emerges which "is defined, therefore, by the principle of equality and fundamental rights, bound together by political choice or by the Legislator's discretion. Also, for the *weak* Constitutional Court is one who does not enjoy the same rights as others, with particular regard to fundamental rights, the limitation of which is subject to a particularly rigorous constitutional legitimacy union" (however, the operation of the principle of equality is not unidirectionally and necessarily aimed at extending the scope of a more favorable and evoked discipline such as *tertium comparationis*, but can also be deployed in the sense of removing the unjustified privilege of a more favorable discipline than that indicated in comparison (Di Maria, 2010, pp.101–102).

4 Equality Is Never "Too Much"

Precisely in the constitutional context, it has long been known that equal treatment – which characterizes the peaceful coexistence of the community of citizens in the liberal era – is no longer sufficient, on its own, to achieve equality: the "universalistic" claims of such principle is badly reconciled, in fact, with a guarantee of a purely legal nature.

It is clear then that the aforesaid "parity" has been assumed to have, precisely, an universalistic nature, through the particular perspective of the s.c. "reasonableness" (of laws); and it is also clear why, in doctrine, it has been argued that the right to equality can be judicially invoked to the extent that discrimination arises with respect to the enjoyment of a specific good in life and in the form of "right to equal treatment" in consideration of that given good[6].

The article 3 of the Constitution therefore represents a "super norm," just because it informs the very notion of constitutional democracy, imbued with the rights that encompass the relations of capitalist production and the relationships between classes and which try to civilize both of them by guaranteeing who – from the relations of production and from the consequent ensuing position – either was and is placed in the situation of not being able to be guaranteed of a free and dignified existence for himself and his family. It is in fact the fight against inequalities that characterizes modern constitutionalism – which arises and is based on the criticism of the s.c. "identity democracy" – aimed at reducing

6 On this subject we suggest the reading – *ex multis* – of Cartabia, M. (2013).

the weight of natural inequalities as well as at defining a "constitutional framework" of the – very cryptic – notion of "merit."[7]

Equality is, therefore, the founding principle of the contemporary constitutional (and social) order; so – paraphrasing Schmitt – it can ultimately be said that never, as in this age, should one be democratic at all costs, that is always keeping in mind the warning of any part of the doctrine that – observing the different characterizing authoritarian systems the twentieth-century history of various nations – clarified that these were caused by the inequalities of a social, political, and economic nature and not, instead, by an excess of equality (Bocchini, 2008). And – in such matter – also significant are the considerations of Alexis de Toqueville (2012), which stated that the dangers to internal democracy do not derive from too much equality but from the fact that, if anything, there is too much little.

In the final analysis – speaking the words of Flaubert – legislation must "tend to maintain the equality that the force of things tends to destroy", which is why the link between the enhancement of equality, the fight against inequalities, and the institutional setup is increasingly evident (Della Morte, 2016, pp. 1–8).

5 Summary and Postponement

Finally, it remains to ask – if anything – what is the rate of "inequality" that a given political system, or legal-social order, can tolerate, which increasingly involves a study and analysis not confined solely to the strict juridical sphere. The answer imposes, in fact, the need to question the outcome of the coexistence between methods of capitalist production and other principles and values, although always recognized by the Constitution, precisely in function of the correction of the distortions produced by the liberal model (Sen, 2010).

It is for this reason that the investigation on the condition of vulnerability of the "migrant" – when conveyed within the channels of "media" and "human rights" – can better explain the connection between the structure of contemporary democracies and the migration phenomenon – both in its essence (i.e., "who are the real traffickers of men?") and in its media representation (i.e., the responsibility of the "media" in the "narration" of the phenomenon) – with respect to the definition of European public policies, inspired by principles and

7 A concept that is indeed often conditioned, in form and effect, by the class or social class to which those who claim some justification for the differences to be put in place or already put in place belong.

values basically shared in the Constitutions of the modern State of pluralist democracy (i.e., "acceptance," "solidarity," "openness," etc.)[8].

It is, therefore, the specific contributions - each for its relative competence profile - that we refer to for the analysis of the multiple profiles implicated by the aforementioned phenomenon, with the premise aware - however - that all these profiles lead back, to the outcome, to the synthesized condition of "vulnerability" as an unavoidable element that distinguishes the *humanitas* itself.

References

Bin R., Pitruzzella G. (2017). *Diritto costituzionale. Turin*: G. Giappichelli.

Bocchini C. (2008). *La teoria schmittiana della democrazia. Il pensiero politico e la teoria costituzionale di Carl Schmitt nel contesto dell'interpretazione delle costituzioni moderne dall'età della Rivoluzione francese alla Repubblica di Weimar*, from www.consiglio.regione.campania.it/cms/CM_PORTALE_CRC/servlet/Docs?dir=docs_biblio&file=BiblioContenuto_761.pdf.

Borelli S. (2007). *Principi di non discriminazione e frammentazione del lavoro*. Turin: Giappichelli.

Cartabia M. (2013). *I principi di ragionevolezza e proporzionalità nella giurisprudenza costituzionale italiana*, from www.cortecostituzionale.it/documenti/convegni_seminari/RI_Cartabia_Roma2013.pdf.

Casadei T. (Ed.). (2012). *Diritti umani e soggetti vulnerabili. Violazioni, trasformazioni, aporie*. Turin: Giappichelli.

Curreri S. (2015). *Lezioni sui diritti fondamentali*. Milan: Franco Angeli.

de Toqueville A. (2012). *Democrazia in America*. Milan: BUR.

Della Morte M. (2016). *Costituzione ed egemonia dell'eguaglianza*. In Della Morte, M. (Ed.), *La dis-eguaglianza nello Stato costituzionale. Atti del Convegno di Campobasso del Gruppo di Pisa*. Naples: ES.

Di Maria R. (2010). *Brevi note sulla tutela dei soggetti deboli nella giurisprudenza costituzionale*. In Andò S., Alpa G., Grimaldi B. (Eds.), *I diritti delle donne nell'area del mediterraneo. Civiltà a confronto, pari opportunità, identità e tutela delle differenze*. Rome-Naples: ESI.

Mackenzie C., Rogers W., Dodds S. (2014). *Vulnerability, new essays in ethics and feminist philosophy*. Oxford: Oxford University Press.

Pastore B. (2003). *Per un'ermeneutica dei diritti umani*. Turin: Giappichelli.

8 For a broad and general discussion of immigration and the related protection of rights, see Verde, G. & Genna, A. (2012).

Sen A. K. (2010). *La diseguaglianza. Un riesame critico*. Bologna: Il Mulino.

Springhart H., Thomas G. (2017). *Exploring vulnerability*. Göttingen: Vandenhoeck&Ruprecht GmbH&Co. KG.

Verde G., Genna A. (2012). *Immigrazione e garanzie dei diritti fondamentali*. Turin: Giappichelli.

Giuseppina Talamo

Chapter Seven Migration, Climate Change and Environmental Degradation

Abstract: In the recent debate, the *nexus* between the study of population movements caused by climate change or occurring for environmental reasons has taken on a new significance in politics and the media and has become a subject for analysis in the scientific world. This chapter takes into account the fact that the decision to migrate is very often conditioned by several factors, which may be of a personal or economic nature, or connected to relationships. The environmental and climatic aspect may be a direct cause or may indirectly affect other aspects very often conditioned by different factors, that is, social, economic, relationships; and the environmental and climatic aspect can be a direct cause or indirectly affect other aspects. An aspect that will be looked at in this chapter is the analysis of the migration phenomenon associated with climate-environmental changes and the concept of vulnerability. Post-disaster migration will also be analyzed as a response to climatic-environmental changes, that is, as one of the possible ways in which populations or individuals adapt to such changes or, alternatively, exploit the opportunities that these events generate. This chapter, therefore, does not simply intend to highlight a current problem, but to demonstrate that climatic-environmental aspects, together with other variables, may also have a role in determining important population shifts.

1 Introduction

In the recent debate, the *nexus* between the study of population movements caused by climate change or occurring for environmental reasons has taken on a new significance in politics, the media, and intergovernmental and non-governmental international organizations[1]. If, on the one hand, the study of environmental migrations considers the link between post-disaster migration and the environment, the study of climate migration, on the other hand, analyzes the impact of climate change on the migration phenomenon. Thus, if, on the one hand, phenomena such as air and water pollution can contribute to determining environmental movements, on the other hand, the increase in temperature, increase in water levels, and desertification can all contribute to determining

1 This chapter refers to the *nexus* between climate change and migration. The literature recognises three main factors that determine migration: the intensification of extreme weather events, drought, and rise in sea level.

population movements due to climatic causes. Migrations due to climatic causes are certainly not a new phenomenon, but they are extremely complex and need to be included within a more global context of migration. Instead, migrations due to environmental causes are placed within more contemporary phenomena, and the pollution of air and water are factors that also pose questions in terms of quality of life standards and have given rise to a series of studies and research[2].

The phenomenon of post-disaster mobility, a recurring motif in all migratory theories of the first half of the 20th century, was first mentioned by Semple (1911), who related it to ecological determinants. Vogt (1948) speaks instead of ecological refugees to describe those who are forced to flee following natural disasters. From that time until the mid-1970s, population displacements linked to environmental causes were partially set aside in the scientific debate to make room for other theories, namely economic theories (*push and pull factors*), theories where the environment was considered a driving factor belonging to deterministic theories matured in the cultural climate of the 19 century, and theories associated with the progressive alienation of nature generated by the idea of the progress of Western societies.

This chapter takes into account the fact that the decision to migrate is very often conditioned by different factors, which may include personal and economic factors, relationships, and also the environmental and climatic aspect may be a direct cause or indirectly affect other aspects. For example, from the studies of Myers (1995, 1997) on environmental mobility, the idea consolidated that rather than environmental degradation, it is the effects of climate change that cause mass displacements of the population and forced exoduses. Thus,

2 For more details see: The relationship between environmental change and the potential human crisis has been covered by: McGregor (Geografia e rifugiati: modelli e processi di cambiamento, Belhaven Press, London, pp. 159–70, 1993), Kibreab (Environment and Population Change, International Union for the Scientific Study of Population, Liège, 1994), Kibreab (Disasters 21 (1): 20–38, 1997), Myers (Bioscience 43: 752–761, 1993), Myers e Kent (Esodo ambientale: una crisi emergente nel mondo arena, Climate Institute, Washington, DC, 1995), Black (New Issues in Refugee Research, Working Paper no. 34, 2001), Lee (Questioni ambientali: conflitto, rifugiati e relazioni internazionali, World Human Development Institute Press, Seoul and Tokyo, 2001), Castles (Environmental Change and Induced Migration: Making Sense of the Dive Working Paper No. 70, 2002), Christian Aid (Human tide: la vera crisi migratoria, Christian Aid, London, 2007) and Massey et al. (http://www.psc.isr.umich.edu/pubs/pdf/rr07-615.pdf, 2007).

environmental mobility is considered the key adaptive measure to mitigating the impacts of climate change.

Population movements due to climate and environmental changes are often associated with catastrophic scenarios. The data presented below shows that every year millions of people are forced to leave their land due to environmental disasters. These events can be of short duration (e.g., earthquakes and droughts) or determined by long-term environmental processes (e.g., sea level rise). The United Nations High Commissioner for Refugees (UNHCR) report states that 21.5 million people a year have left their lands due to natural disasters. Oxfam confirms that in 2017 alone, 15 million people had to leave their lands and 14 million came from low-income countries. From the last report by the World Bank (2018), it is clear that in 2050 there will be 143 million climate migrants[3]. Recently, another strand of literature has also emerged claiming that migration processes can also derive from conflicts caused by the control of natural resources. With this so-called catastrophic vision, other authors, on the other hand (including: Piguet et al, 2011), contrast a so-called minimalist vision and affirm that the catastrophic scenarios according to which hundreds of millions of people will be moving in the 21st century due to climate and environmental changes have no scientific basis.

Even today, despite the fact that the research papers have multiplied on this topic, the attention paid to the study of the relationships between environment, climate, immigration, and development is still modest and, thus, knowledge of the phenomenon remains fragmentary (Piguet et al. 2011).

The chapter is structured as follows: In the first part, the expression environmental refugee and environmental migrant, as proposed by Brown (1976) up to the most recent definition used by the European Parliament, is analyzed. In the second part, the main economic and sociological theories on post-disaster mobility are presented. In the third part, the analysis of the migration phenomenon associated with climate-environmental changes is presented. A detailed examination of the three key elements will be carried out: exposure of the system to the impacts of climate change, sensitivity of the community or of the socioeconomic system to these impacts, and the adaptability of the individuals involved. Finally, we will present a reflection on the polarization of recent studies on the contrast between the North and South of the planet: a non-vulnerable global North and an extremely vulnerable South of the world, with victimisation of the countries that compose it. The conclusions point to the need to come up with

3 Migration is also part of the 2030 Agenda for Sustainable Development.

global policies aimed at preventing and managing the environmental situation and the migration phenomenon.

2 What Definition . . .?

Geographical mobility is a phenomenon that has existed throughout the history of humanity and has profoundly influenced the modernisation of Western societies and the birth of state communities. Especially in today's global society, international migration has established itself as one of the main factors in the transformation of our societies. (Zanfrini, page 5)[4].

Almost daily, media and political attention is focused on the phenomenon of migration and the key players involved. We talk about economic migrants, rather than political refugees, asylum seekers, rather than climate migrants. As stated in Zanfrini (2016, page 3):

> . . .the categories with which migrants are defined do not exist in nature, but reflect political-juridical choices, attitudes and experiences of the population, sentiments held in the collective memory. . .They are "words of state", and they always refer to a certain idea of boundary which, in turn, regulates the processes of inclusion/exclusion.

The author also states that every definition or classification of different migrants is the result of a process of social and political-institutional construction and in particular is the result of the mobility regulating actions by States, which manage immigration as a political problem.

At the international level, there is no single definition to define the migrant forced to move for environmental or climatic reasons. The terms "environmental migrant," "eco migrant," and "environmental refugee" are used which, although referring to individuals who migrate, indicate different starting situations or legal *statuses*.

The expression "environmental refugee," proposed by Brown in 1976, is inspired by a study on the population of Mali, Niger, Senegal, Sudan, and Ethiopia and refers to those individuals who were forced to leave their homes following environmental disasters.

---

4 According to some authors, migration due to the so-called ecological pushfactors is the main form of migration in history, due to man's inability to cope with natural disasters. However, it is also necessary to underline – according to these authors – how it is to be considered "primitive migration", as it belongs solely to past historical periods. In this way, the link between migration and the environment would tend to diminish with human evolution which, over the years, has gradually managed to gain control of nature through technology and progress.

In 1985, the *United Nations Environment Program* (UNEP) report took up Brown's definition and used the following definition to indicate environmental refugees:

> People forced to abandon their traditional habitat, temporarily or permanently, due to a marked environmental degradation (natural and/or amplified by human action) that has jeopardised their existence and /or interferes consistently with their quality of life (El-Hinnawi, 1985, p. 4).

Thus, three types of environmental refugees are distinguished: 1. people forced to move due to a sudden event (i.e. an earthquake or a cyclone), 2. people forced to move due to a radical change in their ecosystem (i.e. the construction of a dam), and 3. people forced to move from a *habitat* no longer able to provide resources necessary for survival.

The United Nations High Commission (1993) has identified four causes that characterise refugee flows: 1. political instability, 2. economic tensions, 3. ethnic conflicts, and 4. environmental degradation. This confirms the approach according to which the environment and its deterioration can cause post-disaster migrations that undermine security inside and outside states, especially in those states that are in the northern part of the world. This approach is also supported by the report of the *Climate Institute* that uses the concept of environmental refugees on the international agenda:

> They are people who are no longer able to obtain safe livelihoods in their original habitat due to environmental factors, in particular drought, desertification, deforestation, soil erosion, water scarcity and climate change, but also natural disasters such as cyclones, sea surges and floods. Faced with these threats, people feel they have no choice but to seek sustenance either within their own country or elsewhere, temporarily or permanently (Myers, 1995, pp. 18–19).

At the beginning of the new millennium, when migration policies became more and more restrictive and states began to limit the cases in which they recognise the *status* of asylum seeker and refugee, there emerged the need to fully define the term "environmental refugee," which appears "simplistic, partial and misleading" (Castels, 2002, p. 8). Precisely because the term "environmental refugee" does not exist in international jurisprudence, we started talking about environmental migrants or eco-refugees to limit the possible misunderstandings about the enlargement of the refugee category provided for by the Geneva Convention[5].

---

5 The 1951 Geneva Convention and its 1967 Supplementary Protocol do not provide for specific laws for environmental refugees; therefore, whenever the environmental change (or natural catastrophic event)–environmental refugees relationship is

Thus the International Organization for Migration (IOM) intervened which, in the absence of a generally accepted definition, uses the term "environmental migrants" and proposes the following definition:

> Persons or groups of persons who, due to a sudden or progressive change to the eco-system that negatively affects their life or living conditions, are obliged to, or decide to, leave their habitual residence, temporarily or permanently, and move within their country or outside it.

The IOM identifies three types of environmental migrants:

- *Environmental emergency migrant*: a person who temporarily migrates due to an environmental disaster such as hurricanes, tsunamis, earthquakes, etc.,
- *Environmental forced migrant*: person forced to leave due to the deterioration of environmental conditions, such as deforestation, salinisation of fresh water, etc., and
- *Environmental motivated migrant* also known *as environmentally induced economic* migrant: those who choose to migrate in response to problems that are intensifying, such as those who leave in response to the decrease in agricultural productivity caused by desertification (Warner and Laczko, 2008, p. 2).

Over time, this proliferation of definitions and the consequent terminological confusion has done nothing but make the concept meaningless (Zetter, 2010) and does not make it possible to identify a single cause of displacement among the different migration factors. On the other hand, the climatic-environmental drivers could represent *proxies* for other determinants such as, for example, demographic growth, socio-political contrasts, and a whole series of relations between man and territory that contribute to promoting mobility (Lonergan, 1998).

From the studies by Myers (1995, 1997) on environmental mobility, the idea consolidated that rather than environmental degradation, it is the effects of climate change that cause mass displacements of the population and forced exoduses. Thus, environmental mobility is considered the key adaptive measure to mitigating the impacts of climate change. One of the main criticisms made by the author of the existing literature, which studies the relationship between the effects of climate change and post-disaster migration, is the failure to give proper attention to a multidisciplinary approach but, on the contrary, to have fragmented the analysis and the *governance* into sub-topics "evacuation,

unequivocally recognised, governments find themselves obliged to recognise the status of refugees and accept them within the national territories. The problem, of course, is very complex.

resettlement and livelihood diversification" (Myers, 1995, p. 116). From this, the definition of climatic refugees is derived; it being held to mean the people subjected to a displacement "that occurred due to climate change: the transfer or resettlement of communities from areas that are no longer habitable due to the environmental consequences of climate change" (Ferris, 2013, p. 2). At the same time, this refugee category has been widely criticised since, as climate change alone is considered as the driving factor, it is seen as restrictive and insufficient, and not sufficient to group together the multiple motivations that lead to post-disaster mobility. Furthermore, concentrating the analysis of mobility only on the climatic variable could represent a form of exemption from political responsibility with respect to policies that are effective from both an economic and a social and legal point of view (McAdam, 2010). Therefore, some authors accuse the previous definition of being a bit restrictive, and the displacements caused by climate change lead to the so-called humanitarian paradox (Rieff, 2002), that is to the dichotomy between the North and South of the globe where there are movements from the South towards a North that is ready to welcome including through international cooperation .

By contrast, following a holistic approach that dispenses with the idea of a single cause, the paper by Renaud et al. (2007) identifies different types of environmental mobility based on the motivations that lead to mobility: the duration of the move, the direction, the level of the migrant's *agency*, funds available, and the sociocultural level of the individual and families.

In 2011, the European Parliament proposed using the term "environmentally induced migration" to indicate forms of forced migration caused by environmental changes and "environmentally induced displacement" to indicate the forms of forced migration caused primarily by environmental stresses. From the report (2011), in the form of both sudden events and slow-onset events, it emerges that climate change will negatively affect migratory pressure, despite the connections being empirically difficult to trace. Starting from this premise, the absence of specific protection mechanisms for environmental migrants is acknowledged but, at the same time, it is emphasised that neither extending the aims of the 1951 Geneva Convention nor expanding *the Guiding Principles* for the IDP of 1998 represent realistically viable scenarios[6].

Some authors maintain that, in the literature, a clear definition of *both environmental migration* and *climate migration* is lacking. McAdam himself (2017)

---

6 For more information, see: http://www.opiniojuris.it/migranti-climatici-ue/#sdfootnote1sym.

states that the lack of a recognised and shared definition at international level also leads to a general confusion in defining who is an environmental migrant, a refugee or a *displaced* person. Two obstacles emerge from this debate: the complex causality of climate migration and the heterogeneity of the phenomenon[7].

Ambrosini (2017, p. 41), for example, recognises that the category of environmental refugees is experiencing a certain fortune because it makes it possible to link growing ecological sensitivity, concern for climate change, and the protection of populations in the South of the world. The author argues that, certainly, there are populations in the world that have to move due to environmental causes, but nevertheless it is very difficult to conclude that these forced displacements translate into international migrations.

Post-disaster mobility would also seem to fuel fears of international conflicts over the hoarding of natural resources, especially in areas already heavily marked by ecological and political instability. Such flows could worsen complex and already vulnerable situations. The United Nations (2009) have compiled a report which shows that 18 conflicts have been caused by the control of natural resources since 1990. Climate change reduces the primary resources necessary for human existence. Those who suffer a reduction in the availability of resources can adopt strategies of resilience and adaptation or can, instead, be forced to leave their land. This type of mobility is often internal and is often directed towards areas that already suffer from scarcity of resources and environmental problems. As a result, there is a risk of exacerbating already difficult situations that can lead to conflicts. Burrows and Kinney (2016) state that despite the strong uncertainty in defining the relationship between climate change, increased migration rate, and subsequent conflicts, there is a strong link between these three events. This uncertainty is due to the particularly complex nature of climate change analyses. Although this topic has been much discussed and widely considered by policymakers to be a topic of national and global security, much uncertainty remains about the role of climate change and the role it could play as a driver of migration and conflict. While the media and recent studies continue to represent climate change as an engine of migration that leads to violent conflict, empirical evidence for such claims is lacking (Vigil, 2017, Gemenne et al. 2014). Although these are not unimaginable future scenarios, this unilinear causality eludes to the fact that environmental changes and concomitant population displacements may actually be the fundamental causes of war and insecurity. Yet, while in some contexts the demographic pressure increases the conflict over scarce resources,

7 For more information, see Hartmann (2009).

it is often in countries like Chad or northern Niger, which are already facing conflicts, that climate change becomes a multiplier of threats rather than the root cause. Migrations and displacements alone will not lead to conflicts if other structural problems are not already in place. The additional stress that climate change brings amplifies an already difficult reality, on which the distribution and access to different resources such as water, land, infrastructure, capital, the rule of law, kinship networks, education, aid, and mobility play decisive roles[8]. However, despite alarmist theories about millions of people expelled by drought and desertification, data is scarce and often leads to contradictory conclusions. Furthermore, many studies have found that long-distance migration to urban and international destinations decreases especially during periods of drought. This is because people tend to use the few resources they have to cover immediate basic needs (mainly food), and do not have the capital needed to undertake long-distance migratory journeys[9].

Furthermore, individuals often move on the basis of their perceptions of environmental changes, rather than on real changes. This is because individuals often have limited access to climate information and data. Research conducted in West Africa, for example, shows that perceptions of environmental changes, such as rainfall variability, do not correspond to the changes observed on the ground.

Once the attempts to summarise what is meant by environmental migrant and/or refugee have been completed, the following section will analyse the main approaches to the study of this category of migrants.

3 Theories on Post-Disaster Mobility

The existing literature on *nexus* climate change, environment, and post-disaster migration is dominated by neo-Malthusian theories and *push-pull* economic

8 For example, with the impact of climate change (among others), nomadic shepherds are now forced to move their herds further south from their usual pastures. The problem in this case is not migration per se, but rather the impact of climate change in weakening the migration strategies that have helped to ensure the livelihood of the populations. Moreover, given the high level of dependence on rain-fed agriculture, it seems reasonable that a lack of rainfall that affects crop productivity also leads farmers to move in search of alternative places in which to base their livelihood.

9 Recent studies have found that people from drier regions were more likely to engage in temporary and permanent migration to other rural areas, but that the likelihood of movement decreased when rainfall was scarcer due to limited domestic resources. This fits with the findings of Van der Geest, who, when studying Ghana, discovered that migration is likely to be reduced in times of more pronounced environmental stress.

theories. The prevailing argument holds that environmental changes deprive people of their livelihood and force them to migrate to better environments, usually permanently. This argument identifies a direct causal relationship between environmental changes and migration. Several authors (e.g. Lonergan 1998; Castles 2002) argue that environmental, economic, social, and political factors are interrelated and must be examined together. Therefore, there is no single and coherent theory of migration, rather it is necessary to consider various economic, social, demographic, environmental, and other factors that can influence migration.

Most of the existing scientific literature on this topic concerns the relationship between environment and migration flows from one country to another. Empirical research shows that migration can be a response to environmental degradation. Environmental degradation (or the so-called vulnerability risk) can contribute to migration by pushing individuals out of the affected areas, so migration could be driven by environmental changes.

Post-disaster mobility scholars are divided into alarmists, also called maximalists who[10] see natural causes as the unique and decisive factor, and skeptics, also called minimalists[11] who consider post-disaster mobility in relation to other geopolitical phenomena.

In the first, the relationship between environmental change and migration is linear, while in the second it is more complex. The expression environmental refugees, in particular, is widely used by the maximalists but rarely used by minimalists.

Among the authors of the minimalist genre consider development as the main factor in the analysis of the refugee issue, among other factors. Thus, migrations can have positive and negative effects on development. For example, remittances can be viewed as a positive element in the development of the receiving country.

To this literature, Mayer adds two opposite spheres of the debate on post-disaster migrations: *descriptive literature* and *normative literature*. *Descriptive literature* is created and develops with empirical studies and is dominated by the minimalist perspective that diminishes the maximalist approach due to the lack of scientific data and bases. *Normative literature*, to which the maximalist approach

---

10 Alarmists, also called maximalists, who refer to a normative literature and consider climatic migrations different from any other form of migration phenomenon (Morrisey 2012).

11 Skeptics, also called minimalists, who refer to descriptive literature.

refers, affirms, instead, that climate change causes post-disaster migrations and that these migrations exclusively concern international migration.

The scientific community seems to agree on classifying environmental changes as a "threat multiplier" for individuals and groups, for both countries that are already disadvantaged from the geographical perspective and from the economic, social-political, and institutional development point of view, as well as for international development and security (CeSPI, 2010).

The study of so-called internal migrations is also of interest. Recent data show a significant increase in movements, above all, of internally displaced people due to sudden natural disasters. These are short-term and short-range movements, with the return as the main expected solution. But they can also give rise to permanent displacements when re-establishing decent, low-risk living conditions in places hit by disasters is difficult, and when families of poor migrants are unable to exercise their resettlement rights. These movements can also be international, when return to the country of origin may be impossible. For example, the borderline case of the small Pacific islands, in particular Kiribati or Tuvalu, whose citizens will be forced to migrate to other countries due to the rise in ocean level, is well known (World Bank, 2014).

5 Conclusions

Despite numerous studies on the link between climate change, the environment, and post-disaster migration, a unique response has rarely emerged. Some results have emerged, however, that show how these migratory movements are modeled and/or conditioned not only by climate change or the environment but also by economic, cultural, demographic, and social factors, etc. At the moment it seems that there is no clear consensus on how significant the relationship between climate change, environment, and migration is. Despite this uncertainty, it is clear that climate-environmental change and its potential impacts are concrete threats that will need to be addressed in the near future. For this reason, analysis of the migration phenomenon, the vulnerability of the territories, the socioeconomic fabric, and conflicts for hoarding resources represent an important area of research and political planning.

This chapter makes it clear scholars agree that climate-environmental changes can potentially lead to an increase in post-disaster mobility. However, the literature diverges on the relative importance of climate, of the environment as the cause of migration, compared with other factors. Over the years, there has been a growing recognition of the complexity of the systems linking climate, environment, and migratory movements and how this system also depends on social, demographic, economic, and political factors.

There are many case studies and a lot of research on this subject, but the research remains fragmented, concentrated above all in developing countries, and it often leads to a great deal of confusion or forced dichotomies.

As stated in the previous pages, for a complete analysis, it is necessary to consider the various causes and motivations that characterize the phenomenon of mobility. Moreover, as the alarmist approach must also be taken into account, it seems necessary to take into consideration the protectionist angle in the study of mobility, in terms of security and peace and the migration policies of the countries traditionally considered as destinations. To date, this alarmist attitude with catastrophic scenarios of incoming floods of migrants is not supported by the data that in fact confirm that most post-disaster mobility takes place within national borders. Finally, as with any other social phenomenon, migration cannot be attributed to a single factor, because it is a very complex phenomenon that also arises from the interaction between different factors, including social, political, economic, environmental, and demographic factors. Consequently, the existing migration dynamics are modified or exacerbated by different climatic-environmental events, rather than being solely caused by them.

Finally, the idea is becoming ever more entrenched that the climatic-environmental factor can only cause mobility for populations coming from socially and economically vulnerable regions, that is, those poor and underdeveloped regions, where it is assumed social, political, and economic measures that could mitigate the impacts of an event do not exist. As a result of this approach, an image will emerge of an increasingly invulnerable North and an extremely risk-exposed South, that is, the already existing dichotomy between the richest and most developed part of the world and, on the other hand, the increasingly poorer and underdeveloped South will continue and grow stronger.

Referring to the most recent literature, I will conclude by observing how great attention to the *nexus* environmental changes and population mobility has focused on developed countries with interregional studies and with analysis of variables related to quality of life, among others. On the other hand, however, when we talk about climate change, studies concentrate the analysis on less developed countries, thus underlining their greater vulnerability due to greater backwardness and poverty. Having said this, following an ex ante approach it is possible to investigate situations relating to rural poverty and post-disaster migration which, if they occur together, contribute to exacerbating social pressures on populations that already experience chronic levels of poverty, economic vulnerability, inequality, and social exclusion. Therefore, policymakers *must* focus their attention and actions not only on mitigating or preventing climate-environmental disasters, but also on addressing the economic and social causes that may have contributed to determining the migration phenomenon, for example, investing more in rural communities, securing land rights for rural populations, strengthening disaster response measures, preparing destination areas, ensuring full enjoyment of human rights, and addressing the root causes of conflicts. Furthermore, post-disaster migration should be seen as an essential strategy for adapting to climate change rather than as a problem to be avoided.

References

Adher N.W. (2006). Vulnerability. *Global Environmentaò Change, 16*: 268–281.

Ambrosini M. (2017). *Migrazioni*. Milano: EGEA.

Black R. (2001). *Environmental Refugees: Myth or Reality?*, Working Paper n. 34, UNHCR, Geneva.

Burrow K., Kinney P. (2016). Exploring the climate change, migration and concflict nexus. *International Jornal of Environmental Research and Public Health. European Parliament, "Climate refugee"*. Legal and policy responses to environmentally induced migration, Bruxelles 2011.

Castles M. (2002). *Environmental Change and Induced Migration: Making Sense of the Dive Working Paper*, 70.

CeSPI (2010). Focus in migrazioni internazionali. Sezione Osservatorio Mondiale.

EL – Hinnawi (1985). Environmental refugees. UNEP (02)/E52. 9280711032

European Parliament. (2011). "Climate refugee". Legal and policy responses to environmentally induced migration. Bruxelles.

Ferris E. (2013). Planned relocation and climate change. UNU-EHS. Publication Series. Policy, N. 8

Gemenne F., Blocher J., De Longueville F., Perrin N., Vigil S., Zickgraf C., Ozer P. (2014). Catastrophes, Changement climatique et Déplacements forcés: Dynamiques régionales de mobilité humaine en Afrique de l'Ouest. Nansen Initiative.

Gomez O. (2013). Climate change and migration: A review of the literature. ISS Working Paper Series/General Series, 572: 1–48.

Heitzmann K., Canagarajah R.S., Siegel P.B. (2001). The sources of vulnerability: A rationale and guideline for the assessment of risks and risk responses. Social Protection Unit Human Development Network The World Bank.

IOM. (2007). "Discussion note: Migration and the environment", Ninety-fourth session, MC/INF/288. IPCC 2007a "Climate change 2007: The physical science basis – summary for policy makers", Contribution of Working Group I to the Fourth Assessment Report of the Intergovernmental Panel on Climate Change, Paris, February.

IOM. (2014). Outlook on Migration, Environment and Climate Change 2014. International Organization for Migration.

McAdam J. (2010). Refusing 'Refuge' in the Pacific: (De)Constructing Climate-Induced Displacement. International Law Migration, Environment and Climate Change. E. Piguet, A. Pécoud and P. de Guchteneire, eds., UNESCO, Paris, UNSW Law Research Paper No. 2010-27

Myers N., Kent J. (1995). *Environmental Exodus: An Emergent Crisis in the Global Arena*. Washington D.C.: The Climate Institute.

Piguet, E., Pecoud A., De Guchteneire P. (2011). Migration and climate change: an overview. Refugee Survey Quarterly, 30(3): 1–23, https://doi.org/10.1093/rsq/hdr006

Renaud F., Bogardi J. J., Dun O., Warner K. (2007). Environmental Degradation and Migration. Berlin Institut Das Online-Handbuch Demografie.

Rieff D. (2002). A Bed for the Night: Humanitarianism in Crisis, New York, Simon & Schuster.

Semple, E. C. (1911). Influences of geographic environment. New York: Holt.

Steve Lonergan S. (1998). The Role of Environmental Degradation in Population Displacement. Environmental Change and Security Project Report, 4: 5–15.

Vigil S. (2017). Climate change and migration: Insight from the Sahel. Out of Africa. Why people migrate. Edited by Giovanni Carbone. Istituto per gli studi di politica Internazionale - ISPI.

Vogt W. (1948). Road to survival. New York: Willian Sloane Associates, Inc.

Warner, K., & Laczko, F. (2008). A global research agenda. A global research agenda. Forced Migration Review, 31: 59–60.

World Bank Report. (2018). Groundswell: Preparing for Internal Climate Migration. World Bank Group. International Bank for Reconstruction and Development/The World Bank https://openknowledge.worldbank.org/handle/10986/29461

Zetter, R.W. (2010). Protecting People displaced by Climate Change: some Conceptual Challenges. Climate change and displacement. Multidisciplinary perspective. Oxford: McAdam J. Hart Publishing.

Ignazia Bartholini

Chapter Eight Manifold Instances of Proximity Violence

Abstract: Over the past few decades and up until 2017, Sicily has hosted increasing numbers of African fugitives into the European Union. Within this markedly multicultural context, the authors carried out a two-part qualitative research project, the first part consisting in participative observation of a number of sub-Saharan women hosted by some of the island's refugee reception centres, victims of abuse, followed by a set of semi-structured interviews administered to them. The aim of the project was to analyse some of the role positions found in gender dynamics among migrants, throwing light on possible processes by which mechanisms of submission to and normalisation of gender violence seem to have been internalised by these victims of proximity violence, emphasising the viscous links existing between vulnerability (Fineman 2008, 2016) and resilience (Bracke, 2016). The project sought, furthermore, *to highlight equivocations surrounding affective action declined in feminine terms and instrumental action in masculine terms, suggesting that proximity may be considered a more* "intimate and deceptive" *declension of gender violence.*

1 Introduction

The extreme variety of migrant women's experiences is reflected in the diversity of the situations in which they undergo discrimination and violence. Gender relations in areas of the Mediterranean cannot be interpreted by means of a single *currently enrolled* paradigm, but are themselves the product of a hybrid cluster of diverse cultural influences. The Mediterranean is, today, a crucible where uninterrupted behavioural patterns favouring interweaves of violent conduct, legitimated by sexist logic and patriarchal reverberations, persist (Edwards, 1987; Garcia-Moreno et al., 2006; Bartholini, 2016).

The most recent migratory arrivals have also contributed to the re-emergence of the "honour-and-shame" paradigm (Peristiany, 1965; Giordano, 1994), expressed primarily through gender-oriented relations founded on control of women (Bimbi, 2015) within marital and parental relationships. As Bimbi wrote recently, the honour-and-shame paradigm is a characteristic of the Mediterranean area (ibidem); even if it seems to represent an archaic residue, it continues to spread through the groups of *newcomers*, in terms of manifest violence too.

One of the most devastating effects of this paradigm is legitimisation of the sexual exploitation of migrants from the African continent (especially Nigeria). Furthermore, it emphasises forms of gender submission found within more traditional marriage-based relationships. The issue of female subordination and exploitation may, therefore, be attributed to the cultural models underlying the socialisation processes experienced by migrant women in their native countries and reproduced in their host countries. The logical, consequential assumption is that there is almost always a continuum between situations of domination and exploitation and the perpetration of violent acts against women (Romito, 2000, 2005; Reale, 2000; Filosof, 2000; Gillioz et al., 2000; Corradi, 2009; Collins, 2008).

To consider violence as belonging to the "normality" of relationships marked by female submission and, in extreme cases, by *outdoor* prostitution becomes sociologically useful to in-depth studies of processes and representations which contribute to the perpetuation of male power within the realm of gender relations, even among social groups that may be identified directly with the marginality or deviance found in some migratory contexts. The more representations legitimising the centuries-old exercise of control by men over women's bodies are shared socially, the more they relegate women to positions of subjugation and vulnerability.

In this brief chapter, the authors analyse some of the role positions emerging from the gender dynamics found among migrants, shedding light on possible processes of submission and internalisation of mechanisms of gender subalternity in the countries where migrants arrive and on the viscous links between vulnerability (Fineman, 2008; 2016) and resilience (Bracke, 2016) characterising women victims who have experienced various kinds of proximity violence. It is also proposes *highlighting equivocations surrounding affective action declined in feminine terms and instrumental action declined in masculine terms, suggesting that the proximity may be considered a more* "intimate and deceptive" *declension of gender violence.*

The chapter also presents the results of a participant observation of 18 sub-Saharan women residing in refugee facilities located in western Sicily, followed by the administration of a non-directive interview to them, with the authors as referents of a European project aimed at favouring the social inclusion of women hosted in refugee reception facilities. The interviews were conducted with the aid of cultural mediators and, above all, that of social workers who had established a relationship of trust with the women interviewed.

2 Proximity Violence, Bodies and Emotions

Violence involves forms of social exclusion, discrimination (Jaji, 2009; Crisp et al., 2012), secondary victimisation (Pinelli, 2011; Tognetti & Rossi, 2016), exploitation of labour (Coin, 2004), forced prostitution (Refugee Law Project 2014; Krause-Vilmar, 2011) and sexual abuse (Crisp et al., 2012). Although recent literature has defined gender-based violence broadly as the exercise of physical and psychological dominion over the victim, highlighting the various modalities (direct, indirect, physical, symbolic, cultural, instrumental, etc.) that explicitly explain it, the issue remains within a cultural paradigm that tolerates, when it does not actually legitimate, gender inequality. Gender differences are the basis of *male domination over* (Bourdieu, 1998) and abuse of women.

The recommendations and conventions that have been drafted at international and European level, and which have subsequently informed national legislation, fail to free themselves from this impasse. Among these we believe it is necessary to mention:

1. General Recommendation n.19, 11th session of the United Nations, art. 1 establishes incontrovertibly that Violence Aagainst Women (VAW) is a form of "gender-based" discrimination and "as that violence directed against a person based on his/her gender. It includes acts that inflict physical, mental or sexual harm or suffering, threats of such acts, coercion and other deprivations of liberty".
2. The Council of Europe Convention on Preventing and Combating Violence (2011 Istanbul Convention) defines gender violence as "any violence directed against a woman as such, or affecting women disproportionately" [Article 3].

What appears, however, to be explored to a lesser degree are the mechanisms that make it possible to continue a violent relationship, whereby categories like "gender", "power" and "domain" prove insufficient. The gender violence experienced during migration throws considerable light on the comprehension of the mechanisms permitting it to perpetrate itself, explain its genesis and construction, normalization, and reproduction and representation.

We argue, in the following pages, that this kind of violence against women or gender violence is specific, distinct, and that, as that it belongs to the realm of proximity relationships, we may well define it as violence of proximity. In similar relationships, the henchman is not a "neutral subject", but the person most intimate and closest to the victim at emotional and life-plan level. Upon the emotional plane we find the dynamics of trust, sentimental closeness, or psychological oppression which determine acceptance of violence on the part of the victim. The hope of a better future is used as a lever by the perpetrator to coerce the victim to accept the squalor of the present as a necessary part of the plan for improvement. The violence suffered by the victim is itself the fruit of a the victims' vulnerability and his/her resistance against putting an end to the relationship with the perpetrator. Vulnerability is a sum of complex factors, calculated mathematically by the trafficker, and exploited to produce a condition of naturally accepted bare necessity, justified by the victim's micro and macro context.

3 Mean of the Proximity Violence

The term "proximus", which means closest, is derived from a Latin superlative absolute indicating "the person closest to another" (in relational sense). And it may refer to a type of relationship where the subjects are linked, in a spatio-temporal dimension, permitting physical contiguity and exploitation of the victim. The "proximus" is the other who, in a rapport of physical proximity, occupies a dominant position. As this dominance is almost always explicitly founded on gender difference, on direct and indirect physical and psychological abuse of the victim, perpetrated in a temporal *dureé*, it may be deemed to belong to the category of proximity. The category of proximity, which illuminates the intimate character of the relationship, makes violence within the victim-executioner dyad and the exploitation of the victim outside the relationship too (as in the case of sexual exploitation), possible. Gender itself may, therefore, be considered "a fluctuating artifice, an incessant work in progress, a practice of improvisation within a scenario of constraint, which does not recuse violence but presupposes it" (Butler 2004: 26) within a mechanism of proximity. Gender is a variable favouring proximity violence which, however, does not justify it completely.

The abuse perpetrated as a result of a voluntary acceptance by the victim is subordinated to the degree of proximity violence that has been metabolized and normalized within the relationship between executioner and victim. Unlike gender-based violence, proximity violence is based on a pact made precisely within a relationship that opacifies instrumental rationality and blurs exploitation within fiduciary bonds. Proximity violence is constitutive of the relationship, self-sufficient self-immune and excludes conflict.

1. Violence is both a tool for regulating relationships and an autonomous social force capable of giving meaning to reality. As a structuring force in the relationship, it gives participants tasks and roles within a commercial pact that has essential emotional values in binding contractors.

2. Because violence – in different forms and in different ways – becomes the bond itself of the relationship, it assumes the characteristics of self-sufficiency. In other words, violence is "enough" to keep the relationship going.
3. The relationship based on violence excludes from inside any other form of resistance to violence, becoming the latter (the same violence) indispensable for maintaining the relationship, it is self-immune, neutralizes, that is, any other tension of a different nature.

Separating the discourse on proximity violence from the patriarchal representations that justify it, as well as from the processes of vulnerability and resistance in place, would therefore mean separating it from any possible interpretation that "naturalizes" it, and this would produce a sort of "racialization" of the migrants (Crenshaw, 1991).

As far as the victim is concerned, the executioner is in an asymmetrical, prevaricating position. From this point of view, the possibility of carrying out violence is subordinate to the behaviour and deeds of the executioner who dominates the victim who finds herself in a condition of absolute vulnerability due to the situation.

4 Proximity Violence Versus Proximity Vulnerability

The woman's body is the "primary place where violence is concretized" (Corradi, 2011: 11). The marriage markets of child brides, the outdoor prostitution of Nigerian women (Siegel, De Roos, 2016; Peano, 2013) or genital mutilation are just some of the aspects of segregationist and patriarchal cultures whose chosen victims are women and girls. Similar practices are an integral part of the established, daily dimension of some migratory cultures, based on simulacra of violence, violence against women in particular. Vulnerability is primarily a physical condition attributed generally to women exposed to bodily violations. It describes the extreme situation in which a person "has no other effective and acceptable choice than to surrender to the abuse of which she is a victim" [art. 4].

The persistence of the victim within a condition of subordination cannot be attributed solely to relationships based on domination, but rather to action based on affection, emotion or trust, which make the victim docile towards or accepting of violence. In other words, it renders the victim resistant within the dynamics of proximity violence.

The sample of women, victims of gender and/or sexual exploitation interviewed here, sems to confirm this hypothesis.

However, vulnerability is not only an intrinsic characteristic of the person (Farmer, 2003), but rather situational characteristic determined by contexts. The subjugation of the weakest person also on an emotional level, and the consequent self-perceiving of one's own vulnerable by the victim, takes place within relationships based on proximity violence. Violence does not act on the bodies, but also through the bodies, in a mix of complicity, consensus and the need for recognition by the victim. The very fact of being bound up with others establishes the possibility of being subjugated and exploited. But it also establishes the possibility of being relieved of suffering, of knowing justice and even love (Butler, 2016).

A wide range of testimonies describes an initial deception by the person closest to the victim, who activates processes of resilience and individual resistance. Resilience is understood as a chance to survive the horror of violence, despite the abuse/mutilations that the body of the victim will suffer. Resistance is understood as a personal interpretation of violence suffered, and it indicates the unconscious will of the victim not to recognize the violence suffered attributing it to causes of "force majeure". Resistance here is a capacity for self-narration of violence in its sweetened form, such as to make it bearable and, in some cases, acceptable. Resilience and resistance are to be understood as compensatory practices which, if on the one hand justify the subordination of the body of the victim to the will of the executioner, on the other hand allow to victim a self-justification of own dependence and subjectum.

There are three main categories of vulnerability that not only depend on the victim's background, but also on the passive and active influence of other factors: 1) pre-existing, basically depending on the victim's background, such as a person's physical or mental disability, youth or old age, gender, pregnancy, culture, language, belief or family situation; 2) situational that is a form that may be created or maintained, such as legal status in a given territory or generated and protracted due to social, cultural or linguistic isolation or 3) circumstantial (also created or maintained: such as unemployment or economic destitution).

As demonstrated, established vulnerabilities are not only those inherent to the victim, normally grounded in age, illness, gender and poverty, but also those created by the trafficker with a view to engendering potential vulnerability in a victim. The balance of passive (inherent) and active (potential) vulnerability (Pascoal, 2017) is based on an attentive analysis of the victim, perceived only through a proxemic type of relationship. Therefore, the persistence of the victim within a condition of subordination cannot be attributed solely to relationships based on domination and violence. Only resilience and resistance, activated within a proxemics relationship, make the violence suffered acceptable. The sample of women, victims of gender and/or sexual exploitation interviewed here, sems to confirm this hypothesis.

5 Marginal Notes on the Research "Method"

Often, a goodly knowledge of their respondents' backgrounds can help researchers maintain a neutral approach and avoid potential "pollution" of the object of their study. This theoretical approach can prove particularly advantageous when it comes to exploring the behaviour and the interactive dynamics (De Wal, 1992) of human beings (Schutz, 1956) and help avoid a priori emphases capable of jeopardising the results of research at various levels.

The qualitative methodological approach employed in this research, which avails itself of the participant observation method, permitted greater interaction between the researcher and the immigrant women, and had the merit of bringing to the fore answers to invisible questions (Raheim *et al.*, 2016) while also counting on the contribution of intermediaries who facilitated direct, though temporary, contact with the interviewees (Gorman *et al.*, 2005). The fundamental aim of the interviews carried out subsequently as a technique typical of qualitative analysis was not to limit it to the mere collection of information, but consisted in gaining access to the "perspective of the subjects being studied" (Corbetta, 2015: 70), that is interpretations of their perceptions, feelings or representations of the world as well as of the motivations intrinsic to their actions.

Despite this, the semi-structured interviews conducted with the sub-Saharan women hosted at the refugee reception centres initially risked reinforcing the vulnerability of the interviews by laying them bare, as it were, despite the flow of spontaneous accounts generated by the semi-structured interviews, which required no precise answers or any stimulation by the interviewer. The spontaneous narration became self-narration which, through a process of self-reflection, brought a negative kind of awareness to the surface. Each interviewee discovered "having been unable", "not having understood in time", having transformed the abuse endured into deception, into veritable delusions, mystifications which, during the interviews, were progressively debunked and revealed in all their painful veracity. However, the aid of the cultural intermediaries present within the reception centres helped lower existing defensive barriers and foster true emotional interaction (Dahlberg, 2008) from an insider-outsider perspective (Pollner,Moscovici, 1984). If the co-presence of interviewer and interviewee highlighted the subjective vulnerability of the women interviewed (Fineman, 2008), this kind of vulnerability cannot be considered a characteristic intrinsic to either sub-Saharan or Romanian accounts, but as a trait characteristic of gender segregation tout court.

Given the heterogeneousness of the two groups of interviewees, the adoption of an intersectional approach Crenshaw, 1991) seemed mandatory to analyse the multiple forms of discrimination produced by the specific positions of the interviewees while, at the same time, it sought to detect similarities and differences between the various processes of acknowledgement undertaken.

6 The Migrant Women

The research carried out between 2016 and 2017 aimed at appraising perceptions of the violence to which migrant women hosted by various immigrant facilities in Sicily were submitted.

A non-directive interview outline was designed and employed with a view to facilitating the interviewees' narratives. The presence of the cultural mediators proved indispensable in order to grasp the cultural, relational and family backgrounds of the women interviewed, as well as their recollections of the violent experiences and traumas to which they had been subjected, as well as the degree of their awareness of the violence undergone. The interview outline was divided into five thematic areas. The first concerned the women's personal, family and sentimental backgrounds; the second referred to the physical violence they had experienced, which was usually the first form of violence acknowledged; the third regarded symbolic violence (Bourdieu, 1998), the cultural devices used to legitimise processes of family socialisation and naturalisation of gender differentiation; the fourth area regarded the process of acknowledgement (or not) of the violence suffered. It was precisely the formulation of a number of specific questions concerning this last-mentioned area which permitted us to comprehend the ways by which normalisation of violence within "affective-emotional" contexts of subordination and normalised suffering was achieved. Some short accounts of the most significant testimonies regarding this fourth area are provided below.

6.1 Ghana and Her Abuse-Ridden Journey

Ghana began by describing the hopes she nourished before boarding the boat she took. She meant to arrive in Italy and find a job to help her family which was in economic difficulty. Once on board, two men approached her asking if she knew how to make love with a man or whether she was a virgin. At this point the interviewee said that,

> Despite not wishing to answer two strange men regarding this overly intimate sphere of my life, I could not but answer and that is how my long journey of pain, hatred and despair began.

The girl spoke very softly, her gaze fixed on the floor, as she told of how she had been raped repeatedly by these two men, whose physiognomies she could not remember, because she had never found the courage to look them in the face. They kept telling her that only constant training could prepare her for the work awaiting her in Italy.

6.2 Foluke and a Post-Journey Scam

Foluke arrived in Italy like many other women in hopes of enjoying a better life style. In reality, she was actually tricked by a female friend, because once she landed in Sicily, she was obliged to become a prostitute. During her paid sexual work, she established a "sentimental" rapport with one her clients, Michele, with whom she also had a child. Despite going to live together, Michele made her continue to work as a prostitute because he had no intention of having a child, much less pay for its upkeep. Furthermore, as Michele was unemployed, he kept telling Foluke that "she had to manage things herself!"

> So, I continued prostituting myself, and with the little money made, I needed mainly to satisfy the needs of Michele who smoked, went to the bar and always liked to have new clothes to cut a good figure. What was left was for my son; for me there was not even a Euro.

6.3 Aziza and the Domestic Violence of an Imposed Marriage

The case of Aziza, a woman from Cameroon, is emblematic. At 14 she was obliged by her own family to marry a man of 35.
This is her story:

> I had no idea what was happening to me. I found myself in the home of an unknown man whom I had married at my father's behest. I had to look after him, cook . . . but worst thing of all . . .the word ugly does not suffice . . . I'm looking for a stronger one . . . the most animalistic thing he did . . . was that he took me to bed continuously against my will. As soon as he came home I shuddered, because whatever I was doing, I had to stop and give myself to him against my will. I could not refuse him, I could not turn back. I don't want to remember, it makes me suffer and I still feel great pain when I think about it.

For Aziza, like the majority of the interviewees, violence is a necessary rite of passage in their life stories.

Male hegemony was considered normal by most of the interviewees as were the non-negotiable rules of family life. Only the violence undergone during their journeys towards the shores of the Mediterranean was considered "abnormal", though necessary for their very survival. In these cases, the abnormality did not reside in the act as such, but identifying the actor an outsider, not an insider, in terms of family relationships. Some of the women told about the ways in which they had been tricked into leaving their own countries only to find themselves entangled in a skein of forced prostitution. For some of the interviewees prostitution was perceived as a "necessary evil", an inevitable, mandatory condition to be spoken about only sotto voce, however.

7 Conclusions

To separate the issue of the proximity violence undergone by the migrant women interviewed from the cultural representations used to explain it or from the processes of resilience and resistance that underscore it would mean disjointing it from possible interpretations which "naturalise" it and lead to a kind of "racialization" of migrant women (Crenshaw, 1991; Razack, Smith, Thobani, 2012). The notion of proxemic vulnerability succeeds in encompassing a broad range of situations where the perpetrator has a close relationship with the victim and where room for consent is blurry.

From the interviews it emerges that for most of the interviewees only physical violence is considered truly violent, while all the other forms of ill-treatment, from economic to symbolic abuse, to sexual exploitation, are frequently perceived as justifiable behaviour on the part of males who are invested with the authority to establish order within the relationship and make instrumental use of women for the very purpose of maintaining their intimate relationship.

Therefore, one of the main problems surrounding gender-based violence and one which makes finding ways of impeding it, difficult, is that for most of the women interviewed, proximity violence is permissible, tolerated and justified thanks to traditional views of the couple or because of emotional dependency. From this point of view, patriarchy (Edwards, 1987; Garcia-Moreno, 2006) is not simply an interpretative category of violence referring to the economic, cultural or religious peculiarities of its actors, but finds its epistemic characterisation in the kind of violence that victims undergo at the hands of close henchmen, as in the cases of Ghana's abuse-ridden journey, the exploitation of Foluke and Aziza's forced marriage. This is substantiated, at present, by means of the cross-grafting and strengthening of cultures of different origins due to the waves of migration, and expressed through the normalisation of violence at a symbolic level. From the interviews conducted, it may be inferred that women perceive violence as a problem only when it degenerates and/or broadens the circle of its perpetrators beyond a proximity relationship which establishes the victim's submission to a sole subject.

The intersectional approach also highlighted how gender is a necessary but insufficient category by which to interpret dynamics and trajectories that are also influenced by the differences that each one of the women interviewed and every woman in general incorporates (Crenshaw, 1991; Nixon, Humphreys, 2010).

Vulnerability is not only inherently embodied by the human being, and "we cannot understand bodily vulnerability outside (. . .) social and material relations" (Butler 2016: 16). Consequently, analysing this phenomenon in terms of the human relations leads to a set of vulnerabilities engendered by interaction and resulting in active and passive vulnerabilities as well as to situational and proximity vulnerability. It is necessary to keep in mind that the interviewees' pathway to self-awareness of their vulnerability was studded with pauses and numerous instances of sudden silence as they narrated their stories. During these pauses and silences they recalled terrible images of abuse, of physical and sexual violence and found it difficult to reveal, even speak of them. Some of them like Ghana burst into uninterruptable floods of tears. For the interviewees, the most common ruse was to pretend being married to a certain man, whom they did not actually know, to avoid having sexual relations with strange men.

By comparing the interviewees' stories, "differences that make a difference" (Crenshaw, 1991) became evident in violent practices themselves and affected the construction of meanings and above all, conditions capable of preventing them from overcoming proximity violence. The Latin word *proximus* is, grammatically speaking, an absolute superlative indicating the person closest to someone in a given space, at a given time (Bartholini, 2013; 2019). For the sub-Saharan women alike, it meant the link with a person close to them (usually a partner, but also the men on the boats, or the pimps with whom a useful link had been established) determining acceptance of the violence undergone within a particular context.

Although it is in no way easy to speak of sexual violence perpetrated by a stranger, the "bitter" contribution made by this survey is that the "friend-enemy" transforms the old dyad which opposed the proximus, who was "entitled to" because of being a husband, father or brother, to him who was "not entitled to" because of being extraneous. So the friend-enemy dyad becomes the authorised-proximus versus the unauthorised-stranger (Bartholini, 2013 and 2015) violating or not a woman's body and with it her personal identity and integrity. The "sweet" contribution is found in this very same vulnerability, which presupposes a certain degree of wife-victim found in the testimonies of the refugees women. This vulnerability, initially discriminating in itself, as the interviews proceeded in an all-female gender-dynamic involving the interviewees and the interviewers, actually favoured a potential kind of caring empathy that identified the vulnerability of the victim for the sole purpose of mitigating it (Butler, 2004) and avoiding any kind of possible resistance.

References

Bartholini I. (2013). *Violenza di prossimità. La vittima, il carnefice, lo spettatore e il "grande occhio"*. Milano: Franco Angeli.

Bartholini I. (Ed.). (2015). *Violenza di genere e percorsi mediterranei. Voci, saperi, uscite*. Milano: Guerini e Associati.

Bartholini I. (2016). Emancipazione pubblica privata. Tratteggi di una gender violence tardo moderna nell'incrociarsi di paradigmi atlantici e mediterranei. *Autonomie locali e servizio sociale, 2*(3): 56–81.

Bartholini I. (2019). *Proximity violence in migration times. A focus in some regions of Italy, France and Spain*. Milano: Franco Angeli.

Bimbi I. (2015). Onore-e-vergogna. Il ritorno di un paradigma mediterraneo nel dibattito europeo. In Bartholini I. (Ed.), *Violenza di genere e percorsi mediterranei. Voci, saperi, uscite*. Milano: Guerini e Associati, pp. 27–44.

Bourdieu P. (1998). *La nomination masculine*. Paris: Edition di Seul.

Bracke S. (2016). Bouncing back: Vulnerability and resistance in times of resilience. In Butler J., Gambetti Z., Sabsay L. (Eds.), *Vulnerability and resistance* (pp. 52–75). Durham: Duke University Press.

Butler J. (2004). *Undoing gender*. Abignton: Routledge.

Butler J., Gambetti Z., Sabsay L. (2016). *Vulnerability in resistance*. Durham: Duke University Press.

Coin F. (2004). Gli immigrati, il lavoro, la casa. Milano: FrancoAngeli.

Collins R. (2008). *Violence. A micro-sociological theory*. Princeton: Princeton University Press.

Corbetta P. (2015). *Metodologia e tecniche della ricerca sociale*. Bologna: il Mulino.

Corradi C. (2009). *Sociologia della violenza. Modernità, identità, potere*. Roma: Meltemi.

Corradi C. (2011). L'amore come istituzione totale. Un modello interpretativo della violenza contro le donne. Spazio Filosofico, 3, 1–12.

Crenshaw K. (1991). Mapping: Intersectionality, identity politics and violence against women of colour. *Standford Law Review, 43*: 124–129.

Crenshaw K. (1991). Mapping the Margins: Intersectionality, Identity Politics, and Violence against Women of Color. Stanford Law Review, *43*(6): 1241–1299.

Crisp J., Morris, T., Refstie H. (2012). Displacement in urban areas: New challenges, new partnerships. Disasters, *36*(1): 23–42.

Dahlberg K., Dahlberg H., Nyström M. (2008). *Reflective lifeworld research.* Lund: Studentlitteratur.

De Wal F. (1992). Intentional deception in primates. Evolutionary Anthropology, *1*(3): 86–92.

Edwards A. (1987). Male violence in feminist theory: An analysis of the changing conceptions of sex/gender violence and male dominance. In Hanmer J., Maynard M. (Eds.), *Women, violence and social control. Explorations in sociology*. London: Macmillan.

Farmer P. (2003). *Pathologies of power: Health, human rights, and the new war on the poor.* Berkeley: University of California Press.

Filosof F. (2000). Violenza economica come contesto alla violenza domestica. In Romito P. (Ed.), *Violenze alle donne e risposte delle istituzioni* (pp. 39–48). Milano: FrancoAngeli.

Fineman M. (2008). The vulnerable subject: Anchoring equality in the human condition. *Yale Journal of Law & Feminism, 20*(1): 1–23.

Garcia-Moreno et al. (2006). Prevalence of intimate partner violence: findings from the WHO multi-country study on women's health and domestic violence. *Lancet*, 1260–1269.

Gillioz L., De Puy J., Ducret V. (2000). La violenza domestica in Svizzera: nuovi dati su un fenomeno antico. In Romito P (Ed.), *Violenze alle donne e risposte delle istituzioni* (pp. 83–96). Milano: FrancoAngeli.

Giordano C. (1994). Der Ehrkomplex im Mittelmeerraum: sozialanthropologische Konstruktion oder Grundstruktur mediterraner Lebensform?. Vogt L. und Zingerle A. (Eds.), *Ehre. Archaische Momente in der Moderne* (pp. 172–192). Frankfurt a.M.: Suhrkamp Verlag.

Gorman G., Clayton P., Shep S., Clayton A. (2005). *Qualitative research for the information professional.* London: Facet Publishing.

Jaji R. (2009). Masculinity on Unstable Ground: Young Refugee Men in Nairobi, Kenya. Journal of Refugee Studies, *22*(2): 177–194.

Krause-Vilmar, J. (2011). Preventing Gender-based Violence: Building Livelihoods. Guidance and Tools for Improved Programming, Women's Refugee Commission, retrieved from https://reliefweb.int/report/world/

toolkit-optimizing-cash-based-interventions-protection-gender-based-violence.

Mackenzie C., Rogers W., Dodds S. (2014). *Vulnerability: New essays in ethics and femminist philosophy*. Oxford: Oxford University Press.

Nixon J., Humphreys C. (2010). Marshalling the evidence: Using intersectionality in the domestic violence frame. *Social Politics, 17*: 137–158.

Pascoal R. (2017). The analysis of the concept of vulnerability on the international legal framework on human trade. *Revista Debater a Europa, 17*, 97–114.

Peano, I. (2013). Opaque loves: Governance and escape in the intimate sphere of Nigerian sex workers'. Etnografia e Ricerca Qualitativa, *3*, 359–384.

Peristiany J.G. (Ed.). (1965). *Honor and shame: The values of Mediterranean Society*. London: Weidenfeld & Nicolson.

Pinelli B. (2011), Attraversando il mediterraneo. Il «Sistema campo» in Italia: violenza e soggettività nelle esperienze delle donne. Lares, *77*(1):159–179.

Råheim M., Magnussen L., Sekse R., Lunde A., Jacobsen T., Blystad A. (2016). Researcher–researched relationship in qualitative research: Shifts in positions and researcher vulnerability. International Journal Qualitative Studies Health Well-being, 11, retrieved from https://www.ncbi.nlm.nih.gov/pmc/articles/PMC4910304/

Reale E. (2000). Vita quotidiana delle donne: rischi di violenza e di disagio psichico. In Romito P. (Ed.), *Violenze alle donne e risposte delle istituzioni* (pp. 49–64). Milano: Franco Angeli.

Refugee Law Project. (2014). From the Frying Pan into the Fire: Psychosocial Challenges faced by Vulnerable Refugee Women and Girls in Kampala. A Qualitative In-Depth Study Report. April 2014. Retrieved on: https://reliefweb.int/sites/reliefweb.int/files/resources/From_the_Frying_Pan_into_the_Fire.pdf

Romito P. (2000). *La violenza di genere su donne e minori*. Milano: Franco Angeli.

Schütz A. (1956). Der sinnhafte Aufbau der sozialen Welt. Eine Einleitung in die Verstehende Soziologie. Frankfurt a.M.: Suhrkamp.

Siegel D., De Roos W. (2016). *Ethical concerns in research on human trafficking*. New York: Springer.

Thobani S. (2012). Racial Violence and the Politics of National Belonging: the Wisconsin Shootings, Islamophobia and the War on Terrorized Bodies. Sikh Formations: Religion, Culture, Theory, *8*: 281–286.

Tognetti, M., Rossi, P. (a cura di) (2016), Salute e inclusione sociale degli immigrati. La sfida dell'accesso ai servizi sanitari. Milano: FrancoAngeli.

Thea Giacobbe

Chapter Nine Women trafficking: a case of sexual exploitation

Abstract: In the context of migration flows, trafficking in human beings continues to have as its main aim – almost 60 % of cases (UNODC, 2018) – sexual exploitation. The methods of recruitment, subjugation, and exploitation of the people involved are very different: there is currently a "system" of Maghreb, Nigerian, Albanian, Romanian, Latin American, Eastern Europe and the former Soviet Union, and also a Chinese system. A common and enduring element is that trafficking in person represents a very serious violation of human rights, which mainly affects women, but also men, minors, and transgender people. In Italy, Nigerian criminal organizations manage all stages of trafficking for sexual exploitation, from the country of origin to the country of destination. A system in which everyone has a specific role: the recruiter, the *baba – loa*, the "connection man" or "trolley man", the *madame*. The women involved have a double role: as victims and executioners. The "victims" are young, very young girls, recruited from the slums, convinced that they can improve their economic and social conditions by skilled mediators, and also subjected to traditional rituals (*woodoo* and *ju-ju*). The recourse to black magic has, in fact, a coercive function, often psychologically stronger than blackmail and threats. The "executioners" are the madame, often former prostitutes who, having managed to free themselves from the debt, become exploiters, recruiters, supervisors, and even leaders of the entire criminal network. They accumulate the capital that will give them social recognition once they return home to perpetuate the system. In Italy, the mafia connotation of the main cells of the Nigerian structures was recognized, called *The Black Axe Confraternity* and *The Supreme Eye Confraternity* (SEC).

1 Trafficking in Sexual Exploitation: Some Data

Trafficking in human beings is considered a grave violation of human rights and a serious form of organized crime, explicitly prohibited at the EU level by Article 5 of the EU Charter of Fundamental Rights and with treaty references in the Treaty on the Functioning of the European Union (TFEU). The EU Charter considers "human dignity" as "inviolable" and central to citizens' rights.

The Anti-trafficking Directive (Directive 2011/36/EU, 2011) defines trafficking in human beings as: "the recruitment, transportation, transfer, harbouring or reception of persons, including the exchange or transfer of control over those persons, by means of the threat or use of force or other forms of coercion, of abduction, of fraud, of deception, of the abuse of power or of a position of vulnerability or of the giving or receiving of payments or benefits to achieve the consent of a person having control over another person, for the purpose of exploitation."

According to the analysis of the data on trafficking victims over the last 15 years, at the global level, human trafficking disproportionately impacts women and girls who make up over 70 % of victims detected worldwide, a group that is particularly vulnerable also to re-trafficking and secondary victimization.

In the context of migration flows, trafficking in human beings continues to have sexual exploitation as its main aim in almost 59 % of cases (UNODC, 2018).

Women and girls primarily experience this form of exploitation: 83 % of adult female victims and 72 % of girls under 18 identified as victims of trafficking had been trafficked for sexual exploitation (UN Global Report on Trafficking in Persons 2018).

In Europe, the most reported form of human trafficking is sexual exploitation (56 % of all registered victims), where the majority of victim (European Commission Data collection on trafficking in human beings in the EU 2018).

2 A Gender-Specific Approach

Trafficking in women and girls is a structural form of violence against women. A violence *directed against a woman because she is a woman*, motivated by her primary and secondary sex characteristics: a violence crosscutting ethnic, cultural, and economic differences.

"Unlike other forms of trafficking in women, such as for the purposes of labor exploitation or forced criminality, that might sometimes contain an element of sexual(ised) violence and/or exploitation, trafficking for sexual exploitation and trafficking for forced marriage have sexual and intimate violence as their *core constituents*, placing these two forms of trafficking firmly on the continuum of violence against women as opposed to other forms of violence and discrimination" (Report EIGE, 2017: p. 11).

Women are particularly vulnerable to trafficking for a combination of root causes: the so-called push factors, which force people to leave their home country, and the pull factors, which bring people to their selected destination. These two factors are combined with others such as poverty, gender inequalities, domestic violence, marginalization, conflict, lack of legal avenues for migration, ineffectual border controls, corruption, and ineffective criminal justice response to the male demand for sexual services.

Moreover, women trafficked for the purpose of sexual exploitation suffer particular types of harm and trauma (vaginal injuries, increased risk of sexually transmitted diseases and HIV, forced pregnancies, high rates of post-traumatic stress disorder, anxiety and depression).

And so "stereotypical ideas of women as mothers also play a role in the experiences of victims for sexual exploitation, hindering the exercise of these women´s right to family life and to be mothers. They are often not considered "fit" to take care of children and, consequently, are deprived of custody of their children [. . .]. Interpretation of the best interests of the child is often based on the stereotypical perception that a victim of trafficking for sexual exploitation cannot be a good mother, because she is seen as a "prostitute"" (European Institute for Gender Equality, 2018:15).

Furthermore, the fear of retaliation from the trafficker is a specific characteristic, because people known and trusted by their victims, such as friends or family, often do the recruitment (Zimmerman et al. 2008, 2011).

In addition, the mistrust in the system is an important factor related to the fear of consequences because of their legal status.

Assistance, support and rehabilitation of victims need to be adapted to different categories of victims and their experiences.

In the EU, Member States are obliged by law to take gender-specific measures to assist and protect victims.

In the same Palermo Protocol (United Nations, 2000), the recognition that trafficking cannot be dissociated from the exploitation of prostitution is reaffirmed, stating that the consent of the victim to the intended exploitation is irrelevant, recognizing that the victim of trafficking should not bear the burden of proof, and providing protection measures for victims.

At the regional level, The Istanbul Convention (Council of Europe Convention on Preventing and Combating Violence against Women and Domestic Violence, 2011) offers a comprehensive framework on violence against women directly relevant to the provisions on victim protection and assistance.

The gender-specific phenomenon of trafficking is recognized by the Anti-trafficking Directive (European Parliament and the Council, 2011) and above all complemented by the Victims' Rights Directive (European Parliament and of the Council, 2012) that establishes minimum standards on the rights and underlines that it is crucial that victims receive continuous support and assistance before, during and after any criminal proceedings.

EU Gender Action Plan 2016–2020 calls for stronger gender-sensitive legislation and to invest in governmental and non-governmental services to survivors, for their empowerment, wellness and a full reintegration into the society.

Crimes remain under-reported and under-investigated globally; overall data on sexual violence against women are missing: there is a great need of a comprehensive analysis in this area.

In order to empower women, barriers such as the non-identification as a victim of trafficking (Lutenbacher, Cohen and Mitzel, 2003), the dependence on the offender and the lack of knowledge about available resources must be demolished. Victims should be taught to view assistance not as an imposition but as a valid resource; they should be taught to eliminate the stigma associated with sex as the only kind of "work" they can offer in order to support their families.

It is very important in this context to promote the cooperation between authorities and establish partnerships, and to provide strategies and structural change in the society (EIGE, 2018).

3 Trafficking in Sexual Exploitation: "The Nigerian System" in Italy

The methods of recruitment, subjugation and exploitation of the people involved are very different: there is currently a "system" in Maghreb, Nigeria, Albania, Romania, Latin America, Eastern Europe and the former Soviet Union, and a Chinese system. A common and enduring element is that trafficking in person represents a very serious violation of human rights, which mainly affects women, but also men, minors and transgender people.

In Italy, Nigerian criminal organizations manage all stages of trafficking for sexual exploitation, from the country of origin to the country of destination, a system in which everyone has a specific role: the recruiter, the *baba – loa*, the "connection man" or "trolley man" and the *madame*.

Controlling migratory flows is "one the typical manifestation of today's criminality, which is related [...] to profit, to gender, to international organized crime" (Militello, 2018).

Landing on Italian territory, southern *lines of Europe*, is just the last part of a more complex and well-planned activity: it is a sequence of illegal behavior.

According to what emerged during recent investigations, coordinated by various national District Attorneys, the "trafficker" is part of a transnational criminal "network" rooted in the countries of origin of the migratory flows, in which extreme poverty or unstable socio-political contexts become factors of attraction for the criminal organizations involved in such illicit activities.

Migration flows from Nigeria to Italy are constantly increasing: from 30,000 presences recorded in 2012 to almost 70,000 presences recorded today.

Nigerian crime has developed outside the motherland, exploiting migration flows: a business estimated to be between 600 million and 4 billion euros and that today is also connected to the phenomenon of migrant smuggling: according to the International Organization for Migration (IOM), 70 % of young people arriving from Lagos follow the routes of boatmen.

Nigerian citizens are settled throughout the country from north to south, mostly in the major islands, in the cities of Palermo and Cagliari: above all, they are illegal immigrants.

Their presence had already been registered in northern Italy in the early 1980s, and it was extended in the early 1990s in the center and south of the Peninsula.

A crime specialized in the traffic of narcotic substances and in the exploitation of prostitution is often connected to the counterfeiting of documents, aiding of the clandestine immigration, trafficking of human beings, and slavery: it branched out into *cult*.

The cultist groups, which emerged as university brotherhoods, are today structured organizations, characterized by the bond of secrecy and connected to the headquarters in Nigeria. They are similar to our *cosa nostra* Palermo-based organization, because they replicate, on a world scale, a confederate state. A sort of anti-state divided into Nigerian summits, regions (with continental dimensions), nest zones (with national dimensions), and inhabitants forum.

In Italy, the main cells of the Nigerian structures are called *The Black Axe Confraternity* and *The Supreme Eye Confraternity* (SEC); they emerged due to the number of their components.

Each cult has an internal structure with well-defined roles, and it is characterized by the use of specific symbols and clothing and by the systematic use of aggression and prevarication: the collective bodies, for example, are appointed to the fundamental choices of the association and to the affiliations of new members (operated through specific rituals)[1].

The Corte di Cassazione, by issuing judgments on first degree[2], have underlined the mafia connotation of these criminal associations. The mafia nature is not

1 Detention orders of suspects of the crime "Disconnection zone" of July 9, 2019, "No fly zone" of March 21, 2019 and "Black Axe" of November 17, 2016 ordered by the District Anti-Mafia Prosecutor's Office of Palermo, for the crimes to which the fundamental choices of the association and the affiliations of new aspirants who follow a specific ritual in relation to the different cult provided by the journalist of Meridio news and the daily Fact Dario De Luca.

2 Supreme Court of Cassation judgment no. 24803 5/5/2010, Supreme Court of Cassation judgment no. 1635301/10/ 2014, GUP judgment at the Court of Palermo 09/0872018.

determined by the purposes pursued, but by the method of intimidation: by using the force of intimidation, the cult produces the condition of subjugation and *omertà*, typical of the case of Art. 416 bis of the Italian Criminal Code.

A consolidated investigative know-how[3] together with recent judicial collaborations have made it possible to outline the typical features of the association.

The Nigerian criminal system is based on *debt bondage*, which forces victims to bear serious forms of exploitation in order to pay very high amounts of money, all in exchange of freedom. The roles are well defined: the recruiter is located in the suburbs of Lago, Benin City and in the Edo State, Delta State, Lagos State, Ognun State, and Anambra State (World Report 2018); the *baba-loas* who operate the ju-ju rite, "retaining" their compatriots with the use of black magic; the *connection man*, who takes care of the Nigerians often until their arrival in Italy: they also give them a phone number to call once they arrive.

This number is the last link of the chain, the one that will bring them to the *Madame* herself, the adult Nigerian who will force them, using blackmail, to prostitution.

4 Women on Moves: Victims and Executioners

Women involved in human trafficking for prostitution are mostly from Nigeria, but also from Ghana, Côte d'Ivoire, and Cameroon. They play a double role: as victims and executioners.

The "victims" are recruited from the slums and convinced, by skilled mediators, that they can improve their economic and social conditions: right after the recruitment they are subjected to a traditional ritual called *ju-ju*, very similar to *voodoo* and *macumba*, typical of the *Yoruba* culture. Magic, now retained superstition, has been considered in different cultures as fundamental to understand and to modify reality. The use of black magic has, in fact, a coercive function often psychologically stronger than blackmail and threats, because it is symbolically linked to the culture of belonging. Psychotic episodes, hallucinations, panic attacks, and insomnia are all symptoms of post-traumatic stress disorders, but Nigerian women consider them proof that *ju-ju* is punishing them as a warning not to break the oath to pay their debts. Debt bondage, or the

---

3 This is testified by the most recent operations of the State Police of Catania ("Norsemen" January 2019), Naples ("Mommy", May 2018), Cuneo ("Voodoo Girls", April 2018), Palermo ("Trafficking" March 2018), and the Guardia di Finanza of Palermo ("Maman" June 2019).

debt that the woman has to pay to the organization, becomes an indisputable and inexhaustible obligation that also includes a fee to pay for food, for lodging, and even for a spot on the sidewalk.

The young women, accompanied by the mediators, begin their odyssey across the continent: some of them start to know slavery even before they have the chance to touch Italian soil.

The "executioners" are the *maman*, often former prostitutes who, having managed to free themselves from the debt, become exploiters, recruiters, supervisors, and even leaders of the entire criminal network. They accumulate the capital that will give them social recognition once they return home to perpetuate the system.

The most recent investigations of the Sicilian prosecution have ascertained the existence and operation in Sicily of the *cult* called Black Axe and Viking Confraternity. The role of the *madams* emerged from the investigations, often at the top of the criminal associations, along with the close connection with the mafia, for the exploitation of young women as prostitutes.

The members of the cult call the prostitutes who rebelled against the *madam* to order often by very violent means (DIA Semiannual Report, 2018).

In some cases, the sexual exploitation occurred within brothels and hotels, but many women and girls testified that *madam* made them solicit customers for forced prostitution in the streets. In a few cases, women and girls were sexually exploited in residential homes, which are more hidden from the scrutiny of the public and from law enforcement.

The *madams* got the profit of the investment made with the purchase of women and invested it through a continuous exchange of girls, thus expanding their range of action. This process is testified by the numerous "connection houses" in the Ballarò district of Palermo (DIA 2019).

Women are often used to recruit other women. There is evidence that many former victims are, at some point, offered the opportunity to recruit new victims, to reduce their debt to traffickers or to end their own exploitation (United Nations Office on Drugs and Crime, 2016). The conviction that their exploitation will end up as time goes by (once they extinguish their debt) and that, therefore, it is not convenient to denounce their torturers putting their lives at risk makes it even more difficult for Nigerian women to get out of the organization. Another important unfavorable factor is the personal link between a woman and her offender, often her spouse or the father of her child, as witnessed by the investigations of Palermo. All of these conditions increase the risk that the offender may further harass the victim in an effort to intimidate her, a vicious circle that feeds itself.

5 Nigeria: Between Vulnerability Factors and Good Practices

As analyzed at the beginning of this brief examination, there are many different factors involved in the phenomenon of trafficking for prostitution. Assuming the method of the "double look" can deepen the analysis of these dynamics: this means not to stop at the "nationalistic" look alone, but to assume another one called "transnational."

Most of the many women victims of trafficking come from Nigeria: the geographical characteristics of this country could be conducive to the spread of crime. Traffickers exploit Nigeria's vast and porous borders – and the free movement of people and goods within the ECOWAS (The Economic Community of West African States) that comprises 15 countries in West Africa, and was formed to promote economic integration across the region – to traffic women and girls.

The state also faces serious economic and social challenges, including low literacy levels, lack of access to education, high rates of unemployment, endemic corruption, ongoing conflict with Boko Haram – a Jihadist terrorist organization set in the north of Nigeria – and exclusion and inequality among social groups, including gender inequality.

Nigeria is a patriarchal society of cultural beliefs that influence women and girls' everyday experiences. According to the World Bank, more than half of Nigerians, most of them women, live in absolute poverty (World Bank, "Poverty & Equity Brief, Sub-Saharan Africa, Nigeria," April 2019).

Women are in many countries disadvantaged when it comes to accessing education and employment opportunities: most of them are employed in the agricultural sector, but they earn less than their male counterparts; most of the young females are more unemployed than young males (Human Rights Watch 2018). This background of socioeconomic disadvantage makes it unlikely for a victim, who has recently escaped a trafficking situation, to support herself. They often suffer a revitalization because the Social Stigma of "prostitutes" and Family Rejection have marked them for having returned home without getting rich.

Women make a significant contribution to West Africa's food economy, perpetuating a long tradition of commerce and participating in cross-border trade and regional outreach. The development of innovative public policies based on the reinforcement of the social capital of women can represent important opportunities: policies should promote better integration of the initiatives undertaken by both governments and international and nongovernmental organizations to empower women and strengthen their resilience (OECD/SWAC, 2019).

Nigeria has made some positive steps to address the widespread problem of trafficking in persons. It has endorsed most international instruments on human trafficking, establishing the National Agency for the Prohibition of Trafficking in Persons (NAPTIP), which has improved awareness, investigation, and prosecution of trafficking cases, and identification, protection, and assistance for survivors.

The Nigerian government has developed national protocols for referral, protection, and victim assistance. There is also a Victims of Trafficking Trust Fund that provides humanitarian and financial aid for victims of trafficking, although its implementation is unclear. Nigeria has also established, with the support of international development agencies, shelters, assisted with medical care, and created skills training and economic support programs for trafficking survivors. There is a strong network of NGOs who provide services to trafficking victims, including shelter accommodation, identification and family tracing, as well as rehabilitation and reintegration.

It is necessary to ensure that no one is detained in the shelter, where respect of survivors' rights is mandatory; no one is being forced to remain there against their will, and all shelter residents are free to leave and return. Developing and providing resources for community-based rehabilitation and reintegration programs for survivors of trafficking (Human Rights Watch 2018) is one of the main goals of the government.

Therefore, the system has to be strengthened and implemented, because there are still a number of factors that impede a rights-respecting response to trafficking in Nigeria.

Trafficking is an extremely complex phenomenon difficult to combat. It is a violation of human rights that has become a global challenge and a phenomenon that must be tackled according to a logic of "network," of cooperation.

References

Council of Europe (2011). *Convention on Preventing and Combating* Violence against Women and Domestic Violence (Istanbul Convention). Retrieved on: https://rm.coe.int/168008482e

Data collection on trafficking in human beings in the EU Final report (2018). Lancaster University.

Directive 2011/36/EU of the European Parliament and of the Council of 5 April 2011 on preventing and combating trafficking in human beings and protecting its victims.

Directive 2012/29/EU of the European Parliament and of the Council of 25 October 2012 establishing minimum standards on the rights, support and protection of victims of crime.

EIGE - European Institute for Gender Equality (2018). *Gender-specific measures in anti-trafficking actions*. Luxembourg: Publications Office of the European Union. Retrieved on: https://eige.europa.eu/publications/gender-specific-measures-anti-trafficking-actions-report

Kelly L. (2003). The wrong debate: Reflections on why force is not the key issue with respect to trafficking in women for sexual exploitation. *Feminist Review*, *73*: 139–144.

Lanza E. (2004). *Stranieri e diritto penale*. Padova: CEDAM.

Lutenbacher M., Cohen A., Mitzel J., (2003). Do we really help? Perspectives of abused women. *Public Health Practice*, Jan-Fe:56–64.

Militello V. (2018). La tratta di esseri umani: la politica criminale multilivello e la problematica distinzione con il traffico di migranti. *Riv. it. dir. proc. Pen.*

OECD/SWAC (2019). *Women and Trade Networks in West Africa*, West African Studies. Paris: OECD Publishing.

UNODC (2018). *Global Report on Trafficking in Persons*. New York: United Nations.

World Report (2018). Human Rights Watch. Retrieved in: https://www.hrw.org/sites/default/files/world_report_download/201801world_report_web.pdf

Yonkova N., Gillan S., Zobnina E. A. (2017). *Protecting Victims: An Analysis of the Anti- trafficking Directive from the Perspective of a Victim of Gender-based Violence*, European Institute for Gender Equality (EIGE).

Zimmerman C. et al. (2008). The health of trafficked women: A survey of women entering post trafficking services in Europe. *American Journal of Public Health*, *98*(1): 55–59.

Zimmerman C., Hossain M., Yun, K., Gajdadziev V., Guzun N., Tchomarova M., Ciarrocchi R.A., Johansson A, Kefurtova A., Scodanibbio S., Motus M.N., Roche B., Morison L., Watts C. (2008). The health of trafficked women: a survey of women entering post trafficking services in Europe. *American Journal of Public Health*, 98(1): 55–59.

Zimmerman C., Hossain M., Watts C. (2011). Human trafficking and health: A conceptual model to inform policy, intervention and research. *Social Science and Medicine*, *73*(2): 327–335.

Yosi McIntire

Chapter Ten Asylum at the Southern US Border

Abstract: The world is rife with economic dilemmas and political conflicts. Climate change into the future will only exacerbate the situation. Post-WWII, Western culture idealized refugees to demonstrate the desirability of democracy and capitalism. Today, in the United States, immigration practices are neither generous nor comprehensive. Public discussion is hampered by general misinformation. This chapter differentiates between economic migrants and "asylum seekers." It outlines the historical cause-factors of asylees approaching the United States primarily from Central America – and the vetting process they face and the human rights violations they are subjected to at the border. We are left with a dilemma: there is an urgent need to deploy practical solutions to the challenges of migration with the clear goal of establishing safe, orderly, and legal migration. But what moral foundations should we uphold? How do we reconcile our humanitarian obligations with our domestic concerns?

1 Introduction

Refugees have always been an ideological symbol within Western culture, particularly in the United States which has demonstrated to the rest of the world the desirability of democracy and capitalism. Americans try to conceptualize themselves – and the nature of the United States – according to an idealized history: as an immigrant nation with the Statue of Liberty welcoming all newcomers regardless of whether they are immigrants, refugees, or asylum seekers.

In fact, however, United States immigration law has been neither generous nor comprehensive. Indeed, as in Europe, we see a growing antipathy for migrants. Opinion polls indicate that in the United States, throughout American post-WWII history, about 30–40 % of the public has consistently opposed refugee admission. It was not until 1980 that Jimmy Carter finally signed the Refugee Act that adopted the UN's definition of refugees that provides an administrative mechanism for admitting refugees. Nonetheless, even before 1980, hundreds of thousands of foreigners were admitted into the United States based initially on an *ad hoc* combination of humanitarian concerns and national interests guided by anti-communist ideology.[1]

---

1 Thus, favoring Soviets, Vietnamese, and Cubans. In the 1970s, concern turned to global human rights – favoring Haitians and, to a lesser degree, anticommunist Hungarians, Poles, and other Eastern Europeans.

The basis for the current dislike of foreigners has been fear of job displacement, ethnic bias (concern about the loss of cultural identity), and more recently security concerns[2]. Confusion still exists over what kind of legal status, if any, migrants deserve. This confusion – or misunderstanding – between the legal terms has hampered public discussion.

It is important to recognize that much of the turmoil and upheaval in Haiti and Central American countries was the result of what we might call US colonialism/imperialism. The United States supported a century of devastating belligerence of autocratic military governments in Central America by pitting them against the national population. It would be an understatement to say that this history has contributed to the horrific circumstances that many are fleeing now.

President Trump has made crystal clear that he is no friend to "brown" immigrants. Perhaps it would be fairer to say that Trump, like Interior Minister Salvini here in Italy, uses the issue of immigration and treatment of national or religious minorities as a hot-button issue to carve out and grow his constituency.

Currently, legal immigration into the United States is restricted to three categories: family sponsorship, asylum status, and work visas. I am going to focus my presentation on current US immigration at the southern border – and specifically how it relates to the process of "refugee status determination" within the asylum admissions program.

Traditionally, persecution is thought to come from one's home government. In Central America, asylum seekers are mostly fearful of violence from private actors. Today, corruption and gang violence are deeply entrenched in El Salvador, Guatemala, and Honduras. Gangs have become part of popular culture. Even children are recruited into gangs. Children fleeing their bloody homelands and arriving at our borders are younger and younger every year, many even under five years of age.

"Illegal entry" is usually defined as entry to US territory by way of open borders as opposed to presenting oneself voluntarily at official entry posts staffed by immigration officers. Most "illegal" immigrants in the United States are individuals who simply overstay their visas.

Between July 2017 and July 2018, "apprehensions at the southern border were up 57 %—family units were up 142 %" (Karen Jacobsen, 2018). In each of the

2 The "Trojan Horse" dilemma: Can you really tell for sure who this person is and whether they are not hostile sleeper-agents?

past two months, that is, March and April, almost ten thousand people were arrested for illegal entry at the border. The chances of approval of an asylum case are significantly reduced with an illegal entry notation on one's record.

In US law, "asylum seekers" are refugees who request protection in the United States from within the US territory. "Asylum seeker" is a future-oriented term primarily characterized by the experiences of "seeking," hoping, and waiting (Jayne Howell, Deborah R. Altamirano, Faedah M. Totah, & Fethi Keles, 2018).

Over the past 10 years the number of asylum seekers on the US-Mexico border has increased alarmingly by as much as ten-fold[3] – putting a major strain on the US legal system. Sixty percent of these came from Honduras (24 %), Guatemala (27 %), and El Salvador (13 %). Currently there are more Hondurans in the United States than in Honduras, and more than 20 % of the Honduran economy is based on remittances from the United States.

The borderlands near the Mexico-US border are the site of hundreds of migrant deaths each year due to heat exhaustion, dehydration, and debilitating injuries commonly accompanying exposure to the trek that involves several days of walking through harsh conditions and extreme temperatures (Jayne Howell et al., 2018). Hoping to find safety in numbers, the migrants travel in caravans.

Research has found that criminalizing unauthorized entry into the United States does not deter those fleeing violence (Hersher (NPR), 2016).

Those who succeed in gaining access at official ports of entry must prove their identity and request asylum to be established by an immigration court. At the border, an agent gives them a preliminary interview referred to as the "credible fear interview." Subsequently, each case is taken to an Immigration Court.

To meet US asylum requirements, the asylum seekers must demonstrate a reasonable fear of future persecution and prove their own state could not protect them. In addition, the asylum seeker must be civilian and not have a criminal record – of even minor crimes. Of the 110,736 filings in 2018, 99,035 asylum seekers claimed "credible fear."

If their case is deemed credible, they are given an "affirmative-track" asylum status. When there is some doubt, they fall into a "defensive-track" status with "temporary parole status" until the time of their court appearance (American Immigration Council, 2018). The term "parolee" refers to any alien who entered the country legally and based on "urgent humanitarian or significant public benefit reasons."[4] Parole provides permission to *temporarily* remain in the United

3 2008: 13.118; 2012: 19.903; 2016: 69.156; 2018: 110.736.

4 For example, to participate in a civil or criminal legal proceeding in the United States.

States under the supervision of the US Department of Homeland Security (DHS)[5]. Parole is reviewed on a case-by-case basis and can be revoked at any time.

2 The Situation in Recent Years

In March of 2018, there were 900,000 asylum cases being processed (Maria Cristina Garcia, 2018).

Requests for asylum are challenging in the best of circumstances: practically impossible for an immigrant who has walked 3000 miles, who rarely understands the legal process. The great majority of asylum seekers do show up for their immigration hearing –89 % in 2017[6].

Affirmative-track asylum seekers can expect a 3 to 5-year process. Immigration Court judges must determine how credible the fear is and how well founded the claim.[7] In that time, most live in the United States and begin their new lives. Court hearings submit applicants to answer multiple questions about multiple years with precision, backed by appropriate paperwork. Often, unfortunately, by the time they get in front of a judge, many have lost corroborating evidence of their asylum claim.

Legal representation is not provided by the US government. Without representation, those with grounds for relief may not know how to advocate for and seek such relief, and ultimately may be coerced into voluntary departure (Jayne Howell et al., 2018).

Success rates are only about 11 % when the asylum seekers are not represented by an attorney, and 55 % when they are represented. Statistically, approval rate is significantly skewed against this geographic group. While the total international approval rate is 33 % – the lowest in 20 years – for the Central American countries, the success rate is somewhere between 18 and 23 %.

When a claim is deemed unsubstantiated, the migrant (and family) is registered as a criminal and is subject to "expedited removal" that can take anywhere from a few hours to a few weeks.

---

5 U.S. Citizenship and Immigration Services (USCIS); humanitarian cases, Customs and Border Protection (CBP); court cases, or Immigration and Customs Enforcement (ICE); ports-of-entry for asylum seekers.

6 In the 2017 fiscal year, about 28 % of immigrants failed to attend their court hearings. Among asylum seekers, 11 % did not show up for legal proceedings.

7 The bottom line is they try to establish that there is at least a 10 % chance the individual would suffer serious harm if deported.

To limit the number of asylum seekers, President Trump has floated a number of policy changes and proposals:

- In August, 2017, he ended the 2014 Central American Minors Refugee Program (CAM) – a program that targeted youth from El Salvador, Guatemala, and Honduras – and gave them the opportunity to be considered for refugee resettlement in the United States while still in their home country.
- Currently, all asylum seekers from Central America are required to present themselves at US ports of entry. Embassies in Central America provide services for work visas, but asylum applications are not serviced.
- New policies might require that asylum seekers remain in Mexico while their asylum proceedings in the United States are pending[8].
- He has raised the burden of proof that is required to pass the "credible fear interview." For example, suggesting that victims of domestic and gang violence – a primary cause for families to leave their homes in search of safety – should not qualify for asylum.
- He has suggested a ruling that would make immigrants who enter "in between ports of entry" ineligible for asylum[9].
- He has placed caps on the number of people who can apply each day – a process called "metering."[10]
- He has suggested asylum seekers wait in Mexico until their cases are heard.
- He has suggested that the US government deny residence status to any migrant who has been a "public charge" in the preceding 3 years – that is, has been primarily dependent on the government assistance such as food stamps, Section 8 housing vouchers, Medicaid prescription drug coverage, etc. – or is "likely" to need government assistance.[11]
- Since last November, counter to the *1878 Posse Comitatus Act*, he ordered active-duty troops to the southern border to take on law enforcement roles.

---

8 The ACLU is challenging this process arguing that it puts the victim at risk.

9 These immigrants typically try to maintain a low profile and usually request defensive asylum only when they have their first encounter with law enforcement.

10 By "metering" asylum seekers at ports of entry to only 60–100 people per day, asylum seekers might have to wait up to months or even years before they would even begin the lengthy asylum process. This unsustainable situation has led to rising desperation and tensions among the many thousands of immigrants holed up south of the border.

11 This would make it virtually impossible for the applicants who are low income or disabled to get green cards and visas. According to a March 2018 survey by the National WIC Association, benefits agencies in 18 states reported "drops of up to 20 % in enrollment" because of "fears about the immigration policy."

- He has presented the "wall" as the "moral and compassionate" response to a national "crisis of the heart and soul" (Sarah Stein Kerr & Ainara Tiefenthäle, 2019).
- Most recently, he ordered the suspension of US government aid to Honduras, Guatemala, and El Salvador and threatened to shut down the US border to Mexico until immigration through Mexico is controlled.

The immigration crisis has shattered the American sense of decency:

- The pushback of asylum seekers is in violation of the most fundamental principles of US and international refugee law: the prohibition on *refoulment* (forcing people to a place where they might be at risk of serious human rights violations).
- It is fair to assume that a significant number of the migrants arriving at our southern border seeking a new life are legitimate asylum seekers.
- Forcibly separating children from their parents is shocking by any standard.
- Leveraging the agony of prolonged detention in order to compel asylees to "voluntarily" give up their asylum claims is disgusting.
- Subjecting immigrants to arbitrary and indefinite detention without parole constitutes cruel, inhuman, degrading treatment or punishment.
- Indefinite detention without criminal charge is in violation of the UN Convention Against Torture, which the United States ratified and integrated into US law.

There is an urgent need to deploy practical solutions to the challenges of migration with the clear goal of establishing safe, orderly, and legal migration. Comprehensive reform will be required.

In conclusion, both in Italy and in the United States, we are left with outstanding questions: What ethical principles should we uphold? How do we reconcile our humanitarian obligations with our domestic concerns?

References

American Immigration Council. (2018, January 24). The Use of Parole Under Immigration Law. Retrieved November 28, 2018, from https://www.americanimmigrationcouncil.org/research/use-parole-under-immigration-law

Garcia M.C. (2018, October 1). Cold War Refugee Policy. Retrieved November 26, 2018, from CSPAN/History website: https://www.c-span.org/video/?452255-1/us-cold-wa refugee-policy&start=102

https://www.documentcloud.org/documents/4551257Hiskey-Understanding-the-Central-American.html

Howell, J., Altamirano, D.R., Totah, F.M., & Keles, F. (2018). *Porous Borders, Invisible Boundaries? Ethnographic Perspectives on the Vicissitudes of Contemporary Migration*. Retrieved from http://sunta.org/wp-content/uploads/2018/11/Porous-Borders Invisible-Boundaries.Nov_.2018.pdf

Jacobsen K. (2018). Refugees and global migration. *Foreign Policy Association, https://fic.tufts.edu/newsroom/karen-jacobsens-article-published/*

Stein Kerr S., Tiefenthäle A. (2019, January 8). Trump's Evolving Rhetoric on the Wall. The New York Times. Retrieved from https://www.nytimes.com/video/us/politics/100000006298111/trump-wall-shutdown.html

Nicola Malizia and Guglielmo Dinicolò

Chapter Eleven The Case of Maltese "Detention Centers": An Analysis

Abstract: The aim of the present work is to highlight the case of Maltese detention centers, born as governmental administrative structures, but which are characterized as "waiting" detention facilities, forcing the occupants to live for a long time in inadequate sanitary and humanitarian conditions. The research investigated the actual knowledge of the situation of migrants by the Maltese, the processes of ghettoization, and the perception of urban security, in the event of a possible closure of these detention centers. The elaboration of a questionnaire allowed the collection of data on the alienation and isolation process of immigrants and the correlation with the detention systems set up at government level. The awareness-raising interventions on the matter are, however, suitable results and useful to moderate the forms of social stereotype. Future research will have to investigate the interconnections present on the topic, increasing the number of variables and subjects involved in the measurement.

1 Introduction

In recent years, Malta has often been the destination of a migratory phenomenon that has affected much of southern Europe.

The aim of the present work is to highlight and analyze the case of Maltese detention centers, which are born as governmental administrative structures, but which are characterized as "waiting" detention facilities, forcing the occupants to live for a long time in inadequate conditions from a sanitary and humanitarian point of view. One of the results that the Maltese government hopes to reach with these structures is also to avoid the social contact between the Maltese people and the migrants present in these centers, for fear that these subjects may prejudice the economic system and urban security.

In this context, however, the phenomenon of intolerance and racism would be strengthened with sociological and emotional connotations based on a stereotyped vision.

Based on the above, the research work carried out investigated the actual knowledge of the situation of migrants by the Maltese, the processes of ghettoization underway, and the perception of urban security, in the event of a possible closure of the detention centers or the implementation of alternative forms of social inclusion.

The research has tried to give relevance to the most significant Maltese urban contexts, both in relation to the definition of the chosen sample and to the representativeness in relation to the perception of safety following the constant focus on this topic by the mass media.

The elaboration and administration of the questionnaire allowed the collection of important data to bring out some evidences related to the dynamics of the alienation and isolation of immigrants and the correlation with the detention systems set up at government level. The awareness-raising interventions on the matter are, however, suitable results, according to the first deductions, and useful to moderate the forms of social stereotype. Future research will have to investigate the interconnections present on the topic, increasing the number of variables and subjects involved in the measurement.

2 The Ethnocentrism Theories and Migrants

Ethnocentrism is certainly one of the significant expressions of lack of hospitality. It represents the tendency to judge the history, social structure and culture of human groups other than the group to which they belong.. According to Adorno et al. (1950), a positive stereotyped representation of one's own group, with attitudes of submission towards it, as well as a hierarchical and authoritarian point of view of the interaction between groups, within which the role of ruler is attributed, by right, to their own group and to subordinates to other groups. The ethnocentric profiles can be identified: a) in the belief that migrations to Europe are the result of economic reasons, as well as choices made also by the desire of individual migrants of a different life (identified as better) characterized by values and lifestyles from the West; b) in the fear of loss of identity; and c) in the anguish of losing one's religious identity.

The ethnocentrism of the host nation, on the other hand, takes shape in the fear of a lack of control over migrant people who, by stabilizing themselves in a given territory, can trigger conflicts and represent a danger for public safety and the safety of people; and this is in relation to the widespread prejudice that the migrant, not having a job, could be willing to do anything to survive, to this is added that the lack of work and the more or less widespread unemployment in many layers of the population of the countries that represent the goals of migratory flows determine fears related to the employability conditions of the natives, to this is added that hospitality requires the respect of norms and rules of behavior that involve expectations of demonstration of gratitude for the hosting country, linked to reciprocity that often do not seem to be respected by migrants.

It should be noted that in our culture the terms "prejudice" and "stereotype" are characterized by a strong negative value and are used to express hostility towards minorities, especially cultural and ethnic ones, to which phenomena such as discrimination and racism are often linked. Despite their similarity, these concepts indicate two very distinct phenomena: if on the one hand, the prejudice consists in an evaluation independently of an actual knowledge, the stereotype represents the set of information and beliefs about a specific category of objects in the form of a stable and consistent image over time. On the other hand, a modern form of prejudice is represented by avoidance and detachment to replace a more explicit and manifest hostility that goes against the principles of tolerance and equality shared socially in modern pluralist Western democracies; the reluctant or aversive racist, therefore, will put in place behaviors aimed at avoiding contact with those who are the object of his prejudice, or, if this is not possible, will tend to keep the relationship at a purely formal level (Dovidio & Gaertner, 2004).

3 The Figure of the Foreigner and Social Distance in a Theoretical Perspective

According to Conahay (1986), the term "racism" refers, on the one hand, to a dissembling attitude of racist beliefs and, on the other, it indicates a hostile attitude towards those social and legislative policies that aim to give minorities the same opportunities as majority groups. Pettigrew and Tropp (2000), based on the assumption that ignorance promotes prejudice, propose a fifth contact condition useful for mediating intergroup relations and favoring the reduction of biases. This condition, called cross-group friendship, consists of four interdependent processes: 1) a more functional knowledge of the outgroup, through the old stereotypes denial given by the acquisition of new information; 2) the role of emotions, according to which initial contact favors the emergence of negative emotions such as anxiety, an emotion that can be reduced through positive and lasting contacts that improve intergroup relations in general; 3) the revaluation of the ingroup, since the contact with members of other groups can help to reevaluate not only the outgroup, but also the ingroup; and 4) behavior change, as repeated and positive behavioral interactions among group members promote the development of new acceptance rules. According to Batson et al.

(1997), empathy can be defined as an emotional response oriented towards the other, congruent with the perception of his well-being. At the beginning of the twentieth century, it was argued that the immigrant had the possibility, as a foreigner, to observe the host society from an external point of view, becoming, unlike the natives, a magnifying glass capable of detecting problems in structures it contains. Sayad (2002) defines the stranger as "doubly absent" because he is not recognized as a legitimate member either by the community he belongs or by the host community; he is considered by both to be a second-class citizen. Also Schutz (1971), in his studies on the condition of the foreigner, emphasizes the presence of possible identity crises due to the lack of reference points in the new cultural context, which, with time, can negatively affect the relations between the migrant and the host society. Elias (2004) was also in charge of the relationships established between the majority group and the minority group, regarding the refusal mechanisms implemented by the dominant group towards the foreigner. The most interesting aspect of this study is not the strategies used by the group to exclude "the other", based mainly on denigration, but on the reaction of the foreigner to such discrimination. Lewin (1972) on the relationship between majority and minority defines the relationship between groups as a two-faced problem, representing the need to study both groups interested in interaction, thus supporting the importance of the bidirectional dimension in the relationships that they established, at a given historical moment, between the majority and the minority. The problems, of one of the two parts in question, once inserted in the group dynamics do not concern only the migrant but the society as a whole, thus becoming a problem of everyone. Numerous sociological currents of thought, over time, have analyzed the problem of the disintegration of social ties and moral density in modern societies: the researchers of the Chicago School and the exponents of symbolic interactionism have studied the forms of social disintegration and the groups defined as anomic, showing that within such groups a new social order is formed and a new social bond is restored. Integration sociologists, taking up the concepts of anomie and social control, have interpreted any deviant behavior as a form of lacking socialization and internalization of the rules (Berzano & Prina, 2003).

The figure of the foreigner has contributed to the analysis of the concepts of social distance, prejudice, marginality, and social integration. Simmel (1908) analyzes the social bond in its microsocial form, specifying that all the phenomena of life are linked together by a relationship of interchange and reciprocal causation: each element cannot be isolated and understood in its singularity, but in its vital interaction with others, in a dynamic of action and feedback (theory of reciprocal action). The poor and the foreigner represent marginal figures in the society, although characterized by a twofold connotation, since, despite being outside the "central" social places, they maintain a bond with society and are in any case part of it. Modern state ensures a position of belonging to society through "guarantees" and "aid" to the poor and the marginalized, despite being such subjects "outside" social boundaries and connected to society itself only by minimal relations and ties. The foreigner of the migration flow, in addition to falling into the category of "internal enemy," penetrates the dynamics of the relationship between "the group and the foreigner," with a social profile linked to his sociocultural condition. Simmel (2006) distinguishes three forms of relationships: 1) when social groups are small, closed with strong cohesion and centripetal unity, the foreigner places himself outside the group and is the object of hostility; 2) when the group is open to the outside or is forced to entertain relations with the foreigner, for example, for commercial reasons, this becomes an intermediary with the world to which it belongs; and 3) when the groups are open and mix with the outside, the foreigner is perceived as omnipresent, inside and outside the group, and is the object of new aversion and hostility. In this last form of relationship, the foreigner is at the same time inside and outside the society, the object of integration and marginalization. Simmel (2006) does not consider the foreigner as an autonomous figure, but as one of the two poles of a permanent social interaction. This relationship can also be found in the norms that each society imposes on its members in a differentiated way depending on their proximity or distance from the culture of the group. Different rules are assigned to those who are integrated or marginalized in society.

Greater cultural conformity is required of those who occupy central positions in society, unlike those who occupy positions of social disadvantage. According to sociologists of the Chicago School, "marginality" finds its roots in the processes of political, economic, and cultural transformation that have given rise to modern industrialized societies. Park (1928) defines the foreigner as "the cosmopolitan" divided between two worlds, the old one he abandoned and the new one he has just adopted, without belonging to either of them. The detachment from these two worlds, and the detachment towards their cognitive and moral bases, makes him an individual open and free from community bonds. This extreme form of freedom is, however, a source of potential identity crises: the cosmopolitan is in danger of not recognizing himself anywhere, of feeling himself a stranger both in the country of origin and in the host ones. Park (1928) hypothesizes a model of permanent integration that is established between the individual and the group, based on its cultural belonging, because following the mass migrations that have led to exchanges of goods and culture, the "foreigner" is on the margins of two cultures and two societies. The marginal man is an individual with a "divided self," a cultural hybrid that manifests itself in the presence of great migrations but also in cities and large metropolises, which has expectations and expectations of integration, existential difficulties, and frustration for the exclusion. He is condemned to live in the culture and tradition of two peoples without, on the one hand, being able to make a definitive break with the society of belonging and, on the other, to be fully integrated into the new society. He is, therefore, "caught" and "victmin" in the conflict between systems of contradictory values and antagonistic normative models.

4 The Foreigner and the Possible Integration Scenarios in the Social and Economic Policies

The evolution of the integration process of foreigner takes place in phases. The first link between the "foreigner" and society is the competition that affects the economic balance and the division of labor: an example is constituted by the workforce at a lower wage, while conflict is the social process through which competition becomes conscious and acquires a collective dimension; minorities produce solidarity within their own group and thus acquire the strength and the possibility of affecting the political order. Competition and conflict are followed by adjustment, which is the adaptation that allows the coexistence of a plurality of groups and minorities; finally, assimilation is the last phase of the "cycle of ethnic relations" where the differences between the groups do not disappear, the traditions remain, but there is the construction of a new common tradition. In the transformations that take place in this cycle, conditions of "maladjustment" and "demoralization" of individuals are created, above all in the second generation, which determine the most dramatic effects of the marginalization of racial and ethnic minorities, such as delinquency, crime, alcoholism, and wandering (Park & Miller, 1921). Schutz (1979) places at the center of his theory the presence of significant structures of daily life. In fact, already from birth, man is inserted in an organized and intersubjective environment, with preestablished meanings that define and limit reality and which provide a set of knowledge that serves to direct its actions (Izzo, 1979). The intrinsic validity of subjective knowledge is destined to falter when tradition is called into question, especially if suddenly, both the cognitive, emotional, moral, and aesthetic references that individual and group possessed disappear (Tabboni, 1990). The foreigner, therefore, finds himself in a new context and must confront himself with a preexisting and consolidated system of knowledge that until that moment did not belong to him: this situation generates the crisis of his own identity, since he does not share the presuppositions (Schutz, 1979). The social fear of foreigners has also been linked to the concept of "race" in the past. The studies of Herskovits (1930) and Hooton (1939) have shown that among black Americans, only a very limited percentage can be said to be "pure race" and that, therefore, the concept of race understood in a biological sense is unusable. The concept of race was followed by the formulation of numerous criminological theories on ethnicity, immigration, and crime; these studies were aimed at verifying, on the one hand, whether blacks and immigrants commit a greater number of crimes than whites and natives and, on the other, whether, for the same crimes there is particular discrimination against blacks and of foreigners by the formal social control system. The analysis conducted by Shaw and McKay (1929) on the condition of the immigrant and on the settlement in the ghettos (criminal areas), characterized by widespread crime, social disorganization, high mobility, and poor social controls, will lead them to conclude that the deviant characteristics are closely linked to the environment and not to people or groups (ecological theory); authors argue and specify, also, that there is no way to predict the crime levels of immigrants, since they are inclined to follow the level and type of deviance of the place where they grew up. Thus, while the first generation of immigrants tends to reproduce the crime rates of the place of origin, the second generation tends to adapt to the type of crime in the area in which they live. The conclusion reached by the authors of the Chicago School is, as is known, that immigrants have higher crime rates than the average rates of autochthonous ones, but not higher than those of the natives living in the same conditions as immigrants (Shaw & McKay, 1942). In the dynamics of the relationship between immigrant and host society, some of the most significant theories like that of Sellin's cultural conflicts (1938) are applied, according to which cultural conflict must be considered as a conflict between norms when three different phenomena occur: 1. the frontier phenomenon, that is, when two groups that are culturally different from one another live in neighboring territories; 2. the phenomenon of colonization, when the culture of a people is imposed by force on another people; and 3. the immigration phenomenon. In this last hypothesis, the immigrants, maintaining as reference standards those of the origin culture, can come into conflict with the cultural norms of the country in which they moved. The work on the cultural conflicts of the Chicago School find value in the concept of "subculture." This concept, which indicates the contrasting nature of certain normative precepts with respect to those of general culture, is developed in the sense of delinquent subculture, around the 1950s, by Cohen (1955) and applied to juvenile criminal gangs, the formation of which are traced by the author to the presence of social inequalities and a conflict with the culture of the middle class, which feel itself as extraneous, a conflict that triggers a reactive formation mechanism, that is, a reversal of the dominant values. The concept of criminal subculture is further investigated by Cloward and Ohlin (1968); in the study on "youth gangs", they theorize that the unfavorable economic and social conditions translate concretely into a limitation of opportunities (theory of differential opportunities); society, characterized by economic liberalism, offers everyone the same opportunities to achieve the goals of social success, but this competition system limits the effective opportunities of those who start from a disadvantaged situation. Race, social class, and origin country or region concretely limit the opportunities of access to the goals, and favor the confluence towards certain subcultures of band. Of particular interest is the analysis relating to the relationship between the penal system and ethnic issues: Vold (1986) emphasizes as the growing contrast between groups creates solidarity among the members of the same ethic group for the defense of the interests of the group and that "the entire process of production, violation and enforcement of laws reflects the deepest conflicts between interest groups and the struggles related to the overall control of state police power." Minorities do not have the strength to influence the legislative process that condemns them to become victims of the criminal regulatory process, criminalizing their behavior. This involves the violation of the principle of equality towards ethnic minorities; this inequality seemed to be explained only by reason of the racial factor and not of the socioeconomic one (Vold & Bernard, 1986). Quinney (1970) explores the racial problem, analyzing the criminal rates relating to the white and the color population: the first ones are lower than the latter. The author reports that being "black" entails a greater risk of condemnation. The probability of being called "criminals" thus varies in relation to racial collocation. Chambliss (1969) analyzes the process of law formation and its application. On the basis of a Marxist reading of society, he analyzes the American penal system noting that the control of the dominant classes over the lower ones was given by the management of the law. This is done in two ways: by implementing criminal laws aimed at criminalizing the behavior of the lower classes and spreading the myth of the law as a tool for everyone, plagiarizing the lower classes because they cooperate in their own control. In this perspective, the black, the foreigner, and the immigrant play the role of a subordinate class, without power, completely victim of the penal system. Chapman (1971) believes that the judicial system, considered as a producer of the true crime, is primarily responsible for social inequalities: identical actions, with identical results, can be criminal or not depending on age, sex, social, and racial position actor. Chapman (1971) underlines, in particular, how the control agencies put strong expression of the criminal stereotype against blacks and immigrants, behaviors that can only reinforce their negative role. The initial process, defined as the stigmatization of the "foreigner", represents both the main cause and the effect of the latter's marginalization.

A significant contribution to the analysis of immigrant deviance comes from the theory of relative deprivation (Runciman, 1966), according to which criminal behavior would be the result of the perception of an inferiority condition by an ethnic group, in a social context that assumes the equality of opportunity as the dominant value. Frustration develops as a result of this evaluation process, as some individuals come to believe that there is little or nothing to do to improve their relative position, and it is from this frustration that violence, or other criminal behavior, can arise. The propensity to delinquency is also fueled by criminal subcultures that form within immigrant groups. These may originate both in the country of departure and in the country of destination, supported by the relative deprivation process. The lack of social and, above all, economic integration therefore seems to be deeply linked to the deviance of immigrants. Where integration occurs, the propensity to commit crime is contained. Goffman (1963), inside the work "Stigma. Notes on management of spoiled identity," provides a clear definition of "social stigma." It is a rupture between the "virtual social identity" and the "actualized social identity" of an individual. In summary, the stigma originates in the asymmetric incongruity between "what seems and what is": this definition is applicable to the presence of the immigrant in our society. In the Social Antagonism Essay, Znaniecki (1931) emphasizes that the stranger can be perceived only through encounter and contact. The latter would allow the individual, or social group, to perceive the commonality or diversity of the value systems they carry and which would contribute to understanding a concordance of meanings or, on the contrary, a non-concordance, even if the contact would be sufficient to explain the foreignness, but not the antagonism, which is a feeling of negative hostility towards the foreigner (Znaniecki, 1931).

Michels (1925), in the essay entitled "*Materialien zu einer Soziologie des Fremden*," collected in the first volume of the German journal *Jahrbuch für Soziologie: eine internationale Sammlung*, analyzes the analysis on the foreigner and introduces a classification in which they are identified in four different types: 1) individuals whose citizenship and nationality coincide effectively; 2) individuals who have adapted to the cultural model of the host society, but without having acquired the juridical nationality of the foreign state in which they find themselves; 3) individuals who have emigrated abroad but who remain psychologically and legally connected to their original nation; and 4) individuals who have completely adapted to the living conditions of a society other than that to which they belong and which arouses the disapproval of their parents and of that part of the family left behind. The theme of the foreigner and deviance is also at the center of Merton's (1938) reflections, who states that a society finds itself in abnormal conditions when its culture proposes goals without providing all institutional and legitimate means to achieve them. Therefore, in some social groups such as the lower classes, immigrants, and ethnic minorities, given the situation of disadvantage and inequality inherent to the same social structure, these goals can be reached only through the use of illegitimate means.

5 The Case of the "Detention Centers" and "Open Centers" in Malta

One of the fundamental characteristics of the migration policies followed by the Maltese government is the institution of administrative detention as a response to fear and distrust of foreigners who have entered the Maltese territory in an "irregular" way. motivating such choices for a general fear and mistrust of Maltese citizens towards the foreigner. Furthermore, the study conducted on administrative detention applied on Maltese case could be more comprehensive and provoke interesting reflections, if related to all those recent philosophical, sociological, and anthropological theories that have tried to find categories to classify and "decode" the current places of concentration and confinement of humans, which often continue to be defined generically as "camps." It should be remembered that the Maltese government exercises its national sovereignty over a territory of just 316 square kilometers and a population of about 400,000 citizens. Malta is therefore one of those called "micro-states," whose peculiarity has long been described by Nairn (1998) in his contribution on European borders. To address and regulate the sudden presence of foreign citizens, the Maltese government decides to fully implement the Immigration Act, a law drafted in 1970. In this act, irregular entry into Maltese territory is not considered a "criminal offense," or a criminally punishable offense. As is the case of most other European countries, in fact, this behavior is evaluated as an administrative violation. But, nevertheless, the same text of law (1970) establishes that in the interest of national security and public order "any person caught on Maltese territory without the right to entry, transit or residence, is considered a prohibited migrant and is detained until his/her deportation," setting the time limit for administrative detention for a maximum period of 18 months. Only asylum seekers, at least formally, are held for up to 12 months pending a decision on their application. The research found that four detention facilities are officially active in Malta where irregular migrants and asylum seekers are held indiscriminately. They all fall under the jurisdiction and responsibility of the Ministry of Justice and Home Affairs. The Safi Barracks and Lyster Barracks centers are directly managed by the army, while those of Ta'Kandja and Floriana are entrusted to the police. To the aforementioned official structures, Rodier and Teule (2005) advised to add also "*le dépôt de l'Aéroport international où sont gardés les étrangers en voie de refoulement et qui n'est donc pas un lieu de séjour, même s'ils peuvent être amenés à y dormir*" and "*l'hôpital du Mont carmel vers le quel sont dirigés les étrangers maintenus lorsqu'ils manifestent des troubles psychiatriques*." Within these centers, the maximum detention limit is 18 months; however, in reality the timing of immigrants' stay is variable according to different conditions. The so-called vulnerable categories (pregnant women, disabled, and elderly) are identified by the Apoġġ, a governmental foundation dependent on the Ministry for the Family and Social Affairs, which proceeds to facilitate their release within a month. According to much more arbitrary criteria, on the other hand, Somalis and Eritreans are on average detained for five months, while migrants from other countries are refused recognition of refugee status and must serve the entire 18 months of imprisonment. To date, all migrants arriving in Malta and who, in the ways we have said, are being held there, after a maximum period of 18 months of detention, therefore, remain on the territory of the Maltese state for different reasons. There are actual political refugees who are a minority; then there are all those who have received temporary protection for humanitarian reasons (with residence permits valid even for six years); and, finally, there are all the migrants who have never requested asylum or who have received a refusal to their request and have not been granted any protection. This last category of people is that of irregular immigrants who have no legal residence permit but who, like others, remain within the territory. To these latter migrants are given a "freedom of movement" document whereby, although they do not occupy a legal position that guarantees them a regular stay or rights, they are allowed to remain on the Maltese territory on the loose, having already served their administrative detention period. In essence, then, all migrants, regardless of their legal status, find themselves, at the end of the detention period, sharing the same condition passing from an overcrowded cell behind bars and barbed wire to a prison that is not too large: whole territory of the Maltese State. Once migrants leave the detention centers, therefore, they move into so-called open centers which become their place of residence for substantially indefinite time, even if, in the Policy Document (2005), we read that for irregular migrants, this condition should only last "until such time as immigrants to find their country of origin." There are currently four open centers in Malta that are home to several thousand people. Some, like the open center of Marsa, a few kilometers from Valletta, are places for men only. Others, like the Catholic center of Balzan, in a small village in the Maltese hinterland, host both families and single men and women. These spaces are more or less self-managed depending on their physical and logistic characteristics. The center of Balzan, for example, is managed by a Catholic community that plays a more canonical role of reception consisting in giving food, lodging, and some language lessons. The one in Marsa, on the other hand, is formally administered by an NGO which, however, provides just four paid operators. Substantially, therefore, in this center the migrants are self-organized, also promoting small commercial activities and opening cafeterias and restaurants: a sort of small African city in the heart of Malta, although not reported in any geographical map, is slowly taking shape. In all the open centers, regardless of how they are managed, the life of migrants flows slowly and without future prospects. Given the difficulty of finding space in a labor market so reduced in variety and extension, almost no one carries a trade, except for small jobs on piecework strictly not registered.

6 Research Methodology and Sample

In order to conduct the investigation of the research, the methodology that was adopted is as follows: 1. Literature review: it provides the context for the research and demonstrates why it is important. In this stage of this research, there is a need to build a theoretical context to determine which previous works have made a significant contribution to understanding the fear of migrants; 2. Data collection methods: two types of data were used in this research: secondary and primary. Secondary data are available and are used in order to obtain the necessary information that will be related to this study, such as documents and reports provided by institutions. Primary data will include two main methods: interviews and questionnaires. Both qualitative (interviews) and quantitative (questionnaires) approaches were used to collect the data. Discussion on the data collected was used to develop a framework for the implementation of new integration policies; 3. Interviews: we used interviews to study the current situation in Malta and to identify the barriers and motivations for implementing new forms of hospitality. These interviews were conducted with a sub-sample to provide practical assistance to the current situation and also to explain the real data on the phenomenon. In this view, interview was useful to better understand the migrants' condition in the detention center; 4. Questionnaire: a questionnaire was used to obtain information about the fear of migrant and also to collect data without bias effect. A Statistical Package for Social Science (SPSS) was mainly used as a method through which to analyse the results of the questionnaire, in a computer password protected to ensure security and privacy.

Modern research is increasingly complex in that it is multidisciplinary, multidimensional, and dynamic. Mixed-methods research offers a pragmatic approach to address this complexity (Johnson and Onwuegbuzie, 2004; Maxcy, 2003); its methodological pluralism can result in superior quality research, compared with mono-method research (Johnson and Onwuegbuzie, 2007). When considered from a public policy perspective, it is difficult to understand why, in appropriate circumstances, the two more-traditional research paradigms should not be combined. The migration flow, and the relative hospitality programme, is, theoretically and practically, a multidisciplinary program of work. Migrants hospitality problems are multifaceted; they tend to be multidimensional with many possible causes and solutions. The problem must be faced in a multidisciplinary and multi-method way, with innovative research that will combine conceptual beliefs and analysis tools in different disciplines. The premise of the mixed-method research approach is that it can draw from each paradigm to maximize strengths and minimize weaknesses of both in single research studies and across studies. In this perspective, mixed-methods research paradigm bridges the schism between quantitative and qualitative research by covering the area in the research continuum that places the quantitative approach at one pole and the qualitative approach at the other (Johnson and Onwuegbuzie, 2004).

The definition of the sample started from the choice of the territorial area, with the aim of giving relevance to different and specific urban contexts in order not to distort the data and conclusions that can be reached. In fact, the most relevant urban contexts of the Maltese territory were chosen, not only in relation to the size but also with reference to the geographical location (proximity/distance with the detention centers); this choice was made since it was assumed that these variables have an impact on the phenomenon under study, namely the knowledge and the dimension of the migratory phenomenon in the Maltese territory, on the one hand, and the perception of safety/insecurity, on the other.

Considering that the Maltese resident population amounts to 493,559 persons (2019), a significant and statistically representative sample was calculated which resulted in 1,789 subjects[1]; the statistically representative sample for our reference universe has been expanded in excess of 1,800 citizens to be compared on the themes, above all, of urban security. In this way we proceeded to construct a sample as balanced as possible, both by gender and by homogeneous cities. It was a stratified sample with random extraction. The sample proportion

1 Applying the formula of the samples for known universes of not very high size, the sample size sufficient for our study was obtained. In the specific case, the formula according to which the search results could be considered valid with a percentage difference of + or – 4 % was applied.

per stratum reflected the proportion of the immigrant population by country of origin on the total number of residents of each of the cities considered. Subsequently, the casual extraction of the male and female population, between the ages of 18 and 81, was initiated. The survey was conducted from January to September 2018 and the response rate was the 78.94 %[2], with a usable questionnaire of 1,421. The sample selected has shown to have a good robustness also following the respect of the theoretically calculated proportions with those reached in the single communities. The topics of the survey were treated with mixed methodology in two phases: in the first, an exploration and reconstruction of the reference context was carried out through semistructured interviews aimed at members of local communities; in the final phase, instead, an in-depth analysis of the results emerged from the questionnaire, with quantitative analysis, was carried out in order to identify proactive actions for the management of the phenomenon and alternative solutions to the "detention center." In the latter case the methodology was differentiated according to the realities and issues to be addressed: from focus groups to individual interviews. A total of 1,421 subjects (756 females and 665 males) were interviewed in ten cities: Birkirkara, Bormla, Qormi, Rabat, Senglea, Siggiewi, La Valletta, Zabbar, Zebbug, and Zejtun. The age of about half of the sample is between 25 and 45; 37 % of young people are under 30 with a percentage of five points higher for women. In both males and females, medium-high schooling prevails: almost half (54 % male and 65.2 % female) have a degree or a post degree.

The data presented and collected in Table 11.1 show a gender difference, which is especially marked for some offensive behavior. If, in fact, men claim to be subjected to greater forms of hostility, women are/have been harassed with insistent compliments (Tab. 11.2).

The total is over 100, because multiple answers were possible.

The following data represent the answers provided by the sample specifically on immigration and perceived social consequences. If we compare the data collected with the aforementioned general data, it is clear how relevant is the discrepancy between the actual presence of foreign citizens and that perceived. The latter is often connected to the feeling of living in a new social and cultural context, prompted by constant changes in which the presence of the other is now indispensable. However, only a small percentage (16.1 %) believe that immigration is a

2 The field survey, through the provision of a questionnaire with closed and open answers, made use of the operational contribution of the entire research group in order to reduce the sample effort and increase the reduction of the error.

Tab. 11.1: Forms of primary victimization suffered

	Recently		*In the past*		*Never*	
	Male	Female	Male	Female	Male	Female
Be observed with mistrust and hostility by foreigners	35.2	29.1	45.7	57.8	42.5	42.5
To be ignored by foreigners	25.7	25.1	40.5	45.5	60.7	67.9
Being treated with arrogance, contempt by foreigners	24.4	28.1	39.8	39.8	71.6	70.9
Being threatened, insulted by foreigners	23.2	22.5	32.2	31.6	74.6	81.6
Receive insistent compliments, be harassed by Maltese	9.8	20.1	14.5	28.2	81.0	78.2
Receive insistent compliments, be harassed by foreigners	7.2	22.4	14.2	24.7	88.2	89.0

Tab. 11.2: Typing of situations that generate anxiety and fear

	Male	*Female*	*Mean*
Walking down the street	6.7	5.5	6.1
Exit the neighborhood	4.6	4.8	4.7
Take the means of transport	5.0	4.8	4.9
Enter bars/restaurants (etc.) of foreigners	12.2	7.0	9.4
News of aggressions and killings by immigrants	67.2	54.8	60.6
Go out at night alone	27.3	65.1	47.5

resource with a score very close to the quota of the sample that defines it first of all a disadvantage (17.3 %) while the vast majority believes it should be controlled and reduced (62.2 %). As regards the immigration phenomenon, gender differences can be observed with regard to the item "should be controlled and reduced" but compared to the opinion that males are at a disadvantage (16.5 %) significantly outnumber women (10.9 %) while the option "should be facilitated" is chosen by 11.6 % of females against 7.8 % of males. The sample is divided into positive and negative immigration judgments. Adolescents are more favorable to it, considering it above all a resource and, as such, they think it should be facilitated.

7 Conclusions

It is a known fact, and often the chronicles confirm it, that there are very deep-rooted ethnic intolerances capable of producing diversified ways of understanding the self from whom the other is. Furman et al. (2007) argued that throughout history masses of people have always moved for the most varied reasons, social, economic, and political. Since the 1990s, immigration has become a very complex phenomenon that has put the host countries, which are not always reacting with inclusion policies, into crisis and caught unprepared. The coexistence on the same community territory with different languages, religions, and ethnic groups, being a phenomenon destined to grow, can be faced either with an approach based on ethnic exclusivity or with another based on multi-ethnic coexistence. This last logic must necessarily be put in relation to identity: cohabitation must guarantee a space for mutual knowledge and moments of ethnic familiarity. In other words, it is based on the balance between protecting individual human rights to safeguard ethnic origin (language, religion, and traditions) and collective human rights. This does not ensure the drastic elimination of conflicts but it is still a case of experimenting with mixed inter-ethnic groups, which put themselves to the test in a sort of cohabitation laboratory, to reach an expansion, without, however, the so-called traitors to ethnic compactness they become "defectors" of their cultural identity.

The mixed-methods research paradigm provided a "best of both worlds" approach intended to generate a fuller understanding of the research problem than a mono-method approach, with minimal compromise. In the context of this research, the mixed-methods approach had the potential to encourage the gathering and use of multiple worldviews, allow the strengths of one approach to offset the weaknesses of the other, and facilitate the generation of more comprehensive and convincing evidence to answer research questions. Additionally, the emphasis on pragmatism stimulated a more practical approach to address the research problem by using multiple techniques and approaches, in line with the recommendation to use "what works" (Howe, 1992). This is particularly good when impact research is needed (i.e., research that brings results useful for defining social policies). The insistence with which the mass media provide news and information relating to crimes and delicts committed by foreigners drastically increases the level of hostility towards migrants detained in administrative structures. It is probable that the extreme negativity of judgment is affected – in addition to the problems related to security and public order – by a cultural aspects: in the eyes of many young Maltese it is difficult to conceive the very existence of nomadic and non-settled people, without its own state. In this sense, the provision of information and intercultural programs that make the real Maltese migration phenomenon known appears necessary. A fact that confirms this aspect is related to the fact that in some questions of the questionnaire, it was possible to provide an open answer and express an opinion on immigrants. Before the awareness-raising paths and knowledge of the phenomenon, the interviewees took extremely negative and intolerant positions, after which the share of these claims was drastically reduced. Also in this case the fundamental role of the information system clearly emerges.

References

Adorno T.W., Frenkel-Brunswik E., Levinson D., Sanford R.N. (1950). *The authoritarian personality.* New York: Harper Book.

Batson C.D., Polycarpou M.P., Harmon-Jones E., Imhoff H.J. (1997). Empathy and attitudes: Can feeling for a member of a stigmatised group improve feeling toward the group? *Journal of Personality and Social Psychology, 72*(1): 105-118.

Berzano L., Prina F. (2003). *Sociologia della devianza.* Roma: Carocci editore.

Chambliss W.J. (1969). *Crime and the legal process.* New York: McGraw Hill.

Chapman D. (1971). *Lo stereotipo del criminale. Componenti ideologiche e di classe nella definizione del crimine.* Torino: Einaudi.

Cloward R., Ohlin L. (1968). *Teoria delle bande delinquenti in America.* Bari: Laterza.

Cohen A.K. (1955). *Delinquent boys. The culture of the gang.* Glencoe: Free Press.

Dovidio J. F., Gaertner S. L.(2004). Aversive racism. In M. P. Zanna (Ed.),*Advances in experimental social psychology*, Vol. 36 (pp. 1–52). Elsevier Academic Press.

Elias N. (2004). *Strategie dell'esclusione. Saggi.* Bologna: Edizioni Il Mulino.

Furman R., Langer C.L., Sanchez T.W., Negi N.J. (2007). A qualitative study of immigration policy and practice dilemmas for social work students. *Journal of Social Work Education, 43*(1), 133–146.

Gaertner S.L., Dovidio J.F. (1986). The aversive form of racism. In J.F. Dovidio & S.L. Gaertner (Eds.), *Prejudice, discrimination, and racism.* Orlando, FL: Academic Press.

Goffman E. (1963). Stigma. Notes on the management of spoiled identity. New York: Simon & Schuster.

Herskovits M.J. (1930). The negro in the New World: the statement of a problem. American Antropologist, 32(1): 145–155.

Herskovits M. (1943). The negro family in Bahia: A problem in method. *American Sociological Review, 7*(8): 394–404.

Hooton E.A. (1939). *The American criminal. An anthropological study.* Cambridge: Harvard University Press.

Howe K.R. (1992). Getting over the quantitative-qualitative debate. *American Journal of Education, 100*, 236–257.

Johnson R.B., Onwuegbuzie A.J. (2004). Mixed methods research: A research paradigm whose time has come. *Educational Researcher, 33*(1), 14–26.

Johnson R.B., Onwuegbuzie A.J. (2007). Toward a definition of mixed methods research. *Journal of Mixed Methods Research, 1*(2), 112–133.

Izzo A. (1979). *Introduzione a Schutz. Saggi Sociologici.* Torino: UTET.

Lewin K. (1972). *Teoria e sperimentazione in Psicologia sociale.* Bologna: Il Mulino.

Maxcy S. (2003). *Pragmatic threads in mixed methods research in the social sciences: The search for multiple modes of inquiry and the end of the philosophy of formalism.* In A. Tashakkori, C. Teddlie (Eds.), *Handbook of mixed methods in social & behavioral research.* California, US: Sage.

Mc Conahay J.B. (1986). Modern racism and modern discrimination: The effects of race, racial, attitudes, and context on simulated hiring decision. *Personality and Social Psycology Bulletin, 9*: 551–558.

Merton R.K. (1938). Social structure and anomie. *American Sociological Review, 3*(5): 119–155.

Michels R. (1925). Materialien zu einer Soziologie des Fremden. In *Jahrubuch fur Soziologie.* Karlsruhe: Ester Band.

Nairn T. (1998). *After Brobdingang: Micro-states and their future.* In M. Anderson, E. Bort (Eds.), *The frontiers of Europe.* London: Pinter.

Park R.E. (1928). Human migration and marginal man. *The American Journal of Sociology, XXXIII*, 6.

Park R.E., Miller H. (1921). *Old world traits transplanted.* New York: Harper.

Pettigrew T.F., Tropp L.R. (2000). *Does intergroup contact reduce prejudice? Recent meta-analytic findings.* In S. Oskamp (Ed.), *Reducing prejudice and discrimination: The Claremont symposium on applied social psycology.* Mahwah, NJ: Eribaum.

Policy Document. (2005). *Irregular immigrants, refugees and integration.* Ministry for Justice and Home Affairs e dal Ministry for the Familiy and Social Solidarity of Malta.

Quinney R. (1970). *The problem of crime.* New York: Dodd/Mead.

Rodier C., Teule C. (2005). Enfermement des étrangers : l'Europe sous lamenace du syndrome maltais. *Cultures & Conflits, 23*: 1-25.

Runciman W.G. (1966). *Relative deprivation and social justice: A study of attitudes to social inequality in twentieth-century*. England: University of California Press.

Sayad A. (2002). *La doppia assenza. Dalle illusioni dell'emigrato alle sofferenze dell'immigrato*. Milano: Cortina Raffaello.

Schutz A. (1971). *Collected papers*. Martinus Nijhoff, The Hague.

Schutz A. (1979). *Saggi Sociologici*. Torino: UTET.

Sellin T. (1938). *Culture conflict and crime*. New York: Social Science Research Council.

Shaw C.R., Mckay H.D. (1929). *Delinquency areas*. Chicago: The Chicago of University Press.

Shaw C.R., McKay H.D. (1942). *Juvenile delinquency and urban areas; a study of rates of delinquents in relation to differential characteristics of local communities in American cities*. Chicago: University of Chicago Press.

Simmel G. (1908). *Soziologie. Untersuchungen uber die Formen der Vergesellschaftung*. Leipzig: Duncker & Humblot (*trad. it*. Sociologia, Milano: Edizioni di Comunitâ 1985).

Simmel G. (2006). *Lo straniero*. Torino: Il Segnalibro.

Tabboni S. (1990). *Vicinanza e lontananza*. Milano: Franco Angeli.

Vold G.B., Bernard T.J. (1986). *Theoretical criminology*. New York: Oxford University Press.

Znaniecki F. (1931). *Saggio sull'antagonismo sociale* (eds. G.J. Kaczynski, 2009. Roma: Armando Editore).

Nikos Kourachanis

Chapter Twelve Forms of Housing and Social Policies for Asylum Seekers in Greece

Abstract: This chapter examines the housing and social policies developed for asylum seekers and refugees in Greece over the last five years. The basic argument is that the way refugees are managed by the European Union (EU) does not promote the goal of social integration. Conversely, inadequate housing and social support conditions serve the purpose of repelling refugee inflows from the territory of the EU countries. The housing and social policies that have been implemented in Greece over the last five years are an example of such a policy orientation. This argument is supported by an overview of the international scholarly literature on the concept of social integration and the EU polices for migration management. It is also supported with quantitative and qualitative data from the databases of international and European organizations, Greek state agencies, and nongovernmental organizations.

1 Introduction

This chapter will attempt to analyze and interpret the housing and social interventions developed in Greece for asylum seekers and refugees as a specific case of the wider EU immigration policy. The focus will be on the last five years (2014–2019), which will highlight the structural deadlock resulting from the available European options. The key argument to be developed is that EU refugee policy has repressive features, designed to discourage the influx of refugees. Therefore, the social policies that it shapes do not promote their social integration, but rather place them on the social margins. The choice of such a practice serves the rationale of preventing new, additional, refugee populations from entering the geographical territory of the EU.

Greek asylum and social housing policies for asylum seekers and refugees can be seen as an example of this repressive logic. The majority of these housing practices results in these individuals remaining in camps in adverse and inhumane conditions. However, even in the minority of housing interventions that aim at the provision of social housing or rent support, the goal of social integration is not substantially and fully advanced. This suggests that the real aim of social policies for asylum seekers is their social marginalization in order to make Greece and Europe an unattractive destination for migrant and refugee flows.

To substantiate this claim, at the level of methodology, this chapter will be based on desk research and quantitative and qualitative data. First, the concept of social integration and the most popular approaches for housing vulnerable groups will be elaborated. This analysis will be undertaken with an overview of the international scholarly literature. At a second level, the relevance and positioning of the EU's dominant refugee policies within the specific dimensions of the theoretical framework will be presented. This will be done by utilizing the international scholarly bibliography and official EU refugee documents. Developing this broader framework further, the chapter will then examine Greek housing and social interventions for asylum seekers and refugees over the last five years. In particular, it will discuss the four different housing schemes that have been developed (hotspots and camps, social housing, rent subsidies, and squats) and the social services that accompany them. The analysis of each subcategory will be based on the findings of previous research efforts (Kourachanis, 2018a; Kourachanis, 2018b), quantitative data, and on the collection of new material from the reports of international organizations, the Greek state, and civil society. The conclusions of the chapter, based on the preceding theoretical and research discussion, will explain why specific housing and social interventions do not favor the social integration of refugee populations.

2 Refugee Housing and Social Policies: Scientific Theory and Political Reality

2.1 The Scientific Theory

The theoretical part of this chapter will examine the policies for housing and the social integration of refugees at the level of theoretical approaches and political reality. A primary claim is that decent housing is a fundamental, but not sufficient on its own, condition for the social integration of refugees. This is because the complex concept of social integration involves broader meanings than simply the provision of accommodation.

The concept of social integration encompasses a wide range of parameters, such as access to material and immaterial goods. Material goods for meeting essential human needs such as food, housing, health, employment, but also immaterial goods such as social acceptance, social relations, and the development of links with society, linguistic and cultural interaction, as well as the formation of a sense of belonging to the political community (Ager and Strang,

2008). Many studies have highlighted individual dimensions of the diverse nature of social integration, such as lifestyle patterns, music and dress choices (Lewis, 2015), and the possibility of participating in community sport and cultural activities. It therefore appears that the achievement of social integration is something complex and broad, based on formal and informal conditions. It deals with complex parameters concerning the socioeconomic, institutional, political, and cultural environments of host societies (Phillips, 2006) that interact with the actions and survival strategies of migrant populations (Berry, 1997). Therefore, in order to achieve social integration, it is necessary for housing services to be accompanied by social support actions.

In the scholarly literature on housing studies, two contrasting approaches to housing for vulnerable groups can be distinguished: the staircase of transition approach and the housing first approach (indicatively Tsemberis and Eisenberg, 2000; Busch-Geertsema, 2013). Both aspire to homeless housing, but with completely different philosophies. The staircase of transition is a traditional form of housing support, the basic philosophy of which is that the homeless must have acquired self-sufficient housing before they can move into an independent home. The structural condition necessary for this to happen is the progressive resolution of the causes that led to their loss of housing, with the help of social services. Housing autonomy is therefore the culmination of housing support procedures and will only be possible when the beneficiaries are judged to be ready (Sahlin, 2005).

In contrast to the staircase approach, modern and dynamic approaches, such as the housing first approach, argue that decent housing should be offered immediately and without conditions, in combination with additional social services. Here, housing autonomy is an inalienable human right. The goal is to provide the homeless with a sense of security and then to utilize the social services they need to empower them. A number of studies have shown that prioritizing housing has a high level of efficacy in terms of beneficiaries remaining in the residence after the intervention has ended (Busch-Geertsema, 2013). The philosophy of these two diametrically different approaches is reflected in the different forms of refugee housing. Housing practices in the host countries vary and many different schemes can be distinguished, such as housing in camps, social housing, and rent subsidy policies.

The camps are designed as specially constructed spaces to accommodate a significant number of displaced households. Often these populations are so large that they are also housed in unsatisfactory housing conditions. Camps have been the form of temporary accommodation provided to asylum seekers for many decades. In these, asylum seekers receive humanitarian aid and basic material support until a definitive solution to their situation is found. The placing of refugees in the camps is a traditional top-down practice. In recent years, new approaches have been proposed so as to establish long-term conditions for refugees in camps by their active participation in their own development processes (Jahre et al., 2018).

Social housing or rent subsidy actions are measures designed to ensure immediate housing autonomy. These are subsidized forms of housing designed to provide housing to households unable to meet the financial requirements of the private real estate market. Such cases are poor households, people with physical or mental disabilities, immigrants, refugees, and other vulnerable groups. More rarely, the general population also has access to social housing. Social housing is often accompanied by additional benefits in kind or in cash, such as subsidies for water, heating or electricity bills, psychosocial services, employment counseling, and more (Kourachanis, 2018c).

Rent subsidies can be a viable solution to ensuring decent housing for asylum seekers and refugees after the initial emergency regime has been surpassed (Fitzgerald et al., 2014). They are a form of cash assistance to beneficiaries intended to cover their housing needs only. For refugees, the granting of housing benefits often goes hand in hand with them fulfilling certain conditions (Csete, 2016) such as the provision of specific supporting documents or their participation in social integration activities (such as learning the language of the host society, cultural familiarization, or vocational training). Such measures, in addition to the immediate benefit of housing, can also help stimulate the local economy through the consumption practices of refugees (UNHCR, 2016). However, there are inherent dangers, such as the distrust on the part of landlords to rent apartments to refugees or even their exploitation by the apartment owner. At the same time, this practice can lead to inflation by increasing rental values (Dewast, 2016).

Having considered the two different approaches to forms of accommodation, it is safe to say that the one used in the camps is more in line with the philosophy of a staircase approach. In contrast, housing policies such as social housing or rent subsidies appear to promote housing autonomy and decent living, and are in fact combined with the use of social services. Therefore, they appear to be more in line with the housing first approach. Based on these findings, in the second part of the discussion on the theoretical framework, an outline will be given of the approach taken by EU housing and social protection policies for asylum seekers and refugees.

2.2 The Political Reality

The efforts made for European integration since the 1990s have put the economy and development at the forefront and degraded social policies (Geddes, 2008). Some scholars even argue that the promotion of these neoliberal policies is accompanied by a sophisticated political vocabulary that mitigates political costs. This objectionable vocabulary constructs antisocial policies as something that is mandatory (indicatively Vis, 2009), thus legitimizing a framework of repression, rather than one of social support.

The inclusion of immigration policy as part of the EU Commission portfolio on "Protecting the European Way of Life" can be considered an illustration of this. More specific to the area of housing is European Directive 2013/33/EU on the material reception of applicants for international protection. In its proclamation, this Directive claims to ensure decent conditions for the material reception and accommodation of asylum seekers. However, as will be shown below, the political implementation of the Directive by the Member States (with the institutionalization of hotspots and camps) means that it is doubtful whether the requirement for decent material reception conditions is fulfilled in practice. These are policies that, in essence, promote the neoliberal political program of market primacy and cover up antisocial policies with a falsified and cleverly worded vocabulary.

EU immigration policies must be viewed through this lens. This framework also includes the close link between migration and the central objective of development since 2000 (Lavenex & Kunz, 2008). In the context of the Europeanization of immigration policy, residual social policies have been strongly intertwined with the control and strengthening of external borders (Balzacq and Carrera, 2006). The ultimate aim has been to limit the influx of migrants into European territory (Levy, 2005; Delanty, 2008). This spirit is reflected throughout the initiatives developed at the community level from the 1990s to the present (Kourachanis, 2019). Indeed, any initiatives, such as the Common European Asylum System, have always been incomplete (Scipioni, 2018), a permanently incomplete process that has led to the failure of migration management and, consequently, to the need for repressive interventions.

The security of external borders is the main concern of these policies, which are shaped by and implemented under repressive, military, and control conditions (Chou, 2009). The policies promoted after the crisis management of refugee flows in the summer of 2015 can be seen in this context. The European Program on Migration (European Agenda for Migration) was adopted in May 2015 [COM (2015) 240FINAL]. The first set of measures was to take immediate action, including a threefold increase in FRONTEX support. The introduction of the concept of the hotspot in cooperation with the European Commission, EASO, FRONTEX, and Europol was also envisaged. Hotspots would help accelerate the identification, documenting, and fingerprinting of new entrants.

At the European Council on Migration, just five months later, 17 additional guidelines on the management of the "refugee crisis" were drawn up. The main axes of these guidelines were cooperation with third countries with the aim of stopping refugee waves, strengthening the protection of the EU's external borders (based on the Schengen acquis), tackling the entry of refugees into Europe (through the creation of more hotspots), and ensuring their return (EUCO 26/15). Deepening cooperation with third countries aimed at tackling refugee flows was promoted by the EU-Turkey Statement in 2016. The main argument is to dismantle irregular migration from Turkey to the EU (EU-Turkey Statement, 2016), and hotspots have been identified as the key point of reception and identification.

In fact, hotspots are utilized as places of detention and exclusion. At the same time, they are used to prevent travel to the countries of central and northern Europe. Hotspots, therefore, act as a double precautionary frontier. On the one hand, they restrict migrants to the southern borders of Europe. On the other hand, through their exclusionary practices they discourage the arrival of new asylum seekers (Tazzioli and Garelli 2018). The operation of the hotspots as asylum seeker identification and registration centers initially began on a small scale in Italian ports. The island of Lampedusa is a prime example, as it has become known worldwide for the thousands of immigrants who have drowned near it. Hotspots, as will be discussed in the next section, have been implemented to a greater extent in Greece, especially after the EU-Turkey Statement (Kourachanis, 2018a).

The political management of refugees with increased external control and expulsion measures and with hotspots as checkpoints and hosts have been identified by many scholars as a kind of death policy. In addition to the natural conditions of social deprivation, refugees are also shunned and lose human dignity through their construction as a danger to health and society (Mulkens, 2017). Davies et al. (2017) point out that shaping these inhumane housing conditions is an EU political option. In this way, Member States exclude people from access to formal/institutionalized social policies.

The focus of the current refugee housing and social policies seems to be limited to accommodating them in camps. Indeed, the efforts of international organizations, such as the UNHCR, focus on improving living conditions within the camps, as long as such a situation cannot be avoided by finding housing solutions outside of them (UNHCR, 2014). According to this argument, the camps are created in emergency conditions. They often have huge deficiencies in, for example, access to water, food, and decent housing. Due to the fact that the majority of their refugee populations end up staying in them for the long term, they should eventually be converted into future cities where refugees will develop a social and occupational cohesion that meets their needs (Idris, 2017). However, even such an approach aimed at converting camps into future cities is extremely limited (Jahre et al., 2018).

The emphasis on housing practices in the camps through the political implementation of the EU framework is more in line with the staircase of transition approach. An approach that does not exhibit high levels of effectiveness and, in particular, does not match so well with the multidimensional content of social integration. The one-dimensional focus on housing practices undermines human dignity as, without the strong interconnection of the refugees with the social support services, it weakens any prospect of social inclusion and keeps refugee populations in the trap of extreme poverty.

3 Housing and Social Policies for Asylum Seekers and Refugees in Greece

Greece has been a transit country for refugees for many years. Any housing and social interventions in the past were short-term and aimed at facilitating refugee populations to continue their travel to their countries of destination (Kourachanis, 2019). Following the EU-Turkey Statement, the Greek Parliament was forced, under urgent and blackmail conditions, to make changes to the institutional framework for asylum. One of the first actions was the establishment of the Reception and Identification Service (RIS) (Article 26, Law 4375/2016) with the aim of establishing inbound reception and identification procedures. Within this framework, RIS is responsible for the creation and operation of hotspots and temporary accommodation structures (camps) (article 8, Law 4375/2016).

Law 4540/2018 sought to adapt the directions of Directive 2013/33/EU to the requirements for the reception of asylum seekers enshrined in Greek law. Article 18 incorporates the provision of housing in kind. In-kind housing can be offered in three different ways: first, by accommodation in a place used for the purpose of housing applicants while their application for international protection at the border or in transit zones is examined. Secondly, by housing in kind in accommodation centers. These centers may operate in publicly or privately owned buildings, managed by public or private nonprofit organizations or international organizations. Thirdly, housing can be offered in the form of social apartments and hotels that are leased under asylum-seeker housing schemes and implemented by public or private nonprofit organizations or international organizations (Articles 21, 22, and 23).

The adaptation of Directive 2013/33/EU to domestic law has so far led to the creation of three (plus one) different forms of housing and social support: firstly, the hosting of hotpots and camps; secondly, in social housing (Emergency Support to Integration and Accommodation (ESTIA) program); and thirdly, in rent subsidies and social empowerment actions for recognized refugees (HELIOS program). The fourth dimension comes from activists who believe that existing policies do not contribute to ensuring decent living conditions for refugees. As a result, they occupy empty buildings in urban centers in order to provide better housing conditions and to demonstrate that the social management of refugees is possible. Each of these different housing practices is discussed below.

3.1 Housing and Social Policies for Asylum Seekers in Hotspots and Camps

The emphasis of the Greek state's housing and social policies for asylum seekers is on housing in hotspots and camps. To date, five hotspots have been launched in the islands of the north and east Aegean. These are in Lesvos, Chios, Samos, Leros, and Kos. In the mainland there are almost 30 camps, the numbers of which are constantly fluctuating. The management of many structures is entrusted to international or domestic organizations, many of which in fact operate without substantial oversight by the Greek state (The Greek Ombudsman, 2017: 42–4).

The findings from field research (Kourachanis, 2018a) and reports from the involved organizations show that the conditions at the hotspots are inadequate in terms of housing and health protection. This is primarily expressed by the phenomenon of housing overcrowding, with many people residing in a few square meters or in the countryside. Many people have been forced to stay in tents near hotspots for long periods of time and in poor weather conditions, expecting that they will get a place to live in them. A second issue raised by informants is the issue of poor living conditions in the hotspots, which pose health risks that directly threaten their lives. A third factor is that these structures do not meet the requirements of adequate living conditions. In other words, they are structures that are unsuitable for medium- to long-term housing. A last important dimension is the lack of specialized social care structures (Kourachanis, 2018a).

Table 12.1 reflects the inhumane living conditions in the hotspots. As it turns out, the population living in the reception and identification structures (29,939

Tab. 12.1: Ratio of housing places to actual population hosted at the hotspots (October 17, 2019)

Island	Lesvos	Chios	Samos	Leros	Kos	Total
Places	2,800	1,014	648	860	816	6,138
Actual population	14,000	4,451	5,968	2,116	3,404	29,939

Source: Ministry of Citizen Protection, https://infocrisis.gov.gr/6462/fwd-apotyposi-tis-ethnikis-ikonas-katastasis-gia-to-prosfygiko-metanasteftiko-zitima-tin-17-10-2019/

people) is six times greater than their capacity (6,138 accommodation places). Moria in Lesvos is the epitome of repressive refugee management, where a structure of 2,800 places accommodates about 14,000 people, many of them outside the hotspot in tents or even without tents. The situation on the island of Samos has also deteriorated lately, where a tenfold number of people currently reside in a hotspot with 648 places.

The housing conditions in the mainland camps are also marked by severe deficiencies and full capacity at 100 %, especially in the urban centers. In a few cases, these living conditions directly threaten human life. According to a report by the International Organization for Migration (IOM) (2019a), 28 camps are currently operating in the mainland in the regions of Attica, Central Greece, Central Macedonia, Eastern Macedonia and Thrace, Epirus, Thessaly, and Western Greece.

In many camps, phenomena of overcrowding are reported. These are housing practices that are unable to meet basic human needs. In addition, there are questions about their legal status and how they are controlled (Council of Europe, 2018: 5). Adverse housing conditions are mainly due to the lack of centralized planning and coordination between stakeholders and services. Also significant are the problems arising from the lack of the implementation of the relevant provisions for dealing with these dysfunctions and the inefficient use of the available financial resources (Tab. 12.2) (The Greek Ombudsman, 2017: 39).

The main dimension highlighted in the case of the camps is accommodation in inappropriate conditions. In fact, this situation has been perpetuated and extended for long periods of time. Their inadequacy goes hand in hand with poor quality logistic infrastructure, poor health conditions, or even being accommodated in tents. These phenomena are also observed during periods of extreme weather in both winter and summer. A serious problem is still the lack of safe accommodation in these areas (Amnesty International, 2018).

Tab. 12.2: Ratio of housing places to actual population hosted in mainland accommodation (September 2019)

Region	Places	Actual population
Alexandria	614	627
Andravida	312	288
Diavata	928	951
Doliana	129	106
Drama	420	325
Elefsina	180	202
Eleonas	1850	1871
Filippiada	625	516
Grevena	742	754
Kato Milia	340	295
Katsikas	1040	976
Kavala	586	461
Korinthos	672	575
Koutsochero	1678	1447
Lagadikia	456	429
Lavrio	269	241
Malakasa	1589	1787
Nea Kavala	2098	1814
Oinofyta	590	508
Ritsona	900	860
Schisto	1100	903
Serres	652	935
Skaramangas	3196	2211
Thermopiles	560	514
Thiva	956	790
Veria	341	325
Volos	150	161
Volvi	1000	993
Total	23,973	21,865

Source: IOM (2019a)

3.2 Housing and Social Policies in Social Apartments

The housing and social support program for asylum seekers in social housing is ESTIA. ESTIA was created with the UNHCR's executive management and EU funding in collaboration with Greek state authorities, local authorities, and NGOs. In its original form, launched in October 2015, it was called the "Accommodation and Relocation Program." The primary objective was to house applicants for relocation or family reunification in other EU Member States, as well as asylum seekers with high vulnerability. Since January 2016, UNHCR has received funding from the Directorate-General for Migration and Home Affairs (DG Home) for its implementation. By the end of the same year it had managed to open 20,055 housing units (UNHCR, 2018a).

Since 2017, the program has evolved into its current version and been renamed ESTIA, with a new goal of reaching 22,000 housing units by the end of December. In this new form, its funding comes from the Directorate-General for European Civil Protection and Humanitarian Operations (DG ECHO). The beneficiaries of the intervention have been extended to include asylum seekers, with priority being given to the most vulnerable, to recognized refugees, and to candidates for family reunification and relocation to other EU countries. In 2018, ESTIA set a target of increasing its hosting capacity to 27,000, under the same framework, while closing several camps, which it achieved (UNHCR, 2018a). The last year of implementation of the program through Emergency Community Fund is 2019. By 2020, the program is expected to be financed by the AMIF national program and responsibility for its management will be transferred to the Greek state.

ESTIA's goal is to ensure adequate housing and social support for its beneficiaries by moving them from camps to social housing. According to the relevant guide to the local authorities issued by UNHCR (UNHCR, 2018b: 2–4), in addition to the housing subsidy, the program includes a range of accompanying services to fulfill the provisions of the Community Directive on "adequate reception conditions."

These benefits include cash assistance, which aims to meet the basic living needs of the beneficiaries. In collaboration with the Greek government, the amount was calculated to be commensurate with the amount of social solidarity income and ranges from 150 to 550 euros depending on the number of members of each family. Financial assistance is provided directly by UNHCR through a single system of prepaid cards to all beneficiaries.

The operation of ESTIA is supported by psychosocial support services. In their current form, they are provided by social scientists who work on the program, who offer their services to beneficiaries at home. More specifically, they are

Tab. 12.3: ESTIA accommodation capacity (October 15, 2019)

Total Number of Places	25,477
Actual Capacity	22,180
Current Population	21,523
Occupancy Rate	97 %

Source: UNHCR (2019) https://data2.unhcr.org/en/documents/download/71778

responsible for the entire stay of the beneficiaries, from reception to retirement (guidance and information provision, regular monitoring of daily living issues, resolution of potential problems, attendance, mediation and referral to organizations and services, compliance file, etc.). The work of the social scientists is supported by interpreters and those responsible for accompanying social services beneficiaries. Finally, hosting supervisors assume responsibility for the stay in the apartments. In addition to the support services provided under the program, referral procedures to specialized social structures are also provided. The implementing partners of ESTIA are responsible for facilitating the access of beneficiaries to health and legal services (hospitals and legal support); municipal services (social solidarity structures, public education structures, and cultural and sports activities); and citizen solidarity initiatives.

The partners in the ESTIA implementation stage were the designated Municipalities and NGOs, which responded to the call for interest in the program. Each partner involved in the project had to staff a project team. For each of the 10 beneficiary apartments, there was a social scientist and an interpreter. For each of the 20 apartments, an escort and a hospitality supervisor were hired. The apartments that were selected had to meet a number of technical specifications to ensure decent living conditions (UNHCR, 2018b: 2–4).

A total of 18 partners were involved in the implementation phase of the current phase of ESTIA. Ten of these are Municipalities, either acting on their own or through their public or development companies, and eight are domestic or international NGOs. At the geographical distribution level, nearly 15,000 housing units have been created in Athens, nearly 4,000 in Thessaloniki, and the rest in other geographical areas of the Municipalities involved (UNHCR, 2018a). An important factor in ESTIA's overall operation to date was the advance payment of financing tranches to the partners, which ensured liquidity (Tab. 12.3).

Field research around the design and implementation of the ESTIA program (Kourachanis, 2018b) has produced useful findings. The planning phase highlights the emergency situation in which the program was designed and the inadequate link between housing and social integration. In general, its connection to the social services of the Greek state is not satisfactory. On the contrary, it encounters the wider dysfunctions and weaknesses of the Greek social protection system. The implementation part highlights the need for additional support initiatives by the implementing agencies. The initiatives primarily concern the development of social actions for the beneficiaries, burnout of program employees, the selection criteria for the beneficiaries, as well as the overcrowding of the program due to the lack of a satisfactory output (exit strategy) (Kourachanis, 2018b).

The Ministerial Decision of March 12, 2019 (Government Newspaper No. 85212.03.2019) set the framework for the exit strategy of recognized refugees from ESTIA. Those who were recognized refugees by the end of 2017 would have to leave their social apartments. The eviction would have temporarily exempted those families that had members with asylum decisions still pending. Also subject to temporary eviction were those families with a pregnant female member, families with children enrolled in school, and those with members who had serious health reasons or were beneficiaries on humanitarian grounds. It is noteworthy that refugees leaving the program will not be able to return to the camps as they apply for asylum. Beneficiaries who agreed to leave the program by the deadline would receive the cash assistance for another three months. Also, 3,000 of them would have the opportunity to participate in a vocational training program designed by the Ministry of Labor (UNHCR, 2019).

3.3 Housing and Social Policies for Recognized Refugees

HELIOS is a newly established rental subsidy program for recognized refugees, to be implemented by the International Organization for Migration and its partners with the support of the Greek Government and funded by the Directorate-General of the European Commission for Migration and Home Affairs. It is a pilot project aimed at supporting refugees and beneficiaries of subsidiary protection to be integrated into Greek society.

According to the HELIOS Project Regulations Handbook (IOM, 2019b), three eligibility criteria have been set: first, to be refugees or beneficiaries of subsidiary protection; second, to be recognized as a beneficiary of international protection after January 1, 2018; and third, be officially registered and reside in an open reception and identification structure or hotel in the IOM FILOXENIA program or in the ESTIA program.

The main purpose of HELIOS can be divided into two parts: the development of actions to support independent living and the monthly rental subsidy. HELIOS beneficiaries receive information, assistance, and financial support to improve their independent living skills. In particular, there is support for finding an apartment to rent that will be leased in the name of the beneficiaries. The rental period of the apartment should be at least 6 months and a maximum of 12 months. With the official renting of the apartment, the beneficiaries receive one-off financial assistance paid into a bank account. The amount of the one-off financial assistance varies from 440 euros for a single person to 1,490 euros for households of six or more. Along with the one-off financial assistance, there is also a rent subsidy ranging from 162 euros per month for one person to 630 euros per month for a household of six or more.

In addition to the HELIOS financial support, six-month mandatory integration seminars are also planned. These seminars will be divided into 280 hours of Greek language learning and 80 hours of soft skill modules (cultural orientation, life skills, and job readiness). In addition, HELIOS beneficiaries are expected to be able to make use of guidance services and other services related to their ability to be employable. Finally, social workers and interpreters will be used to monitor the social integration process of HELIOS beneficiaries and to provide psychosocial support whenever necessary (IOM, 2019).

3.4 Squat Practices for the Housing of Asylum Seekers and Refugees

Activists and groups in solidarity with refugees also gave their own solid response to the mainstream hotspots and camp policies in the form of squat practices, with political actions that seek both to promote social support for refugees and to attempt to highlight the stalemate created by the repressive EU refugee policy. The crisis in the efforts to manage refugee flows in recent years, as a result of the repressive EU immigration policy, has resulted in the mobilization of solidarity groups to support refugees. The wave of solidarity has sought, among other things, to separate political solidarity from NGO-funded humanitarian interventions (Maniatis, 2018). In housing terms, this support was expressed in the form of occupying empty buildings, that is, squatting. Dozens of squats have been created over the last three years in Greece to meet the housing needs of refugees on decent terms. Through such practices, solidarity organizations aim to raise the issue of the inhumane living conditions of asylum seekers and refugees in camps throughout Greece (Kotronaki, 2018). The bulk of the squats are geographically located mainly in Athens and Thessaloniki, while some others have been reported in provincial cities.

The national elections on July 7, 2019, brought the center-right New Democracy party to power and the new government of Kyriakos Mitsotakis has high on its political agenda the issue of security. The refugee issue is the most striking example to date. From August 2019 until today the government has evacuated many of the refugee squats in Athens (especially in the Exarchia area, where many activists are concentrated). All of the refugees who lived in squats (i.e., in otherwise empty buildings), many of them families with minors, were relocated back to the camps, that is, to worse housing conditions compared to those offered by the solidarity groups. The fact that small groups of activists, without funding and financial support, are able to provide better housing and social inclusion for some individuals than those offered by large international and Greek host programs suggests that this particular form of refugee management is intentional and the aim is precisely to discourage the entry of new refugee flows.

4 Conclusions

The analysis and data presented show that the policies developed over the last five years for housing and social support for asylum seekers and refugees do not serve the aims and values of social integration. Theoretical analysis has shown that social integration is much broader than the mere provision of accommodation. It includes access to a range of material and immaterial goods, such as food, housing, health, employment, but also social acceptance, social relations, and the development of social bonds, language, and cultural interaction, as well as the formation of a sense of belonging to the political community.

Modern European political reality is far removed from the development of social policies with such a target. This divergence is not due to the inability or inadequacy of refugee management but to a conscious political decision. The EU's asylum-seeker reception policies are designed to prevent refugee flows to the geographical borders of Europe. The security of the external borders is the main concern of these policies, which are shaped and implemented under repressive, militaristic, and controlling conditions. The establishment of hotspots as a key mechanism for managing refugee flows serves this broader purpose, as they are a double precautionary border: refugees are trapped in the southern border of Europe, while through the exclusionary practices of hotspots they discourage the arrival of new asylum seekers.

Shaping a policy of reception with an emphasis on hotspots and camps, therefore, serves the aims of social exclusion and repression rather than that of social integration. Greece is an indicative example of this way of managing refugees. The urgent establishment of structures and processes and the repressive nature of EU policy have resulted in the formation of a reception policy focusing on hotspots and camps. The overwhelming majority of asylum seekers and refugees are housed in hotspots and camps, and only a minority of them reside in social housing. Social support services are extremely inadequate in both hotspots and camps and in social apartments.

Accommodation in hotspots and camps violates human rights and does not guarantee adequate housing conditions, as stipulated by EU Directive 2013–33 EU. The housing inadequacy of hotspots and camps results in asylum seekers living in inappropriate housing conditions that threaten human life. At the same time, many of them lack access to fundamental human needs, such as potable water or basic hygiene and safety standards. The most important issue related to hotspots is that of housing overcrowding. At the time of writing, the population in the hotspots is five times as high as their housing stock. It is precisely to serve a political plan that Europe seeks not to be an attractive destination for refugee flows.

The development and operation of the housing program in the social apartments is a very positive step, which needs to be further supported by the Greek state. It is necessary to provide more housing in order to eliminate the practice of people living in camps. In addition, social integration policies, as well as housing subsidies, should include cultural familiarization and social awareness practices, as well as interventions to enhance training and employment, in order to increase the prospects for the beneficiaries' empowerment and social autonomy. This can only be achieved through the development of a holistic social integration plan, of which ESTIA will be a vital central component.

The housing subsidy for recognized refugees comes with a long delay. The formulation of a housing subsidy program for landlords themselves, for a certain period of time, in combination with integration measures, is an intervention that will enhance the empowerment and social autonomy of refugees. However, the length of time (from 6 to 12 months) probably cannot be considered sufficient to ensure their ability to live independently thereafter. It remains to be judged in practice.

The existence of squats created by activists shows to a large extent that the specific form of the formal housing and social policies for refugees is not due to administrative incapacity but to political decisions. Because when activists with scarce resources and intervention means manage to house refugees in better conditions than in the camps, it is clear then that the goal of official policies is not social integration, but repression. Refugee squats are connected to the search for an alternative model of political action against repression and with a focus on solidarity. Reinforcing claims in this direction is important for social movements and refugee scholars towards the process of deconstructing dominant repression policies.

References

Ager A., Strang A. (2008). Understanding Integration: A Conceptual Framework. *Journal of Refugee Studies*, 21(2): 166–191.

Amnesty International (2018). *Amnesty International Report 2017–18*. London.

Balzacq T., Carrera S. (2006). Introduction: Policy Convergence in Migration, Borders and Asylum. In Balzacq T. & Carrera S. (Eds.), *Migration, Borders and Asylum. Trends and Vulnerabilities in EU Policy.* Brussels: Center for European Policy Studies.

Berry J.W. (1997). Immigration, Acculturation and Adaptation. *Applied Psychology*, 46: 5–34.

Busch-Geertsema V. (2013). *Housing First Europe. Final Report*. Brussels: European Commission.

Council of Europe (2018). *Report of the Commissioner for Human Rights of the Council of Europe Dunja Mijatović following her Visit to Greece from 25 to 29 June 2018*. Strasbourg.

Chou M.H. (2009). The European Security Agenda and the 'External Dimension' of EU Asylum and Migration Cooperation. *Perspectives on European Politics and Society*, 10(4): 541–559.

Csete E. (2016). *Cash-Based Programmes for Shelter and NFI. Implications upon Shelter Cluster Information Management Services*. Global Shelter Cluster. https://www.sheltercluster.org/sites/default/files/docs/cash_based_programmes_for_shelter_and_nfi.pdf

Davies T., Isakjee A., Dhesi S. (2017). Violent Inaction: The Necropolitical Experience of Refugees in Europe. *Antipode*, 49(5): 1263–1284.

Delanty, G. (2008), "Fear of Others: Social Exclusion and the European Crisis of Solidarity", Social Policy and Administration, 42(6): pp. 676–690.

Dewast C. (2016). *Literature Review for Cash in Shelter.* Global Shelter Cluster. https://www.sheltercluster.org/sites/default/files/docs/literature_review_of_cash_in_shelter.pdf

Fitzgerald E., Corsellis T., Vivo G., Debomy S. (2014). *Rental Support Cash Grant Programs: Operational Manual*. Washington: World Bank.

Geddes M. (2008). *Immigration and European Integration: Beyond Fortress Europe?*. New York: Palgrave Macmillan.

Idris I. (2017). *Effectiveness of Various Refugee Settlement Approaches.* K4D Helpdesk Report 223. Brighton, UK: Institute of Development Studies.

IOM (2019a). *Improving the Greek Reception System through Site Management Support and Targeted Interventions in Long-Term Accommodation Sites. Factsheet September 2019*. Athens.

IOM (2019b). *HELIOS. Hellenic Integration Support for Beneficiaries of International Protection. Project Regulations Handbook*. Athens.

Jahre M., Kembro J., Adjahossou A., Altay N. (2018). Approaches to the Design of Refugee Camps: An Empirical Study in Kenya, Ethiopia, Greece, and Turkey. *Journal of Humanitarian Logistics and Supply Chain Management*, 8(3): 323–345.

Kotronaki L. (2018). Outside the Doors: Refugee Accommodation Squats and Heterotopy Politics. *South Atlantic Quarterly*, 117(4): 914–924.

Kourachanis N. (2018a). Asylum Seekers, Hotspot Approach and Anti-Social Policy Responses in Greece (2015–2017). *Journal of International Migration and Integration*, 19(4): 1153–1167.

Kourachanis N. (2018b). From Camps to Social Integration? Social Housing Interventions for Asylum Seekers in Greece. *International Journal of Sociology and Social Policy*, 38(11/12): 1–15.

Kourachanis N. (2018c). The Housing Policy as a Social Policy. In Sakellaropoulos T., Economou C., Skamnakis C., & Angelaki M. (Eds.), *Social Policy*. Athens: Dionicos (in Greek).

Kourachanis N. (2019). *Refugee Housing Policies*. Athens: Topos (in Greek).

Lavenex S., Kunz R. (2008). The Migration–Development Nexus in EU External Relations. *Journal of European Integration*, 30(3): 439–457.

Levy C. (2005). The European Union after 9/11: The Demise of a Liberal Democratic Asylum Regime?. *Government and Opposition*, 40(1): 26–59.

Lewis H. (2015). Music, Dancing and Clothing as Belonging and Freedom among People Seeking Asylum in the UK. *Leisure Studies*, 34(1): 42–58.

Maniatis G. (2018). From a Crisis of Management to Humanitarian Crisis Management. *South Atlantic Quarterly*, 117(4): 905–913.

Ministry of Immigration Policy and UNHCR (2019). “Information Regarding the Exit of Beneficiaries of International Protection from “ESTIA” Programme”, Athens.

Mulkens S. (2017). *The Dehumanization of Refugees: A Framework. An Analysis of How Dehumanization Affects the Lives of Refugees in Two Different Refugee Camps/Centers*. RMA Thesis, Utrecht: Utrecht University.

Phillips D. (2006). Moving towards Integration: The Housing of Asylum Seekers and Refugees in Britain. *Housing Studies*, 21(4): 539–553.

Sahlin I. (2005). The Staircase of Transition: Survival through Failure. *The European Journal of Social Science Research*, 18 (2): 115–136.

Scipioni M. (2018). Failing forward in EU Migration Policy? EU Integration after the 2015 Asylum and Migration Crisis. *Journal of European Public Policy*, 25(9): 1357–1375.

Tazzioli M., Garelli G. (2018). Containment beyond Detention: The Hotspot System and Disrupted Migration Movements across Europe. *Environment and Planning,* 1. https://journals.sagepub.com/doi/abs/10.1177/0263775818759335

The Greek Ombudsman (2017). *Migration Flows and Refugee Protection. Administrative Challenges and Human Rights Issues.* Athens.

Tsemberis S., Eisenberg R.F. (2000). Pathways to Housing Supported Housing for Street-Dwelling Homeless Individuals with Psychiatric Disabilities. *Psychiatric Services*, 51(4): 487–493.

UNHCR (2014). *Policies Alternatives to Camps.* Geneva.

UNHCR (2016). "Regional Refugee and Migrant Response Plan For Europe", Report, Geneva.

UNHCR (2018a). *Managing Cooperation Agreements in the Framework of the Asylum Seeker Housing Program.* Athens.

UNHCR (2018b). *Framework for Asylum Seekers and Refugees. Local Authorities Information Guide.* Athens.

Vis B. (2009). Governments and Unpopular Social Policy Reform: Biting the Bullet or Steering Clear? *European Journal of Political Research*, 48: 31–57.

Maria Bottiglieri

Chapter Thirteen Decentralised Cooperation and Global Education in Turin

Abstract: Decentralized cooperation and Global education are an important support in defense of Human Rights, empowering innovative Local public policies and changing the narrative on Migration. They both represent two processes that link the local issues with the global ones and contribute to localize the SDGs of Agenda 2030. Decentralized cooperation and Global education both use the Public-Private Partnership (PPP) approach to improve the *glocal* change processes. According to the Italian law (L. 125/2014), the PPP is empowered by the Migrants' associations that are recognized as new actors of international cooperation. This chapter would like to show those topics through the case study of the Turin municipality. Turin is one of the most relevant Italian municipalities that has been working on Decentralized cooperation and Global education since many years. Furthermore, Turin is one of the few Italian municipalities that approved the strategic guidelines on international cooperation and intercultural policies.

1 Introduction

Decentralized cooperation and Global education help fulfilling Human Rights, improving innovative local public policies and changing the narrative on migration[1]. They represent two processes that link the local issues with the global ones and contribute to localize the Sustainable Development Goals (SDGs) of Agenda 2030.

Both decentralized cooperation and Global education use the positive approach of the public/private partnership that is one of the most important bricks in the *Agenda for Change* processes[2].

---

1 About the alternative narrative see the work of The Council of Europe through The Intercultural cities programme (ICC), in particular Del Felice, C., Ettema, M. (Eds.) 2017, *WE CAN! Taking Action against Hate Speech through Counter and Alternative Narratives,* Council of Europe Publishing (online https://www.coe.int/en/web/no-hate-campaign/we-can-alternatives).

2 The Agenda for Change, adopted in 2011, is the basis for the EU's development policy for the 2014–2020 period. See more Agenda for Change – COM(2011) 637 final, 30 August, 2017 on https://ec.europa.eu/europeaid/agenda-change-com2011-637-final_en.

The Italian law improves this partnership by recognizing the Diaspora and Migrants Associations as new actors of international cooperation.

Moreover, the new Italian law on international cooperation (L. 125/2014[3]) allows the migrants' associations to act in the framework of Development cooperation as the other traditional actors – for example, the historical ones and the NGOs (Bottiglieri, 2017B).

The aim of this chapter is to discuss these topics through the case study of the municipality of Turin, one of the Italian municipalities most engaged in decentralized cooperation and Global education.

Furthermore, Turin is one of the few Italian municipalities that approved Strategic Guidelines on these issues with the administrative act (named *Delibera di Giunta*) on "International cooperation and peace activities planning 2017–2021." It states that in the framework of the Italian international cooperation strategies and guidelines, the Turin Municipality establishes local criteria to identify geographic priorities, development partnerships, and areas of intervention[4].

2 The Decentralized International Cooperation

Territorial or decentralized international cooperation, together with international bilateral cooperation (promoted at governmental level) and multilateral cooperation (promoted in the framework of international organizations), are part of the Development sustainable cooperation. This in turn is one of the international cooperation dimensions, together with economic, industrial, and cultural cooperation.

Territorial or decentralized cooperation in particular consists of international cooperation actions for Sustainable Development "carried out by Regional and Local Authorities in the framework of territorial partnership relations with the local Counterparts of the partner countries. These actions are aimed at establishing and strengthening a mutual and equal sustainable development. Public and private stakeholders located in the partner countries are actively involved in the realization of decentralized cooperation actions"[5].

---

3 Legge 11 agosto 2014 n. 125 – *Disciplina generale sulla cooperazione internazionale per lo sviluppo.*

4 Delibera di Giunta n. 2017-04952/001 approved on November 21, 2017 about *International cooperation and peace activities planning 2017–2021,* on http://www.comune.torino.it/giunta_comune/intracom/htdocs/2017/2017_04952.pdf.

5 Directorate General for Development Cooperation, *Linee Guida sulla cooperazione decentrata,* approved by Act on March 15, 2010 (www.cooperazioneallosviluppo.esteri.it/pdgcs/documentazione/PubblicazioniTrattati/2010-03-01_LineeGuidaDecentrata.

International development cooperation's core objectives are the expression of the Italian Republic Foreign Affairs, as established in article 2, law n. 125/2014:

a) Eradicating poverty and reducing inequalities, improving people living conditions, and promoting a sustainable development;
b) Protecting and consolidating human rights, individual dignity, gender equality, equal opportunities, and principles of democracy and legality;
c) Preventing conflicts, supporting processes of pacification, reconciliation, post-conflict stabilization, consolidating and strengthening democratic institutions.

Italian development cooperation's goals are coordinated with the European and international goals, particularly with the *17 Sustainable Development Goals* included in the *2030 Agenda* approved by the UN Assembly[6] (Bottiglieri 2017B). In this framework Local Governments are asked to contribute to the achievement of these Goals. In particular Sustainable Development Goal 11, *Make cities and human settlements inclusive, safe, resilient and sustainable*, entrusts local authorities with a double task: on the one hand, local authorities are requested to promote sustainable development of their territories, and on the other they are expected to achieve all the other Goals at local level.

The main feature of SDGs is their universal validity, that is: all countries without distinction are expected to achieve the goals according to their capacities. Therefore, all players are requested to contribute: governments (at local and central level), private sector and civil society.

In this framework – with regard to the achievement of the SDGs – local authorities' activities should be dual, impacting from both the *inside* and *outside*.

From the inside local authorities are expected to provide public services ensuring that all citizens living in their territories may fully benefit from the fundamental rights related to each Goal (e.g. Right to Food, related to Goal number 2, Right to Water, Right to the City related to Goal n. 11, Right to education related to Goal n. 4, etc.).

From the outside, local authorities can cooperate with other cities in the world through international decentralized cooperation activities.

---

pdf); about this topic see Bottiglieri, 2017A; Magarini, Nicolareu, Dansero, Bottiglieri 2017.

6 General Assembly, *Resolution adopted by the General Assembly on September 25, 2015 – Transforming our world: the 2030 Agenda for Sustainable Development* – A/RES/70/1, October 21, 2015 (www.un.org).

According to the Italian law and case law, Italian local authorities can collaborate with the government to carry out international cooperation activities in the frame of the legality principle when they have a "local public interest Main interests and topics concerning decentralised cooperation are: enhancement of immigrants communities as well as emigrated communities, global solidarity co-development, governance of commons, internationalization and "glocalization" (Ferrarese, 2006).

Partners of local authorities in this activity are all the actors of international solidarity active in the territory: NGOs, profit and non-profit bodies, associations, cooperatives, universities, institutions, public companies and religious bodies.

The Italian legislation has recently expanded the typology of the actors of international cooperation, recognizing a pre-existing and consolidated practice of decentralized cooperation arranged by local governments; for instance, the art. 26 of law n. 125/2014 recognizes the new actors of international cooperation as the fair trade associations, microfinance bodies, companies and, as the first law in Europe, it recognizes a role to diaspora associations in international cooperation processes[7].

This recognition meets the needs of the "co-development" that was already practiced for years in many international cooperation activities promoted also by local authorities (Mezzetti & Ceschi, 2019; Bottiglieri, 2017C; Ambrosini, & Berti, 2009)[8].

---

7 Art. 2 co. 6 – Law n. 125/2014: "6. The Italian cooperation policy, by promoting local development and also thanks to the role of the immigrant communities and their relations with their countries, gives an important contribution to migrant policies shared with the partner countries and inspired by the protection of human rights and by the respect of the european and international laws." Art. 26: the subjects of cooperation are "d) the migrants' organisations and associations that still have a liaison with the communities in their countries on the topics of cooperation and support to their development or that work with those subjects who have the previous requirements and are active in the involved countries; a *diaspora* representative is a member of the cooperation national council established by Art. 16 as a permanent tool for participation, consultation and proposal."

8 For example, the Turin Municipality experience started with Teranga project in 2006. See more on http://www.comune.torino.it/cooperazioneinternazionale/uno-sguardo-complessivo/scheda_louga.shtml. The co-development is a trend of thought and a development strategy in development studies which considers migrants to be a developing factor for their countries of origin.

The diaspora has a relevant role in the processes of Development Cooperation much as in those of Global Education. Both activities can contribute to contrast the bad image on migration and changing the narrative on migration.

The measures used by public administrations in order to give relevance to diaspora associations vary from public calls for projects to political processes.

The first public calls launched by AICS (the new Italian Agency of Development Cooperation, born thanks to Law 125/2014) gave specific relevance to the candidate projects in which local authorities or NGOs included such migrants' associations in their partnership (Bottiglieri, 2018).

At the same time, the process of building a regional and national network of Migrant Associations active in development cooperation is leading to a greater awareness by the diasporas about the role they should play in development cooperation policies.

This process is called *Diaspora National Summit* (Stocchiero, 2019). The training courses promoted by its team in local and regional territories aim to strengthen the capacity of these associations in managing and planning international and cooperation projects[9].

Local and national meetings organized in many Italian cities aim to give a political role to diaspora's associations.

The specific role that regions and local authorities have in the path of the *Diaspora National Summit* is well evidenced by the experiences promoted by the municipalities like Turin and Milan, or Bologna and Rimini. In fact, they all have hosted their first local diaspora meetings.

The municipalities are changing the narrative on migration through international cooperation processes and projects.

In terms of processes, we highlight that diaspora partnership is part of the strategy promoted by the City of Turin which, according the legislative framework, expressed criteria and objectives of decentralized cooperation activities of the municipality, through specific guidelines.

In particular, the diaspora partnership is a criterion to identify:

a) The geographical areas suitable to launch or to strengthen international relations with partner cities focused on migration (the *Delibera* talks about citizens of Turin coming from the partner-municipality);
b) The partnership for development and to find the project partners (the *Delibera* talks about associations of migrants and diaspora communities that promote co-development in the geographical area of origin).

---

9 See more on https://summitdiaspore.org/.

c) The main thematics and priorities of Turin decentralized cooperation, with particular focus on the connections between migration and development cooperation policies.

3 Decentralized Cooperation and Migration Experiences in Turin

Some specific projects have been promoted and launched within this programmatic framework.

In this chapter, we will highlight three projects that specifically link the new narrative on migration with international cooperation:

- *XARIT – Friendship between Louga and Torino Youth Centers;*
- *MENTOR – Mediterranean Network for Training Orientation to Regular migration;*
- *PAISIM – program to support social enterprise and migrant initiative in Saint Louis, Louga and Thiès regions project.*

The regional project XARIT aims to strengthen the network of services for young people in Louga (Senegal), in order to create synergy between the promotion policies and services active at a territorial level regarding the youth.

An exchange platform has been created through the strengthening of a cultural center dedicated to the young people of Louga, as well as through the opening of two new outlying front desks targeted to collect youth information's needs. This platform presents a virtual front desk (inspired to the TorinoGiovani model), targeted to the improvement of current services.

A particular focus is dedicated to the training (*front office and back office*) of the operators in charge of managing both center and front desks. The exchange with the Torino InformaGiovani Center empower the skills as well as the promotion of a new culture of solidarity and institutional friendship.

The project partners are: Torino Municipality (project Leader), Louga Municipality, RE.TE. NGO, CISV, AST, ENAIP, and CEFAM. Project beneficiaries are students, young people, and local administrators.

The XARIT project is quite relevant, for it is the project led by the City of Turin in which a diaspora association is not only a beneficiary, but also an official partner.

The City of Turin has been promoting development projects on migration since 2006. This was the case of the Teranga project (2007–2009). However, in the Teranga project the partner was an association of intercultural mediators, whose associates were both Italian and new Italian citizens. The direct partnership of an association of migrants (in this case, the Association of the Senegalese community from Turin) has completely changed the perspective. Moreover, this association becomes the direct interlocutor of the local authority on several levels: institutional, political, contractual, and accounting (Bottiglieri, 2017c; Bottiglieri, 2018).

In this frame, the crisis of co-development, highlighted by many doctrines (Mezzetti, 2019), seems just a political-sociological issue, while in terms of administrative and juridical practices co-development is yet to be invented and experimented.

The *MENTOR* project was aimed to: 1) strengthen cooperation among the services' providers related to train employment and youth policies in Italy (Milan and Torino), Morocco (Beni Mellal, Khouribga, and Fquih Ben Salah), and Tunisia (Gran Tunis territory); 2) improve the skills of employment mentors and local operators of the targeted territories that work with young people to promote circular and temporary migration; 3) increasing information availability for Moroccan and Tunisian citizens about the legal migration opportunities both in Italy and EU; and 4) enhancing young Moroccans and Tunisians' access to employment in their country of origin by following their training or professional experience in Italy (Torino and Milan). The main activities are: raising awareness campaigns on temporary and circular migration targeted at young people in Tunisia and Morocco, selection of young candidates in Morocco and Tunisia, listing of companies in Italy and *matching* candidate/company, professional internships including pre-stage training and post-stage *mentoring*, and publishing of guidelines and recommendations targeted to the realization or to the improvement of procedures related to professional internships both in Italy and the EU, with focus on circular migration and local development[10]. Project partners are municipality of Milan (project leader), municipality of Turin, Agenzia Piemonte Lavoro (Piedmont Region agency for employment), and ANOLF (technical partner). Beneficiaries are 20 young Moroccans and Tunisians, local authorities, enterprises, and citizens.

This project is relevant because not only is it the first circular migration project promoted in Europe by local authorities but also it shows that their role in

---

10 See more on the website: https://www.networkmentor.org/home the video https://www.facebook.com/136603537090607/videos/305626626889029/ About Mentor see also the Video MORE – Mobility Opportunities and REgular Migration on https://www.youtube.com/watch?v=pTwqf_ppRgE.

migration processes is not only a role of implementation of emergency activities related to reception of immigrants, but also a preventive and proactive role in promoting legal migration paths that correspond to the public and private interests of the territories of the south and north shores of the Mediterranean Sea (Bottiglieri, 2018).

The PAISIM project aims to fight poverty and the primary reasons of irregular migration by supporting rural economy in the Louga, Saint Louis, and Thiès regions (Senegal).

Its main objectives are: in Senegal, to create employment opportunities in the agricultural sector, prioritizing young people, women, and "social" as well as "green" initiatives, by supporting 200 rural microenterprises and 10 migrant initiative enterprises; in Italy, to enhance the migration experience of Senegalese population in Italy by supporting investment projects in Senegal; and to provide public opinion with a new point of view about migrants living in Italy. Project partners are CISV (project leader), IPSIA, RE.TE. NGO, Sunugal Italia, Etimos Foundation, CreSud, Asescaw, Fapal, Sunugal Senegal, municipality of Turin, municipality of Milan, and CISAO. Project beneficiaries are young people, women, Senegalese entrepreneurs, Senegalese migrants, Italian and Senegalese local authorities, and citizens.[11]

PAISIM is an important project not only because it supports rural entrepreneurial initiatives originated by migrants in the region (collaborating with institutional and financial actors in the area), but also because the project provides a rating system for microenterprises' access to credit with social and environmental value, and the launch of an investment fund.

4 Global Education

The Italian law calls Global Education: "Education to Global Citizenship (ECG)." ECG is a specific dimension of international cooperation policies and – with development cooperation and humanitarian aid – is one of the objectives of the Italian foreign policy in this field[12].

---

11 About the project, see website: http://cisvto.org/cisv/cosa-facciamo/progetti/04-impresa-sociale-e-iniziative-migranti-paisim – On the micro-enterprises experience see more of the following short videos: https://youtu.be/r9E6kDkNP5g; https://youtu.be/UM3VLWg8j_w?list=PL7DqYwpp-oTrrzVosA3ds6in09ArdH4sZ; https://youtu.be/Ith8ghC2ydM; https://youtu.be/LVgAmAyijBs.

12 See 4 art. 1 L 124/2015: "Italy promotes education, awareness and participation of all citizens to international solidarity, cooperation and sustainable development."

Recently ECG has been rediscovered as a central measure against intolerance and terrorism and as a lever to untie stereotypes and prejudices.

The Italian ECG guideline gives many different meanings to global education:

1) From the NGOs' point of view: an *education capable of the future, which focuses on human rights, commons, and sustainability.*
2) The Italian local authorities' point of view, expressed in a document approved by the Conference of Regions and Autonomous Provinces, underlines the community approach: ECG is based on the concept of interdependence between the local and the universal level and is based on a sustainable, empathetic, and supportive behavior.

In the practices of ECG, educational policies, environmental and international cooperation migrations, and social cohesion are strongly linked to each other.

The Italian cooperation guidelines on ECG adopt the UNESCO approach, that is to say ECG is "a training process that arouses people to be committed for a change in social, cultural political and economic structures that has an influence on their lives."[13]

It considers ECG as an action for change, based on the use of innovative teaching methods, related to both formal and informal education, based on dialogue and thought, in which the learner is placed at the center[14].

According to the art. 4 and art. 26 of Italian law on international cooperation, the local authorities and diaspora's associations are also actors of ECG process and strategy.

The Italian ECG strategy is part of the global and European strategy.

Educating to global citizenship is in fact first and foremost one of the Goals of the global agenda for Sustainable Development 2030. The Goal n. 4 commits the

---

13 Global Education Monitoring Report Team, *Global education monitoring report, 2019: Migration, displacement and education: building bridges, not walls,* 2018 on https://en.unesco.org/gem-report/.

14 See AICS, *Strategia italiana di Educazione alla cittadinanza globale,* 2018 on https://www.aics.gov.it/wp-content/uploads/2018/04/strategia-ECG-2018.pdf. This report, written by all the cooperation subjects, has thrree parts: in the first one, the main subjects involved in the strategy are presented and ECG are contextualized globally, in Europe and in Italy's last 50 years' history. In the second one, there are definitions and the strategy follows the United Nations' point of view. This document then explains objectives, topics, and main issues; its role in the framework of formal and nonformal education, and sensitization. It explains its educational role and lists the subjects that must apply the strategy, their roles, interactions, and synergies.

international community to "provide quality, fair and inclusive education and learning opportunities for all." Indeed, obtaining a quality education is the core to create sustainable development.

With this framework, global education is directly named in paragraph 4.7 which requires to "ensure that all learners acquire the knowledge and skills needed to promote sustainable development, including, among others, through education for sustainable development and sustainable lifestyles, human rights, gender equality, promotion of a culture of peace and non-violence, global citizenship and appreciation of cultural diversity and of culture's contribution to sustainable development."[15]

The European Union, through the program DEAR (Development Education and Awareness Raising Program) also contributes to improve global education. According the EuropeAid view,

> the Development education and awareness raising (DEAR) aims to inform EU citizens about development issues, mobilise greater public support for action against poverty, give citizens tools to engage critically with global development issues, to foster new ideas and change attitudes.

Its objectives are: informing EU citizens about development issues and foster awareness and understanding of global development and recognition of interdependence; mobilising greater public support for action against poverty and fairer relations between developed and developing countries; changing attitudes, provide the European public with tools to engage critically with global developments and supporting the emergence of new ideas on development issues"[16].

The EU provides funding for DEAR projects through a dedicated program.

The DEAR program also involves the local authorities, as stated by art. 14 of *Regulation (ec) no 1905/2006 of the European parliament and of the Council* of December 18, 2006, establishing a financing instrument for development cooperation: "The objective of the thematic programme on non-State actors and local authorities in development supports initiatives proposed and/or carried out by civil society organisations and local authorities originating from the Community and partner countries in the area of development [...]. The programme is implemented in consistency with the objective of this Regulation and to strengthen the capacity of non-State actors and local authorities in the policy making process, so as to: increasing the level of awareness of the European citizen regarding development issues and mobilising active public support in the

15 See note number 5 about Agenda 2030.

16 About DEAR programme, see more on https://ec.europa.eu/europeaid/node/655_fr.

Community and acceding countries for poverty reduction and sustainable development strategies in partner countries, for fairer relations between developed and developing countries, and reinforce civil society and local authority roles for these purposes."[17]

Based on this regulatory framework and local, national, European, and international policies, some specific financial programs and measures, at each level, aim to strengthen the actions of local authorities and civil society in order to enhance the global education processes.

The City of Turin, as many other European municipalities, promotes or adheres to global education process and projects that aim at the protection of all fundamental rights and, in particular, of the ones of people in conditions of greater fragility, such young people, women, and new citizens.

In the administrative act on international cooperation and peace of the City of Turin, the education for global citizenship is the second strategic priority expressed by the resolution approved by the Turin guidelines, where migration policies are the first priority.

The consequence of the combination of these two political priorities is that the activities of global education promoted with the contribution of the diaspora associations and migrants constitute a central and utmost commitment of the municipality[18].

5 The Global Education Experience in the Projects of the City of Turin

The level of commitment of the City of Turin is well expressed by three specific projects about Global Citizenship Education (GCED): the European and AICS project *Recognize and Change*, the AICS project *Recipes for dialogue*, and the AICS project *Our invisible cities. Meeting and new narrative of the world in the city*.

Recognize and Change project aims to enhance among citizens of the involved countries, in particular young people, the diffusion of a culture based on the plurality of identities and on their mutual recognition by fighting all forms of discriminations and violence, mainly those based on gender and cultural diversity.

17 See the text of *Regulation (ec) no 1905/2006 of the European parliament and of the Council* of December 18th on https://eur-lex.europa.eu/legal-content/EN/ALL/?uri=CELEX:32006R1905.

18 See more supra note 3.

The main activities are: 1. Actions in schools realized through mutual learning and *peer education* on three themes (once every year): 1.1. relationships: personal and social identity; 1.2. diversity and discrimination: equal and different; 1.3. violence: action and reaction; 2) raising awareness campaign realized through events, contest, and a multimedia platform; and 3) promotion of actions of local public policies (local and international workshops, meetings with the policy makers that dialogue with youth associations).

Project partners are Prefeitura Municipal de Fortaleza (Brazil), Caritas Ruse (Bulgaria), Delphi Association for Strategic Management (Bulgaria), Câmara Municipal da Praia (Cape Verde), Ville de Dunkerque (France), Vardakeios School for Indigent Children – Ermoupoli (Greece), Collegno Municipality (Italy), ISCOS Piemonte NGO (Italy), Comunidade Intermunicipal do Alto Alentejo – CIMAA (Portugal), Serviciul Public Asistenţă Socială Baia Mare (Romania), Direcţia Generală de Asistenţă Socială a Municipiului Bucureşti (Romania), Asociaţia Caritas Bucureşti (Romania), Diputación Provincial de Huelva (Spain), and Diputación Provincial de Jaén (Spain). Project beneficiaries are students, young people, schools, parents, youth associations, researchers, and local administrators[19].

The *Recipes for dialogue* project aims to promote dialogue and meeting through the "language of food," as the social element and contact point among people coming from different countries, tool of fusion and knowledge, economic growth, and employment. Indeed according to an Arabic saying "You really can't get to know a person 'till you haven't eaten together."

The project involves different sectors of the Piedmont region society, both improving the critical comprehension of plural society and increasing social and labor inclusion of the foreign population.

Main activities are: 1) a formal and informal education plan in the Piedmont provinces' schools and communities, mostly involving young people; 2) a path planned for migrants to promote social and labour inclusion through training; the set-up of entrepreneurial ideas based on the theme "food and intercultural dialogue"; 3) specific support for job placement; and 4) launch of institutional roundtables and calls, the participation at relevant territorial events.

19 See more the official website on www.recognizeandchange.eu; see also the video promos: (https://recognizeandchange.eu/PromoRCShort.mp4), the videos made by young people involved in the 2019 video contest: (https://videowall.recognizeandchange.eu/contest/), and the game Choose and change (https://game.recandchange.eu/).

Partners are LVIA (project leader), Slow Food, Renken Onlus, Cooperativa Colibrì, Panafricando, Asbarl, municipality of Turin, and Piedmont region. Beneficiaries of this project are young people, students, women, diaspora communities, and *nonprofit* associations[20].

The project "Recipes for dialogue" is part of the process towards a Turin food policy "Right to food oriented" (Ziegler, Golay, Mahon, Way, 2011), in which Turin has been engaged for many years (Bottiglieri, 2015; Bottiglieri, 2016).

Our invisible cities project aims to fight against false and discriminatory representations of migration and cultural diversity. In response to the dominant negative narrative of the migration phenomenon, the project wants to contribute to the spread of a new narrative based on *the others'* equal dignity and on the enhancement of the contribution that past and present migration processes have given to our society, through the realization of migration walks. *Migrantours* are guided visits of Italian city areas that are strategic from a cultural point of view. They are led by a migrant guide, or by a person living in our territory but coming from another country, able to talk about our city from a different perspective.

Project partners are Foundation ACRA (project leader), Oxfam Italy, Foundation Pubblicità Progresso, Foundation ISMU – Iniziative e Studi sulla Multietnicità, Viaggi Solidali Società Cooperativa Sociale, Casba Società Cooperativa Sociale, Cooperativa Sociale Progetto Con-Tatto, Next Generation Italy, Volunteering Association Amici di Sardegna, Association Trame di Quartiere, municipality of Milan, municipality of Turin, and International Research Centre on Global Citizenship Education – Bologna University[21].

These three projects are interesting for reasons of merit and method. First of all the target: in the two AICS projects, target is not young people, as in most

---

20 About the project, see more the website: http://old.lvia.it/italia/Le-Ricette-del-dialogo and the following videos: Young people at Terra Madre: https://youtu.be/ghLMYyy00JM The migrants' training: https://youtu.be/uFiy9do3gjI?list=PLaFrlDyz_DqdDg7-JABABIN1qD3hWJRHw, interculture and fair trade: https://youtu.be/Yef_C7Z_1II, African recipes: https://youtu.be/QdsZhbMW910?list=PLaFrlDyz_DqdDg7-JABABIN1qD3hWJRHw, recipes from food schools: https://youtu.be/MG2xiE1OMYE, and home restaurants https://www.youtube.com/watch?v=A2TRtQZwNtI. The Turin associations in "Paper Arcades" https://www.youtube.com/watch?v=w2i4WXeWRp0 &list=PLaFrlDyz_DqdDg7-JABABIN1qD3hWJRHw&index=15&t=0s.

21 See more on website: https://www.acra.it/index.php?option=com_content&view=article&id=1195&Itemid=1723&lang=it. See more the video about the Migrantour Experience on https://youtu.be/h2d9vEEpyjw and the video of the Project Campaign named "Adults and kids" on https://vimeo.com/328611339.

development education projects, but adults: food consumers or travelers, who approach a vision of global citizenship by using two very different, particular and popular languages: food and the urban landscape.

Another added value of the two AICS projects is the fact that in both the new citizens or second generations citizens are actors of the change, either because they cook the recipes for dialogue or because they are the "intercultural guides" guiding Italian citizens to visit the cities in which they were born make them see those cities from a different point of view. The new citizens in this case are not beneficiaries but co-actors of change.

The Recognize and Change project (R&C) is relevant for the methodology: peer education becomes a cascade peer education. With this approach young people involved in the project are not only beneficiaries of the project, but they are the first actors and protagonists of the change scenario.

Finally, a special mention should be given to the POPP project since it also contributes to change the narrative on asylum seekers and refugees. The POPP (*Progetto Organico Porta Palazzo*: Towards Circular Markets), through circular markets, focuses on multiple environmental, social, and economic topics related to food waste. POPP is focused on the food waste generated by Porta Palazzo, the largest and most culturally diverse food market in the city (and the largest open air market in Europe). An efficient waste collection system developed by a private partner and the collection of food waste by many volunteers organized by an NGO are primary partners of the city government. Interactions between vendors and volunteers extend far beyond efficient waste management to include greater food access to the poor and homeless, civic engagement and inclusion of new asylum seekers or new city residents, public education and awareness raising about the benefits of waste collection, composting, and food recovery. After just a few months from inception, organic matter collected for compost increased enormously. The volunteer brigade is the backbone of the program and its services have been extended to other areas that needed support, even beyond the food market to the second-hand market. Ongoing multisector public and private management of the program is made possible by the political commitment of the city and strong engagement of civil society[22].

22 See more about the project on the website: http://www.ecodallecitta.it/notizie/macro/15/sentinelle-dei-rifiuti/torino/ and http://www.milanurbanfoodpolicypact.org/2018/09/05/ghent-lima-win-mpa-2018-monetary-prizes/; see also the video on https://youtu.be/aQMNnhmtM_c.

This Turin municipality experience in the field of the development cooperation and global education, promoted with the diaspora and migrant associations, shows that local authorities have many tools to act in order to change the narrative on migration and to promote more intercultural cities, *human rights* oriented.

References

Ambrosini M., Berti F. (Eds.) (2009). *Persone e migrazioni: integrazione locale e sentieri di co-sviluppo*. Milano: Francoangeli.

Bottiglieri M. (2015). The Protection of the Right to Adequate Food in the Italian Constitution. In *Novità dal Forum – Rassegna 11/2015 (08.12.2015)* (on-line http://www.forumcostituzionale.it/wordpress/wp-content/uploads/2015/11/bottiglieri.pdf).

Bottiglieri M. (2016). The Turin Food Autonomy for a "Right to Food oriented" Urban Food Policy. In M. Bottiglieri, G. Pettenati, & A. Toldo (Eds.), *Taward the Turin Food Policy: Good Practices and Vision* (pp. 15–22). Milano: Francoangeli, (on-line http://ojs.francoangeli.it/_omp/index.php/oa/catalog/book/156).

Bottiglieri M. (2017a). Da cooperazione decentrata a partenariato territoriale. La cooperazione allo sviluppo degli Enti locali nelle prime attuazioni della nuova "Disciplina Generale sulla cooperazione internazionale per lo sviluppo" (L. 11 agosto 2014 n. 125). *Labsus 2017 (3)* (on-line https://www.labsus.org/wp-content/uploads/2017/03/Cooperazione_Internazionale_Bottiglieri.pdf).

Bottiglieri M. (2017b). La cooperazione internazionale decentrata: agire locale pensare globale. *Labsus 2017 (3)* (on-line https://www.labsus.org/2017/03/la-cooperazione-internazionale-decentrata-agire-locale-pensare-globale/).

Bottiglieri M. (2017c). Turismo responsabile e cooperazione decentrata. Il caso della Città di Torino. In G. Belli, F. Capano, & N.I. Pascariello (Eds.), *La città, il viaggio, il turismo. Percezione, produzione e trasformazione/The City, the Travel, the Tourism Perception, Production and Processing* (pp. 2029–2034). Napoli: Cirice Edizioni.(on-line http://www.fedoabooks.unina.it/index.php/fedoapress/catalog/view/96/78/492-1).

Bottiglieri M. (2018). La cooperazione decentrata o territoriale. Il ruolo delle Autorità locali nelle politiche europee di cooperazione allo sviluppo sostenibile e di *governance* del fenomeno migratorio. In A. Morelli, A. Iannuzzi, & C. Aliberti (Eds.), *Autonomie territoriali e Unione Europea. Fonti*

Istituzioni Diritti (pp. 345–370). Napoli: Editoriale Scientifica (Università degli Studi Roma Tre, collana CRISPEL, Sezione di diritto pubblico italiano ed europeo, F. Modugno (Series Ed.), Collettanee 9).

Ferrarese M.R. (2006), La "glocalizzazione" del diritto: una trama di cambiamenti giuridici. In C. Amato, & G. Ponzanelli (Eds.), *Global law V. Local law. Problemi della globalizzazione giuridica. XVII Colloquio biennale Associazione Italiana di Diritto comparato Brescia, 12–14 maggio 2005* (33–48). Torino: G. Giappichelli editore

Magarini A., Nicolareu Y., Dansero E., Bottiglieri M. (2017). Urban Food Policies: Decentralized Cooperation and African Cities. In B. Husson, S. Soukouna, & Y. Viltard (Eds.), *Revue internationale des études du développement, 232, 2017 (4),* monographical issue: *Stratégies internationales des collectivités territoriales*, pp. 67–93.

Mezzetti P. (2019). Migrazione e sviluppo tra crisi e rinnovamento. In P. Mezzetti, & S. Ceschi (Eds.), *Ripartire dall'Africa. Esperienze e iniziative di migrazione e di co-sviluppo* (pp. 3–8). Roma: Donzelli.

Mezzetti P., Ceschi S. (Eds.) (2019). *Ripartire dall'Africa. Esperienze e iniziative di migrazione e di co-sviluppo.* Roma: Donzelli.

Stocchiero A. (2019). Gli spazi di democrazia delle diaspore nel co-sviluppo. In P. Mezzetti, & S. Ceschi (Eds.), *Ripartire dall'Africa. Esperienze e iniziative di migrazione e di co-sviluppo* (pp. 165–179). Roma: Donzelli.

Ziegler J., Golay C., Mahon C., Way S. (2011). *The Fight for the Right to Food.* London: Palgrave Macmillan.

Part Three Migrations in the Media System

Antonia Cava, Gino Frezza and Gevisa La Rocca

Chapter Fourteen New Migrations in the Media Communication System

Abstract: The purpose of this chapter is to introduce the third section of the essay collection. So here we show – in short form – the importance of the media system in providing a representation of migrations and migrants.

1 The Media: Tools to Cross Borders

What is happening in Europe? What is going on in the world?

We know well that one way to get to know something physically distant from us – and thus form an opinion about it – is to ask the media. Be told by media what is happening. Each of us, then, in the silence of his screen decides which source to attach importance to and how and whether to express his opinion.

There is no doubt that, over the past few years, Europe has again acquired a central position in migratory geography, if it had lost it. Indeed, it has gained this central position again for obvious reasons, such as geographic location and socio-demographic structure, for example. Europe is, therefore, exposed to spontaneous migrations which are sometimes even unwanted, and which signal the need for planned flows and common policies. It is here, in this difficulty, that is, in the complexity of matching what is the migratory reality of today, with what are, instead, the aspirations and needs of Europe and above all of the individual member countries, one of the central challenges must be taken for European companies and institutions themselves. It is a complex challenge, no doubt. But it is precisely the complexity of these new challenges that call social sciences, communication scholars, and the organization of news in the media system to deal with European society and how it has transformed and how it is – still – transforming itself. Because if the solutions adopted by single societies are unsatisfactory to us, it is we who must strive to improve them, through the creation of a security that is dictated by inclusion and that fades threats to cultural identity through a process of knowledge of cultural identities themselves. To do this, perhaps, we should start thinking differently about the society and the societies in which we live.

The reflections on the role of the media and the communication system in the processes of generating integration or mechanisms of fear originate from here. Dealing with the narrative of new migrations in the media system means taking responsibility because the media produce effects. Media "effects" are simply the consequences of the activity – intentional or not – of mass means of communication. The expression "media power" indicates instead the ability of media to induce, provoke effects. "Media efficaciousness" concerns their efficacy in reaching a certain objective and implies in any case intention or a prearranged goal (McQuail, 1983). Media can facilitate or slow down change (McQuail, 1983) determining repercussions individually, collectively, institutionally, or culturally. By facilitating change, a role of mediation is attributed to the means of communication, which exercise it in the construction of meanings and of the most general processes of change in society. Media impact and penetration are felt not only by the single individual who is exposed to them reading a newspaper, watching television, or putting a post or tweet on social media. In the long term, the effects of media produce a cultural change. Media are able to produce a change of the cognitive structures, and, therefore, of the perception individuals have about what is happening around them because they not only bring closer and to the attention of their users events which otherwise would be distant, but they also provide a frame of interpretation, thanks to which the users can read and understand what is happening. Thus, information is not an amorphous object of communication; it is already interpreted by the media and its interpretation orients the users' reading (La Rocca, 2017).

In her human rights story, Hunt (2007) points out the importance of the role of the media in spreading knowledge of respect for others. The tools that Hunt uses are: individual autonomy and empathy, both in the author's "history" become evident, and therefore they develop thanks to one mass media, which today we would define as old or traditional: the printed paper, the books. The circulation of ideas, which is essential for change to take place, needs both a public sphere, an arena that can use them, and a tool that can convey their requests, which can express them (La Rocca, 2015). According to Melucci (2001), public speeches are stories that individual and collective actors make to someone for someone else.

We are going to draw on this subtle and strong importance of the media in narrating migrations and migrants, hoping to say well that the role of the media in crossing borders is not a secondary role.

2 The New Migrations in the Media Communication System

The central role that international migrations have gained in the contemporary debate leads us to rethink the interpretative paradigms that we have used so far to understand storytelling in migratory dynamics. In the process of social construction of migrations, the media have a relevant role, contributing to shape public representation of the "other" and the agenda of issues and problems felt by citizens and brought to the attention of public decision-makers. Migration as "total social fact" too often – as demonstrated in the chapters in this volume – has been defined as cultural emergency. The chapter form a mosaic of pieces held together, in our opinion, by the idea of border.

The word "'border" has a significant meaning: a porous limit, almost permeable, and from a cultural point of view it must be conceived as a place of continuous processes of translation: a filter between internal and external, a meeting/clash among different cultures, a place of crisis where production of sense is continuously redesigned. Dealing with migration obliges to rethink about the issues of borders (inside/outside) and about the relation with the other (us/them); therefore. it does not just mean how to handle the umpteenth "emergency."

Definition and classification of migrations do not apply to objective criteria but they are social constructs. Too often media and political actors take part in the process of social construction of immigrants, creating forms of labelling (extracomunitarian, refugee, illegal immigrant, etc.) that affect citizens' perception of migrants. The lens through which migrants are observed is a "us" defining "the other", often leading to an interpretation of the phenomenon as a problem. Above all in the periods of higher unrest, migrants are projected with intolerance and discomfort, and the community often ends up compacting itself against the threat coming from outside.

The analysis contained in this work goes deep into details in this crucial topic casting light on the problem of reinterpreting cultural maps that over the time have become more and more obsolete.

In media representations, migrants' point of view is almost totally absent, overwhelmed by a thematization that can be connected to concepts of legality, deviance, safety, criminality, and illegal migration. Chiurco, through the analysis of the European Social Survey (2016–2017), reports that discrimination and anti-immigration feelings are rising in public opinion. Mystification of information related to immigrants – generating a xenophobic rhetoric – determines a gap between perception and reality. In perceptions almost all phenomena are amplified and those more worrying, as migration, are felt like social emergencies.

The "normal" side of migration does not hit the headlines and extreme icons, labelling immigrants as victims or criminals, are more and more popular, while the process of stereotyping keeps on nurturing on repertoirs of images that are always the same. The portrait of immigration provided by the media appears like frozen and motionless, always anchored to the same narrative styles (Binotto, Bruno & Lai, 2016). The features of exceptionality that have so far characterized the tales of immigrants' lives become a daily representation generating what we could define an aesthetics of piety (Chouliaraki, 2006; Cava, Parito & Pira, 2018).

The rise of the web and the radical transformation of communicative flows from lines to nets, apart from having put into crisis the system of institutional information, strengthens narrative distortions regarding the topic of migration. Connections have transformed individuals from simple content users into content producers, although this mostly does not occur through an original act of creation, but through the activity of commenting and sharing. Pira, Fobert Veutro, and Fragapane and Mortara through their research point out the risk that the net can exacerbate the atmosphere of permanent emergency that generates fear. Disintermediation, in fact, can contribute to the acceleration of the process of narrative distortion. On the one hand, there is the extraordinary wealth that the abundance of information can offer, and on the other, the risk of the impossibility to handle this inflation of continuous messages.

Social actors are more and more taking advantage of digital platforms and providers that allow them to overcome mediations. Public actors are not any more stuck in places of consumption, utilization contexts become mobile, and even the activities of cultural consumption are multiplied. This has consequences on the content transmitted by digital technologies. With a contemporary audience that is more and more participatory, the web can become even the space for efficient counter-narrations. Many of the writers of the following pages underline the urgency of giving life to new narrations on migration in terms of cultural creativity. It is necessary to abandon the idea of immigration as ontological condition and the conviction that these lives are marked by an origin writing an infinite destiny. Because every difference, actually, should be contextualized, should be reversible. The presence of diversity reminds us, in fact, that other worlds are possible. Only in this way it is possible to move from the symbolic violence of hetero-definitions to the freedom of self-definitions (Cava, 2014). As well explained by Pasanisi and by Moralli, Parmiggiani and Paltrinieri in their analysis of drama and performative arts as spaces of social inclusion, drama can deconstruct distorted narrations through different strategies of acknowledgement of otherness, aiming at a new policy of being together and at a new culture of participation. Art, in other words, as a form of emancipation. As Bernardi has written (2014:13), the new frontier of drama is the dramaturgy of human relations and above all where there are difficulties and tragedies. The rhetoric of liability can be overcome if art becomes an instrument, physical and symbolic space, where it is possible to develop intercultural participation.

It is therefore crucial, in this sense, the issue of how to regenerate the relation among migration cultures and shared imagery. In the last decade, a mix of sociopolitical dynamics has fulfilled a sort of competitor-like approach: migratory processes are perceived, in a first step of the rebuilt imagery, as undermining coherence and solidity in the social organization, or at least putting it in front of risks for which there are no reliable and definite answers. And it is therefore undeniable that this approach feeds on a negative imagery, strongly oriented by political decisions made in muddy waters. Notwithstanding this, it is necessary to report a significant fact: there is no direct connection between, on one hand, critical situations for which migratory processes require tangible operational solutions and long-sighted decisions, and, on the other, visions and projections of threat taking over in the media (which in Italy are, for example, poorly regulated and, for this, easily influenceable).

It is therefore fundamental to take action so that that first step of collective imagery, rebuilt according to instrumental views, strategical for "negative" policies, is definitely contradicted by a new, different step in collective imagery connected to migratory processes.

It is a lengthy and hard job, but not impossible. There are antibodies present in current social and political forces working against considering how migratory processes can support an overall operation of reclassification of collective imagery. The target is supporting a coherent vision with perspectives of sustainable development and integration among far and different cultures; for this goal, in terms that are not short, but not even decades, knowing how to work well on imagery involved in social practices can accelerate the solution of issues connected to migratory processes.

Regarding the physical space, non-verbal communication gains particular relevance as Turco and, after, Polizzi explain. Turco points out that there are many reading keys of social phenomenon about migration because it is complicated and perpetually current. In existential-phenomenological view it is possible to look the reality through a relationship between autochthonous and Other, which takes place in physical spaces, such as streets, houses, and cities. In these places the first form of "silent" interaction takes place.

In fact, in the study of the migratory phenomenon it is undoubtedly fundamental to understand its impact on local realities, balancing the democratic principle of hospitality with the processes of integration and social inclusion (Colombo, 2017).

Polizzi accurately describes how the level of metacommunication gets complicated in intercultural relations. In the analysis of face-to-face interaction, it is necessary to pay attention to what is said and what is not said, to the uttered speech and to what is left unsaid. This is the reason why communication is always saying and not saying, a continuous series of words and silences creating proximity and distance (Pacelli, 2014). It must be acknowledged that as soon as – as observing subjects – we get an idea or an impression about anyone in front of us, we are almost involuntarily using a set of information provided by their non-verbal behaviour (Carzo 1992).

When we really start to feel the transfer and we get into touch with a new cultural space, the challenge to meet is to grasp the meanings of the new cultural frame comparing, mixing, and hybridizing them with the cultural features of their land of origin. Approaches to life are therefore modified; ways of thinking produce new results. In this process, immigrants' cultural consumptions can be spaces of connection favouring the interaction between country of origin and country of immigration, as pointed out in the essay by Cava, Carzo and Cava. Access to cultural consumption is in fact strategic to define the relation between culture of belonging and culture of origin. In this process, schools, as pointed out by Centorrino and Pellegrino, play the role of central institutions in looking for new strategies to handle multiculturality; schools can become a bridge between Country of Origin and Host Country, although Italian schools, object of their analysis, show some resistance in this sense.

New insights are needed to build Otherness without stereotypes, insights like the ones by Moravia and Pasolini narrated by Cutrona. New stories are needed as a place that is at the same time imaginary and real, where experiences can be shared. Marini's work closes this section presenting a critical view of the role played by the news media in the shaping of immigration, connecting the issue of migration with the concepts of post-welfare policy, uncertainty, and risk.

References

Bernardi C. (2014). *Il teatro sociale. L'arte tra disagio e cultura*. Roma: Carocci.

Binotto M., Bruno M., Lai V. (2016). *Tracciare confini. L'immigrazione nei media italiani*. Milano: Franco Angeli.

Carzo D. (1992). *Il diritto come retorica dell'interazione*. Milano: Giuffrè Editore.

Cava A. (2014). *Ombre migranti. Pratiche discorsive sullo straniero*. In P. Musarò & P. Parmiggiani (Eds.), *Media e migrazioni. Etica, estetica e politica del discorso umanitario*. Milano: Franco Angeli.

Cava A., Parito M., Pira F. (2018). Beyond aesthetics of pity. Italian media representation of migrants and emotional audience. *ICSR Mediterranean Knowledge*, 3: 49–81.

Chouliaraki L. (2006). *The spectatorship of suffering*. London: Sage.

Colombo M. (2017). Flussi migratori e integrazione, due ferite aperte nel cuore degli europei. Introduzione all'annuario CIRMiB 2017. In M. Colombo (Ed.), *Immigrazione e contesti locali. Annuario CIRMiB 2017* (pp. 9–26). Milano: Vita & Pensiero.

Hunt L. (2007). *Inventing human rights.* New York-London: Norton & Company.

La Rocca G. (2015). *Percorsi di comunicazione sociale. Teorie, strumenti, idee.* Roma: Carocci.

La Rocca G. (2017). Media, migrants and human rights. *International Review of Sociology*, 27(2): 225–229.

McQuail D. (1983). *Mass communication theory. An introduction*. London: Sage.

Melucci A. (2001). Su raccontar storie e storie di storie. In G. Chiaretti, M. Rampazi, C. Sebastiani (Eds.), *Condizioni, storie e discorsi* (pp. 123–34). Roma: Carocci.

Pacelli D. (2014). Il posto del silenzio nella teoria sociale: da forma relazionale a strumento di esclusione. M@gm@ Rivista Internazionale di Scienze Umane e Sociali, 12(2).

Lucia Chiurco

Chapter Fifteen Immigration and Discrimination: A Focus on Italy

Abstract: The study explores a range of issues covered by the most recent survey of the European Social Survey (ESS), Round 8 (2016–2017), concerning discrimination and attitudes towards immigrants and immigration. Country-level elements and international studies are used to try to link the main findings to the potential factors triggering anti-immigrant attitudes. The overall results show that attitudes are relatively homogeneous concerning levels of support, or lack thereof, for immigrants, while there are wider cross-country differences in opinion about the impact on society, international protection and access to social services. Anti-immigration sentiments are growing across European societies, and immigration flows are likely to increase in the coming years. It is therefore imperative to promote legislative measures against the use of hate speech along with measures addressing the conditions conducive to its use. It is also necessary to strengthen social cohesion and ensure equal opportunity for all, turning to the strategy of "mainstreaming" integration.

1 Introduction

International migration, defined by Castles and Miller (2014) "as a key dynamic within globalization" (p. XII), is increasingly perceived by public opinion in the host countries as a threat. In the ongoing economic and social crisis, the potential effects of immigration on the economic and political-institutional spheres, on social relations (in particular those between gender and generations), the labour market and welfare trigger fear and frustration. Furthermore, as Zanfrini (2016) explains, immigration represents a challenge to the idea of ethnic homogeneity on which the nation state is based. As a result, the level of politicization concerning the immigration issue has increased in Europe. In recent years, the topic of international mobility has received a high level of mediatization, whilst alarming levels of hostility, discrimination, racial harassment and violence towards immigrants and asylum seekers is growing in many countries, including Italy.

Regarding immigration-related news, media monitoring reports say that Italian media coverage leads to the perception of immigrants as a threat[1]. The

1 The Association Carta di Roma says that media coverage has increased rapidly in Italy since 2015. The annual reports in 2016 and 2017 show that representation of migrants

mainstream and digital media, often using discriminatory language[2], influences social representation. Consequently, hostile narratives converts opinion into fact. In Italy, the figure of *the immigrant* in the public discourse is represented as male, in an irregular situation, or asylum seekers, black, and/or Muslim. However, actual statistics differ from this. The vast majority of immigrants are long-term residents, Europeans and/or Christian. The gender composition is balanced, with a slight majority of women. At the end of 2018, there were 5,255,503 foreigners in Italy, corresponding to 8.7 % of the Italian population (Italian National Institute of Statistics [ISTAT], 2019); and according to the United Nations High Commissioner for Refugees (2018), refugees numbered 189,000 (3 refugees per 1,000 people), whilst the Foundation for Initiatives and Studies on Multi-ethnicity (ISMU) (2018) estimates immigrants in an irregular situation accounted for 533,000 people. Although the focus has primarily been on asylum seekers in recent years (ISTAT reports 130,000 new applications for refugee status in 2017 and less than 60,000 in 2018), family reunification and work are the two most common reasons for settling in Italy.

Many sources collect data on public opinion regarding immigration and immigrants via standardized surveys across countries[3]. The main European polls, Eurobarometer (Standard and Special editions) and European Social Survey (ESS), collect information on public opinion across EU member states on different topics, including migration-related issues. However, these surveys have their limitations because they principally report the opinions of the population's national majority with few respondents from an immigrant background due to the difficulty of reaching them. Consequently, the cross-national analysis on perceptions held by immigrants remains an understudied field.

This lack of data (especially comparable data) makes it difficult for policymakers at national and EU levels to develop and target integration mechanisms aimed at the immigrant population in order to fight discrimination. Moreover, data on how people with an immigrant background experience everyday life can be useful to build indicators of integration in the areas of social cohesion, discrimination and active citizenship. For these reasons, it is important to refine research

---

and refugees were often negative. The issues most frequently connected to immigration were security, invasion, suspicion, threat and illnesses.

2 See Chiurco, Gentile and Monaldi (2014).

3 Gallup World Poll, International Social Survey Program (ISSP), World Values Survey (WVS), Pew Global Attitudes Survey, Ipsos Global Trends and Observatory of Public Attitudes to Migration (OPAM).

methodologies for sampling and surveying hard-to-reach groups, such as people with an immigrant background.

Misinformation and fake news about immigration have plagued the public debate for years, fostering an anti-immigrant sentiment. Only a minority of Italians (2 %) say they are well informed regarding immigration, and 46 % think that the media presents immigrants objectively. Italians (as Europeans) tend to largely overestimate the number of non-EU immigrants as a proportion of the population. Half of them think that immigration is more a problem than an opportunity. Italians say immigrants are a burden on the welfare system (63 %), worsen crime problems (75 %) and take jobs away from workers (58 %) (Special Eurobarometer 469, 2018). Immigration is the main concern at the European level (39 %), and outstrips concern over the economic situation (17 %) and unemployment (13 %) (Standard Eurobarometer 88, Autumn 2017).

Contrary to the current perception of immigration, according to the Organisation for Economic Co-operation and Development (OECD) and European Union (EU), facts show that people from an immigrant background face numerous obstacles accessing the labour market, accommodation, health care and education (OECD & EU 2018). Surveys can be useful to highlight how erroneous people's perceptions are about immigration, and measuring the differences between perceptions and facts on this issue can be useful in determining the development of integration and media policy. Bearing in mind the definition of integration as being a two-way process of adaptation between the immigrant and the host society, the attitudes, values and opinions of both nationals and immigrants become relevant factors to be explored given their influence on integration outcomes.

This descriptive research provides an overview of attitudes towards immigrants and immigration using data from eight countries sampled in the most recent survey of the ESS[4], Round 8 (2016–2017). The main aim of the study is to highlight how nationals in eight European countries (Austria, Belgium, France, Germany, Italy, the Netherlands, Portugal and Spain (hereinafter the *EUG8*)[5]) differ in their opinions. The study explores a range of issues covered

4 ESS is an academically driven cross-national survey that has been conducted across Europe since its establishment in 2001. Every two years, face-to-face interviews are conducted with newly selected, cross-sectional samples. The survey measures the attitudes, values, beliefs and behavioural patterns of diverse populations in more than 30 nations. The main aim of the ESS is to chart stability and change in the social structure, conditions and attitudes within Europe.

5 Those countries were selected because they were the eight original group members that signed the Schengen Agreement. Despite different migratory histories, different

by the ESS concerning perceived discrimination, attitudes towards immigrants and refugees and opinions on the effects of immigrants on a country's economy, cultural life and quality of life. Furthermore, opinions on the access to social benefits and services for immigrants are analysed.

In order to also give a voice to immigrants, the study considers the concept of *country of citizenship* because it allows the division of population samples into the following groups: *nationals* (citizens of the country where they were surveyed) and *foreigners* (citizens of another State residing in the surveyed country)[6]. Foreign respondents in the ESS do not reflect the relative size of the foreign population in a country[7]; however, it is worth analysing their opinions about two relevant topics: perception of discrimination and international protection, especially since the start of the "refugee crisis"[8].

The information originating from the ESS is integrated with data from other surveys, namely, the Eurobarometer, EU-MIDIS, IPSOS and Gallup. In addition, international studies and country-level elements as integration policy and migration and migrant population statistics originating from other data sets[9] are used to try to link the main findings to the potential factors triggering anti-immigrant attitudes.

2 Background

Since 2015, when the so-called refugee and migrant crisis reached its peak, the immigration issue has dominated the political agenda of the EU and its Member States. Since then, Europe has been experiencing a new political climate that has led to a rise in xenophobic populism and anti-European sentiment. Across

---

concepts of integration and national integration policies, they adopted common rules regarding visas, right of asylum and checks at external borders to allow the free movement of people.

6 Out of all the people with a migrant background, foreign citizens residing in EU Member States, especially if non-EU citizens, are in a different situation with regard to their legal rights. Moreover, they face more difficulties in the labour market and in overcoming social exclusion than people holding citizenship from their country of residence, either from birth or naturalization.

7 The respondents in the EUG8 number 16,220, including 857 non-national individuals. Even if samples are representative of everyone aged 15 and over and resident in each country, regardless of their nationality, citizenship or language, unfortunately, it is difficult to sample and survey immigrants because they are harder to reach.

8 Foreigners could perceive refugees as competitors for housing, welfare and/or jobs.

9 Migrant Integration Policy Index (MIPEX), Statistical Office of the EU (EUROSTAT).

Europe, the issue of immigration has been politically sensitive; and security concerns, due to the high flows of asylum seekers and terrorist attacks, play an important role in changing immigration policies. Protecting external borders in Europe, and internal borders within the Schengen Area, has become an urgent matter[10]. In 2016, the EU experienced another year of intense migratory pressure at its external borders[11], in particular from Africa, and "Italy saw the highest number of arrivals ever recorded (about 182,000), with a significant increase in the number of immigrants from West Africa" (European Border and Coast Guard Agency [Frontex], 2017 p. 6). During the period of ESS data collection, from 2016 to 2017, migration continued to be a "hot topic". According to Eurostat (2018), a total of 4.3 million people immigrated to the EU during 2016. Examining the eight countries analysed, Germany reported the largest total number of immigrants (about 1 million) in 2016, followed by Spain, France and Italy. Relative to the size of the resident population, Austria recorded the highest rates of immigration (15 immigrants per 1,000 people) in 2016, ranking sixth in EU-28. Italy was only 23rd (5 immigrants per 1,000 people). In absolute terms, Germany recorded the largest numbers of non-nationals (9.2 million people), followed by Italy (5 million), France (4.6 million) and Spain (4.4 million). In relative terms, among the EUG8, a high proportion of foreign residents (10 % or more of the resident population) was observed in Austria (ranking third in EU-28) followed by Belgium and Germany. In Italy, foreign citizens accounted for 8.3 % of its total population (Eurostat, 2018).

European Union countries have also experienced an increase in the movement of large groups of displaced people over the last few years. The number of asylum applicants was approximately double the number recorded during the previous peak of 1992, more than 1.2 million in both 2015 and 2016. In 2016, the main countries of destination were Germany (60 % of all first time applicants in the EU Member States), followed by Italy (10 %) and France (6 %).

This extraordinary situation, amplified by the media, may have had multiple repercussions on attitudes towards immigration, and it is likely to have polarized opinions. The public is likely to have felt empathy or fear towards the immigrants.

---

10 Since 2015 some Schengen countries (included France, Germany, Austria and, for a brief period, Belgium) have reintroduced border controls at their internal borders. In 2016, the EU-Turkey Statement was adopted with the purpose of deterring refugees from arriving in Europe. In 2017, Italy reduced migration flows from Africa thanks to an agreement with Libya.

11 A total of 4.3 million people immigrated to any one of the Member States during 2016. There were an estimated 2 million citizens from non-EU countries.

2.2 People with an Immigrant Background Surveyed in Italy

Out of all people surveyed in Italy (2,626 in total) during ESS Round 8,231 were foreign-born people. Most of them were Romanians, Albanians and Moroccans, the largest groups of foreigners living in the country (ISTAT, 2017). Most of the foreign-born respondents had been residents in Italy for a long time. About a half of them arrived in 1998 to 2007 whereas new immigrants, who arrived in 2014 to 2016, account for a very small share of the respondents. It is worth noting that a high share of those polled (one out of three) were Italian citizens, probably due to their long residence in the country[12]. Among respondents with an immigrant background, only non-nationals (159 people) are considered in the analysis. Specifically, their opinion about two relevant topics, discrimination and international protection, are analysed. Even if those polled do not reflect the relative size of the foreign population, it should be pointed out that some socio-demographic elements reflect the national data collected by ISTAT[13] concerning the characteristics of foreigners living in Italy.

3 Perceived Discrimination

EU-MIDIS II, the survey carried out between 2015 and 2016 by the European Union Agency for Fundamental Rights (FRA) across all 28 EU Member States, shows high levels of discrimination based on ethnic or immigrant background (especially skin colour and religion as related characteristics). According to the FRA Report (2017), "respondents who have experienced discrimination, harassment or violence motivated by hatred show significantly lower levels of trust and feel less attached to the country in which they live. Discrimination and hate crime can undermine integration and social inclusion policies, affecting the social cohesion of our societies". Considering ESS data, among the EUG8 surveyed, the highest rates of discrimination based on ethnic or immigrant background are related to nationality, religion and skin colour.

As expected, perceived discrimination on these grounds is very widespread among foreign respondents. When considering other grounds of

---

12 According Eurostat, Italy had the highest number of people acquiring citizenship in 2016, at 201.6 thousand (or 20 % of the EU-28 total).

13 Information about the area in which those polled live (the vast majority live in country villages and only a quarter live in a big city), the household composition (more than an half of those polled indicated a household composed of three to five members) and education (only one in ten has a tertiary qualification) reflects data collected by ISTAT.

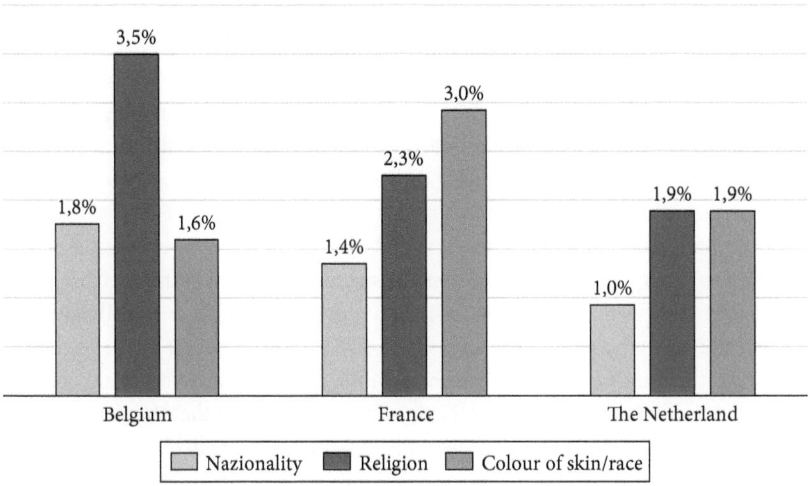

Fig. 15.1: Perceived discrimination based on *racial* and *ethnic* origin, by citizens of the country where they were surveyed (%). *Source:* Data processed by Inapp based on ESS results

discrimination prohibited by specific legislation (Council Directive 2000/78/EC, the Employment Equality Directive), such as gender, disability, age, etc. the proportion of foreigners who indicate some form of discrimination is very low.

Although the number of foreigners surveyed is not representative of foreign populations, it should be pointed out that the highest levels of perceived discrimination are reported in Belgium and Italy: one in three of those polled in Belgium, and one in four in Italy, consider themselves part of a group at risk of discrimination[14].

Unsurprisingly, the share of national respondents reporting discrimination on the basis of racial or ethnic origin is low; however, nationals mentioned religion, skin colour and nationality as grounds of discrimination, particularly in Belgium, France and the Netherlands – see Fig. 15.1.

This finding could be explained by the population heterogeneity in these countries in terms of ethnic background. Discrimination on these grounds is likely to be mentioned by naturalized immigrants of the host country, included in the samples as native-born nationals. Indeed, having host-country nationality,

14 Foreign respondents are 159 in Italy and 141 in Belgium.

in itself, cannot be considered as an element sufficient for integration into the host-country society. The integration of immigrants has other fundamental elements in relation to the social, economic and cultural role they play in their host countries. On its own, the status of citizenship (the political element) is not sufficient to guarantee equal opportunities for new citizens with an immigrant background. This could explain why they think of themselves as belonging to a group at risk of discrimination.

While national respondents, as expected, do not perceive language-based discrimination[15], surprisingly some of them answered that they belong to a group that experiences discrimination on the basis of nationality (around 2 % in Belgium). It is worth noting that although the terms *nationality* and *citizenship* have two distinct meanings, they are often used interchangeably. Nationality is an ethnic concept, while citizenship is a legal concept. Nationals that answered that they are part of a group at risk of discrimination on the basis of nationality are likely to refer to their origin, language or ethnicity. Moreover, race and ethnicity are different, but they are overlapping concepts that are often used synonymously. They are multidimensional concepts and therefore subject to varying interpretations because of different sensitivities, cultures and values across countries. All these considerations show how difficult it is to measure attitude and self-perception.

3.1 Discrimination Perceived and Anti-discrimination Policy

In this section, data on perceived discrimination is analysed in relation to national anti-discrimination policy. Using the ESS data and MIPEX (country-specific anti-discrimination scores), no strong relationship between level of self-identification with a discriminated group and anti-discrimination policy is observed across the EUG8. According to the MIPEX score, Belgium (78), France (77) and the Netherlands (73) have slightly favourable anti-discrimination policies (see Fig. 15.2). According to the ESS, these countries share high levels of respondents identifying as a member of a discriminated group on the basis of racial or ethnic origin. Portugal and Spain share very low levels of self-identification with discriminated groups, but in the former, anti-discrimination laws, enforcement mechanisms and equality policies are among the strongest

15 Knowledge of the country's official language is one of the stated requirements not only to apply for citizenship but also for long-term residence permit.

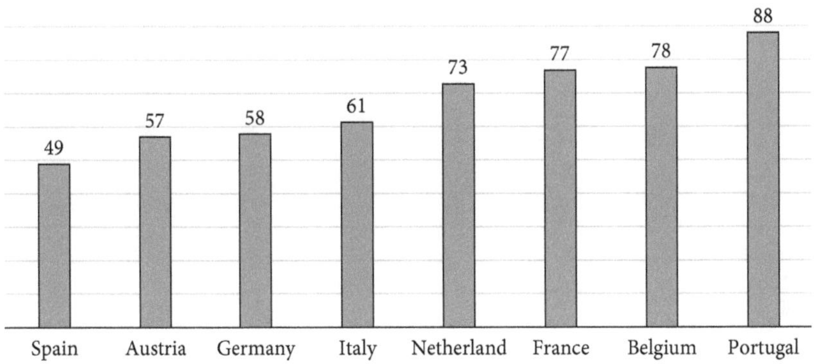

Favourable (80–100)
Slightly favourable (60–79)
Almost favourable (41–59)

Fig. 15.2: Anti-discrimination policy, MIPEX score by country (2015). *Source:* Data processed by Inapp based on MIPEX data

internationally. By contrast, Spain has very weak anti-discrimination laws and equality policies, nearly 20 points below the average for western Europe[16].

On the basis of these considerations, the strangeness or weakness of anti-discrimination laws and equality policies do not have a significant effect on the general perceptions of discrimination. It is most likely that the social and political climate plays a more important role in affecting the perception of being at risk of discrimination.

3.3 Self-Perception of Foreigners Surveyed in Italy

Italy and Belgium, in comparison to other countries, have the highest rates of perception concerning discrimination on the grounds of nationality. Foreigners polled in Italy (one in five) mention nationality-based discrimination as the

16 Ziller (2014) found that people in countries with stronger anti-discrimination laws are more aware of discrimination and know more about their rights than those from countries with less effective policies. The author says that "For the most part, policy differences across countries are unsystematically related to discrimination-related outcomes. However, an increase in knowledge levels over time is associated with higher reports of witnessed discrimination, and less individual self-identification with a discriminated group".

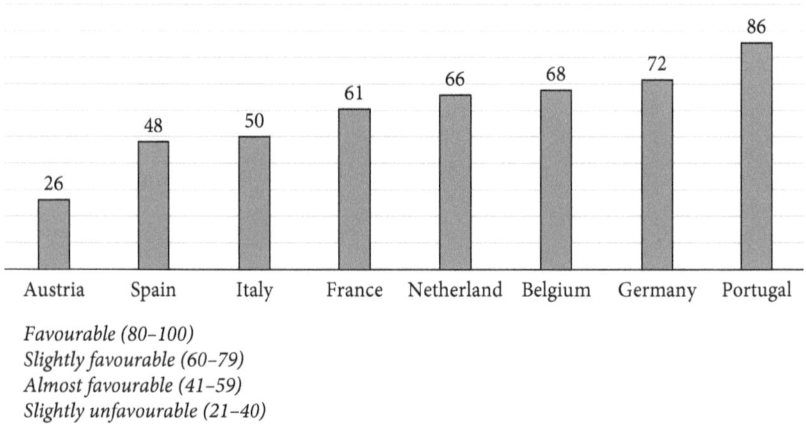

Fig. 15.3: Access to nationality policy – MIPEX score by country (2015). *Source:* Data processed by Inapp based on MIPEX data

most widespread form. In this regard, it is worth mentioning that the Italian legal framework against discrimination does not precisely cover the ground of nationality[17]. Skin colour is the second most common factor mentioned by foreign respondents in Italy (one in ten). Moreover, within the EUG8, Italy records the highest level of discrimination based on skin colour. Even if those polled do not reflect the relative size of the foreign population, it is interesting to try to explain why nationality and skin colour discrimination are prevalent among foreigners in Italy.

Using the Migrant Policy Index within the EUG8, once again only weak relationships are found between perception of nationality-based discrimination and naturalization policies (see Fig. 15.3). Italy and Belgium share similar perceptions of discrimination on this basis but, according to MIPEX, their nationality policies are quite different: a more restrictive one in Italy and a more inclusive one in Belgium.

In order to find an explanation behind the high levels of perceived discrimination, elements related to social and political climate need to be taken into account. Considering the Italian case, as reported by the European Commission against

---

17 The difference in treatment based on nationality is not covered by the Directive 2000/43/EC and its implementing Italian law although a pre-existing set of statutory rules on discrimination has been in force in the labour law field since 1970.

Racism and Intolerance (ECRI), established by the Council of Europe, "political extremism in Italy with strong xenophobic and islamophobic connotations has become a source of concern in the current migration context" (ECRI, 2016 p. 18). Additionally, the website for the Office for Democratic Institutions and Human Rights of the Organization for Security and Co-operation in Europe (OSCE/ODIHR) indicates, in the hate crime category, a marked increase of racist and xenophobic offences in 2017 compared with 2016 (from 494 to 828 offences) in Italy.

4 Attitudes Towards Immigrants and Immigration

Studies on immigration report considerable cross-country differences in attitude towards immigrants and immigration in Europe. These differences depend on a number of individual characteristics[18] and country-level factors that drive public opinion on immigration. The level of social cohesion and inclusion, the level of economic development and the level of perceived corruption may potentially affect attitudes (Messing & Sàgvàri, 2018). Moreover, many studies show how immigration issues presented in the media impact public opinion (Kosho, 2016), while some evidence shows that good-quality immigrant inclusion policies have a positive impact on the public (Callens, 2015). A striking finding is that a higher value for immigrant acceptance is linked to greater happiness for both immigrant and native-born individuals, by almost equal amounts. (UN, 2018).

4.1 Immigrants of the Same Race or Ethnic Group as the Majority Are More Welcome than Others

The ESS measures levels of support for immigration, with a number of questions concerning the respondents' opinions on whether people from different countries, or backgrounds, should be allowed to come and live in the host country. The questions in the survey distinguish between immigrants from poorer countries outside Europe and those of the same ethnic group as the majority of the population, or of a different group.

Data from the EUG8 reveal a hierarchy of preferred types of immigrants. In each country, *ethnic affinity* plays an important role in determining higher desirability of immigrants (see Fig. 15.4); however, there are some differences between them. More specifically, in Italy, there is a less immigrant-friendly attitude even towards

18 Among individual factors, education, age and economic situation play an important role in shaping attitudes (Heath, Richards, Ford, 2016).

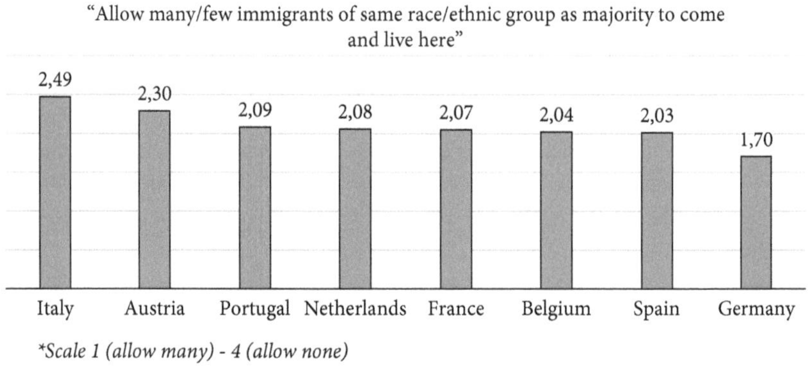

Fig. 15.4: Nationals' attitude towards immigrants of the same ethnic group, by country (average value*). Source: Data processed by Inapp from ESS results

immigrants of the same ethnic group. On average in Italy, people say that *some or a few of them should be allowed to come and live in the country* (average score 2.49 on a scale of 1–4 with 1 indicating "allow many" and 4 "allow none"). By contrast, in Germany there are higher levels of support (score 1.70) for these immigrants groups (on average respondents indicate *allow many* and *allow some to come and live here*).

Similarly to ethnic affinity, other surveys show how opportunities to interact with immigrants promote more positive attitudes. The Gallup World Poll, when surveying data from 140 countries, showed that the strong relationship between interpersonal contact and attitudes toward immigrants is near-universal (Fleming, Esipova, Pugliese, Ray & Rajesh, 2018). In the case of Italy, Pagnoncelli (2019) writes that while Italians consider immigration as the leading problem at the national level, they think that immigration is not an important issue at a local level. This contradictory representation depends, on the one hand, on the low level of knowledge about the issue, the low level of education and the way people obtain the news (online and/or from television). On the other hand, the author states that a more positive attitude about immigration at a local level depends on increasing contact with immigrants in such a way that they are perceived as "good people" (for instance, contacts with those employed as care assistants and in home-help positions).

On the basis of these considerations, it seems interesting to observe the positions of the EUG8 according to Gallup's Migrant Acceptance Index[19] based

19 Gallup created the Migrant Acceptance Index to gauge people's acceptance of immigrants based on increasing degrees of personal proximity (social distance).

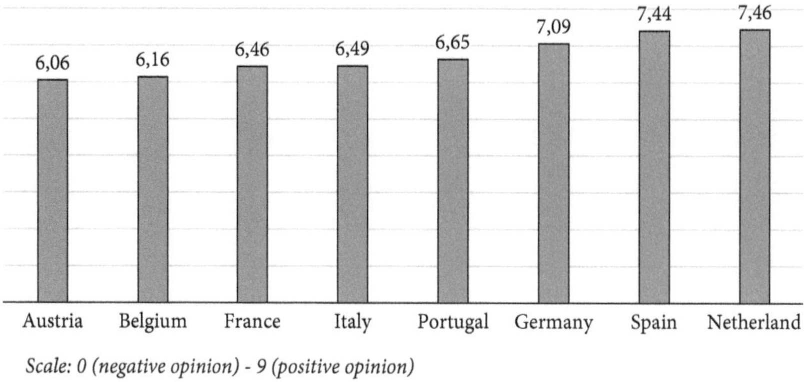

Fig. 15.5: Migrant Acceptance Index (Gallup 2017). *Source:* Data processed by Inapp on Gallup results

on increasing degrees of personal proximity (top possible score is 9.0) (see Fig. 15.5).

4.2 Diversity and Poverty Trigger Negative Attitudes

Immigrants of a different ethnic group than the majority, and from poorer countries outside Europe, are positioned as less desirable compared to other immigrant groups. This is true across the EUG8. On average, nationals feel that *some or a few of these immigrants should be allowed to come* (see Fig. 15.6).

On a scale from 1 (allow many) to 4 (allow none), average scores vary from 2.73 in Italy to 2.12 in Germany.

On the basis of these results, an ethnocentric view seems to be shared by nationals: *ethno-racial diversity*, *poverty* and *non-European origins* are perceived as indistinct and problematic elements. According to the Social Identity Theory, members of an *in-group* (nationals) tend to exaggerate the differences between groups, and to find negative aspects of an out-group (foreigners) through social categorization. It is worth noting that social categorization is one explanation for prejudiced attitudes and discrimination. In order to better understand this finding, it could be useful to use the *boundary-making approach* as an analytical

---

https://news.gallup.com/poll/216377/new-index-shows-least-accepting-countries-migrants.aspx.

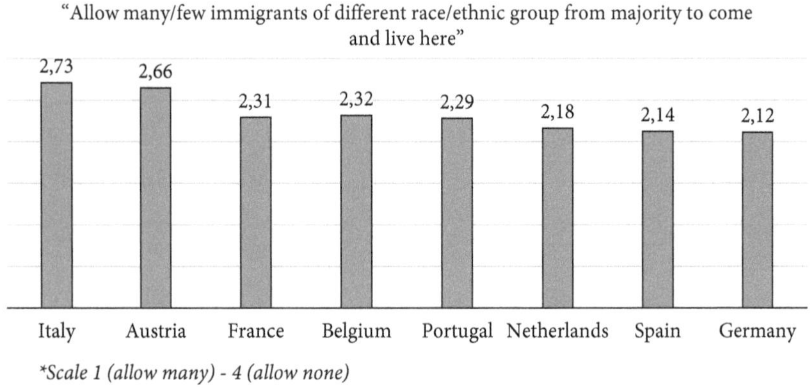

Fig. 15.6: Nationals' attitude towards immigrants ethnically different to the majority group, by country (average value*). *Source*: Data processed by Inapp from ESS results

lens. Heizmann and Böhnke (2018) speak about *symbolic boundaries* in the form of negative public opinion towards immigrants. The authors show that "the rights non-citizens enjoy determine the strength of the *social boundary* that separates them from the European majorities (Bail 2008). Greater legal inequality leads to higher exclusion and, as a consequence, immigrants are more strongly perceived to be distinct and different when compared to natives" (p. 2). Social boundaries (institutionalized differences) and symbolic boundaries (attitudes) define separation between foreigners and nationals. According to this approach, given that third-country nationals enjoy far less rights compared to EU citizens, people from countries outside EU are a less preferred type of immigrant.

5 The Right to Asylum

Since 2015, when the refugee crisis reached its peak, and during the period of the ESS data collection (2016–2017), the international protection issue has dominated public debate and political agendas at national and European levels. Since then, a key issue has been the need to secure Europe's internal and external borders and to reform the European asylum system.

5.1 *The Right* to *Asylum* Triggers a Combination of Feelings

Within the EUG8, nationals in Portugal, Spain and France are more homogeneous around a relatively supportive average position towards international

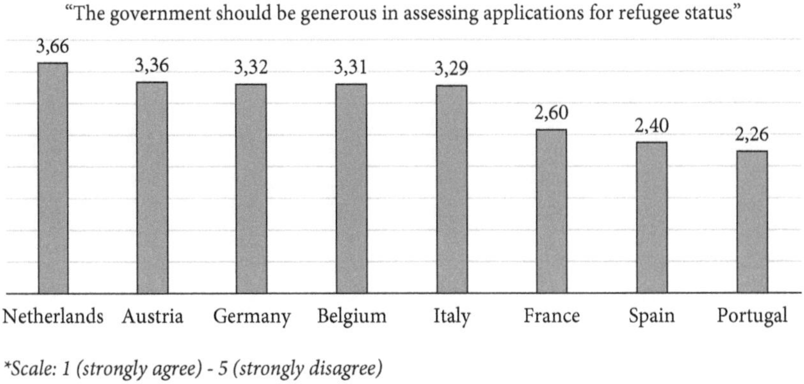

Fig. 15.7: Nationals' attitude towards refugee status by country (average value*).
Source: Data processed by Inapp from ESS results

protection (see Fig. 15.7). On a scale of 1 (*strongly agree*) to 5 (*strongly disagree*), the average scores of these countries vary from 2.26 to 2.60. Nationals from Austria, Germany, Belgium and Italy do not express an opinion on this issue (average scores from 3.36 to 3.29). Nationals in the Netherlands are on average less favourable towards international protection (3.66). In most of the countries (see Fig. 15.8), respondents do not express an opinion about asylum seekers' real fear of persecution (average scores around 3, *neither agree nor disagree*).

Italy is more positive than might have been expected towards asylum seekers. In this case, opinions are not as polarized as towards other immigrants. Another survey (IPSOS, 2018) has also observed that Italians are slightly more refugee-friendly than immigrant-friendly[20]. However, attitudes towards asylum seekers are not coherent; their fear of persecution is found not to be genuine by Italians. The ESS data show the same findings (see Fig. 15.8).

By contrast, in Germany there is more support for immigrants and less support for asylum seekers. This difference may reflect the fact that, in 2015, the highest number of first-time applicants for refugee status was recorded in Germany (with 441,800 first time applicants, or 35 % of the EU total). Moreover, with 424,800 pending applications at the end of 2015 (or 46 % of the EU total), Germany had the largest share of asylum applicants in the EU (Eurostat 2017). The *open-door policy* on refugees led to resentment in the German society and

20 According Ipsos only 9 % of Italians do not support the right of asylum.

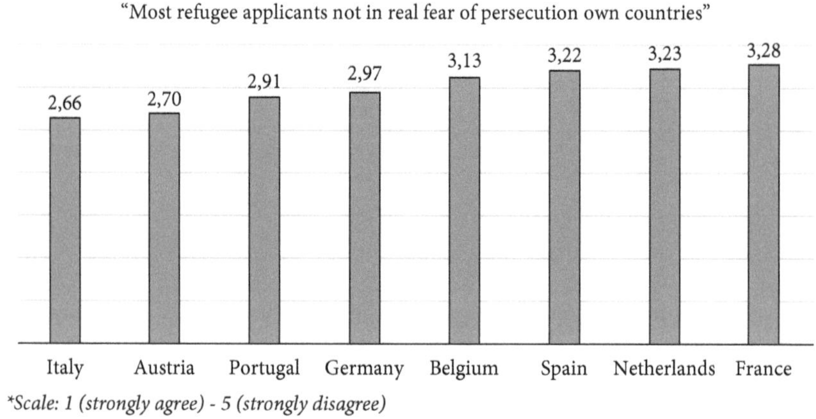

Fig. 15.8: Nationals' opinion about asylum seekers' real fear of persecution (average value*). *Source:* Data processed by Inapp from ESS results

dissent amongst the ranks of government. By 2016, the government had moved to a less welcoming stance and had reintroduced border controls.

Among foreigners surveyed, those residing in Portugal, Spain and France are on average the most favourable towards asylum seekers. Those residing in the Netherlands and Germany are more homogeneous around a less supportive average. On average, foreigners surveyed in each country do not express an opinion about asylum seekers' real fear of persecution (*neither agree nor disagree*). A possible explanation about the lack of a supportive attitude is that foreigners may perceive newcomers as competitors for jobs, housing and welfare.

5.2 Family Reunification Is Not a Divisive Issue

Attitudes concerning family reunification for refugees are not hostile across countries. Nationals in Austria, Belgium and the Netherlands do not express an opinion on the issue (average scores around 3, indicating *neither agree nor disagree* on a scale of 1 (strongly *agree)* to 5 (strongly *disagree*)). Those in France, Italy and Germany are slightly more favourable (from 2.78 to 2.67). A greater favour for reunification is observed in Spain (2.14) and Portugal (2.42). With regard to this issue, it should be noted that the two Iberian countries have the most inclusive family reunion policy in the EU-28 (see Fig. 15.9).

The foreigners surveyed are, on average, sensitive to the family reunion issue. Those most favourable reside in Spain. In each country, excluding the Netherlands

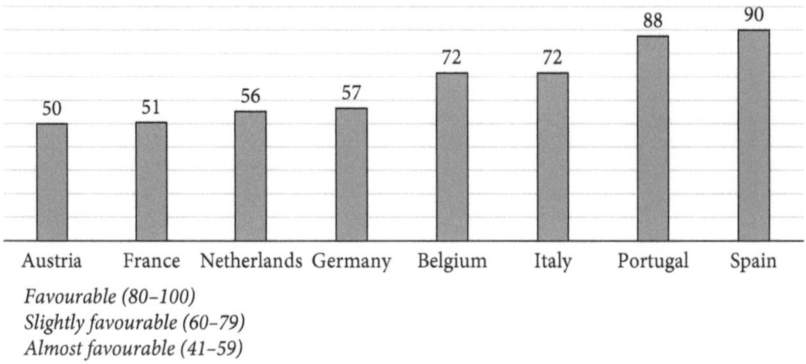

Fig. 15.9: Policy on family reunion – MIPEX score by country (2015). Source: Data processed by Inapp on MIPEX data

(where they do not express an opinion), foreigners agree that refugees should be entitled to bring in their close family members.

6 General Perceptions About the Impact of Immigrants on the Host Societies

Considerable attention by researchers, policymakers and the public has been directed towards the effects of international immigration on host countries. There are economic, social and cultural arguments, as well as security concerns, used to argue for and against immigration. The ESS survey asked a number of questions about people's perceptions of the effects of immigration on European societies.

Even though most studies show that the economic effect of immigration on the host countries is usually positive, the perception that immigrants cost more than they yield is widespread (OECD & the International Labour Organization [ILO], 2018).

Among the EUG8, respondents in Italy are the most concerned (3.99) about the effect of international immigration on the economy – on a scale of 0 (*bad*) to 10 (*good*) – while those in Germany have the most positive view (5.82) (see Fig. 15.10).

One reason for this may be that the high unemployment rate, growing poverty and social exclusion have increased perception of competition for jobs and services between nationals and foreigners in Italy. This perception may have led to a more negative attitude towards immigrants. By contrast, Germany has

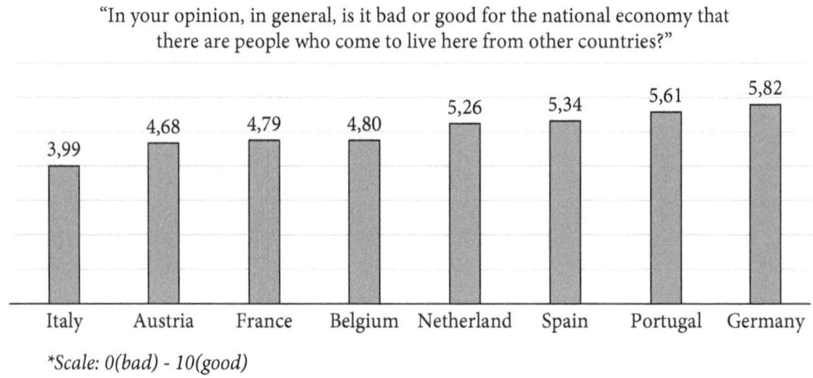

Fig. 15.10: Nationals' opinions on the effects of immigrants on a country's economy (average value*). Source: Data processed by Inapp from ESS results

been enjoying a strong economic performance in recent years and a flow of highly skilled immigrants is considered, in a functionalist way, as a means to meet labour demands. It could explain why international immigration is considered more an opportunity than a problem in Germany. According to the Special Eurobarometer (2018) in Italy, more than an half of the respondents think that immigrants take jobs away from workers (58 %) while in Germany only 21 % perceive competition for jobs (39 % is the average in the EU). In Italy, 37 % of respondents say immigrants have a positive impact on the economy, whereas, in Germany, more than half of those surveyed share this view.

Compared to opinions about the impact on the economy, in all eight countries perceptions about the impact of immigration on cultural life are less negative. Among these countries, in Italy and Austria, cultural concerns are on average the most pressing ones for the public (respectively 4.25 and 4.58), while at the other end of the scale, people in Spain are on average the least concerned (6.32) – see Fig. 15.11.

Finally, people are asked to consider whether a country is made a better or worse place to live in due to the presence of immigrants. The countries where, on average, the national population have a positive view are Spain, the Netherlands, Germany and Portugal (the range is from 5.49 in Spain to 5.19 in Portugal). By contrast, Italians (3.53), more than Austrians, are the most concerned on this issue.

Concerns on this element are often linked to security and quality of life issues and, on an urban scale, these concerns are taking on an ever more alarming

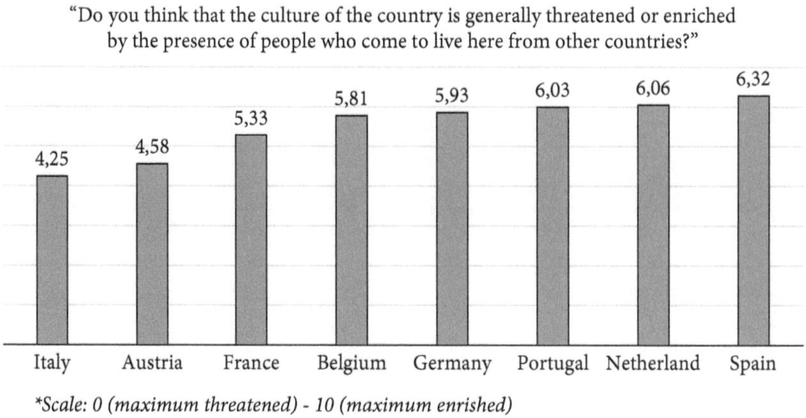

Fig. 15.11: Nationals' opinions on the effects of immigrants on a country's cultural life (average value*). Source: Data processed by Inapp on ESS results

dimension. Increasing inequalities and socio-spatial segregation are well visible in suburban areas. These areas are characterized by urban and social decay, informal settlements and visible phenomenon (drug dealing, prostitution, begging, etc.) that, especially when involving foreign citizens, could lead to a worse perception of quality of life, and to a growing perception of the "immigrant" as a threat to security (Ricotta, 2017).

7 Equal Access to Social Benefits and Services

In the last few years, the perception of immigration as a burden on the welfare system is becoming more and more relevant to public opinion in Europe. The ESS measures public opinion on this matter, asking whether foreigners coming to live in the country should obtain the same rights to social benefits and services as citizens already living there.

Figure 15.12 shows that the five countries are polarized in their opinion: 50 % of respondents in Belgium, France, Germany, Spain and Portugal think that *only after immigrants have worked and paid taxes for at least a year* should they have equal access to social benefits and services. By contrast, about a half of the respondents in the Netherlands indicate *acquisition of citizenship* of the host country as a prerequisite for enjoying welfare rights.

Austrian and Italian people share a very similar attitude with 38 % and 37.2 %, respectively, saying that they are favourable to granting these rights only *after*

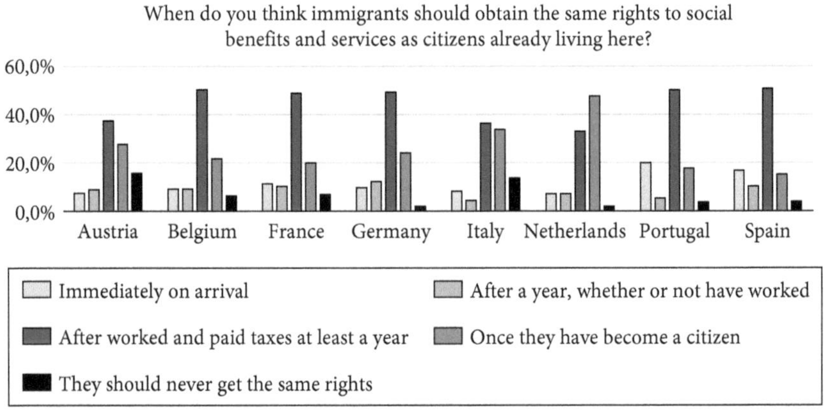

Fig. 15.12: Nationals' attitude concerning access to the right to social services and benefits (%). Source: Data processed by Inapp from ESS results

working and paying taxes for at least one year. In these countries, there is reported a high proportion of respondents (28 % and 34.5 %, respectively) supporting it only *after acquiring citizenship*. Additionally, a significant proportion (16.5 % and 14.6 %, respectively) believe that immigrants *should never obtain the same rights as citizens*, a view shared by very few respondents in the other countries (the range is from 2.4 % in Germany to 7.2 % in France).

A look at the results with regard to the EUG8, it is apparent that Italy, over Austria, is on average the least in favour of offering equal access to welfare rights, while the highest proportion of those that agree with more inclusive services and benefits are in Spain and Portugal (see Fig. 15.13).

Italian concern about pressure on public services are shown by the survey *Global Views on Immigration and the Refugee Crisis*, carried out in 2017 by IPSOS[21] (prior to Italy reducing immigration flows owing to an agreement with Libya), indicating that concern about the welfare system is greater than preoccupation about the impact of immigration on the labour market. More specifically, 61 % of Italians say immigration has placed too much pressure on public services

21 https://www.slideshare.net/IpsosItalia/global-views-on-immigration-and-the-refugee-crisis-79771961/ La rilevazione ha avuto luogo prima della contrazione degli arrivi via mare e dei flussi di immigrazione a seguito degli interventi promossi dal Ministero dell'Interno in accordo con la Libia.

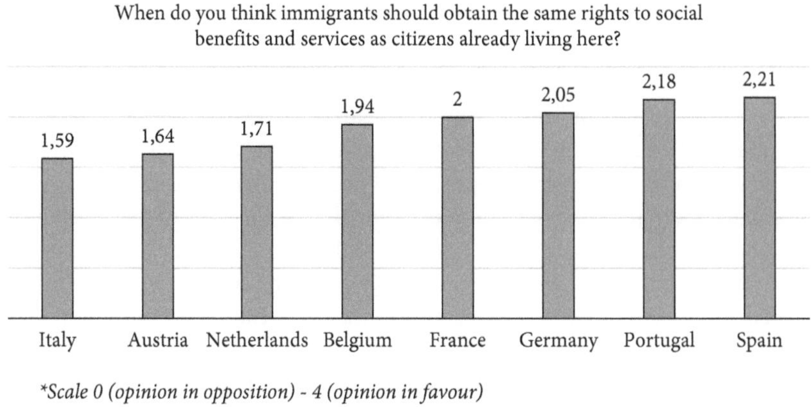

Fig. 15.13: Nationals' attitude towards access to the right to social services and benefits (average value*). Source: Data processed by Inapp from ESS results

in the country, and more than a half (58 %) think that social welfare expenses are too high.

Contrary to widespread public belief, immigrants are not a net financial cost to the Italian economy.

Figures say immigrants contribute more in taxes and social contributions than they receive in benefits. According to the International Organization for Migration (IOM) (2017), in 2016, foreign workers produced almost 9 % of the total GDP; they "pay taxes and sustain Italy's social security system (with an estimated net contribution of 241.2 billion euros between 1960 and 2016)".

8 General Results and Conclusions

The overall results of the study show that attitudes are relatively homogeneous concerning levels of support, or lack thereof, for immigrants, while there are wider cross-country differences in opinion about the impact on society, international protection and access to social services and benefits. With regard to the first point, findings show a clear hierarchy of the preferred type of immigrant, with *ethnic affinity* playing an important role, for nationals, in determining the level of desirability towards immigrants. Concerning the second point, findings highlight how, within cross-national differences in attitudes, some countries are highly polarized in their opinions. On the one hand, in Germany, Spain and Portugal, the public is on average more favourable towards immigration. On the other hand, the Italian public has the most opposing view towards immigrants and immigration. The main concerns of Italians are related to ethnic diversity and immigrant origins. In addition, the Italian public is worried about the *effects* of *immigrants* on the country's economy and quality of life. The same polarized view on immigrants and immigration is shared by Austria. Respondents surveyed in these countries are the least favourable to equal access to social services and benefits, with the highest proportion of people who believe that immigrants should never obtain the same rights as nationals. On the basis of these results, it could be confirmed that *identity* (cultural conflict), *civil security* (crime and terrorist attacks) and *social security* (competition for jobs and services) (Battistelli, 2016) are the main topics triggering anti-immigrant attitudes in the countries.

It should be noted that on the topic of international protection, there are mixed feelings. It seems that emotions tend to blend together into newer and more complicated sentiments. Italians are slightly more refugee-friendly than immigrant-friendly. By contrast, in Germany, there is less support for asylum seekers than for economic immigrants. Opinions are, in fact, not as polarized as they are towards other immigrants, but attitudes are not always coherent. Italians believe most applicants for refugee status are not in actual fear of persecution in their own countries.

In relation to foreigners' attitudes towards international protection, it could be observed that where the public is more hostile (Austria, the Netherlands and Germany), foreign respondents seem to share the same scepticism. They probably perceive an intolerant climate and, consequently, they are likely to fear competition from *newcomers* towards access to rights and services. In general, it could be observed that they do not express an opinion about suspicious that asylum seekers are abusing the system and the positions of foreigners and nationals are substantially aligned on this point.

Findings related to discrimination show that the highest level of discrimination based on ethnic or immigrant background are related to nationality, religion and skin color. Surprisingly, a look at the results for national respondents shows that they also mentioned these three sorts of discrimination. This result reveals how solely the status of citizenship is insufficient to guarantee equal treatment and opportunities for new citizens. In this respect, the choice to divide populations into groups of nationals and foreigners has allowed this interesting finding to be highlighted. Additionally, findings confirm that policy differences across countries are unsystematically related to perceived discrimination. Social and political climate might have a more significant role in affecting self-identification with a discriminated group.

The cross-country differences in the level of support, or lack thereof, for immigration do not depend on the extent of immigration or the size of the immigrant population. However, the new levels of migratory pressure emphasized by the media is likely to have influenced public opinion. According to the ECRI, "As in previous years, 2017 has witnessed a rise in fear and resentment in European societies, largely due to high levels of migration, religious extremism, and terrorist attacks. The austerity-driven socio-economic climate has exacerbated these sentiments, leading to a rise in populism in Europe". ECRI has observed how social media "encourages self-segregation and deepens social divides. Similarly, a considerable number of media outlets either knowingly or unintentionally spread xenophobic rhetoric". Considering the ESS results, it could be said that *symbolic boundaries* play a significant role in shaping self-perception in belonging to a group that experiences discrimination. Over the last decade, increased unemployment and vulnerability have been among the dominant social impacts of the financial and economic crisis. This situation has triggered among native populations anti-outgroup sentiments and, consequently, have increased hostility towards immigrants. Basso and Pesole (2019) wrote that media-reinforced fears and insecurity of people who are already facing difficulties are more likely to turn to aggressive behaviour. According to the authors, *distortion of information* and *sense of injustice* due to *increasing inequality* are the main reasons of the current success of populist parties. It could be observed that these factors have similarly triggered xenophobic rhetoric and racism across European societies.

Anti-immigration sentiments are growing across European societies, and migration flows are likely to increase in the coming years. Against this backdrop, having reliable facts is a prerequisite for a better informed public debate, and for better targeted policymaking. It is therefore imperative to promote legislative measures against the use of hate speech along with measures addressing the conditions conducive to its use. It is also necessary to strengthen social cohesion and ensure equal opportunity for all, turning to the strategy of "mainstreaming" integration.

Acknowledgement

Data processed by Sergio Ferri and Claudia Tagliavia (INAPP).

References

Bail C. (2008). The configuration of symbolic boundaries against immigrants in Europe. *American Sociological Review*, 73, 37–59) 1.

Basso R., Pesole, D. (2019). *L'economia percepita. Dati, comunicazione e consenso nell'era digitale.* Roma: Donzelli editore.

Battistelli F. (2016). *La sicurezza e la sua ombra. Terrorismo, panico, costruzione della minaccia.* Roma: Donzelli editore.

Callens M. S. (2015). *Integration policies and public opinion: In conflict or in harmony.* Luxembourg Institute of Socio-Economic Research – University of Leuven, 2015, Working Papers n°2015–02, 28 p., from https://www.liser.lu/?type=module&id=104&tmp=3886

Castles S., De Haas H., Miller M. (2014). *The age of migration. International population movements in the modern world* (5th ed.). London: Palgrave Macmillan.

Chiurco L., Gentile L., Monaldi G. (2014). *Riflessioni per un linguaggio non discriminatorio: alcune proposte per la redazione di avvisi pubblici di Fondo sociale europeo.* Roma Isfol Occasional paper; 15, from http://bw5.cilea.it/bw5ne2/opac.aspx?WEB=INAP&IDS=20159

European Border and Coast Guard Agency (Frontex) (2017). *Risk analysis for 2017* Warsaw, February 2017 Risk Analysis Unit Frontex reference number: 2133/2017.

ECRI - European Commission against Racism and Intolerance (2016). *Ecri report on Italy (fifth monitoring cycle)* 2016. Council of Europe Strasbourg.

ECRI - European Commission against Racism and Intolerance (2018). *Annual report on ECRI's activities covering the period from 1 January to 31 December 2017*, Council of Europe Strasbourg.

European Union Agency for Fundamental Rights (FRA) (2017). *European Union Minorities and Discrimination Survey (EU-MIDIS II).*

EUROSTAT (2017). *Asylum in the EU Member States.* Newsrelease 46/2017. Retrived from: 16 march 2017 https://ec.europa.eu/eurostat/documents/2995521/7921609/3-16032017-BP-EN.pdf/e5fa98bb-5d9d-4297-9168-d07c67d1c9e1

EUROSTAT (2018). *Migration and migrant population statistics. Statics Explained.* Retrived from https://ec.europa.eu/eurostat/statistics-explained/index.php/Migration_and_migrant_population_statistics

Fleming J. H., Esipova N., Pugliese A., Ray J., Srinivasan, R. (2018). *Migrant acceptance index: A global examination of the relationship between interpersonal contact and attitudes toward migrants*, Border Crossing – Transnational Press London, 8.

Foundation for Initiatives and Studies on Multi-ethnicity (ISMU) (2018). *XXIV Rapporto sulle migrazioni* 2018.

Heath A., Richards L., Ford R. (2016). *How do Europeans differ in their attitudes to immigration?* Centre for Social Investigation, Nuffield College Oxford, University of Manchester. Retrived from: https://www.europeansocialsurvey.org/docs/about/conference/HEATH_FORD_how-do-Europeans-differ.pdf

Heizmann B., & Böhnke P. (2018). Immigrant life satisfaction in *Europe: the role of social and symbolic boundaries. Journal* of Ethnic and Migration Studies, 45(7): 1027–1050, 2019. Published Online: 15 Feb 2018.

IOM (2017). *Migrants' contributions to Italy's welfare.* IOM Italy BRIEFING Issue n.2, October 2017.

IPSOS (2017). *Global views on immigration and the refugee crisis.*

IPSOS (2018). *Un'Italia frammentata: atteggiamenti verso identità nazionale, immigrazione e rifugiati in Italia.* More in common, Social Change Initiative.

ISTAT (2017). *Bilancio demografico nazionale.* Anno 2016.

ISTAT (2019). *Indagine conoscitiva in materia di politiche dell'immigrazione, diritto d'asilo e gestione dei flussi migratori,* Commissione Affari Costituzionali della Camera dei Deputati. Roma, 18 settembre 2019. Audizione parlamentare.

Kosho J. (2016). Media influence on public opinion attitudes towards the migration crisis. *International Journal of Scientific & Technology Research,* 5(5), May 2016. Retrived from: https://www.ijstr.org/final-print/may2016/Media-Influence-On-Public-Opinion-Attitudes-Toward-The-Migration-Crisis.pdf

Messing V., Sàgvàri B. (2018). *Looking behind the culture of fear. Cross-national analysis of attitudes of attitudes towards migration,* Friedrich-Ebert-Stiftung (FES). Retrived from: https://cps.ceu.edu/sites/cps.ceu.edu/files/attachment/article/3014/messing-sagvari-fes-study-march-2018.pdf

OECD/EU (2018). *Settling In 2018: Indicators of immigrant integration.* Paris/EU, Brussels: OECD Publishing, doi:10.1787/9789264307216-en.

OECD/ILO (2018). *How immigrants contribute to developing countries' economies.* Geneva/OECD Publishing, Paris: ILO, doi:10.1787/97892642887 37-en.

Pagnoncelli N. (2019). *La Penisola che non c'è. La realtà su misura degli italiani.* Milano: Mondadori.

Ricotta G. (2017). Esclusione sociale e sicurezza. In Federci M.C., Romeo A. (Eds.), *Sociologia della Sicurezza. Teorie e problemi* (pp. 197–208). Milano: Mondadori.

Special Eurobarometer 469 (2018). *Integration of immigrants in the European Union.*

Standard Eurobarometer 88 (2017). *Public Opinion in the European Union,* Autumn 2017.

UN (2018). *World happiness report 2018.* Retrived from: https://worldhappiness.report/ed/2018/

UNHCR - United Nations High Commissioner for Refugees (2019). *Global trends. Forced displacement in 2018.*

Zanfrini L. (2016). *Introduzione alla sociologia delle migrazioni.* Roma-Bari: Laterza.

Ziller. C. (2014). Societal implication of antidiscrimination policy in Europe. *Sage Journals.* Retrived from: https://journals.sagepub.com/doi/full/10.1177/2053168014559537

Francesco Pira

Chapter Sixteen Fake News Interference on Media and Social Media

Abstract: In Italy the mystification and distortion of reality have been used constantly by politicians when they speak of migrants. The information remains centered on the theme with the same anxiogenic tone as a permanent emergency, so the perception that people have of the migratory phenomenon generates fear, hate racism. And that perception based on the distortion of reality marks the victory of the algorithm and reaffirms the very strong weight by the disinformation system. We are facing a challenge of global relevance that must be achieved through a new autonomous construction of meaning. This means getting out of the dynamic click response, to use technology as part of an evolutionary process that does not simply generate interconnections but is able to give life to new relational models in a real integration between real and virtual.

1 Introduction

The role of the State has been greatly weakened as it has been theorized in modern society according to the classics of sociology (Durkheim, Weber, Pareto, Marx). "To the State is assigned a central role as regulator and guarantor of citizenship towards citizens, organizations, civil society in general, towards which a substantially asymmetrical relationship is established. This asymmetry is in fact an expression of a society that is gradually invested in the process of division of labor and functional specialization, with a consequent differentiation of tasks and in various areas of work and non-working life " (Ducci, 2017: 20). The role of guarantee has been diluted and at the same time the asymmetrical relationship has also entered into crisis in face of the disintegration of the process of division of labor resulting from globalization and a different organization of tasks and competences. The State seems to have lost the capacity to answer to the needs of citizens in a strategic perspective, bound to the search for electoral consensus.

The data published by the Oxford Internet Institute (Bradshaw, Howard, 2018) show that in 30 countries out of 48 surveyed, government agencies and political parties are exploiting social platforms to alter informational environment, spreading misinformation and fake news, to promote skepticism and mistrust with the aim of polarizing the processes of voting, nurturing populist drifts, and undermining the democratic processes of political participation. In such a social and political context, objective truth becomes secondary for a political communication centered on emotivism, which exploits the power of the algorithm to modify the perception of the real, the cognitive bias (Nickerson, 1998) according to which individuals define the cultural frame of reference and attribute veracity to the contents to which they are exposed, a manipulation that has deep effects on the cultural and cognitive models of individuals, distorting the mechanisms of building trust and credibility. The representation of the migratory phenomenon is grafted into this process by spreading in the citizens a feeling of insecurity and rejection of migrants.

The polarization of the public opinion that derives from this kind of representation of the migratory phenomenon generates violence and fear and crystallizes opinions and positions, making difficult debugging and credibility's reconstruction processes based on the search for objective truth.

Disintermediation, today, is one of the dominant processes and has become the ideal terrain for the development of fake news, because there is no longer control over news, which are shared more and more quickly, giving rise to virality and personalization of content. In this sense, the phenomenon of fake news has taken on a global dimension that shows its pervasive capacity through six characteristic elements: appeal, virality, speed, cross-media, flow, and strength (Pira, Altinier, 2018).

So if: disintermediation, sharing, and personalization are becoming the drivers of the new communication trends, it is also imperative to work so that these processes become key elements in the construction of new formats capable, within a digital media system, of conveying quality information and contents that can disrupt the mechanisms of dissemination of mass disinformation processes.

The progressive crisis of values is contributing to the weakening of the European identity and bringing about the evident emergence of an individualistic and self-representing component of society.

As Bauman states "we feel vulnerable: on an individual level, singularly, and all together as a nation, or rather as a human species" (2015: 5). Globalization and the web society seem to have contributed to widening the sphere of individual freedoms and to predicting a new participatory potential, but at the same time it has weakened those boundaries which generated an apparent safety in the following way "we move as a pendulum between the exhausting search for greater freedom and the exhausting search for greater security. [. . .] the terrible misfortune from which we hoped the governments would liberate us and which instead torment us nowadays is a result of their initiative, with their active participation or with their resigned indifference, it is in substance the sense of the insecurity of our life" (Ibidem: 7).

The crisis of social organizations, social movements, and political parties has made the individuals who perceive their lessening social roles weaker, and thus they withdraw evermore into themselves as exteriorization. This general weakening gives rise to fear and violence, because the individual feels left alone and perceives everything not under control as dangerous and insidious to his own status. Groups whose objective is the defense of their own borders, whose members often tend to keep their distorted vision prevails over reality or making realistic image according to their own needs and expectations.

2 Informational Environment Versus Disinformation System

In the description of the framework of reference illustrated in the introduction, it seems interesting to propose again as a starting point of the analysis on the representation of migration, which focuses on the contrast between the information system and the disinformation industry, a concept clearly expressed by Carzo (2011), that is that of the meaning of frontier. The frontier, the overcoming of the limit, of the physical barrier is the thrust that has driven millions of people for centuries to reach places, cities, and nations where they imagine they can conquer a better life. But the frontier also becomes a cultural limit, where information and tools for reading reality and understanding it are lacking, thus giving rise to a real communicative short circuit based on the alteration of reality and manipulation.

This is more evident in the Italian society that has built up prominently on the unifying action of the media where:

> The power of TV action, which generates modernity and cultural uniformity, and together with anomie [. . .] on the other hand, has caused imbalances in a country where there is no medium capable of counterbalancing them: in a firstly, this applies to press that is read by a small percentage of the population and conditioned also for this by the weight of the interventions of banks and large companies on the one hand, and public subsidies on the other. The coincidence of the golden age of television with the most acute phase of internal migration, and with the full implementation of compulsory education, has nonetheless given rise, from the second half of the fifties, to a system of media authentically national, centered not so much on abstractly patriotic values as on the most banal nationalism sentiment, that of the unified audience (Ortoleva, 2011: 53).

This with the consequence that the media have and are continuing to play a catalyst action incapable of conveying high values but rather of being a mirror of society (Pira, 2011), a drift that the advent of social media has sharpened. The principle of cultural uniformity and a unified audience have been strengthened as a result of the power of penetration of the disinformation system. It is clear that in a society so weakened and with a fragile national identity, today at the mercy of sovereign and populist pressures, the understanding of the migration phenomenon and the capability of reading reality encounter obstacles that are difficult to overcome, especially if migration represents one of the items most conveyed by the disinformation industry. In this sense, the data published by the AGCOM Observatory in February 2019 show that in the period January–August 2018 among the 30 most recurrent terms in the disinformation sites, the words "migrants" and "immigrants" had over 10,000 occurrences. To this we can add that on a sample of 1,358 individuals aged between 14 and 74 representing the Italian population, it appears that: considering the issues relevant to the EU identified by Eurobarometer, immigration is indicated among the three most important by almost 60 % of citizens. The issues related to the country's economic situation and unemployment follow with shares close to 50 %. These data set, collected in the period that preceded and followed the electoral campaign for the Italian general elections until the launch of the European campaign, shows a political communication strongly centered on emotivism. Messages constructed to exploit the power of the algorithm, to modify the perception of reality, alter the cognitive bias on the basis of which individuals define their own cultural frame of reference and attribute truthfulness to the contents to which they are exposed. It is quite clear that if representation prevails over the reality of facts in a media-driven society, we trigger a mechanism in which the imaginary prevails over reality. In this sense, the process is charged with an emotional content that threatens to alter one's understanding.

The way itself in which information and communication are built creates deception, confuses the interlocutor through the manipulation of frames, mean as all those operations and strategies with which individuals try to make false frames or exploit their ambiguity (Gili, Colombo 2012: 341).

An exploitation that benefits from the weaknesses of the information system. In fact, if immigration covers 25 % of the disinformation offer, while it represents only 9 % of the journalistic information one, the imbalance, associated with the viral force of the disinformation system, produces profound consequences on the processes of public opinion building.

After all, as already mentioned in other works (Pira, Altinier, 2018), modernization has led to the prevalence of democracy in the economy over the democracy of culture, transforming it into a mass industrialized market of culture, thus subtracting tools to the ability to interpret reality and reducing more and more the space for the creation of a collective culture in favor of a "cultural" consumerism (Bauman, 2015). Individuals take refuge in echo chambers, groups, and environments where they meet only with other individuals who tend to be already aligned on the same opinions, so the de-ideologization of society has led people to search for new points of reference.

Thus, the fake news, as the most evident manifestation of post-truth (Gili, Maddalena, 2018) thanks to their ability to spread in digital environments, is the most evident demonstration of how confused the margin between fact and opinion is now. The result is that the public receives information and, even if this does not correspond to the reality of the facts, but it is consistent with the idea that the individual has developed himself, he shares it. The media have become tools for governing power, as expressed in the definition of bias introduced by Innis, that circumscribes the specific property of the medium such as: influence, tendency, deformation, and prejudice. In this sense, this bias is reinforced in a monopoly when some groups take control of this form of communication that identifies their religious and political interests with it (Miconi in Innis, 2001). In an era in which the pervasiveness of the media involves every sphere of individual action, we are witnessing the transformation also of social mechanisms of exchange and sharing of information that are increasingly based on the concept of homophilia: the architectures of online platforms favor communicative exchanges among like-minded people with whom cognitive dissonance is not generated but rather are more interesting due to social similarity. As underlined by Gili and Maddalena in the analysis of factoids and their ability to influence and distort the reality of facts with reference to war conflicts as an ideal theater:

> [. . .] for the flourishing of this form of lie: the confusion generated in these contexts, combined with the difficulty for impartial witnesses to access the theater of events, favors the possibility of boasting victories never obtained, of attributing atrocities to the enemies that strike negatively public opinion, often making use of the "evidence" of skilfully forged photographic or audiovisual images. Next to this first nucleus there is a much wider area that includes all the different forms of falsification and omission of information, united by a certain degree of intentionality in wanting to hide or distort the truth of the facts. (2018: 4)

It is the same process that takes place in the representation of migration, where we witness the constant alteration of reality. In this way, a manipulation is carried out able to generate profound effects on the cultural and cognitive models of individuals, distorting the mechanisms of trust and credibility. The representation of the migratory phenomenon is grafted into this process by spreading a feeling of insecurity and rejection in the citizens. An example of these types of reactions is illustrated in the report of the nongovernmental organization Avaaz, who in May 2019 identified and reported about 500 suspicious pages on Facebook identified in Germany, France, UK, Spain, Poland, and Italy, which spread misinformation through a language that praised hatred, racism, and anti-migrants. In Italy 23 pages have consequently been closed (Agi.it 05/12/2019). Then there is the propagandistic use of images manipulated, as happened for the video then removed by Facebook because in contrast with company policy, appeared on the page of Matteo Salvini, leader of the La Lega party, describing an attack to a train conductor by a black boy. It was a false post, published for fee, and seen by quite around 10,000 boys and girls under the age of 18 (La Repubblica 05/24/2019). In 2018, 628 cases of verbal and physical violence, discrimination, and damage of a xenophobic and racist nature were recorded. These are not official data, but those documented in the database of the Organization for Ordinary Racism reports based on direct reports by witnesses or victims or by monitoring of the press (Lunaria, 2019), which however show how communication dynamics in action feed Italian citizens vis a vis to immigration, the construction of a model of resistance identity based on the idea that it is easier to "build trenches for resistance and survival on the basis of different principles or even opposed to those that inform the institutions of the society" (Castells, 2003: 7–8).

Access to information occurs partially, only through some channels and not others; and the social environment conveys data flows through the use of increasingly sophisticated algorithms and increasingly intuitive applications. It is quite clear that disintermediation, today, is one of the dominant processes and has become the ideal ground for the development of fake news, because there is no longer control over the news, which are shared more and more quickly, giving rise to virality and personalization of the contents. The fake news phenomenon has taken on a global dimension that shows all its pervasive capacity through six characteristic points: appeal, virality, speed, cross-media, flow, and strength:

- Appeal: Mechanism of attraction and distortion of the *agenda setting*. An apparent contrast between journalism and SNS companies. Big news broadcasts take advantage of app and algorithm developing an *agenda setting* in line with people tendencies.
- Virality: The proliferation of informational cascades makes it easy for fake news to be relaunched through the web. They also remain in digital environments. This is the demonstration of how difficult it can be to identify them and how difficult it is to unmask the misinformation because it confuses the boundaries between fact and opinion.
- Speed: Exploiting speed is a key element in the connection and in the way in which communication processes are implemented in the digitalized society. The distortionary power of disintermediation.
- Flow: *fake news* represent a flow. A set of information spread to demonstrate a thesis or to direct public opinion towards a position that does not reflect reality.
- Crossmediality: This kind of news is able to be transversal. To cross different media platforms. A news posted on Facebook is immediately relaunched by other media.
- Strength: The Business of Social Manipulation (Pira, Altinier, 2018: 60).

A structured and planned phenomenon in which:

Cyber troops use a variety of communication strategies to disseminate computational propaganda over social media platforms. They create their own content, including fake videos, blogs, memes, pictures, or news websites. These content strategies involve more than simply posting forum comments or replying to genuine user posts; they are important sources of junk news and conspiratorial or polarizing information that can be used to support a broader manipulation campaign (Bradshaw, Howard, 2018: 12).

Fake news have an enormous power, and they risk influencing the construction of the collective imagination, because, as Lippman stated, "we do not see what our eyes are not used to considering. We are struck, sometimes consciously, more often without knowing it, from those facts that fit our philosophy," that is," a series more or less organized images to describe the world that is not seen." It is clear that today social networks combine to form this interpretation and overlap with a function performed, in the past, only by classical media. And it is in this process that fake news confirms itself as a dangerous instrument because "what the individual does is based not on a direct and certain knowledge, but on images that are formed or given to him" (Lippmann, 1922, tr. It. 1999: 395). The fake news, however, before being a hoax represent for those who are communication professionals an uncontrolled news. In this sense, fake news is a threat not only to the credibility of the media, but also and above all to the reputation of companies or institutions. It is true that today false information lurks everywhere, but there is certainly a deficit in the control of sources and contents (Ivi). The proliferation and dissemination of *fake news* is no longer an episodic phenomenon but is an integral part of a well-defined strategy that also involves politics and that exploits social dynamics to build consensus and manipulate public opinion. It is a fact of an industry of global influence and that crosses all sectors of society.

3 Social Fragility and the Impact of the Representation of the Migration Phenomenon

We have indicated above what are the elements in function of which fake news are so effective in penetrating and persisting in the net, but these are not sufficient to make people understand why individuals believe in false news. Gili and Maddalena (2018) identify three factors that help define the profiles of the individuals most likely to succumb to the "fascination" of disinformation. A first factor concerns the fact that "he believes more in fake news who" wants "to believe, because in those news – even when they are suspicious or patently false – he finds confirmation of his previous ideas, opinions and beliefs" (2018: 12). Then there is another risk, that of self-referentiality, "in some ways opposed to the previous one, [. . .] which arises from the fact that we are usually not very aware of the influences we suffer. We are therefore led to believe and prefer to believe that others are more vulnerable than us to deceptive and manipulative messages" (Ibidem: 12). The third factor concerns the attitude that false news very often stimulates, that is, that "the fake news lend themselves perfectly to feeding conspiracy theories to which the loser can resort to justify their own insufficiencies and defeats" (Ibidem: 12).

The picture is particularly complex; the structure of the fake news and the attitude of individuals are grafted into a social dimension that is deeply fragmented as a result of the crisis of social organizations, social movements, and political parties that has weakened the individuals who feel less of their social role and they close more and more in the experience of the Self as an exteriorization. Added to this is the general crisis in the media system, the increasingly click-based technology that has revolutionized the way we communicate. Today, journalism is undergoing a profound crisis that has become increasingly acute and that the advent of social media has made more evident, further weakening its mediation role and contributing to the proliferation of distortive processes of representation of reality.

The making of social networks on the web, which feed on and find their own dimension within contexts of mobilization, represents one of those elements that are contributing to undermine the relationship between the media and public opinion, as it is happening for politics and institutions as a whole.

The digital society has overcome and almost annihilated the mediation role of journalism: Facebook, Twitter, Instagram, and WhatsApp are the new places of narration of reality or of what is believed to be reality (Pira, 2017). Thus also the proliferation of false profiles during the electoral campaign influenced the vote, in the sense that it served to increase the visibility of the populist candidates on search engines and on social networks, effectively creating an indirect advantage that exploits the individuals' poor ability to identify the false or distorted news, as highlighted by the data that Ipsos MORI – Social Research Institute (2018) – detected in 27 countries showing a false perception on the part of individuals on the impact that false news, post-truth, and engine filters of research and social networks have on their own lives and those of others. About 65 % think that other people live in a bubble on the Internet, mostly in search of opinions with which they already agree, but only 34 % say they live in their own "bubble," 63 % is confident of being able to identify false news, but only 41 % think that others are able to do it; 58 % think they are better than average in identifying false news, only 28 % think they are unable to identify them; 60 % think that other people do not care about the facts anymore, they just believe what they want, 59 % think they have a better understanding of social realities like crime rates than the average person, and only 29 % think they do not.

For some years now, migration has proved to be a subject capable of responding perfectly to the need to feed the frame of fear that creates consensus and therefore power over public opinion. To propose the accounting of flows, to show landings and reception centers, to associate those unnamed faces with countries crossed by war and terrorism, to associate albeit indirectly the economic crisis to migrants who are trying to enter Europe, to emphasize the facts of petty crime widespread involving foreigners, they are all useful elements to outline a very precise framework, capable of generating an attitude of fear and insecurity that in some cases evolves into hostility and violence towards those who are perceived as "intruders," disturbing our relative security and threatening our well-being.

In the information production process the world must be transformed to be adapted to the logic of the media and to respond to public expectations at the same time. Thus events are de-contextualized, removed from the context in which they occurred, isolated from their meanings and their causes, to be arbitrarily re-contextualized in a new frame – the media format – on the basis of associations and relationships to them completely extrinsic (Altheide, 1976, tr. it .: 24–28). This particular structure of information not only does not allow us to understand the developments of events, their antecedents, contexts, and the scenarios they open, but also prevents us from understanding their logic and direction (Gili, 2001: 191).

The immigration theme fits perfectly into Gili's thesis, even the data that emerged from the sixth Report on the application of the Charter of Rome published in October 2018, outlining a precise picture of the way in which the migration question finds representation through TV and printed paper.

> An information that feeds on itself, that has no predisposition to listen and produces obvious consequences [. . .] It is striking, among all the data contained in the report, that on television the voices of immigrants, refugees and asylum seekers are present in the 16 percent of immigration-related services, more than double 7 percent last year. It seems an important progress, we listen to them more. In reality, the analysis of those rumors reveals that these are testimonies relating to racially motivated attacks. We listen to them more not to understand who they are and where they come from, but why they are attacked. [. . .] Pacchia, cruise, clandestine, the pocket money of the 35 euros, invasion, are the words with which politics makes its propaganda, but which bounce on all the newspapers and on all the newscasts, without contradictory. We have seen television

> broadcasts in which politicians spoke of billions of Africans ready to leave, when billions of Africans do not even exist. All this happened in television studios in which those words, those numbers so far from reality were not placed a barrier, no clarification was requested.
> Words like invasion are very far from objective reality. Even putting together the arrivals of the last 5 years in Italy it would not be possible to fill Piazza San Giovanni as it can do a mediocre live concert of May 1st.
> The perception we have of the migratory phenomenon changes moods, generates fear. And that perception is based on the distortion of reality conveyed by words like clandestine, as an invasion (Rome Charter Report, 2018: 6).

Therefore, the perception that generates fear makes manifests the dichotomy between the real country and the perception that citizens have of it. This is an altered perception that clashes with the photograph taken by ISTAT, and contained in the report on the condition and social integration of foreign citizens residing in Italy in 2018, which analyzes from different perspectives the presence of foreigners in the country: "5,144,440 foreign residents, equal to 8.5 percent of total italian citizens, with an increase of less than 10 thousand compared to the previous year. Feeding the number of foreigners in Italy there are not only migrations from abroad, but also the many born in the country from both foreign parents, the so-called second generations" (ISTAT, 2018: 18).

An evident contradiction, the reality represented by almost 10 % of the Italian population made up of foreigners living and working in the peninsula and the imagery of an invasion of potential terrorists and criminals who threaten the security of the lives of Italian citizens. But the data also show that there is a progressive slow down of the presence of non-EU immigrants since 2011 in relation to the requests for permission in the face of a growth in the number of non-EU foreigners due to the acquisition of Italian citizenship. And still in the total of foreign residents 30 % come from the EU as a whole of over 200 nationalities (ISTAT, 2018: 20). As indicated by Bauman:

> We fear what we do not know how to handle. We call this incapacity "misunderstanding": "understanding" something is in fact the know-how that allows one to face that same thing. The knowledge of how to treat something, that *understanding*, is a "tribute" offered together with the tools with which one can perform that treatment, or rather incorporated in them. As a rule, this knowledge arrives a posterior: it requires, we can say, first of all the instruments, and only afterwards it is established in the mind through reflection on the effects of their use. In the absence of the tools and practices that they make possible, this knowledge or "understanding" hardly appears. *Understanding comes from the ability to manage.* What we cannot handle is "unknown" to us; and the "unknown" is scary. *Fear is another name we give to our being without defences* (Bauman, 2006: 119).

To combat fear, the ability to manage information and have the cultural tools that make us understand is necessary. If partial information prevails, the representation of migration remains something other than us, it does not promote questions, it does not make us overcome the barrier constituted by the immigrant's imagination, and makes him a real person. Above all, it does not show us the interdependencies that bind us to them, it does not explain to us that the increase in the economic gap between the north and the south of the world is the trigger for migratory flows, that the economic exploitation of which our Western society benefits is the cause, and that the same technology that has opened us to almost infinite possibilities is the same one that shows the gap and that motivates the excluded to try not to be anymore. The phenomenology of the migrant as a representation through the media is what, in Castells' vision, determines an excess of anxiety in the environment that compromises learning abilities, "the situations that awaken the fear are those that attract the largest audience (Graber, 2007: 267). These are reactions to events that threaten survival, and these reactions mobilize cognitive resources that activate attention. [. . .] The news (and in particular the images) can operate as sources of stimuli equivalent to the lived experience" (Castells, 2009: 193). So images with a high rate of drama, de-contextualized, arouse emotions in the public and influence their decisions. Thus the processes of construction of public opinion are altered by modifying the way in which consciousness and knowledge act. Consciousness because it operates on the processes of the mind and knowledge, acquired through consciousness because it increases the individual's ability to process events and build ever more complex mental models. A fundamental aspect in the digital society characterized by a continuous and growing flow of information that forces an effort to understand, metabolize, and eliminate this is considered as not necessary or as an obstacle to one's own survival and well-being and which also defines social behavior. Precisely in relation to the ways in which social behaviors are realized, Castells recalls Damasio's studies aimed at demonstrating the prominent role of emotions and feelings in social behavior. "Experimental research shows that the work of these emotions can be related to specific systems in the brain. The six basic emotions are: fear, disgust, surprise, sadness, happiness and anger. Species or individuals that are not equipped with the correct emotional perception system are unlikely to survive. Emotions are perceived in the brain as feelings. [. . .] Feelings derive from mutations activated emotionally in the brain, which reach a level of sufficient intensity to be consciously processed" (Ibidem p. 173).

In this sense, the path of identity construction becomes a representation of the self that makes us feel part of the network. The imperative is not to be excluded, the critical conscience is threatened by the need to be accepted and live in conditions of false security.

4 Conclusions

At the end of this analysis, some aspects of particular relevance on the way in which the disinformation industry alters the representation of the migration phenomenon through the media are highlighted. We have described the feeling of insecurity that runs through European and Italian society in particular. A framework from which it emerged with great evidence how emotions are now prevailing in the interpretation of facts and in the processes of construction of public opinion. This led us to analyze how the media system has evolved, stressing the growing crisis of journalism and the loss of credibility and reputation of traditional media, which has been grafted into a wider crisis that is sweeping institutions, governments, and basics of democracy as we had lived at the turn of the second half of the twentieth century and the beginning of the twenty-first century.

This has a direct consequence on the communicative and relational processes in an intrinsically mediated society that is giving life to a complex interweaving of interferences between the media system, institutions, and social networks that is able to produce manipulative actions through the transmission of false or distorted information. Also in this area we are witnessing an evolution in the use of the factoid scheme "which in the sphere of social phenomena and mass media constitute what hallucinations represent among the disorders of the individual psyche: they are in some respects collective hallucinations. [. . .] not events, events that never happened, that the mass media present as "real". These are pure inventions of rumors, gossip, which are treated as true news and, as such, can produce effects on the public" (Gili, 2001: 250).

Migration presents multiple critical aspects: a high level of complexity of its narration, its own chronicle if not accurate and thorough can generate altered or partial visions of the world. It is fundamental to define the geopolitical, cultural, and social framework, as well as the use of an appropriate and correct terminology in the description of individuals and situations of evident drama.

Thus the false and partial representation of the migratory phenomenon feeds the frame of fear and clearly conditions in depth the society and the individuals, who find themselves crushed between the continuous flow of news and an unscrupulous use of some specific keywords and, and a politics that in the obsessive search for consensus facing of a crisis of credibility, exploits this theme as an element to polarize the different ideological positions.

Cross-media becomes an element that promotes the rooting of polarized opinions that are consolidated, thanks to a communicative construction focused on the feeling of fear. Moreover, the emotional component is also pervading the areas of political communication in which it has taken on an increasingly important aspect (Cepernich, Novelli, 2018), particularly in relation to those "political" discourses that have seen the prevalence of positions connected to the anti-politics. A process that began over ten years ago with the first internet election campaigns until the last time, the European elections. If in 2011 Facebook in Italy had 20 million users, of which many were under 18, in 2019, after almost ten years, that generation of adolescents has grown up growing within the dynamics of a scandal policy. A policy that has not recovered its ethical dimension, and the populist language has become deeply rooted in bringing out a public ignorance (Morcellini, 2011). Thus, the process of building public opinion focuses on the concept of silence of citizenship (Pira, 2012), which has turned into non-participation and increasingly episodic participation. In the media-driven society where the plurality of media and information sources had contributed to the affirmation of democratic societies, through the main function of the journalistic system of conveying facts and controlling power, it became a society that shows all the signs of a profound disintegration, in which the core values of democracy seem strongly threatened. The society in the net and the globalized economy have, precisely through the power exercised over the communication flows, profoundly modified the system of rules of society. The progressive weakening of the institutions and the lack of political and social representation have deeply destabilized the individuals who, in an attempt to reconstruct an at least apparent riverbed, join forces in closed communities in which they recognize each other in function of primary needs or common enemies. It is quite clear how urgent it is to rewrite the rules of communication. As Jenkins argues: "We are in the midst of a profound and prolonged media change, which is impacting the ways messages are generated and circulated. The communications and marketing industries are now facing pressure to rewrite the rules around branding and strategic communication" (Jenkins, 2015).

Jenkins identifies some key concepts on the basis of which it is possible to create a new shared and participatory culture model (Jenkins, 2006), concepts that clash at present with the deviations that the media and relational system generated by social media produces. The possibility of giving life to a participatory culture, including the ability to produce media, and that somehow promote or modify the messages produced by the media, by advertising agencies, by corporate communicators, it clashes with the proliferation of misinformation and instrumental use of information. Thus, the affirmation of transmedia branding and the dissemination of key information and experiences across multiple media platforms with the aim of intensifying the relationship with the customer, are overwhelmed by, as Bauman states, a pervasive consumerism that "in our society liquid-modern consumer eviction industry – replacement – disposal – evacuation is one of the few commercial activities that is guaranteed to continue growing and that is immune to the bizarre consumer markets" (2012: 50). In the same way, social networks do not yet play a central role in spreading messages through cultures that adapt and diversify when they enter a spectrum of ongoing conversations. While we observe the effects of echo chambers and information cascade, we are shown that we are witnessing an amplification and stereotyping of information that gives life to polarized communities, where emotion prevails over reflection, hyper simplification over reality, leading to populist thought and to the extremes of positions. Thus they create networks in the connected but separate networks. Exactly the opposite of the concept of crowdsourcing associated with those organizations that cultivate online communities to find solutions to common problems, to innovate products, and to give inputs that communities can benefit from accompanying collective intelligence in reaching new opportunities. Individuals show a growing inability to select, analyze, and understand the flow of information they receive; consequently, the social dimension of our lives is characterized by becoming more and more homogeneous, outlining a process of construction of social action based on the paradigm of the choice made depending on what is more similar to me or in line with my positions. Politics is losing its ethical dimension to slip towards a logic of the exercise of power also using the use of communication strategies focused on the manipulation and construction of alternative truths. We are facing a challenge of global relevance that must be realized through a new autonomous construction of meaning (Castells, 2009). A process that is possible only if the relational dynamics and the construction of comparative skills on different opinions can prevail over the perverse dynamics arising from the distorted use of confirmation bias and the hyper-generation of polarizing effects. This means getting out from the dynamic click response, to use technology as part of an evolutionary process that does not simply generate interconnections but is able to give life to new relational models in a real integration between real and virtual, as opposed to the dissolution of reality and to the precariousness of identity.

References

AGCOM - Autorità per le Garanzie nelle comunicazione (2019). *Osservatorio sulle comunicazioni,* n.2/2019, published (July 23 2019) on Agcom.it: https://www.agcom.it/documents/10179/15564025/Documento+generico+23-07-2019/1cbb6f48-034f-417b-a57f-35650b070622?version=1.0

Agi.it (May 12 2019). *Facebook Italia chiude 23 pagine, published on Agit.it*: https://www.agi.it/politica/fake_news_facebook_italia_chiude_23_pagine-5474800/news/2019-05-12/.

Altheide D.L. (1976). *Creating Reality. How TV News Distorts Events*. Beverly Hills: Sage.

Bauman Z. (2006). *Liquid Fear*. Cambridge: Policy Press.

Bauman Z. (2012). *Conversazioni sull'educazione*. Trento: Edizioni Erickson (original work published 2012).

Bauman Z., Mauro E. (2015). *Babel*. Bari: Laterza.

Bradshaw S., Howard P.N. (2018). *Challenging Truth and Trust: A Global Inventory of Organized Social Media Manipulation*. Oxford: Oxford University Press.

Carzo D. (Ed.) (2011). *Narrare l'altro. Pratiche discorsive sull'immigrazione* (pp. 93–108). Roma: Aracne Editrice.

Castells M. (2003). *L'età dell'informazione*. Milano: Università Bocconi Editore.

Castells M. (2009). *Communication Power*. Oxford: Oxford University Press.

Cepernich C., Novelli E. (2018). Sfumature del razionale. La comunicazione politica emozionale nell'ecosistema ibrido dei media. *Comunicazione Politica*, Anno XIX, 1, Bologna: Il Mulino.

Ducci G. (2017). *Relazionalità consapevole. La comunicazione pubblica nella società connessa*. Milano: FrancoAngeli.

Gili G. (2001). *Il problema della manipolazione: peccato originale dei media?*. Milano: FrancoAngeli.

Gili G. (2005). *La credibilità. Quando e perché la comunicazione ha successo*. Soveria Mannelli: Rubettino Editore.

Gili G., Colombo F. (2012). *Comunicazione, Cultura, Società. L'approccio sociologico alla relazione comunicativa*. Brescia: Editrice La Scuola.

Gili G., Maddalena G. (2018). *Post-verità e fake news: radici, significati attuali, inattesi protagonisti e probabili vittime*. Media Education Studi e Ricerche (Vol. 9, pp. 1–16). Trento: Edizioni Centro Studi Erickson.

Graber D. (2007). The road to public surveillance: breaching attention thresholds, in W. Russel Neuman, George E. Marcus, Ann N. Crigler, Micheal MacKuen, The Affect Effect: Dynamics of Emtion in Political Thinking and Behavior, Chicago: University of Chicago Press.

Jenkins H. (2006). *Convergence Culture*. New York: New York University.

Jenkins H. (2015). *Back to School Special: Transmedia, New Media, and Strategic Communication*, published January 14 2015 from henryjenkins.org: http://

henryjenkins.org/blog/2015/01/back-to-school-special-transmedia-new-media-and-strategic-communication.html

Innis H.A. (2001). *Impero e Comunicazioni.* Roma: Meltemi.

IPSOS MORI Social Research Institute (2018, September). *Fake News, Filter Bubble, post.truth and trust. A study across 27 countries,* published September 6 2018, on site: https://www.ipsos.com/ipsos-mori/en-uk/fake-news-filter-bubbles-and-post-truth-are-other-peoples-problems.

ISTAT (2018). Vita e percorsi di integrazione degli immigrati in Italia, published May 2019 on site: https://www.istat.it/it/files/2019/05/Vita-e-percorsi.pdf

La Repubblica (24 may 2019). *Elezioni europee, meno fake news condivise su Facebook e Twitter,* pubblicato su Repubblica.it: https://www.repubblica.it/tecnologia/social-network/2019/05/24/news/europee_populis_fake_news_meno_condivise-227093200/

Lippmann W. (1999). *L'opinione pubblica.* Roma: Donzelli.

Lunaria (2019). *Il razzismo nel 2018 tra rimozione ed enfatizzazione*, Focus n.1 published on site cronachediordinariorazzismo.org: http://www.cronachediordinariorazzismo.org/pubblicazioni/

Morcellini M. (Ed.). (2011). *Neogiornalismo. Tra crisi e rete come cambia il sistema dell'informazione.* Milano: Mondadori Università.

Nickerson R.S. (1998). Confirmation bias: A ubiquitous phenomenon in many guises. *Review of General Psychology*, 2(2): 175.

Ortoleva P. (2011). Sintonizzare la nazione. Media e identità nazionale. *Rivista Comunicazione Politica*, Anno XII, n.1, Bologna: Il Mulino.

Pira F. (2011). Multiculturalità nella società web 3.0. Comunicare e comprendersi. . .con chi viene da lontano. In Carzo D. (Ed.), *Narrare l'altro. Pratiche discorsive sull'immigrazione* (pp. 93–108). Roma: Aracne Editrice.

Pira F. (2012). *La net Comunicazione Politica. Partiti, movimenti e cittadini-elettori nell'era dei social network.* Milano: FrancoAngeli.

Pira F. (2017). De la post-verdad a la desinformación. La mutación en el sistema de los Medios. In Martínez Paricio J. Y., Moreno Carrillo J.M. (Eds.), *Comprender el presente, imaginar el futuro: nuevas y viejas brechas sociales* (pp. 388–402). Roma-Messina: CORISCO Edizione.

Pira F., Altinier A. (2018). *Giornalismi. La difficile convivenza con fake news e*

Rapporto Carta di Roma (2018). *Notizie di Chiusura* (December 2018). Published on Cartadiroma.org: https://www.cartadiroma.org/wp-content/uploads/2018/12/Notizie-di-chiusura.pdf (http://www.cronachediordinariorazzismo.org/pubblicazioni/).

Maria Fobert Veutro

Chapter Seventeen Migration Images: in Newspapers of Different Orientations

Abstract: The subject of the study are the images of the migration that can be taken from the articles published in 2019 in two online Italian newspapers, each with a different political orientation, the first on the right, the second oriented towards the center-left. In each article I identified: *frame, theme(s), declarations/assessments/descriptions of facts, tone* and *terms particularly connoted*. Among the results: the most widespread frame in the first newspaper can be defined as *Sovereignism*; and in the second *Strength and centrality of associationism, of the European Union and of International humanitarian organizations*. The first newspaper tends to consider migrants as an *indistinct category*; conversely, in the second *customization* is quite frequent. On the positions of the Catholic Church in this matter, the first newspaper claims its *transcendent* character: the Church should not deal with "worldliness" but with the "spiritual sphere"; the second, on the contrary, with the *immanent* trait: good and justice must be achieved in this world and the prelates have this objective.

1 Introduction

As widely argued in communication studies, the mass media – directly or through a third party, addressing viewers or readers with varying levels of passivity depending on the different theories (see a review in Paccagnella, 2004, pp. 100–163[1]) – participate in the "social construction of reality" (Berger and Luckmann, 1966; Perrotta, 2005).

In order to interpret social events, Goffman (1974) proposed the concept of *frame:* a key to reading, looking at things on a metalevel that highlights certain aspects of situations and neglects others; and Zerubavel proposed that of *framing*: "an act that consists in enclosing situations, gestures or objects in mental brackets" (1993, p. 11).

With regard to media content, "frames focus on what will be discussed, how it will be discussed and, above all, how it will not be discussed. Certain themes

1 The theories differ according to whether the effects of the media are considered strong (Hypodermic needle, Knowledge differential theories; Frankfurt School; agenda setting) or weak/limited (Uses and gratifications; Two-stage communication flow, Cultural Studies).

become appropriate if particular frames are adopted ... [for example] within the *criminal justice* frame, which implies a speech of punishment, issues of concern for health, which include treatment, intervention and even education, seem quite out of place" (Altheide, [1996] 2000, p. 49).

The social figure of the foreigner has been the object of reflection of scholars since the beginning of the 20th century. Among the classical authors, we can mention (see a review in Cipollini, 2002): Thomas e Znaniecki (1918–20), Simmel (1921), Park (1928), and Schutz (1944). Among the most recent ones, there are: Kaczynski (2008), Romania and Zamperini (2009), Colombo (2011), and Ambrosini (2011).

In Italy, the migration phenomenon has long been in the limelight of the media[2]; it is mostly considered to be a social problem and its "definitions" are varied. Griswold points out that social problems can be seen as situations that originate from structural causes and/or as cultural objects: "more or less shared meanings and incorporated into a form" ([1994] 1997, p. 26). The status of the cultural object is not intrinsic to the object itself but is given by the observer who interprets events. Considering social problems as cultural objects draws attention to the fact that the possible solution to a problem is implicit in the way it is defined, which is usually the one considered to be the easiest and/or fairest by the broadcaster. For example, using expressions and terms of war, such as "border protection", "siege," "fight," and "contain flows" about immigrants, suggests that the legitimate (and unique) solution is rejection, even with the use of force.

Cohen (1987) coined the expression "moral panic" to underline how, in particular moments, society is affected by concerns about people considered threatening to common interests and shared values. Becker ([1963] 1991, pp. 115–126) traces the figure of the "crusader" who, indignant about evil, is committed to oppose it and eradicate it. But along with the crusader, convinced of the ethical value of his enterprise, there are also "moral entrepreneurs" whose initiatives may have objectives that have little to do with the problem reported: the moral panic serves to aggregate a consensus that will then be exploited to obtain economic benefits or to acquire power.

---

2 In view of the news reports: "The monitoring of the news concerning immigration which appeared on the prime-time news programmes of the Rai, Mediaset and La7 networks reveals that in twelve years the references to immigration have increased more than tenfold, rising from 380 news items in 2005 to 4.268 in 2017." (Caritas Migrantes, 2018).

There is now a wealth of literature on the representations of migrants (among others see Macioti, 1995; Dal Lago, 1998; Perrotta, 2000 and 2002; Toscano, 2009; Fobert Veutro, 2010), and also specifically on the images portrayed by the press, some references to which I have reported below.

Maneri (1998) analyzed articles from seven Italian national newspapers[3], comparing them in two periods between 1988 and 1993: in the first period, the themes of racism and xenophobia prevailed, and in most cases no generalizations appeared and in-depth studies were proposed; in the second period, there was the strengthening of the theme "crime" with generalizations that are based on the dichotomy us–them. To this regard, Perrotta noted that "in the case of immigrants, the stigma related to ethnic origin is accompanied by that related to belonging to a low social class because they live, in general, in situations of economic poverty and are mostly placed in employment roles considered inferior" and that in Italy, since the 1990s "next to the binomial immigrant = incivil, the binomial immigrant = enemy" has tended to assert itself (2000, p. 658).

Following a qualitative approach and using interviews, official documents, press, and media speeches, Dal Lago pointed out that in one of the most widespread frames, "foreigner" is the equivalent of "outsider," a term in which a potential threat is enclosed, and coined the expression "tautology of fear" (1999, p.73): "I define this mechanism as tautological when the simple statement of the alarm demonstrates the reality it denounces. These autopoietic mechanisms are known in sociology, at least starting from the concept of Definition of the situation (coined by Thomas), according to which if men define situations as real, they are real in their consequences."

In the 2007 report of the *Fondazione* iniziative e studi sulla multietnicità (ISMU), which reported the analysis of the articles of one week in each month from January to September 2006 of four Italian newspapers[4], it was pointed out, among other things, that the section in which the article appears is a first frame that indicates the areas in which the image of the migrant is relevant. In this study, 50 % of the articles on the subject appeared in the *news* section and only 4 % in *opinions*; the most recurrent point of view was that of politicians, and the direct voice of migrants was almost absent.

Also the study of Sciortino and Colombo in two national newspapers[5] (2004) noted that the overwhelming voice was that of politicians, especially those

3 Il Corriere della sera, La Repubblica, La Stampa, L'Unità, Il Giornale, L'Indipendente, Il Manifesto.

4 Il Corriere della sera, La Repubblica, Il Giornale and L'avvenire.

5 Il Corriere della sera and La Repubblica.

belonging to the majority, and that attention peaks were linked firstly to legislative measures on the subject, and secondly to news items related to landings or crime.

2 Textual Corpora and Method of Analysis

For this study, I chose to analyze articles published in 2019 in two online newspapers[6] in Italian, with a high digital readership, each with a different political stance, the first on the right, the second oriented to the center-left: ilgiornale.it. and repubblica.it (to be precise, the paper newspapers of reference are *Il Giornale* and *La Repubblica*).

As I have noted, the editorial policy of online newspapers is to offer almost exclusively news articles, excluding pieces of background, opinion, and/or in-depth analysis, perhaps to induce readers to pay a fee for reading this type of article or for a subscription, or for the purchase of the paper newspaper. Therefore, the articles I have collected concern exclusively the news; moreover, as mentioned above, previous studies point out that the topic of immigration is mainly dealt with in the news section.

In fact, newspapers express the ideology and editorial line especially in in-depth and background articles mentioned above, and in the dossiers, but, albeit less evident and sometimes hidden, they are also found in the news sections, where more or less deliberate tactics are used, as well as in the headlines, photos (both usually with a sought-after effect), in format, in the description of facts and news, and in the definition and setting of events in a frame.

I carried out the research using the keywords "immigration," "immigrants," and "migrants" and examined all the articles published on the subject in the specific periods below.

I started collecting the pieces on April 1, 2019, which was roughly the same date as the government's choice of "closed ports," and I did not set a precise closing date.

6 Regarding the information that can be collected on the internet, Airoldi (2017, 331) proposes this classification: digitized data (such as online newspapers): in this case, the internet is used as an immaterial archive; virtual data (surveys, interviews, and focus groups): the internet is used as a means of recruitment and data collection; and finally digital data (spontaneous comments from digital surfers on Facebook or other social networks, more searched keywords, online reviews, etc.): the internet represents a "social universe."

Subsequently, following the political events that led to the fall of the first government led by Conte[7] and the establishment of the second government also led by Conte, in which the government members changed significantly due to the exclusion of the Lega and the inclusion of the Democratic Party ("yellow-red" or "yellow-pink" government), I thought of distinguishing the text corpus into two time intervals. The first falls in the period of the first government members and the other in that of the second. I decided to analyze the two corpora also to check if significant differences emerged in the presentation of the news regarding the phenomenon of immigration.

I examined all the articles on the subject published between 1st and April 30, 2019, and all those published between 14 September and 14 October of the same year. The choice of the second period is linked to the date of the start of the second government headed by Conte: September 5, 2019. In total, I collected 115 articles: 71 from ilgiornale.it (24 of which were published in the first period and 47 in the second) and 44 from repubblica.it (29 of which were published in the first period and 15 in the second).

I opted for a qualitative analysis of the documents[8] and, in particular, I was inspired by the principles of ethnographic content analysis (ECA) proposed by Altheide. In ECA "the reflective and highly interactive nature of the investigator[is of great importance] ... in ECA the investigator is continually at the center ... Categories and variables initially guide the study, others are allowed and expected to emerge to be taken into account in the course of the study, including an orientation towards constant discovery and constant comparison of relevant situations, settings, styles, images, meanings and nuances" ([1996] 2000, p. 27).

I devised some sort of protocol, partly inspired by Altheide: "protocol: a way to ask question of a document; a protocol is a list of questions, items, categories, or variables that guide data collection from documents" (ivi, p. 43).

It was a guide to identify in each article – in addition to title/subject, author, and date – the following characteristics:

---

7 So-called yellow-green government, composed of 5-star Movement and the League.

8 The contributions dealing with the analysis of documents according to this approach are numerous: see, among others, Schwartz and Jacobs (1979), Denzin and Lincoln (1994, 2011), Cipolla and De Lillo (1996), Altheide (1996 and subsequent publications including Schneider), Corbetta (2003), Cardano and Ortalda (2017), and Fobert Veutro (2008 and 2019).

a) *Frame:* a background in which one or more topics are set. Often it escapes our notice and is taken for granted; it focuses attention on what is appropriate and legitimate to discuss and neglects other perspectives. Certain themes become appropriate if certain frames are adopted.
b) *Theme(s):* object of the speech; what is being talked about.
c) *Declarations/assessments/descriptions of facts.*
d) *Tone*: for example, neutral/emotional/hostile/denigrating.
e) *Particularly connoted terms.*

While collecting, "the investigator goes back and forth between protocols when the data of a category show similarities or differences from those just read a moment before" (ivi, p. 86). In fact, as usual in the recursive process of qualitative research, I considered the probability that subsequent and repeated examinations would suggest other significant elements and perhaps the importance attached to those originally chosen would be weakened. "Meanings and patterns . . . rarely appear all at once; rather, they emerge or become clearer through constant comparison and examination of documents over a period of time . . . the emergence refers to the gradual taking of shape of meaning through understanding and interpretation" (ivi, p. 17).

Table 17.1 shows an excerpt from the protocol that helped me with the analysis:

3 Results

a) Frames and Frequent Themes

In the period between 1 and 30 April, the *frame* in which many articles of ilgiornale.it are set can be defined as *sovereignism*[9].

For example, the *theme* of the piece *Ngo's it forces Salvini's blockade: Sea Eye sets sail on Lampedusa* (G. De Lorenzo, April 4) is the ships of nongovernmental organizations (Alan Kurdi, Mediterranea Saving Humans) and, reporting the words of the Minister of the Interior, *descriptions* and *assessments* of this kind are formulated as follows:

---

9 A political position which advocates the defense or reconquest of national sovereignty by a people or a State, in antithesis to the dynamics of globalization and in opposition to the supranational policies of consultation (A. Manzella, *La Repubblica*, November 13, 2002, p. 1).

Tab. 17.1: Extract from the analysis protocol

	Title/topic and author	Date	Frame	Theme/s	Declarations/ assessments/ descriptions of facts	Tone and connotated terms
1	The Pope on immigration (F. Bernasconi)	1/4	Spiritual, otherworldly view of the phenomenon	Immigration and solidarity	Solidarity is divine quality, difficult to realize among humans	Affective/ emotional
2	Border guards and repatriations (C. Sarra)	1/4	Bellicose view	Sovereignism	The individual state is sovereign in directing operations	Fighting, attacks, military corps, protection, limiting
3	Migrants, changed the laws regarding the ships (B. Dall'orto)	2/4	sovereignism	ONG	Holland limits the possibility of rescuing immigrants	A bit emotional
4	Do not touch him, even if he is a murderer (S. Rame)	2/4	Violence of immigrants	Aggression towards the police	Violence of immigrants towards the police is daily	Emotional and violent
5	Demographic crisis (F. Boezi)	3/4	The drop in the birth rate is a problem	1. Transfer solution 2. Different views of coalition parties	1. Transfer is not a solution 2. Delegitimising of 5 stelle minister (Di Maio)	Emotional and alarmistic
6	Going around armed with a Katana sword (C. Certaldo)	4/4	Violence of the immigrants	Insecurity in the suburbs despite law enforcement interventions	Strengthening repression of immigrant violence in the suburbs	Heavily worried, alarmistic

1) NGOs help traffickers and states must stop them ("The French minister also confirmed that NGOs help traffickers. Immigration management cannot be left to private organisations");
2) There is a link between immigration and terrorism ("combined provisions proven by investigations and facts").

The theme (foreign NGOs), the descriptions and assessments above appear natural because the supremacy and defense of national sovereignty are taken for granted from the sub-headline ("they must go to Hamburg") and then in the text ("Our government has written to the German government ... The position of the Viminale is clear ... But a long tug of war is expected ... Salvini is in Paris for the G7 ..."). Moreover, the unfavorable prediction in the phrase "Other lives put at risk by a foreign NGO" gives the term "foreign," therefore not national, reprehensible connotations.

Sovereignism also often appears as a *theme*. For example, the article *Border guards and repatriations: this is how Europe is changing Frontex* (C. Sarra, April 1st) is about defending the national territory, and this is linked to the phenomenon of immigration ("10,000 border guards, repatriations and agreements: this is how the fight against illegal immigrants is changing"). The main *declaration* is that the individual State is sovereign in directing operations ("Member States will retain primary responsibility for the management of their borders") and, like the *theme*, is set within a *frame* that I have called *The bellicose view of the phenomenon*, reinforced several times by terms and expressions such as "fight," "military corps," "besieged countries," "contain flows," "border protection," "deployed personnel," and "use of force and weapons."

Another recurring *frame*, which confirms some of the results of the studies of the last two decades, is the assumption that the immigration phenomenon is a social problem in terms of violence and crime. Even a *theme* of domestic violence (N. De Angelis, *England, does not want to help him with a visa and he stabs his foreign wife*, April 5) is set in the frame *Violence of immigrants* (the murderer is "a pedophile and irregular immigrant").

Moreover, as Perrotta noted (2002, p. 126), when it comes to immigrants from Islamic countries, there is often a tendency to take for granted that they are religious and that the religion they profess is the Islamic religion[10], which appears to be violent. However, "the automatic combination of Islamic religiosity danger does not allow us to see how religious observance has positive implications for the host country. Religion offers a legitimising apparatus that helps to keep the visions of the world and of life firm. Referring to family routines and conversations with subjects who share one's own definitions serves to preserve

10 Yet in Italy "immigrants of the Muslim religion are about 1.7 million, less than a third of the total." Moreover, with regard to the perception of the prevailing gender, it is significant that "52 per cent are women" (E. Di Pasquale, A. Stuppini, C. Tronchin, 2019).

daily reality" (ivi, p. 132). Therefore, it is useful in order to prevent possible discomfort with possible consequent deviant behavior.

The fact of constituting a social problem also manifests itself in other, nonviolent forms. Inscribed in a *frame* that I have called *Immigration creates new phenomena/problems,* in three articles there are declarations/descriptions/assessments on three themes. Immigration:

1) *has made a business out of reception,* in an article, the theme of which is the protest against the cuts to the reception system (M. Indelicato, *No more business with migrants and now cooperatives and unions take to the streets,* April 8);
2) *accentuates the demographic crisis,* which can instead be solved by helping Italian families and "real" Italian people, and not immigrant families (F. Garau, *Meloni versus Bonino: "Helping Italians to create a family",* April 10);
3) *is a source of political conflict.* For example, the representatives of humanitarian organizations hurl themselves against the right and the left (A. Scarano, *Gino Strada attacks Salvini: "Racist". On the Pd: "He declared war on NGOs",* April 9).

One of the themes that can often be found in ilgiornale.it is the risk of the "racial transfer," or "demographic transfusion," which is instead to be desired in one of the articles by Emma Bonino, currently leader of a Europeanist party (*Meloni versus Bonino: "Helping Italians to create a family"*). It is interesting to note that the danger of the invasion, of *Le grand remplacement* (Renaud Camus, 2011), has been constantly repeated in history[11]. Even a writer, F. Scott Fitzgerald, got a wealthy young man living on Long Island (N.Y.) to declare in 1925:

> "Civilization is breaking down! Have you read The Rise of the Coloured Empires? It says that if we don't look out, *the white race will be pushed under by the coloured races* – said Tom – Our race has produced all the things that make up civilization – oh, science and art and all that. And if we don't watch out, these order races will take control of thing. Do you see?" (The Great Gatsby) (my italics).

In the same period (from 1 to 30 of April), in repubblica.it, the frame *Violence of immigrants* does not appear, and it seems that the episodes of deviance described are occasional, sometimes with responsibilities shared with Italians and set in different frames.

11 "Also in France, in 2015, the dystopian novel by Michel Houellebecq *Submission* caused a sensation (and sales success), where it is imagined that at the 2022 presidential elections Marine Le Pen will be defeated by the first Muslim president. The same debate, however, has also taken hold in the United States, focusing in particular on Mexican immigration" (E. Di Pasquale, A. Stuppini, C. Tronchin, 2019).

For example, in an article entitled *Oulx, a passeur with seven people in the car was stopped* (C. Rocci, 6 April), about a 20-year-old Pakistani boy arrested for aiding illegal immigration, it is stressed that "the car was not registered to a compatriot but to a 40-year-old Italian who owns seven other cars," in a frame that I called *The illegal immigrants tend to leave Italy*, also because it is stressed several times that the car was headed to France, anyway "certainly across the border" and "the young passeur lives and resides in France." This *frame* therefore suggests the inevitability of this type of crime (illegal immigration) and thus mitigates its seriousness. Another article concerning the facilitation of illegal immigration (*Van with 12 migrants blocked in Udine: getaway started in Slovenia*, April 7) refers to "alleged Bengali irregular migrants" in a framework that underlines the efficiency of the police ("managed to block the means") and the presence of medical staff: "Together with the police forces of Duino, Udine and Gorizia, the rescuers who ascertained the condition of the migrants arrived on the spot: none of them was seriously injured"; therefore, in describing the event, there is also concern for the health of the migrants and there is no insistence on the crime.

In a piece on a topic concerning the criminal behavior of illegal migrants (*Migrants, Libya warns the NGOs "Do not enter our waters,"* April 2) the critical statements of the Libyan authorities about the NGOs and the European Union (EU) are referred to but placed in a frame of *Difficulty in the relationships between states, the European Union and the UN*, rather than violence of migrants, which is reported nonetheless.

As one may expect, the opposite evaluation – immigration as a resource – is not presented.

The prevailing frame is rather the *strength and centrality of associationism*, the seriousness and reliability of *international humanitarian organizations* (such as the UN) and/or the recognition of the importance of *the European Union*, therefore, the legitimacy of bodies that are smaller or larger than the national state: ultimately, an opposite stance to that of sovereignism.

Here are some examples where this frame can be found: in an article entitled *Trapani, the "Ionian Sea" that helped 50 migrants is applauded at the port of Marsala* (G. Ruta, April 1st), the results achieved by NGOs and other humanitarian associations are praised. In the piece *Citizenship the "new Italians" of the second generation* (V. Polchi, April 1st) we read: "while large organizations [including trade unions of various orientations] . . . relaunch a movement on the *ius soli* . . . a series of associations meet for a big event . . . To relaunch the theme today are associations (from *Cara Italia* to *Neri italiani*) and many children of immigrants." In another, entitled *German NGO Sea Eye rescues 64 migrants off the coast of Libya* (April 3), the relief operation is applauded and "the importance of the intervention of the civilian fleet off the coast of Libya" is underlined. This frame is apparent in a number of other articles, the subject of which is the rescue of migrants and/or the decision of the Ministry of the Interior not to allow the docking of rescue ships.

Mediation skills for solving difficult situations are in some cases identified in the EU institutions, and this recognition constitutes the frame of the speech. For example, in the article entitled *Immigration, the Mayor of Lampedusa tells Tajani: "Help us"* (G. Ruta, April 5), in which he calls for measures to support municipalities and border islands, the authority of the President of the European Parliament in Brussels, who is also a political representative of a right-wing party, is legitimized. In the same way, the choice not to split up the families (women and children from the adult men), hoped for by the staff of the ship (of a German NGO) responsible for the rescue and stuck at the mooring of the Italian coast, is entrusted to the EU: "the government of Berlin has asked the European Commission to find a shared solution . . . We have asked the EU Commission to assume the coordination . . . We have asked for a control room of coordination between the member States" (A. Ziniti, *Migrants, mothers and children refuse to get off the Alan Kurdi. In the night the ship goes to Malta*, April 5).

On September 5, 2019, a new government took office with the same prime minister but a different ally of the 5-star Movement: the Democratic Party (PD) in place of the Lega.

As was to be expected, in the period between 14 September and 14 October in many articles of ilgiornale.it, the *statements* and *assessments* insisted that the wind had changed, in some cases from the sub-headlines: "the wind has already changed: the government assigns the island as a safe haven. It is the first NGO to enter Italy without any problems" (A. Scarano, *The migrants of the Ocean Viking will land in Lampedusa*, September 14). It is clear that the policy of containing migratory flows and "closed ports," implemented by the previous Minister of the Interior Salvini, was quickly repudiated.

Analyzing many articles, it seems that the communicative tactic based on irony now appears to be more effective than the one based on bellicosity. In fact, the tones are mostly not aggressive but mocking or, at worst, sarcastic and disparaging as in this excerpt: "The mayor of Lampedusa, always of the idea that 'we open our ports to all', now doesn't agree and says he is not an idiot . . . And he thinks along the lines of 'yes to open ports but not in my house'. But where did his theory of 'let's welcome them all' end up? But above all, has the great 'war' fought for 14 months against Matteo Salvini been forgotten?" (S. Pizzi, *The NGO lands in Italy and the do-gooder mayor gets shirty: "Why here? We are not idiots"*, September 14).

The *Sovereignism* frame remains but now it is more like the one of *Threatened sovereignty*. In fact, the renewed alleged invasion of migrants may be allowed by the overwhelming power of the EU over the decisions of individual states, by the impunity of foreign NGOs that are no longer held back by restrictive legislation, and by the failure to comply with agreements on the redistribution of migrants, in particular by Germany and France. For example, with regard to the European Frontex Agency, "The problem is that among the 'specific objectives' of the Agency there is not only border control, but also search and rescue activities. And so, border defence is often transformed into a rescue service for immigrants"; moreover "as a police officer from Samos bitterly explains: Frontex brings all the migrants to the islands. The ships of France and Germany docked here are very happy to rescue immigrants. They say: 'Welcome to Europe'. And then they leave them here" (G. De Lorenzo, M. Di Piazza, *Frontex does not defend borders. So, they bring us all the migrants*, October 1st).

However, now the most recurrent *frame* seems rather closely linked to a *contingent electoral strategy*. There are different themes and problems in the various articles – the new "migratory crisis," the pressures for the approval of laws on *ius culturae* and *ius soli*, the renewed flourishing business of reception, the theft of jobs intended for Italians by immigrants, the "culture of NGOs," and the danger posed by the presence of immigrants – but, it is suggested, they are all attributable to the policy of a government in which the hegemonic party is the Democratic Party, which also has a parliamentary representation significantly lower than that of the 5-star Movement.

In essence, the latter is presented as a succubus of the government ally, which would represent the real "danger for the Italians." An example is the following excerpt: "even if we change partners, the result is the same: the 5-Star supporters are overshadowed by the ally. At the end of the film, there is another protagonist, that is, the one that, at least according to the numbers, should have been the side-kick. Now the new left government has reopened the doors … But it is not just a question of numbers. The Pd has collected the seats that count" (F. Angeli, *Migrants. Grillo followers without a direction. All the democrats decide*, September 15). Another example shows the subordination of the leader of the 5-star Movement: "Now even Luigi di Maio has figured it out … he tries to talk tough on immigration. An attempt that seems to go in the direction of that hard Salvinian fist on immigration that … can certainly not please the red Democrat allies of the government" (F. Franchini, *The last promise of Di Maio: Repatriation of migrants in four months*, October 3).

In other articles, reporters of ilgiornale.it accuse high representatives of the left-wing party (PD) of being ambiguous and fraudulent in their communication, with regard to the new Minister of the Interior of the second government headed by Conte, one of the headlines: *Here's the latest from Lamorgese "More landings?The situation in Tunisia is to blame"* (M. Indelicato, October 1st); and the comment: "But this appears to be only a half-truth." Quoting data provided by the Viminale, and reported as misleading, here are other headlines: *Deception about empty hotspots. Here is the government's trick* (M. Indelicato, October 2); *Lamorgese uses Salvini's data to hide the "open ports"* (A. Scarano, October 2). And regarding the work of a well-known exponent of the PD, the mayor of Bergamo Giorgio Gori: *The last trick of the left to keep the illegal immigrants in Italy* (S. Rame, October 2). As you can see, the terms used are: half-truth, deception, trick, and hide.

Therefore, this frame – which can be called *Delegitimization of the government* – disqualifies the political and decision-making power of the 5-star Movement and presents the Democratic Party's communication as mendacious. Therefore, it can induce the voters of the party that previously received more support than its allies (the 5-star Movement) to reflect and bring their votes to a party (the Lega) that showed that it could wield the baton in the previous government (the Leghist minister Salvini was called "The Captain") even with a smaller parliamentary representation than the other party, and furthermore that would be free from ambiguity. All this, obviously, took place with the forecast of new elections in the short/medium term.

After the new government took office, in the period from 14 September to 14 October and using the same key words, only 15 articles on the subject of "immigration" appeared in repubblica.it: a smaller number than in the previous period and much fewer than the number of articles – 47 – that appeared in ilgiornale.it on the same subject in the same period.

In repubblica.it the most common *frame* is the renewed recognition of *The importance of the European Union and supranational organizations* such as the UN and within this recurring *themes* are framed such as the meeting of 23 September in Malta – in which the Interior Ministers of some European countries and the European Commission participated – and the redistribution of asylum seekers and so-called economic migrants. Here are two headlines of articles where this frame can be found: *The EU: Italy will never be left alone again but no automatisms* (T.C.A. Ginori, September 15); *Syria and migrants, Mattarella's concern "Europe is marginal, so it will be overwhelmed"* (C. Vecchio, October 12) in which he reads that the head of the Italian state "makes a heartfelt speech: 'Solidarity is the founding value of the Union, it is the reason that started the process of integration seventy years ago, and it is the reason for the enlargement that has been progressively achieved in integration'. The alternative risks being terrorist violence."

The importance of *humanitarian associations* such as the International Organisation for Migration and the United Nations High Commissioner for Refugees (UNHCR) continues to be recognized, but the role of NGOs in rescuing migrants is not mentioned so often as before.

The change in the *weight of information* is underlined: for example, in the piece *Migrants, the alarm regarding autonomous mini landings* (A. Ziniti, September 20) we read: "The phenomenon of the landings, explained Salvatore Martello, mayor of Lampedusa, is just the same as before, but with a difference: before it could not be discussed. No one could tell if there had been a landing or not. Today, however, arrivals are communicated to all Italians ... There was an absence of information in 2018 and 2019. Now that the government has changed, everyone wants to record information, everyone wants to know. But the problem of the landings has remained the same, it is the same as before."

In two articles the concern for the protection of human rights extends to those violated at the border between Mexico and the USA by the agreements promoted by the government of Trump. The sub-headlines are as follows: "UNHCR denounces Trump's new anti-immigration policies" and "Mexico and Honduras: the violence in the Central American nation has not prevented the agreement of cooperation that obliges asylum seekers to a forced stay" (V. Negro, September 22 and 30).

As for the attitude towards *the new government*, almost only one of the two allied parties is mentioned, the Democratic Party, and its work is valued. There is a tendency to present this party as the deciding factor, probably, like in the other daily newspaper, in anticipation of elections in the short term from which they hope it will gain strength. However, unlike in the other newspaper, this is not the prevailing frame of this textual corpus.

b) The Church and the Pope

As is to be expected when we analyze the contents of the Italian mass media, both newspapers dedicate some articles to the position of the Pope and individual priests. In the frame that I have called *The opinion of the Church is relevant*, the two newspapers use different tones that are close to their respective political positions on the subject: repubblica.it. is mostly emotional and positive, while ilgiornale.it is critical and denigrating.

The piece in repubblica.it *Depressed refugee takes his own life. The Archbishop of Turin says: "Reflect on the wounds of migrants"* (April 6) presents the attitude of the prelate as merciful and charitable: "he was followed by a team of people, this commitment was not enough ... We followed closely this boy who had repeatedly shown signs of depression . . . we tried to help him in every way . . . they are wounds that mark many immigrants in our country." And in the same way in the article *Migrants, the bishop of Palermo Lorefice meets Casarini: "I am with you from the Ionian Sea"* (G. Ruta, April 13); the statement of the head of mission is: "the head of the archdiocese of Palermo had taken a strong position against what is happening at sea . . . I told him that I was horrified to see people left in the water. And he replied that that term, 'horrified', would be the right translation of the 'moved to compassion' that Jesus felt when he encountered injustices . . . I pointed out to him that I would hate to let him get into the debate that involve us, I was surprised by his response: every life saved is a hymn to God."

The commentary therefore also reveals the attribution of a courageous, almost transgressive behavior to the bishop.

In the second period, when the new government had already taken office, the tone did not change, but rather strengthened and attributed a role of "political" stimulus to the Catholic Church: two articles reported with appreciation the "strong support of the Church" for the promotion of *ius culturae* and the attribution of citizenship to migrants who go to school and obtain qualifications.

The presentations of ilgiornale.it are very different in tone. In an article entitled *The bishop of Bologna defends immigration and relaunches ius soli* (G. Aloisi, April 5), as in others, the tone is ironic and denigrating and it is worth reporting a large excerpt:

> Let's go ahead with the reception of migrants and the promotion of *ius soli*. The Archbishop of Bologna . . . is one of the consecrated progressives who have distinguished themselves for their criticism of the restrictive management of migration phenomena. Immigration, for the prelate, must become an 'opportunity', while in terms of citizenship it would be enough to look at the case of the footballer of Juventus . . ... who, according to the bishop, cannot only be considered a citizen of Italy when he kicks the ball into the net with the national team . . ... The prelate does not say it openly, but there is a clear reference to the extension of citizenship.

However, in another article (F. Bernasconi, *The Pope on immigration: "Whoever builds walls remains a prisoner there"*, April 1st), the *theme* of which I called *Immigration and Solidarity*, the position of the Pope is presented in a socially desirable way (the right-wing party of the yellow-green government – the Lega – is notoriously critical about this). This piece suggests an interpretation as "solidarity is a sublime divine feeling, but difficult to implement among human beings" in a *frame* that I called *The spiritual, otherworldly vision of the migration phenomenon*. To make this representation clearer, here is a quotation from it:

> Already in the past the Pope condemned the raising of walls to stop migrants. 'We need bridges, not walls', Pope Francesco forcefully reiterates, confessing the pain he feels when he sees 'people who prefer to build walls'. And he warns: 'Those who build walls will end up as prisoners of the walls they have built. Instead, those who build bridges will go a long way forward'. *But the Pope knows that it is not easy to reach beyond the wall, so much so that, to explain the almost divine gesture of building a bridge, he retrieves a metaphor from the novel by Ivo Andric, The Bridge over the Drina: 'He says that the bridge was made by God with the wings of angels.* (my italics).

In essence, the daily newspaper maintains a critical but not oppositional position, and therefore is also appreciated by right-wing Catholic readers (and voters), possibly admirers of the Pope.

In the second period considered (14 September–14 October), in the articles of ilgiornale.it ironic and devaluing tones are still found about some prelates who express approval for the "turnabout" of the government, more inclined to welcome migrants than the previous one: "the head of the bishops of the *Belpaese* has reasoned openly on the microphone about the need for full integration" (G. Aloisi, *At the IEC open ports are not enough*, September 27). Another comment (my italics): "They have already renamed him the 'welcoming tortellino'. The idea, pursued by one of the most *extreme supporters of immigration*, the Archbishop of Bologna, recently awarded by Pope Francesco with the office of cardinal, is yet *another in favor* of Muslim migrants" (S. Rame, *Bologna, on the feast of the patron saint tortellini without pork "for the sake of integration,"* October 1st).

At the same time, however, a more clearly oppositional and ideologically delineated line emerges which presents members of the clergy as standard-bearers: "Cardinal Francis Arinze … expressed himself as follows: 'Europeans must stop encouraging the departure of young Africans. Africa needs them. These are different tones from those usually heard … we would dare to say Ratzingerians', 'the right not to emigrate' also of Ratzingerian origin" (G. Aloisi, *The Cardinal thunders at the do-gooders: "Don't tell the migrants to leave,"* October 1st). Even stronger and clearer are the statements in an article (G. Aloisi, *The priest criticizes the Pope: "He is obsessed with migrants,"* October 8) of which I report some excerpts:

> He strongly accuses the Pope, 'he has little faith'. And also the continuity with which Bergoglio refers to migrants … for Tedoldi it is 'an obsession' of the Argentinean … This parish priest does not seem in line with the common feeling of a good part of the Catholic clergy around the world … '*Many men of the hierarchy, and even priests have little or no fait … But I have confidence,* God does not let his boat sink, he saves it'. Once *again the words that Benedict XVI wrote* at the funeral of Cardinal Meisner resound, those according to which the Ecclesia, in some circumstances, may seem on the verge of being overturned … 'The great problem… is not paedophilia in the clergy, which

is certainly an offence, but the fact that faith is scarce. We are constantly talking about migrants, politics, the environment. *In short, worldliness, and we forget God, the great absentee, transcendence, the sacred and therefore the salvation of souls that is the true purpose of the Church' ... Too much political interventionism, therefore, while reducing the space for the spiritual sphere* (my italics).

The sharp opposition to the thinking of the present pontiff is clear but this time it is presented with the chrism of the presumed orientation of a no less authoritative prelate: Pope Ratzinger.

c) Homologate and Customize

In general, and in both periods, ilgiornale.it tends to consider migrants as an indistinct category, with little reference to different ethnic groups regarded as interchangeable.

The lack of differentiation can favor generic stereotypes (for example, regarding women in general, men, children, Germans, Americans, Muslims, Jews, etc.). Among other things, cultural models vary not only in relation to the countries of origin but also "to the historical period in which immigration took place ... It is then possible to identify a continuum at the ends of which there are immigrants who ... arrive already knowing the language of the place and being familiar with the patterns of behaviour of the host context, and immigrants for whom, instead, everything is new ... There are immigrants who find themselves living in a completely different context from that from which they left, and immigrants who, instead, find in the host country elements that bring them somehow closer to the places from which they come" (Perrotta, 2000, p. 660).

In the articles of ilgiornale.it.it that I have selected, the nationality is indicated above all when it comes to crimes: "gang of Ghanaian immigrants," "Nigerian mafia." For some time, as Dal Lago (1999) also noted, in these cases the mass media have not neglected to underline the ethnic origins.

Conversely, in the pieces of repubblica.it there is quite frequent customization, which can also promote empathy: "a 20-year-old Pakistani boy," "a Gambian student," "a 28-year-old Ivorian," "citizens of Bangladesh," "Bengali migrants," "Syrian girl," and "Nigerians and sub-Saharan Africa."

Empathy can also be facilitated by narrations inserted in *familiar frames*: for example, in the piece *Palermo, two migrants ask for a roof for the night: arrested for stalking* (R. Marceca, April 17), you can see a *frame* that we could call *Dilemma of Antigone*, the heroine of the famous tragedy of Sophocles: "From the judicial point of view, the story makes perfect sense. Those who manage the E.r.c. (Exceptional reception centres) had to comply with the security and immigration decree of Minister Salvini . . . But . . . no one put aside the protocol . . . the law of the code was respected but not that of the heart."

d) Parts of Speech, Styles, and Connotative Terms

In ilgiornale.it you can find connections, which may seem tendentious, between terms concerning immigration and other terms or behaviors: "a paedophile *and* illegal immigrant," "terrorism *and* illegal immigration" (my italics); in one passage (V. Dardari, *Illegal Immigrant attacks the whole family*, September 27) begging is incorrectly associated with an act of violence committed by an immigrant.

These are variations of a cognitive process linked to the categorization called "illusory correlation" (Chapman, 1967), that is, the tendency, conscious or otherwise, to present (or grasp) relations between two or more aspects of the same object – or between two or more events – which are not necessarily connected, or are connected to a much lesser or sporadic extent than that perceived subjectively, a tendency which usually favors the overestimation of the co-occurrence between a behavior/event and belonging to a group.

There are also qualifications that can be indicative of an orientation (sovereignism): "lives put at risk by a *foreign* NGO" (my italics).

The "delegitimizing use of quotation marks" can also be underlined (Altheide, [1996] 2000, p. 51). Here are some examples: the term "opportunity" in inverted commas for immigrants, in the context of an article with an ironic and critical tone on the statements of a prelate on the subject, suggests that the migration phenomenon is, on the contrary, a harbinger of problems; and in the same article, the term "embarrassment" in inverted commas, felt by the priest for the bread intended for the Roma gypsies and trampled underfoot with contempt by some citizens of a deprived neighborhood of Rome, undervalues his feeling of unease in the face of the war between the poor; the expression "lack of the bare necessities" in inverted commas referred to migrants in a controversial piece on the protests for cuts in funds for facilities for migrants, cuts that instead – according to the journalist – would reduce the "business of reception," stresses that migrants are used as a commodity; the expression "European solution" in inverted commas relating to agreements between states for the redistribution of migrants devalues the role of the EU in addressing the problem.

Moreover, highlighting in bold organizes a certain frame at a glance: for example, in an article already mentioned (V. Dardari, *Illegal Immigrant attacks the whole family*, September 27), the only terms highlighted are "foreigner," "drunk," "irregular immigrant" and "fist."

Finally, in line with the trend of the mass media, especially TV, in both newspapers the use of expressions and terms that arouse strong emotions is frequent: "dilapidated boats," "rust buckets," "traffickers of death," "traffickers of human flesh," "horrified," "a sacred battle," "tug of war," "war," "invasion," "spreading hatred with the spray," "the real Italians," "the new Italians," "only mentally handicapped people can declare . . .," "the party's over," "scenes of daily violence," "the immigrant shouts in the face of the agent," "demographic transfusion," "the NGOs help the traffickers," "journeys of hope," "demographic crisis," "Taliban reception," and "Euro-trashcan."

4 Further Concluding Considerations

In general, a given *frame* persists in the readers' minds and is quickly recalled, in the presence of different *themes* and *assessments*, probably also as a result of a practice that, with Altheide, we could call "encapsulation" ([1996] 2000, p. 30): an event is connected to a similar event or to a series of services over a certain period of time through verbal and/or conceptual connections: terms, expressions, and/or similar ideas.

In ilgiornale.it there is a limited range of frames and themes: they concern almost exclusively sovereignism, violence, and crimes or at least trouble on the part of immigrants, due to the threat of physical and cultural siege, means of consensus, source of political conflict, and alteration of the labour market and welfare. As for the combination of violence and immigration, "not only is the event distorted by this combination, but also our ability to deal with it in different ways is compromised . . . we can imagine that from this comes part of the difficulty of convincing people that violence committed in the family is 'real violence' and also a 'crime'. Until not so long ago, the notions of 'family' and 'crime' and 'violence' rarely appeared very close to each other in the usual news" (ivi, p. 111).

Compared to the other newspaper, in repubblica.it there is a little more: in addition to the strength of associationism and the legitimacy of supranational organizations, the frames and themes also concern human rights in general, integration initiatives, policies reception (good and bad), social benefits, racism, and cultural activities related to immigration. For example, in the piece *Monterotondo, in the theater the voice of migrants between hope and death* (April 2) the theme is the play "The islands of the soul" created to "let people listen to the voice of migrants who seek a new life in a foreign country often encountering death." The sub-headline of the article *Festival of journalism, the power of those selfies of migrants on the boat* (L. Malà, April 3) sums it up like this: "First day of the Perugia kermess. The most exciting narration in the award-winning photo by Massimo Sestini, that of the migrants' boat seen from above, 25 miles from the Libyan coast. Then the anti-corruption words of Raffaele Cantone, the etiquette of Vladimir Luxuria and the sick football." It is significant that in a cultural event the theme "migration" is mentioned before the other themes.

Comparing the two reporting periods considered – the first during the government whose allies were the 5-star Movement and the Lega, and the second during the government headed by the same premier in which the Lega party was replaced by the Democratic Party – it seems that:

- When the Lega was in government, ilgiornale.it used more often the '*Fear*' frame[12] (of immigrants) probably to legitimize the implementation of restrictive migration policies: "Various studies on newsmedia .... have revealed that one of the most important frames within which many services are built is 'fear'... often leads people to seek solutions that can reduce it, generally resorting to the use of force by the State" (Altheide, ([1996] 2000, p. 106). And that in the second period, when the Lega was no longer in the government structure, it concentrated more on an electoral strategy: the most widespread frame is the delegitimization of the executive to obtain a greater consensus in favor of the right-wing party (the Lega) at the expense of the 5-star Movement, presented as ineffective and succubus of a dangerous and fraudulent left party.
- Maybe in a way suited to this change, ilgiornale.it in the second period dampened the tones: a little less warlike and more ironic or sarcastic.
- In the second period, the number of articles of repubblica.it decreased, perhaps because the focus was on other government policy issues (mainly financial) now that the party of reference of this newspaper is in government, and it no longer seems so necessary to denounce the opinion of a party (right), which is not in government, on the subject of immigration.
- In this newspaper, the main frame is still the *Importance of the European Union and supranational organizations*, but it is underlined that now, in general, the information about the theme "immigration" is more adherent to the phenomenon, as if it had previously been subject to restrictions, and a legitimization frame (partial) the new government seems to appear, in which various themes not strictly of governmental policy are framed.
- With regard to the positions of the Catholic Church on the subject, in the passage from the first to the second period in the articles of repubblica.it the *immanent* trait of religion is enhanced even more: good and justice must be

12 In Cohen's terms "moral panic": see above in the Introduction.

achieved in this world and the prelates have this objective. On the other hand, ilgiornale.it strongly claims its *transcendent* character: the Church should not deal with "worldliness" but with the "spiritual sphere."

References

Airoldi M. (2017). I metodi digitali. In M. Cardano, F. Ortalda (Eds.), *Metodologia della ricerca psicosociale* (pp. 329–342). Torino: UTET.

Altheide D. (1996). *Qualitative Media Analysis.* New York: Sage.

Ambrosini M. (2011). *Sociologia delle migrazioni.* Bologna: il Mulino.

Becker H. S. (1963). *Outsiders. Studies in the Sociology of Deviance.* Glencoe: The Free Press of Glencoe.

Berger P., Luckmann T. (1966). *The Social Construction of Reality.* New York: Doubleday.

Cardano M., Ortalda F. (2017). *Metodologia della ricerca psicosociale.* Torino: UTET.

Caritas Migrantes (2018). XXVII Rapporto immigrazione 2017–2019. Un nuovo linguaggio per le migrazioni, https://www.caritas.it/caritasitaliana/allegati/7824/Sintesi%20per%20 giornalisti.pdf

Chapman L. J. (1967). Illusory Correlation in Observational Report. *Journal of Verbal Learning and Verbal Behaviour*, 6: 151–155.

Cipolla C., De Lillo A. (1996). *Il sociologo e le sirene. La sfida dei metodi qualitativi.* Milano: Franco Angeli.

Cipollini R. (2002). *Stranieri: percezione dello straniero e pregiudizio etnico.* Milano: Franco Angeli.

Cohen S. (1987). *Folk Devils and Moral Panics. The Creation of the Mods and Rockers.* Oxford: Basil Blackwell.

Colombo E. (2011). *Le società multiculturali.* Roma: Carocci.

Corbetta P. (2003). *La ricerca sociale: metodologia e tecniche.* Bologna: il Mulino.

Dal Lago A. (Ed.). (1998). *Lo straniero e il nemico. Materiali per l'etnografia contemporanea.* Genova: Costa & Nolan.

Dal Lago A. (1999). *Non-Persone. L'esclusione dei migranti in una società globale.* Milano: Feltrinelli.

Denzin N. K., Lincoln Y. S. (1994, 2011). *The Sage Handbook of Qualitative Research.* New York: Sage.

Di Pasquale E., Stuppini A., Tronchin C. (2019). *Errori e orrori della teoria della "grande sostituzione"*. https://www.lavoce.info, march, 26.

Fobert Veutro M. (2008). Qualità e quantità: una sintesi del dibattito. In R. Cipriani (Ed.), *L'analisi qualitativa. Teorie metodi applicazioni* (pp. 29–38). Roma: Armando Editore.

Fobert Veutro M. (2010). Donne musulmane immigrate fra tradizione ed emancipazione. In S. Andò, G. Alpa, B. Grimaldi (Eds.), *I Diritti delle donne nell'area del Mediterraneo. Civiltà a confronto, pari opportunità, identità e tutela delle differenze* (pp. 187–200). Napoli: Edizioni Scientifiche Italiane.

Fobert Veutro M. (2019). An Interactionist Approach to Document Analysis: Hidden Values in Advertising Images. *Italian Sociological Review*, 9(2): 317–344.

Fondazione iniziative e studi sulla multietnicità (ISMU) (2007). *Dodicesimo rapporto sulle migrazioni '06*. Milano: Franco Angeli.

Goffman E. (1974). *Frame Analysis: An Essay on the Organization of Experience*. Cambridge, MA, US: Harvard University Press.

Griswold W. (1994). *Cultures and Societies in a Changing World*. Thousand Oaks, CA: Pine Forge Press.

Kaczynski G. J. (2008). *Processo migratorio e dinamiche identitarie*. Milano: Franco Angeli.

Macioti M. I. (Ed.). (1995). *Per una società multiculturale*. Napoli: Liguori.

Maneri M. (1998). Lo straniero consensuale. In A. Dal Lago (Ed.), *Lo straniero e il nemico. Materiali per l'etnografia contemporanea*. Genova: Costa & Nolan.

Paccagnella L. (2004). *Sociologia della comunicazione*. Bologna: Il Mulino.

Park R. E. (1928). Human Migration and the Marginal Man. *American Journal of Sociology*, 33(6): 881–893.

Perrotta R. (2000). Interagire con gli immigrati: definizione della situazione e sentimento del noi. In G. Barone (Ed.), *Una Facoltà nel Mediterraneo* (Vol. II, pp. 655–671). Milano: Giuffrè.

Perrotta R. (2002). Immigrati islamici e costruzione della realtà. In D. Melfa (Ed.), *Islam. Frammenti di complessità* (pp. 121–139). Catania: Bonanno.

Perrotta R. (2005). *Cornici, specchi e maschere. Interazionismo simbolico e comunicazione*. Bologna: Clueb.

Romania V., Zamperini A. (2009). *La città interculturale*. Milano: Franco Angeli.

Schutz A. (1944). "The Stranger", An Essay on Psycology. *American Journal of Sociology*, 49: 499–507.

Schwartz H., Jacobs J. (1979). *Qualitative Sociology*. New York: The Free Press.

Sciortino G., Colombo A. (2004). Semir, il questore e la sardina. In M. Barbagli, A. Colombo, G. Sciortino (Eds.), *I sommersi e i sanati. Le politiche di regolarizzazione degli immigrati in Italia*. Bologna: Il Mulino.

Simmel G. (1921). The Sociological Significance of the 'Stranger'. In R. E. Park & E. W. Burgess (Eds.), *Introduction to the Science of Sociology* (pp. 322–327). Chicago: University of Chicago Press.

Thomas W. I., Znaniecki F. (1918–20). *The Polish Peasant in Europe and America*. Chicago: University of Chicago Press.

Toscano G. (2009). Identità creole. Lo sguardo meticcio di una scrittrice italo-somala. In M. Santoro (Ed.), *La cultura come capitale. Consumi, produzioni, politiche, identità* (pp. 223–247). Bologna: il Mulino.

Zerubavel E. (1993). *The Fine Line. Making Distinctions in Everyday Life*. Chicago: The University of Chicago Press.

Stefania Fragapane and Ariela Mortara[1]

Chapter Eighteen Migration & Social Media: the Closure of Italian Harbours

Abstract: In the last few years, immigrants and immigration have gained a prominent place both in the public debate and in the news. The paper analyses the reaction of public opinion to the decision of the Italian Ministry of the Interior to close the Italian harbours to ships carrying migrants. Since the growing role of digital media in reducing the barriers to information, the research was conducted on Twitter. Researchers have carried out a content and sentiment qualitative analysis of Italian tweets. T-lab software was used analyze the prevailing headwords, the co-occurrences and the word associations. The most relevant results highlight two opposing narratives concerning the Sea-Watch story, referring to two different positions about the migration phenomenon. Both narratives depend on different political orientations. These results reflect the narrative spread by traditional and non-traditional media, which highlights an increasingly politicized framework of the narration.

1 Introduction

In the last few years, immigrants and immigration have gained a prominent place both in the public debate and in the news. However, according to ISPI data (Villa, Corradi, Villafranca, 2018), in the first months of 2018 the number of migrants landing on the Italian coasts was down on the previous year, yet Italy and Europe are still struggling with the absorption of the almost two million migrants who have landed in the last five years. These landings have unsettled the reception system and have fostered the onset in the public opinion of mixed feelings including intolerance, fear, rejection and indignation, but also solidarity and understanding.

"The 4th Report Associazione Carta di Roma declared 2016" (p. 2)the year of the "great immigration" in the media, since articles on this topic occupied 10 % more news space than the previous year. Since then, the association with the theme of fear has become increasingly relevant, as confirmed by a quite recent survey (Osservatorio Europeo sulla Sicurezza, 2017). According to this source,

1 Although the chapter is the result of a common work, it is possible to attribute to Stefania Fragapane paragraphs 1 to 4, and to Ariela Mortara 5 and 6.

the use of alarmist tones in dealing with the issue of immigration amplified the feelings of fear, as testified by the 10 % increase in the respondents' concern index, compared with 2010 data.

Furthermore, in 2018 almost half (47 %) of the news on immigration on the front pages of newspapers concerned the migration flows (Associazione Carta di Roma, 2018). Despite the current reduction in migrant arrivals, the topic is growing in importance compared to previous years, since the rejection policies of the Italian ports have filled the news. The reports on containment, harbor closures and border controls, and the debate on how to manage the migrants have replaced the news about arrivals, shipwrecks, and tragedies at sea.

June 2018 recorded the highest peak in immigration news, in conjunction with the forming of the new government, with Giuseppe Conte as Prime Minister and Matteo Salvini and Luigi Di Maio as Vice Premiers. The most visible media events were the closure of Italian harbours to NGOs, international political tension, and the proposal to launch a census of Roma (Associazione Carta di Roma, 2018).

According to the same source, over the last four years, the issue of reception has receded from occupying 54 % of news in 2015 to 17 % in 2018. Stories about reception, both the positive ones of efficiency and collaboration, and the more complex and conflicting ones, are progressively less newsworthy. Many are the reasons for the decrease in interest, ranging from the normalization of reception policies, to the lower number of arrivals in Italian regions and municipalities, to the attention shift from the territories to border controls, from the reception to the blocking of migrant flows.

In recent years, according to Binotto and Bruno (2018), the two prevailing frames shaping the media discourse are fear and landings. Besides these two predominant dimensions, a third one has appeared presenting an alternative position, centred on the humanitarian theme, sometimes leading to pietism. Furthermore, the growth of migration flows – and the correlated frequency of articles on the subject – fostered the "normalization" and the stabilization of the phenomenon in the traditional and non-traditional media. Recently, the narrative of the migratory phenomenon is passing increasingly through politics and the exponents of the various parties, thus becoming a hot topic of political debate.

Both traditional and new media have referred to the three prevailing frames favoring one position over another according to the events, thus reinforcing the attitude of refusal towards the migrants (Panichella & Ambrosini, 2018). Within the new media, social media contributed to radically changing both the production and distribution processes of news (news-sharing), and those of the construction of their meanings and interpretations (frame building) (Binotto & Bruno, 2018).

Indeed, several studies (Pew Research Center, 2016; AgCom, 2016) confirm that not only young people, but also more mature segments of the population rely on Facebook and Twitter as information sources instead of drawing on television and the press.

Social media have therefore given voice to an ever-increasing number of actors (Chadwick, 2013; Sorrentino, 2016) influencing news creation and dissemination. Nowadays, not only journalists and politicians but also anyone accessing the new social showcases can affect public opinion. Indeed, digital media have increased the possibilities of participation, fostering the grassroots debate, reducing the barriers to information (Shirky, 2011) and encouraging the development of the phenomenon of citizens' journalism (Altheide, 2013). At the same time, the diminished importance of gatekeepers has led to a strong increase in the spreading of often poorly verifiable information (Mocanu, Rossi, Zhang, Karsai, & Quattrociocchi, 2015) thus fueling the well-known phenomenon of fake news (Gili & Giovanni 2018).

In this context, the chapter analyses the reaction of public opinion to the decision of the Italian Ministry of the Interior to close the Italian harbours to ships carrying migrants. The news in itself is misleading, because the ports have never really been closed since, according to Article 83 of the Italian Navigation Code, a provision of the Ministry of Infrastructure and Transport should have been issued.

Following on from a previous analysis carried out on Twitter posts between June and September 2018, during the well-known story of the Aquarius (Mortara & Fragapane 2019), the aim of the research is to monitor the evolution of the debate on social media, considering the events that have taken place since June 2018, from the Aquarius story up to the recent Sea-Watch story.

2 The Timeline from Aquarius to Sea-Watch

On June 9, 2018, the Aquarius ship of SOS Méditerranée and Medici Senza Frontiere rescues 629 people in the Mediterranean. The Aquarius heads for Sicily waiting for the authorization of the Italian government to disembark migrants. In the meanwhile, the Interior Minister Matteo Salvini launches the hashtag "closeharbours" on social networks. Despite no decree being signed by the Minister of Infrastructure Danilo Toninelli, the Interior Ministry denies the landing rights to the Aquarius. Eight days later, Valencia welcomes the 629 migrants, despite the aid being coordinated directly from Rome, and the nearest safe port to the Libyan coast not being the Spanish one.

On August 10, 2018, the Aquarius rescues 141 people from the sea. The consequences of the Italian government's political choices begin to be evident when the migrants report claiming help from five merchant ships before being rescued. Ships in the Mediterranean are no longer willing to help people at sea, despite violating international maritime law, to avoid the risk of being stranded and denied access to a safe landing location. The ship will land in Malta six days later and migrants will be redistributed among five European countries, including Italy.

On August 14, a boat carrying 190 migrants is sighted near the coast of Malta. Maltese authorities do not rescue it because they do not assess danger. The Italian Coast Guard rescues the ship 17 miles off Lampedusa, when it enters the waters of Italian SAR. Thirteen people in poor health land in Lampedusa, while the other 177 remain on the ship waiting for permission to disembark, which the Italian Interior Minister Matteo Salvini does not grant. It is the first time that an Italian military boat is denied entry to the port. The night between 25 and 26 August, 11 days after, the remaining migrants can finally disembark. The Catania Ministers' Court will request authorization to proceed with charges against the Minister of the Interior for the aggravated kidnapping of people and underage persons.

On December 22, 2018, the civil aircraft Colibrì of Pilotes Volontaires and of the German NGO Sea Watch sights a boat in difficulty. There are 25 people on board. The Sea Watch 3 ship intervenes to carry out the rescue. The Coordination Center of the Italian Coast Guard (MRCC) and the Maltese Coast Guard (RCC) instruct the Sea Watch 3 to contact the so-called Libyan Coast Guard (LYCG) and to wait.

While waiting, Sea Watch 3 rescues seven other people. Not receiving any news from the LYCG, the captain decides to contact Madrid to find out whether they can transfer passengers to the Open Arms ship bound for Spain, which is already carrying on board 311 rescued migrants. The request is denied. In order to find a safe port to disembark, Sea Watch 3 sends the request to all the coast guards involved and to all the States bordering the Mediterranean.

Five days later, the Sea Watch 3 is informed of another SAR case from the Rome MRCC on behalf of the Libyan coast guard. Meanwhile, no one responds to the request for a safe port. After two days of searching, the ship suspends all efforts on the reported SAR event.

Meanwhile, the ship Professor Albrecht Penck of the German NGO Sea Eye rescues 17 people.

While the weather conditions are worsening, the doctors on board issue a statement stressing the critical situation of migrants and crew. On January 2, 2019, after the mediation of the Dutch coastguard, the Maltese authorities allow ships to enter Maltese territorial waters but not to disembark.

On January 4, during the refueling and change of crew of the Sea Watch 3, a migrant throws himself into the sea hoping to be able to swim to Malta, and is rescued a few minutes later. The ship's captain refuses to make the change, deciding to complete the rescue mission. Despite the critical situation and the very high level of stress on board, no European country will welcome the 49 migrants on board the two ships. Sea Watch and Sea Eye migrants will finally be disembarked in Malta after 20 and 13 days at sea, respectively, and will then be redistributed among eight European countries, including Italy.

3 Methodology and Sample

The research was conducted through a content and sentiment qualitative analysis of Italian tweets. Twitter, among the social networks, is the one most oriented to the sharing of information and opinions (Kwak, Lee, Park & Moon, 2010) and is also the most used for political communication (Tumasjan A., Sprenger Timm O., Sandner Philipp G., Welpe Tumasjan et al., 2010; Kim & Park, 2011; Bekafigo & McBride, 2013), as recent studies show (Zimmer & Proferes, 2014).

Researchers collected tweets using the tools provided by the advanced Twitter search, after having set some hashtags deemed significant for the analysis. Specifically, they identified #seawatch as the most relevant hashtag, and then they selected relevant themes and keywords, such as #nonsiamopesci. Moreover, in order to allow some comparison with their previous research on Aquarius, they decided to use also the most important hashtags of that research, such as #apriteiporti and #chiudiamoiporti.

After collecting tweets, researchers manually selected the relevant ones, excluding posts by politicians, journalists and NGOs, in order to identify the prevailing semantic areas.

Specifically, the analysis was carried out on tweets included in the period between January 1 and April 1, 2019, the three months following the announcement of the closure of the ports. The three-month period allows researchers to highlight some comparisons with the results of the previous research on the topic of the Aquarius encompassing the period between June 10 and September 10, 2018.

Tables 18.1 and 18.2 show the number of posts and the selected hashtags highlighting similarities and differences between the two samples.

Tab. 18.1: Research sample: Analysis January 1–April 1, 2019

#	Number of posts
#seawatch	308
#chiudiamoiporti	47
#apriteiporti	228
#nonsiamopesci	87
	670

Tab. 18.2: Research sample: June 10–September 10, 2018[2]

#	Number of posts
#aquarius	321
#chiudiamoiporti	195
#apriteiporti	158
#umanitaaperta	105
	458

Researchers imported the selected posts into the T-lab software[3], generating a corpus on which they carried out the analysis of the prevailing headwords, of the co-occurrences and of word associations[4].

2 Before the selection, researchers collected 1900 posts concerning the topic of the Aquarius and 436 concerning the hashtag #seawatch.

3 T-lab includes a set of linguistic, statistical and graphical tools for text analysis allowing us to perform content analysis, sentiment analysis, semantic analysis, text mining, discourse analysis, network text analysis and other analyses useful for understanding contents and for their graphic representation (Lancia, 2004, 2012).

4 Specifically, using T-lab, researchers performed automatic lemmatization, the segmentation of the text (sentences, fragments and paragraphs) and the automatic selection of keywords using statistical methods. The selected threshold frequency of the headword has been set to four occurrences. While importing the texts, the program performed a corpus segmentation in elementary contexts (the post), followed by the analysis of co-occurrences, to measure the number of times two or more lexical units were present simultaneously within the same elementary contexts. As part of the co-occurrence analysis, the word associations tool was used to verify co-occurrence and similarity relationships and determine the specific meaning of the selected keywords. The proximity analysis, which identifies the most commonly associated words, generates a radial graph with the keyword in the centre and the length of the radius is inversely proportional to the force of the association between the headwords. Researchers adopted the cosine coefficient or association index, which is an association measure used as a weighted measure of co-occurrences. This coefficient is defined as the relationship

Fig. 18.1: Word cloud – Seawatch

4 The Textual Analysis

The word cloud generated on the corpus through T-Lab (Figure 18.1) shows how the most present words are "migrate", "Italy" and "Salvini" (at the time the Minister of the Interior).

The posts containing the word "migrate" refer mainly to migration policies and to the role of Europe needing to review these policies in order to guarantee a more equitable distribution of migrants. The headword "migrate" is also present in the posts of those who emphasize the urgency of saving lives. Other posts, however, refer to illegal immigration and amplify the themes used by the government, such as the need to keep the ports closed and to avoid security problems in the country. The word "people" (persone) occurs many times in the corpus and reflects the position of those who prefer to characterize migrants first as human

between the number of co-occurrences between each pair of words (X, Y) (Lancia, 2004, 2012). The coefficient ranges between 0 (minimum) and 1 (maximum value).

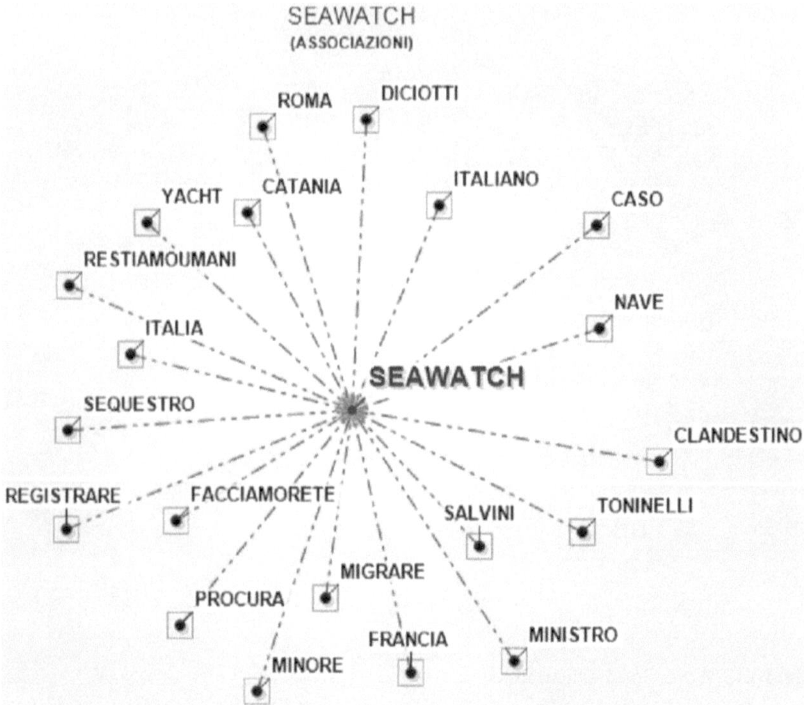

Fig. 18.2: Seawatch word associations

beings with universal rights. Two other headwords deserve a mention, although they are less frequent: "diciotti" and "underage" (minori). The first is connected with other recent events in Italy following the Aquarius case and before the Sea-Watch case. Twitter users citing the "diciotti" case essentially ask not to repeat the same mistake, highlighting the presence of young underage people on board. The word "underage" occurs, however, also among those questioning the presumed age of declared underage persons, recalling the question of identification and assuming a position of closure.

Figure 18.2 shows the words associated[5] with Sea Watch and highlights a few strong associations, including Salvini, "letsnetwork" (facciamorete), "ship"

5 Graphs are the output of the analysis of co-occurrences, i.e. quantities resulting from the count of the number of times in which two or more lexical units are simultaneously present within the same elementary contexts (the post).

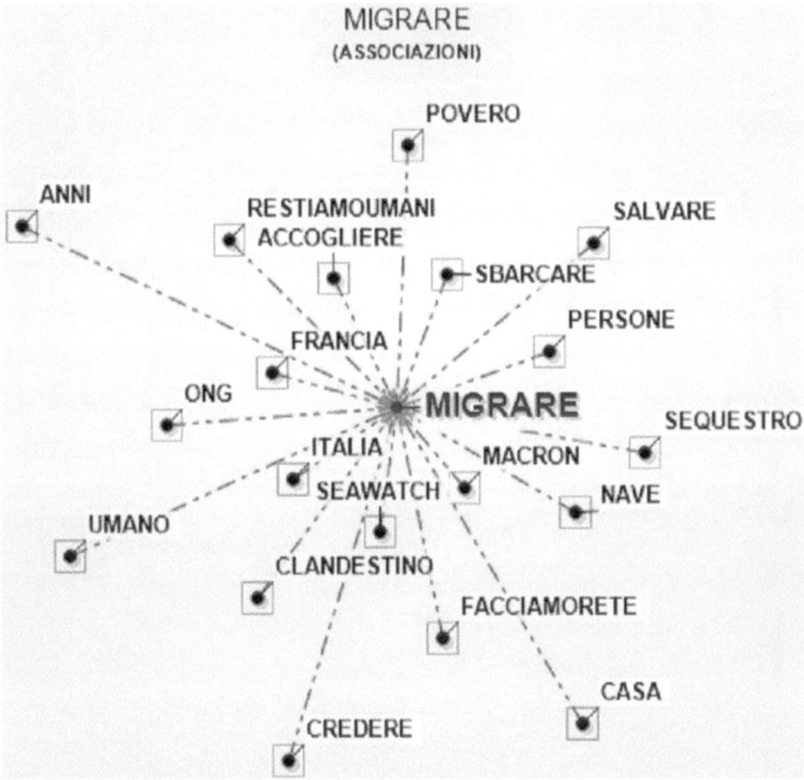

Fig. 18.3: To migrate (migrare) word associations

(nave) and "Italy", and many distant words. As the following sentiment analysis will discuss, users both for and against the government's measures refer to Salvini in their tweets, thus making the association very powerful. The same happens to the lemma Italy, since the country appears strongly connected with the ship's name. The distance between Sea Watch and "remainhuman" (restiamoumani) could signify that most posts are indeed in favour of the harbour closure, despite the strong connection to "letsnetwork" (facciamorete).

Figure 18.3 shows the words associated with "migration" (migrazione). As expected, the headword is mainly associated with the issue of landing and with "ship" (nave). Nearby connections are also Macron and France. Indeed, some posts refer to the critical positions of the French government towards Italy in dealing with Aquarius and Sea Watch, and in general towards Italian reception

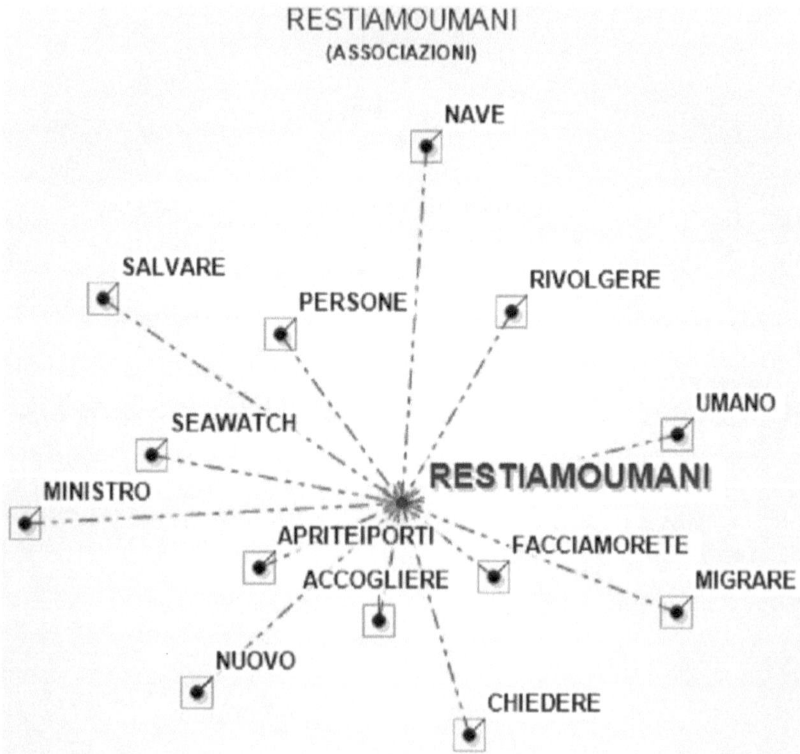

Fig. 18.4: Stayhuman (restiamoumani) word associations

policies. Nevertheless, the Macron government refused to accept the migrants aboard the ships. Other words close to the main lemma are people (persone) and clandestine (clandestine). The last word testifies that some users perceive and discuss migration in terms of security/securitization, public health and the migrants' propensity to crime. Moreover, the corpus analysis reveals that migration is discussed more as a political problem than as a social problem closely linked to migrants to be saved, since words such as rescue (salvataggio), reception (accoglienza) and human (umano) are more distant.

Finally, Fig. 18.4 shows the words associated with "stayhuman" (restiamoumani) and show that remaining human is essentially associated with opening ports, welcoming (accoglienza) and "letsnetwork" (facciamorete). In this graph, the lemmas "ship" (nave) and "minister" (ministro) are more distant, probably because it is more urgent to save, to open ports and welcome people into the community, postponing strictly political questions to later.

5 The Sentiment Analysis

The frame of migrant representation on Twitter reflects what traditional media have built up in the last few years. In fact, traditional media play a central role in the process of the symbolic and social construction of reality, and their greater power consists in framing events, providing a clear picture of responsibilities as well as a set of metaphors and feelings connected to them. In the Italian and European experience, according to Binotto and Bruno (2018), the frames and the social representations reverberate feelings of fear and chaos, conflict and oppression. In the present analysis, these frames highlight two prevailing positions for and against the government policy of harbour closure. Those in conflict with the institutional position embrace a humanitarian position. The following post analyses highlight the different narratives opposing the interest and the alleged security of the nation and the citizens to the common sense of belonging to the human race, since those who migrate and ask to be welcomed in a safe harbour are not migrants, but rather "people".

The hashtags related to #seawatch reveal both the humanitarian position (#facciamorete, #nonsiamopesci; #restiamoumani, #fateliscendere #apriteiporti #apritelacostituzione, #sindaci, #senzadime, #salvininonmirappresenta, #siamotanti, #siamoveri #disumani, #razzisti, #antirazzista, #antifascista and #dirittiumani) and the defensive position (#salvininonmollare, #portichiusi, #buonisti, #dirottamento #migranti, #ong, #macron, #francia and #clandestini).

5.1 The Humanitarian Position

5.1.1 #we are not fish

The humanitarian position revolves around the concept #Nonsiamopesci. "We are not fish" is the headline of the manifesto signed by representatives of the world of entertainment and journalism fostering the welcoming of migrants after the vicissitudes of the Sea Watch and Sea Eye ships. It refers to a phrase pronounced by Fanny, who escaped from the war in the Congo, commenting the prolonged period at sea on board the Sea Watch and asking to be treated as human beings.

POST 1
Jan 4 2019
Ho freddo….

ho freddo, perché 49 persone hanno freddo
Ho freddo, perché la disumanità è agghiacciante
Ho freddo, perché non si può giocare con delle vite umane
Ho freddo...
e finché non apriranno i porti, le menti e i cuori, io avrò freddo.
#ApriteiPorti
I'm cold...
I'm cold because 49 people are cold.
I'm cold because inhumanity is chilling.
I'm cold because you can't play with human lives.
I'm cold ...
and until they open harbours, minds and hearts, I'll always be cold
#Openharbours

POST 2
Jan 26 2019
Porti chiusi. Cervelli chiusi. Cuori chiusi. Barricatevi in casa armi in pugno e fra i denti e soffocate e regredite nelle vostre misere paure. A vivere davvero ci pensiamo noi altri- W i porti aperti, w l'umanità aperta!
Prima gli esseri umani! U-MA-NI
#SeaWatch
#apriteiporti
Closed harbours, closed minds, closed hearts. Barricade yourself at home with arms in your hand and between your teeth and suffocate and regress in your miserable fears. We shall truly live. Cheers to the open harbours, cheers to open humanity. Human beings come first! H-U-M-A-N
#SeaWatch
#openharbours

5.1.2 The Need to Integrate

People against the government's position also highlight the necessity to embrace a multicultural approach and foster the idea of receiving and integrating people. The future generations should be prepared to live in a truly multicultural society. Thus, some posts report the family circle story, seeing in the closure towards migrants a society that is impoverished and moving away from the values of a welcoming community.

POST 3
Jan 28 2019
Risposta cumulativa: ma io li voglio a casa mia.
Casa mia è l'Italia. Pago un fracco di tasse per renderla più bella e accogliente.
#nonsiamopesci #Scendeteli #SeaWatch #RestiamoUmani
Cumulative answer: but I want them at home.

Italy is home. I pay a lot of taxes to make Italy beautiful and welcoming #nonsiamopesci #letthemgetoff #SeaWatch #Remainhuman

POST 4

Jan 6 2019

Forse non piacerà a tutti, ma quando scrivo #Apriteiporti, non penso solo a quella povera gente. Penso anche a mio figlio, al suo futuro, alla società in cui crescerà, ai valori che avrà. Perché non dipenderà solo da me, ma anche dalle mille persone che incontrerà nella sua vita

Maybe somebody will not like it, but when I write #opentheharbour I do not only think about those poor people. I think about my son, about his future, about the society in which he'll grow up, about his values. Because all that will be influenced not only by me, but also by the thousands of people he will meet in his life

For some users, Twitter and social media are useful tools not only to express their opinion, but also to pressure both political actors and public opinion, trying to awaken the conscience of other users.

POST 5

Jan 4 2019

E comunque io ho iniziato a scrivere assiduamente su Twitter per legittima difesa.
Cioè quando questi imbecilli sono andati al governo. E ho fatto bene.
#ApriteiPorti sono esseri umani e bambini prima che stranieri.
In any case, I began to use Twitter a lot in order to defend myself. When these idiots won the elections. And I was right.
#opentheharbour they are human beings and children more than foreigners.

Some posts suggest that the focus on the migratory phenomenon is actually diverting the attention from Italy's real problems in order to gain more political consensus. Other users support the position of some Italian mayors, opposing government measures and supporting the opening of harbours, and the statements of exponents from the world of entertainment, who publicly contested the Interior Minister.

POST 6

Jan 30 2019

Abbiamo:

- *bombe davanti ai negozi come se piovesse*
- *maestre che picchiano i bambini*
- *imprenditori che inquinano come se avessimo un pianeta di riserva*
- *evasione fiscale, furbetti del cartellino, falsi invalidi*
- *6 mod ISEE su 10 sono falsi*

Eppure il problema è la #SeaWatch

We have:

– bombs in front of the shops, like it was raining.
– school teachers beating up children.
– entrepreneurs who pollute as if we had a spare planet.
– tax evasion, people misbehaving in the workplace, false invalids.
– six out of ten tax forms are fraudulent.

And the problem is #SeaWatch.

POST 7
Feb 22 2019
Grande la Sindaca di Ancona #mancinelli. #Salvini non sta risolvendo il problema immigrazione ma sta solo scatenando l'odio verso l'immigrato per avere consenso politico.
#iostoconemma #apriteiporti #emmamarrone #ottoemezzo
Hurray for the mayor of Ancona #mancinelli. #Salvini is not solving the immigration problem, he is triggering hatred towards immigrants to gain political consensus. #Iamwithemma #openharbour #emmamarrone #ottoemezzo.

5.1.3 Against Neo-totalitarianism

Moreover, some posts focus on the rise of the neo-fascist movement and racism, expressing concern for the future of the country and of Europe, with its nationalist and populist tendencies.

POST 8
Jan 2 2019
Mi vergogno. Non è questa l'Europa che sognavo. Se l'Italia ha un governo razzista e fascista, non è possibile che nessuno in Europa si prenda la responsabilità di salvare 49 esseri umani. Così muore l'Europa e vincono i populisti.
#ApriteiPorti
#RestiamoUmani
I'm ashamed. This is not the Europe of my dreams. If the Italian government is racist and fascist, it's not possible that nobody in the EU is taking the responsibility to save 49 human beings. So, the EU is dying and the populists are winning.

POST 9
Mar 2 2019
PRIMA GLI ITALIANI? NO! PRIMA LE PERSONE! Una marea colorata e antirazzista in piazza a Milano che ci riempie di speranza. Finiranno i tempi bui!
#PrimaLePersone #apriteiporti #SavingHumans #stayhuman #antifa
Italians first? No! People first! A colourful and antiracist tide takes to the streets in Milan and that gives us hope. The dark times will end!
#Peoplefirst #openharbour #SavingHumans #stayhuman #againstfascism

5.2 Pro-government Positions

5.2.1 The Anti-ONG Position

One of the main themes in favour of the government's decision revolves around the role of the ONGs, accused of aiding illegal immigration.

POST 10
Jan 31 2019
#seawatch in porto a Catania, dove non avrebbe voluto andare perché "porto non sicuro".
(!) Attendiamo le decisioni di #Zuccaro per indagine e sequestro della nave.
MAI PIÙ ONG, gli schiavisti del mare vanno fermati definitivamente.
#seawatch in Catania harbour where it should not dock because it's not a safe harbour. We are waiting on #Zuccaro's decision about the inquiry and the seizure of the ship.
ONG NEVER AGAIN, the sea slave traders should be stopped for good.

POST 11
Mar 19 2019
La conversazione tra ong e scafisti deve esser più o meno così: siamo partiti, tra un paio di giorni arriviamo. Caricate il gommone e fatelo partire bello pieno di clandestini paganti, che quando arriviamo facciam finta di salvarli.
#chiudiamoiporti #portichiusi #iostoconsalvini
The conversation between ONGs and smugglers should be more or less the following: we departed and we'll arrive in a couple of days. Load the boat and let it leave full of paying clandestine passengers. When they arrive, we fake their rescue.
#closeharbour #closedharobours #Imwithsalvini.

5.2.2 The Underage Rhetoric

A second critical topic involves the underage rhetoric. According to these posts, the media system insists on the young age of some migrants, but the picture shows young adults with cell phones and designer clothing, not underage passengers and children that should be rescued. Sometimes the real age of migrants on the boats becomes an issue involving the government's incapacity and indifference towards the violation of children's rights.

POST 12
Mar 19 2019
#Bersani "Ci sono 49 persone che ballano in mare, con 10 bambini". Mi sfuggono i BAMBINI... forse "minori" (autodichiarati, naturalmente... magari come quelli di #SeaWatch tutti nati 1/01/2002) ma non bambini.
Menzogne senza contraddittorio a #dimartedi

#Bersani "There are 49 people dancing at sea and 10 children". I can't grasp the idea of children . . . maybe they are underage (they obviously declare they are. . . maybe like the ones on the #SeaWatch all born on 01/01/2002) but not children.
Lies without contradiction on the TV programme #dimartedi

POST 13
Jan 11 2019
Le disavventure dei bambini malnutriti della #SeaWatch giacca a vento Lacoste.
Grazie a @cassius_151 per la segnalazione
The misadventures of undernourished children on #SeaWatch Lacoste anorak. Thanks to @cassius_151 for the report.

5.2.3 Italy Versus EU

Among the posts in favour of the harbour closures, the topics of nationalism, sovereignty and anti-European positions emerge. Many users highlight the critical conditions of Italian families that should be the focus of political interest, despite some politicians fostering the welcoming of migrants' families. Indeed, Italian newspapers emphasized the threat and the emergence of an out-of-control phenomenon, using headlines such as "immigration chaos", "immigration bomb", "immigration emergency", "continuous invasion", "security alarm", "illegal immigrants" who commit crime, the "murderous hypocrisy" of NGOs, welfare crisis due to "baby bonuses for immigrants" and "free treatment for illegal immigrants" (Associazione Carta di Roma, 2018).

Within the discussion, France is judged to be unjustifiably critical towards Italy and guilty of leaving the question of migration to other European countries.

POST 14
Jan 9 2019
Famiglie italiane povere che vivono in macchina ma @GiuseppeConteIT pensa alle "famiglie" clandestine sulla #seawatch che sbarcando avrebbero vitto e alloggio gratis e zero spese. Vergogna. #SalviniNonMollare
Poor Italian families living in their cars, but @GiuseppeConteIT thinks about clandestine families on board the #seawatch who upon landing will have free food and housing and no expenses at all. Shame. #Salvinidontgiveup.

POST 15
Feb 2 2019
L' immagine della sopraffazione della nostra sovranità. Questo è. Pensateci. #SeaWatch,fuorilegge per loro stessa ammissione, affermano che le nostre leggi non li riguardano. I fuorilegge esultano, Conte li ha fatti attraccare. Bene. ALLORA IN GALERA. #SalviniNonMollare

The image of the oppression of our sovereignty. That's what it is. Think about it. #SeaWatch they declare themselves outlaws, they say that our laws don't affect them, Outlaws exult. Conte let them dock. Fine. THEN IN JAIL. #Salvinidontgiveup.

POST 16

Feb 8 2019

LA #Francia NON SI PRENDE PIU' GLI #IMMIGRATIS DELLA ONG #SeaWatch, QUINDI TUTTI GLI "SFORZI" DI #Conte e #DiMaio (che in realtà volevano solo farli scendere) SONO INUTILI.HA RAGIONE #Salvini:

#portichiusi E BASTA! #leuropa ESISTE SOLO PER SPILLARCI SOLDI

France is not going to take the #immigrants of the ONG #SeaWatch. So all the efforts of #Conte and #DiMaio (who only really wanted them to disembark) are useless. #Salvini is right: #harboursclosed and that's it! #Europe just wants to steal our money.

5.2.4 The Narrative of Racism and Prejudice

Finally, a bunch of posts highlight the racist position of their authors and their prejudice towards migrants. In these contributions, the topic of people presented as underage is heavily discussed, as is the status of those asking for humanitarian protection.

POST 17

Jan 9 2019

Perdono sempre i documenti con molta facilità, ma il cellulare sempre bello carico (di soldi) mai! Guardate Ad esempio questo povero bambino, affamato e ancora sul volto il terrore della guerra #SalviniNonMollare #portichiusi #iononmivergogno #chiudiamoiporti #clandestini

They always lose their documents, but they never lose their cell phone full of money! Let's look at this poor child, he is hungry and shows his fear of war (ironic) #Salvinidontgiveup #closedharbour #Imnotashamed #harbourclosure #illigal

POST 18

Jan 2 2019

Ma se ci tenete tanto ad essere invasi da extracomunitari, andate voi da loro. Aiutateli a casa loro. Non aspettano altro. #chiudiamoiporti #SeaWatch

If you are so keen on being invaded by non-EU citizens, you should go to their country. Help them at their home. It's what they're waiting for. #harbourclosure #SeaWatch

6 Conclusions

The sentiment analysis of the posts highlights two opposing narratives concerning the Sea-Watch story, referring to two different positions about the migration phenomenon. Both narratives depend on different political orientations.

These results reflect the narrative spread by traditional and non-traditional media, which highlights an increasingly politicized framework of the narration.

Those assuming an unwelcoming position towards migrants are mainly favourable to the measures adopted by the government. In these discussions a clear contraposition between "us" and "them" prevails, Italians versus migrants, Italians versus foreigners. The textual analysis graphically shows the polarization of the posts highlighting the closeness between the anti-government position and the humanitarian one, as the proximity of "welcoming" (accogliere), "openharbours" (apriamoiporti) with "stayhuman" suggests.

On the other hand, people assuming a welcoming position oppose the government decisions, and their discussions essentially revolve around the need to "remain human".

The evolution of the debate over time highlights the emotional involvement of posts closer to the news (around Christmas holidays) that are generally in favour of the landing of migrants and against the government. The main issues refer to the emergency of saving human lives. Over time, posts criticize the government's work introducing issues that emerge in the following weeks and recalling the debates around the previous cases (Diciotti, Aquarius, etc. for the accusation of kidnapping by the Interior Minister).

The comparison with the first step in the research shows similarities and differences. As for similarities, the presence of the polarized positions between opening and closing ports, as discussed above, and the wrong assessment of the number of migrants who actually landed in Italy (Villa et al., 2018). However, compared to the analysis on the Aquarius story, this research step highlights a stronger presence of humanitarian positions, and the references to the fascism/anti-fascism positions solicited by the International Holocaust Remembrance Day.

The analysis highlights how the perception of the migration phenomenon relies on poor knowledge of data referring to the actual presence of migrants in the country, and of the consequences and implications for the host countries. Poor knowledge is sometimes associated with prejudices.

These distorted perceptions are also fostered by the news spreading a diffused narrative reinforcing the emergency logic (Altheide, 2002; Bauman, 2014, 2015; Rizzuto, 2018), thus eliciting immediate and emotional reactions. However, the emotive reaction means there is no necessary fact checking, and it prevents the rational analysis of the causes or the search for possible solutions to the problems.

Nowadays, the predominant media system presents the migratory phenomenon, as well as its relevance for humanitarian needs and health, as a challenge for national and supranational governments, which needs coordinated responses to ensure the citizens' security. Saving migrants seems to have become an attack on national security and sovereignty, while closing harbours is associated with defending the State against an enemy invasion.

References

AgCom (2016). *Il consumo di informazione e la comunicazione politica in campagna elettorale.* Autorità per le Garanzie nelle Comunicazioni.

Altheide D.L. (2002). *Creating Fear: News and the Construction of Crisis.* New York: Aldine de Gruyter.

Altheide D. L. (2013). Media logic, social control, and fear. *Communication Theory, 23*(3), 223–238.

Associazione Carta di Roma (2016). Quarto Rapporto: "Notizie oltre I muri", retrieved October 2, 2019 from: https://www.cartadiroma.org/wp-content/uploads/2016/12/Rapporto-2016_cartadiroma.pdf

Associazione Carta di Roma (2018). Sesto Rapporto: "Notizie di chiusura", retrieved October 10, 2019 from: https://www.cartadiroma.org/wp-content/uploads/2018/12/Notizie-di-chiusura.pdf

Bauman Z. (2014). *Il demone della paura.* Roma: Laterza.

Bauman Z. (2015). *Il secolo degli spettatori.* Bologna: CED.

Bekafigo, M.A. and McBride, A., 2013. Who tweets about politics? Political participation of Twitter users during the 2011gubernatorial elections. Social Science Computer Review, 31(5), pp. 625–643.

Binotto M., Bruno M. (2018). Spazi mediali delle migrazioni. Framing e rappresentazioni del confine nell'informazione italiana. *Lingue e Linguaggi, 25*, 17–44.

Chadwick A. (2013). *The Hybrid Media System: Politics and Power.* Oxford: Oxford University Press.

Gili G., Giovanni M. (2018). Post verità e fake news. Radici, significati attuali, inattesi protagonist e probabili vittime. *Media Education, 9*(1), 1–16.

Kim M., Park H. W. (2011). Measuring Twitter-based political participation and deliberation in the South Korean context by using social network and Triple Helix indicators. *Scientometrics, 90*(1), 121–140.

Kwak H., Lee C., Park H., Moon S. (2010). What is Twitter, a social network or a news media? In *Proceedings of the 19th international conference on World Wide Web,* pp. 591–600. ACM.

Lancia F. (2004). *Strumenti per l'analisi dei testi. Introduzione all'uso di T-LAB.* Milano: FrancoAngeli.

Lancia F. (2012). *T-Lab pathways to thematic analyses*. Retrieved October 2012 from: http://www.mytlab.com/tpathways.pdf

Mocanu D., Rossi L., Zhang Q., Karsai M., Quattrociocchi W. (2015). Collective attention in the age of (mis) information. *Computers in Human Behavior*, *51*, 1198–1204.

Mortara A., Fragapane S. (2019). Immigrazione e Social media: il caso della "chiusura dei porti" italiani su Twitter. *Comunicazionepuntodoc*, *21*, 51–60.

Osservatorio Europeo sulla Sicurezza (2017). *Sondaggio Demos &Pi – Immigrazione e sicurezza.* Retrived October 2, 2019 from: http://www.demos.it/a01427.php

Panichella N., Ambrosini M. (2018). Between fears, contacts and family dynamics: The anti immigrant attitudes in Italy. *Journal of International Migration and Integration*, *19*(2), 391–411.

Pew Research Center (2016). *The Modern News Consumer. News Attitudes and Practices in the Digital Era*. Pew Research Center. Washington, DC

Rizzuto F. (2018). *La società dell'orrore. Terrorismo e comunicazione nell'era del giornalismo emotivo*. Pisa: Pisa University Press.

Shirky C. (2011). The political power of social media: Technology, the public sphere, and political change. *Foreign Affairs*, Jan. (90)1, pp. 28–41.

Sorrentino C. (Ed.). (2016). *L'integrazione delle notizie. Come le testate giornalistiche televisive italiane si preparano alla sfida del digitale. Focus in Media*. Fondazione per la Sussidiarietà: Milano.

Tumasjan A., Sprenger T. O., Sandner P. G., Welpe I. M. (2010). Predicting elections with twitter: What 140 characters reveal about political sentiment. In *Fourth international AAAI conference on weblogs and social media*, May 16, pp. 178–185.

Villa M., Corradi E., Villafranca A. (2018). *ISPI. Fact checking: Migrazioni*. May 7, 2018. Retrieved October 20, 2019 from https://www.ispionline.it/it/pubblicazione/fact-checking migrazioni-2018-20415.

Zimmer M., Proferes N. (2014). A topology of Twitter research: Disciplines, methods, and ethics. *Journal of Information Management*, *66*(3), 250–261.

Chiara Pasanisi

Chapter Nineteen Limits and Possibilities of Social Theatre

Abstract: *La trilogia del naufragio* by Lina Prosa and *La trilogia del deserto* by Riccardo Vannuccini are two of the most representative Italian productions on migration. On the one hand, Lina Prosa portrays the distress of immigrants. Her dramaturgy is lyrical, but it is also able to decry one of the most traumatic events of contemporary history. On the other hand, *La trilogia del deserto* is remarkable in that some refugees become involved in a workshop run by Vannuccini, and that they begin to become actors in their own stories. In Vannuccini's production, the text ceases to be the core. It emerges how the interaction with the experience of the refugees becomes an integral part of the production by way of "a sort of" text as context. The main goal of this chapter is to investigate how contemporary drama continues to involve itself in social and political reality and why, consequently, it calls for new forms and techniques. According to Prosa and Vannuccini, the tales of immigrants aim to mirror the multiple complexities of our times; the analyses of their works also highlight how and why the concept of inclusion has undoubtedly become a fundamental theme of our times.

1 Introduction: An Encounter with the Other

The growing increase in the phenomenon of migration has brought about a continuous exchange between individuals and the transformation of cities that intersect in terms of culture, ideas and character. In this changing context, the theatre being extraordinarily capable of questioning reality, of translating it and acting upon it, assumes a role of fundamental importance, both as regards the possibility of recounting the condition of man as a migrant, and when it becomes an instrument for implementing strategies aimed at inclusion.

La trilogia del naufragio by Lina Prosa and *La trilogia del deserto* by Riccardo Vannuccini are two remarkable examples of the encounter between theatre and the phenomenon of migration. In the first work, it is a purely dramaturgical and poetic encounter, where the author-director, taking advantage of the theatrical narrative, stages the distress of migrants through a production. In the second work, refugees, after having participated in a workshop, have become actors and able to interact with the professional actors on stage. The text ceases to be the fulcrum around which the representation unfolds, becoming a tool capable of giving life to an experience of confrontation and interchange, which can be translated into performance. Migrants are represented, and represent themselves, as identities hanging in suspense waiting to find a place in a society that often reveals itself to be hostile to any encounter with the Other, and with the consequent impossibility of establishing any real dialogue, intended as a source of enrichment, interaction and integration. Thus, both trilogies could be considered a good starting point in outlining both the process of narrating the migrant condition and the social practices aimed at the inclusion of refugees.

As it is closely connected to the acts of gazing and watching, the dramatic art of the theatre can be a useful means of triggering an improvement in the quality of relationships between individuals. In fact, it is by looking at another human being in the face that it is possible to fully recognise their identity, suppressing any kind of urge to prevaricate or be selfish. As Emmanuel Lévinas (1986) maintains the "visage" is endowed with a potential that goes far beyond its external peculiarities, and which resides in the unveiling of identity, understood as a distinctive trait of human beings. In fact, material objects, being devoid of a "visage" (and so of an identity), offer themselves to us in a depersonalized way (p. 58). Although the attempt of the art to "give a face to things" determines its "greatness" on the one hand and constitutes the implementation of a "lie" on the other, the theatre, being a live art-form, could be considered beyond this categorisation (p. 58)[1].

Some psychological studies (Ekman, Friesen 2007) consider the face a "multi-message system" (p. 21) able to communicate by way of a whole range of emotions, including surprise, fear, disgust, anger, happiness and sadness. In fact, the face is that part of the human body that more than any other is connected to the subjectivity of each individual and to his/her feelings. This is the reason why it can turn out to be a double-edged sword; both are able to reveal an emotional

1 However, this position is countered by some anthropological studies that come to conclusions far removed from this thesis. For example, Alfred Gell (1988), starting from the desire to define an anthropological theory of art, notes that objects can be configured as "social agents". This is the case, for example, where a girl considers her doll a "best friend", or the relationship between human beings and cars. In the course of the twentieth century, it is possible to find a form of "vehicular animism", where a personality is "attributed" to cars that end up having nicknames or are a source of concern for their respective owners, who feel guilty if their vehicle is parked in the street late at night and is not safely parked in a garage. With this in mind, the works connected to the visual arts, precisely because they are subject to the eye, appear "equipped with physiognomy" and, through abductive reasoning, are viewed as if they were human beings (pp. 14–19).

truth and to deceive the person that looks at it by way of the triggering of a mechanism in order to create an illusion. However, being able to control facial expressions in an attempt to hide emotions, or alter them, is a very difficult task; facial expression, unlike words, is involuntary and automatic, as well as extremely quick (pp. 179–180)[2].

In the specific case of *La trilogia del deserto*, migrants act in the production, narrating in the first person their lived experiences; and the expressive means of the theatre (set design, costumes, drama, acting and lighting design) that they use allow them to amplify the potential of the encounter with the "visage" of the Other. A double effect is generated that involves both actors and spectators, where the former, by recounting their experiences to each other dramatise a lived trauma, and the latter, in the act of meeting, have the chance to discover the value of Otherness.

Thus, the theatre could be viewed as:

> a large gymnasium, as such for the acceptance of the Other; provided, however, that it is no longer presented as a 'mirror of reality' but, quite differently, as a 'dual culture', that is – precisely – as a journey towards and into Otherness, as a discovery, as an exploration and comparison with Otherness, starting from one's own, and therefore also as a journey towards and within ourselves, or more precisely as work on oneself (De Marinis 2011, p. 170)[3].

The encounter with the Other, besides being a necessary and dual/bivalent moment, reveals itself as an opportunity to meet ourselves. Starting from the presupposition that Otherness is already present in each of us, a simultaneous dialogue with multiple voices can be triggered, favoured by the expressive forms of contemporary theatre – and in particularly by the *Teatro Sociale*[4], which allows us to

---

2 The attitude that human beings have developed, for cultural reasons, is to lie mainly through the use of words, rather than through the camouflage of facial expressions. In this regard, Ekman and Friesen (2017) affirmed that "we were explicitly taught to speak; we learnt vocabulary and grammar. We can consult a dictionary or even a lexical repertoire and write in advance what we want to say [. . .]. We have nothing similar to a vocabulary of facial expressions, nor have we ever been taught to speak with the face: what we have learnt is not which muscles to contract to obtain the mimicry of each emotion, but only that it is appropriate to control it" (pp. 180–181).

3 My translation. All the essays mentioned here have been translated from Italian to English by me.

4 Fiaschini (2013) pointed out that social theater has a vast field of action, it can in fact turn to various areas of distress: "psychiatric disorder, handicap, social marginalization, prisons, drug addiction, such as children, adolescents and the elderly; from school to business, of cultural animation and interventions in traumatic situations of war and

leave the logic of intransigence aside, giving life to a fertile human and cultural exchange. In this sense, theatrical production is configured as a possible place to face the challenges posed by the contemporary world, bringing forth numerous questions.

2 *La Trilogia del naufragio* by Lina Prosa – a "Theatrical Composition of Inclusion"

As regards the narrative of the migrant condition, Lina Prosa[5] elaborates "writing with resonance" (Mayette 2013, p. 7) on the plight of refugees who landed in Lampedusa; it unfolds in three stages: *Lampedusa Beach*, *Lampedusa Snow* and *Lampedusa Way*[6]. From a chronological point of view, the development of the

post-war". However, "the extreme breadth and mobility of this range of applications obviously excludes the hypertrophic idea of a super-method, valid for all situations, highlighting on the contrary a propensity of social theater aimed above all at promoting the value and effectiveness of theatrical language in a complex and integrated community perspective" (pp. 154–155). For a more extended analysis on Social Theatre see: Bernardi, Cantarelli (1995); Bernardi, Cuminetti, Dalla Palma (2000); Bernardi, Perazzo (2001); Bernardi, Dragone, Schininà (2002); Fiaschini (2003); Bernardi (2004); Schechner, Thompson (2004); Ghiglione, Pagliarino (2007); Fiaschini (2007); Perina (2007); Fiaschini (2008); Jennings (2009); Ghiglione (2013) and Pontremoli (2014).

5 A playwright and director, Lina Prosa has been active in Sicily since the 1990s, together with Massimo Verdastro, in the redevelopment of abandoned theatrical spaces. She is active, together with Anna Barbera, in the *Amazon Project* (*Myth-Science-Theatre*), aimed at research in the theatre, with particular attention to issues related to the female situation (the project also includes support for women with breast cancer). Lina Prosa also conducts dramaturgy workshops focused on rewriting myths in a contemporary tone. In 2015, she won the Italian theatre critic prize for dramaturgy. The recurring themes in her productions are the encounter with Otherness, illness and diversity. Her works include: *La stanza del tramonto* (2016), *Migrazioni* (2006), *Una cellula al tour de France* (2001), *Cassandra on the Road* (1998) and *Artrosi* (1991).

6 *La Trilogia del naufragio* (The Shipwreck Trilogy) was performed for the first time in its entirety on 31st January 2014 at the *Théâtre Vieux Colombier*, Paris directed by Lina Prosa; translated by Jean-Paul Manganaro and interpreted by Céline Samie (Shauba), Bakary Sangaré (Mohamed), Cécile Brune (Mahama) and Gilles David (Saif). In Italy, the *Trilogy* was produced at the *Teatro Biondo*, Palermo (2014–2016). The following are details relating to each staging: *Lampedusa Beach*, directed by Lina Prosa; cast: Elisa Lucarelli (Shauba); scenes, lights and images: Paolo Calafiore; costumes: Mela Dell'Erba; date and place of the debut: Teatro Biondo, Palermo, 21st March 2014. *Lampedusa Snow*, directed by Lina Prosa; cast: Federico Lima Roque (Mohamed), Bakary Sangaré (griot, off-screen); scenes, lights and video design: Paolo

three works is separated by a long interval, given that *Lampedusa Beach* was written in 2003, while one has to wait until 2013 for the drafting of the other two dramaturgical texts. The word, like the act of writing, appears to be the central element of the *Trilogy*, and tends to assume a political value, as the author herself declares, in the form of a poetic style.

In this instance, to delineate the continuous flow that determines the narration of the physical and existential drama of the migrant protagonists to whom Lina Prosa gives a voice, she chooses to begin from the end, that is, analysing some aspects from the play *Lampedusa Way*. Mahama and Saif seem to share the same fate, even if they never met. Indeed, it is a coincidence that allows them to meet on the beaches of Lampedusa, while they search for their missing grandchildren. Shauba and Mohamed, after having arrived illegally on the Sicilian island, are already protagonists in *Lampedusa Beach* and *Lampedusa Snow*, and so are no longer in contact with their respective families. The two elderly uncles, who in a capitalist society would be viewed as those "left behind" but who, for this very reason, still have the privilege of having "time to gaze at the stars" (Prosa 2013b, p. 76), are the protagonists of a dialogue in which hopes, fears, realisations and scars[7], real and metaphorical, intersect to create a stream of consciousness that recalls the presence and absence of their two now-deceased nephews (respectively victims of a shipwreck and an avalanche). Both could be considered as two identities held in suspense, becoming emblems of a condition that could be extended to all those who make the journey by sea, risking and often losing their lives. Far from their country of origin, catapulted into a new world that neither sees or recognises them, they do not find a place in which to place themselves; they only seem to exist when they speak on the beach of Lampedusa, which is represented as a redemptive "non-place" in which to find a real possibility of expression. From the discussion of the two protagonists, it clearly emerges that "the impetus" that drives them lies solely in the act of longing, which consists both in the desire to meet Shauba and Mohamed again, and in an "absolute act", and so distinguished from any type of desired object. However, this desire assumes the semblance of a dream, and therefore endows itself with the risk of being

Calafiore; video-mapping: Alessio Bianciardi; costumes: Mela Dell'Erba; assistant director: Claudia Brunetto; vocal preparation: Miriam Palma; date and place of debut: Teatro Biondo, Palermo, 26th February 2015. *Lampedusa Way*, directed by: Lina Prosa; cast: Maddalena Crippa (Mahama), Graziano Piazza (Saif); scenes, lights and costumes: Paolo Calafiore; assistant director: Claudia Brunetto; and place and date of debut: Teatro Biondo, Palermo, 3rd February 2016.

7 Saif's abdomen is covered with numerous scars.

unattainable to the point of colliding with the harshness of reality, imprisoned in the fixed image of the shipwreck that, in the end, resounds like a threatening echo in Mahama's questions, which begin with a reference from Shakespeare's *The Tempest*, one of the most notable shipwrecks of Western drama:

> Can one be shipwrecked, drowning, have the same subject from which the dream is made?
> Can those who dream of tuna fish stink,
> Even if, like me, you don't believe you have been in the tuna fish trap?
> Did I dream of tuna?
> Or is it the tuna that dreams of me and doesn't stop?
> You can, shipwrecked, drowning,
> Not know who the meat is anymore,
> The one who gets away,
> To make dreams come true,
> And let pass at the bottom of the water
> A mass of tuna? (Prosa 2013, p. 97)[8]

The shipwreck, intended as an emblem of disorientation and loss of identity, as well as the island, understood as a non-place, are theatregrams, also strongly present in *Lampedusa Beach*. A monologue in which the drowning is recounted in the first person by those who experienced it, in what, at first glance, might seem like an *anabasis*, but which is actually the result of an act that has no conclusion, where the shipwreck becomes a permanent condition. Shauba, who only has a pair of sunglasses[9] as a raft to which he can cling in order to try not to drown,

---

8 My translation of: "Si può naufragando, annegando, avere la stessa materia di cui è fatto il sogno? / Può chi sogna puzzare di tonno, anche se non crede come me di essere stata nella gabbia del tonno? / Ho sognato il tonno? / Oppure è il tonno che mi sogna e non la smette? / Si può, naufragando, annegando, / non sapere più di chi è la carne, /quella che se ne va, / per fare sì che si sogni, /e lasciare passare in fondo all'acqua/ una marea di tonni?". In her review of the production that appeared in *Avvenire*, Angela Calvini (2017) traces an analogy between *Lampedusa Way* and *Waiting for Godot* by Samuel Beckett (1952). As one can see from this brief snippet, the atmospheres suggested by the text also refer to Peter Handke's dramaturgical and poetic production and, in this specific case, to the proposals of the *Lied Vom Kindsein* (1986). Remaining within the sphere of Sicilian drama, there are also recognizable echoes of the poetic style of Franco Scaldati as regards the character types, and the choice of an indefinite space in time that takes on the characteristics of an eternal present.

9 The pair of sunglasses to which Shauba clings in an attempt not to drown are represented by Prosa as an anthropomorphic object endowed with "agency" (see footnote n. 1), which goes beyond the strict sense of its usual function, resisting the "weight of the body" and trying to "pull up" Shauba to keep her from drowning. In a cruel paradox,

tells of his tragic experience as it happens; as if it were an event that has already occurred. Along with the shipwreck, she also tells of the harshness, often the subject of media attention, of which migrants are victims in the stage prior to boarding and during the sea voyage, as in this excerpt where the girl describes the stage of "berthing" aboard the boat, which takes place in a climate of violence and abuse:

> Mahama, they did it.
> Mahama they did it anyway.
> They forced four men and four women to lie in pairs, one on top of the other.
> Then the others. A human stack.
> The young smuggler pulled me hard against him
> Forcing me to walk on bellies and heads,
> To reach the top.
> I held the bowl tight.
> He slapped me and told me, foaming at the mouth:
> What do you have to defend little dirty nothingness,
> you are illegal, there is nothing here that is worth defending (Prosa 2013, pp. 25–26)[10].

On the other hand, *Lampedusa Way* comes to life at a higher altitude, on a mountain located in the Bergamasque Alps, and focuses on the theme of waiting. Mohamed, while waiting to know the outcome of his request for political asylum, will be destined to encounter an "upward" shipwreck (Prosa 2013, p. 11), that is, an avalanche of snow that will sweep him away and so kill him, along with a myriad of unfulfilled aspirations.

With her *Trilogy*, Lina Prosa escapes from the theatre that Alessandro Pontremoli (2007) defined as a "museum, cemetery-like and dying" (p. 8), in an attempt to create a truly inclusive dramaturgy. However, the author-director acts in a traditional context, closely connected to the demands of the theatre, where the text is the pivot around which the production unfolds and is the fruit of the

---

by acting as a "lifeboat", the object also illustrates that it knows more about being in solidarity with the girl than human beings.

10 My translation of: "Mahama, l'hanno fatto. / Mahama l'hanno fatto lo stesso. Hanno obbligato quattro uomini e quattro donne a stendersi a coppie le une sulle altre. / Poi gli altri. Una catasta umana. / Lo scafista giovane mi ha tirata con forza contro di sé / Obbligandomi a camminare sulle pance e sulle teste, / fino a saltare sulla cima. / Io mi tenevo stretta la ciotola. / Lui mi schiaffeggiava e mi diceva con la bava alla bocca: / «"cos' hai da difendere piccola sporca nullità, / sei fuori legge, qui non c'è nulla che vale la pena difendere»".

imagination of an author rather than the result of a collective and co-authorship process. The *Trilogy* offers the viewer the opportunity to reflect on the theme of immigration, and lays bare the existential truth of the migrant protagonists.

An opportunity is also given for "different voices" to be heard, albeit within a representative process that has professional actors playing the protagonists. Prosa uses "an evocative and poetic language capable of transforming the chronicle into myth" (Calvini 2017), transforming reality into poetry and performing a political act which, by means of the word, is inscribed in the sphere of dramaturgy and theatrical representation in the most canonical sense of the term.

3 *La Trilogia del Deserto* by Riccardo Vannuccini: Dynamics of an Encounter Between Theatre and Migrants

La Trilogia del Deserto (The Desert Trilogy), conceived by Riccardo Vannuccini[11], is the conclusive moment of a process aimed at inclusion in which migrants are protagonists; in fact, they speak in the first person and are involved as actors in the theatrical production. The operation is part of the *Teatro in fuga* (Theatre in Flight) project, sponsored by the *Associazione Culturale ArteStudio*, which envisages a dual action both within the Italian Reception Centres for Asylum Seekers (C.A.R.A.) and in war zones such as Lebanon and Jordan. The *Trilogy* is made up of the plays *Sabbia, Respiro* and *Africabar*, and is presented as an anthological collection of texts.

As Lucia Medri (2015) points out in her review of a performance of *Sabbia*[12], the power of suggestion evoked on stage is vast and ranges from *Pina Bausch* to *Romeo and Juliet* by Shakespeare. Vannuccini gives life to a "choral" production, where "it is the mob that advances to become the protagonist". The power of suggestion already explored will continue to manifest itself in *Respiro*, the second

11 Artistic director of the company *Artestudio*, director, actor, playwright and scholar Riccardo Vannuccini runs theatrical workshops in areas such as Lebanon and Jordan, and is active in the Roman suburb of Corviale with the project *Il teatro del rammendo*. For several years, he has been working alongside migrants, and in 2005 he founded the multi-ethnic company *Il cane pezzato* in Rome, making integration one of the main focuses of his theatrical research.

12 The production, staged on 12th and 13th of June 2015 at the Teatro Argentina in Rome, featured the guests from the C.A.R.A. refugee centre in Castelnuovo di Porto who were involved in a ten-month workshop. One also witnesses the interaction with professional actors, such as Alba Bartoli, Caterina Galloni, Elisa Menon, Maria Sandrelli and the same Vannuccini, author and director of the product.

play in the *Trilogy*, in which the narrative takes on the connotations of "a collective stream of consciousness" (Daddario, 2016). Finally, *Africabar*, using a title that is both "ironic and dramatic" (Bendettini, 2017), allows migrants to tell of the waiting time before embarking on their journey by sea.

The *Trilogy* could be individualised as one work, where it presents recurring characteristics that ascertain a strong similarity between the plays, both in terms of stylistic and aesthetic aspects, and with regard to the processes underlying the creation of the theatre props. In fact, the refugees, all guests of the Reception Centre for Asylum Seekers in Castelnuovo di Porto, Rome, participate in workshops where each performance is the final, but not the exclusive, end, aided by professional actors and cultural mediators. The productions, written entirely by Vannuccini, also include a strong performative dimension and place bodily expression at the centre of the performance. Thus, the reiterated references to *Pina Bausch* do not only consist of the scenographic installation that in *Africabar*, with its swarm of chairs, links to *Café Müller*, but in the appearance within the production of several sequences from *Tanz Theater*[13]. Therefore, it is far from the monologues of Lina Prosa, and from the double dialogue, in which the "word" headlines as the protagonist, becoming the preferred method of evoking the power of suggestion and so provoking reflection. In this case, it is the body that acquires a "authorial capacity", as noted by Renata Mazzanti (2007):

> The body is the principle condition of theatrical creation; I show myself through what I am – my body. One of the founding principles of social theatre is totality, that is, body, mind and emotion are involved in learning, in change, in the search for harmony between the parts; all of which are painfully split in our culture. A body that is no longer an instrument of interpretation, is still capable of representing and transmitting moods with its own authorial capacity (p. 55).

During the workshops that took place prior to the *Teatro Sociale* productions, the corporal dimension is explored through exercises that involve its totality, with the dual purpose of knowing oneself and others, developing both attitudes related to non-verbal communication and a high degree of trust in all the members of the group and in the director[14].

---

13 In the performances at the *Teatro Sociale*, dance theatre, as well as puppet theatre and clowning, are often predominant.

14 As regards the management of the social theatre workshop, Giulia Innocenti Malini (2007) points out that this "action is very complex", escaping any kind of consequentiality from the point of view of single acts implemented. In this way, "care" and "paying attention" are fundamental components, both towards individual members

Standing on stage to talk about oneself, exploring the expressive potential of languages that are not necessarily verbal or semantic, represents a new possibility for the refugees hosted by the refugee centre in Castelnuovo di Porto. In this context, the dramaturgical text ceases to be the cornerstone of representation and is inserted within it as a code that, like the others (and sometimes even to a lesser extent than the others), contributes to the final outcome. The experiences endured by the refugees from the C.A.R.A. refugee centre in Castelnuovo di Porto have several points of contiguity with the dynamics that characterize the processes developed in all the theatrical experiences that place the encounter with Otherness at their centre. For example, Pippo Delbono involves subjects who experience poverty or marginality in his productions, getting them to interact with professional actors. For people like Bobò, a psychiatric patient suffering from deaf-mutism, involved by Delbono in the famous show *Barboni*, the theatre has become a "necessity" (Dragone 2000, pp. 85–86) in order to exist and live. Standing on stage to talk about oneself, exploring the expressive potential of languages that are not necessarily verbal or semantic, represents a new possibility for those who have been left out. In this context, the dramaturgical text ceases to be the linchpin of the production, and is inserted within it like a code that, like others (and at times, to a lesser extent than others), contributes to the final outcome. These days, this element characterizes theatrical productions in an increasingly marked manner, where we witness:

> the phenomenon of the release of much of contemporary staging from the increasingly constrictive and narrow confines of text-centrism, to rethink itself in opposing terms, which by analogy one could call "scenographic", meaning a creative process that radically shifts its centre of gravity from the written text to the setting and its languages (De Marinis 2014, p. 262).

4 Practices of Inclusion – between Reality and Theatrical Production

The two trilogies under consideration present, and can help one to understand, the possibilities and limits of the theatre as a tool for social inclusion, even when the inclusion, and the wish for its implementation, is only represented or evoked.

Starting from the beginning, first of all it is possible to consider that dramaturgical writing cannot act alone in a direct way on reality in the same way as a process that puts into practice procedures and deploys strategies that involve the

---

and towards the whole group, where "in the social theatre workshop the director looks after the subject group in exactly the same way as an individual person" (pp. 32–39).

group and the corporeality, and that encourage experimentation and exchange. However, *La Trilogia del Naufragio* has the power to represent a situation and to draw out reflections from the audience on the theme of forced migration. In this way, the positive repercussions could also influence the behaviour of civil society; a cultural and poetic formula provided by the theatre could undoubtedly foster an attitude of openness towards the Other. By undermining prejudices, more or less rooted, the distorted narrative concerning migrants is deconstructed to outline the contours of a new image. Listening to these "different voices", the distance between civil society and those who are protagonists in a process of integration is shortened in favour of the rediscovery of a fraternity that links the speakers (the migrant-actors) to those who listen (the spectators). "Dramaturgy" can only help "to limit the damage caused by the homogenisation of the cultural industry and of the global market, reducing the asymmetries between the centre and the peripheries of the world and redistributing wealth and symbolic powers to peoples, groups and individuals" (Bernardi 2000, p. 59)[15].

As one can see, the workshop is conversely the gestational stage that precedes the staging of *La Trilogia del deserto*. In his studies on the *Teatro Sociale*, regarding the transition from the workshop phase to the production stage, Claudio Bernardi (2004) has highlighted the risks that can be encountered from the moment when "the theatre is no longer at the service of the group and the people, but rather the participants are at the service of the theatre". It is highly probable that "rivalries, jealousies, hierarchies and frenzies" will occur and that

15 De Marinis (2008) has highlighted that as far as the viewer is concerned, it should be stressed that some studies developed since the 1980s have focused on theatrical reception, understood as a "cognitive process", in an attempt to escape a "naive, neo-romantic conception of theatrical emotion". While not considering the watching of a performance as an exclusively intellectual activity, it is nevertheless possible to assert that the spectator is the protagonist of a serious "experience of conceptual knowledge" (p. 354). It was precisely the aesthetic forms of contemporary theatre, and its practice, which allowed the theoretical shift from the notion of the public, understood as an indistinct entity of users of a physical event, to that of spectator, an essential element of the "relationship" with the actor and thanks to which the production can become a "performance" (Giacché 2004, p. 9). As early as the 1950s, an era in which studies on theatrical reception processes had not yet been developed, Silvio d'Amico (1954) had felt the need to emphasise that the theatre determines a relationship between the author, the spectators and the actors. He strived to ensure that messages with a strong ethical value could be conveyed by way of theatrical dramaturgy, in an attempt to give life to a "collective art" (p. 10) that could supplant those forms of entertainment aimed only at being mere instruments of amusement.

"competition within the production will mount up so that what has been painstakingly built up over time will be destroyed" (p. 95). Moreover, when the experience with the community comes to an end, it is housed in a hall of memories; its effect on the present weakened.

In this specific case, asylum seekers, guests of the C.A.R.A. refugee centre in Castelnuovo di Porto, have experienced transition whereby, from members of the workshop group, they were transformed into the actors of a production, interacting with professionals during the performance, and finding themselves inhabiting the world of a professional theatre, that is, the *Teatro Argentina* in Rome that, moreover, is a theatre that represents part of the official theatre circuit *par excellence*.

Thus, the process of integration that takes place is twofold, since it determines both a possible dialogue with civil society, which in the act of "meeting" becomes aware of Otherness, and working in close contact with a specific category of professionals. However, after the performance, new risks can arise, whereby, in the experience of the *Teatro Sociale*, on the cessation of the workshop stage the positive mechanisms, which such a collective moment has been able to build, are in danger of withering away, especially as regards the relational aspects. For this reason, "the workshop system needs to expand in the first instance to the core of people who professionally deal with the users of the service, their relatives, friends and acquaintances, and finally to the widest possible social circle" (Bernardi 2004, p. 107).

Respiro, by Vannuccini, went on tour in several Italian cities and enabled refugees to continue their journey and distil it into various progressive stages, being introduced to and experimenting with new realities and various possibilities of integration. However, the tour is a smokescreen that has the effect of delaying the end of the experience; before or after the "clash" with reality, together with the difficulties that this entails, the end is destined to happen. On balance, the various attitudes that have developed on the journey can still aspire to lend considerable weight. Self-knowledge, confidence in oneself and in others, the ability to act in a group context, respect for shared rules and the encouragement of creative abilities are likely to continue to endure and so be redeployed in society, especially in terms of resilience. Finally, the encounter with the public emerges as a significant act, since the experience gained during the workshop, interacting with the spectators' gaze, is revealed as a completed event. The detailed changes that the productions of social theatre can trigger involve the spectators, the actors, the operators, those who live in a state of poverty and marginality and the institutions. However, it is necessary to implement a means that will enable a double transformation, where both society and the theatre are protagonists. The latter, when implemented with a "social" function, has the possibility to redefine itself, rediscovering its original dimension, connected to rituality and sacredness. Becoming an instrument of the collective good, it also allows one to meet the Other and to inhabit a dimension in which so many different worlds can meet and aspire to co-exist.

Hence, the procedure devised by Vannuccini combines the reasons for inclusion with those of the production, illustrating that they can operate at the same pace and nourish each other reciprocally.

A relationship of give and take is born, where the theatre reaffirms itself as an effective and, at times, even indispensable instrument for dealing with situations of distress and marginality that, in turn, can provide a vital boost to the theatre in its rebirth.

References

Bendettini A. (2017). Africabar, i migranti a teatro diventano attori: una soglia divide la quotidianità. *Repubblica*, 13 maggio 2017.

Bernardi C., Cantarelli L. (Eds.) (1995). *Emozioni. Riti teatrali nelle situazioni di margine*. Milano:Euresis.

Bernardi C., Cuminetti B., Dalla Palma S. (Eds.) (2000). *I fuoriscena: esperienze e riflessioni sulla drammaturgia nel sociale*. Milano: Euresis.

Bernardi C., Perazzo D. (Eds.) (2001). Missioni impossibili. Esperienze di teatro sociale in situazioni di emergenza. *Comunicazioni Sociali. Numero monografico,* 23.

Bernardi C., Dragone M., Schininà G. (Eds.) (2002). *Teatri di guerra e azioni di pace. La drammaturgia comunitaria e la scena del conflitto.* Milano: Euresis.

Bernardi C. (2004). *Il teatro sociale. L'arte tra disagio e cura.* Roma: Carocci.

Calvini A. (2017). Al piccolo di Milano si conclude la trilogia dedicata ai migranti. *Repubblica*, 23 aprile 2017.

Daddario A. (2016). Respiro – Uno spettacolo di Riccardo Vannuccini. *Sipario*, 31 luglio 2016. (Accessed August 22, 2019. http://www.sipario.it/recensioniprosar/item/10130-respiro-uno-spettacolo-di-riccardo-vannuccini.html).

D'Amico S. (1954). *Rinascita del dramma sacro.* Officine grafiche Carlo Ferrari.

De Marinis M. (2008). *Capire il teatro. Lineamenti di una nuova teatrologia.* Roma: Bulzoni.

De Marinis M. (2011). *Il teatro dell'altro.* Firenze: La Casa Usher.

De Marinis M. (2014). Il processo creativo nel teatro contemporaneo: trionfo e trasmutazioni. *Teatro e storia*, 35: 353–379.

Dragone M. (2000). "Esperienze di Teatro sociale in Italia". In C. Bernardi, B. Cuminetti, S. Della Palma (eds.), *I fuoriscena. Esperienze e riflessioni sulla drammaturgia nel sociale* (pp. 61–123). Milano: Euresis.

Ekman P., Friesen W.V. (2007). *Giù la maschera. Come riconoscere le emozioni dall'espressione del viso* (Gabriele Noferi, Trans.). Firenze: Giunti.

Fiaschini F. (2003). Il laboratorio teatrale di comunità. *Itinerari mediali*, 5: 65–69.

Fiaschini F. (2007). L'utopia praticabile. Teatro e comunità nel '900. *Itinerari mediali,* 2: 4–15.

Fiaschini F. (2008). Parole che non vanno più di moda: riflessioni sulla nozione di teatro educazione. *Itinerari mediali*, 6: 9–14.

Fiaschini F. (2013). Di cosa parliamo quando parliamo di teatro sociale. *Biblioteca teatrale*, 105–106: 153–171.

Gell A. (1988). *Art and Agency. An Anthropological Theory.* Oxford: Clarendon Press.

Giacché P. (2004). *L'altra visione dell'altro: una equazione tra antropologia e teatro.* Napoli: L'ancora del mediterraneo.

Innocenti Malini G. (2007). Come un seme. La conduzione del gruppo nel laboratorio di Teatro Sociale. In Rossi Ghiglione A., Pagliarino, A. (Eds.), *Fare teatro sociale.* Roma: Dino Audino.

Jennings S. (Ed.) (2009). *Dramatherapy and Social Theatre. Necessary Dialogues.* London: Routledge.

Lévinas E. (1986). *Difficile liberté* (Giancarlo Penati, Trans.). Brescia: Editrice La scuola. (Original work published 1963).

Mayette M. (2003). ". . . mai loro senza te(tto)". In Prosa, L. (Ed.), (2013). *Trilogia del naufragio* (pp.5-7). Spoleto: Editoria & Spettacolo.

Mazzanti R. (2007). Il corpo: dalla consapevolezza al training. In Rossi Ghiglione, A., Pagliarino, A. (Eds.), *Fare teatro sociale* (pp. 55-79).. Roma: Dino Audino.

Medri L. (2015). I rifugiati insegnano: Sabbia è il racconto. *Teatro e critica*, 16 giugno 2015. (Accessed August 20, 2019. https://www.teatroecritica.net/2015/06/i-rifugiati-insegnano-sabbia-e-il-racconto).

Perina R. (Ed.) (2007). *Teatro al limite. La passione dell'incontro e la mediazione socioeducativa.* Verona: QuiEdit.

Prosa, L. (2013a). Tre monosillabi, tre testi, tre storie- Introduzione. In Prosa, L. (Ed.), *Trilogia del naufragio* (pp. 9-11). Spoleto: Editoria & Spettacolo.

Prosa L. (2013b). *Trilogia del naufragio.* Spoleto: Editoria & spettacolo.

Pontremoli A. (2007). Introduzione. In Rossi Ghiglione, A., Pagliarino, A. (Eds.), *Fare teatro sociale* (pp. 7-9). Roma: Dino Audino.

Pontremoli A. (2014). *Teorie e tecniche del teatro educativo, sociale e di comunità.* Torino: Utet.

Rossi Ghiglione A., Pagliarino A. (Ed.) (2007). *Fare teatro sociale.* Roma: Dino Audino.

Rossi Ghiglione A. (2013). *Teatro sociale e di comunità. Drammaturgia e messa in scena con i gruppi.* Roma: Dino Audino.

Schechner R., Thompson J. (2004). Why "Social Theatre"?. *The Drama Review*, 3: 11–16.

Melissa Moralli, Roberta Paltrinieri and Paola Parmiggiani[1]

Chapter Twenty Performing Arts, Diversity and the Right to the City

Abstract: The chapter proposes a reflection on how performing arts can produce alternative representations on migration and "otherness", challenging the humanitarian and securitarian emergency frame conveyed by contemporary mediatic and political rhetoric. These sensationalist and stereotyped images depict migrants as "victims" and/or "potential criminals", influencing public opinion. Within this context, arts, and particularly performing arts, can play a role in challenging these forms of representation, overturning the spectacle of the migration into collective performances. Drawing upon these conceptual premises, the chapter starts with a general reflection on how arts can promote alternative representations of migration. It will, then, continue with a reflection on the role of performing arts in enhancing spaces of intercultural conviviality, experiencing different languages and narratives, new communicative spaces and alternative perspectives on experiential citizenship.

1 Enhancing an Alternative Perspective on Diversity

In the last decades, Europe is experiencing a crisis of the liberal order and its related integration processes. Under the pressure of globalization, digital revolution and multiculturalism, the European Union is not adjusting to its promises of well-being, inclusive democracy and security, and is liable to become less egalitarian, democratic and open to cultural diversity than it was envisaged. Political leaders who are overtly inspired by illiberal principles – from Hungarian Prime Minister Viktor Orbán to sovereign populist forces in Austria, Bulgaria, Czech Republic, Finland, Greece, Italy, Latvia and Slovakia – formulate the political debate by riding the wave of general discontent with the negative effects of economic globalization, distrusting the so-called establishment (including the European one). Populist parties and movements, sometimes xenophobic, which make division and separation out of their main programme, fuel the hatred of others and profit from fears.

1 The authors worked together to the conceptualisation and construction of the chapter. Although, Paola Parmiggiani wrote paragraph 1 and 3, Roberta Paltrinieri paragraph 2 and Melissa Moralli paragraphs 4 and 5.

A particular characteristic of this period is the obsession with immigration, even in the case of a radical reduction in arrivals. The "migration crisis", instrumentally constructed and amplified by those who politically benefit from it, feeds on the fears of citizens, strengthens them and presumes to provide simple (static) answers. Answers made of walls to block immigration, undermining respect for human rights both in domestic and foreign policies, as demonstrated by the outsourcing of the management of migrants to third countries such as Libya or the failure to sign the Global Compact on migration by various European countries. These recent facts clash with intra-European solidarity, which envisages that maintaining the free movement of people in the Schengen Area is the fundamental bond of the Union.

The media and their imaginary play a key role in this process. In fact, the strategies of representation and discursive practices conveyed by the mediatic and political rhetoric describe migration as a perpetual emergency, as a cyclical phenomenon (Calhoun, 2010; Vaughan-Williams, 2015; La Rocca, 2017; Musarò & Parmiggiani, 2017) that must be managed in terms of "crisis", often represented by boats trying to reach an increasingly distant Europe. Thus, the negative portraits of migration influence public opinion (Pastore, Monzini & Sciortino, 2006; de Haas, 2007; Musarò & Parmiggiani, 2014), as the gap between perceptions of the number of migrants within a country and their actual presence show.[2] In a context where freedom of movement becomes the main factor of social stratification (Mezzadra & Neilson, 2013;Wihtol de Wenden, 2013; Bauman, 2016), the negative representations of migrants depict them as unwelcome "invaders" (Albahari, 2015), crystallizing the imbalances of power between those who have the opportunity to narrate and those forced to be narrated, promoting a rhetoric of passivity (Ahmed, 2004). Images (and imaginaries) that dehumanize migrants, helping to legitimize the imperialist gaze of those who have established the rules of the game of mobility (Mirzoeff, 2011).

Based on the above considerations, it is nowadays necessary to make room for imagination so that it can produce a vision of solidarity that goes beyond the idea of the "ironic spectator" (Chouliaraki, 2014). It is therefore required to enhance

---

2 For further information visit: http://www.cattaneo.org/wp-content/uploads/2018/08/Analisi-Istituto-Cattaneo-Immigrazione-realtà-e-percezione-27-agosto-2018–1.pdf. Thus, the negative portraits of migration influence public opinion (Pastore, Monzini & Sciortino, 2006; de Haas, 2007; Musarò & Parmiggiani, 2014), as the gap between perceptions of the number of migrants within a country and their actual presence show (Ipsos, 2018).

an alternative vision of solidarity, no longer based on compassion, capable of recognizing the other as a human being, despite the harsh oppressive conditions of the global and local structures of injustice.

Within this context, in this chapter we propose to widen the reflection to the role that theatre and performing arts can play in the production of different representations of migrations, as privileged tools to foster conviviality and processes of transformation of everyday practices. Our research is focused on specific questions: What is the role of culture in challenging the narrative structures that characterize the European imaginary on migration? And, specifically, how can performing arts become a tool to promote diversity and political participation for migrants and asylum seekers in European cities?

Starting from a more general reflection on the social, political and symbolic role of art in promoting alternative representations of migration, in the following sections we will investigate on some of the most significant aspects that emerged during an action-research based on a European project, *Atlas of Transitions*, which involves artists, researchers, experts and communities of action from seven countries in order to experiment with new languages, spaces of conviviality and innovative self-expression. A project that, as we will have the opportunity to emphasize, aims to create alternative social imaginaries on the migration phenomenon through the use of artistic devices of different types. Our analysis will shed light on how to promote an intercultural encounter based on the enhancement of diversity, but also on the re-conceptualization of citizenship and justice in an increasingly Eurocentric political space.

2 Arts as a Political Space for the Negotiation of Diversity

The expressive power of performing arts, conceptualized both as a process of knowledge and as a dynamic concerning the living experience of bodies, is not only able to intervene within the processes of negotiation of the meanings related to the migratory phenomenon. It also represents a space of inclusion, recognition, belonging and citizenship. Indeed, a space where to experiment and promote new citizenships, individual and collective, as Mouffe (2008) suggests when she mentions the "agonistic" dimension of artistic practices capable of subverting the dominant hegemony through a conflictual approach in the management of public space. According to the author, in fact, the negation of the controversial dimension typical of the liberal approach implies an idea of consensus based on reason, determining a political hegemony which creates, at the same time, the exclusion of certain groups: "According to the agonistic approach, critical art is art that foments dissensus, that makes visible what the dominant consensus tends to obscure and obliterate. It is constituted by a manifold of artistic practices aiming at giving a voice to all those who are silenced within the framework of the existing hegemony" (Mouffe, 2008, p. 11). From this perspective, therefore, art can be a valid tool to counteract hegemonic discourses such as the Eurocentric discourse, based on an exclusive identity and aimed at cancelling out diversity when perceived as being too distant from European values.

In this way, art can represent a privileged means to foster conviviality and transform everyday practices, since it is a pedagogical as well as a political tool able to reshape the existing imaginary around migration and its impacts on territories. First of all, art can become an instrument, but also a physical and symbolic space where migrants and refugees can develop processes of intercultural participation (Martiniello, 2016), stimulating the creation of alternative narratives that lie beyond the dominant, dichotomous and stigmatizing vision promoted by contemporary media and political representations (Musarò, 2018).

Among the devices that artists, researchers and activists use to provide an unconventional, dissonant and counter-hegemonic image of migration and its protagonists, there exist movies, street art, documentaries, web-series, exhibitions, photographs and installations. These tools strive to create a sympathetic identification between European citizens and "Strangers at Our Door" (Bauman, 2016), cementing a cosmopolitan solidarity increasingly challenged by the populist and sovereign political instrumentalization. For example, contemporary art becomes an instrument of criticism of unequal geopolitical relations and the way in which the migratory phenomenon is managed and represented. Among the most famous cases is Mion's mural "European Programme for Migration", which transforms the tragedies of the Mediterranean into a naval battle played by a child in an ironic and provocative way. Another example is Banksy's works "Floating Bodies" or his project "Dismaland-Bemusement Park"[3]. A similar aim is shown in Ai Weiwei's numerous works on the dramatic situation of refugees at the borders of Europe and, above all, the fate of those drowned in the Mediterranean, such as the two temporary installations "Reframe" at Palazzo Strozzi (Florence) and "Rettungssäulen" at the Konzerthaus (Berlin).

In the copious production of recent years on the theme of migration, films like Ai Weiwei's documentary entitled "Human Flow" (2017) open intimate insights

---

3 "Floating bodies" shows bodies floating in a sea forming the European flag, whereas in "Dismaland-Bemusement Park", Banksy proposed a "game" in which visitors could make overcrowded refugee boats sail. See the video: https://www.youtube.com/watch?v=V2NG-MgHqEk (last access on 24/09/2019).

into the complexity of a phenomenon – migration – strongly conditioned by international geopolitical balances and stigmatizing visual representations (Abruzzese, 2001). Even more interesting are the film productions that amplify the voice of migrants, such as "Midnight Traveler", a documentary shot on a mobile phone by an Afghan family trying to reach Europe, or "L'ordine delle cose" (2017), which fosters the emergence of public resolve, encouraging the audience to advocate the migrants' rights. These movies, directed by or engaging migrants, not only lead us to reflect on the need to overcome the dominant rhetoric that portrays migrants as a number and not as people with a story to tell, but amplify their stories and voices.

These are only some of the many artistic projects that try to challenge the contraposition between "us" – Europeans guided by *rational* – and "them" – subjects characterized by over emotional reactions. As Ahmed (2014, p.3) suggests, in fact, "the association between passion and passivity is instructive. It works as a reminder of how 'emotion' has been viewed as 'beneath' the faculties of thought and reason. To be emotional is to have one's judgment affected: it is to be reactive rather than active, dependent rather than autonomous". As the following paragraphs show, in fact, arts, and especially performing arts, can break this perspective, making emotionality and expressiveness a form of mutual recognition and, in some cases, of shared belonging that challenges this dualistic rhetoric.

Among the artistic forms that enhance a collective mobilization towards the freedom to move, we focus here on theatre. Political art *par excellence*, as Aristotle or, more recently, H. Arendt claimed, the idea of theatre is not simply associated with entertainment, but it is seen as a form of moral education, capable of stimulating forms of solidarity based on mutual universal rights (Chouliaraki, 2014). These principles and values are particularly important when dealing with the migration phenomenon. However, if theatre was developed as an instrument of education and sensitization to the values of the public sphere of the polis, it became explicitly a political tool with directors such as Brecht, Piscator, Stanisvlaskij and Artaud. For example, by reintroducing the concept of catharsis, Brecht proposed an idea of theatre that pushed to action, a collective awareness that, beyond any reactionary expedient, turned into some sort of political participation. If until the end of the 19th century theatre was considered as the "Temple of the Muses" (Piscator, 1929), in Piscator and Brecht "the search for a political theater has become the search for a new theater, which was identifying its own political function. Political theater, a term that represents a fascinating and provocative concept because of its versatility of meanings, it rightly meant as the theater that wants to participate, with its own specific means, in the general attempt to contribute to the process of transformation of social reality [. . .]"

(Fazio, 2001, p. 4).[4] In this view, performing arts also constitutes a political space where new instruments of participation, inclusion, recognition and belonging can emerge (Belfiore, 2002). This is the case of the project "Atlas of Transitions – New Geographies for a Cross-Cultural Europe" which shows how art can facilitate an intercultural dialogue between participants, the audience and, more generally, the local community (Lo & Gilbert, 2002; Musarò & Moralli, 2019; Paltrinieri & Gemini, 2018). In fact, as we will illustrate in the next paragraphs, these experiments of performing arts, political interventions, intercultural theatre and creative installations, played a significant role in the process of negotiation between different cultural sensibilities and in the enhancement of diversity.

3 The "Atlas of Transitions" Project

Co-financed by the European programme "Creative Europe", "Atlas of Transitions"[5] is a European project which includes ten partners in seven countries – Italy, Albania, Belgium, Poland, France, Greece and Sweden – and a network of university stakeholders that investigate the relationship between migration and performing arts through the methodology of action-research (McNiff, 1998; Trombetta & Rosiello, 2000; Levy, 2017). The project intends to challenge the stereotypical imagery conveyed by the mediatization of contemporary migratory phenomena through an innovative use of performative practices, working on new ways of perceiving public spaces and experimenting creative conviviality between European citizens and newcomers.

The project alternates theatre performances with urban itineraries, public meetings on the theme of borders and the right to mobility, participatory DJ-sets in peripheral neighbourhoods, but also installations, workshops on body archives and actions of political activism. Since the activities developed by the European partners in the first two years are numerous, our analysis will focus on some transversal aspects that emerged from the analysis of the artistic projects proposed in the city of Bologna, which have seen a collaboration between Emilia-Romagna Teatro Foundation[6], Cantieri Meticci collective[7]and the University of Bologna[8].

---

4 Translated by the authors.

5 For further details on the project, please visit: http://www.atlasoftransitions.eu/(last access on 29/08/2019).

6 http://bologna.emiliaromagnateatro.com/ (last access on 29/08/2019).

7 http://www.cantierimeticci.it/ (last access on 29/08/2019).

8 Specifically, the departments included in the project were the Department of Sociology and Business Law and the Department of Arts.

Adopting an approach aimed at co-creating some of the performative practices and processes from the earliest stages of our investigation, action-research seemed to be the most appropriate methodology not only to better understand the relationships between migration and arts, but also to develop other narratives on the migration phenomenon through the voice, ideas, creativity and skills of migrants themselves. Therefore, the action-research was not limited to try to blur disciplinary boundaries, enriching the perspectives on the phenomenon, but also to promote, through different ways, a mutual collaboration between artists, researchers and participants of the workshops proposed throughout the duration of the project. Hence, many of the projects mentioned are to be considered as the result of a process of cooperation that has alternated moments of theoretical reflection with performative interventions, research in the field with opportunities for interdisciplinary and transdisciplinary dialogue, developing results in which the theoretical, practical and analytical dimensions are strictly interrelated.

The action-research started with an exploratory phase of context analysis – at national and local level – on the phenomenon of migration, as well as with ethnographic observations of the artistic workshops developed in Bologna by the artistic collectives Cantieri Meticci and Zimmerfrei[9]. The ethnographic research was integrated by in-depth interviews with artists, curators, participants and activists. On the basis of this first level of analysis, the action-research included different tools, such as meetings between all stakeholders involved, interdisciplinary conferences and seminars on project issues, public debates open to citizens, art workshops, training in high schools and university courses, debates with the communities of migrants living in Bologna and its surroundings. The participant observations took place during the overall project but mostly in the first months (November 2017–May 2018). In total, 47 in-depth interviews were conducted.

The framework of analysis was completed by a questionnaire addressed to the public of the two festivals held in 2018 (230 questionnaires in total[10]). The first festival, "Right to the City", took place in the city of Bologna from 15 to 24 June 2018, and developed the theme of the right to participate and

9 Zimmerfrei is an artistic collective that combines different languages ranging from documentary films to video art, sound and environmental installations, capable of conveying unconventional representations of public space and, in general, cities: http://www.zimmerfrei.co.it/ (last access on 29/08/2019).

10 The results of the quantitative analysis will be presented in a forthcoming paper.

re-appropriate of symbolic and physical urban spaces. The second festival, "Home", animated the city from 1 to 10 March 2019 and dealt with the feeling to be at home or being away from home, starting from the reflection of Ahmed (2014), who suggests to overcome a representation of migrants as "ontological uprooted". Based on a feminist and post-colonial approach, this perspective tries to challenge the ethnocentric narratives that depict migrants as an indefinite community that belongs nowhere, and primarily to a Europe with borders remodelled and fortified by the Schengen agreements. These two conceptual nodes – the right to the city and the concept of home – were primarily used as narrative and design expedients to reflect on issues such as identity, belonging, inclusion and citizenship.

4 Reconfiguring Imaginaries on Migration and Diversity

The primary objective of the project was to try to deconstruct the imagery conveyed by stigmatizing media and political rhetoric, which represents the migrant, as mentioned in the introduction, as a victim to be saved – fuelling imbalance of power and conveying pietism – or an invader to be rejected – fuelling a generalized criminalization of growing episodes of "everyday" racism. Indeed, one of the crucial elements adopted to activate this process of deconstruction of the imaginary linked to the migratory phenomenon consists in the fact that "Atlas of Transitions" does not directly address the issue of migration or social inclusion. Rather, it seeks to enhance diversity in two main ways. The first one refers to the direct involvement of people from different backgrounds in the artistic workshops. The second one refers to the ability of most of the projects to address issues that are transversal to the migration phenomenon – issues capable of stimulating connections, cognitive effervescences, direct or indirect references stimulating a reflection on the social inequalities linked to the right to move, but also collective experiments of new forms of social integration capable of enhancing diversity.

The artistic project developed by the famous Moroccan choreographers and dancers Taoufiq Izeddiou and Said Ait El Moumen is a clear example of how performing arts can become a tool for re-appropriation of space and intercultural dialogue without necessarily explicitly addressing these topics. The performance "100 Pas Presque"[11] invited a hundred people of different origins, ages, genres,

11 http://bologna.emiliaromagnateatro.com/laboratorio-gratuito-100-pas-presque/, visited on 04/02/2019.

educational and professional backgrounds to participate in a series of dance and theatre workshops in order to create two collective performances within the festival "Right to the City". The performances were realized in two different areas of Bologna: one in the city center, the other in the periphery, and more precisely in Piazza dei Colori in Croce del Biacco, a district characterized by continuous social conflicts due to the coexistence of migrants hosted in the regional hub of Emilia-Romagna and the inhabitants of the neighbourhood – many of them retired/unemployed or families with low and middle income.[12]The performance, which at the beginning consisted in a dance for 100 metres in public space by the workshop participants, subsequently opened to the audience, making participants and spectators plunge into a rhythmic spiral, capable of creating a discontinuity in the perception of the rhythms of the city. According to the choreographer, "dancing across 100 meters very slowly is likely to provide another way to occupy a place together, to ask questions about listening, about the other, as well as to revisit their relationship with time and space".[13] Therefore, if the dimensions of integration, dialogue and interaction in urban space were not directly discussed by the choreographer, neither with the participants of the workshops – nor with the audience itself – it was conveyed through forms of communication that were not verbal but visual. This mechanism is also explained by a workshop participant:

> Through the workshop, I have realized to what extent the 'other' can stimulate a dance move like for other things. It was a dance workshop, so I'm talking mainly about that, but in my opinion, this is also true for many other things. This is the message for me, the message I got from the workshop. They are now common words, but never reminded enough. . .zero walls and zero constructions of barriers, absolutely! (Vittorio, 27 years old, Italian).

It is, therefore, through the artistic space that processes of dialogue with diversity were activated, without being directly questioned, but through relationships facilitated by doing things with different people. By activating processes of

---

12 In June 2019, the regional hub was closed and several protests aroused to highlight the social and economic consequences for the migrants and the people who worked there (https://www.radiocittadelcapo.it/archives/bologna-chiude-hub-via-mattei-centro-accoglienza-migranti-presidio-prefetto-avvocati-diretta-204395/, last access on 24/09/2019).

13 The interviews were conducted in Italian and translated by the authors from Italian into English. The interviews were translated by the authors providing, in some cases, a youth spoken text. Some of the translation choices, therefore, have been adopted in order to be loyal to the oral source text.

Verfremdung, of estrangement in the Brechtian sense (Brecht, 1957), these projects thus reminded the need for more complex, alternative stories, challenging the "sympathetic understanding evoked by traditional feelings of piety and terror" (Fazio, 2001, p. 35).

A second important element concerns "Atlas of Transitions" effectiveness to avoid the exploitation of arts as a mere tool to promote social inclusion. Here, the artistic device is not a simple "medium" (Piscator, 1929). In these projects, on the contrary, artistic skills and competences are positively integrated with the desire to enable inclusive processes, without generating imbalances between the aesthetic/artistic dimension and the social dimension. In other words, the importance of realizing performances with a high artistic value is not overshadowed by the need to facilitate forms of conviviality and dialogue through arts, and vice versa. This perspective is well clarified by a teacher of the company Cantieri Meticci:

> Here you come to learn how to perform, you are not in a social center, you are not in a recreational club, we are not here to carry out social activities, we must not entertain someone or have a pietist gaze such as 'poor Africans, poor migrants'. You are here to learn how to perform and I often use theatrical techniques that constitute my educational background. So, theater – the traditional one – has a strong influence, I give artistic indications to students. For example, I say that they have to move in a certain way, and I give suggestions on how to do it. . . (Francesco, Cantieri Meticci).

By promoting valuable artistic performances, aesthetically elaborated in every detail, and not explicitly dealing with the theme of migration, "Atlas of Transitions" helped to deconstruct the pietistic imagination of migrants as "silent victims" (Chouliaraki, 2014), vulnerable and suffering people in need of protection and help. Narratives that ignore their stories and personal experiences, and that end up in legitimizing the reproduction – rather than the change – of dominance relations between the North and the South of the world.

In the project "Atlas of Transitions", migrants, asylum seekers and refugees do not appear as "victims" or as people to be helped, who do not have their own will, becoming the fulcrum of our humanitarian thought. On the contrary, performing arts become "an authentic revolutionary alternative to the dominant language" (Fazio, 2001), generating new and unexpected imaginaries and forms of mutual recognition. Hence, those who are usually represented as "non-persons" (Dal Lago, 2009) participate in a performance of high aesthetic and artistic value with their skills and experiences, de-coupling themselves from the common imagination that combines the practices of inclusion to charitable works, linked to "sad" or "poor" contexts, where there is no room for self-expression.

5 Supporting Relations Beyond Artistic Performances

Besides promoting unconventional narratives on migration, most of the projects developed in "Atlas of Transitions" became not only didactic and expressive, but also symbolic and physical spaces of de-territorialized relationships (Massey & Jess, 1996).

The workshop entitled "Unleashing ghosts from urban darkness", for example, worked on the perception of movements and the relationship between individual and collective urban space. These aspects were materialized through the body of the participants and their interpretation of the characteristics of the objects mapped in the public space. Hence, the workshop, developed by Alessandro Carboni, a researcher artist who works in the field of performance and critical geography, not only presented itself as an opportunity to critically rework the relationship between the individual and the city. It also proved to be an opportunity for creating social relations among the participants, most of them coming from different areas of the world (Bangladesh, China, Romania, Italy, Brazil, etc.).

A similar example was offered by the collective Zimmerfrei, which organized three workshops dedicated to Italian and foreign young people (15–22 years old). The groups developed some practices of storytelling, transposing their personal experiences into sounds and images in order to realize a three-episode documentary, "Saga", with the aim to give an unconventional vision of the city of Bologna. The tools adopted ranged from individual stories to scripts for images, from interviews to informal conversations, passing through examples of collective storytelling, auto-fiction, urban legends and domestic narratives. In addition to providing technical knowledge of the use of filming tools and documentary techniques, the workshops promoted forms of encounter, confrontation and intercultural but also intergenerational dialogue that enhanced diversity as a source of the creative process. Being different, having particular stories to tell and to transform into sources to be used in the artistic production process, allowed the participants not only to break down interpersonal barriers (of origin, gender and age), but also to feel part of a community of action (Kaufmann, 2004). The artistic/creative device has therefore, in this case, conveyed a sense of belonging based on "integral relationships" which, unlike the "community of belonging" (*Ivi*), maintain the collective sense of acting together, valorizing diversity. These aspects were underlined several times by the participants, as Marta (18 years old, Albanian) suggests:

> "This project made me grow, it was a good thing to meet new people . . . I was one of the youngest and others were much older than me, but despite this we got along very well, it was a very positive thing".

Similarly, Enrica (16 years old, Italian) admits:

> "It was great to meet such different people... there were many university students... normally I could never have the possibility to meet them, it was nice. In the second workshop, we had times of great chats between all of us. And on these occasions, everyone started to talk about what they liked, where they wanted to go... So, it was a significant exchange. Then it was nice because they also described cities that are completely different from Bologna. But they did it very well, it was like having experienced it a little... Being able to have this exchange on people's experiences and stories was very nice".

Many of the artistic projects had the capability to create new relationships, to increase – according to a Bourdieusian vision (1979) – the "social capital" between people who, for various reasons, rarely share spaces and experiences. In other words, these projects conveyed new forms of conviviality, even beyond the workshops. This aspect has also contributed to overcome the temporariness and the "ephemeral" dimension of the artistic workshops. In all those cases where the final performance was preceded by a workshop, in fact, direct relations were created between the participants. As an example, Haroon (29 years old, Pakistani) told us that, after the workshop, he often stayed with other participants "to eat together or drink a beer". But also Lea (20 years old, Chinese), who invited some of her group to share a "real Chinese dinner"; and Maria (23 years old, Brazilian), who was able to "meet new people, also because I have just moved here", thanks to her participation in the workshops.

In some cases, these new relationships were incorporated into other artistic and creative interventions, which developed outside "Atlas of Transitions". As, for example, in the case of a participant of the Cantieri Meticci workshop, who explained to us during an interview:

> It was fantastic to involve some of them in the presentation of my personal artworks. And this is incredible, it is not because I want to show off, absolutely. One thing I noticed with my creative work is that the choral, collective dimension is increasingly important. In the last event, I managed to involve 7–8 people from Cantieri Meticci, and it was an honor for me, not only to enter this world, but to make this world enter my life. A transversal exchange, an important reciprocity. I bring them into my world where there are other people, and it becomes a successful exchange. It seems like a multiplication of loaves and fishes at a relational level (Vittorio, 42 years old, Italian).

By expanding relational possibilities and generating a dialogue that does not repress but enhances diversity and direct confrontation, "Altas of Transitions" has therefore promoted a new idea of integration based on direct relationships, capable of de-constructing stereotypical imagery that confines the possibilities of confrontation with diversity only in certain spaces and times, entering the dynamics of everyday life (Moralli, 2016).

5 Arts, Migration and the Right to the City

As explained above, the project "Atlas of Transitions" aimed at deconstructing Eurocentric narratives, promoting mutual recognition and spaces of collective participation. Hence, the artistic interventions represented physical spaces and processes of knowledge that developed plural and various forms of conviviality. These aspects are particularly interesting in urban contexts, where diversity emerge more strongly than in other contexts (Wood & Landry, 2007). In these contexts, the declination of citizenship goes beyond its legal meaning and can be expressed through the concept of the "right to the city". In fact, the way in which people can live the city, have access to its resources and can transform urban space, is a central issue for contemporary societies.

In this regard, Harvey (2012) suggests that the right to the city is primarily the right to change ourselves with the city, and refers not only to the economic dimension and the (re)distribution of resources, but also to the relational and political dimension, which concerns the right of those who can be included and excluded from urban life. In the city, all these plans intertwine and overlap, creating a political and social geography that conditions the individuals' lives. These subjects develop a sense of belonging also through the ways in which they live and act within public spaces. Resorting to Lefebvrian's conceptualization of the right to the city (Lefebvre, 1968),, we agree that it is based on two strongly interrelated processes. The first process relates to the "(re)appropriation" of physical and symbolic spaces where social relations are established on the basis of common values. The second process refers to "participation", which concerns not only the tools through which people can participate in urban life, but also the opportunities that are created to redefine the norms on which exclusion is founded, supporting what Appadurai (2004) defines the "capacity to aspire".

One of the projects developed by "Atlas of Transitions" can represent a paradigmatic example of this alternative declination of citizenship. The project, entitled "EXIL #17/Terra rossa", was presented by the collective Strasse within the first Festival. Here, the right to the city emerged as a form of participatory DJ set that involved asylum seekers hosted in the regional hub and the inhabitants of the Croce del Biacco district. Some days before the performance, the artistic collective entered the hub and involved the asylum seekers in the creation of a playlist to be used for an evening DJ set that took place in the local park. During the performance, the right to the city was expressed through the movements of the participants and their spatial relations. At the beginning of the DJ set, in fact, we experienced an overt spatial polarization: the asylum seekers sat all together on the left of the stage, whereas the inhabitants of the neighbourhood sat on the opposite side. A physical polarization that reflected the social and cultural polarization that characterizes the contemporary European debate on migration, usually associated with the rhetoric of the opposition between "we"/ Europeans vs. "them"/others. Nevertheless, through the performance (the participatory DJ set), at the end of the evening this polarization was completely dissolved, transforming the park into a collective and shared space: migrants, elderly residents, children and adolescents danced together to the rhythm of the music from different areas of the world. By sustaining a participatory process, the performance has therefore not only helped to redefine the daily practices of coexistence in urban space, but also to mediate between citizens and newcomers, while promoting an alternative definition of doing politics in public space. Within the performative process, therefore, the park transformed into a "competitive space" (Mouffe, 2008), thanks to a new relationship between actors and spectators, between participants and audience, equally active in deconstructing and re-constructing meanings linked to a space where they could experience diversity. In other words, the performance has generated alternative "acts of citizenship" (Isin & Nielson, 2008).

Like "EXIL #17/Terra rossa", other projects developed within "Atlas of Transitions" have conveyed an idea of citizenship that goes beyond the mere legal framework. These projects promoted a more articulated idea of citizenship through daily practices of belonging, encouraging a wider right to the city within the spaces of "everyday life" (de Certeau, 1984). In fact, a similar process took place within the laboratory "Unleashing Ghosts from Urban Darkness". Starting from the perspective of critical cartography, but involving elements linked to dance and contemporary art, the project has been able to represent a different image of Bologna. This image wanted to be closer to the rhythm experienced by its inhabitants than to the traditional cartographic representation. As the artist himself states, the project was able to develop a sort of collective resemantization from below: "I have approached those practices that use the city as a rhythm and not as a stage, those practices that interact with the rhythms of the city, that enter into its dynamics" (Alessandro Carboni). Similarly, the project "100 Pas Presque" allowed the re-appropriation of the public space through dance, in the centre as well as in the periphery of the city of Bologna. As a participant of the artistic laboratory suggests, in fact:

> I tell you something important, I had this impression there, in that space, in that street I always walk in, with all those unknown people around me. . .I had the impression of appropriating something mine, and it's important. I keep on thinking about it a lot. One of the things I was asking myself before the workshop started, being loaded with all that is happening now in Italy, was that I would have participated in it because it also

> responded to principles that are part of my – and certainly other people's – background now, but they are no longer popular among those who are in power now. And, also, this idea of appropriating a space together with other people, of being together with a person who comes from a different country, who has a different culture, a different religion and a different dance style was very important. For me it was also a political act and not just a cultural one (Carlo, 27, Italian).

Thanks to its innovative methodology, "Atlas of Transitions" challenged the social conventions and power relationships that lie behind the ways in which different people are represented. Using the performers' body – a body with an aesthetic and performative value but also a strong political meaning – as a way of participating and re-appropriating urban space, the projects have acted both on an aesthetic and emotional level (Ahmed, 2004), as forms of (inter)cultural political interventions. Moreover, they intervened on a relational level, modifying social practices. In other words, the projects have shown how art can become a "narrative of change" (Wittmayer et al., 2015), capable of fighting "against pre-existing cultural and institutional narratives and the structures of meaning and power that they transmit" (Davis, 2002, p.25). In fact, it is precisely through the creative and cognitive activation of new forms of urban coexistence and shared reflection that – as already suggested by the theorists of social movements at the end of the last century – new models of action and negotiation processes can be activated. These alternative forms of identity and citizenship propose a new idea of justice as "mutual recognition", which aims to integrate and overcome both the idea of justice as "non-domination" – which recalls the need to manage complex phenomena such as migration through international governance – and the idea of justice as "impartiality" – which emphasizes the role of institutions in guaranteeing fundamental rights (Eriksen, 2016). These are important processes that aim to stimulate, beyond the normative codes of official politics, new "architectures of listening" (MacNamara, 2016) and a renewed sense of solidarity and coexistence.

By doing this, the participatory approach of the "Atlas of Transitions" projects partially solved some limits that may concern these types of artistic interventions, such as the lack of involvement of specific social groups or the transitory temporariness of the performances. By selecting the stage venue outside the traditional places where culture is produced, involving the centre as well as the periphery, institutional places but also streets and reception centres, and encouraging the participation of different people, the project has included and amplified the voice of those who usually are not heard. An experiment that showed how performing arts can have both an aesthetic and political value, promoting a broader idea of citizenship (Mouffe, 2008; Martiniello, 2016).

References

Abruzzese, A. (2001). *Forme estetiche e società di massa. Arte e pubblico nell'età del capitalismo*. Venice: Marsilio.

Ahmed, S. (2004). *The Cultural Politics of Emotion*. New York, London: Routledge.

Ahmed, S. (2014). *Willful Subjects*. Durham: Duke University Press Books.

Albahari, M. (2015). *Crimes of Peace: Mediterranean Migrations at the World's Deadliest Border*. Philadelphia: PENN.

Appadurai, A. (2004). The Capacity to Aspire: Culture and the Terms of Recognition. In V. Rao & M. Walton (Eds.), *Culture and Public Action*. Stanford: Stanford University Press.

Bauman, Z. (2016). *Strangers at Our Door*. Cambridge: Polity Press.

Belfiore, E. (2002). Art as a means of alleviating social exclusion: Does it really work? A critique of instrumental cultural policies and social impact studies in the UK. *International Journal of Cultural Policy*, 8(1): 91–106.

Bourdieu, P. (1979). *La Distinction. Critique sociale du jugement*. Paris: Les Éditions de Minuit.

Brecht, B. (1957). *SchriftemzumTheatre*. Frankfurt: Suhrkamp.

Calhoun, C. (2010). The Idea of Emergency: Humanitarian Action and Global (Dis)Order. In D. Fassin, & M. Pandolfi (Eds.), *Contemporary States of Emergency*. New York: Zone Books.

Chouliaraki, L. (2014). *The Ironic Spectator: Solidarity in the Age of Post-Human itarianism*.Cambridge: Polity.

Dal Lago, A. (2009). (original edition 1999). *Non-persons*. Vimodrone: IPOC di Pietro Condemi.

Davis, J.E. (2002). *Stories of Change. Narrative and Social Movements*. Albany: State University of New York Press.

De Certeau, M. (1984). *The Practice of Everyday Life*. Berkeley: University of California Press.

De Haas, H. (2007). *The Myth of Invasion. Irregular Migration from West Africa to the Maghreb and the European Union*. Oxford: IMI Research Report.

Eriksen, E. O. (2016). Three Conceptions of Global Political Justice. *GLOBUS* Research Paper 1/2016. Available at SSRN: https://ssrn.com/abstract=2878745 orhttp://dx.doi.org/10.2139/ssrn.2878745.

Fazio, V. (2001). *Il teatro come politica, la politica come teatro*. Degree thesis in Sociology of Communications, University of Bologna, Faculty of Political Sciences, a.a. 1999/2000.

Harvey, D. (2012). *Rebel Cities: From the Right to the City to the Urban Revolution*. New York: VersoBooks.

Ipsos (2018). Perils of Perception. Research Paper. Available at: https://www.ipsos.com/sites/default/files/ct/news/documents/2018-12/ipsos-mori-perils-of perception-2018-slides.pdf.

Isin, E., Nielson, G. M. (2008). *Acts of Citizenship*. London: Zed Books.

Kaufmann, J. C. (2004). *L'invention de soi. Une théorie d'identité*. Paris: Armand Colin.

La Rocca, G. (2017). Media, migrants and human rights. *Revue Internationale De Sociologie*, 27 (2): 225 – 229.

Lefebvre, H. (1968). *Le droit à la ville*. Paris: Anthropos.

Levy, P. (2017). *Handbook of Arts-Based Research*. New York: Guilford Press.

Lo, J., Gilbert, H. (2002). Toward a topography of cross-cultural theatre praxis. *The Drama Review*, 46(3): 31–53.

MacNamara, J. (2016). *Organizational Listening: The Missing Corollary of Speaking in Public Communication*. New York: Peter Lang.

Martiniello, M. (Ed.) (2016). *Multiculturalism and the Arts in European Cities*. New York, London: Routledge.

Massey, D., Jess, P. (Eds.) (1996). *A Place in the World?: Places, Cultures and Globalization*. New York: Oxford University Press.

McNiff, S. (1998). *Art-Based Research*. London: Jessica Kingsley Publishers.

Mezzadra, S., Neilson, B. (2013). *Border as Method or the Multiplication of Labor*. Durham: Duke University Press.

Mirzoeff, N. (2011). *The Right to Look: A Counterhistory of Visuality*. Durham: Duke University Press.

Moralli, M. (2016). Fostering interculturality in urban ethnic neighbourhoods: Opportunities and limits of the responsible tourism approach. *Journal of Mediterranean Knowledge-JMK*, 1 (2): 165–183. Available at: http://www.mediterraneanknowledge.org/publications/index.php/journal/article/view/29.

Mouffe, C. (2008). Art and democracy: Art as an agonistic intervention in public space. Open, 14, 6–15.

Musarò, P. (2018). Performing metaphors into a physical space. The role of participatory theater in promoting social coexistence between citizens and newcomers. *Media@LSE Working Paper*, 52, 1 – 27.

Musarò, P., Moralli, M. (2019). De-bordering narratives on tourism and migration. A participatory action-research on two innovative Italian practices. *Italian Journal of Sociology of Education*, 11, 147–173.

Musarò, P., Parmiggiani, P. (Eds.) (2014). *Media e migrazioni: Etica, estetica e politica della narrazione umanitaria*. Milan: FrancoAngeli.

Musarò, P., Parmiggiani, P. (2017). Beyond black and white: The role of media in portraying and policing migration and Asylum in Italy. *Revue Internationale De Sociologie*, 27(2): 241–260.

Paltrinieri, R., Gemini, L. (Eds.) (2018). I pubblici dello spettacolo dal vivo e museale. Tra audience development, audience engagement e audience reception. *Sociologia della Comunicazione*, 56(2).

Pastore, F., Monzini, P., Sciortino, G. (2006). Schengen's soft underbelly? Irregular migration and human smuggling across land and sea borders to Italy. *International Migration*, 44: 95–119.

Piscator, E. (1929). *The Political Theater*. New York: Avon.

Trombetta, C., Rosiello, L. (2000). *La ricerca-azione. Il modello di Kurt Lewin e le sue applicazioni*. Trent: Erickson.

Vaughan-Williams, N. (2015). *Europe's Border Crisis: Biopolitical Security and Beyond*. New York: Oxford University Press.

Withol de Wenden, C. (2013). *Le droit d'émigrer*. Paris: CNRS.

Wittmayer, J. M. Backhaus, J., Avelino, F., Pel, B., Strasser, T., Kunze, I. (2015). *Narratives of change: How social innovation initiatives engage with their transformative ambitions* (TRANSIT working paper; 4). Available at: http://www.transitsocialinnovation.eu/resource-hub/narratives-of change- how-social-innovation-initiatives-engage-with-their-transformative-ambitions.

Wood, P., Landry, C. (2007). *The Intercultural City: Planning for Diversity Advantage*. New York: Routledge.

Benedetta Turco

Chapter Twenty-One Cohousing to Get to Know Each Other

Abstract: There are many reading keys of social phenomenon about migration because it is complicated and perpetually current. In existential-phenomenological view it is possible to look the reality through a relationship between Other and I. It is a continually present relation that in its manifestation in everyday life (micro) takes up the complexity of global phenomenon (macro). This is a dialectic. One way to observe migratory flows, and its protagonists, is through the Sartrean concept of *rareté*. It is absence which emerges when each individual understands condition of things in society and therefore perceives what is lack. Some citizens felt the *need* to react to the *rareté* of State towards system of reception of migrants. Since 2014 many projects have been created to improve the well-being of migrants and reduce *inertia* and *rareté* in hospitality centers. There are paths that begin with host family to help the migrant achieve autonomy. It is a domestic hospitality.

1 Why Stay in Africa?

The migratory phenomenon is a widely complex social fact in which a multiplicity of factors are inserted and chained together in a space and in a time. In this migratory framework, in which different populations, cultures, and identities coexist, individual stories emerge of those who choose to embark on a journey into the unknown.

What are the motivations that drive an individual to leave their country, their home, their affections, and their certainties in order to set out on an unknown path? In the 21st century, why do citizens of Africa and the Middle East cross lands and deserts, get on makeshift boats to find themselves in the immensity of the Mediterranean Sea? What drives them to make this choice? What is missing in these realities so as to make it impossible to live there?

Choosing which behavior to adopt, what action to put into effect among the infinite possibilities, allows the human being to express their own singularity with the awareness that in front of them there is not a destiny already written but a void to be continuously filled.

Choosing means having possibilities. Human beings find themselves in the daily condition of making a decision even when they think they are not doing it or they are being forced by events caused by the choices of others.

Looking at the phenomenon of migratory flows, we realize that it is not possible to insert it in a well-defined framework governed by a single trigger. Every choice, every action, and every circumstance has a world behind it with which it is important to come to terms in order to understand the social reality of reference and its complexity. So why do we do what we do? Why do we emigrate?

By reopening the scenarios of the past we can better understand the current dynamics and the causes of human mobility in some countries.

The philosopher Tzvetan Todorov (1992) gave voice to one of the first protagonists of colonization, Christopher Columbus, through the analysis of his diaries. Todorov highlights how Europeans have assumed attitudes and behaviors based on the perception they had from meeting the Other. This condition, however, does not take a positive perspective as, if on the one hand the differences emerge and one feels in a position to underline one's own superiority, on the other hand the perception of the stranger as equal to us places us in the condition of recognizing it as identical and, therefore, similar. Both these aspects produce an image of the otherness that arises from European egocentrism and from the identification of one's own values as absolute values. This brings assimilationism towards a slavery ideology, a passage that highlights the thought of those who call themselves a divulger of the word of God and a re-populator who "does not recognize them the right to have their own will; in short, he considers them to be living objects" (1992, p.58).

The presence of Europeans in the game of colonization within the African continent connotes a *bitter* reading of slavery. The European rulers demanded the presence of African slaves constrained to forced labor to complete their constructions, not always paid and, in some cases, forced to military service as, for example, during the First World War where half a million African slaves was sent to European borders (Pietrostefani, 2000). In this regard, Hannah Arendt recalls in one of her works, *The Origins of Totalitarianism*, a famous phrase of the then president of the French Republic, Raimond Poincarè, in those years of conflict:

> France is not a country of 40 million, it is a country of 100 million [. . .]. [An] economic form of cannon fodder, obtained by mass production methods (Crozier, 1924 in Arendt, 2009, p.180).

Europeans attempted to implement, starting from the first half of the 16th century, a new slave trade, the Atlantic section, which allowed the exploitation of Africans on large American areas rich in agricultural and mining potential. In this way, the long journey from the Black Earth to the New World caused the destruction of entire ethnic groups, erased pieces of history, of social and cultural life with its own languages and traditions. The African territory, in itself battered by the tropical climate, suffered further demographic mutilation due to this Atlantic route, which interrupted the development of the population for about two centuries. Moreover, this continuous demand for slaves became ever more insistent, leading to the emergence of new social and political organizations, of inhuman behaviors towards those considered inferior and preventing Africa from its socioeconomic development (Pietrostefani, 2000).

On January 20, 1949[1], the new president of the United States of America – Harry Truman – spoke for the first time, in his speech to the White House, of developed areas of the world that should have been in a phase of scientific and industrial progress which, as a consequence, should have supported underdeveloped areas. With these statements, President Truman gave a definition of what was later called the Third World which, within this vision, was identified and classified through its economic limits (Tognonato, 2014).

From a sociological point of view, Karl Marx, already in the previous century, was interested in the concept of *progress*, considering it fundamental in order to overcome the evolution of production and the rise of capitalism. A Marxist imprint is also present in his "Eurocentric vision [in which they emerge] presumptuous statements, such as the one where he considers that many countries of the world would not be able to achieve development without the positive contribution of colonialism" (Tognonato, 2014, p.146).

Between 1815 and 1914 colonial expansion began with a first phase in which the intervention of the European state aimed at the military conquest of the chosen African territory, while in a second phase, it saw the presence of industrialists and traders, of the same State, for the exploitation of raw materials and their natural products (Strangio, 2017).

> The fundamental causes of European colonialism in the nineteenth century were: 1. economic development: industries [...] went to acquire raw materials (coal, oil, cotton, etc.) in ever greater quantities and at lower cost in the Asian and African continents; 2. the imperialist spirit: the European states, animated by a strong desire for conquest, not being able to enlarge their territories in the Old Continent, expanded in Africa and Asia, also to demonstrate their power (Strangio, 2017, p.51).

1 *Inaugural Addresses of the Presidents of the United States: Grover Cleveland (1885) to Barack H. Obama (2009)*, Harry S. Truman, Inaugural Address. Thursday, January 20, 1949. Applewood Books, River Road, Carlisle, Massachusetts 2009, pp. 109–115.

We can better understand how in this phase of colonization, and therefore of encounters and "contaminations" between very different cultures and realities, an economic dependence of Africa emerged that was subalternally inserted into the global capitalist system. In this dynamic came into play a new dialectic, which was defined world-system: it consisted in the exploitation of the underdeveloped areas – better known as the Third World – perpetrated by the self-imposed "Centre" (Wallerstein, 2006).

Is it therefore through power games and deprivation of raw materials that the First World countries want to bring help and support to the underdeveloped countries?

In this scenario, of continuous exploitation, a strong sense of lack and *rareté*[2] is generated in the Black Continent that has led many to undertake a "makeshift journey."

From Africa migrations have multiple causes and are often not aimed at reaching the Western world but at the natural attempt to have some chance of survival. The reasons for this type of mobility vary according to the country of origin of the migrants. People escape from Mali because it is one of the poorest countries in the world with severe political instability, a strong environmental crisis, and the siege of Islamic terrorists. Nigerians escape from their homeland because the great interest of the First World on the oil fields present in the territory causes disastrous consequences for the environment, for the balance of the ecosystem, and also for the inhabitants who live on the products of these lands. People make their getaway from Central African Republic as it is torn by continuous civil wars: the last one began in 2012 between the anti-Balaka Christian government coalition and the Muslim-majority rebel Sèlèka, a war in which rape is used as a weapon and massacres are on the agenda (Furlanetto, 2019).

From the Middle East, on the other hand, the migratory flows arriving in the West are mainly made up of Afghans, Pakistanis, and Syrians who try to escape from the attacks of the Taliban, from the sudden bombings and cruelty of terrorist groups such as Al Qaida and ISIS. Bangladeshis are also part of these streams which leave their land and their family mainly due to poverty and exploitation of rich countries: they are mostly "unaware victims of our well-being." They, like all those who leave, are not only in search of better conditions in which to live but

---

2 Jean-Paul Sartre deals with category of the *rareté* is "lack of…", "scarcity, of…"; it is the insufficient of indispensable goods to life. In this perspective the human being understands the condition of matters and, consequently, what is lacking them.

also in the hope of being able to be of help and sustenance for those who remain. They will then be labeled as "economic migrants."

In the *Bel Paese* this figure is considered an individual to be discarded and not worthy of protection by the European continent. But what makes a human being "worthy" of our humanity? Why do European countries impose a classification on who, among migrants, is in the worst condition? Why do they not accept their responsibilities in the face of these migratory flows? Why do they not see in the eyes of these people the same eyes of the many Italians abroad who feel that their country brings them more *rareté* than work?

We find ourselves having to deal with a world divided in half, between rich and poor, a world where the exploitation and the logic of capitalist progress have led some countries to be underdeveloped and to perceive their shortcomings even more in the face of their ostentatious opulence. This spread of *rareté* arises from the need for the First World to follow development models based on economic growth and power. The *rareté*, therefore, is not created by Nature but given by the human being who holds the reins of neoliberal globalization; the latter has increased the gap between countries through the concentration of wealth, thus increasing the motivations that lead to the decision to migrate.

2 Arriving in Italy, What Is Next?

The arrival in the countries bordering the Mediterranean Sea of those escaping from the many "hands of terror" in Africa and the Middle East – through small makeshift boats – has led Europe to find ways to face this situation.

Italy – along with Spain, Greece, Malta, and Cypro – is one of those countries that, from a geographical point of view, is at the forefront of the rescue and hospitality of these human beings (Breen, 2019).

When they encounter the unknown, their "Other", that is, the Italian in his various roles of first aid and care, begins a whole procedural process within the structures deemed most suitable. The hospitality system in Italy operates, in fact, on two levels: the first concerns the entry into the Hotspots and the first hospitality centers (CAS), while the second refers to a stay in the SPRAR centers (protection system for asylum seekers).

What is the situation for the beneficiaries of these systems? In addition to the care of basic needs, does it allow a real integration within the company? Does it provide the tools to understand the culture, the new reality in which they find themselves living in, and the ways in which Italians socialize? Does the surplus of people within the centers lead to shortcomings in this State hospitality?

The intent of these pages is not to discredit this type of planning but to highlight the existence of critical issues and inertias that limit the process of entry of the foreigner into the new society.

Schooling and professionalization are, for example, the main elements that increase the possibilities of socialization by reducing the obstacles and barriers that the fear of the Other can generate. The political choices of the last few years, however, inserted within a continuous debate on the risks of "opening our doors" has not simply increased the perception of *rareté* in this system, but may have created it.

The 2019 dossier presented by the Authority for Childhood and Adolescence (AGIA) together with the UN agency for refugees (UNHCR) highlighted the multiple risks and vulnerabilities that emerge within the centers of the first and second hospitality in Italy. Throughout the monitoring period of the 22 structures, located in 11 regions, *focus groups* and participation and listening activities were carried out with about 200 subjects. Paying attention to their voices, what resonates are the problems linked to the ever more present deficiencies in these increasingly crowded places less and less interested in creating possibilities for coexistence with the Other[3].

> I worked for so many years in migrant communities, my hands have tightened the shoulders of many and my eyes have seen everything, especially the critical ones. These places fail to meet the needs of these people, they do not allow to reach those goals that led them to stay alive throughout the trip. If the law protects, why would a boy who arrived as an MSNA and placed in the special center for minors as soon as he is eighteen years old be thrown out at any time? Why are integration and inclusion projects lacking? It is not enough to have room and board, a path is necessary.
>
> (Cultural mediator of Pesaro and mother of a host family)

In the Italian state hospitality system limits can be identified because the reaction to landings is a response to a situation that is still defined as an "emergency." In this reality the subjects are not considered in their individuality, in their being singularity with specific needs and requirements, with the desire to invest the hospitality's resources to try to reach autonomy. An approach of subsistence and support of the State given to third parties, so that they can "manage" migrants,

3 Comunicato stampa UNHCR – AGIA: *Dossier sui minorenni stranieri non accompagnati nei centri di accoglienza: «Chiediamo inclusione»*, 9 luglio 2019 – www.unhcr.it/news/comunicato-stampa-unhcr-agia-dossier-sui-minorenni-stranieri-non-accompagnati-nei-centri-accoglienza-chiediamo-inclusione.html.

constitutes inertias that increase again the dependence previously defined "center-periphery."

An example of inertia is related to *pocket money* (so 2.50 euros per day per migrant up to a maximum of 7.5 euros per family unit provided by the State[4]) which can be perceived for the individual migrant as a constraint to the hospitality centers and the cooperatives that manage them. This choice of state, of control, diminishes the possibilities of individual choice and mobility of these human beings. Furthermore, the diversity of the Prefecture's projects, which are not aimed *ad personam* but are generic, hinder a concrete and organic provision of established benefits.

> It is we who place these human beings in refugee status, we choose to place them in a condition of beneficiaries and subsistence, but not all projects in this regard offer the same possibilities. Before leaving the world of hospitality, I ran a facility in Genova where there were 50 places for first and second hospitality migrants: I tried to increase the quality of the Cas to make it closer to the Sprar level. To equate the possibilities ... but it's not easy! In one room there were 3 migrants from Cas and 2 from Sprar, how could I make them understand why they did not have the same rights? How could I tell him that one was entitled to the work grant, to cover the costs of the residence permit and so on while the other was not? In my structure I was trying to manage the budget so that everyone could have the same things but there are many other situations in which this concern does not exist.
>
> (Referent of domestic hospitality project)

From the point of view of existential sociology, the *rareté*, or scarcity and the need to fill it converge. But what is the *need*? The need is "the first relationship that the human being has with the material exteriority that surrounds him, configures the point of contact between organic and inorganic" (Tognonato, 2018, p.33). Among the latter there is a strong dialectic since the existence of the organic derives from its need for the inorganic: this means that when we feel the presence of a void in front of us, the need to fill it emerges. We find ourselves in a continuous attempt to reach completeness and this is what drives us to act and react to the limits of society.

According to Jean-Paul Sartre (1982) "everything is revealed in need: it is the first totalizing relationship of this material being, a man, with the material whole of which he is part" (p.206). In fact, need is the main element between the subject and the thing, whether it is material as an object the individual needs or intangible as the bureaucracy related to migration flows and hospitality methods.

4 www.unhcr.it/risorse/carta-di-roma/fact-checking/rifugiati-4-luoghi-comuni-smentire.

Furthermore, Sartre, focusing on the concept of *rareté*, goes so far as to say that this lack is a human construction, a human fact that is part of human history. The *rareté* therefore is not given by "Stepmother Nature" (Sartre, 1982, p.371) as, on the contrary, it is previously considered by Adam Smith, a natural and incontestable limit to be respected.

Taking into consideration the economic and political dynamics imposed by a neoliberal globalization and the increasing attention on oneself and on one's own advantages, the limits and criticalities present within the state hospitality system are not due to the impossibility of managing such situation as an invasion of migrants, but arise from the choices of the First World, choices that generate large forms of *rareté* for the Other.

3 The Reaction of Citizens to the State's *Rareté*: "I Welcome Them to My Home!"

The mass media tell what happens in the world by looking at real facts, but at the same time manipulating them. History is a narrative of the real and for this reason, being perceived, it takes on multiple interpretations.

Paul Ricoeur (1986), in his work *Time and narrative*, faces the *aporia*[5] of time by affirming that, "Time becomes human time to the extent that it is articulated in a narrative way; on the other hand History is significant to the extent that it draws the features of the temporal experience" (p.15).

For Ricoeur, history outlines an event, gives it form and a meaning in that "a *praxis* is needed that brings together elements scattered in a totalization of meaning and gives them a meaning" (Tognonato, 2018, p.47). Language is therefore the tool used to describe an "object" that otherwise could not be expressed. The subject, recounting, takes up the substance of the object, of the real fact, which becomes different because it is *altered* every time.

From this perspective it is possible to understand how a phenomenon, such as migration, can be perceived in different ways and how this can lead each individual to choose to act differently in front of the Other.

In this perspective, the Other can take the form of the "enemy" because it could cause an increase in the sense of *rareté* for those who live in a welcoming

5 The *aporia*, in philosophy, is the difficulty faced by the thought in his research, whether the solution is considered to be achievable or whether it appears intrinsic to the nature of the thing and therefore unavoidable (Encyclopedia *Treccani*) – http://www.treccani.it/vocabolario/aporia/.

reality. It can be seen as a further competitor of the assets available within the social reality, and this develops the fears and suspicions that accompany everyday life. Furthermore, through the narrative altered by the political and mass media debate, there is an amplification of the real on the theme of immigration and of hospitality enough to find a solid basis in the economic and social difficulties of the country. This could contribute to the emergence of discriminatory and prejudicial ideas that could lead to racist behavior and attitudes.

This way of perceiving reality, however, is not experienced as normal by all individuals. But what is normal and what is not? Should we give in to the normality that can become the norm and law? In a society "ordering means defining the threshold that separates the normal from the abnormal, "relegating" the differences and strengthening the idea of an identity understood as a consolidated normality" (Tognonato, 2018, p.135). This, however, must not favor and constitute rigid forms of conformism even if it is complex for the human being to manage not to submit to praxis, as Gabriel Tarde (2012) recalls in his work *The Laws of Imitation*.

> The modern citizen boasts about making a free choice between the proposals that are made to him; but, in reality, the one he prefers, the one that follows, is the one that best responds to his needs, to his pre-existing desires and which derive from his customs, his habits, all his past of obedience (p.250).

Referring to the thought of Tarde, just some common citizens have felt the need to react to the *rareté* of a state that does not accept migrants, and it is precisely this need that moves the action leading to choices that do not conform to the *praxis*. They miss something and look for the conditions to fill that void. Even if it is impossible to fill, as it is impossible to reach the absolute, that is, to individually fill a global problem, citizens have an expectation, to be able to heal this deficiency through their actions, through a social dispute that takes shape in domestic hospitality projects.

The need to fill the shortcomings of the state hospitality system finds its starting point in the *desire* – which in turn originates in the *rareté* – which "is not something that inhabits the conscience, because the conscience has no content, it is not a storage area" (Tognonato, 2006, p.71). Desire, however, is not enough because it is necessary to go beyond it, "beyond the idea that consciousness is inhabited by objects that push to be realized" (Tognonato, 2006, p.71). The desire, for some individuals, is to be able to find themselves in the forms of help to the Other produced by public policies, a reflection in which they can mirror and recognize themselves. Not being so, they feel the desire to reduce this distance by trying to reach their being. It is a continuous search for oneself in things and in this case the search for oneself takes place in the domestic hospitality projects in which the citizens find themselves as social workers, volunteers, or activists of the project or, in the position of host subject. But this *rareté*, and the constant search for oneself, is not lived only by those who belong "to the fortunate part of the world" but also by those who try to enter this reality, the foreigner, the Other. The latter, as aforementioned, can find themselves in a state of failures that makes them "requesting" subjects and unprepared for achieving autonomy in the country of arrival.

Furthermore, the migration issue, in its multiple dynamics, is as a matter of fact a phenomenon that has long been inserted into a global (universal) dimension. This does not distance us from the problems that concern us but, on the contrary, we are interested in and live in everyday life. The domestic hospitality (singular) is the example of a small part of reality that captures and re-proposes the limits and difficulties of immigration: micro and macro are in a constant dialectic[6].

> Already in 2017 there were public policies that included a hospitality system with SPRAR projects but they were not functional in the concrete practice of hospitality in terms of integration on our territory. Now, in May 2019, we are "at the feet of Pilate" precisely because there is a «disused» policy for the hospitality system that is even more distant from the SPRAR project, which, at least, was widely disseminated in terms of the quality of primary needs. This was fundamental because through this first step of provisional food and lodging there was the possibility, or at least there was time for an attempt, to access secondary assets, which are not so secondary! Health care is important for these children who embarked on a «journey of hope» that lasted months and months, who walked uninterruptedly, who were locked in trucks, who were held prisoners in the camps, who crossed the sea on a dinghy. Learning the Italian language is important for these young people who want to enter our territory, who need to develop a network of relationships and that will probably allow them to enter the world of work. So, from my point of view, it was still not a sufficient hospitality because it didn't look at the integration processes in an effective way but now the migrants don't even have that minimal support! The hospitality network has been dismantled today and the signals given to us by the current government in the last year are signs of strong disincentive to any integration process because when this sense of invasion and intolerance towards the migrant grows, the migrant goes from

6 The unity is, for existentialism, the origin that through the choice materializes in the moment in which the subject and the object are joined, and therefore every time that the universal becomes singular.

> swearing to insults, from insults to beatings! There is a growing declination towards non-hospitality policies and practices of intolerance towards the different.
>
> (Host family of Palermo)

Faced with the awareness of this *rareté* and the provocations that emerged in the political debates, some citizens have realized, as mentioned, alternative forms of hospitality and welcoming, giving the possibility to some migrants to insert themselves in their everyday life and in their own family dynamics.

But what is domestic hospitality? These projects were born in Europe in the two-year period 2014–2015 as a political and social challenge to the lack not only of concrete materials, routes, and opportunities but also the lack of humanity. In life we often find ourselves at a crossroads and it is inevitable to make a choice. From this point of view, it could be said that the world of politics has chosen to identify the Other, the foreigner, as the enemy that must be far from its borders and, in case of presence on the territory, must be excluded. On the contrary, with the socialization of hospitality a new way of acting emerges, made up of openness, meetings, and daily clashes. It is not possible to deny the existence of the Other, to deny the otherness that is in us and around us, to deny a globalized reality that has already overtaken the imaginary walls of nations.

According to Ricoeur (1993), Other and I, identity and otherness, cannot be thought of as two disjoint realities but, on the contrary, complementary because by means of this continuous dialectic it is possible to conceive one's Self through the Other.

Emmanuel Lévinas has a different view on this duality which takes on more ethical nuances: Io and Other come into contact through the concept of responsibility. The Ego, which Levinas calls Oneself, receives a considerable boost that puts him outside his circumscribed reality when perceiving the Other and his condition. This will make him "one-for-the-other" (Pinzolo, 2015). A choice of responsibility comes along, as Jean-Paul Sartre would say.

> When you feel you «belong» as a presence, knowledge, coexistence in a context made of sociality, of politics – in the sense of polis and not of party politics – it is natural to protect it and fight for it! We are not going to harm someone's rights, but privileges are broken because you understand that your rights also belong to the Other. It is, in my opinion, a somewhat romantic vision of anarchy, one tries to undermine the privileges to confront oneself on one's rights and on the universal rights of the human being, you recognize yourself as belonging to the human category! I think back to Foucault and to the Sovereign State, today we live a spectacularization of the death of migrants in the Mediterranean Sea and we are increasingly oriented towards a devastating perspective

> supported by security decrees, by the crime of solidarity . . . then one wonders: what is the population that can be sacrificed?
>
> (Referent of domestic hospitality project)

In Italy, the domestic hospitality projects have the most disparate origins; and this indicates how, despite the differences, humanity is still the most important prerogative. This is the engine that drives individuals to join in a shared project, giving life to what Sartre calls a *fused group*. This group "is not an autonomous body, has no life of its own, was established and its existence is *derived* because in addition to being created, it must be supported [. . .], its existence is the result of the interaction of individuals who make it necessary" (Tognonato, 2018, pp.55–56).

The domestic hospitality projects are mainly designed to help the most vulnerable, those who are of legal age who leave the hospitality centers for unaccompanied foreign minors (UAMs). Foreign adolescents begin a path of adequate insertion within the appropriate center but, as soon as they reach the age of 18, they must abandon these more protected environments to fit into those for adults. The realities of hospitality at home are numerous, for example, the project "Protected, refugee at my home" by Caritas, *Refugees Welcome Italia*, the project "Between us" of the *Farsi Prossimo* consortium of Milan, the "Vesta" project of the municipality of Bologna-Ferrara, and others. Moreover, addressing only one age group is not the rule for these new realities; in fact there are other projects such as "WelcHome," implemented by the municipality of Modena, which is aimed at minors well away from the age of majority.

The strength of domestic hospitality projects is not just to provide hospitality, a bed to sleep in, and a hot meal, but to be a solid base for those who have come to Europe alone and are looking for their own autonomy. The achievement of this condition could be achievable starting from a protected environment, from a place that stands as a bridge between them and the world. The domestic hospitality could limit the dimension of vulnerability, discomfort, isolation, and passivity – lived in the large state centers – allowing an improvement and an enhancement of the individual's individual and personal capacities. This creates the conditions for getting to know the territory, the culture, the implicit meanings of the relationships, and thus developing new opportunities for *encounter-clash*. It is a socialization of hospitality.

4 First Considerations

Migration flows are part of a phenomenon that is widely debated and very complex. It is precisely for this reason that it is possible to try to understand it through different interpretations such as the labor issue, discrimination, the relationship between the first and second generations, the scholastic context, the hospitality, and many others.

None of the aspects mentioned is more important than the others; it simply offers a particular look to those who choose to dwell on a part of reality.

In this chapter, a key to the interpretation that was born from the existentialist thought of some scholars, such as Martin Heidegger and Jean-Paul Sartre, was chosen, who face the human being of modern society, aware of that continuous sense of emptiness that distinguishes them.

On the basis of what has been said, the *rareté* is one of the elements that allows us to approach complexity through that sense of lack that unites all the actors of the phenomenon and that leads to acting in different ways. The circumstances in which each individual lives are defined by themselves as insufficient and limited: this is fueled by their continuous desire to capture the absolute and to reach totality.

As stated in the first lines of this contribution, modern society has contributed, through the race to economic power and domination over the weakest, to increase competition at every level of social life and, consequently, to focus our attention on what we lack, on things that we do not have. From this point of view, everyone becomes possible competitor capable of further depriving the others of what, on the contrary, is believed to come as one's own right. The Other, understood both as "near" and as "distant", carries the clothes of the enemy; and in this way human relationships give way to relationships regulated by the *laissez faire* of economic rationality.

What are the consequences of this logic? Is it possible to get out of this *rareté* circuit? Are we condemned to see the Other as an enemy for our shortcomings?

Sartre, observing a reality in which there are more and more *serial relationships*[7] between individuals, offers us an almost catastrophic image of mankind, an image in which exteriority rules. From this point of view, human beings become a risk to each other, a threat.

> Nothing, in fact, neither the great ferocious beasts nor the microbes, can be more terrible for the man of an intelligent, carnivorous, cruel species, able to understand and to foil human intelligence and whose purpose is precisely the destruction of 'man (1982, p.257).

7 The serial relationships are defined by Jean-Paul Sartre as failed relationships, devoid of any interest that may constitute a link between the parties involved.

The *rareté* is, therefore, understood as a conflict that becomes the rule. This lack becomes the florid basis for the inhuman social and political organization inserted in a globalized and neoliberal reality. *Rareté* is in everything, we perceive it at all times "because it is created by a social order that generates relationships of exclusion, violence and fragmentation, designating who will be saved and who will be excluded and destroying any social project" (Tognonato, 2018, p.40).

It is difficult not to see the Other as an enemy, to free oneself – even if in part – from the weight of competition and economic rationality. However, in an existential perspective human relationships can be defined as such only in a relationship of reciprocity "that is realized in the recognition of the Other as freedom, as a project and not as an object" (Tognonato, 2018, p.173).

References

Breen D. (2019). UNHCR Regional Bureau for Europe staff, Desperate Journeys. *Refugee and Migrant Children arriving in Europe and how to Strengthen their Protection*. January to September 2019, UNHCR, online, 2019.

Crozier W. P. (1924). *France and Her Black Empire*. In New Republic, 23 gennaio 1924 in H. Arendt (2009). *Le origini del totalitarismo*. Torino: Piccola Biblioteca Enaudi.

Furlanetto V. (2019). *Perché i migranti scappano da casa loro*, Il Sole 24ORE online, www.ilsole24ore.com/art/perche-migranti-scappano-casa-loro-ACPcrai, articolo del 8/09/2019.

Pietrostefani G. (2000). *La tratta atlantica: genocidio e sortilegio*. Milano: JacaBook.

Pinzolo L. (2015). *Emmanuel Lévinas: etica dell'altro uomo*. In U. Eco e R. Fedriga (a cura di), *La filosofia e le sue storie* (pp.391–393). Bari: Laterza.

Ricoeur P. (1986). *Tempo e racconto* (Vol. 1). Milano: Jacka Book.

Ricoeur P. (1993). *Sé come un altro*. Milano: Jaca Book.

Sartre J. P. (1982). *Critica della ragione dialettica, Tomo 1, Teoria degli insiemi pratici*. Milano: Il Saggiatore.

Strangio D. (2017). *Globalizzazione, disuguaglianze, migrazioni. introduzione alla storia economica contemporanea*. Roma: Carocci.

Tarde G. (2012). *Le leggi dell'imitazione*. Torino: Rosenberg & Sellier.

Todorov T. (1992). *La conquista dell'America. Il problema dell' "altro"*. Torino: Einaudi Editore.

Tognonato C. (2006). *Il corpo del sociale. Appunti per una sociologia esistenziale.* Napoli: Liguori Editore.

Tognonato C. (2014). *Economia senza società. Oltre i limiti del mercato globale.* Napoli: Liguori Editore.

Tognonato C. (2018). *Teoria sociale dell'agire inerte. L'individuo nella morsa delle costruzioni sociali.* Napoli: Liguori Editore.

Wallerstein I. (2006). *Comprendere il mondo. Introduzione all'analisi dei sistemi-mondo.* Trieste: Asterios.

Gabriella Polizzi

Chapter Twenty-Two Managing Non-verbal Communication to Facilitate the Reception of Migrants

Abstract: Face-to-face communication plays a fundamental role in any human interaction. Interactions between people working in the migrant reception system and migrants themselves are not exceptions to this type of communication because effective face-to-face communication with migrants is a prerequisite for safeguarding their stay in the host country. However, managing interpersonal interactions in this field merits special attention since hosts and migrants often belong to different cultures. This management, therefore, requires that people providing services to migrants possess appropriate knowledge and intercultural communication skills. Intercultural communication can serve as a tool which law enforcement officers, medical and paramedical staff as well as social workers may use in different ways to meet with migrants and to develop interactions, which respect the various cultures they will encounter. Departing from this premise, the aim of this chapter is to explore how the adoption of an intercultural approach to the management of non-verbal communication (NVC) codes can facilitate the reception of migrants.

1 Introduction

Despite the growing importance of computer-mediated communication in the field of human interaction in recent years, interpersonal communication via face-to-face interaction continues to play a fundamental role in establishing, maintaining and strengthening human relationships. Face-to-face interaction is a specific type of human interaction whereby various key elements have been identified by sociologists and psychologists in a given time period. According to Thompson (1995), face-to-face interaction is characterized by at least three elements: a) it occurs in a *context of co-presence*, which means that the participants in the communication process share the same place and time; b) it is *dialogical* in nature and characterized by a bidirectional communication process since the roles of *producer* and *recipient* of a message are not predetermined but, rather, interchangeable during the process and c) face-to-face interaction deploys a *multiplicity of symbolic cues*, which consist of verbal and non-verbal elements.

Departing from these considerations, this chapter will focus on face-to-face interaction between people working in the migrant reception system and the migrants themselves. This is consistent with the assumption that effective face-to-face communication with migrants is a prerequisite for managing and safeguarding their stay in the host country. Moreover, this has been proven by studies in the strategic fields of migrant integration into the host country; these include the provision of healthcare services (Pauwels, 1995).

As research by Mehrabian (1981) has demonstrated, on occasions when other people's feelings and attitudes (i.e., like or dislike) are interpreted, the most influential element regarding perceptions is other people's *body language*, followed by *tone of voice*; *utterances* exert the smallest influence of all the human communication codes. The substance of this chapter has arisen because people coming from different cultures use non-verbal codes differently (Andersen, 2012). Since hosts and migrants often pertain to different cultures, the management of interpersonal interactions in the field of face-to-face communication with migrants merits special attention. It requires that those providing services to migrants possess appropriate knowledge and intercultural communication skills, as well an enhanced level of awareness regarding inherent challenges.

From such a perspective, a further aim of this chapter is to focus on the non-verbal dimension of face-to-face communication and to explore how the adoption of an intercultural approach to the management of non-verbal communication (NVC) codes can facilitate the reception of migrants. As part of this aim, Section 2 will deal with the role and main features of NVC in human interaction. Section 3 will focus on eight non-verbal codes, which human beings can deploy during their encounters, and it will analyse each code from an intercultural perspective. The ultimate aim of the chapter is to provide those working in the migrant reception system with suggestions and recommendations regarding the management of NVC codes in order to establish effective and respectful relationships with migrants.

2 The Role and Main Features of Non-verbal Communication in Human Interaction

Non-verbal communication plays an important role in human interactions. Samovar, Porter, McDaniel and Roy (2012) have written a stimulating review of its main functions:

a) *NVC expresses internal states*. Since it has been demonstrated that human beings are not as capable of controlling their own bodies as their utterances, NVC can convey information relating to the "real" thoughts and emotions of people. "Be it fear, joy, anger, or sadness, your posture, face, and eyes can convey your feelings without you ever uttering a word. For this reason most people rely heavily on what they perceive through their eyes. In fact, research indicates that you will usually believe nonverbal messages instead of verbal messages when the two contradict" (Samovar et al., 2012, p. 268).

b) *NCV forges one's identity*. "Nonverbal communication is important in human interactions because it is partially responsible for establishing identity. The nonverbal inferences people use to construct their identities are drawn from a variety of messages. From personal experience you know how judgments are often made about another person based on such things as skin color, use of makeup, facial expression, manner of dress, accent, jewelry, and even the type of handshake offered" (Samovar et al., 2012, p. 269).
c) *NVC regulates interaction*. Non-verbal actions, such as gaze direction and head movements, can be used as an organizing guide by which to conduct the communication process in a comprehensible way. Gestures termed *regulators* (Ekman & Friesen, 1975) may indicate the starting point of a conversation, who is supposed or permitted to take their turn and at which precise moment, including the termination of the interaction.
d) *NVC can repeat the message*. Non-verbal actions, such as facial expressions and hand gestures, can be used to reinforce messages which are simultaneously conveyed via verbal communication.
e) *NVC can substitute utterances*. On occasions when utterances do not satisfy the communicative intent, non-verbal actions can be used as substitutes.

In order to further our understanding of the nature and role of NVC in human interaction, three of the five and well-known axioms of human communication, as conceptualized by Watzlawick, Beavin and Jackson (1967), will now be analysed: the first, the second and the fourth.

The first axiom, which states that "One cannot *not* communicate" (Watzlawick et al., 1967, p. 51), contains an indirect reference to the importance of NVC in human interaction: even in those situations in which human beings are not making utterances, their bodies are still conveying meaning intentionally or not. Consequently, people working in the migrant reception system should be aware that their body language (e.g., eye contact and hand gestures) could risk conveying meaning which might be misinterpreted by migrants. This will be discussed in greater detail in the next section of the chapter.

The impact of non-verbal elements on the effectiveness of the communication process can also be highlighted by the second axiom, which asserts that "Every communication has a content and a relationship aspect such that the latter classifies the former and is therefore a metacommunication" (Watzlawick et al., 1967, p. 54). Ruesch and Bateson (1951, p. 179) have termed this *report* and *command*, respectively. Usually, the specific content of a message is defined particularly by verbal communication with NVC mostly contributing to defining the type of extant relationship or that which might be established between the participants in the communication process.

Of the five axioms describing human communication, the fourth can be said to refer more directly to the importance of NVC in human interaction. This axiom specifies that: "Human beings communicate both digitally and analogically" (Watzlawick et al., 1967, p. 66). This can be explained by the fact that "In human communication, objects – in the widest sense – can be referred to in two entirely different ways. They can either be represented by a likeness, such as a drawing, or they can be referred to by a name (…) These two types of communication – the one by a self-explanatory likeness, the other by a word – are, of course, also equivalent to the concepts of the analogic and the digital respectively. Whenever a word is used to *name* something it is obvious that the relation between the name and the thing named is an arbitrarily established one (…) In analogic communication, on the other hand, there is something particularly "thing-like" in what is used to express the thing. Analogic communication can be more readily referred to the thing it stands for" (Watzlawick et al., 1967, pp. 61–62).

Within the scope of this chapter, the main difference between digital and analogic communication is that analogic communication "is virtually all nonverbal communication. This term, however, is deceptive, because it is often restricted to body movement only, to the behaviour known as kinesics" (Watzlawick et al., 1967, p. 62). Rather, the term should also include "posture, gesture, facial expressions, voice inflection, the sequence, rhythm, and cadence of the words themselves, and any other nonverbal manifestation of which an organism is capable, as well as the communicational clues unfailingly present in any context in which an interaction takes place" (ibid.).

Other non-verbal manifestations may include elements such as *physical appearance* (e.g. sex, age, weight, height, etc.), *manner of dress* and *body odour*, whereas "the communicational clues unfailingly present in any context" may refer to *objects, furniture arrangement and colours*. Whilst it may be said that "there is something particularly "thing-like" in what is used to express the thing" (ibid.), it should also be noticed that this *something particularly* "thing-like" can possess wide-ranging and arbitrary (i.e. digital) components. That is, these components can be defined, transmitted and learned by means of culture and, of greater importance, they depend on cultural characteristics. As a consequence, people belonging to different cultures can use NVC codes in a different manner (Andersen, 2012): this, therefore, can necessitate that those providing services to migrants are in possession of the appropriate knowledge and skills of intercultural communication. This will be developed below.

3 Managing NVC from an Intercultural Perspective: Key Codes and Challenges

Adopting an intercultural perspective, with which to manage NVC, necessitates clarification regarding the term *intercultural communication*. The latter has been defined as: "the symbolic exchange process whereby individuals from two (or more) different cultural communities attempt to negotiate shared meanings in an interactive situation within an embedded societal system" (Ting-Toomey & Chung, 2012, p. 24). In a similar vein, Samovar et al. (2012) have stressed that "Intercultural communication occurs when a member of one culture produces a message for consumption by a member of another culture. More precisely, intercultural communication involves interaction between people whose cultural perceptions and symbol systems differ enough to influence the communication event" (p. 8). Both definitions underline the reciprocal relationship between culture and communication since "You 'learn' your culture via communication, while at the same time communication is a reflection of your culture (ibid.)". That is, the manner by which people communicate depends on the symbolic frames adopted by each culture, and, as these frames differ across cultures, it follows that the way people communicate can vary markedly from culture to culture. This fact should be taken into account when those working in migrant reception systems attempt to establish effective and respectful relationships with those migrants.

According to Andersen (2012), people of different cultures differ in their use of the following eight NVC codes: physical appearance, proxemics, chronemics, kinesics, haptics, oculesics, vocalics and olfactics. These will now be briefly analysed. *Physical appearance* includes: "stable physical features of human beings such as gender, height, weight, skin color, and body shape, as well as the strategic use of artifacts associated with one's physical appearance like clothing, jewelry, make-up, hairstyles, and accessories. All of these elements play an important role during initial encounters" (Andersen, 2012, p, 295). An example of physical appearance is the traditional garment of Indian women, known as a sari (or saree). The different patterns, colours, materials and manner of dress can indicate different ages, and the sub-castes and regions to which Indian women belong. People working in the migrant reception systems should be aware that migrants of different cultures use all these elements according to specific meanings and habits, which are specific to their own culture.

Proxemics refers to the use of physical space between two or more people. Cultures define an appropriate distance between people in an interaction. As research by Hall (1966) has demonstrated, the specific physical distance between people can reflect the social distance characterizing their relationship. Four discrete proxemic zones have been identified by Hall: *intimate* (0–50 cm), *personal* (0.50–1 m), *social* (1–4 m) and *public* (4 m or more), all of which vary along a continuum from "extremely intimate" to "not at all intimate" relationships. Differences exist in the way by which people from different cultures manage physical distances and proxemic zones. As Andersen (2012) has highlighted, numerous studies agree that "people from Mediterranean and Latin cultures maintain close distances, whereas people from Northern European and Northeast Asian cultures maintain greater distances" (p. 296). In addition to external differences *between* cultures, there may also exist internal differences *within* the same culture, affecting the way by which different genders as well as ages allocate and manage proxemic zones in their daily interactions. As Ting-Toomey and Chung (2012, p. 146) have commented: "Any violation of these zones can result in feelings of anxiety or discomfort".

Since space is intrinsically correlated with time, another important non-verbal code of communication is *chronemics*, which "concerns how people in different cultures structure, interpret, and understand the time dimension" (Ting-Toomey & Chung, 2012, p. 148). Temporal regulation, "as the attitudes we have about time" (ibid.), depends on culture. According to Hall (1959, 1983) and Hall and Reed Hall (1990), cultures can be characterized as possessing elements of two patterns of time orientation: *monochronic* and *polychronic*. The monochronic (M-time) orientation is typical of the cultures of the USA, Canada, the UK, Germany, Switzerland, Austria, Sweden, Norway and Finland. People living in accordance with a monochronic time orientation "do one thing at a time; concentrate on the job; take time commitments (deadlines, schedules) seriously; are low-context and need information; are committed to the job; adhere religiously to plans; are concerned about not disturbing others; follow rules of privacy and consideration; show great respect for private property; seldom borrow or lend" (Hall & Reed Hall, 1990, p. 18). The polychronic (P-time) orientation is said to be typical of Arab, African, Latin American, Asian and Mediterranean cultures. People with this time orientation "do many things at once; are highly distractible and subject to interruptions; consider time commitments an objective to be achieved, if possible; are high-context and already have information; are committed to people and human relationships; change plans often and easily; are more concerned with those who are closely related (family, friends, close business associates) than with privacy; borrow and lend things often and easily" (ibid.).

In conclusion, "In monochronic cultures, time is experienced and used in a linear way – comparable to a road extending from the past into the future (. . .) P-time is characterized by the simultaneous occurrence of many things and by a *great involvement with people*" (Hall & Reed Hall, 1990, pp. 16–17). People working in the migrant reception system should be aware of the existence of different conceptions of time and be sensitive to that which they expect to encounter. Thus, the risk emphasized by Samovar et al. (2012, p. 297) may be avoided: "When cultures employ time in dissimilar ways, misunderstandings and even antagonisms can occur".

When people interact, their bodies move across space in ways which are associated to culturally pre-coded meanings: "*Kinesics* behavior is communication of the body in motion and includes aspects of people's facial expressions, body movements, gestures, and conversational regulators (. . .)" (Andersen, 2012, p. 296). Similarly, Ting-Toomey and Chung (2012), focusing on *facial expressions*, have noted that "there is consistency across cultures in our ability to recognize at least seven emotions in an individual's facial expressions. We can refer to these recognizable facial emotions by the acronym SADFISH: Sadness, Anger, Disgust, Fear, Interest, Surprise, and Happiness (Richmond & McCroskey, 2000). People are able to recognize not only the emotion but also the intensity of emotion and often the secondary emotion being experienced (. . .) However, the ability to recognize specific emotions on the SADFISH list may vary from one specific culture to the next" (p. 138). In this regards, Ting-Toomey and Chung recalled the difference between students from the USA and Japan emerging from several studies, which showed that the former "are better at identifying anger, disgust, fear, and sadness than are Japanese students (Matsumoto & Juang, 2003; Safdar et al., 2009). The reason is that Japanese students learn at a very young age to suppress their facial emotions because this display can be threatening to others and also create disharmony in their everyday relationships" (Ting-Toomey & Chung, 2012, p. 138).

Body movements include a wide range of actions, which may be classified into two main categories: *posture* and *gestures*. As Samovar et al. (2012) have stressed, "slouching, being stiff, slumping over, crouching, kneeling, pulling back one's shoulders, twitching one's legs, putting one's hands in pockets, bowing, and the like (. . .)" (p. 280) are cross-cultural examples of posture-related actions. However, the meaning of each of these elements displays significant variability across cultures, with implications when this variability is underestimated by those working in the migrant reception system. An effective example of this variability can be found in the meaning and management of the action of bowing. Unlike that generally inferred by Americans, bowing for the Japanese "is not a sign of capitulation, but rather it mirrors their value of status and respect. Actually, the Japanese have a wide range of uses for the bow. It can be a nonverbal way of expressing 'thank you', a greeting, an apology, a congratulatory gesture, and much more" (ibid.).

The same multiplicity of interpretation can also be applied to *gestures*, especially those of the hand: its use might lead to misunderstandings and confrontation between people of different cultures due to the marked variability in meaning. An example of this variability has been reported by Samovar et al. (2012, p. 282), who noticed that in the USA "making a circle with one's thumb and index finger while extending the others is emblematic of the word 'okay'; in Japan (and Korea) it traditionally signifies 'money' (*okane*); and among Arabs this gesture is usually accompanied by a baring of teeth, signifying 'extreme hostility'" (Harper, Wiens & Matarazzo, 1978, p. 164, as cited in Samovar et al., 2012, p. 282). Specifically, "To a Tunisian, the gesture means 'I'll kill you'. And in some Latino cultures the circle with the thumb and index finger is 'an obscene gesture'" (Samovar et al., 2012, p. 282).

Another important non-verbal code is *haptics*, which refers to the meaning and management of *touch*. "Every culture has a well-defined set of meanings connected with touching. That is, each culture defines who can touch whom, on what parts of the body, and under what circumstances" (Ferraro, 2006, p. 147). That is, each culture defines precise rules regarding touch which vary depending on variables such as sex and age. In this regard, Ting-Toomey and Chung (2012, p. 144) have noted that "same-sex touch and handholding in Malaysia, China, Sudan, Japan, Nepal, and Saudi Arabia are considered acceptable and part of daily life because contact among the opposite sex is inappropriate. This is better known as 'PDA', or the public display of affection. In the United States, same-sex handholding pertains to the gay/lesbian/ bisexual community. However, opposite-sex handholding is an appropriate PDA in the United States. Latino/as from Latin American cultural regions tend to engage in more frequent touch behaviors than do U.S. Americans and Canadians. But it is important to remember that the touch behaviors in both the Arab and the Latin American cultures are usually confined to same-sex touching, not opposite-sex touch". As reported by Samovar et al. (2012, p. 289), "So prescriptive are these 'cultural definitions' regarding touch that in the United Arab Emirates a British couple was sentenced to one-month in prison for kissing in public. You may recall the upheaval created in Great Britain when First Lady Michelle Obama was introduced to Queen Elizabeth and touched the queen as part of her greeting. Shaking hands and even hugging dignitaries is common in the United States; it is taboo in Great Britain". The author of this chapter reiterates the suggestion that people working in the migrant reception system should learn how to modify their own tactile behaviour to that of people coming from different cultures.

Of the different types of non-verbal behaviour, there is a further type of contact, that of *eye contact*, which belongs to the field of *oculesics*. As defined by Andersen (2012, p. 297), *oculesics* is "the study of messages sent by the eyes, including eye contact, blinks, eye movements, and pupil dilation (. . .). Because eye contact has been called an 'invitation to communicate', its variation cross culturally is an important communication topic. In North America and Western Europe direct eye contact communicates interest and respect, while Japanese people may look away from another's eyes almost completely to be polite" (Samovar & Mills, 1998).

When referring to contact – be it mediated by the hand or the eye – a well-known distinction is that between *high-* versus *low-contact* cultures. To quote Andersen (2012) once more: "Cultures that display considerable interpersonal closeness or immediacy have been labeled 'contact cultures' because people in these countries stand closer together and touch more (Hall, 1966). (. . .) Research has shown that high contact cultures comprise most Arab countries, including North Africa; the Mediterranean region, including France, Greece, Italy, Morocco, Portugal, and Spain; Jews from both Europe and the Middle East; Eastern Europeans and Russians; and virtually all of Latin America (. . .) low-contact cultures comprise Northern Europe, including Scandinavia, Germany, and England; British Americans; white Anglo-Saxons (the primary culture of the United States); and virtually every Asian country (. . .)" (p. 307). Other scholars in the field, like Ting-Toomey and Chung (2012), have emphasized that people from high-contact cultures "often look each other in the eye directly, face each other, touch and/or kiss each other, and speak in rather loud voices. East Asians and Asian Americans, such as Chinese, Japanese, and Indians, are members of low-contact cultures. Low-contact cultures often engage in little if any touching, preferring indirect eye gazes and speaking in a lower tone. The United States, Canada, and Australia are moderate-contact cultures, which is a blend of both" (pp. 144–145).

Ting-Toomey and Chung's reference to *voice volume* leads to another non-verbal code, that is, *vocalics*. Also known as *paralanguage*, *vocalics* "includes all the nonverbal elements of the voice (. . .) Research reveals that how a person's voice sounds can influence perceptions related to the individual's emotional state, social class, credibility, comprehension, and personality" (Andersen, 2012, p. 297).

As highlighted by Samovar et al. (2012), paralanguage can be divided into three categories:

1. *Vocal qualities* comprise volume, rate, pitch, tempo, resonance, pronunciation and tone. For example, "Arabs speak with a great deal of volume because for them it connotes strength and sincerity (…) For the Japanese, a gentle and soft voice reflects good manners and helps maintain social harmony—two important values in Japanese culture" (p. 291).
2. *Vocal characteristics* refer to non-verbal vocal behaviour including laughing, giggling, crying, moaning, whining, yawning, sneezing, etc, which are "vocalizations that convey a learned meaning for members of a specific culture. In both France and Argentina it is considered rude to yawn in public. And in much of Europe whistling during a public performance is a message of disapproval and ridicule. For many Muslims the simple act of sneezing is interpreted as 'a blessing from God'" (p. 292).
3. *Vocal segregates* include sounds like "uh", "oooh", "um", "mmmh", "shh", etc. They are "sounds that are audible but are not actual words. These sounds are used as substitutes for words. A case in point is the 'shh' sound produced by Americans when they are asking someone to be silent" (p. 292).

Even silence can have communicative value. "Intercultural miscommunication can thus often occur because of the different priorities placed on talk and silence by different groups. Silence can serve various functions, depending on the type of relationship, the interactive situation, and the particular cultural beliefs held. Silence can also serve as a powerful means of sharing or persuasion" (Ting-Toomey & Chung, 2012, p. 128). Substantial differences in the meaning and management of silence have been identified between people from Western and Eastern cultures. "In most Western cultures talk is highly valued, and it is often difficult to determine the meaning behind someone's silence, because it can be interpreted as an indication of agreement, anger, lack of interest, injured feelings, or contempt (…) It seems that there is a link between cultures that emphasize social interaction (Jewish, Italian, French, Arab, and others) and their perception of and use of silence. In fact, talking in these cultures is highly valued (…) In the Eastern tradition the view of silence is much different from the Western view" (Samovar et al., 2012, pp. 301–302). An apposite example of the complexity of silence can be observed in Japanese culture, in which the "emphasis on silence serves a variety of purposes. First, among family members, silence is actually seen as a way of 'talking' (…) Second, silence in Japan is linked to credibility (…) Finally, the Japanese also use silence to avoid both conflict and embarrassment" (Samovar et al., 2012, p. 303).

As physical contact between two or more people increases, not only individual non-verbal cues hitherto analysed can be noted but also body odour, whose study is termed *olfactics*, that is, "interpersonal communication via smell" (Andersen, 2012, p. 298). Many scholars agree that the perception of odour and odour preferences can depend on cultural factors such as familiarity. For example, Ayabe-Kanamuura et al. (1998) have observed significant differences regarding the perception of everyday odours between Japanese and German people. This study included a ranking of 18 odours according to intensity, familiarity, pleasantness and edibility. The results of this cross-cultural study demonstrated that "Significant differences were found between the two populations on all measures. Better performance by the Japanese in providing appropriate descriptors for 'Japanese' odorants and by the Germans for 'European' odorants supported the pre-selection of stimuli as culture-typical. Particularly clear differences between the two populations were found in pleasantness ratings. In general, a positive relationship was found between pleasantness and judgement of stimuli as edible, suggesting that culture-specific experiences—particularly of foods—may significantly influence odor perception" (p. 31). Similarly, in their comparative study investigating which feelings were associated with special odours between Swiss, British and Singaporean sample groups, Ferdenzi et al. (2011) observed more similarities between Swiss and British people but a greater number of differences between the two European and the Asian cultures. Indeed, Andersen (2012) has stated: "Olfactics, interpersonal communication via smell, has been virtually ignored in intercultural research despite its importance (. . .)" (p. 298). However, odour perception, classification and preference can be important aspects of intercultural communication since they can affect interactions in a variety of ways ranging from pleasantness to embarrassment or even avoidance.

In conclusion, a review of the literature relating to the culture-dependent differences of the meaning and management of eight NVC codes (physical appearance, proxemics, chronemics, kinesics, haptics, oculesics, vocalics and olfactics) suggests that the observations of McDaniel, Samovar and Porter (2012) regarding their research into intercultural communication also applies to the migrant reception system: "Nonverbal facial and body expressions, like language, form a coding system for constructing and expressing meaning, and these expressions are culture bound. Through culture, we learn which nonverbal behavior is proper for different social interactions. But what is appropriate and polite in one culture may be disrespectful or even insulting in another culture. People engaging in intercultural communication, therefore, should try to maintain a continual awareness of how body behaviors may influence an interaction" (McDaniel et al., 2012, p. 16).

4 Conclusion

This chapter has explored how adopting an intercultural perspective to managing the non-verbal codes of interpersonal communication can facilitate the reception and treatment of migrants. Despite the growing importance of computer-mediated communication in human interaction in recent years, interpersonal communication in the form of face-to-face interaction continues to play a fundamental role in establishing, maintaining and strengthening relationships. It has been widely acknowledged by many scholars that when other people's feelings and attitudes are interpreted, non-verbal cues are significantly more influential when compared to verbal messages. And interactions between those working in the migrant reception system and migrants themselves are not exceptions to this observation.

Many researchers contend that the managing of interpersonal interaction when dealing with migrants merits special attention since hosts and migrants often belong to different cultures, and this necessitates appropriate knowledge and skills relating to intercultural communication. Culture influences the way people interpret and use several categories of NVC codes, i.e. *physical appearance*, *proxemics*, *chronemics*, *kinesics*, *haptics*, *oculesics*, *vocalics* and *olfactics*. "Misinterpreting the nonverbal actions of people of different cultures is commonplace" (Samovar et al., 2012, p. 267), a fact which can also be applied to those working in the migrant reception system whenever they have not been sufficiently well trained in intercultural communication. In order to avoid this issue and develop effective relationships with the migrants, appropriate training should be made available to identify how each NVC code is framed by the culture of specific ethnic groups and the challenges associated with the use of a particular ethnic group's communication code. To quote McDaniel et al.: "Every day we encounter an overwhelming amount of varied stimuli that we must cognitively process and assign a meaning to (...) The volume of environmental stimuli is far too large for us to pay attention to everything, so we select only what we consider relevant or interesting (...) we see, hear, feel, taste, and even smell the world through the criteria that culture has placed on our perceptions (...) Thus, it is important to be aware of the more relevant socio-cultural elements that have a significant and direct influence on the meanings we assign to stimuli" (McDaniel et al., 2012, pp. 13–14). The adoption of an intercultural perspective to the interpretation and management of non-verbal codes of communication could lead those working in the migrant reception system to be more respectful and mindful and to form more fruitful intercultural relationships, ultimately facilitating the process of migrant integration into a given society.

References

Andersen P. A. (2012). The Basis of Cultural Differences in Nonverbal Communication. In L.A. Samovar, R. E. Porter, & E. R. McDaniel (Eds.), *Intercultural Communication: A Reader* (13th ed., pp. 293–312). Boston, MA: Wadsworth.

Ayabe-Kanamuura S., Schicker I., Laska M., Hudon R., Distel H., Kobabyakaw T., Saito S. (1998). Differences in perception of everyday odors: A Japanese-German cross-cultural study. *Chemical Senses*, *23*(1): 31–38.

Ekman P., Friesen W. V. (1975). *Unmasking the Face: A Guide to Recognizing Emotions from Facial Clues*. Englewood Cliffs, NJ: Prentice-Hall.

Ferdenzi C., Schirmer A., Roberts S. C., Delplanque S., Porcherot C., Cayeux I., Velazco M., Sander D., Scherer K. R., Grandjean D. (2011). Affective dimensions of odor perception: A comparison between Swiss, British, and Singaporean populations. *Emotion*, *11*(5): 1168–1181.

Ferraro G. (2006). *Cultural Anthropology: An Applied Perspective* (6th ed.). Belmont, CA: Thomson Higher Education.

Hall E. T. (1959). *The Silent Language*. New York: Doubleday & Company, Inc.

Hall E. T. (1966). *The Hidden Dimension* (2nd ed.). Garden City, NY: Anchor/Doubleday.

Hall E. T. (1983). *The Dance of Life: The Other Dimension of Time*. New York: Anchor Press/Doubleday.

Hall E. T., Reed Hall M. (1990). *Hidden Differences: Doing Business with the Japanese* (Reprint. 1st. ed. 1987). New York: Anchor Books.

Harper R. G., Wiens A. N., Matarazzo, J. D. (1978). *Nonverbal Communication: The State of the Art*. New York: Wiley.

Matsumoto D., Juang, L. (2003). *Culture and Psychology* (3rd ed.). Belmont, CA: Wadsworth.

McDaniel E. R., Samovar L. A., Porter R. E. (2012). Using Intercultural Communication: The Building Blocks. In L. A. Samovar, R. E. Porter & E. R. McDaniel (Eds.), *Intercultural Communication: A Reader* (13th ed., pp. 4–19). Boston, MA: Wadsworth.

Mehrabian A. (1981). *Silent Messages: Implicit Communication of Emotions and Attitudes*. Belmont, CA: Wadsworth.

Pauwels A. (1995). *Cross-Cultural Communication in Health Sciences: Communicating with Migrant Patients*. Melbourne: Macmillan Education Australia.

Richmond V., McCroskey J. (2000). *Nonverbal Behavior in Interpersonal Relations* (4th ed.). Boston: Allyn & Bacon.

Ruesch J., Bateson G. (1951). *Communication: The Social Matrix of Psychiatry*. New York: Norton.

Safdar S., Friedlmeier W., Matsumoto D., Yoo S. H., Kwantes C. T., Kakai H., Shigemasu, E. (2009). Variations of emotional display rules within and across cultures: A comparison between Canada, USA, and Japan. *Canadian Journal of Behavioural Science/Revue canadienne des sciences du comportement*, *41*(1): 1–10.

Samovar L. A., Mills J. (1998). *Oral Communication: Speaking Across Cultures*. Boston, MA: McGraw-Hill.

Samovar L. A., Porter R. E., McDaniel E. R., Roy C. S. (2012). *Communication Between Cultures* (8th ed.). Boston, MA: Wadsworth.

Thompson J. B. (1995). *The Media and Modernity. A Social Theory of the Media*. Cambridge, UK: Polity Press.

Ting-Toomey S., Chung L. C. (2012). *Understanding Intercultural Communication* (2nd ed.). New York: Oxford University Press.

Watzlawick P., Beavin J. H., Jackson D. D. (1967). *Pragmatics of Human Communication. A Study of Interactional Patterns, Pathologies, and Paradoxes*. New York: Norton.

Domenico Carzo, Antonia Cava and Gaetana Cava[1]

Chapter Twenty-Three Consumption of Culture by Young Migrants

Abstract: This study, with young migrants as its object, aims to examine the field of consumption of culture. Our attention focused on a wide range of cultural consumption, from reading to music, from cinema to use of various technological devices. The picture we will show is drawn from the actual corpus of semistructured interviews carried out with members of Messina's Chinese, Sri Lankan, and Filipino communities in the context of an ongoing research project. Part of our field study was dedicated to cultural consumption by young people who are children of migrants resident in Messina, both those born in Italy or those who came here to join their family. The hypothesis would be that fashions, rituals, and consumption filter down, at least in part, from the particularly receptive category that teenagers form to their immigrant contemporaries, who, in turn, are made permeable by the desire for integration they experience in addition to the typical characteristics of the age group.

1 Introduction

Cultural objects make a specific contribution to the definition of both individual and collective social identities, to the dynamics of economic and political groups, and to the structures of social inequality (Hesmondhalgh, 2002; Visconti & Napolitano, 2009). Thus, the cultural needs and consumption of immigrants give signals about how our identity is evolving: we believe that a better understanding of immigrants' lives enables to better understand what Italy, and in our case study, Messina, is like now (Corti & Sanfilippo, 2012).

Styles of consumption, viewed as styles of behavior and of self-expression, play an important part in the process of reconstruction of identity and relationships. Consumption has a role in how social identities are expressed and established: consumption is a constituent as well as an expressive act. By means of their consumer experiences, social actors create themselves and help to establish a series of cultural classifications, and in this way, they reorganize their

1 The chapter is the result of pooling of thoughts from the three authors. However, academically speaking the paragraphs should be attributed as follows: Domenico Carzo para.1, Antonia Cava paras. 2 and 5 and Gaetana Cava paras. 3 and 4.

identity and the world around them (Alberoni, 1964; Bourdieu, 1979; Veblen, 1899; Sassatelli, 2004).

There are some fundamental questions underlying this study. What does these young foreigners' cultural consumption consist of? Is it different to that of the Italians'? How does it change when they emigrate? Is there a particular preference for products of the culture of their home country? What are the significant variables in the consumer choices?

Our study, with immigrant citizens of foreign origin as its object, aims to examine that field of cultural production which "includes all those sectors of the contemporary economy which respond to the demand for entertainment, self-realization, identification, promotion and presentation of self, as well as information" (Santoro, 2008, p. 12–13). Our attention focused on a wide range of cultural consumption, from reading to music, from cinema to use of various technological devices. Television and the internet were objects of particular interest since these, like many cultural objects, act as a link with the home country and play the important role of maintaining a space for interaction between the latter and the country of immigration (Bonerba, 2013). The picture we will show is drawn from the actual corpus of semistructured interviews carried out with members of Messina's Chinese, Sri Lankan and Filipino communities in the context of an ongoing research project in cooperation with the Doctorate School of Migratory Studies of the University of Granada (Cava, Cava & Penna, 2018).

The specific survey objectives of the main project are: understanding the significance that immigrants attach to their television viewing habits, studying the relationship between immigrants' television viewing and their social interpretation of the definition of integration, and analyzing the effects that television images may have on their everyday life. The interviewees are Asian men and women between 30 and 50 years of age, given that the data at our disposal (Salanitro, 2012) indicates that this age group is the largest present in the area (31.96 % of foreigners).

Part of our field study was dedicated to cultural consumption by young people who are children of migrants resident in Messina, both those born in Italy or those who came here to join their family.

Asking oneself questions about second generations is a particularly useful way of looking at the future of Italian society, at the forms of social cohesion it needs, and at the production of new cultural identities which are being negotiated daily (Ceravolo & Molina, 2013).

We therefore met with male and female subjects, both those born in Italy whose parents had immigrated several years earlier and adolescents who had spent their infancy in their country of birth and who joined their parents in Italy when the latter had attained stability in their jobs and daily life.

This category of young people has specific characteristics which are in part different to the adult subjects involved in the study. Young migrants are indeed exposed to a deeper, more constant contact with the reality of life in Italy through their experiences at school and the friendships they establish with their Italian peers (Caneva, 2011; Ricucci, 2010; D'Ignazi, 2008). The hypothesis would be that fashions, rituals, and consumption filter down, at least in part, from the particularly receptive category that teenagers form to their immigrant contemporaries, who, in turn, are made permeable by the desire for integration they experience in addition to the typical characteristics of the age group. They are a constantly growing young and vibrant target, part of the most dynamic and active contexts of Italian society and, from the viewpoint of brands and the media, present important parallels with the Italian population.

We believe that research on young Italians of foreign origin should be seen as a valuable resource for study in the field of sociology of transnational migrations (Basch, Glick-Schiller & Szanton-Blanc, 1992).

2 Cultural Diets and Integration Processes

It is only recently that, thanks especially to the striking progress made with means of communication and the fall in communication costs, it has become possible for a migrant to be almost continuously and actively present within two physically separate societies. The migrants' access to cultural consumption occupies a significant place in the field of the complex relationship between the culture they live in and the culture they come from (Etchegaray, Correa & Portales, 2015; Giusiti, 2015). Cinema, theater, sporting events as well as traditional ethnic events which a territory offers to its citizens go to make up a corpus of entertainment resources and access to the symbolic culture within which individuals trace their own path based on the needs which spring from their life story and on negotiation with the subjects who make up the network of social relationships (Vittadini, 2008). The composition of their cultural diet thus corresponds to a choice of position with respect to their social surroundings and to the two cultures they belong to, the culture of origin and the culture of arrival.

This task is more complex for minors of foreign origin. After migration, adults preserve a sense of belonging to their culture of origin which is revealed in their maintaining habits of religion, of language, and of their life view. Adolescents, who are caught up in the migration process through a decision made by their parents, do not possess such clear and rooted references to their culture of origin because they construct their identity on models which belong to more than one culture (Bolognesi, 2008). On the one hand, then, they are obliged to keep up a constant dialogue with the traditions, the language, and the rules of their culture of origin, while on the other they construct other references which help them to understand the social and scholastic context and the symbolic languages of the territory they live in. Besides the difficulties which derive from having to face an evolutionary phase which is complex in itself – the transition to adulthood – there are the two-way stereotyped viewpoints (those of native Italians towards migrants and those their co-nationals have towards native Italians) and the limited opportunities of their context regarding access to services, regulations concerning citizenship and residence, availability of housing, and opportunities for qualified jobs (Spanò, 2011).

Is this dual sense of belonging a fracture or an opportunity?

We will see how it is almost possible to speak of a plural identity which is the fruit of this plurality of belonging. The adolescent migrants encountered in our study fluctuate between the lifestyles, values, and roles of the various groups they feel part of at the time and are continuously redefining their knowledge and experience. Young migrants belong to cultures in movement, which are plural and open. Indeed, their identity appears ever more defined by conditions of difference, multiplicity, and intersectionality (Sokefeld, 2002).

The young children of immigrants can, in a sense, be seen as pioneers. Indeed, the conditions in which they have to build their adult identity, made up of references, values, models of consumption, and behaviors which extend over a wider space than the mere local context, are beginning to be typical not only of children of immigrants, but of all young people in a globalized world. They are therefore – especially the privileged sector made up of young foreigners with greater cultural capital – a vanguard, precursors of situations and experiences which will presumably become common, a potential nucleus to refer to for the development of narratives, practices, and models of relationship with Italian society which will become more widespread. The daily lives of these young people are inhabited by intersecting practices, habits, and references to different cultural worlds (Eve, 2013).

We will proceed to identify cultural consumption as a method used by individuals to relate to the culture they live in and as strategies for importing an "ethnic dimension" into construction of their identity (Calabrò, 2013; Daher, 2012). We will attempt to analyze the plurality of their sense of belonging and their ability to combine diverse cultural references in their daily life, including through media experiences.

3 Methodology

The study aimed to examine some particularly significant aspects of contemporary integration processes (Bramante, 2011; Sciortino, 2015), such as media use by immigrants, the ways in which the migrants themselves acquire information about the reality surrounding them and about their country of origin. More specifically, the aim was to analyze the goods and services which migrants use to satisfy their cultural needs.

The initial phase of the study mainly involved collection and analysis of the existing literature, studies, and data. This contributed to the choice of the survey tools to be used and to selecting the men and women to be interviewed (Patton, 1980). The second phase consisted in field work comprising 60 semistructured interviews with migrants who belong to the Chinese, Filipino, and Sri Lankan communities at present resident in Messina. The interviews aimed to identify the migrants' cultural diets as a means to gaining a deeper understanding of cultural participation by a young population which will have an ever-stronger impact on the socio-urban fabric of Italian cities. Our interpretations of data took into account the presence of some differences linked to the migrants' specific cultural origins: the social and political conditions, the state of the media in their country of origin, and the reasons for migration (economic or political motives, whether they were single individuals or whole families, etc.).

The subjects for the interviews were selected using an "intentional sampling" method. This involves non-probabilistic sampling procedures and, as such, does not guarantee the statistical representativeness of its results. It would, however, have been impossible in any case to guarantee statistical representativeness because of both the limited number of interviewees and the type of survey tools used.

Although our study examines media consumption by migrants between 30 and 50 years of age, some interesting aspects of their children's media consumption emerged during the interviews. These adolescent migrants were frequently present during the interviews and took part in the conversations.

We felt, then, that the scenario of our analysis would be enhanced by including the most interesting data that came to light concerning adolescent migrants and cultural consumption.

4 Young Migrants' Cultural Consumption

In the past, it was easier to reconstruct the makeup of people's media consumption, which had definite time outlines. In the contemporary scenario, however, the all-pervasiveness of the media and their continuous use by "always-on" users makes it difficult to distinguish a moment when a person is not exposed to some kind of media stimulus (Di Fraia & Risi, 2018). Our interviews confirmed this pervasiveness of media exposure and the vast quantity of information channels available to young people. These channels include both information from the internet and news from mainstream media, and from television in particular. The interviewees name the television programs they watch and news sites with local information. The adolescents we encountered showed a prevalently recreational use of the social media, which are the main channels for the circulation of information among their peers (Riva & Scarcelli, 2016).

Our interviewees' cultural reference points and relationship systems vary across a sheaf of possibilities, ranging from a prevalent orientation towards Italy to a prevalent orientation to the country of origin. Hybridized forms of typical cultural reference points and relationship networks of the two societies can emerge, especially in the intermediate positions of the range.

In their daily life, the majority of young migrants relates to the country of origin – in the broadest sense, both as a physical location and as a set of relationships and cultural practices – as well as to Italy. However, in their personal experience, the two realities of reference may remain distinctly separate[2].

So, the point of contact between the two possible worlds of reference for these young people sometimes does not exist outside of their individual experience as migrants. Thus, they themselves are the linking and mediating element between the two different realities.

4.1 Television Consumption

Television plays a significant part in young migrants' organization of their free time. But what television do immigrants to Italy watch? The significance of television's role as an "ethnic anchor" is often overestimated, especially when considering the opportunities offered by satellite television. The research results do not necessarily indicate such a tendency, but rather show how Italian

2 At least three examples can demonstrate this. The first is the case of those who say they have friends here in Italy who form two separate groups, their fellow nationals and Italians, with the two groups never, or practically never, coming into contact. The second is the case of those who say they have relational contact with both Italians and non-Italians, but who use different tools – social networks, for example – for each of the two groups. The third is those who say they usually eat typical food from their country of origin at home and Italian food outside the home.

television can act as a powerful agent for socialization (in a positive sense) and for comparison-mirroring (often negatively) on the part of migrants to Italy. It is therefore necessary, when analyzing the integration dynamics that immigrants to Italy employ, to bear well in mind that these fellow citizens of ours are in close contact with the imagery of Italian television and, to a certain extent, show that they willingly absorb it.

Almost all the young migrants said they watch television. They seem more interested than adult immigrants in watching television, and this could be explained by their greater knowledge of the language and their higher levels of social and family integration, both deriving from the fact that all the young immigrants go to school. Consumption levels are high also in terms of frequency. It is important to note, though, that these high levels of television consumption are not indicators of scant use of other media; on the contrary, the young immigrants have a rich media diet, so this notable television consumption could indicate an interest in television as a means for acquiring knowledge of aspects of Italy which may seem obvious to Italians, but which are not so to them. The most popular consumption times are, first, lunch time, followed by early morning and early afternoon. Consumption levels fall perceptibly at supper time and after supper. Young boys and girls are more interested in entertainment, music, escapism and having fun.

Digital cable television is very popular because it offers wider variety, ranging from coverage of important public events to the niche programs of the numerous free monothematic channels (Censis, 2017).

The most popular channels are Italia 1 and Canale 5[3]. Entertainment/variety programs are the most popular genre, followed by TV series, sport and films, while there is very little interest in news and information programs. The most popular programs are Le Iene[4], Amici[5], Big Brother[6] and The Simpsons[7].

---

3 Commercial broadcasting networks on Italian non-specialist television.

4 An entertainment program whose hallmark is its irreverent style. It uses reporting and satire to examine Italian and international news.

5 This is the longest-lasting talent show on Italian TV: a school with a class of about 20 young students who hope to become dancers or singers.

6 A reality show based on the Dutch *Big Brother* format, broadcast in Italy from 2000. The participants are people who are unknown, or almost unknown to the general public, equal numbers of men and women of various social extraction and from various regions of Italy who live a communal daily life in a house where cameras follow them 24 hours a day.

7 A United States product with extremely satirical content and essentially based on Western middle-class themes.

A conclusion can be drawn from this: cultural integration actually comes about through pop culture. Pop culture is often criticized, because people do not realize that the "glue" of integration is hidden right there in the melody of a song heard on television. Although family habits do shape those of young people, consumption of films, TV series and entertainment programs exists and expands precisely because these provide currency for creating peer relationships, albeit in competition with internet use.

4.2 Use of Computers, Smart Phones and the Internet

The tendency to being permanently connected is encouraged by the diffusion of portable and personal computers and by the possibility of going online from ever more numerous devices. Internet use is becoming more and more individualized, personalized, private and mobile (Livingstone, 2011). The internet is an important element in responses to relational and social functions, as well as gaming. Features such as speed of access, flexibility of use, connection to global networks, digital disintermediation, personalization of schedules and breakdown of space and time barriers have become part of these adolescents' daily lives, just as they have for their Italian peers. The young migrants organize their communication activities through an interdependent combination of digital contexts. Use of the internet is certainly central, but it is combined with other means, both digital and non-digital. There are already 1 million children of immigrants in Italy and they are more "digital" not only than their parents, but also than their peers with Italian parents. Young people with a migrant background appear to be the high point of the internet generation, their behaviors tending towards a more intense use of new technologies (Istat, 2016).

The internet offers outstanding opportunities for learning and knowledge, but also and above all for mediation and socialization, and this has particular significance when processes of integration and cultural hybridization are involved.

There are high levels of self-declared competence in computer use: the young migrants are competent users, or competent enough to search for various types of information on the internet; to download music, films, and TV series; shop; and read online newspapers. Smart phones – cult objects with a strong symbolic, as well as functional, impact – are the most widely used device for managing online relational dynamics through social networks. Adolescents view social networks as their optimal relational universe, by means of which they put a personal filter on the outside world and share self-expression. Their identity becomes public because it is created for the web, their emotions travel through their smart phone keypad, and apps and digital technology can exponentially increase creative potential when they are used in a careful and positive way (Gardner & Davies, 2013). WhatsApp, Facebook, Instagram and Twitter have evolved from mere messaging networks into multichannel platforms for content distribution.

The internet has also become an essential tool for young migrants in the creation of a sociocultural space which links their country of origin to the country they have migrated to.

Of course, one of the main reasons for accessing the internet is to make contact with relatives and friends in the country of origin (or in other countries). The internet has given transnational families, with their physically and emotionally long-distance relationships scattered across nations and continents, a hitherto unknown frequency band closeness of contact. Desynchronized time, as a result of the many time zones, is re-synchronized thanks to digital technologies. Stratified living spaces, spread across various geographical locations, are reunified by the possibility of inhabiting analogous spaces online.

Our study revealed a continuous quest for dialogue through social networks and instant messaging services. The internet is used to keep in touch with peers through chat services or a personal profile on a social network.

4.3 Music Consumption

Music is an integral part of an adolescent's life – the communicative punctuation of growing up, of love stories and of disappointments. So it has great emotional significance.

Music consumption by second-generation migrants seems to give preference to music from their country of origin. It is music, rather than films or books, which expresses sentimental links to the country of origin.

Mp3s or Ipods are preferred devices; alternatively they listen to music on the internet or YouTube.

There is also appreciable interest in international and Italian music. They are assiduous participants at live music events at popular locations in town, particularly when these are free events organized by public or local institutions.

Among adolescent migrants, there is also a prevalence of choices linked to sharing music from radio channels, such as Radio 105 and Radio DJ, with peers. Native Italian peers are included in the sharing. Listening to the radio is, however, not very frequent and occurs mainly in leisure time and through the internet on a PC. Data show that, like their native Italian contemporaries, they prefer rap to Italian pop music (Osservatorio sulle Tendenze e Comportamenti degli Adolescenti, 2016). It is important to highlight the marked identification with the music of a country of origin where these young migrants have never actually lived; this is an opposite trend compared to use of other media, where Italian products are preferred, and to consumption habits among adolescents in general.

4.4 Books, Theaters, and Museums

The adolescent immigrants show no great affinity with books and their preferences definitely lie elsewhere. This is not to do with difficulties with the language, but simply a question of personal taste. The books they read are generally those recommended by their teachers, mainly novels or nonfiction, and are preferably read in Italian.

Going to school in Italy has enabled young migrants to have access to theater through their school. Thus theater becomes included in their experience of cultural consumption, and its inclusion in their extra-domestic cultural diet becomes more likely. Musicals and comedy shows are the most popular genres and are frequently seen together with native Italian peers. The structure of schooling in Italy also promotes visits to art exhibitions. Museum visits are part of their cultural diets as they are included in the extra-domestic activities of families with pre-adult children. Ethnic events provide opportunities for cultural consumption and enjoy ample participation. These events make possible consumption of products linked to the culture of origin (food, music, etc.) and let the young migrants come into contact with typical ways of socializing in their country of origin. Festivals organized by associations (often with a social purpose, such as aid to people in difficulty in the country of origin) and religious festivals are perceived as opportunities for meeting up and for consumption of cultural products, where the more regulated forms of participation generate greater trust and positive judgments in second-generation migrants. This second type of gathering also offers forms of theater, which seem to be preferred to more widespread theatrical forms.

4.5 Cinema Consumption

Second-generation migrants prevalently define watching films as an escape from reality, where there is less attention to content and more to sharing consumption with peers.

The choice of film is generally made on the basis of word-of-mouth information and on advertizing campaigns centered on mainstream consumption. Choices within peer groups (which tend towards action and horror films, or thrillers) are a relational resource and a resource for integration. Cartoons occupy a significant place in the field of cinema consumption, both for their intergenerational appeal and because the generic themes they deal with enable them to respond to emotional or other needs linked to the experience of migration. Reasons for choices then are linked to different definitions of the consumer experience, where the idea of cinema as an emotional experience or an escape from reality is dominant.

5 Conclusions

While the learning process for digital technology conforms to that of the host culture, we must examine those differences in the practical use of technology, which can be attributed to the existential condition of dual cultural belonging, and especially to the double structures of social networks, in Italy and in other countries.

The web presence of migrant communities in Italy is increasingly organized and may indeed be viewed as a sort of counterforce to the stereotyping processes through which traditional media have contributed to creating specific social representations of immigrants. Digital media have a decisive role in structuring the relationship immigrants have both with Italian society and with the society of their country of origin. For first-generation migrants this duality derives from a fairly basic interpretative template. On the one hand, means of communication and information are the main tool used by migrants for acquiring the knowledge and symbolic resources – including the language itself – which are necessary for interaction with the diverse cultures the migratory experience brings them into contact with, and with the final destination in particular. On the other hand, means of communication and information are the tool migrants use for maintaining contact and relationships with their country of origin and its culture. In the light of this, the greater consumption of country of origin media by first-generation migrants should not be seen as a sign of ghetto-ization and isolation, but rather as an indication of the migrants' ability to create a transnational space that amalgamates diverse elements of their daily lives.

When considering second-generation migrants, however, this interpretation is too limiting; any problems arising must take into account the age at migration. Non-Italian children born in Italy or who arrived in Italy at a very young age need to encounter and learn about the reality of their country of origin. Their parents and close relatives play a decisive part in this learning process through their storytelling and habits. At the same time, the internet makes it possible to create contacts and friendships with contemporaries of their own nationality, whether resident in Italy, in the country of origin, or in other countries, and to maintain and consolidate in the long term those relationships which have originated in long, short, recent, or more remote visits to the country of origin. Social networks can further contribute to defining and strengthening a sense of belonging to one's original society and culture. They also provide spaces where this sense of belonging finds expression – web communities with ethnic connotations. These communities can bring together – in a genuinely transnational perspective – people with a common nationality residing in various parts of the world. The foregoing in no way detracts from the fact that digital media have a key role in shaping the relations that immigrants have with Italian society and native Italians. The social media are able to sustain very intense and broad relational networks, which include both native Italians and migrants of different nationalities .

Young immigrants undoubtedly have a specific characteristic – the transnational nature of their life history. This is true whether they have had an actual experience of migration in their early life or whether they live, albeit as stable residents of Italy, the experience of belonging to more than one culture. At the same time, though, they are adolescents who are members of a specific youth culture, a "system of values and beliefs which permeates the behaviors of a specific age group and which exhibits distinctive characteristics" (Castello, 2008, p. 145). Young people are particularly open to more intense forms of integration because of their greater tendency to socialize and of their greater interest in and attraction to Italian cultural models (Santucci, 2004). Indeed, success in their own process of integration is what makes young migrants remain in Italy and give up any idea of returning to their country of origin. Italy is undoubtedly an attractive destination, both because it is a western country and is permeable (accessible borders) and offers a good quality of life: the integration process in Italy appears less complex and onerous than in other western countries. The young migrants involved in our survey have grown up in Messina – our field of observation – and their assimilation of behaviors and "signs" of the "locals" seems to be a "natural" process, in the positive sense of being in the nature of the things of life, a valuable part of integration, which is a premise for the best possible future for new generations (Caselli, 2009). Traditions from the country of origin are not viewed as a reality to be accepted or rejected wholesale, but rather as a range of opportunities and options to be taken – or not taken – into account according to the context or one's own personal inclination or personality[8]. Links

8 Another element to be highlighted is how maintaining some specific links with the culture of the country of origin, which may as has been mentioned combine with

are created, among other things, through use of a language, preparation of food, musical tastes, access to sources of information, and through forms of entertainment. These links are not an alternative, but indeed often coexist within limited fields of action, such as the close family. The experience of the children of the immigrants we interviewed reveals a combination of typical elements from the culture of the country of origin, from Italian culture, as well as hybrid cultural elements (Menotti Conti, 2004). The result is neither Italian culture nor the culture of the country of origin; it is the specific culture of these young people, second-generation culture, the culture of these young people suspended, as it were, between two diverse social and, of course, cultural contexts.

Appadurai (2001), for example, highlights the existence of diasporic communicative landscape, a space in the imagination where images, cultures, consumption models, references, and languages circulate and can, thanks to the new ways of communicating and transmitting information, be re-appropriated, whatever context one lives in. It is a polygamy of place (Beck, 2003), an open world which goes beyond the political borders of nations. In a global scenario, the whole concept of culture is reformulated. In a context of generalized movement and change, it cannot be considered an object which is external to an individual, predetermined, compact, integrated, and firmly fixed in place and time. Hybridization, blending, and liminality form the new lexicon applied to how we view culture today. The consequence is a profound change in what is meant by difference. In situations of everyday multiculturalism (Colombo & Semi, 2007), that is to say, concrete everyday relational situations in which difference is considered to be significant by at least one of the actors involved, the children of migrants often have an active role in giving a sense to their difference and their specificity, without this becoming a binding or un-modifiable essence or dissolving into a continuous flow that lacks stability or consistency. Difference is no longer a totally imposed entity, but is rather a result of dialogues and conflicts, the outcome of strategic action which may be orientated to various ends, such as influencing others, resisting dominant discourse, demanding recognition, and opposing discrimination (Colombo, 2011). The cultural transformations in a

---

elements of Italian culture to create new forms, depends in a significant way on the nature of the relationship parents or other important adult figures have with their culture of origin. Many young people listen to or watch news programs concerning their families' country of origin and listen to its music because their parents talk about the news at home, watch the news broadcasts and listen to this type of music. Similarly, young people often know and appreciate the traditional food from the country of origin because their parents keep these traditions alive in everyday family life.

global society are leading to a new view of identity – no longer something of fixed character, but a process of reconstruction of self. Ethnic origin is becoming a fluid, porous, and plural dimension of identity. The binary logic of belonging, which assumes that an individual can belong to one group only (Beck, 2004), is out-of-date; and spaces are opening up for multiple forms of belonging based on mediation, combination, and negotiation of diverse cultural codes in the field of interpersonal and social relations.

The principal aim of this chapter is not so much to present research results, but rather to develop reflections about the specific aspect of culture consumption as it relates to the lives of these adolescents, these young migrants. While they are decidedly anchored to the first-generation immigrants, they are also launched into a process of inclusion steeped in uncertainties.

Immigrants are no longer mere "objects" of media communication and representation, but are now above all real "subjects" on the multimedia stage, with their specific needs and tastes which are of increasing significance for cultural and editorial equilibriums in Italy.

For second-generation migrants, the internet is a resource for home entertainment, mainly 2.0 web services (music downloads, online shopping, watching YouTube videos, etc.), and for relational use (e.g., Messenger and Facebook) to keep in touch with their Italian or migrant peers.

Since habits of cultural consumption from within the culture of origin are absent, certain types of consumption are more easily absorbed into the cultural diet, as in the case of theater. Choices of cinema genre seem to tend more towards entertainment needs than towards seeking answers about forms of dialogue with Italian culture. Indeed, this kind of dialogue seems to be mediated far more by interaction with peers and by the choices of entertainment and cultural consumption made within this context than by more personal paths towards construction of a cultural diet.

Asking oneself questions about the second generation thus becomes the best method of discussion about the future of Italian society and new forms of social cohesion. It also lets us enter into the life experiences of these youngsters and so understand how family and social relations and the diverse cultural points of reference can come into play in the definition of identity and of relations with others.

References

Alberoni F. (1964). *Consumi e società*. Bologna: Il Mulino.

Appadurai A. (2001). *Modernità in polvere*. Roma: Meltemi.

Basch L., Glick-Schiller N., Szanton-Blanc C. (1992). *Transnationalism: A new analytic framework for understanding migration*. New York: Annals of the New York Academy of Sciences.

Beck U. (2003).*Un mondo a rischio*. Torino: Einaudi.

Beck U., Grande E. (2004). *Das kosmopolitische Europa. Gesellsschaft und Politik in der Zweiten Moderne*. Frankfurt: Suhrkamp Verlag.

Bolognesi I. (2008). Identità e integrazione dei minori di origine straniera. Il punto di vista della pedagogia interculturale. *Ricerche di Pedagogia e Didattica*, *3*, 1–13.

Bonerba G. (2013). *Da uomo marginale a cittadino globale*. Roma: Carocci.

Bourdieu P. (1979). *La distinction. Critique sociale du Jugement*. Paris: Minuit.

Bramanti D. (2011). *Generare luoghi di integrazione*. Milano: Franco Angeli.

Calabrò A. R. (2013). Di che parliamo quando parliamo d'identità? *Quaderni di Sociologia*, 63, 85–104.

Caneva E. (2011). *Mix generation. Gli adolescenti di origine straniera tra globale e locale*. Milano: FrancoAngeli.

Caselli M. (2009). *Tra due mondi e tra due culture: l'esperienza degli adolescente figli di immigrati a Milano*. Milano: FrancoAngeli.

Castells M.(2008).*Mobile communication e trasformazione sociale*. Milano: Guerini.

Castells M., Fernandez Ardevol M., Qiu J. L., Sey A. (2008). Mobile communication and society: A global perspective. *Economic Geography*, *84*(1), 119–120.

Cava A., Cava G., Penna, A. (2018). La televisión de los inmigrantes en Italia. In G. Tardivo & R. Barbeito (Eds.), *La sociología y el Sur de Europa. Italia y España ante el cambio climático y el fenómeno migratorio* (pp. 101–110). Barcelona: Editorial UOC.

Censis (2017). *14° Rapporto sulla comunicazione. I media e il nuovo immaginario collettivo*. Roma

Ceravolo F. A., Molina S. (2013). Dieci anni di seconde generazioni in Italia. *Quaderni di Sociologia*, *63*, 9–34.

Colombo E. (2011). *Le società multiculturali*. Roma: Carocci.

Colombo. E., Semi G. (2007). *Multiculturalismo quotidiano. Le pratiche della differenza*. Milano: Franco Angeli.

Corti P., Sanfilippo M. (2012). *L'Italia e le migrazioni*. Roma-Bari: Quadrante Laterza.

D'Ignazi P. (2008). *Ragazzi immigrati. L'esperienza scolastica degli adolescenti attraverso l'intervista biografica.* Milano: FrancoAngeli.

Daher L.M. (2012). *«Migranti» di seconda generazione. Nuovi cittadini in cerca di un'identità.* Roma: Aracne.

Di Fraia G., Risi E. (2018). Sbarchi mediatici. Pratiche di consumo mediale e rappresentazioni socio-narrative del fenomeno migratorio. *Mediascapes journal, 11*, 95–120.

Etchegaray N., Correa T., Portales D. (2015). Media consumption and immigration: Factors related to perception of stigmatization among immigrants. *International Journal of Communication, 9*, 3601–3620.

Eve M. (2013). I figli degli immigrati come categoria sociologica. *Quaderni di Sociologia, 63*, 35–61.

Gardner H., Davies K. (2013). *The APP Generation. How Today's Youth Navigate Identity, Intimacy and Imagination in a Digital World.* New Haven: Yale University Press..

Giusti M. (2015). *Immigrazione e consumi culturali. Un'interpretazione pedagogica.* Roma-Bari: Laterza.

Hesmondhalgh D. (2002). *The Cultural Industries.* London: Sage Publications.

Istat (2016). *Rapporto annuale. La situazione del Paese.* Roma.

Livingstone S., Haddon L., Görzig A., Ólafsson K. (2011). EU *Kids Online final report 2011.*

Menotti Conti G. (2004). La comunicazione come luogo e opportunità di integrazione. *Micro &Macro Marketing, 2*, 445–452.

Patton M. Q. (1980). *Qualitative Evaluation methods.* Beverly Hills: Carl-Sage.

Ricucci R. (2005). La generazione «1.5» di minori stranieri. Strategie di identità e percorsi di integrazione fra famiglia e tempo libero. *Polis*, XIX(2), 233–261.

Ricucci R. (2010). *Italiani a metà. Giovani stranieri crescono.* Bologna: Il Mulino.

Riva C., Scarcelli M. (2016). *Giovani e media. Temi, prospettive e strumenti.* Milano: McGraw-Hill Education.

Salanitro A. (2012). *L'immigrazione a Messina. Ricerca sugli stranieri residenti.* Messina: Anolf Cisl.

Santoro M. (2008). *Cultura in Italia. Media vecchi, media nuovi.* Bologna: Il Mulino.

Santucci C. (2004). I percorsi e i nodi dell'integrazione. *Micro &Macro Marketing,* 2, 11–25.

Sassatelli R. (2004). *Consumo, cultura e società.* Bologna: Il Mulino.

Sciortino G. (2015). *È possibile misurare l'integrazione degli immigrati? Lo stato dell'arte*. Trento: Università degli studi di Trento, quaderno 63.

Sökefeld M. (2002). Reconsidering identity. *Anthropos*, *96*(2), 527–544.

Spanò A. (2011). *Esistere, coesistere, resistere. Progetti di vita e progetti di identificazione dei giovani di origine straniera a Napoli*. Milano: Franco Angeli.

Veblen T. (1899). *The Theory of Leisure Class*. London: Macmillan.

Visconti L. M., Napolitano E. M. (2009). *Cross Generation Marketing*. Milano: Egea.

Vittadini N. (2008). Diete di consumo culturale e migranti. *Ikon-Forme e processi del comunicare*, 56/57, 13–37.

Marco Centorrino and Lilia Pellegrino[1]

Chapter Twenty-Four The Relationship Between School and Immigrant Families

Abstract: Our contribution intends to investigate, in the dimension of everyday life, one of the aspects through which – in our opinion – it is possible to analyze the dynamics of integration of immigrants in Italy. In fact, the increasing presence in recent decades of children of immigrant families within the Italian school has highlighted the need for constant and effective communication and interaction between the family and the school. The contribution focuses on the first results of a study, dedicated precisely to this aspect, carried out in a city in Southern Italy, in a lower secondary school that every year records a significant increase in pupils of foreign origin. Our work analyzes the perceptions of the teaching staff regarding the participation and involvement of immigrant families in the school context.

1 Introduction

In recent years, Italian society has witnessed a complex process of transformation in which immigration is a central factor[2] that has involved many spheres of social life, recalling the attention of all institutions. The school is one of those most interested in the search for new strategies to manage the changes generated by multiculturalism, also due to the fact that increasing number of pupils who attend the school are children of immigrants[3].Furthermore, the increase of pupils of immigrant families has further highlighted the importance of establishing points of interaction and communication between the family and

---

1 The work is the result of a common reflection among the authors. However, the Introduction, paragraph 2, and the Conclusions are to be attributed to Marco Centorrino and to Lilia Pellegrino pararaphs 1 and 3.

2 Between 2001 and 2011, the number of resident immigrants rose from one and a half million to 4.5 million. According to the most recent estimates, there are now fewer than 6 million (De Santis & Strozza, 2017). In 2016, almost 70,000 children of foreign-born children in Italy, or 14.7 % of all births registered in the country, but if we consider those born to foreign mothers, the percentage rises to 19.7 (Bonifazi, 2017).

3 In Italy, from 196,144 non-Italian students in the 2001–2002 school year (2.2 % of the school population) to 802,844 in 2015–2016 (9 %) (Dandolo, 2018).

the school. “The relational dimension is the engine of a process of renewal, the founding element of every intercultural educational project aimed at developing in all the students and their immigrant families the feeling of a multiple belonging that allows us to live harmoniously in societies as they are the current ones” (Silva, 2009, p.24). However, the school cannot be considered the only institution dedicated to the education of children and young people; at the same time, one cannot think that the family is solely responsible for this process. Both are essential parties in the socialization[4] processes of children and young people[5].This situation is even more important and often difficult to manage with regards to a foreign immigrant child who, accompanied by his family, experiences his first contact with the host country through the school. In this phase, the school has a fundamental role in supporting the processes of integration in the new reality, both with regard to families and towards students, and could be very effective if it were able to act as a “bridge” between the culture of the country of origin and that of the host country. Therefore, the involvement of immigrant families in schools could bring benefits for children who find themselves immersed in a foreign culture for them (Bolognesi, 2016). According to Cartei (2008), parents are the fundamental resource for achieving scholastic success: the different cultures they belong to require the school to identify the best tools for dialogue and the sharing of educational choices. Our research aims to investigate the state of family-school relations, focusing above all on the analysis of the perception by the teaching body of the participation of immigrant families.

As a point of observation, a lower secondary school in a southern Italian city, Messina[6], was chosen, characterized by a conspicuous presence of foreign

4 To be understood, obviously, as the primary channel of transmission of culture between generations.

5 Although the vision of educational responsibilities is not always shared between the figure of the teacher and that of the parent. For further information, see Molinari L. & Bertocchi S. (2007).

6 Messina is certainly the protagonist of the growing multi-ethnicity that now characterizes the country. The growth of the foreign population residing in the Messina area has changed considerably in a period of ten years. If in January 1, 2008 the total number of foreigners residing in the area was 6,991 (2.9 % of the resident population), on January 1st 2018 the numbers almost doubled: the foreigners living in the city are 11,885 (the 5th, 1 % of the resident population). As for their origins, Asia (58.4 %) is the continent from which most of them originate, followed by Europe (25.04 %) and Africa (14.2 %). There is also a minority of people from the American continent (1.9 %) and from Oceania (0.03 %). Now, like ten years ago, the most numerous foreign community

students of immigrant origin. Obviously, what emerges cannot be defined as a comprehensive picture, nor does the object of the research assume the value of a representative sample. However, ours can be interpreted as a pilot study, able to contribute to drawing up guidelines for a large-scale survey, which may also include an adequate deconstruction of the analysis with respect to the countries of origin of the immigrants.

2 State of the Art

In the family-school correlation the teaching body plays a very important role. It must do so in order to develop, encourage, and stimulate the participation of the families of its students and also to establish good communication with them to obtain positive and useful results for the development of the students' education. However, in the relationship with immigrant parents, teachers are often measured with educational styles different from their own. Certainly it is appropriate to state that the life that these families face is rather complex and in many cases merge a series of factors that do not facilitate their educational work and, consequently, affect the relationship between families and teachers.

Within this context, the inclusion of these students is often problematic: "MIUR data show cases of repetition that are much higher than those of Italian students, with a tendency much more evident in proceeding from elementary school to secondary schools" (Dandolo, 2018, p. 180). Added to this are higher scholastic dispersion rates compared to Italian pupils and peculiar problems regarding certain disciplines (Di Bartolomeo, Bonifazi & Strozza, 2017). On the other hand, however, "the majority of immigrant parents [...] consider the possibility of sending their children to school as one of the most positive aspects of their life in Italy: the school as a vehicle for social promotion" (Abis, 2004, p. 426). The factors that condition direct communication between teachers and families are in particular interpersonal ones. This "communication includes the ability to listen, exchange and share information, as well as the ability to collaborate around specific tasks" (Granata, Mejri & Rizzi, 2015, p.79).

is formed by individuals originating from the Sri Lanka with 32.9 % of all foreigners present in the Messina area. In second place was the Filipino community: in 2008 they represented 26.2 % of the foreign population and today they have fallen to 19.8 %, followed by Romania (12.9), Morocco (9.7), Greece (3, 3 %), the People's Republic of China (3.2 %), Poland (2.6 %) and the remaining percentage (15.6 %) concerns other communities (Demographic statistics, 2018). Istat 2018 data (http: // www.tuttiitalia.it/sicilia/38-messina/statistiche).

However, families do not always understand the demands of the school, often do not have clear objectives and educational goals and tend to see it as a place of mere transmission of disciplinary knowledge. For this reason, in many cases, families delegate to the school all the education of their children (Silva, 2009). “Interpersonal factors also include the emotions, attitudes and relational styles of the parent or teacher that can affect the family-professorsrelationship” (Granata, Mejri & Rizzi, 2015, p.79). The detached attitude on the part of most immigrant families is mainly due to the lack of knowledge of the Italian language[7]. However, it is not only a question of linguistic difficulty, but in broader terms the language of the school, whose codes and vocabulary are not always easily understood (Favaro, 2010). According to Grasso (2015, p. 211) “the cultural implications of which the educational models implemented are dense and the indecipherable and extreme specificity of the language used, sometimes make families’ sense of the actions and educational choices made by the school incomprehensible. Very often ambiguity and difficulty lurks precisely in the unsaid and in the misunderstood, compared to what on both fronts seems obvious and shared.”

Moreover, as already underlined by other studies, when faced with words such as “portfolio,” “primary school,” “educational credits,” or even acronyms such as “pof” or “invalsi,” families are in difficulty. These are terms that often convey the idea of a system that is difficult to interpret, even more so for those families from other countries (Zoletto, 2007). “This linguistic barrier has emotional implications for the relationship between parents and teachers, in a context that favors little or no plurilingualism and communicative exchange on multiple linguistic registers” (Granata, Mejri & Rizzi, 2015, p. 82). Therefore, there is a basic communication problem that is often not addressed by the school. The language barrier thus creates misunderstandings “sometimes even trivial, but which, if protracted, degenerate to the point of inducing parents to assume a detached attitude towards educational institutions and, on the other, teachers to build themselves a stereotypical image of immigrant families” (Silva, 2009, p.25). Then there are structural factors that greatly affect the participation of these

7 A factor that, of course, also strongly affects the educational performance of children. In this regard, it should be considered that the procedure for enrollment in the Italian school system of foreign students is not strictly bound to a certain degree of knowledge of the language, although an assessment test is required. Therefore, even students who do not speak Italian are included in the system and, at most, their path starts in one (and not more than one) previous class compared to the one that would have been assigned based on the correspondence of the title achieved in the country of origin. The schools, in this case, must include special recovery routes.

immigrant families in school life: problems concerning their socioeconomic situation, cases of social hardship, families in which parents do not work, and poor housing conditions. "Immigrant families belong more easily to a lower social class and this condition of theirs sometimes also affects the reality of school and the educational performance of their children" (Granata, Mejri & Rizzi, 2015, p.83). Structural factors include the working hours of immigrant families (often incompatible with school opening hours), their level of schooling insufficient to help their child with homework, as well as apathy, lack of interest towards the educational path of their child, and/or lack of motivation to participate in school life as it is not a priority (Bochaca, 2008). The framework is completed by those structural factors that refer to "the absence of an extended family network in the territory, in particular in a welfare system such as the Italian one based on the informal support of the extended family in the care of children" (Granata, Mejri & Rizzi, 2015, p.82). Finally, cultural factors[8] are those that bring together values, visions and imaginaries, lifestyles, and educational cultures, linked in some way to both individual and group cultural backgrounds that characterize both family and school actors and which can influence the relationship between them (Granata, Mejri & Rizzi, 2015, p.79).

In the background, the climate of the insertion of foreign families in the Italian context must obviously be considered. That of imitation is now – from the point of view of cultural and communicative processes – above all a field of increasingly saturated and "high-voltage" relationships: a network of interactions in strong evolution, whose energy intensity is destined over time to increase quantitatively and qualitatively for individuals and the community. We are dealing with an issue of primary social relevance, around which – not surprisingly – the space of public opinion appears to be inflamed by divergent orientations, points of view and polarities, and with respect to which the political decision-makers themselves continue to demonstrate blatant uncertainties and contradictions in governing the now irreversible multicultural transfiguration of the Italian society (Carzo, 2011).

3 Methodology

This study is part of a wider research, whose objective is to analyze and learn about the participation of immigrant families in a secondary school in the city

8 In this contribution, we consider as cultural factors those attitudes and behaviors that concern foreign families, according to the view that culture is not "only that of others" (Rogoff, 2003).

of Messina, "Manzoni-Dina and Clarenza,"[9] and to understand if this participation could give rise to processes of integration or exclusion. This chapter analyzes teachers' perception of the participation of immigrant families in the school environment. The techniques used to collect the information were: participant observation carried out through an observation table, document review, and semistructured interviews, in which anonymity was guaranteed and whose answers were recorded and transcribed textually. In each interview, an identification code was used for each teacher. These interviews took place one part within the school[10]and another good part outside[11]. The selected sample includes 36 teachers (8 men and 28 women). They are qualified teachers, who teach in the lower secondary school with heterogeneous years of experience (from 8 to 40 years). The faculty interviewed teachers in different classes[12], and their students have an age ranging from 11 to 14 years. The duration of each interview was between 40 and 60 minutes. This type of interview allowed the interviewed teachers to express their opinions, their attitudes, their concerns freely based on their own experience, and also giving interesting additional information[13].

---

9 The institute, consisting of the headquarters of the Manzoni Secondary School and including the complex of the First Degree Secondary School "L. Pirandello", welcomes 49 teachers, distributed in 19 classes and 7 sections. It is located in a central area of the city. The school population is heterogeneous (Table 24.1), only a small part of the students attending the institute does not reside in the surrounding area. The context of origin is varied and, broadly speaking, can be defined as medium. More sociocultural realities coexist: alongside the multi-income and single income families, there is a reality of families with youth unemployment, groups of unemployed, underemployed and precarious, there is no lack of cases of poverty. The lack of social and cultural services in the area, as well as of relevant productive activities, is the source of widespread discontent. Resources are not lacking, not always obvious and sometimes dormant, in terms of skills, traditions, historical-cultural assets, moral and civil values, which, in the synergistic commitment of institutions and communities, can promote concrete territorial development processes, of cultural elevation and mature civic-social participation. *La carenza di servizi sociali e culturali nella zona, come pure di rilevanti attività produttive, è fonte di un diffuso scontento. Non mancano le risorse, non sempre evidenti e talvolta sopite, in termini di competenze, di tradizioni, di beni storico-culturali, di valori morali e civili, che, nel sinergico impegno delle istituzioni e delle comunità, potranno promuovere concreti processi di sviluppo territoriale, di elevazione culturale e di matura partecipazione civico-sociale.*

10 Exactly in the auditorium.

11 In a public place, near the school.

12 Classes I, II and III. Sections A / B / C / D / E / F / G.

13 Four teachers refused the interview, justifying their refusal as follows:

4 Results

4.1 Family Participation at School and the Language-Relational Barrier

From the interviews with the teachers, the need for interest, dialogue, listening, sharing, and involvement from both parties, family and school, emerges as important, so that a positive relationship can be generated that can lead to an effective participation by families.

> P06: In my opinion these two important institutions have a common goal, namely the development and growth of the student. This is why both must work in the same direction. Therefore I believe that this union is important, collaborative and that it represents one of the variables that most influences school performance, especially for adolescent pupils. (Music teacher).
> P07: In my opinion these two realities symbolize an educational alliance. The teacher can get to know the students better, especially if he has the opportunity to meet with their parents. So, between teachers and parents, a real pact must be developed that will allow both of them to get to know the paths at school and at home, so that they can "build" their future together. (French teacher).

School life develops not only during class hours, but also consists of occasional interaction between teachers and parents, as well as certain shared appointments (such as, e.g., the election of representatives on Class Councils and in the Council of the Institute). In this regard, a teacher (P025) who has several immigrant pupils in the classroom told with a hint of bitterness about the experience of the last elections, in which for a class there was the participation of only two parents, which never happened in the past. If it is true that a certain number of Italian families did not participate, it is also true that the absence of foreign families was dictated by the fact of being excessively busy in the workplace.

The words of the teacher lucidly photograph the situation:

> P025: Within our Institute Council, we were thinking of proposing to some foreign parents to joint, because very few are currently part of it (and are even less those willing to be part of it). We were looking for a way to involve them more. We still

---

- P08: I don't have time to dedicate to your interview because I have other things to do after school! (Literature teacher)
- P018: No, absolutely not if he talks, I'm ashamed. (Technology teacher)
- P020: I'm sorry but I have absolutely no time to devote to your research. (support teacher)
- P026: Excuse me, but I had a series of commitments and problems that did not allow me to present myself at the appointment. (Spanish teacher)

> have to understand how these parents live and see the school and what do they think. By involving them in the moment of choice and decision, they would help solve the problems of the school. But thinking about their participation also means providing them with the tools to be able to participate actively. So they need to know and understand the Italian language at a conversational level or they must be joined by people who explain the dynamics to them. The matter is rather difficult, but the school must do something to bring them closer and make them an integral part of it. (Italian teacher).

According to this teacher and many others, the low presence of immigrant parents is due, in general, above all to the low knowledge of the Italian language. Therefore all the professors refer to the need to provide more resources from the school. They refer in particular to the need to train people who act as mediators, to facilitate communication and sharing with and between new families, since most teachers do not feel formed from a linguistic point of view and, therefore, there are limitations in the communication field.

> P021: Many immigrant families do not speak Italian well, we must take into account the language or languages of origin, age upon arrival in Italy, socio-economic situations and, of course, motivations with respect to the new language learn. There is therefore a communication problem that has not been taken over by the school. An Italian course for certain immigrant families would certainly facilitate their integration and consequently their participation [...]. However, the desire to learn is relevant. Unfortunately in this school or, better, in all the schools of this city, the figure of the linguistic and cultural mediator is absolutely absent. (Literature teacher).
> P027, P030: [...] The mediator would be the perfect figure that would allow a greater involvement of immigrant families. (both teachers of Religion).

The multiple testimonies[14]refer first of all to the vision of communication as a relational system, centered on the theses of the School of Palo Alto. The language barrier affects the contents and these, in turn, on the relationship. This happens

14 The answers of other teachers are also indicative:

- P014: It is necessary that there is a professor or an association that favors communication between the school and the immigrant families and that, therefore, has an understanding of interculturality. (physical education teacher)
- P019: What would help facilitate the integration of these families is the figure of the mediator that is lacking in the Messina school, also because we teachers do not have the linguistic preparation to be able to [refer them to parents] welcome and accompany during the school path of your child. (Literature teacher)
- P05: [...] the faculty at a cultural level seems to me to be quite prepared, but on a linguistic level it could encounter serious difficulties in expressing and understanding. I, for example, had two Chinese students last year, brother and sister had been here for a very short time. With the boys I used a Chinese vocabulary, I transcribed the

despite many families, apparently, showing a positive attitude towards the Italian language and culture:

> P04: They have been striving since their first entry into school to use the Italian language perhaps wrongly, initially monosyllabic, but the commitment is truly remarkable, indeed they are often ashamed, in the sense that they do not express themselves for fear of linguistic mistakes [. . .]. (English teacher).

The figure of the mediator could certainly have a relevant role, however – referring to the results achieved in the field of studies on intercultural communication (Gudykunst and Mody, 2002; Baraldi, 2003) – it is necessary to intervene on multiple fronts. On the one hand, in fact, it is necessary to keep in mind the concept of communicative competence, that is, the possession of the "sensitivity, knowledge and skills necessary to be able to interact effectively and appropriately with people of different cultures" (Chen &Sarosta, cit. In MucchiFaina 2006, 102). In this perspective, in terms of effects, uncertainty in interaction and miscommunication become central (the misunderstandings that can influence the order of the interaction itself). On the other hand, however, it is necessary to remember how – recalling the dynamic model of intercultural sensitivity (Bennett, 2002) – the acquisition of intercultural competences takes time and is closely connected to the exposure of the individual to experiences of cultural otherness, but also to his willingness to develop assessment and observation systems that can change according to the diversity of contexts. This obviously applies to both teachers and families. It is essential to complete a path that, starting from the ethnocentric phases of the experience, leads to the ethnorelative ones (through, in fact, a dynamic model). The scheme that allows progress to be made through the various phases involves the recognition of difference (acceptance), the development of empathy and closeness (adaptation), and, in the end, internalization (integration).

4.2 The Degree of Family Involvement

With reference to involvement in the school, different degrees and forms can be distinguished, as shown by the words of the teachers:

---

word in Chinese, I wrote in Italian and I put the symbol. In Sciences, in the same way, the image and, therefore, the word in Italian with the image. Then, another colleague did literacy, as if they were in first grade; just with the syllables and things, little by little we managed to get them expressed in Italian, let's say precisely that the first year with them we did not follow the same programming. (Mathematics and Science teacher).

P09: Surely the involvement is medium-low for immigrant families. Even willing, they cannot cooperate due to time, work, and money; instead Italian families are more present and willingly get involved, but perhaps because they have more time available or are helped by relatives. (Literature teacher).
P013: [. . .] The overall involvement is medium-high for Italian families, but medium-low for foreign families, probably because they can spend less time at school for work reasons. (English teacher).
P014: In my opinion, the immigrant families who come to us are all busy, have a lot of work and little time to spend with their children. But there are those families belonging to ethnic groups who care more about their children's schooling, so we are faced with a diverse range of families and heterogeneous involvement. (physical education teacher).

On the sidelines, it is interesting to note how the variable of work commitments seems to underline an almost exclusive participation of mothers at school-family meetings[15], giving us a picture that is in line with the overall picture of our country[16].

P01: [. . .] mothers are more present, probably because not all of them work, especially the native mothers (teacher of Art Education)
P02: Mothers are more present at interviews, meetings and various meetings because they have more time to spend within the school. (Literature teacher, referent of the multicultural area).

More generally, the aspect of work commitments that, according to the scenario outlined by the teachers, see immigrant families more involved refers to a broader reflection. First of all, we need to start from the role of immigrants in the Italian labor market and the differences with respect to the natives. Consider, for example, that 31.3 % of non-EU residents are employed in the collective

15 On this point, a teacher offers an alternative view:

- P06: Surely the mother participates more in school because above all in some cultures and / or by tradition the husband attributes this exclusive role to the woman, who is more interested in the education of her own child or children probably because she is the one who feeds more cultural expectations towards one's child (s). (Music teacher).

16 Mencarini (2018) notes that in Italy the "female employment rate (from 20 to 64 years) remains among the lowest in Europe: despite rising after the years of the Great Recession, it reached only 52.5 % in 2017, with a gap with male employment among the highest, although – thanks to a higher male unemployment rate – it fell below 20 %. In the same year the female employment rate was almost 60 % in Spain (with a gender gap below 11 %), in France almost 67 % (with a gap below 8 %), in Sweden almost of 80 %, with a 4-point gap " (p. 766).

services sector and to people (mostly caregivers, domestic helpers, babysitters, and domestic workers), while Italians working in the same sector register a percentage equal to 5.2 %[17]. And, again, one migrant out of three (36.5 % of the total) accepts humble jobs, generally underpaid, a percentage that among Italians is reduced to 8 %[18]. The issue of economic inequalities not only continues to be relevant in our country, but it should also be remembered that engages immigrants mostly. An inequity that can only be partially corrected by policies of redistribution and welfare (Saraceno & Saraceno, 2019). On this front, the school can partially affect, if not through a formative function which, it is hoped, can implement, albeit indirectly, opportunities for social mobility also for students coming from immigrant families. At present, however, it is called above all to adapt, perhaps providing services and facilities that give, in logistical terms, greater opportunities for participation by all parents. The physical presence, however, is not the only variable on which to measure the involvement of families. Another form of sharing – for most teachers – is represented by the social and emotional support that these express towards their children.

The most common strategy is enrollment in extracurricular activities, so that the students relate to their companions even outside the school.

> P017: The young people who receive support immediately notice each other, in the meantime because they come to school, hence the motivation for learning, integration are stimulated at home because they have to study, they have to go on. Then you see these very attentive boys, very fearful if something didn't take place, participate, try not to make mistakes. Parents, some and not all, show interest and try to ensure that their children attend extracurricular activities so that they can relate to all the other companions. (Music teacher).
> P011: [. . .] It is important to motivate the learning process of the students during the school journey and to help them to the extent that they can, to encourage them more and more. This is especially true for those children whose parents are little involved in their children's lives. (Physical Education teacher).

According to several teachers, the family must undertake to develop the social relations of their children through various initiatives, in particular by enrolling them in extracurricular activities that are organized at school (sports,

17 For an overall picture, see the VII Annual Report "Foreigners in the labor market in Italy" (2017) available online at: http://www.lavoro.gov .it / news / Pages / Presented-the-seventh-annual-relationship-Foreigners-in-market-work-Italy.aspx.

18 The figure is taken from the "XXVI Immigration Report 2016" by Caritas and Migrantes, available online at the site: http://s2ew.caritasitaliana.it/materiali/Rapporto_immigrazione/2017/Sintesi_RICM2016.pd.

linguistic-cultural, and educational excursions in which they participate together with families).

> P027: [. . .] Very often parents, too involved in their work, do not think what is right or not right for their children, so I believe that families should better solicit, encourage their children to engage in extracurricular activities that they certainly do well from a cultural, relational and, therefore, social point of view. (Religion teacher).
> P028: I believe that parents should know more about their children and for this reason it is important to have a dialogue followed by perhaps non-assiduous participation by the family in school, even if only to know the companions of their child, the school performance. Unfortunately, alas, some boys feel abandoned, little considered by the family. (Literature teacher).
> P030: In my opinion, the integrative aspect is the most important and it is precisely this that acts as a glue and that should be developed more. I say this because I happened to notice with some of my colleagues the fact that several foreign boys tend to have curricular and extracurricular relationships only among themselves 20 and, on the other hand, assuming this attitude they move away from other native boys. Consequently it happens that on the occasion of birthday parties Italian children do not invite them because they already perceive that it would not be a pleasure for them. Let's say that in this case the family should intervene, making it clear to these foreign students that it is important to relate to everyone without differences, but often this does not happen because families also tend to talk more with those belonging to their nationality. [. . .] (Religion teacher).

The teachers' observations, therefore, tend to emphasize the *responsibility for what to do* (Jonas, 1979) which obliges actions designed for the well-being of others, which the family must assume. In recent school years, to allow greater involvement of families, a series of inclusive initiatives have developed in which the families themselves have intervened in a varied manner. In this regard, we report some of the statements made by the interviewed teachers:

> *P04: Many families, more local than foreign, have participated in activities, laboratories, work for school projects, thanks to the stimuli dictated by the school. (English teacher)*
> P05: [. . .] From the various conversations I have had, I know that several immigrant parents have some very creative ideas, but they never take the initiative to expose them for fear of making mistakes, of not feeling up or of not being adequate to the context. (Mathematics and Science teacher).
> P02: [. . .] The activities promoted by the school are not so many, but those carried out try to make families participate, collaborating with each other and bringing their own ideas and, even better, linked to different cultural traditions. I remember that last year the school decided to promote a day dedicated to ethnic multiculturalism, in which each family cooked a typical dish of their country at home and took it to school, placing it on a well-laid table. You could taste many different foods and this allowed many families to get to know each other, to exchange their ideas and traditions, not only gastronomic. I clearly remember that that day was really appreciated by both children and families

> and ended with the performance of Italian boys who honored immigrant families with a song in English. Conversely, foreign boys sang a song in Italian. From there I really understood that the school represents an important institution, aggregating and therefore acting as a common thread between the various cultures, languages, religions and that barriers do not exist, but if they are created by those who have never experienced similar situations. (Literature teacher, referent of the multicultural area).
> P022: Since the beginning of last year we have had the pleasure of starting the intercultural project called "The rainbow of cultures", represented by a series of different laboratories [image and theater; sculpture, drawing and manual work; music; English language; Italian language, the rediscovery of poetry]. This project is mainly aimed at pupils, but is also open to families and their collaboration. In fact, I have to say that several families have created a WhatsApp group to organize and coordinate with each other. They are interested in the material to be purchased, they have always contacted us teachers for some doubts or even thoughts and advice. These workshops were held and held every 15 days, [...]. However, both the day and the timetable have always undergone changes depending on the availability of families, so that those who had greater job difficulties could participate. The immigrant families, however, were and are in a strong minority [...]. (Literature teacher).

Another obstacle that prevents the involvement of immigrant families, and not so much of indigenous ones, refers to the presence or not of public services linked to welfare policies and social inclusion. These are elements that greatly influence the family-school relationship. As already mentioned, one of the structural factors intended as an obstacle concerns the absence of an extended family network. In fact, according to some teachers:

> P09: [...] Families of foreign children do not often come to interviews, not because they are uninterested in their child's education, but because they do not have the support of the extended family network: grandparents, uncles, etc. Several parents do not they often participate because they do not know materially to whom to entrust the boys. Contrary to what happens in native families where the support of the family network is really wide. (Literature teacher)
> P012: [...] Almost always many immigrant families do not know who to entrust their children even just to go for a medical examination and, therefore, are forced to take them with them. Others, indeed, leave them alone at home even though they are still minors.

Some interviewed teachers stress the importance of enhancing the parents' cultures of origin, as a factor that can facilitate relationships and collaboration.

> P031: [...] Some immigrant families want to talk about their provenance of origin, their studies, their graduation, the chance they had of being able to live in a splendid house equipped, do not like to be considered just for the current precarious situation that they live in Messina, but for all their life experience, like an Albanian father who

> works in Villafranca, in the province of Messina as a bricklayer and in his country he was a teacher. (Support teacher).
> P032: Based on my scholastic experience I have always noticed that there are some families such as Albanians and Arabs who are very keen to let people know that they too have studied in their countries, but unfortunately personal education was not enough for them to be able to go ahead and, therefore, often begin during the reception hours to tell me about their experiences, what they had and then lost. This is why they have high expectations of their child. (Literature teacher).
> P024: [. . .] but it would also be right to enhance the cultures of each family, because they represent a strength. In fact, the school would never allow itself to cancel their culture and, therefore, their identity, indeed for the school the cultural diversity represents an added value, otherwise we could not talk about our school as an inclusive school under the different points of view. (Mathematics and Science teacher).

Therefore, it is clear that cultural factors are not only obstacles, but often act as a resource in the family-school relationship.

5 Conclusions

From the interviews carried out we realized how important and sometimes difficult it is to be able to establish a reciprocal relationship that allows a full involvement of immigrant families within the school context. Behind the efforts put in place to encourage the development of this relationship, there is the goal of making the pupil feel good, of fostering his development, and making sure that he can integrate into society in the best way. According to the teachers, the communicative aspect of listening and sharing is important to make a relationship effective. Even Garreta and Maciá (2017) state that communication must be two-way to achieve effective participation. According to Dubet (1997), it is necessary to establish a new agreement between families and school to lead back to a situation in which the school should enhance involvement, teachers maintain their right to exercise freely, and parents to defend their interests and those of their children. From what we can see from our survey, an important result shows a greater participation of local families and less than immigrant ones. The obstacle factors that emerged from the statements of the teachers and that prevent the involvement of these families within the school context can be summarized as follows:

- The lack of a linguistic and cultural mediator that facilitates integration and participation starting from the knowledge, understanding, and correct use of the Italian language;
- Lack of adequate training in foreign languages among a large number of teachers;

Tab. 24.1: Distribution of foreign and indigenous pupils in the first, second, and third grade of secondary school classes of the "Manzoni-Dina and Clarenza" Institute of Messina.

	First Grade		**Second Grade**		**Third Grade**	
	2018–2019		***2018–2019***		***2018–2019***	
Nationality	*N*	*%*	*N*	*%*	*N*	*%*
Romanian	3	2,08	1	0,80	0	0,00
Philippine	4	2,78	2	1,60	2	1,94
SriLankan	2	1,39	3	2,40	1	0,97
Chinese	1	0,69	0	0,00	2	1,94
Senegalese	0	0,00	0	0,00	0	0,00
Bangladeshi	0	0,00	1	0,80	0	0,00
Italian	129	89,58	111	88,80	96	93,20
Maroccan	3	2,08	3	2,40	1	0,97
Gambian	0	0,00	1	0,80	0	0,00
Ivoriana	0	0,00	1	0,80	0	0,00
Sierra Leonean	0	0,00	1	0,80	0	0,00
Ukrainian	0	0,00	0	0,00	0	0,00
US	1	0,69	1	0,80	1	0,97
Brazilian	1	0,69	0	0,00	0	0,00
Total	***144***	***100,00***	***125***	***100,00***	***103***	***100,00***

Source: Own processing
Key: N= number of scholars; %= percentage of the total

- The socioeconomic instability of families and, therefore, the difficulty to sustain some expenses;
- The incompatibility of working hours with school opening hours that do not allow immigrant families to participate in meetings, school activities, and/or other meetings;
- The absence of an extended family network in the territory, which allows families to be more present and participatory in school.

Certainly, these factors take on a strong weight in making the relationship of participation and therefore of involvement with immigrant families more or less effective. Alongside all this, some considerations related to functionalist sociological studies dedicated to the concept of education, which can constitute a further obstacle, must obviously be taken into account. Thanks to educational systems, in fact, individuals acquire the knowledge and skills necessary to live in society. Moral and social values are therefore found in the school training programs. But what we have to deal with are the inflexible social values. A society in which resistance to broadening the sphere of fundamental values is recorded – the many episodes of intolerance that we witness every day – is also reflected in the scholastic institution and on morals and social values that it proposes. In the wake of conflicting thought, it should be pointed out that, in societies marked by social inequalities, educational systems actually strengthen them and school education makes the interests of dominant social groups.

References

Abis M. (2004). Background e motivi della ricerca: fra integrazione e integrazioni. *Micro & Macro Marketing*, 2, 421–427.

Baraldi C. (2003). *Comunicazione interculturale e diversità*. Roma: Carocci.

Bennett M. J. (a cura di) (2002). *Principi di comunicazione interculturale.* Milano: Franco Angeli.

Bochaca J. G. (2008). Escuela, familia de origeninmigrante y participación School, Immigrant Families and Participation. *Revista de Educación*, 345, 133–155.

Bolognesi I. (2016). Coinvolgere i genitori nella scuola multiculturale. Un progetto di ricerca azione per la costruzione di una cultura della partecipazione. *Rivista Italiana di Educazione Familiare*, 2, 81.

Bonifazi C. (a cura di) (2017). *Migrazioni e integrazioni nell'Italia di oggi*. Roma: Consiglio Nazionale delle Ricerche, Istituto di Ricerche sulla Popolazione e le Politiche Sociali.

Cartei C. (2008). Una Scuola dell'infanzia accogliente, tra aspettative delle famiglie immigrate ed esperienze in atto. *Rivista Italiana di Educazione Familiare*, 3(2), 73–85.

Carzo D. (2011). Discorsi e narrazioni sull'Altro: un'introduzione sul fenomeno immigratorio. In D. Carzo (a cura di) *Narrare l'Altro. Pratiche discorsive sull'immigrazione*(pp. 11–18). Roma: Aracne.

Dandolo F. (2018). Una rassegna sui temi dell'immigrazione in Italia. *Rivista economica del Mezzogiorno*, 1–2, 167–186.

De Santis G., Strozza S. (a cura di) (2017). *Rapporto sulla popolazione. Le molte facce della presenza straniera in Italia.* Bologna: Il Mulino.

Di Bartolomeo A., Bonifazi C., Strozza S. (2017). Figli degli immigrati e riuscita scolastica. In C. Bonifazi (a cura di) *Migrazioni e integrazioni nell'Italia di oggi* (pp. 171–182). Roma: CNR IRPPS e-Publishing.

Dubet F. (1997). *École, familles: le malentendu.* Paris: Les Editions Textuel.

Favaro G. (2010). Una lingua "seconda e adottiva". L'italiano delle seconde generazioni. *Italiano LinguaDue*, 1, 1–14.

Garreta J., Maciá M. (2017). La comunicaciónfamilia-escuela. In J. Garreta (coord.) *Familias y escuelas: discursos y prácticassobre la participación en la escuela* (pp. 71 – 98). Madrid: EdicionesPirámide.

Granata A., Mejri O., Rizzi F. (2015). Non è solo questione di cultura. Fattori di ostacolo erisorse nella relazione famiglia-scuola dell'infanzia. *Rivista Italiana di Educazione Familiare*, 10, 77–91.

Grasso M. (2015). Il successo scolastico dei giovani figli dell'immigrazione: il ruolo della famiglia come capitale sociale. *Rivista italiana di educazione familiare*, 10(1), 201–216.

Gudykunst W. B., Mody B. (Eds.) (2002). *Handbook of International and Intercultural Communication.* Thousand Oaks: Sage.

Jonas H. (1979). *Das PrinzipVerantwortung.* Francoforte: Verlag (trad. it. *Il principio di reponsabilità. Un'etica per la civiltà tecnologica.* Torino: Einaudi, 1990).

Mencarini L. (2018). Padri e madri, lavoro e famiglia: un Paese non al passo coi tempi. *il Mulino*, 5, 766–773.

Molinari L., Bertocchi S. (2007). La responsabilità a scuola e in famiglia. Una ricerca su insegnanti e genitori.*Giornale italiano di psicologia*, 4, 901–920.

Mucchi Faina A. (2006). *Comunicazione interculturale. Il punto di vista psicologico sociale.* Roma-Bari: Laterza.

Rogoff B. (2003). *The Cultural Nature of Human Development.* Oxford: Oxford University Press (trad. it. *La natura culturale dello sviluppo.* Milano: Raffaello Cortina, 2004).

Saraceno P., Saraceno C. (2019). Contro le disuguaglianze insostenibili: non solo Welfare. *il Mulino*, 2, 254–261.

Silva C. (2009). La relazione tra genitori immigrati e insegnanti nella scuola dell'infanzia. *Rivista Italiana di educazione familiare*, 3, 23–36.

Zoletto D. (2007). *Straniero in classe. Una pedagogia dell'ospitalità.* Milano: Raffaello Cortina.

Alessandro Cutrona

Chapter Twenty-Five "The Other" in the perspective of Moravia and Pasolini

Abstract: This chapter examines the perspectives of two of the 20th-century's greatest Italian and European authors, Pier Paolo Pasolini and Alberto Moravia, as well as certain markedly topical elements within their autobiographical and literary work. In particular, it will focus on the relationship they both developed with Africa, each playing their part constructing a creative and symbolic dimension. On this basis, it will be possible to study the Other from a perspective devoid of ethnocentrism and stereotypes of any kind, thanks especially to the method of "going native" (Brugnolo, 2017). It will be essential to analyse the development of the figure of the Other in the literary and visual work of the two authors and essayists: an essential step towards understanding and sharpening our focus within a multicultural and inclusive society.

1 Introduction

A literary text, despite striving to describe the forms of Otherness that threaten a civilisation from the inside or outside, also allows us to see ourselves reflected in these forms of Otherness from a safe distance (Brugnolo, 2017). Western, or even better, globalised man, in the borderless stories that he reads, finds in them a part of himself and of the other, and therefore of a certain "us", in equal measure imaginary and universal. The theme in question is very common in 19th- and 20th-century Western literature, and one that has never been studied systematically: that of "going native". "Going native" is a term coined to describe the phenomenon of Western explorers of a certain geographical and anthropological Otherness "losing themselves" in this Otherness. No longer identifying with "their own" people, they associate more closely with the "Others", and assimilate with their ways of life and thinking.

Literature is an edifying component of human consciousness, an educational image of a personal mental heritage created to inspire a sense of civilisation that makes the reader feel actively part of their community. At the origin of it all is the underlying question of how to understand our individuality within a wider whole, and how this subjectivity relates to the human condition and interpersonal relations: finite entities in relationships with other finite entities. Literature, however, "*è il luogo del finito che parla all'infinito*" ["is the space within which the finite speaks to the infinite"][1]. Stories are the space within which the narrating subject recognises himself and asks to be recognised. As Paul Ricoeur posited: through stories, we can combine our multiple experiences, recognising meaning in them. Ricoeur interpreted the identity of the self as a "narrative identity", shaped through the art of telling stories, modes of telling stories and creating fiction, as part of a project that brings both the self and the Other into play. Even when it takes us back in time, literature can provide answers and possible inroads towards valid discussion about social relations and multicultural exchanges in the post-modern age. The focus here is on the Other, Third-Worldism and the African dream of a certain non-circumscribable pan-meridionalism at the frontier of democratic culture. All of these are central themes in Pasolini's work. His work consistently addresses social issues and features marginalised people and minorities. He frequently depicts the rural, dialectal world of the South in a broad sense (Southern Italy and Africa included): fully fledged poetic and political universes, self-contained whilst, at the same time, interconnected.

His visit to Kenya in 1961 with Alberto Moravia and Elsa Morante was only the first of a dozen such African journeys[2]. On these trips, the act of circumnavigating foreign lands represented "poetic survival": a strange, primigenial space in which to salvage words by then overcontaminated by the European man. Important features of Pasolini's work are the transnational and Third Worldist perspectives, and the political role of African Americans; aspects somewhat overlooked by the existing literature, which identifies him primarily as an "Orientalist".

Several works and projects were dedicated to Africa: prose, poetry, articles, travel memoirs, the screenplay *Il padre selvaggio* ["Primitive Father"] and the films *Un'orestiade africana* ["African Orestes"] and part of *Mille e una note* ["A Thousand and One Notes"]. Luca Caminati described Pasolini's observation of Africa as a form of "ethnographic experimentalism"[3].

It is, therefore, clear that the incorporation of Otherness is not an invasive operation. On the contrary, it is a comparison with "the Other", regardless of

1 Raimondi, E. (2002). *Letteratura e identità nazionale*. Milano: Bruno Mondadori.

2 (It should be noted that Pasolini makes no reference to the Indian subcontinent, as is often mistakenly believed. Instead, Africa is the recurrent macro-region of the Southern world in his work) cf. Trento, G. (2009). *Pasolini e l'Africa. L'Africa di Pasolini. Panmeridionalismo e rappresentazioni dell'africa coloniale*. Milano: Mimesis.

3 Caminati, L. (2007). *Orientalismo eretico. Pieri Paolo Pasolini e il cinema del Terzo Mondo*. Milano: Bruno Mondadori.

whether this figure is represented by the marginalised inhabitants of the Roman suburbs or the pre-bourgeois society of the East.

Alberto Moravia's perspective is enlightening, as is his journalism in Africa, which pertains more to the essence of this chapter: the discovery of a civilisation as a one-way mirror reflecting the present Western condition in its humanistic relations with the foreigner. Two aspects of Africa interested Moravia: its archaism or primitivism, and the way in which it enabled one to experience the degradation of modernity, the civilised modernity in which we live. Enzo Siciliano associates Moravia's journey, as a walk back into prehistory, with the concept of archaism and primitivism; a path far removed from the aggression of the known world[4]. Far from the neo-capitalist frontiers, Moravia, according to Roberto Tessari, "*cerca se esiste, un altro uomo o meglio ancora, l'altro dell'uomo europeo. L'Africa è quello che Moravia chiama natura*" [is seeking, if he exists, a different man or, more precisely, "the other" from the European man. Africa is what Moravia calls nature][5]. Moravia's use of imagery is a more fruitful interpretative lens for the purposes of this study. For instance, his use of metaphor to associate, from a critical, international perspective, a state with a figure: India as the negation of all Western conditions, "an immersion in the irrational", that illustrates the degradation of words as a disease afflicting European languages; or the Soviet Union as the monster of the West. Therefore, both in Pasolini and in Moravia, Africa represents an escape from "history" toward nature.

Whilst the approach of the West has been increasingly to rationalise and homogenise the world, literature has almost exclusively made space for that which resists such processes of standardisation: for the "Other", for the bizarre, for the idle, for archaic environments and unspoilt nature. It is as if modern literature were a vast photographic negative of the progress of modern rationality. The Other is not unattainable; we can experience him, we can identify with him or imagine him through literature. One need not travel or seek out primitive peoples, the Other is everywhere and nowhere, if we recognise that beyond our ways of thinking and our societies, which distinguish us from the rest of the universe, we are not radically different from others, particularly if we also recognise that we are part of a single cosmos, and if we are capable of mutual forgiveness.

---

4 Cf. Siciliano, E. (1982). *Alberto Moravia, vita, parole e idee di un romanziere*. Milano: Bompiani, pp. 229–232.

5 Tessari, R. (1975). *Alberto Moravia, introduzione e guida allo studio dell'opera moraviana*. Milano: Mondadori, pp. 147–149.

Brugnolo posited the following hypothesis in his essay: "*che una grande opera contraddice necessariamente e anzi supera l'ideologia che lo scrittore come uomo ha eventualmente abbracciato*" [that a great work necessarily contradicts and even transcends any ideology that the writer, as a man, may have embraced][6]. This is indeed the case since a work transcends the boundaries for which it was written and conceived. Space is made, within a text, for the norm and for transgression, for identity as well as diversity; we then apply that which literature contemplates to multicultural and social inclusion contexts. "*Ma se la letteratura ci interessa è proprio perché è s-quilibrata, perché ci racconta le nostre imperfezioni e soprattutto le contraddizioni che sempre si danno tra i nostri principi e le nostre concezioni da una parte, e dall'altra la vita reale che sempre li scuote, di qualunque tipo essi siano*" [But if literature interests us, it is precisely because it is unbalanced, it shows us our imperfections and, above all, the contradictions that always emerge between our principles and concepts on the one hand and, on the other, our real lives which always undermine the former, whatever their nature][7]. In short, a text must question and touch on several critical aspects, and open the reader up to a mobile and multi-faceted point of view. Acceptance of the Other also involves the complexity of social and ideological frameworks, that is, a system of thought well suited to its own vision: Western rather Eastern.

The opening of Kipling's *Beyond the Pale*, published in Italy by Adelphi under the title *Oltre il limite* (in Id., *La città della tremenda notte*, Adelphi, Milan 2007, pp. 57–64), suggests the impossibility of crossing the threshold of race, caste and gender barriers: "A man should, whatever happens, keep to his own caste, race, and breed. Let the White go to the White and the Black to the Black" (Kipling, 1965)[8]. The story describes an impossible love between an English man and an Indian woman: the theme is the impossibility of coming together, in this case, of union with the Other. The repudiation of such a possibility dehumanises and impoverishes the underlying issue. Thus, a conflict of Western thought emerges or, more precisely, the impossibility of crossing the threshold, as in the above-mentioned colonial writer.

As writers, Pasolini and Moravia were interested in the Other, but in fundamentally different ways; a distinction we shall attempt to examine. On the one hand, Pasolini – considered "the intellectual of the most vulnerable" – is set on idealising the Other. Consider his dramaturgy and films: his cinema is based

6 Brugnolo, S. (2017). *La tentazione dell'altro*. Roma: Carocci, p. 24.
7 Ibid.
8 Ibid.

on reality and dream, made using street actors; not professionals, but shyly sincere improvisers and amateurs. On the other hand, Moravia acutely portrays the Other within a simple and direct vision of the world, and the instant he "strays" from his own highly active role in the field of cultural and artistic criticism, during his African travels, for example, he feels renewed, refreshed and "switched on", fully engaged in describing the situation (the African question). We shall examine the perspectives of these two intellectuals to shed more light on the theme of multiculturalism.

2 Alberto Moravia and Reporting on the Other

Alberto Moravia was a travel writer, or rather, he produced the type of literature that makes us "discover" unknown practices, customs and languages. His is a literature that "builds bridges" between geographically remote worlds, and therefore one that is endlessly fascinating, precisely because it instils a certain curiosity about other peoples. This type of literature makes the invisible visible. It offers a solution to our incomplete perceptions of our places, our conditions. In short, "it ignites", "illuminates" and "records" events that stimulate the mechanism of thought.

In *Lettere dal Sahara* ["Letters from the Sahara"] 1981), Moravia gazes admiring on a still unknown or not entirely known reality, and presents the reader with an image of desert life, not a tableau of loss and death. The point is that as soon as we attempt to speak of the Other without respect for their traditions and their cultures, we Westernise them, or "cloak" them in stereotypes that do not belong to them. Moravia, here, does not need to invent anything, but simply provide snapshots of a non-European people through his critical and convincing notes.

> Ed è proprio la presenza di questa intelligenza che apprezziamo nel Moravia dei viaggi e, in particolare, in queste Lettere dal Sahara. Si tratta di una intelligenza finalmente restituita alla libertà dei suoi movimenti autonomi e non inceppata dai propositi troppo facili di lettura ideologica del mondo. Una intelligenza del genere ha e non può non avere riscontro in una scrittura affatto particolare, dotata di un grado di trasparenza eccezionale, lucida e insieme fragile, spavalda e attenta, limpida e densa, autorevole e leggera. In questo senso le Lettere dal Sahara rappresentano un Moravia inedito, decisamente altro da quello che incontriamo nei romanzi
> [And it is precisely this intelligence that we appreciate in Moravia the travel writer, particularly in his Lettere dal Sahara: an intelligence that has finally regained its freedom of movement, unshackled by the facile, ideological views on the world. An intelligence of this kind has and cannot but be reflected in a very particular writing, endowed with an exceptional degree of transparency, lucid and at the same time fragile, bold and careful,

limpid and dense, authoritative and light. In this sense, Lettere dal Sahara is a new Moravia, decidedly different from the writer we encounter in his novels].[9].

The letter *Il ragno del deserto* ["The Desert Spider"] begins with Moravia finding himself lying on a camp bed, beside a wall in the middle of the desert: first, he has a dream in which he sees modern, glass offices that look so much like sterile, futuristic cages; then, he stumbles upon a member of the Tuareg tribe (a nomadic people of the Sahara), whom he finds fascinating. The following day, whilst waiting to be received by the Sultan, he observes, delightedly and with close attention, the palace, the three Tuareg who welcomed him and, above all, a battered text full of dates and writings, given to him by the head of the guards. The moral of this story – and it does read like a fairy tale – is the importance of the text, not as a text *per se*, but as an inestimable, universally recognised treasure: "*infatti quel libro così prezioso e così malridotto è un segno eloquente dell'impossibilità di qualsiasi rapporto altro che visivo*" [indeed, that book, so precious and so battered, is an eloquent sign of the impossibility of any relationship other than visual][10]. Perhaps, Moravia would go on to say, we will transition from illiteracy to television without the interim step of printed text, highlighting the capacity of visual contact to "unite". Moravia's testimony is also a paradigm. As Brugnolo noted, the works by authors such as Conrad and Kipling paint us a picture of other ways of being human, other modes of relating with the world.

Said, a key point of reference for post-colonial literature, theorised that it was more accurate to consider the Other by exploring the variety within ourselves, one's own inner wealth, through an ethical as well as cognitive lens. Brugnolo (*La tentazione dell'altro*, 2017) notes that our adopted existential approach to the exotic, the foreign, the unknown, whether derived from artistic or literary poetics, is an essential component of any literary study. Something necessary, visionary and subjective that allows the reader to find, therein, features agreeable to him; in a rigorously objective critical study, one cannot entirely discard the existentialist perspective.

Insomma la domanda che dobbiamo porci ogni volta davanti a questi testi è: di cosa stanno parlando Conrad, Kipling, Maugham, Loti, Malraux quando parlano id africani, indiani, samoani, turchi, cinesi? E la risposta è che gli artisti non parlano mai solo e proprio di quei certi popoli e territori e culture, bensì che, parlando di quei popoli e di quelle culture, essi mobilitano altri sensi, altri significati, più universali. In altre parole, se queste immaginarie avventure oltre il confine sono così interessanti è perché non si

9 Guglielmi, A. (ed.) (1981). *Il piacere della letteratura*. Milano: Feltrinelli, p. 265.
10 Idem, p. 277.

> svolgono solo lontano da "noi", ma anche, se non soprattutto, dentro di "noi". L'Oriente, allora, non è tanto un luogo geografico, ma anche e più che mai un luogo della mente o, se si preferisce, dell'inconscio culturale della civiltà occidentale (e cose simili si potrebbero dire dell'Africa e di altri luoghi). Come a dire che all'Altro incontrato lontano da "qui" corrisponde un Altro che è vicino e anzi dentro la nostra civiltà, anche se non sempre di esso si ha consapevolezza.
> [In short, the question we must ask whenever approaching these texts is: what are Conrad, Kipling, Maugham, Loti and Malraux talking about when they speak of Africans, Indians, Samoans, Turks and Chinese people? And the answer is that artists never speak solely and entirely of those specific peoples, lands and cultures; rather, by talking about those peoples and cultures, they mobilise other, more universal senses and meanings. In other words, if these imaginary adventures across the border are fascinating, it is because they not only take place far from "us", but also, and perhaps most importantly, inside us. The East, then, is not just a geographical location, but also, and more so than ever, a place in the mind or, if you like, of the cultural subconscious of Western civilisation (as one could also say of Africa and other places). As if to say that the Other, whom we meet far away from "here", corresponds to an Other who is close by and indeed in our civilisation, even if we are not always aware of its presence][11].

Literature is never only about its subject matter. It goes further, dissolving into multiform shapes and identities. As Sergio Antonielli explained, Moravia's gift to 20th-century literature was a form of realism derived from neorealism itself: "*così possiamo dire che si è reso rappresentativo della stagione saggistica della narrativa degli ultimi anni: oggi il romanzo-saggio è un genere, o meglio un sottogenere abbastanza diffuso*" [so we can say that he has come to represent the essay season of narrative over the last years: today the novel-essay is a genre, or rather a fairly widespread sub-genre][12]. Moravia demonstrated that the novel was not, in fact, dead. Indeed, he proved as such with *Gli indifferenti* [*The Indifferent Ones*] (1929), and the "new" and "dangerous" themes it employed in its thorough diagnosis of social and political mores.

In *A quale tribù appartieni?* [*Which Tribe Do You Belong to?*] (Einaudi 1972), Moravia offers us a broader vision of Africa: in tackling topics omitted by economists, by highlighting the spread of neo-capitalism, he deals with non-rational but no less important issues.

> Faccio queste riflessioni passeggiando per la Main Street di Accra, tra la folla più multicolore che abbia mai visto in vita mia. Che spettacolo allegro e incredibile: tra le due file di edifici sgangherati e ineguali della strada principale, brulica una moltitudine vestita delle stoffe dai colori più smaglianti e dai disegni più arditi che si possano

11 Brugnolo, S. (2017). *La tentazione dell'altro*. Roma: Carocci, pp. 31–32.
12 Antonielli, S. (1987). *M'illumino d'immenso*. Milano: Mursia, pp.163–164.

immaginare. Gli uomini si avvolgono queste stoffe intorno il corpo alla maniera delle toghe romane, dalla testa ai piedi, lasciando il collo, una spalla e un braccio ignudi. Le donne se le stringono intorno ai fianchi e il petto come abiti da sera per la Scala o il Metropolitan un fazzoletto della stessa stoffa fascia loro il capo con certe enormi cocche da far pensare che portino sulla testa un vaso da fiori. Le stoffe, come ho già detto, sono barbaricamente colorate e disegnate; ma a un occhio esperto non può sfuggire che questa barbarie è un prodotto di secondo grado, ossia è una barbarie filtrata attraverso le esperienze pittoriche delle avanguardie europee.

[I think all this whilst walking down Main Street in Accra, among the most colourful crowd I have ever seen in my life. An incredible and uplifting spectacle: between the two rows of dilapidated and irregular buildings on the main street bustles a multitude of people dressed in fabric with more dazzling colours and bolder designs than you could possibly imagine. The men wrap their bodies in this cloth like Roman togas, from head to foot, leaving the neck, one shoulder and an arm uncovered. The women tie it round their hips and chest like evening dresses for a night out at the Scala or the Metropolitan, a handkerchief of the same fabric wraps their heads with certain enormous ends that it looks as though they have a flowerpot on their heads. The fabrics, as I have already said, are barbarically coloured and drawn; but it cannot escape an expert eye that this barbarism is a second degree product, that is, it is barbarism filtered through the pictorial experiences of the European avant-gardes][13].

Moravia was much admired for his enraptured descriptions of dazzling colours and outdoor markets in shabby streets. A direct testimony that retains all the charm of crossing the bridge, going beyond and not stopping at appearances. For Moravia, travelling through Africa was like stepping back into prehistory; a prehistory, which, as he specifies:

è la savana che fascia l'Africa per migliaia di chilometri da ovest a est, cioè dall'Oceano Atlantico all'Oceano Indiano. La savana è una sterminata steppa color verde pallido sparsa, a perdita d'occhio, di una sola specie di albero, la piccola acacia africana, irta di spine, coi rami disposti a ombrello, e di una sola specie di cespuglio di forma rotonda, color verde scuro. Si corre e si corre, in macchina, per strade o per piste, per centinaia di chilometri e la spetta non finisce mai, non fa che ripetere se stessa, ossia i due motivi che le sono proprio, l'acacia e il cespuglio.

[is the savanna surrounding Africa for thousands of kilometres from west to east, that is, from the Atlantic Ocean to the Indian Ocean. The savannah is an immense, pale green steppe, scattered, as far as the eye can see, with a single species of tree, the small African acacia, bristling with thorns and branching out into an umbrella shape, and a solitary species of round, dark-green bush. You can drive and drive, by car, on roads or tracks, for hundreds of kilometres and it goes on and on, simply repeating itself, or rather its two motifs, the acacia and the bush.][14]

13 Moravia, A. (1972). *A quale tribù appartieni*, Torino: Einaudi, pp. 10–11.

14 Idem, pp. 14–15.

Moravia's travel literature is like an unchartered corner of the map. Somewhere to discover wonders previously misunderstood and places that seem suspended in time, in that they retain a primitive charm, a charm that is perhaps not, as yet, entirely lost. The silence, the colours of the vegetation, the animals, the movements of the sun: Moravia's work was that of an explorer able to do justice to his own perceptions. Africa's prehistory resides not only in its landscape, but also in its single and sole native religious belief: magic. Magic is part of the notorious fascination that Africa inspires: a certain fear, fear of prehistory and hence of the irrational. As such, it is controversial.

In his expansive reportage-style prose, Moravia focuses on African dance. Probably the most obvious example of a primitive ritual, dance represents a rhythm that has entered the modern world and become part of its contemporary fabric: *"esso è il dono più prezioso che l'Africa abbia fatto all'umanità e, al tempo stesso, il segno più chiaro dell'influenza degli africani sul costume contemporaneo"* [this is Africa's most precious gift to humanity and, at the same time, the clearest sign of the influence of African people on contemporary culture][15]. Dance is a metaphor for life. This is the conclusion Moravia reaches when recalling how, whilst travelling along a strip of red earth leading from Lagosto Benin, between two walls of dark forest, he witnessed a group of Africans abruptly leave the path to dance in the stillness of the forest. In short, Africans do not know what the dance will bring, somewhat like life: you simply experience it, perhaps opening yourself up to encounters with others. *"La danza è anche per l'africano un mezzo per associarsi o meglio per disfarsi della superficiale forma individuale e fondersi con gli altri allo stesso modo che si fondono in un solo crogiuolo diversi pezzi di diversi metalli"*. [For Africans, dance is also a means of associating with others, or better discarding the superficial individual shape and merging with others, much like different metals melt into one another in a crucible][16]. Body language as a universally recognised expression, a blaze of energy and vitality, a sign of freedom but also an individual event: in a sort of carefree and happy engagement with others, we forget the misery that surrounds us.

> Dove ho veduto quelle figure sottili, filiformi, nere ed eleganti, quelle teste tutt'occhi e tutta bocca nelle quali la pelle ha l'untuosità, la rugosità, la lucentezza e il colore fosco del bronzo? Diamine, al museo nelle cui teche sono esposte le sculture misteriose degli artisti di Benin. In Europa quelle sculture danno talvolta l'impressione della caricatura. Ma qui, in questi night club di Lagos, si vede che sono realistiche, addirittura quasi

15 Idem, p. 22.
16 Idem, p. 24.

fotografiche. È la natura che nel golfo di Guinea è espressionistica, soggettiva, delirante, caricaturale, non gli artisti. Gli uomini danzano e, attraverso la danza, esprimono la stravaganza della natura.
[Where have I seen those slender, filiform figures, black and elegant, their heads, all eyes and mouth, with skin as unctuous, rough, glossy and sombre as bronze? That was it! At the museum. Those mysterious sculptures in display cases by Benin artists. In Europe, these pieces sometimes have an air of caricature about them. But here, in these Lagos night clubs, you realise they are true to life, photographic even. Here, in the Gulf of Guinea, it is nature that is expressionist, subjective, delirious and caricatural, not the artists. Men dance and, through dance, express the extravagance of nature.][17]

Migration, the wayfarer, the traveller, the foreigner, the Other: these are the representations of Africans in the collective imagination. In Moravia's reportage, he suggests this endless wandering, driven by economic factors and subsistence requirements, is in fact a conscious approach to life. The people moving for economic reasons are selling products made by their family, a sort of small business powered by a sort of entrepreneurial zeal from which one could take inspiration, and that, for Africans, constitutes a *raison d'être*, a way of manifesting their own existence: "*perché gli africani, pur nel loro modo bislacco, fantasioso, irrazionale e danzante, sono una delle razze più traffichine che ci siano al mondo*" [because Africans, even with their dancing, their outlandish, fanciful and irrational ways, remain one of the most bustling races in the world][18].

Vista sotto questo profilo, l'Africa nera appare non già un'accozzaglia di stati e staterelli imitati dall'Occidente e più o meno ritagliati sui confini delle antiche colonie francesi ed inglesi, come si vede sulla carta geografica, ma come un solo organismo nel quale, di contro all'infinito spezzettamento tribale, si contrappone, equilibrante e integrante, l'unità economica[19]
[From this perspective, Sub-Saharan Africa seems a world away from the jumble of states and city states modelled on the West and carved up along more or less the same old French and English colonial lines, as seen on the map. This is a single organism in which, amid the patchwork of tribal divisions, we find equalising and integrating economic unity].

These extracts confirm Moravia's great descriptive skill and capacity to rationalise with empathy. His work recalls such authors as Hemingway or Kipling, who brought certain images of misunderstood continents to the surface of the

17 Idem, p. 27.
18 Idem, p. 30.
19 Ibid.

collective imagination: for example, Hemingway's fiction brings to mind certain East African lands, prowling beasts and safaris.

As Brugnolo asserted:

> Solo i testi che partono dal presupposto che l'Altro ci disturba e sfida riescono poi a raccontarci convincentemente i casi in cui nonostante ciò il soggetto si fa tentare dalla diversità. È appunto la rappresentazione della lotta tra questa pericolosa e imprevista tentazione e le resistenze, le paure, i pregiudizi che si oppongono a essa che rende interessanti questi racconti e romanzi universalmente leggibili. . .
> [Only texts that start with the assumption that the Other disturbs us and challenges us are then able to convincingly describe cases in which, despite all this, the subject is attracted by diversity. It is precisely the representation of the struggle between this dangerous and unexpected temptation and the resistances, fears and prejudices that arise to oppose it that makes these universally relatable stories and novels interesting. . .][20]

Brugnolo also commented that, although it would be more appropriate to speak of "micro-otherness", in the globalised world, than major anthropological differences, when faced with these differences, we still react in essentially the same way as the colonial-age writers.

This perspective translates into a certain approach to studying the Other, one based on a very specific hypothesis: there are "relative differences" within a single humanity, unique in space and time: "*apparteniamo tutti a una comune specie e per quante differenze si diano tra culture, lingue e nazioni le nostre esperienze restano comunque confrontabili*" [we are all part of the same species and, whatever differences exist on the level of culture, language and nationality, our experiences are always comparable][21].

Literature and its constituent genres provide readers with a figurative, indirect image of the places and landscapes they depict, sometimes intercepting clichés, or even questioning them: nevertheless, such images may be true, but they would be true as representations of certain ways of life, windows onto the world and studies on how we can relate to it. Literature draws us in, it is devoid of textual boundaries and engages readers in an intimate relationship, taking them around the world. Said invites us to "observe" the Other in light of the inherent variety in our own difference. Therefore, we could define difference as complexity and multiplicity; something to discover, not to avoid. Ultimately, the cultural and anthropological diversity we learn about and study through literature enables us to recognise ourselves in these forms of Otherness: "*assumerle immaginariamente*

20 Brugnolo, S. (2017). *La tentazione dell'altro*, Roma: Carocci, p. 26.
21 Idem, p. 27.

in noi, invece che provare a espellerle definitivamente. Si direbbe anzi che questa sia la sua funzione principale" [assimilating them within ourselves imaginatively, rather than trying to expel them definitively. In fact, you might say that this is its main purpose][22]. The fascination of literature and, in this case, the potential tool of cosmogonic knowledge in the broad sense, is the sense of being immersed in the stories that we read, in our encounters with the people we meet. In short, we become as one with the Other in and by means of narratives, and are thereby able to "re-view" our perspective. Narratives, here, understood as *media*, places to populate with one's mind, horizons to explore with words or perhaps even confines to sweep away with knowledge.

> Le storie possono diventare il luogo immaginario, ma contemporaneamente reale, dove è possibile cambiare pelle e going other, dove esperienze, credenze, memorie possono essere scambiate, condivise e salvate. È, dunque, solo come narratori o ascoltatori di narrazioni che si può diventare altri da sé, che ci si può convertire ad altre culture e tradizioni
> [Stories can become imaginary and simultaneously real locations in which we can change our skins and "go Other"; a place where experiences, beliefs and memories can be exchanged, shared and recorded. Therefore, it is only as storytellers or listeners of stories that we can become other than ourselves; that we can convert to other cultures and traditions][23].

In Moravia's travel writing, we perceive all the realism and authenticity of a land rooted in the purity of its own tribal culture. His work paints a picture of an Africa between prehistory and the future.

Enzo Siciliano wrote:

> Attraverso l'Africa Moravia mette a fuoco qualcosa di perdutamente personale. Moravia ci suggerisce che l'Africa lo affascina per un duplice aspetto: la sua arcaicità, il suo primitivismo, e per il modo in cui essa fa sperimentare la degradazione della modernità, quella civile modernità nella quale siamo immerse
> [Through Africa, Moravia brings something desperately personal into focus. From his work, it would appear that two aspects of Africa fascinated him: its archaism, primitivism, and the way in which it enabled one to experience the degradation of modernity, the civilised modernity in which we live].[24].

In his travels in Africa, Moravia journeyed beyond the bounderies of time and history. He immersed himself in an "a-historical", almost religious dimension with no personal god.

---

22 Idem, p. 35.
23 Idem, p. 216.
24 Siciliano, E. (1982). *Alberto Moravia*. Milano: Bompiani, p. 230.

> Il richiamo che l'Africa – terra emblematica come nessun'altra – esercita su lui indica. "nel momento storico non precisamente positivo che sta conoscendo la nostra civiltà, una atavica nostalgia per l'antica e così feconda contraddizione di un tempo fra paganesimo e cristianesimo, tra politeismo e monoteismo, tra particolarismo e universalismo". Tale nostalgia ha volto filosofico: è senza dubbio una forma di religione
> [Moravia's attraction to Africa – the emblematic land par excellence – evokes, "in the somewhat troubled period of history that our civilisation is currently experiencing, an atavistic nostalgia for the ancient and the highly fertile contradiction found in an age between paganism and Christianity, between polytheism and monotheism and between particularism and universalism". Nostalgia such as this has a philosophical face: it is most certainly a form of religion].[25]

3 Pasolini and the Image of the Other as an Archaeological Discovery

Pier Paolo Pasolini used his art for the simultaneous purposes of creation and exegesis. Angela Biancofiore observed a number of constants in his work:

1. The combination of poetics and ideology;
2. The relationship between literature and culture;
3. The analysis of how a work functions (be it a poem, novel, essay, play, etc.), including language and stylistic models and
4. Observations on the author-character and author-reader/audience relationships[26].

Breaking down Pasolini's work in this way helps focus our gaze on this multi-faceted intellectual, whose oeuvre is vast and imposing (here we shall examine the "African project").

In 1970, Pasolini made a documentary film intended as preparatory notes for a future project. This was an idea that never came to fruition, poised in the realm of the potential, still communicating its message today: borrowing its title from Aeschylus' tragedy, he called the piece *Appunti per un'Orestiade Africana*, translated into English as *Notes Towards an African Orestes*. The voiceover narrator in the film presents a survey of Tanzania and Uganda, with a view to adapting the Greek tragedy for a modern African setting. As if conducting some primordial form of casting study, Pasolini moves the camera as though it were a hungry wild animal: he frames faces, landscapes or forms of these, seeking out every kind of

---

25 Idem, p. 212.
26 Biancofiore, A. (2003). *Pasolini*. Palermo: Palumbo, p. 118.

emotion, even the most bitter. He observes, just as Moravia did, that the only way these people know is laughter and living life as though it were a never-ending party. This constant smile leaves no room for feelings such as pride and revenge. In their eyes, the camera looks like a technological insect recording fragments of daily life.

The idea at the heart of the project was to make a popular film, one dominated by the chorus. Perhaps because it is important to glorify action, collective acts, sharing: the basis of communication. Pasolini's gaze falls between poetry and archaeology. Bodies must be rediscovered because they have been buried under a layer of dusty indifference. Customs, however fascinating in their own right, must be understood in the context of a certain archaic contemporaneity. The film has a maieutic objective, seeking to shed light on a reality drowned out by prejudice, smothered by blinkered intellectual perspectives that tribalise the communities even more.

Diversity is in the eye of the beholder. One sequence depicts the most modern area and, in particular, workers leaving a factory: a sight replicated anywhere else in the world. Such images point towards a way of thinking, a ritual, a sociological act that does not recognise ethnicity. It also features school, and students who work and study, depicting a vision with echoes of modern pedagogy: it cuts from fields to books. Exterior shots are followed by interior shots: books on a shelf or a classroom, accompanied by Pasolini's paternalistic voiceover noting the importance of education for African students, almost as though it were a gift to savour in religious silence and humility. These shots have a pedagogical character, because the prevailing message here is a pedagogical one.

Later in the documentary, Pasolini films himself in discussion with African students at Sapienza University of Rome. He presents his ideas and asks the audience questions, in a dynamic reminiscent of a talk show offering a platform to "foreign" voices. In doing so, he creates a historical and political sort of realism, since this is a project with philosophical rigour, seeking to reconstruct the map of formal democracy: the moment Orestes arrives in Athens and Athena establishes the first human court, so that, for the first time, a man may be judged by people and not by the Gods. African tribal civilisation is similar to ancient Greek civilisation. One of the most predictable criticisms to arise from this meeting with the students is that Africa is losing its own identity and assuming European characteristics.

According to Pasolini, in this changing nature, with its monstrous forms, reside beasts that he compares to Aeschylus' Furies, identifying, in them, the more primitive dimension destined to disappear. The documentary also includes material on the Biafran War: metaphorical images of death, pain and tragedy;

searingly present images associated with the fantastical ones of the ancient Greek tragedy.

Another part of the documentary presents an original idea of Pasolini's: a jazz version of the Oresteia sung by black Africans.

In the final part of the film, Pasolini returns to Africa, to the city of Kampala. He imagines it as a representation of ancient Athens and considers using the University of Dar es Salaam – a structure strongly influenced by the architecture of typical neo-capitalist of universities in the English-speaking world – to represent the Temple of Apollo. He takes a critical approach to the university, filming the contradictions he finds in its bookshop: neo-capitalist titles on religion, American education and nationalism.

The university students Pasolini interviews are driven by a desire for knowledge and progress. Above all, the West is a new world. Whether it is a better or worse world is of little concern. Later, the documentary considers two fundamental aspects: conserving a magical and timeless primitiveness and pursuing growth and cultural development without falling into the grip of magmatic and ferocious neo-capitalist consumerism.

Notes Towards an African Orestes is an anthropological testament of imagination, a precious record of cinema in Africa. It offers no conclusion, because it is suspended in the poetic creation of a future and the future lies in apprehension about the future itself (cf. Pier Paolo Pasolini, Bazzocchi 1998).

Those ones who have chosen the method of going native progress by means of an osmotic process of "going Other", a sort of cultural tandem where one meets the other without nullifying or cancelling each other out in a "new place", a democratic, independent and free place, as we read in Aeschylus' text.

> La forma del film-saggio è sostenibile quando l'opera ha una sua coerenza formale, cioè «funziona», non è immediatamente moralistica, didattica o edificante. Lo spessore ideologico dell'opera non compromette la sua dimensione estetica né la trasforma in un manifesto propagandistico: da qui la possibilità di intraprendere, da parte dello spettatore, diversi percorsi interpretativi. Attraverso il cinema, Pasolini è stato capace di affrontare le questioni scottanti del nostro tempo: il rapporto tra cristianesimo e marxismo (Il vangelo secondo Matteo), la crisi delle ideologie (Uccellacci e uccellini), il genocidio e il nuovo fascismo (Salò), la nuova morale sessuale (Comizi d'amore), la nascita della democrazia (Appunti per un'Orestiade africana), le origini della vita collettiva e la transizione verso nuovi valori culturali (Medea).
>
> [The film-essay format is tenable when the piece is formally coherent i.e. when it "works"; it is not directly moralistic, didactic or edifying. The profound ideological depth of the film does not harm its aesthetic dimension: Whilst the film never becomes a work of propaganda, ideology finds embodiment in the formal structure along with other interpretative paths of the work. The ideological depth of the work does not compromise its

> aesthetic dimension, nor does it transform the work into a propaganda manifesto: hence the possibility of undertaking, on the part of the viewer, different interpretative routes. Through cinema, Pasolini tackled the pressing issues of our time: the relationship between Christianity and Marxism (Il vangelo secondo Matteo), the crisis of ideologies (Uccellacci e uccellini), genocide and neofascism (Salò), new sexual morality (Comizi d'amore), the birth of democracy (Appunti per un'Orestiade africana), the origins of collective living and the transition towards new cultural values (Medea)[27].

In the film-essay format, Pasolini becomes a sort of interpreter of his own works, linking and embodying the respective roles: thus, the poet engages with the novelist, the artist with the essayist and the critic with the director. In short, you could argue that Pasolini represented, in flesh and bone, all the power of the syncretic language of cinema, a clear manifestation of visual and auditory polyphony. His own artistic practice is a critical and conscious response to power. His objective is to modify reality, or at least to try.

> C'è poi quell'esperimento splendidamente fallito che sono gli Appunti per un'Orestiade africana, dove Pasolini, dopo aver costruito una formidabile ipotesi di film, infrange per eccesso di onestà intellettuale un tabù estremo, interrogando i segni reali che avrebbero dovuto esprimere la sua realtà di un Eschilo nero. E, naturalmente, gli studenti africani che popolano Roma nei tardi anni Sessanta, in tale realtà non si riconoscono e si sottraggono alla purezza geometrica di un poema che ormai, in quella forma, esiste solamente nell'immaginazione di Pasolini.
> [Then we have Notes Towards an African Orestes, a spectacularly flawed experiment. After setting up an impressive concept for a film, he breaks a great taboo due to excessive intellectual honesty, by interviewing the real signs that should have expressed his reality of a black Aeschylus. Naturally, the African students in Rome in the late Sixties did not recognise themselves in this reality, and distance themselves from the geometric purity of a poem that by that point, in that form, existed only in Pasolini's imagination][28].

Great literature, like great cinema, can play a fundamental role in multi-ethnic societies: it can unite and bring people together. In conclusion, through the work of both Pasolini and Moravia, we can know the story of the Other through the eyes and souls of individuals able to take the time to listen and listen to themselves.

References

Antonielli A. (1987). *M'illumino d'immenso*. Milano: Mursia.

---

27 Cf. Idem, p. 140.

28 Manzoli, G. (2001). *Voce e silenzio nel cinema di Pier Paolo Pasolini*. Bologna: Pendragon, p. 58.

Bazzocchi M. A. (1998). *Pier Paolo Pasolini*. Milano: Bruno Mondadori.

Biancofiore A. (2003). *Pasolini*. Palermo: Palumbo.

Brugnolo S. (2017). *La tentazione dell'altro*. Roma: Carocci.

Caminati L. (2007). *Orientalismo eretico. Pier Paolo Pasolini e il cinema del Terzo Mondo*. Milano: Bruno Mondadori.

Guglielmi A. (Ed.). (1981). *Il piacere della letteratura*. Milano: Feltrinelli.

Manzoli G. (2001). *Voce e silenzio nel cinema di Pier Paolo Pasolini*. Bologna: Pendragon.

Moravia A. (1972). *A quale tribù appartieni*. Torino: Einaudi.

Raimondi E. (2002). *Letteratura e identità nazionale*. Milano: Bruno Mondadori.

Siciliano E. (1982). *Alberto Moravia*. Milano: Bompiani.

Tessari R. (1975). *Alberto Moravia, introduzione e guida allo studio dell'opera moraviana*. Milano: Mondadori.

Trento G. (2009). *Pasolini e l'Africa. L'Africa di Pasolini. Panmeridionalismo e rappresentazioni dell'Africa coloniale*. Milano: Mimesis.

Rolando Marini

Chapter Twenty-Six Immigration Emergencies: a Possible Praise to the Media

Abstract: This chapter discusses a critical view of the role played by the news media in the shaping of the immigration issue. For this purpose, the context around the issue is reconstructed, especially referring to the concepts of post-welfare politics, uncertainty and risk. It is argued that an interdependence framework is needed to understand the media/politics relationship. Moreover, the impact of trigger events seems to be determinant for an effective methodological approach. Then, selected results of a survey on the immigration coverage by the two main Italian newspapers, in 2014 and 2017, are used to illustrate the complex of factors that act in modifying the issue, starting from some key events and trying to explain the reasons why emergency persists across time. Since 2014 it is possible to observe the increase of the management frame, through which newspapers – although in a contradictory way – highlight the weakness of the government action.

1 Discussing About the Claims Against the Media

The most recent contributions in the social sciences about the transformation of the public space, and the underlying relationship between politics and media, have dealt with the replacement of traditional instances – related to social justice – by other categories, which seem to hold up the new frame of politics and public discourse, especially risk and fear. As in other fields in different ages, social scientists look divided: we can find who pay the major attention on the central powers in society and their pervasive ideology, and who prefer a multi-dimensional reading, based on systemic changes.

One of the emerging issues which involve such typical feelings of threat and fear is immigration, showing a peculiar "ability" to gather basic attitudes (mainly xenophobia), cultural disorientation (regarding globalization) and new kinds of sensitivity (about identity), as a result of accelerated transformations occurred even in the composition of the social aggregates (Norris & Inglehart 2009; Risse 2010; Norris & Inglehart 2019). Being a matter of cultural change, news media are inevitably considered as a relevant part of the whole scenario. This connection is made especially because in the social science a solid tradition survives, which considers social alarm, emergency and fear as a typical product of the mediatized construction of reality.

Looking at the way social sciences in Italy have been studying the formation of the immigration issue so far, it can be said this field has shown a certain difficulty in bringing out a critical reflection about the perspective and therefore the methodology through which that process has been observed and investigated. In particular, a long series of research works on the relationship between media and immigration in the Italian context, which can be considered as the predominant stream, strongly advances a reading scheme according to which the media would be the driving force of a negative vision of migrants, through the stubborn "artificial" construction of emergency situations related to contemporary migratory phenomena. Once again, in accordance with the way the consequences of globalization on the public sphere's dynamics are being studied, media become the centre of the attention: they are held to be the main culprits of this distortion, while the components of the more general context are not taken into consideration.

In this chapter, an attempt to question this scheme is carried on, in order to propose an alternative approach, in an interdisciplinary key, that can redesign the epistemological perspective from which to observe and to analyse the connection between emergency and immigration. The argumentation will proceed by facing, in sequence, the following problematic nodes: a) the critical analysis of the approach in question, looked at in a larger manner; b) the interplay between the contextual conditions that, in the field of immigration, have co-generated a crisis and diverse emergency situations; c) the inconsistency of the separation of media responsibilities; d) the nature of emergencies and their role in the social construction of the immigration issue; and e) a discussion about some selected results of a survey on the immigration coverage.

The discussed approach is typical of a social science branch firmly oriented to link the problems of public order to the voracity of profit and political-cultural influence of the media, both in the European and in the North American context. The news media have been blamed for spectacularizing and trivializing that theme and the connected social situation, using it for their own ends. A classical issue of this connection is crime, whose media coverage has been the subject of studies that have become milestones of this same branch (Hall et al. 1978; Manning 1998; Altheide 2002), also spreading their importance far beyond their specific object. These studies utilize a predominantly media-centric framework to explain political-cultural processes – being a neo-critical front with a technological footprint – and have been subsequently articulated in various paths, mainly with reference to the use of the terrorist threat for social control and consensus purposes (Chomsky 2002; Altheide 2006 and 2009).

News media are seen in the increasingly solid position of monopolists of the social construction of reality; they are blamed for a cognitive twist of society, because of which it loses the essential value references of a social and democratic life based on solidarity and inclusion. This degeneration is read in various but similar ways. A simple overview might start from the *moral panic* caused by the insistence on the crime waves during the 1970s in Great Britain (Hall et al. 1978), up to the over-perception of crime and violence as a result of their representation on television in the USA (Gerbner et al. 1986), getting to the fear of terrorism, which becomes the shared justification of a securitarian and belligerent order, still in the USA, but after 2001 (Altheide 2006).

Despite the proximity to the issues of crime and terrorism, at international level immigration has not been brought into this scheme. One of the most renown surveys about the immigration news, set as a long-term and comparative analysis (France-USA), has shown a notable differentiation of the frames within which the phenomenon is read: not only the frame of threat, but also that of management, the humanitarian one and still others. More interestingly, it has categorized frames that cross and shape media representations, coming from several contexts of the public space. This does not exclude that commercial media tend to simplify and dramatize the issue (Benson 2013).

The combination of the negative image of the migratory phenomenon and the moral degeneration of the media has emerged very significantly in the Italian case. Dealing with the growth of this issue in the political sphere, in the media and in public opinion, many studies, mostly longitudinal and therefore able to highlight the main tendencies (Dal Lago 1999; Sciortino & Colombo 2004; Binotto & Martino 2004; Colombo 2007; Binotto, Bruno & Lai 2012 and 2016), have reported and emphasized some of the main features of the media's attitude that should create a not favourable opinion climate toward migrants.

This perspective is well synthesized by the concept of *media tautology* (Dal Lago 1999; Binotto, Bruno & Lai 2016); it expresses a set of criticisms shared by all the authors:

a) news-media are responsible for having created the correspondence of immigration with increase of crime and insecurity;
b) they largely use stereotypes when reporting news about migrants;
c) they construct feelings of emergency and alarm, emphasizing deviance events;
d) they are unable (or do not want) to represent the process of positive integration;
e) there are no relevant differences within the media system.

It seems that these evaluations have derived from the concern by a considerable number of Italian sociologists for two processes: the growing commercialization of the media content and the legitimization of the right-wing political culture, both taking place in the 1990s and considered as strongly interrelated. So the emergency character of the immigration issue should be the result of this mixture of sensationalism and partisanship, as a typical feature of the Italian media landscape. The information system has been reputed totally unable to promote any kind of positive value within the multicultural transformation of the society.

Beyond the worried perception of a xenophobia spreading, that perspective is to be traced back to the view shared by the many studies on media and public order, playing the role of a platform able to offer a solid interpretation key: it seems that this scheme has become a cumbersome *scientific rhetoric*. It places a legitimate civil ethos between the gaze of the researcher and the analysis of the object of study, but – doing so – inhibits itself the possibility of a lucid understanding of the problematic relationship between media and immigration.

So, it looks more fruitful asking ourselves what is the nature of the context factors which can be considered responsible for having co-generated such a correspondence between emergency (or social alarm) and the migratory flows in the Italian society.

First of all, a reflection may be developed about the fact that migrations are *one* of the numerous aspects that manifest the deep transformation of the Western post-industrial societies characterized by a growing uncertainty, driven by the gradual loss of the previous relative stability of the societal condition (Beck 1986 and 2007; Bauman 2009; D'Alessandro 2010). This is connected with the persistent ineffectiveness of politics in managing what causes this new instability. On the one hand, there is a bias between the culture of government and control of uncertainty, which has been shaped across the last century, and the conditions that explicit the *perception of risk* in contemporary societies. On the other hand, not only old answers (or even no answers) have been given to new questions, but this contradiction also has pushed politics and political communication into a renovate ideological conflict.

It is worth to investigate whether there are reasons, independent on the media behaviour, by which immigration has become the ground of a neo-ideological confrontation.

2 Emergency and the Immigration Issue: A Context Reconstruction

To discuss the thesis according to which emergencies are artificially created by the news media's sensationalism (even if this serves their partisanship), it is necessary to enlarge the scope of the analysis.

Trying to broaden our gaze, we can reason about four fundamental points, which draw the reference framework to correctly evaluate the media strategies.

1. Post-welfare policies are inadequate to respond to emerging needs, corresponding to new social problems.
2. Security has become a "need" and a growing political demand.
3. Contemporary xenophobia should be seen through a revised perspective.
4. A divisive conflict about immigration expands as it is not counterbalanced by a debate on policies.

The first point regards the decline of the welfare model of government and of social right defence. At least in Europe, the scarce availability of additional means strongly limits the development of new State intervention lines (Armigeon & Bonoli 2007; Saraceno 2013): this affects the response to emerging needs, such as those of migrants, inhibiting reception and integration projects (Ambrosini 2008 and 2014).

The counter-trend of immigration and welfare-state resources shows in a simple and hard way what are the two fundamental problems of the project of society called multiculturalism: the weakness of State programs to make the migratory phenomenon *sustainable* and, at the same time, the tendency to reduce migratory policies to a series of declarations of principle (see point 4), becoming vain *rhetoric* (Ambrosini 2008). Not only a defence of human rights would be needed, but also an extension of substantial citizenship should be realized. In the meanwhile, immigration policies chase the problem and implement only partial adaptation to the various contingencies (Tusini 2017). Middle- and long-term programs are not being proposed.

In the European Union (EU) context, post-welfare policies are realized through a combination of public and non-profit activities, following a subsidiarity logic which strongly values solidarity networks, both formal and informal (Rossi & Boccacin 2012). This model has been acquired into the migrants' reception policy as well, giving the local level great importance and responsibility. A typical differentiation raises, due to the not homogeneous degree of cooperation between the two sectors. But many positive results have been documented in the press and in local reports. Although it has revealed to be generally effective (within the limits of the initial support to migrants), that scheme is inevitably fragmented and therefore subject to a difficulty of communication, not helping the public legitimacy of those policies and their actual outcomes.

The sentence at the second point refers to the Beck's concept of *human condition* in the society of uncertainty (Beck 2007; D'Alessandro 2010): a new type of request for social protection emerges with globalization. If redistributive social rights have dominated political action up to the end of the twentieth century, in the third millennium there appears a set of new needs and connected rights, those related precisely to *security*, which promises to be the core of a new politics, going from personal to urban security, environmental and food security, etc. In other words, a new cycle is appearing, despite various cultural and political resistances, based on old and new reasons, which in any case bring security back to state authoritarianism and social control, as previously mentioned.

This tendency is directly connected with the large debate on populism. Despite this theme not being the purpose of the present contribution, it is to be underlined that the most recent analyses on the changes in public opinion and political culture highlight the growth of the demand for protection from the risks brought by globalization (or, better, perceived as such), like in the attitude of the so-called cultural losers, who are prone to defend their "local" identities (Norris & Inglehart 2009; Risse 2010; Norris & Inglehart 2019).

But the point here is that security should be meant as a broader concept, able to comprehend old-type social guarantees regarding labour, education, health, family, etc. and newly conceived forms of protection, in the fields of environment, cyberspace, privacy, mobility, food, technology, *but also* fields that are traditionally thought of as typical of an authoritarian approach, such as terrorism, crime, urban security and immigration (Armigeon & Bonoli 2007; Beck 2016).

This discussion brings to the third point. No doubt that attitudes in this field are complex and not easily detectable. But, so far the peculiar nature of attitudes towards the migrant foreigner has been considered pathological and a sign of undemocratic residues, returning from the past (Balbo & Manconi 1990). Studies about the two conflicting hypotheses of, on the one side, nativism and the cultural threat and, on the other side, self-interest and economic threat clearly come to define the primacy of the first one (Fetzer 2000a and 2000b). Hence – third point – xenophobia should be seen under a different light: not as a result of the effectiveness achieved by the populist discourse, but as a consequence of a political-cultural tension between changing public opinion's attitudes and the general disorientation of the democratic politics. Therefore, contemporary xenophobia could be interpreted as the result of the lack of political answers to neglected demands, which may be advanced by citizens not necessarily identifiable with the cultural loser's profile.

From the considerations made by illustrating the previous points, it can easily be deduced that the immigration issue has formed and shaped within an unbalanced process on the side of ideologies and symbols, giving rise, like an epicentre, to a neo-ideological reorganization of politics as a whole (Cotesta 2009; Risse 2010; Ambrosini 2014; Norris & Inglehart 2019). This new organization of the ideological space is exactly based on the polarized instances of acceptance or refusal of migrants, with their background of values, such as universal solidarity against national identity defence.

To the lack of a policy praxis in favour of reception and integration has corresponded a hypertrophic confrontation on the symbolic field; this kind of conflict has anyway produced, even more easily, policies thought and realized as anti-migration ones.

3 Crisis and Emergencies in the Immigration Issue

This reconstruction of the many co-factors working along the formation of the immigration issue already offers an answer to the hypotheses that concentrate on the news media the full responsibility of the shape of this problem and surrounding cultural and political degeneration.

Having discussed on the neo-ideological conflict, we may say that in the genesis of the imbalanced relationship conflict/policy, the media also play an important role, due to their spectacular inclination, which regards the various types of journalism. This is due to their preference for an "agonistic" representation of politics, which has been advancing since the 1990s in Italy too (Roncarolo 2009).

Then an additional and complementary factor intervenes, the reinforcement that can come, even indirectly, from social web platforms to this type of staging, preferred by the mainstream media (Sunstein 2009; Papacharissi 2010; Sunstein 2017).

But, as said so far, it is advisable to hold an interdependence framework. This relationship between media and politics is to be considered a form of exchange of symbolic resources, between systems that have developed over time a reciprocal collaboration, which appears to be a mixture of cohesion and autonomy (Entman 1989 and 2012; Marini 2017a).

Within the "mix" by which the political-media circuit survives, some factors can play a transformative role within pre-existing balances: these are crisis processes, of the type above described, mainly related to destabilization phases that come to constitute *critical moments* (Tarrow 1990 and 2018; similarly Baumgartner & Jones 1993, with their theory of punctuated equilibrium), like the one that in the last decade has combined economic crisis, cultural consequences of globalization and the impact of the new migratory flows.

Here we can come to the question, not always adequately considered, of what actualizes the crisis in the time flow, and how the reactions of the actors on the field take shape. In other words: having already discussed the contextual aspects of the emergency, we are now talking about the recurrent emergencies that the interaction among the main actors in the public space comes to define as such. We face the research question of the extraordinary events (or critical events or key events). This perspective is particularly important in the analysis of the way the immigration issue has developed. This issue, in fact, has shown to be "sustained" in its evolution by repeated "relaunches" and revivals of attention, following events whose relevance and newsworthiness were defined not only by their intrinsic nature of not being ordinary facts in the social life, but also by their connection with the context of suspension and unresolved emergency described above.

Such key events do not embody the same level of importance; nevertheless in the attention dynamics they are reinforced by the common reference to a critical and controversial issue. We are speaking of murders, rapes, aggressions and other crime or deviance events; but also of the numerous sea tragedies. Their journalistic relevance is clearly linked to the fact that immigration is already in a high position on the political agenda, but they themselves contribute to enforce its relevance. In fact, in most cases, these are events whose genesis is not under the control of the media or of politics (think of the tragedy of Lampedusa, the rape of Rimini, the Macerata case, not to mention the terrorist attacks as events in a collateral position). Precisely because they are characterized by the typical "requirements" of events that should be judged as highly newsworthy in any democratic media system, they attract considerable attention in the processes of extensive mediatization (involving various type of media and of public).

The public debate thus tends to move and concentrate around these events and the related "crises". The deriving storylines become capable of occupying the discursive space with impacts of variable intensity, depending on their durability.

From the theoretical and above all methodological point of view, the contributions of the agenda building offer a general framework for understanding the role of the *trigger events* in the redefinition of issues (Baumgartner & Jones 1993; Dearing & Rogers 1996; Boydstun 2013). More exactly this theory recovers and develops the previous idea of Downs about the attention cycles, especially that of *alarmed discovery*, according to which only events of great emotional impact make people aware of the existence of a social problem, within the frame of a perceived emergency (1972). In the cycle model proposed by Downs, the so-called discovery may happen when indicators used by scientists to monitor that phenomenon are showing a decrease of its impact, in comparison with the phase that Downs define as "pre-problem". This further proposes the frequent dis-alignment between collective perception and the "real-world indicators", showing the centrality of the dynamic going from the trigger event to the collective awareness of a social problem (or political issue).

In the Italian case too studies have been realized about environment and food emergencies in the 1990s (such as the BSE European crisis), demonstrating the strength of disruptive and extensively worrisome events in reorganizing the public agenda, and in starting to sensitize the public opinion about such risks (Bucchi 1999). In an analogous manner, a recent Italian historical research work reconstructs the escape by Albanians to Italy in 1990, during the communist regime crisis, and the reaction in the public debate confronting about the idea of an invasion (De Cesaris 2018).

Some agenda-building studies in particular (Boydstun, Hardy & Walgrave, 2014; Boydstun, 2013) underline the ability of such shocking events, which cannot be controlled in their genesis by political elites, to produce media "storms" or "explosions". In that sense they become *focusing events* (Birkland 1997), capable of opening new phases in the evolution of an issue, as factors of re-framing and renewed agenda conflict: hence they represent an opportunity for the diverse political actors – conventional or not – to intervene and have a standing in the news media arena (Reese, Gandy & Grant 2003; D'Angelo & Kuypers 2010).

This dynamic increases the newsworthiness of the discussed issue, assigning "value" to minor but similar or related facts, so creating sequences that maintain a certain degree of tension upon the focused question. Re-mediation comes into play (Chadwick 2013), as a process of trans- and cross-media multiplication that expands the volume of attention and the need for interpretations.

Such readings may not be framed using rational concepts: this explains how, particularly in phases of crisis and disorientation, controversial issues are framed through ideological and symbolic patterns (Edelman 1964; Marini 2017b). Here we touch the core question in the debate about the role of emotionality in political communication; it is clearly related to the role played by the contemporary media in determining a cognitive shift in favour of non-rational and non-cooperative ways of thinking (as stated by the theses discussed in the first paragraph). Nevertheless, this does not exclude that some forces within the public space try and represent the opposite tendency: this is exactly the problem involving those journalism sectors which are supposed to supply a "quality" information, as it is going to be analysed in the following paragraphs.

4 A First Step of an Unresolved Emergency: The Desperate Journeys Discovery

Previous literature on the coverage of the immigration issue shows that it is highly responsive to extraordinary and shocking events: this kind of news attracts intense attention by the Italian news media, owing to the political climate around the issue itself: the conflict among party representatives increases the already high level of newsworthiness assigned to events involving migrants such as crimes, murders or sea tragedies (Sciortino, Colombo 2004; Belluati, Gargiulo and Seddone 2015; Binotto, Bruno, Lai 2016; Marini, Gerli 2017b). This dynamic designs a framework made of the interplay among three salient elements: the force of events, the political conflict and the subsequent production of storylines that contribute in creating the diffuse perception of an emergency situation. These phases, however, are to be inscribed into a more general frame the issue has acquired: the one of uncertainty, of suspension and lack of resolution.

Now, two emblematic situations will be shortly described, in order to demonstrate how emergency has been able to reshape the way news media – within a system of co-factors – have represented the issue, somehow reflecting the debate within the public sphere and intervening with their logic as well. These are two crucial passages: the years 2014 and 2017[1].

During the year 2014, Italian news media and public opinion *discover* the "desperate journeys"[2] across the Mediterranean Sea. The new trend of migratory

---

1 In order to pursue these research objectives, the two most circulated and influential Italian newspapers, "*Corriere della Sera*" and "*la Repubblica*", have been analysed, choosing three years (2008, 2014 and 2017) to (De Cesaris & Diodato 2018) realize an across-time comparison. Within each year a six-month sample has been selected, from June to November. The three analysed periods may be considered as three different settings of the determinant factors that shape the issue. The chosen technique is the "traditional" content analysis, in which a questionnaire is "submitted" to the news text by a team of analysts-coders. The analysis unit is every news dealing with immigration as the prevalent referring issue of events, declarations, comments, etc. around which the news is narratively organized. Four main research objects are addressed: sub-issues, actors in the news, interactions and scenarios. The two "biggest" newspapers have been chosen exactly for this purpose: they are particularly inclined to a multi-perspective construction of the public issues coverage, as a specific way of expressing an independent profile, while not rejecting (especially "la Repubblica") to use a strong advocating approach, even mixed with a clearly visible compromise with the spectacular style.

2 *Desperate journeys* will be the expression UNHCR will be using from 2017 to label the increase of danger in the crossing of the Mediterranean sea by refugees and migrants.

flows (which was not new at all at that moment) was "discovered" owing to the media "explosion" related to the Lampedusa shipwreck in the early October of 2013: the most serious maritime accident since the beginning of the 21st century in that sea. Actually, it has been the most impressive event among many other similar accidents, though smaller, in the sea crossing that boats with *passeurs* make from Africa to the South European coasts, including landings in extreme conditions, shipwrecks with numerous victims and very difficult rescues, which occupy the year 2014 as well. *Sea tragedy* begins to be a recurrent media label, indicating an ensemble of typical characteristics of such events: exploitation of migrants by crime organizations that make obsolete and overfilled boats to start, and the almost inevitable accident in the Sicily Channel or near the Southern Italy coasts. They affirm the new centrality of the refugee figure.

In 2014 both the Italian government and the EU commit to intervene in rescue activities (respectively with the Mare Nostrum and the Triton missions).

From a descriptive viewpoint, news media reporting registers or even amplifies the emotional charge of those events. The analysed quality newspapers take part in a sort of *ritual* of "pity and pain", while first assistance and registration activities begin to outline the new policy frontier, that of the refugees management.

From a quantitative viewpoint, the most treated sub-issues, detected in the six-month sample period, are[3]: "human rights, racism, reception" (34.8 % of the news items); "landings and sea tragedies" (16.5 %) and "European and international policy/intervention" (16.1 %). Compared with the one of the previously analysed year (Tab. 26.1), the picture looks sensibly changed, especially considering that 2008 fully represents the Berlusconi's era: security is no longer so newsworthy. International actors are more frequently protagonists in the news stories; the international non-EU scenario increases its prominence (see Tabs. 26.2 and 26.3). The level of conflict inside the domestic political sphere is stable (Tab. 26.1), but the domestic scenario percentage registers a drop of about 25 points (Tab. 26.3), also because of the involvement of the EU, which de-nationalizes the domestic political field.

Facing sea tragedies, the Italian quality-newspapers' strategies have a significant change, somehow acquiring a profile that will be developed along the following years. First of all, the drop of the standing offered to the civil society and the Catholic Church is noticeable (Marini & Gerli 2017a). This seems to indicate

3 To access a complete description of this survey results about the years 2008 and 2014, see Marini and Gerli (2017a) and Marini and Gerli (2017b).

Tab. 26.1: Sub-issues of immigration: Percentage variations

Sub-issues of immigration	2008–2014	2014–2017
Conflicts among domestic political actors	-0,1	0,0
European and international politics/intervention	12,0	-5,6
Human rights, racism and reception	-13,1	12,6
Work and economy	-1,2	-2,4
Security and illegal entrances	-9,6	-1,0
Landings and sea tragedies	11,8	-5,2
Others	0,2	1,5

Tab. 26.2: Principal actors in the news: Percentage variations

Actor category	2008–2014	2014–2017
Ordinary people	4,1	2,0
Immigrants	16,8	-6,1
Domestic politicians (local ones included)	-12,0	-9,2
Domestic state officials	-2,9	0,4
EU institutions and representatives	0,6	-2,7
EU Member States, governments and leaders	5,5	1,1
Foreign non-EU States, governments and leaders	0,5	2,0
Civil society	-10,6	6,6
Catholic Church	-4,5	-1,8
Corporations, unions and interest groups	2,5	0,6
Terrorists	-	5,3
Others	-	1,

Tab. 26.3: Main scenario of the news: Percentage variations

Scenario category	2008–2014	2014–2017
National/domestic	-24,8	0,2
International inside the European borders	6,2	1,6
European Union institutions and competences	10,9	-9,1
International outside the European borders	13,2	16,3
Local	-5,4	-8,9

a decreasing *advocacy* attitude, while a dramatization of the sea accidents begins to provide the *emotional frame* both of a unceasing pressure and of a humanitarian crisis.

Further, an *accountability* control of government is realized, as said, in the field of hospitality policies, inevitably looking at the wider European scenario and the international one. Within this new perspective, domestic conflicts seem to be mitigated by the implication of much more actors who seem to play a considerable role in a larger, though complicated, political horizon. This represents a different pathway of pluralizing their own arena, but Italian journalism is not still familiar with those non-domestic actors (Marletti, Mouchon 2005; Cornia 2010; Koopmans, Statham 2010) who take the floor and are increasingly determinant, not allowing the adoption of the usual staging schemes.

This behaviour, that could be called *de-domestication*, implies two consequences: on the one hand, it detaches journalism from the close relationship with domestic politics, breaking consolidated practices; on the other hand, it seems to call those same domestic politicians to face the new interdependence in an accountable way (see also Marini & Gerli 2017b).

Finally, news items seem to be spread over a *multilevel* setting and variable scenario from the local to the international, each policy level is involved, but also investigated about what is at stake. So, in the most influential Italian newspapers – alongside the humanitarian frame – refugee flows begin to outline *a multilevel crisis of sustainability.*

5 A Second Step of an Unresolved Emergency: Rescue Activities and Terrorist Threat

In 2017 the situation in the Mediterranean Sea appears further modified: while crossing attempts and landings increase, various NGOs engage in rescue activities (MSF, SOS Mediterraneé and others), provoking the reaction by a part of the Italian political forces that accuse the volunteers to act out of rules and to mine the official missions. Later, an agreement will be established between the Italian and the Libyan governments aimed to contain flows.

Compared with the picture of 2014, the situation in 2017 differs also because of the chain of terrorist attacks (that have been continuing from January 2015) in many European cities (among which Paris, Manchester, London and Barcelona, respectively, in April, May, June and August), realized by radicalised immigrants or second-generation citizens, thus questioning the relationship between European societies and the impact of immigration, in a historical perspective too. Attacks often show a strongly symbolic meaning: they are not only claimed by ISIS, but they are also realized in emblematic places of the various nations. This relaunches the security problem in the immigration issue.

The most frequently treated sub-issues in the news during the sampled period are: "human rights, racism, reception" (47.4 %); "security and illegal entrances" (18.6 %) and "landings and sea tragedies" (11.3 %). In comparison with 2014 (Table 26.1), however, only the large category of "human rights and racism" shows a rising percentage, that is the result of the many ways values and world views are under discussion in the above-mentioned situation, made more complex by rescue activities and by the attempt to block flows. Alongside human rights, landings and tragedies at sea seem to be more marginal, placed in the background of a much more conflictual landscape.

As for the "principal" actors in the news, Tab. 26.2 shows there is a further drop of the centrality of the domestic politicians, combined with a diminished importance of immigrants and an upswing of civil society (due to the discussed activism by the non-governmental organizations in the Mediterranean Sea). Terrorists (individuals and organizations) gain salience as well.

The news stories maintain a multilevel setting, but with a slightly modified configuration (Tab. 26.3). The journalists' sight is pushed beyond the European borders, owing to the involvement of countries such as Libya, Turkey and African ones; echoes from the United States' new situation get to the attention focus of Italian newspapers. So, both the EU and the local scenarios lose ground in favour of an international (extra-European) scenario (Tab. 26.3).

An attempt to better understand the composition of the sub-issue "human rights, racism, reception" has been carried out regarding the 2017 news stories, through a new classification. Results show a division in two blocks: "problems and discussions about reception" reaches the 75 % of the news stories in the sub-issue aggregate and other and disperse themes occupy the remaining 25 % (violence, protests, racism acts, heroic actions, etc.). This evidence reinforces what was observed in the 2014 news production, though at a beginning stage: reception policies (regulation, structures, effectiveness and costs) gain a notable level of newsworthiness and seem to be the ground on which newspapers exercise their pressure on politics about accountability. Considering the conflict government/NGOs, it can be said that the emergency that surrounds the immigration issue is characterized by two questions without a plausible answer: "who rescues?" and "who hosts?", emblematic of a stalling situation. Within this suspension a new frame affirms, the one of the management of immigration, that is going to outline as the frame of the unresolved emergency.

6 Conclusions

The articulation of the present chapter started from the discussion about a critical judgement by some scholars toward the news media behaviour in the treatment of the immigration issue. Those studies emphasize the spectacular nature of the media representation, that produces a distortion in the phenomenon perception by the public opinion. A first observation has been proposed, regarding the reproduction – by these readings of the news media production – of a previously defined scheme, related to crime and public order. That scheme is based on relevant assumptions, such as the legitimation strategy adopted by the media and the application of a non-neutral frame on reality. But it seems to manifest a normative perspective, which does not allow those scholars to lucidly analyse the cultural transformations that should be considered as the general context of the news organizations' strategies concerning all those issues related to perceived threats.

Consequently, an analysis about the concepts of uncertainty and risk has been conducted, in order to underline the new relevance of this socio-psychological condition in the contemporary post-industrial societies, as stated by some eminent authors, among whom the most important is, no doubt, Ulrich Beck. A specific reconstruction has been proposed about the characteristics of the post-welfare politics, and its gaps in facing new needs, both because of a resources deficit and because of some cultural lags, especially regarding the raising of security instances. The thesis here advanced is that while immigration has assumed the features of an emergency, no adequate and effective policy measures have been adopted. The consequence has been the hypertrophic development of an ideological and conflictual discourse, in which the immigration issue plays the role of a new cleavage. The shape of the immigration issue has been designed by various emergency cycles, symbolically managed by the political forces on the ground, with a relevant help by the news media.

Therefore, a view of the media/politics relationship based on the key idea of interdependence looks preferable in comparison with those that privilege the strength (and thus the responsibility) of only one of the partners; at least because it is able to explain the mutual influence through which the issue is shaped.

On the base of this reciprocity dynamic, a factor is to be taken in more serious consideration whilst it is read as a typical product of the news media sensationalism: this is the role of those extraordinary events whose genesis cannot be under the control of any actor in the public space.

The agenda-building theory holds that these disruptive events are the starting point of a process of change within the agenda construction. In this process, when an upsetting event attracts a huge attention, the related is re-framed, as the outcome of a renewed debate or conflict. Actually, a new agenda "game" starts, exactly around the new meanings which the actors (media included) want to assign. This vision interprets the emergency situation not as the mere product of the artificial construction by the media, but as the result of the intertwining of multiple strategies and behaviours. Of course, their impact may not be the same in every circumstances, depending on, as said, the variable characteristics of the context.

The thesis of the crucial role of such critical events has been tested through the analysis carried out about the representation of the immigration issue by the two most influential and most circulated Italian newspapers, in 2014 and 2017. The coverage has shown a notable responsiveness to this kind of events, which trigger a sequence of modifications in the issue structure.

In 2014, sea tragedies deeply influence the way immigration is framed as a social problem: the desperate journeys have been discovered and the refugee – the new image of the migrant – needs to be helped and hosted, but a general uncertainty pervades the scene. The humanitarian frame and the securitarian frame still compete, but there begins to appear the frame of the difficulties in managing the crisis, whose development is not foreseeable.

In 2017, the conflict about the rescue activity and the terrorist attacks in Europe further change the picture. The problem of the immigration management even more spreads upon a multilevel scenario and the ineffectiveness of the first assistance and hospitality raises evidently. Within the human rights sub-issue, this praxis question advances in the two papers' representation. At the same time, terrorist attacks by radicalised young people question the future of integration.

This all shows that the analysed media representations are a joint product of historical contingencies, triggered by events possessing an autonomous force, and managed by multiple actors' strategies. Hence, is it possible to state that this way of representing the immigration issue is compatible with the ideal function of a consistent social responsibility? In other words, is it possible to, even partially, to praise the two elite papers?

Italian quality newspapers, though with a different profile, look to follow three combined strategies. Dramatization: when they narratively and emotionally report the most disruptive events; but also when they stage the conflict among leaders. Advocacy: when they defend values, as universal guidelines, but overtly put in discussion in the political struggle. Accountability control of politics (watchdogging): when they highlight the weakness of policies.

This three-fold way of operating seems to show the ambiguity of a transformation process, that of the crisis of the progressive-liberal model of journalism in Italy and abroad. Along this process, different and sometime contradictory attitudes in conceiving journalism become visible. The focus on the inadequacy of policies would look as the full realization of the primary function of the government control, also enlarged toward a supra-national scenario. But, the persistent centrality in the news of the domestic political actors can be read as a renewed form of close linkage with the political sphere, with its inclination for tactics or ideological conflict, adapting the staging to the rules of commercialism. Responding to this last imperative may be considered more cogent than in the past, because of the rapidly increasing importance of the digital environment in the distribution and consumption of news.

References

Altheide D. L. (2002). *Creating Fear. News and the Construction of Crisis.* New York: De Gruyter.

Altheide D. L. (2006). *Terrorism and the Politics of Fear.* Lanham: AltaMira Press.

Altheide D. L. (2009). *Terror Post 9/11 and the Media.* New York: Peter Lang.

Ambrosini M. (2008). *Un'altra globalizzazione. La sfida delle migrazioni transnazionali.* Bologna: Il Mulino.

Ambrosini M. (2014). *Non passa lo straniero? Le politiche migratorie tra sovranità nazionale e diritti umani.* Assisi: La Cittadella.

Armigeon K., Bonoli G. (Eds.) (2007). *The Politics of Post-Industrial Welfare States: Adapting Post-War Social Policies to New Social Risks.* London: Routledge.

Balbo L., Manconi L. (1990). *I razzismi possibili.* Milano: Feltrinelli.

Bauman Z. (2009). *Paura liquida.* Roma-Bari: Laterza.

Baumgartner F. R., Jones B. D. (1993). *Agendas and Instability in American Politics.* Chicago: University of Chicago Press.

Beck U. (1986). *Risikogesellschaft. Auf dem Weg in eine andere Moderne.* Frankfurt am Main: Suhrkamp.

Beck U. (2007). *Weltriskogesellschaft. Auf der Suche nach der verlorenen Sicherheit.* Frankfurt am Main: Suhrkamp.

Beck U. (2016). *The Metamorphosis of the World.* Cambridge: Polity Press.

Belluati M., Gargiulo E., Seddone A. (2015). *Politiche pubbliche e frames nei giornali italiani.* In Bobbio L., Roncarolo F. (Eds.), *I media e le politiche. Come i giornali raccontano le scelte pubbliche che riguardano la vita dei cittadini.* Bologna: Il Mulino.

Benson R. (2013). *Shaping Immigration News: A French-American Comparison.* New York: Cambridge University Press.

Binotto M, Martino V. (2004). *FuoriLuogo. L'immigrazione e i media italiani.* Roma: Rai-Eri.

Binotto M., Bruno M., Lai V. (2012). *Gigantografie in nero. Ricerca su sicurezza, immigrazione e asilo nei media italiani.* Raleigh: Lulu Press.

Binotto M., Bruno M., Lai V. (2016). *Tracciare confini. L'immigrazione nei media italiani.* Milano: Franco Angeli.

Birkland T. A. (1997). *After Disaster. Agenda Setting, Public Policy, and Focusing Events.* Washington: Georgetown University Press.

Boydstun A. E. (2013). *Making the News. Politics, the Media, and the Agenda Setting.* Chicago: University of Chicago Press.

Bucchi M. (1999). *Vino, alghe e mucche pazze. La rappresentazione televisiva delle situazioni di rischio.* Roma-Torino: ERI.

Chadwick A. (2013). *The Hybrid Media System: Politics and Power.* Oxford–New York: Oxford University Press.

Chomsky N. (2002). *Media Control. The Spectacular Achievements of Propaganda* (2nd ed.). New York: Seven Stories Press.

Colombo A. (2007). Gli immigrati nella stampa nazionale quotidiana, in *Primo rapporto sugli immigrati in Italia* (cap. XIV). Roma: Ministero dell'Interno.

Cornia A. (2010). *Notizie da Bruxel. Logiche e problemi della costruzione giornalistica dell'Unione europea.* Milano: FrancoAngeli.

Cotesta V. (2009). *Sociologia dei conflitti etnici. Razzismo, immigrazione e società multiculturale.* Roma-Bari: Laterza.

D'Alessandro R. (2010). *La società smarrita. Quattro letture del presente fra paure, crisi e migrazioni.* Milano: Franco Angeli.

Dal Lago A. (1999). *Non-persone. L'esclusione dei migranti in una società globale.* Milano: Feltrinelli.

D'Angelo P., Kuypers J. A. (Eds.) (2010). *Doing News Framing Analysis. Empirical and Theoretical Perspectives.* Routledge: New York.

Dearing G. W., Rogers E. M. (1996). *Agenda-Setting.* Thousand Oaks: Sage.

De Cesaris V. (2018). *Il grande sbarco. L'Italia e la scoperta dell'immigrazione.* Milano: Guerini.

De Cesaris V., Diodato E. (Eds.) (2018). *Il confine mediterraneo. L'Europa di fronte agli sbarchi dei migrant.* Roma: Carocci.

Edelman M. (1964). *The Symbolic Uses of Politics.* Urbana: University of Illinois Press.

Entman R. M. (1989). *Democracy Without Citizens. Media and the Decay of American Politics.* New York-Oxford: Oxford University Press.

Entman R. M. (2012). *Scandal and Silence: Media Responses to Presidential Misconduct.* Cambridge: Polity Press.

Fetzer J. S. (2000a). Economic Self-interest or Cultural Marginality: Anti-immigration Sentiment and Nativist Political Movements in France, Germany and the USA. *Journal of Ethnic and Migration Studies,* 26(1): 5–23.

Fetzer J. S. (2000b). *Public Attitudes Toward Immigration in the United States, France, and Germany.* Cambridge: Cambridge University Press.

Gerbner G., Gross L., Morgan M., Signorielli N. (1986). *Living with Television. The Dynamics of the Cultivation Process.* In J. Bryant, D. Zillmann (Eds.), *Perspectives on Media Effects* (pp. 17–40). Hillsdale: Lawrence Erlbaum Associates.

Hall S., Critcher C., Jefferson T., Clarke J., Roberts B. (1978). *Policing the Crisis: Mugging, the State and Law 'n' Order.* London: Palgrave-Macmillan.

Koopmans R., Statham P. (Eds.) (2010). *The Making of a European Public Sphere. Media Discourse and Political Contention.* Cambridge: Cambridge University Press.

Manning P. K. (1998). *Media Loops.* In F. Bailey, D. C. Hale (Eds.), *Popular Culture, Crime and Justice* (pp. 25–39). Belmont: West/Wadsworth.

Marini R. (2017a). Potere dei media, interdipendenza tra poteri e pluralismo dell'informazione. *Problemi dell'informazione,* 1: 3–30.

Marini R. (2017b). Fuori dalle *issues*. Poteri e politiche simboliche della paura nell'analisi dei "classici". *Sociologia della Comunicazione,* 54: 40–63.

Marini R., Gerli M. (2017a). Le variazioni del tema immigrazione nei media italiani: tra cambiamenti del fenomeno e pluralità degli attori. In M. Marchegiani (Ed.), *Antico Mare e identità migranti: un itinerario interdisciplinare.* Torino: Giappichelli.

Marini R., Gerli M. (2017b). Le forme di un tema. L'immigrazione nell'arena dei quality papers Italiani. *Comunicazione Politica*, 3: 479–504.

Marletti C., Mouchon J. (Eds.) (2005). *La costruzione mediatica dell'Europa.* Milano: Franco Angeli.

Norris P., Inglehart D. (2009). *Cosmopolitan Communications: Cultural Diversity in a Globalized World.* Cambridge: Cambridge University Press.

Norris P., Inglehart D. (2019). *Cultural Backlash: Trump, Brexit, and Authoritarian Populism*. Cambridge: Cambridge University Press.

Papacharissi Z. (Ed.) (2010). *A Networked Self: Identity, Community, and Culture on Social Network Sites*. New York: Routledge.

Risse, T. (2010). *A Community of Europeans? Transnational Identities and Public Spheres*. Cornell: Cornell University Press.

Reese S. D., Gandy O. H., Grant A. E. (Eds.) (2003). *Framing Public Life. Perspectives on Media and Our Understanding of Social World*. Mahwah: Lawrence Erlbaum Associates.

Roncarolo F. (2009). *Leader e media*. Milano: Guerini.

Rossi G., Boccacin L. (2012). *L'associazionismo multilivello in Italia. Reti relazionali, capitale sociale e attività prosociali*. Milano: FrancoAngeli.

Saraceno C. (2013). *Il welfare. Modelli e dilemmi della cittadinanza sociale*. Bologna: il Mulino.

Sciortino G., Colombo A. (2004). The flows and the flood: the public discourse on immigration in Italy, 1969–2001. *Journal of Modern Italian Studies*, 9(1): 94–113.

Sunstein C. R. (2009). *Going to Extremes: How Like Minds Unite and Divide*. Oxford: Oxford University Press.

Sunstein C. R. (2017). *#Republic: Divided Democracy in the Age of Social Media*. Princeton: Princeton University Press.

Tarrow S. (1990). *Democrazia e disordine. Movimenti di protesta e politica in Italia*. 1965–*1975*. Roma-Bari: Laterza.

Tarrow S. (2018). Il 1968 come "momento critico": tra cambiamento sinottico e graduale. In D. della Porta (a cura di), *Sessantotto. Passato e presente dell'anno ribelle* (pp. 39–56). Milano: Feltrinelli.

Tusini S. (2017). Temporal Apartheid as Italian Response to Global Migration. In M. Caselli e G. Gilardoni (Eds.), *Globalization, Supranational Dynamics and Local Experiences*. London: Palgrave Macmillan.

Part Four Additional Points

Michele Nicotra

Chapter Twenty-Seven Imagery Techniques in Restructuring Social Prejudice

Abstract: Social prejudice determines the self-affirmation of each individual or of a single group. The use of imagery techniques leads to observe what people idealize at the level of vision on a given social dynamic. The present study focuses on what imagery is.

1 Introduction

Imagery is part of the most eclectic and revolutionary visions, and many psychotherapists know marginally all the new frontiers that fall within this field.

In the 1950s and 1960s of the last century, this technique was used as a way of excellence in the behavioural treatments of systematic desensitization and flooding. The beginning of the twenty-first century has brought great developments in the study and practice of this technique, and precisely for this reason the treatments have increased exponentially.

According to Achterberg (1985), "The use of imagery in the psychotherapeutic setting has a complex and articulated history that is still very timely today" (p.722). The images are the tangible demonstration of how human thoughts manifest themselves to consciousness. Imagery holds all the mental representations endowed with sensory characteristics.

Beck (1971) has always affirmed that imagery played a fundamental role in understanding emotional distress; the meanings we give to experience represent the main focus of cognitive therapy. Beck (1971) has suggested that images, fantasies, memories and dreams were the main means to access them.

Imagery techniques are peculiar in anxiety disorders and in post-traumatic stress disorder; Beck et al. (1985) introduced the "double beliefs system" (p.32).

Anxious people tend to have ambivalent beliefs about certain situations: when they are far from a source of danger, the possibility of a catastrophe seems minimal to them; if they get close to it, it seems so much bigger. Therefore, they begin to imagine the feared consequences.

Precisely for this reason, imagery can be stimulated by environmental processes with real definition and it can be manifested in different ways in addition to the visual one. Imagery is often accompanied by intense and perfectly real deep emotions. The new frontiers of imagery in the psychopathological field turn out to be in rapid development. Excellent resources are now available for clinicians and researchers.

Imagery appears to have well-defined main characteristics. It turns out to be true and distressing and can have a positive or negative value. It affects the cognitive sphere and involves different sensorial spheres, and it can define a certain vision and redefines emotions. Through the use of imagery, people can define new emotions.

Imagery has a peculiarity that defines its strategic importance: it assumes different images according to the disorders that affect people, and very frequently it takes back past autobiographical images.

However, positive images may not always have advantageous implications. A possible example could be that of a person who every day imagines winning on scratch cards. This image generated in a constant way can lead to the mania to reach the desired result. In depressed subjects the imagination of their own suicide and the consequent creation of that image determines a sense of contentment and serenity intensifying the desire and the suicidal behaviour.

Conway and Pleydell-Pearce in 2000 distinguished two types of image recovery, one of a deliberate type in which the patients voluntarily recall an image and a type of spontaneous recall in which the image re-emerges spontaneously. The fundamental importance of imagery is that of having a symbiotic relationship with emotions and, not by chance, emotional recalling is central in every therapeutic treatment.

Kosslyn (1980) emphasized the importance and the need to pay attention to emotions, given that "imagery seems to play a fundamental role in the representation of emotionally charged material" (p. 405). Consequently, imagery is a tool of excellence to open and access emotions and redefine them. However, it is fundamental to remember how certain statements happen through a clinical and not an empirical experience.

The emotional nature of memories is defined by the perspective assumed during the use of the imagery. The first-person perspective gives the patients the possibility to observe their memories through "their eyes" while the second possibility is that of the external observer who allows the patients to explore the image from another perspective.

Imagery holds an innate power, that is, to highlight itself in different sensory modalities. These are auditory, visual, olfactory, gustatory and somatic. These sensations become interoceptive, cutaneous, tactile and kinesthetic. However, the visual perception is the predominant one. The exploration of all the patients' sensations through the professionalism of the therapist is fundamental.

Jung (1935) said: "when we focus on a mental representation, it starts moving to enrich itself with details, it grows and develops" (p.193). Thanks to this sentence it is possible to deduce that if introduced intentionally, imagery is very vivid and well defined, and it often creates unexpected emotions and permits to recognize and live experiences that have previously been ignored, and often holds aspects that people were not aware of.

2 Clinical Vision

The therapists who use imagery techniques use certain approaches which can be used according to the therapeutic direction they intend to pursue. The difference depends on two visions: the first is to use the technique in a direct manner in order to help the patients to bring out the evocative image; the second is indirect that is to evoke the image through reflections with a strong emotional impact. There are different imaginative possibilities between the direct and the indirect choice that could be identified considering their positive or negative emotional value.

The direct techniques can be distinguished into different classifications and can be used to reduce negative imagery through: the metaphorical approach; the possibility of transforming images, memories, and dreams; the evocation that is the possibility to explain and the manipulation of imagery.

The direct techniques to promote positive imagery use it to define goals and abilities and to develop new ways of being. In contrast, to reduce negative imagery, therapists use the cognitive therapy based on mindfulness and other metacognitive approaches. With the aim of promoting positive images, is - instead - useful to apply a workout that uses imaginative techniques.

To define an optimal and effective imagery intervention, a main aspect must be underlined, namely that of elaborating and transforming disturbing emotions in a constructive manner.

Rachman (1980) states that emotional processing can be considered effective if it is able to reduce emotional disturbance (p. 51).

Through clinical observations it is clear that to be able to set an ideal work with imagery there must be two essential elements: the first is the evocation of the disturbing image or explicitly the absence of positive imagery and the second is the use of incompatible information. The learning cycle of Kolb (1984), which was used in a superlative way by Bennett-Levy et al. (2004), is fundamental. To build up imagery it is mandatory to maintain a reflective attitude, but it is also necessary to remember that patients often experience feelings and emotions so intense that they are unable to maintain a reflective attitude. Moreover, patients often have magical or superstitious beliefs that make it very difficult to define the goals of imagery.

The therapists should possess a strong emotional intensity so that through their figures, the patients can process all the relevant information and reconstruct their ideas. However, it must be remembered that too strong or stressful emotions can cause the therapeutic abandonment or question a good therapeutic alliance. The capacity of the evocation of the disturbing image clinically brings out emotionally charged information. When patients describe imagery it is possible to detect and define emotions which permit to access a large number of major data compared to a simple verbal discussion. Two types of assessments are identified through a cognitive behavioural therapy: hot and cold. Hot cognitions light up automatically and are complementary to intense emotions and they often influence behaviour. The repetition of unstructured thoughts on a conscious level offers the possibility to highlight their content and to restructure and contextualize them. Often patients do not fully understand imagery and consider mental images as something inadequate or potentially dangerous or not real or even as a sign caused from madness.

It is very useful and important for the therapists to define well what the patients think about imagery before starting to use this technique in order to explain its real use and disconfirm the false beliefs. To achieve this result, the therapists can use phrases that lead to a reflection, for example: "when we are in crisis our mind is struck by many disturbing thoughts and these thoughts can take different forms of sentences, words or images. Has it ever happened to you?"

These kind of sentences induce the patients to think and they almost immediately develop kinaesthetic, visual and gustatory images. As a result, the patients recognize how imagery is part of normal everyday experience. It is very important to ask questions about imagery to understand if the patients are aware or unaware of its presence.

When psychotherapy is based on language the use of imagery is unusual, because the therapists rarely ask their patients to close the eyes and to define specific places and images or sensations of the body. This is the substantial difference. The patients are often suspicious and the therapists have to provide further rational explanations that convince the patients.

3 A Possibility of Restructuring the Prejudice Through the Mind Lab Set

Monitoring electrodermal activity can guarantee a certain reputation and holds the record for the widest literature in the field of psychophysiology. We must remember that the epidermis of our hands, especially of the fingers, constantly comes into contact with the outside world (Scrimali): "For Homo Sapiens, touching and manipulating means knowing and acting" (p.116).

The Mind Lab Set is an instrument of excellence in experimentation of the restructuring of the prejudice, and it is composed of an integrated system and of a unit for the acquisition of the elliptic dermal parameter that is the Psycodata Acquisition Unit, of a software called MindSCAN & Psychofeedback and of a Katane reference database that allows a clear normative reference for the data comparison.

The cutaneous functioning needs that the flexibility and the resistance of the skin are always regulated at best, and this condition is obtained with a constant hydration of the corneal layer of the epidermis that occurs through the sweat glands. The modulation of the micro-sweating activity of the hands forms a crucial process to recognize, manipulate, act and relate to each other. The execution and analysis of a track consists in recording the tonic and spontaneous electrodermal activity carried out with the Mind Lab Set for a period of four minutes during which three phases can be highlighted: the first are two minutes of baseline, the second a minute of cognitive activation and the third a minute of recovery; this recording can be simply implemented.

In clinical practice the use of the Mind Lab Set requires a structured setting. After having carried out the first interview, the MindSCAN & Psychofeedback program is activated. In this phase the monitor that observes the patient is switched off. The therapists explain the functioning of the Mind Lab Set in order to reassure the patients. Two electrodes are connected to the dominant hand of the patients in the index and middle finger. At the beginning of the collection of the data, the patients have to relax. In the second part they will be given a number, and they will have to make calculations for a minute and then, after the calculations, they will have to relax and try to eliminate all the thoughts from the mind. The test at a practical level takes place after having cleaned the index and middle finger of the subjects of the dominant hand through a dry wipe, then the therapists turn on the instrumentation and proceed with the recording. The acquisition value is set to 0.25 so the graph has a four-minute abscissa.

One of the most significant aspects is the restitution of the track to the people. After having printed the graph, it is shown to the patients in order to comment it together. In this way, the patients observe the morphology of the track, and they can comment on what happened during the tracking. Instrumental psychodiagnostics has the objective to make possible the assessment of procedures capable to define the functioning of mental processes.

The trial is being studied, and the research data will be published as soon as they are reviewed.

References

Beck, A. T. (1971). Cognition, affect, and psychopathology. *Archives of General psychiatry*, 24(6): 495–500.

Beck, A. T. (1991). Cognitive therapy: A 30-year retrospective. *American psychologist*, 46(4), 368–375.

Bennett-Levy, J. E., Butler, G. E., Fennell, M. E., Hackman, A. E., Mueller, M. E., & Westbrook, D. E. (2004). *Oxford guide to behavioural experiments in cognitive therapy*. Oxford: Oxford University Press.

Hackmann A., Bennet-Levy J., Holmes E. A., Marsigli N. (2018). *Le tecniche immaginative in terapia cognitiva: strategie di assessment e di trattamento basate sull'imagery*. Trento: Erickson.

Jung, C. G. (1935). "Principi di psicoterapia pratica". In C.G. Jung, *Opere*, vol. XVI: Pratica della psicoterapia, Torino: Bollati Broinghieri.

Kolb, B. (1984). Functions of the frontal cortex of the rat: a comparative review. *Brain Research Reviews*, 8(1): 65–98.

Kosslyn, S. M. (1980). *Image and mind*. Cambridge: Harvard University Press.

Noll, R., Achterberg, J., Bourguignon, E., George, L., Harner, M., Honko, L., ... & Siikala, A. L. (1985). Mental imagery cultivation as a cultural phenomenon: The role of visions in shamanism [and comments and reply]. *Current anthropology*, 26(4): 443–461.

Rachman, S. (1980). Emotional processing. *Behaviour Research and Therapy*, 18(1): 51–60.

Scrimali, T. (2009). *Neuroscienze e psicologia clinica. Dal laboratorio di ricerca al setting con i pazienti: Dal laboratorio di ricerca al setting con i pazienti*. Milano: FrancoAngeli.

Gevisa La Rocca and Tiziana Ramaci

Chapter Twenty-Eight Employees Working with Refugees and Asylum Seekers

Abstract: Training employees is maintained throughout life-long learning, and it is not an easy task. It is difficult to upgrade skills when employees are called to face new scenarios. In this emergency, there are social workers. Hundreds of thousands of migrants, in the last decade, put their lives at risk to reach the European coast (IDMC, 2016). Many organizations have started to engage (also) in the hospitality sector, and this has involved a necessary questioning and redefinition: *In what way, social professions need to evolve and which are the priority needs to be strengthened through training and support?*This chapter represents the First Intellectual Output of a transnational project named "Teaching Partnership Addressed to Refugee's Instances Strengthening" (PARIS, 2016–2019). PARIS is financed with the support of the ERASMUS + Programme of the European Union – Strategic Partnership in the field of Higher Education; it aims to strengthen University's curriculum in the field of refugees, through the creation of a closer linkage between not-for-profit organizations active in the field and the academic sector.

1 Introduction[1]

This chapter represents the First Intellectual Output of a transnational project named *Teaching Partnership Addressed to Refugee's Instances Strengthening* (PARIS). PARIS is a three years' project financed with the support of the ERASMUS + Programme of the European Union – Strategic Partnership in

1 The content of this chapter comes from the first intellectual output realized in the Paris project "Teaching Partnership Addressed to Refugees's Instances Strengthening". Gevisa La Rocca was the scientific coordinator of the Paris project (2016–2019). The first intellectual output produced a volume with the results of the research edited by Di Liberto A., La Rocca G. (Eds.) (2017). *Current models for the management of refugees and asylum seekers in Italy, Spain and Romania: training needs for working with this group.* Palermo: Unione degli Assessorati Comunali e Provinciali alle Politiche Socio-Sanitarie e del Lavoro. The authors of the volume are all members of the project teams (the names are listed on the first pages of the volume). The authors of this chapter have summarized some main activities and results with the aim of increasing their diffusion. The source of the data and tables is therefore that volume.

the field of Higher Education. The project, started in 2016, aims to strengthen University's curriculum in the field of refugee management, through the creation of a closer linkage between not-for-profit organizations active in the field and the academic sector.

Hundreds of thousands of migrants, in the last decade, put their lives at risk to reach the European coast (IDMC, 2016). Over 65.6 million people worldwide need protection and humanitarian assistance as a result of forced migration (UNHCR, 2017). Many organizations of the third sector have started to engage (also) in the hospitality sector, and this has involved a necessary questioning and redefinition: *In what way, social professions need to evolve and which are the priority needs to be strengthened through training and support?*

The innovative aspect of the present work is the focus on training needs of social workers working with this target group. Research findings outline relevant features belonging to such professional sector that will be taken into account for a proper prosecution of the PARIS project. In addition, practitioners (both academic professors and social workers) working in this field could find interesting the conclusions here presented in order to gather new knowledge on this topic as well as to exchange good practices.

2 The Training Needs Analysis

In the knowledge society, knowledge has an increasing value, but it is not stable over time, and if it is not updated and shared, it may become obsolete and therefore "useless." The individual's process of training does not end with entry into adulthood, but is maintained throughout life (life-long learning).

To keep up with a company that grows and transforms itself faster and faster, individuals are forced to increase their knowledge to face the challenges of the labor market. This request for skills upgrade has already been acquired by businesses enterprises and industrial organizations, which now become "learning organizations."

The more difficult it is to upgrade skills when workers – social or non-social – are called to face new challenges and scenarios. This is what is happening to social workers dealing with refugees and asylum seekers. We live in alarmism, caused by the use of catastrophic headlines and words on major means of communication, which describe a recent situation and our inability to deal with this phenomenon (La Rocca, 2017). On the forefront, in this emergency there are social workers.

It is clear how difficult it is, especially for social workers, to face this scenario. In this research, we wonder what are the skills needed to face these changes in the world scenario, changes that redefine skills of social workers. To answer this need of skills, the present Training Needs Analysis (TNA) was realized.

Training employees effectively is not an easy task. Training is an investment and it is not viewed as a cost by human capital theory (Bliss, 2014). Research acclaimed the importance of training by which organization can be developed, enhancing organization profitability (Sung et al., 2014; Tharenou, 1991). We know very well the TNA for business or social workers involved in family or child care, but a little less about the social workers' needs in relation to refugees and asylum seekers, because they represent a new target, a less explored professional sector.

As with a TNA that takes care of employees, even in this, there are some factors that need to be taken into account when designing or screening training programs (Fleck, 2014). These factors will determine if the transfer of learning actually takes place. One of the very important factors is the process of TNA.

To this scope, the PARIS survey was preceded by an exploratory analysis conducted through focus groups on privileged witnesses, representing the target groups facing this humanitarian emergency.It is the condition by which training would make effective and approachable in the start. Furthermore, it includes attentive consideration towards the accuracy of the recognized "needs" and the fulfillment of these "needs." If these "needs" are correctly recognized while using right process, then the probability of success of the training is high. Training must be approached systematically in order to enjoy the benefits on training investment.

From a theoretical point of view, this analysis starts with the identification of training needs, the designing and also developing suitable training solution, implementing this training, and evaluating the training programs' effectiveness whether the original needs have been achieved (Arshad et al., 2015). These steps are popularly known as the "training cycle," and many training researches agreed that these steps are necessary to ensure training effectiveness (Leat & Lovell, 1997). According to that, the first PARIS research was addressed to the execution of focus groups conducted on five target groups: social workers, school teachers, psychologists, intercultural mediators, and mentors and volunteers involved into the project with refugees refugees/asylum seekers; University professors, researchers, doctoral course tutors, master programs coordinators, managing training subjects addressed to prepare students in working in the refugee's sector; managers of communities and services directors; and university students.

Thanks to this activity, an integral part of the training cycle, it was possible to identify targeted training needs, ensuring at the same time the effectiveness of the overall training process. The identification of the most relevant skill/competence areas to be used in the survey was made possible through this activity.

3 Aim of the Study

The aim of the study, conducted as part of the PARIS project (Teaching Partnership Addressed to Refugees' I Strength Staging), is to investigate on training needs and on the new skills required of social workers (Di Liberto A., La Rocca G., 2017) useful for facing the changes that affect the European scenario and not only (EURSOSTAT, 2017) of the three countries participating in the project: Italy, Spain, and Romania. A number of 413 professionals have been involved in the survey: social workers, teachers, psychologists, mediators, and volunteers; refugees/asylum seekers; managers and coordinators of reception services; service managers; and students.

A survey has both advantages and disadvantages, and TNAs based solely on these could be questionable. Surveys are beneficial because many people can be polled in a short period of time. They can be easily analyzed and be quite cheap to administer.

For this task, we decided to use an online tool, Google questionnaire, to create the project questionnaire. Through e-mail, the link to the questionnaire was sent to the potential respondents of the PARIS networks (as well as mapped organizations identified in the previous task).

Survey return rates can be low; it is difficult to design an online questionnaire and many people do not complete them. Surveys should take the form of a questionnaire and should include close-ended or open-ended questions, or a series of both. Close-ended questions require the respondent stay within certain parameters set by the person who created the survey. As the answers are limited, tabulating the data is quite simple. Open-ended questions allow the respondent to provide more feedback and introduce new ideas that may not have been considered initially, although tallying the results may be more difficult. A good option during the creation of a survey is to include a combination of both close-ended and open-ended questions.

For that reason, the questionnaire included a combination of both close-ended and open-ended questions, and was also divided into three areas: personal information; information about the organization and the professional role of the respondent; and trainings needs, divided into educational background and learning needs.

The element in the trainings needs' section is rated along a 7-point scale in two different ways – what is the level of competence owned (rating A) and how useful can the skill be in carrying out their work (rating B).

Interpreting the ratings: rating A provides an index of how useful the skills are the respondent has in carrying out his/her work, while rating B provides an index of which skills are needed for the respondent to do his/her job. Comparing the scores for importance/performance provides an assessment of where the greatest training needs lie (Martilla & James, 1977).

At a later stage, we have tried to evaluate the level of importance of the skills according to the position held within the organization and the professional experience in the humanitarian held (seniority). We analyzed the dataset by a univariate and a bivariate point of view.

The first analysis aims to describe the subjects' responses to each item of the questionnaire. The second one, instead, aims to investigate if and how some given subjects' characteristics or responses act on other item responses.

4 Sociodemographic Characteristics of the Respondents

The third activity included a survey aimed at identifying the training needs related to the field of refugees' reception. For this purpose, a questionnaire was delivered online in the three partner countries of the project. A number of 413 professionals has been involved in the survey, people who are currently working in this field, in order to explore: perceptions, shortcomings, and needs connected to the real fieldwork experience with refugees and asylum seekers. Those who responded to our survey have a clear and direct view of the migration phenomenon because they work in the reception of refugees and asylum seekers.

The first part of the questionnaire was aimed at tracing a basic profile of the respondents, and it detected general information on gender, age, qualification, and knowledge of foreign languages.

The majority (70,7 %) of those who answered the online survey consisted of women with an average age of 37.3 years, and the remaining 29,3 % of men with an average age slightly higher, 40.4 years. In most of the cases (87,0 %) the level of qualification field is high.

In fact, 49,2 % of respondents state to hold a degree and 37,8 % own a postgraduate degree. Only 13,0 % of the respondents have a lower academic qualification. Most of the qualifications belong to the scientific disciplinary sector of social sciences (26,6 %), although significant percentages are found in other fields: 15,4 % fall into the psychological area, 12,0 % in the pedagogical area, and 10,2 % in that one of foreign languages. Percentages between 5 % and 7 % are detected for other areas.

It was verified how respondents perceived the relevance of their educational background to the professional field in which they currently work and the role they hold ("In your current work experience, how useful is your educational background?"). It turns out that 55,0 % of the respondents believe it to be "very relevant," 18,2 % consider it "absolutely relevant," and 21,3 % "relevant enough." Percentages for the other two possible options ("not relevant" and "little relevant") are not significant.

About 87,4 % of respondents speak English (361 respondents, out of which 130 speak only English), 45,5 % know French (188 respondents, of whom 19 know only French), and 21,6 % Spanish (89 respondents, of which 2 speak just Spanish). Thus, 36,6 % of the respondents speak only one foreign language, while the majority of respondents (63,4 %) more than one. Irrelevant percentages of respondents declare to know other foreign languages, in addition to those mentioned above.

5 The Organization and the Professional Role of Respondents

The second part of the questionnaire was aimed at gathering information about the organization and the professional role played by the respondents. The majority of respondents (40,4 %) work within the "operational" level category. This one includes different profiles, who have in common the direct contact with migrants; they are the ones who spend their every day time with refugees and asylum seekers. Among these profiles, we can find: social workers, educators, social animators, and cultural mediators.

The "operational"-level category is well separated from that one related to coordination and that one of leadership. This last one (leadership level), according to the already mentioned criterion (of more or less direct contact with migrants), collects executive and administrative professional roles who do not have a direct contact with migrants. Furthermore, 27,9 % of the respondents play a coordinating role within the organization, while 15,0 % are presidents, managers, or play a more general or technical role. The last category (other professional role), that is present among the respondents with a percentage of 16,7 %, brings together all the pro les that could be defined as "professional": pedagogues, sociologists, psychologists, psychiatrists, anthropologists, health workers, and legal assistance staff.

Respondents are mainly working (71,4 %) for "nonprofit organizations," while a far lower percentage works for "public institutions" (17,2 %) and for "profit organizations" (11,4 %). Over the last year, 29,5 % of these structures have received, on average, more than 100 migrants. The remaining 70,5 % show a very varied situation with regard to the number of migrants hosted every year. A remarkable position is held by small structures that act as a counterpart to those structures with more than 100 users: last year, 16,7 % of the organizations from which respondents belong to hosted refugees/asylum seekers and/or provided services to no more than 10 migrants.

Most respondents (53,7 %) have been working in the humanitarian field ("seniority") for refugees and asylum seekers for less than 3 years (23,7 % for a year or less and 29,5 % for 2–3 years). Percentages decrease as the work field experience increases: 17,4 % for 4–5 years, 17,9 % for 6–10 years, and 11,4 % for more than 11 years. Within the organization 91,5 % of respondents carry out paid work and only 8,5 % receive no remuneration.

6 Training Needs

The third part of the questionnaire was devoted to the recognition of the training needs of the pro les involved in the reception/assistance of refugees/asylum seekers.

The first aspect that has been taken into consideration is that of the specific skills and knowledge that respondents believe to own.

Respondents were asked to state what skills/knowledge they possess and then assess – using a scale from 1 to 7 – their level of own of those skills/knowledge: "On a scale from 1 to 7, which of these skills and specific knowledge do you think to possess and to what extent?" (Tab. 28.1).

In general, the majority of respondents ranks a score of 5 and 6, with higher peaks at 7 that implies a more expertise in such areas, and more significant peaks at 3, pointing out possible shortcomings.

Assuming that self-assessment is often distorted by the subjectivity of the response, the highest score (7) was attributed from 31,7 % of respondents to "team work" skills and from 25,9 % of them to "problem-solving" skills, the latter being more generic skills usually linked to teamwork of an organization, but not necessarily relative to the humanitarian field. Compared to these two areas, the majority of respondents (33,7 % for team work and 37,8 % for problem-solving) ranked 6. Distribution of respondents on linguistic, cultural, and intercultural communication; advocacy; and gender equality skills/knowledge appears to be more skewed towards 4 and with most significant percentages on score 3. For example, for the linguistic area there is a 19,9 % on 4 and a 9,2 % on 7; for the cultural area 20,8 % is on 4 and 7,5 % on 7; for the advocacy area score 4 makes a percentage of 20,3 % and 7 a percentage of 11,4 %. A slight imbalance, though less

Tab. 28.1: Skills/knowledge owned and assessed*

Skills and knowledge	**1**	**2**	**3**	**4**	**5**	**6**	**7**
Linguistic	9,4	10,9	11,6	19,9	23,5	15,5	9,2
Legal/legislative	6,0	7,0	12,6	16,2	20,8	20,3	17
Cultural	4,6	6,8	14,3	20,8	24,5	21,6	7,5
Intercultural communication	3,2	6,1	10,7	15,5	23,7	27,9	13,1
Mediation/conflict resolution	3,6	4,8	9,0	11,4	24,2	30,2	16,7
Team work	1,7	3,4	2,4	10,2	17,0	33,7	31,7
Problem-solving	2,9	2,7	3,2	9,2	18,4	37,8	25,9
Advocacy	4,4	6,5	11,6	20,3	21,6	24,2	11,4
Gender equality	4,4	7,5	11,1	17,2	13,0	23,7	13,1

**Row percentages*

pronounced, is registered for the area of intercultural communication (15,5 % on 4 and 13,1 % on 7) and for the area of gender equality (17,2 % on 4 and 13,1 % on 7). For the areas mentioned here, 3 scores between 10,7 % and 14,3 % indicate the tendency to rank higher towards the lowest scores.

The second aspect taken into consideration was the relevance attributed from respondents to the same skills/knowledge. Also in this case, the sample was asked to assign a score on a scale from 1 to 7: "On a scale from 1 to 7, how relevant do you think the above-mentioned skills and knowledge are in the work context in which you operate?" (Tab. 28.2).

For all expertise and knowledge, the sample is distributed, in higher percentage, around the value being 7. The area that recorded the highest percentage on the highest score was that of team work (62,7 %), followed by problem-solving (57,9 %), intercultural communication (57,4 %), mediation/conflict resolution (55,7 %), legal/legislative (49,4 %), and the cultural area (47,9 %). The last three areas (linguistic, gender equality, and advocacy) show fewer than 45 %.

The most interesting evidence can be drawn from the comparison between what you believe to possess and what you think you need.

A significant correspondence is noted: those areas that seem to be deficient are also those that are considered less relevant (compared to others and in relation with their workplace) by large percentages of respondents (e.g., the linguistic or cultural area). Contrary to the areas where respondents felt they had greater expertise are also the most relevant ones (e.g., team work or problem-solving). Only two areas seem to deviate from this trend. One is that of intercultural communication, to which 57,4 % of the respondents attributed the score 7,

Tab. 28.2: Relevance of the skills/knowledge owned*

Relevance of skills and knowledge	1	2	3	4	5	6	7
Linguistic	2,9	2,4	9,0	8,2	15,3	24,2	38,0
Legal/legislative	2,4	1,0	3,2	5,8	13,6	24,7	49,4
Cultural	1,9	1,0	2,7	5,6	14,0	26,9	47,9
Intercultural communication	1,0	1,5	2,9	2,9	10,2	24,2	57,4
Mediation/conflict resolution	1,2	1,9	2,7	5,3	10,0	23,5	55,7
Team work	0,5	1,2	1,2	3,6	10,2	20,6	62,7
Problem-solving	1,2	1,0	2,4	4,1	9,0	24,5	57,9
Advocacy	1,9	1,5	3,9	8,5	13,8	27,1	43,3
Gender equality	1,45	1,2	3,6	7,8	15,5	27,4	43,1

**Row percentages*

and, the other one is the area of mediation/conflict resolution, which has similar percentages to the previous one.

The other one is the area of mediation/conflict resolution, which has similar percentages to the previous one.

The third point examined in the survey was the relevance attributed by the respondents to the single subjects covered during their own studies. The academic discipline that was awarded higher scores by the vast majority of respondents is that related to the study of asylum seekers legislation and integration as well as that of human rights law (58,4 % rated scores 7 and 25,4 % score 6) (Tab. 28.3).

The next to follow are: social sciences (with a percentage of 35,3 % on score 7 and 31,5 % on 6), migration studies (with 36,8 % on 7 and 26,4 % on 6), psychological studies (with 34,9 % on 7 and 29,1 % on 6), cultural studies (with 30,0 % on 7 and 30,3 % on 6), equal opportunities studies (31,5 % on 7 and 28,3 % on 6), and Indo-European languages (with 27,4 % on 7 and 30,3 % on 6). On the other hand, communication sciences (with the majority of respondents, 52,3 % exactly, between 5 and 6, and 18,2 % on 4), academic disciplines related to the theory and the history of international relations (with 53,3 % between 5 and 6 and 14,8 % on 4), but especially economics and management sciences (with 50,6 % between 4 and 5) are those considered of less importance.

The fourth point assessed by respondents was the importance attributed to the ability to promote positive relationships in the context of humanitarian field (refugee and asylum seekers); in particular, among those social actors specified in the questionnaire most of respondents attribute great relevance to the

Tab. 28.3: Relevance attributed by the respondents of academic disciplines*

Relevance of academic disciplines	1	2	3	4	5	6	7
Social sciences	1,2	1,7	3,2	9,4	17,7	31,5	35,4
Psychological studies	1,0	0,7	5,3	9,2	19,9	29,2	34,9
Asylum integration	0,7	1,2	1,7	4,6	8,0	25,4	58,4
Indo-European languages	1,5	2,9	6,8	12,4	18,9	30,3	27,4
Afro-Asian languages	3,4	5,6	9,0	15,3	17,2	25,9	23,7
Cultural studies	0,7	2,2	4,8	8,5	22,8	31,0	30,0
Communication sciences	1,9	5,3	8,7	18,2	27,1	25,2	13,6
International relation	3,4	4,4	10,2	14,8	29,1	24,2	14,0
Migration studies	1,0	1,5	5,1	9,2	20,1	26,4	36,8
Equal opportunities	1,0	1,5	4,1	13,6	20,1	28,3	31,5
Economics/management sciences	3,9	7,3	12,4	22,8	27,9	16,7	9,2
Social planning	2,4	2,4	5,1	10,9	19,9	31,0	28,3

**Row percentages*

promotion of positive relationships between migrants and citizenry (68,0 % of them think it is absolutely essential and 28,3 % very important), between social workers and migrants (66,3 % think it absolutely essential and 30,8 % very important) and between organizations and public institutions (49,6 % think it is absolutely essential and 44,6 % very important). Instead the promotion of positive relationships between migrants from different nationalities is considered somehow less remarkable (40,4 % think it is absolutely essential and 48,7 % very important).

Even less importance is given by respondents to the promotion of positive relations between their own organization and other similar organizations (37,1 % think it is absolutely essential and 28,3 % very important).

Finally, the last aspect investigated was the relationship between theory and practice aimed at making interventions more effective in the humanitarian field, and achieving a real and positive impact on those who are the target of the services provided. It has emerged that practice tends to give it more space and importance than the theory. In fact, 34,6 % believe that the relationship between practice and theory should be slightly unbalanced towards practice (in a proportion of 60 out of 40), 32,2 % of the respondents equal the importance between them (50 out of 50), while the remaining 24,5 % believe that practice should play a more leading role than theory (70 out of 30) (see Tab. 28.4).

Tab. 28.4: Ratio between theory and practice in the courses

Theory and practice ratio	N	%
30 theory – 70 practice	101	24,5
40 theory – 60 practice	143	34,6
50 theory – 50 practice	133	32,3
60 theory – 40 practice	27	6,5
70 theory – 30 practice	9	2,2

7 Training Provided

The fourth section of the questionnaire was designed to identify the characteristics of a new training course. This new training course could respond to the training needs that we have discovered with this survey. First, respondents were asked to express their opinion on the need for specific professionalism of staff currently providing assistance to refugees and asylum seekers. It has emerged that this requirement exists for 91.8 % of our respondents, who have different roles within the organizations – it is important to recall it. This data is interesting and reinforces the idea that a need to invest in the training of all those who are facing this new migratory phenomenon is really existent. The other important aspect of this data is that it tells us how those who are engaged in this sector feel themselves unprepared to face with it. Although newspapers continue to call it an emergency, since it has been so for many years now, it cannot be defined as such. The new migration wave is a "crystallized emergency."

It is therefore desirable to start thinking about the creation of training courses specializing in the reception of refugees and asylum seekers. This is a must, since even all those who work in this area and who need to increase their professional pro le need to have more skills in this area.

For 90,8 % of the respondents such professionalism should be guaranteed by creating a specialized training course focused on providing humanitarian aid to refugees and asylum seekers. Those who deem it necessary to set up a specialized training course in providing assistance to refugees and asylum seekers have been asked to motivate their response. The majority of the sample (42,9 %) considers it an essential path since the peculiarity and heterogeneity of the problems faced by refugees/asylum seekers once they arrive in the landing place can only be addressed through a specific training. Another significant percentage (37,3 %) motivated this need, believing that the quality of knowledge and skills of staff working in this field could be improved by the combination of well-documented theory and case studies selection/best practice presentation. The remaining

Tab. 28.5: Reasons for choosing*

	N	%
A) A combination between a well-documented theory and a case study selection/best practice presentation would improve the quality of the knowledge people involved in this field need	140	37,3
B) The diversity of the problems refugees face needs a specialized approach and also an integrated one. So, a course would be welcome	161	42,9
C) The refugee crisis is becoming more and more a serious phenomenon and needs a specialized workforce that could be obtained only by a training course	68	18,1
D) Other motivation	6	1,6
Total	*375*	*100,0*

**Percentages are calculated on the total of those who consider it necessary to create a specialized training course, i.e., 375 respondents. About 9,2 % of the sample does not think it necessary*

18,1 % links this need to the emerging and widespread character of the phenomenon ("The refugee crisis is becoming more and more a serious phenomenon and needs a specialized workforce that could only be obtained through a training course") (Tab. 28.5).

The 54.9 % of respondents believe that the most suitable path to providing specialized training to staff is an advanced training course. Within the "advanced training" label, there are many levels of courses: as an upgrade course, specialization course, high education course, etc. Significantly smaller but still significant percentages suggest the "summer school" (11,5 %) or the "master's degree" type (14,4 %). The other offered training courses (bachelor, master, and summer courses) have been judged to be insufficient for training needs. For what concerns teaching methods, 44,1 % of the respondents indicated the blended mode (face-to-face and online) and 39,0 % the face-to-face training modules.

If e-learning is born to free up the didactic intervention from the limits imposed by physical presence, blended – that comes from the verb 'to blend,' meaning to mix – is a mode of training that involves the combined use of traditional classroom, WBT – Web-Based Training with platforms for e-learning – and knowledge management systems.

Less significant percentages are recorded for the other two teaching methods: 13,1 % for face-to-face tutorials and only 3,9 % for the online training.

Also in this section, we have tried to deepen the practical aspect. The hypothesized training paths should include a period of internship. The sample was asked to indicate how many hours of internship they consider necessary in comparison to the hours of theory.

Again, the trend already highlighted to give greater weight to practice has been confirmed.

In fact, although the majority of respondents, 29,5 %, believe that theory and internship should be both equally present, significant percentages of the sample consider that the amount of time devoted to the internship should be greater, 27,9 % believe that the ratio between the hours of internship and those devoted to theory should be slightly unbalanced towards practice (in a proportion of 60 out of 40), and then 19,9 % believe that the hours of internship should prevail over theory (70 out of 30). Another interesting result is that 97,6 % affirms that NGOs operating in this area could be actively involved in a potential specialized training path for providing assistance to refugees/asylum seekers.

There are several possible ways to involve NGOs. Classroom activities seem to have found greatest acceptance, as indicated by 64,5 % of respondents. NGOs could be involved in seminars or workshops or to put into practice their fieldwork experience by analyzing case studies or describing best practices.

Internship opportunities are chosen by 60,9 % of the respondents who would give students the opportunity to work directly in the field. It is also noteworthy to mention (i.e., from 58,4 % of respondents) the format that contemplates meeting for offering some real cases and the way to deal with them, throughout the whole course. Finally, fewer preferences are recorded for a more modest way of involvement, that is, the mode of the testimony within some specific modules, indicated by only 38,1 % of the respondents.

Finally, it has emerged that some available online support could be useful to operators in order to make their role more effective within the organizations and especially towards the recipients of the assistance.

The current models for the management of refugees and asylum seekers in Italy, Spain and Romania highlight the necessity to address training related issues. Therefore, we need expert training for working practitioner, to increase their role within the organizations and especially towards minorities, including asylum-seekers.In particular, 81,3 % of the respondents declare themselves in favor of the availability of online legal advice that could facilitate the activity of social workers in order to obtain detailed and up-to-date information on the management of national practices related to refugee status requests, against 18,7 % who do not consider it necessary.

Another support deemed useful in this area is an online linguistic interpreter (70,4 % of respondents agree) that could facilitate communication between service providers and refugees/asylum seekers. A restrained agreement (68,5 % vs. 31,5 % at odds) is recorded for video interviews in which refugees/asylum seekers (according to their country of origin) talk about their own cultural, religious, and culinary traditions.

8 Brief Evaluation of One's Own Experience

The questionnaire ended with a Likert scale aimed at drawing the attention of the respondents on their fieldwork experience and, with this in mind, to express the real needs they felt daily in their work. These needs are not necessarily limited to the field of training.

Among the proposed items, the one who reported a lower level of agreement (50,8 % of the respondents say they are "strongly disagree" or "disagree") was the proposal to hire a fellow countryman of the refugees/asylum seekers (local entrepreneurs of the same nationality) within the organizations, someone adequately trained to facilitate the entry of migrants into the labor market. More approval is given to the support of an employment counsellor, hypothesis shared by 89,0 % of the respondents. Obviously, the expedient of the fellow countryman aroused some perplexity and not the support for job placement itself.

Continuous updating and strengthening of their expertise is the item that records the highest percentage of agreement: 65,1 % declare to strongly agree and 33,9 % agree. About 92,5 % of respondents agree (49,6 % agree and 42,9 % strongly agree) with the statement that "all they need to know is learn in the field." The training of social workers is not necessary once they are inserted into the reception structures. A significant agreement is also made with respect to other two items, one related to internal mediation and the other related to integration with city life. Specifically, 85,0 % of respondents agree (50,9 % agree and 34,1 % strongly agree) with the proposal to include professionals specialized in mediating internal relations and conflicts within the structures providing services to refugees/asylum seekers. Finally, 84,0 % of respondents declare themselves favorable (53,2 % agree and 30,8 % strongly agree) to hire a professional engaged in the integration of these structures into city life, under the assumption that the structures providing services to refugees/asylum seekers are increasingly perceived as foreign bodies to the rest of the city.

9 Conclusion

In the last decade, hundreds of thousands of refugees, asylum seekers, and migrants have put their lives at risk to reach European shores. The Internal Displacement Monitoring Centre (IDMC) assesses that what is occurring in the European territory is just a tip of an iceberg. Indeed, according to the last available data, over

65.6 million people worldwide are in need of protection and assistance as a consequence of forced displacement. Forcibly displaced populations include refugees, internally displaced persons (IDPs), and asylum seekers. Globally in 2017, over 40.3 million people are internally displaced as a result of conflict, while 22.5 million are refugees and 2.8 million are asylum seekers. Around 51 % of the global refugee population are children under 18 – the highest proportion in a decade. Voluntary repatriation to their home countries is the preferred long-term outcome for refugees, but the lack of political solutions to conflicts prevents many from doing so.

In this context, the PARIS project starts its mission: an intense activity, achieved as first result of the gathering of new knowledge about what the University sector is currently offering to their students and to which extent the actual academic offer fits with the real work context where future students will play as social workers. To achieve this result, specific and interconnected tasks were carried out and properly described and commented in this chapter.

The performed analysis allowed to highlight needs by respondents. The set of these needs not only outlines training needs but can actually draw three distinct training paths.

The needs that emerge in terms of skills, especially according to the information provided by the social workers, are the following.

In general, about the skills and knowledge owned (on a scale from 1 to 7), the majority of respondents ranks a score of 5 and 6, with higher peaks at 7 (teamwork and problem-solving) which implies a more expertise in such areas, and more significant peaks at 3, pointing out possible shortcomings (linguistic and cultural for skills/knowledge). In respect of the relevance attributed to the abovementioned skills and knowledge, the majority of the respondents placed themselves along all the areas of competence/knowledge of score 7. The area that recorded the highest percentage on the highest score was that of team work (62,7 %) followed by problem-solving (57,9 %), intercultural communication (57,4 %), mediation/conflict resolution (55,7 %), legal/legislative (49,4 %), and the cultural area (47,9 %). The last three areas (linguistic, gender equality, and advocacy) show fewer than 45 %.

The most interesting evidence can be drawn from the comparison between what you believe to own and what you think you need. A significant correspondence is noted: those areas that seem to be deficient are also those that are considered less relevant (compared to others and in relation with their workplace) by large percentages of respondents (e.g., the linguistic or cultural area). Contrarily, the areas where respondents felt they had greater expertise are also the most relevant ones (e.g., team work or problem-solving). Only two areas seem to deviate from this trend: intercultural communication and mediation/conflict resolution.

As regards the relevance attributed to the single academic disciplines covered during their own studies, the academic discipline that was awarded higher scores by the vast majority of respondents is related to the study of asylum seekers legislation and integration as well as that of human rights law (58,4 % rated scores 7 and 25,4 % score 6). The 91,8 % of the respondents involved in the survey believe that there is a need for a specific professionalization of the staff currently providing assistance to refugees and asylum seekers. And for 90,8 % of the respondents such professionalism should be guaranteed by creating a specialized training course in providing humanitarian aid to refugees and asylum seekers.

Then 54,9 % of the respondents believes that the most suitable type of course, in order to provide a specialized training to the staff, is an advanced training course. In respect of the teaching methods, 44,1 % of the respondents indicated the blended mode (face-to-face and online) and 39,0 % the face-to-face training modules. About 97,6 % believe that NGOs operating in this area should be actively involved in a potential specialized training path for providing assistance to refugees/asylum seekers, especially in classroom activities which seem to have found greatest acceptance, as indicated by 64,5 % of respondents. In addition, it has emerged that some available online supports (legal advice approved by 81,3 % of the sample or linguistic interpreter approved by 70,4 %) could be useful for social workers in order to make their role more effective within the organizations and especially towards the recipients of the assistance.

Lastly it has emerged, in expressing the real needs felt daily in their work, that in addition to the training, which records the highest percentage of agreement (65,1 % strongly agree with and 33,9 % agree), there are also other needs to consider, above all the need to hire within the humanitarian organizations some professionals that cooperate in the mediation both within the organization and with the hosting country. Noteworthy for most respondents is relevant the importance attributed to the ability to promote positive relationships in the context of humanitarian field (refuge and asylum seekers) between migrants and citizens (68,0 % consider it essential and 28,3 % very important) and between social workers and migrants (66,3 % think it is absolutely essential and 30,8 % very important).

This analysis has a double value: firstly, it presents a quite good picture of the status quo of the refugee workforce; secondly, it represents an important input for the PARIS academic partners in order to go on with the University curriculum updating scope.

References

Bin Arshad M.A., bin Mohamad Yusof A.N., Mahmood A., Ahmed A., Akhtar S. (2015). *A Study on Training Needs Analysis (TNA) process among manufacturing companies registered with Pembangunan Sumber Manusia Berhad (PSMB) at Bayan Lepas Area, Pe- nang, Malaysia. Mediterranean Journal of Social Sciences*, 6(4): 670–678.

Bliss C. J. (2014). *Capital theory and the distribution of income* (Vol. 4). U.S: Elsevier Science Publishing Co Inc.

Di Liberto A., La Rocca G. (Eds.) (2017).*Current models for the management of refugees and asylum seekers in Italy, Spain and Romania: Training needs for working with this group*. Palermo: Unione degli Assessorati Comunali e Provinciali alle Politiche Socio-Sanitarie e del Lavoro.

EURSOSTAT (2017). *Asylum and first time asylum applicants by citizenship, age and sex Annual aggregated data*. Last update: 02-04-2020 Retrieved from:https://appsso.eurostat.ec.europa.eu/nui/show.do?dataset=migr_asyappctza&lang=en

Fleck S. J., Kraemer W. (2014). *Designing resistance training programs*. Champaign: Human Kinetics.

IDMC, *Global Report on Displacement International*, May 2016. Retrieved from: http://www.internaldisplacement.org/assets/publications/2016/2016-global-report-internal displacement-IDMC.pdf.

La Rocca G. (2017). Media migrants and human rights. *International Review of Sociology*, 27(2): 225–229.

Leat M. J., Lovell M. J. (1997). Training needs analysis: Weakness in the conventional ap- proach. *Journal of European Industrial Training*, 21(4): 143–153.

Martilla J., James J. (1977). Importance performance analysis. *Journal of Marketing*, 41(1): 77–79.

Sung S. Y., Choi J. N. (2014). Do organizations spend wisely on employees? Effects of trai- ning and development investments on learning and innovation in organizations. *Journal of organizational behavior*, 35(3): 393–412.

Tharenou P. (1991). Managers' training Needs and Preferred Training Strategies. *Journal of Management Development*, 10(5): 46–59.

UNHCR (2017). *Tendenze globali*. Spostamento forzato nel 2016, June 2017. Retrieved from: http://www.unhcr.org/statistics/unhcrstats/5943e8a34/global-trends-forced-displacement-2016.html.

About the Authors

Fabio Aiello is associate professor at the Faculty of Economics and Laws Sciences at Kore University of Enna. He is main research fields of study are related to the methods and model for the construction of statistical indicators, the meta-analysis, the school dropout, the migratory flows in Europe, and, finally, the mobility of the students in higher education. E-mail: fabio.aiello@unikore.it.

Liborialinda Ardizzone is a Ph.D student in Economic, Business and Legal Sciences at Kore University of Enna. E-mail: liboria.ardizzone@unikore.it.

Roberto-Luciano Barbeito is Profesor Titular (senior lecturer/associate professor) of Sociology at the Department of Applied Economy I, Faculty of Law and Social Sciences, University Rey Juan Carlos, Madrid. He is Executive Secretary of the Spanish Federation of Sociology (FES) and Vice-Coordinator of the Spanish Research Committee on Political Sociology (CI8 FES). His current main research interests include democratic innovation – especially at the local level – and political communication, with special attention to digital technologies and problems related to socioeconomic and knowledge inequalities, work, consumption, welfare, immigration and climate change. E-mail: roberto.barbeito@urjc.es.

Ignazia Bartholini is associate professor in Sociology and Social Policies at University of Palermo; principal investigator of national and international projects (REC 2017-2019, FAMI 2017-, Marie Curie 2008-2010, Prin 2007–2010); visiting professor in many European Universities (Alicante in 2019, Sheffield in 2018, Ljubljana in 2016, Belgrade in 2014) and board member of ISA RC 32 (Gender and Society). Her main research subjects are focused on gender violence, migrations, poverty and citizenship. Among her recent publications are: Proximity violence and Migration Times (ed., Franco Angeli 2019), *Gender and Work-Life Balance: a Context Analysis on Nursey Schools* in Palermo, Springer Nature Switzerland 2018; *Migrations. A Global Welfare Challenge: Policies, Practices and Contemporary Vulnerabilities* (Edition Corunamerica 2017). E-mail: ignazia.bartholini@unipa.it.

Maria Bottiglieri is coordinator of the International Cooperation and Peace activities for the Turin Municipality and holds a Ph.D in "Local self-government, public services and citizenship rights" from the University of Eastern Piedmont. Graduated in Law at the University of Salerno, she attained a Specialization in

Commercial Law at the University of Naples Federico II, a Master in Public Administration at the University of Turin. She obtained full admission to the Bar and she qualified to teach legal-economic disciplines in Italian High schools. She is also Speaker at national and international conferences, author of scientific publications and project manager in international cooperation projects funded by national and international donors. E-mail: maria.bottiglieri@comune.torino.it.

Domenico Carzo† is full professor of Sociology of Communication at the Department of Cognitive Sciences, Psychology, Education and Cultural Studies at the University of Messina. His activity of research mainly involves legal culture, communication and semiotics. These studies resulted in the production of several articles and essays printed in different languages. Among his publications are *Il diritto va in scena. Analisi della trasmissione televisiva Verdetto Finale* (Aracne 2010); *Droit, retorique et interaction sociale* (Bruylant 1994).

Antonia Cava is associate professor in Sociology of Communication at the Department of Cognitive Sciences, Educational and Cultural Studies at the University of Messina. Her activity of research mainly involves two main branches: Media Imaginary Analysis and Dynamics of Audiences fruition. Above all her studies have focused on strategies of media consumption of audiences and on interactions with mass media which take place in everyday life. Among her publications are *#FOODPEOPLE. Itinerari mediali e paesaggi gastronomici contemporanei* (Aracne 2018), and *Una rassegna sul diritto rappresentato. Racconti mediali e interazioni giuridiche a confronto* (Sociologia del Diritto, 1–2011). E-mail: acava@unime.it.

Gaetana Cava holds a postgraduate in Migration Studies at the University of Granada. Her field of study focuses on migrants' use of TV. Among her publications are *Los inmigrantes como audiencia televisiva* (Illuminazioni, 45–2018) and *La televisión de los inmigrantes en Italia*, in G. Tardivo, R. Barbeito, *La sociología y el Sur de Europa. Italia y España ante el cambio climático y el fenómeno migratorio*, Editorial UOC 2018. E-mail: gaetanacava@correo.ugr.es.

Marco Centorrino is associate professor in Communications Sociology at the Department of "Civiltà antiche e Moderne", University of Messina, Italy. His publications concern mass media, new communication technologies, perception and representation of social phenomena. He has also carried out research on Albanian immigration in Italy, the phenomenon of cultural integration in Spain and the representation of migrants by the mainstream media. E-mail: centorrinom@unime.it.

Lucia Chiurco is a technical research assistant at the National Institution for the Analysis of Public Policy (Inapp). In the past, social inequality and discrimination have been the main topics of work activity carried out within European Programmes. The most recent work and publications are related to disability and migration, analyzed with a focus on discriminatory language and social representation. The migration-related researches concern the influence of the media in spreading of stereotypes and prejudices based on ethnicity and the implementation of non-discrimination principles within programmes financed by the European Social Fund. E-mail: l.chiruco@inapp.org.

Lucia Corso is associate professor of Philosophy of Law, Department of Economics and Law, at Kore University of Enna. Her research interests include: vulnerability theory, constitutional democracy, populism and the rule of law, legal sentimentalism, Aristotle and the natural law tradition. Her latest publications are: Corso L. (2019) 'Vulnerabilità e concetto di diritto', in Corso L., Talamo Giuseppina, *Vulnerabilità di fronte alle istituzioni. Vulnerabilità delle istituzioni,* Giappichelli, Torino, pp. 3–14; Corso L. (2019) "When Anti-Politics Becomes Political: What Can the Italian Five Star Movement Tell us about the Relationship between Populism and Legalism". *European Constitutional Law Review* 15(3), pp. 462–487; Corso L. (2019), "Populismo, limiti al potere e giudici costituzionali" *Ragion Pratica*, 52, giugno: 211–232; Corso L. (2018), 2018. "Vulnerabilità, giudizio di costituzionalità e sentimentalismo", *Ars Interpretandi,* 2: 57–76; Corso L. (2018), 'Natural Law in the Middle Ages'. In: Sellers M., Kirste S. (eds) *Encyclopedia of the Philosophy of Law and Social Philosophy*. Springer, Dordrecht. E-mail: lucia.corso@unikore.it.

Alessandro Cutrona is a Ph.D student at Kore University of Enna. He studies contemporary italian literature, also drawing on its relationships with cinema and the media. His published work includes the book *L'attualità della mise en abyme nelle opere di Peter Greenaway e Charlie Kaufman* (Mimesis 2017); and the essay *Biblioteche come agenti di inclusione sociale* ("inTrasformazione", Vol 7, No. 2 2018). More recent studies, for upcoming publication, include: Andrea Camilleri between novels and televisionand From feuilleton to series narrative. He is collaborating with the European project Horizon (2020) *DETECt – Detecting Transcultural Identity in European Popular Crime Narratives,* coordinated by the University of Bologna. E-mail: alessandro.cutrona@unikorestudent.it.

Graziella Di Marco, Ph.D, is a social psychology Research Fellow at Department of Educational Sciences, University of Catania (Italy). Her main interests are: social identity and inter-group relations, acculturation strategies of host and guest community and attitudes towards disability. His recent publications are: Hichy, Z., Coen, S., & Di Marco, G. (2015). The interplay among religious orientations, State secularism, and gay rights issues. *Journal of GLBT Family Studies, 11*, 82–101. Di Marco, G., & Hichy, Z. (2018). Gestione dello stress in genitori con figli autistici: gli effetti dell'autoefficacia e del supporto sociale [Stress management in parents with autistic children: the effects of self-efficacy and social support]. *Annali della Facoltà di Scienze della Formazione, 17*, 75–84. Di Marco, G., Hichy, Z., Coen, S., & Rodriguez-Espartal, N. (2018). The Effect of Values and Secularism on Attitude towards Pre-Implantation Genetic Diagnosis of Embryos. *Social Sciences* 7 (11): 216. E-mail: grazia.dimarco@unict.it.

Roberto Di Maria is full professor of Constitutional Law at University Kore of Enna. His main topics include: *Constitutional Justice, Regionalism and Federalism, Local Economy and Finance, Lobby and Political Representation*. His last most recent publications are: Di Maria, R., Napoli, C., & Pertici, A. (2019). *Manuale di diritto delle autonomie locali. Turin*: Giappichelli. Di Maria, R. (2018). *Le "lobby dei federalismi": brevi considerazioni sulla organizzazione e sulla attività territoriale dei gruppi di pressione nel multilevel system of government*, from www.federalismi.it, n. 7/2018. Di Maria, R. (2018). *Breve ricognizione degli elementi costitutivi della ordinanza di rimessione in Corte di una questione di legittimità costituzionale: sulla (attuale) rilevanza della "rilevanza"*. In D'Amico, M., & Biondi, F. (Ed.). *La Corte costituzionale e i fatti: istruttoria ed effetti delle decisioni. Naples*: ES. Di Maria, R. (2017). *Il proverbiale "rigore a porta vuota": la Consulta si pronuncia sulla l. r. Sicilia n. 17/2017 in materia di ordinamento degli Enti di area vasta (breve nota a Corte cost., sent. 168/2018)*, from www.dirittiregionali.org, vol. 3/2018. E-mail: roberto.dimaria@unikore.it.

Guglielmo Lucio Maria Dinicolò is a Ph.D candidate on Business, Economy and Law, at Kore University of Enna, Faculty of Economics and Law and also an expert in economic statistics and experimental statistics applied to social and economic phenomena. The main research and study topics are characterized by an interest in social policies and their impacts on the main demographic and sociological events. In this sense, some of the latest published works concern: 1. Il sistema di welfare state italiano tra tendenze e percorsi evolutivi e sostenibilità di lungo termine, Rivista Italiana di Economia, Demografia e Statistica, vol.72(4) pp.137–149, 2018; 2. Drivers of brain drain phenomenon: Possible association between macroeconomic variables in the international framework. Rivista Italiana di Economia, Demografia e Statistica, vol.72(1), pp.87–98, 2018; 3. Social Indicators to measure the well-being of the population. Benchmarking countries (working paper no.1); 4. Environmental Management System (EMS), industrial pollution and well-being: Possible association (working paper no.2). E-mail: guglielmo.dinicolo@unikore.it.

Maria Fobert Veutro is a researcher in Sociology at Faculty of Human and Social Sciences, at Kore University of Enna. She has a Ph.D in Methodology of Human Sciences, and her main research topics focus on social research and methods, sociology of knowledge and gender studies. Her latest works concern research methods in the field of: *Women's immigration* (Donne musulmane immigrate fra tradizione ed emancipazione. In *I Diritti delle donne nell'area del Mediterraneo.* Napoli: ESI, 2010); *Analysis of advertising images* (An Interactionist Approach to Document Analysis: Hidden Values in Advertising Images. *Italian Sociological Review*, 2019); *Non-traditional techniques to detect social values* (*When I hear the word migrant... A Research on Images and Stereotypes with Sentence Completion Technique*, in the process of publication). E-mail: maria.fobertveutro@unikore.it.

Stefania Fragapane holds a Ph.D in Sociology and Methodology of Social Research. Her main research activities concern media and online information, with particular reference to young people and migrations, critical consumption and sustainable lifestyles. Among the latest publications are "Territory, borders and local care homes" in M.T. Consoli (a cura di), *Migration towards Southern Europe. The case of Sicily and the separated children*, Milano, FrancoAngeli, 2015; (con G. Minaldi), *Migration policies and digital technologies in Europe: a comparison between Italy and Spain,* Journal of European Integration, 11 June 2018 and (with A. Mortara), "Net-activism on twitter. Mcdonald's and Coca cola @ Expo2015", in Net-Activism. How digital technologies have been changing individual and collective actions, Roma Tre-Press, 2017, pp. 97–107. E-mail: stefania.fragapane@gmail.com.

Gino Frezza is full professor of Sociology of Cultural and Communication Processes at the University of Salerno. President of the Section of Cultural Processes and Institutions of AIS (Italian Association of Sociology) in the three-year period 2017–2020, he is Coordinator of the Doctorate in "Social Theory, Digital Innovation and Public Policies" of the University of Salerno. He studies the forms of cultural evolution of audiovisual media between analog and digital technologies, in particular the relationship between cinema, comics and fiction, and he has recently published the following books: *Nuvole Mutanti. Visual Writings and Imaginary of Comics* (2017); *Figures of the Imaginary* (2016), *Endoapocalypse. The Walking Dead, the Digital Imaginary, the Post-Human* (2016). E-mail: frezza@unisa.it.

Thea Giacobbe has a Ph.D Human Rights Protection, Specialist on Criminology and Penitentiary Science, "Cultore della materia" (IUS17) of the Department of Social and Political Science of the University of Catania. Her research interests are: punishment, gender studies, urban security and human rigths and her publications include: "Le donne in esecuzione penale. Analisi di una marginalità in Sicilia" (2014). In Rassegna penitenziaria e criminologica (n. 3); "La dimensione concreta del reinserimento dei detenuti" (2014) in "Lavoro ed emancipazione: l'inclusione sociale dei condannati. Un'esperienza a Catania". In S. Aleo: Wolters Kluver, CEDAM. E-mail: theagiacobbe@gmail.com.

Valentina Giuffrida is a student in cognitive neuroscience at Sapienza University of Rome (Italy). Her field of interests include: cognitive neuropsychology, behavioral psychology and cognitive neuroscience and her research interest is: study on pathological aging conducted by Sapienza University of Rome in collaboration with the Policlinico Umberto I. E-mail: valentina.giuffrida@ymail.com.

Zira Hichy is associate professor of Social Psychology at the Department of Educational Sciences, University of Catania (Italy). Her main topics are: social identity and inter-group relations, acculturation strategies of host and guest community, methodology and statistics, political psychology and psychology of religion. Recent publications include: Hichy, Z., Coen, S., & Di Marco, G. (2015). The interplay among religious orientations, State secularism, and gay rights issues. *Journal of GLBT Family Studies, 11*, 82–101. Hichy, Z., Halim Helmy Gerges, M., Platania, S., & Santisi, G. (2015). The role of Secularism of State on the relationship between Catholic identity, Political orientation, and gay rights issues. *Journal of Homosexuality, 62*, 1359–1373. Di Marco, G., Hichy, Z., Coen, S., & Rodriguez-Espartal, N. (2018). The effect of values and secularism on attitude towards pre-implantation genetic diagnosis of embryos. *Social Sciences* 7 (11): 216. E-mail: z.hichy@unict.it.

Nikos Kourahanis teaches Social Policy at Panteion University of Social and Political Sciences (Athens, Greece). His research interests focus on the theory of social citizenship, as well as on social integration policies. He is the author of four books (in Greek) and many scientific articles in international journals on housing, migration and social policy issues. He has worked with various European institutions on planning and evaluation of social policy programs. E-mail: n.kourachanis@gmail.com.

Gevisa La Rocca is associate professor at the Faculty of Human and Social Sciences, Kore University of Enna, where she teaches and works. She is the coordinator of the international research group *Rischio, communication e società/*

Riesgo, comunicación y sociedad. She was the scientific coordinator of the Paris project "Teaching Partnership Addressed to Refugees's Instances Strengthening" (2016–2019). Her research interests cover social media and social relations, risk communication, mediatization and emotions. Among her publications: Martínez Torvisco, J. and La Rocca, G. (eds.) (2019). *En torno al riesgo. Contribuciones de diferentes disciplinas y perspectivas de análisis*. El Sauzal: PASOS. La Rocca, G. (2018). *Nuove forme di comunicazione sociale. Antifragilità, communication voice e studio di caso*. Roma: Carocci. In 2017 she was the editor of the themed section "Media, Migrants and Human Rights", for the *International Review of Sociology/Revue Internationale De Sociologie*. E-mail: gevisa.larocca@unikore.it.

Nicola Malizia is associate professor of Sociology of Law, Deviance and Social change at Kore University of Enna, Faculty of Human and Social Sciences. She is a expert in Sociology of Deviance, Criminology and Sociology of Law. The main research and study areas concern the issues related to the most relevant deviant phenomena and behavior present in society, both of individual and collective value. The last publications related to this issue are: 1. The fear of immigrant between stereotype and stigma: an empirical survey on immigrant perception, *International Journal of Scientific and Research Publications*, vol. 8(2), 2018; 2. Boredom and social deviant behavior: An empirical study, *Advances in Applied Sociology*, vol.8, p. 174–187; 3. Cannabis use and deviant behavior among university student: An empirical research, *International Journal of Scientific and Research Publication*, vol.8, p. 269–277. E-mail: nicola.malizia@unikore.it.

Rolando Marini is associate professor at the University for Foreigners in Perugia (Italy), where he teaches Media Sociology. His research interests are related to journalism and public issues, communication theories, youth civic culture and the European public space. Among the main volumes are: *Mass media e discussione pubblica* (2006); *Altri flussi. La comunicazione politica della società civile* (2011), *Media Logic. La logica dei media* (2017); *Società, potere e influenza* (2017). E-mail: rolando.marini@unistrapg.it.

Jo (Yosi) McIntire is Unitarian Fellowship. His recent publications are: The Conflict of Narratives (Foreign Policy Association) and Liberation Theology (for presentation to Great Decisions). E-mail: mcintire.jo@gmail.com.

Melissa Moralli, Ph.D, is a Research Fellow at the Department of Sociology and Business Law, University of Bologna, visiting scholar at IPK, New York University and at CRISES, Université du Québec à Montréal. Her main research interests are: social innovation, tourism, migration and action-research processes. Among her publications: *Innovazione sociale. Pratiche e processi per ripensare le comunità*

(Franco Angeli, 2018); *De-bordering narratives on tourism and migration. A participatory action-research on two innovative Italian practices* ("Italian Journal of Sociology of Education", 2019, 11); *Fostering Interculturality in Urban Ethnic Neighbourhoods: Opportunities and Limits of the Responsible Tourism Approach* ("Journal of Mediterranean Knowledge", 2016, 1). E-mail: melissa.moralli2@unibo.it.

Ariela Mortara is a tenured assistant professor at IULM University of Milan. Her research topics are sociology of consumption, corporate communication, advertising, branding and new media. She has published many papers on national and international journals and chapters in national and international books; she has also co-authored some national books. Among her recent publication Mortara A., Sinisi V. (2019), "Behind and Inside the Screen. Different Research Methods for Social Research", *Micro&Macro Marketing*, anno XXVIII, 2, Agosto, pp. 231–245; Mortara A., Roberti G. (2018), "From celebrities to influencers and back. Web 2.0 and the emerging trends in the celebrity system", in Antonella Mascio, Roy Menarini, Simona Segre Reinach, Ines Tolic, *The Size Effect*. A Journey into Design, Fashion and Media, Mimesis International, pp. 217–227. E-mail: ariela.mortara@iulm.it.

Michele Nicotra is a Ph.D student at Kore University of Enna. E-mail: michele.nicotra@unikore.it.

Roberta Paltrinieri is full professor at the Department of Arts of the University of Bologna where she is the scientific director of DAMSLab and the Director of Ces.Co.Com (Advanced Studies Centre on Consumption and Communication). Her main research interests are: participation, cultural consumption, cultural policies, sustainability and tourism. Among her most recent publications: *Partecipazione e collaborazione negli interventi di comunità. L'esperienza dei laboratori di quartiere del Comune di Bologna*, con Giulia Allegrini («Sociologia Urbana e Rurale», 2/2018); *Pratiche di riduzione dello spreco alimentare e inclusione sociale*, con P. Parmiggiani (FrancoAngeli, 2018); *Collaborative Consumption and trust building processes in the emerging new food economy, with S. Spillare* (Springer VS, 2018). E-mail: roberta.paltrinieri@unibo.it.

Paola Parmiggiani is full professor at the Department of Sociology and Business Law of the University of Bologna, where she coordinates the master's degree in Sociology and Social Work. Her main interests of study and research concern: social and humanitarian communication, media and migration, consumption practices and sustainability. Among her most recent publications: *Taxis or sea ambulances? Politiche dell'immagine nella crisi dei migranti nel Mediterraneo,* with P. Musarò ("Problemi dell'informazione", 2/2018); *Pratiche di riduzione dello spreco alimentare e inclusione sociale*, with R. Paltrinieri (FrancoAngeli, 2018); *Beyond Black and White: The Role of Media in Portraying and Policing Migration and Asylum in Italy*, with P. Musarò, "Revue Internationale de Sociologie" (2017). E-mail: paola.parmiggiani@unibo.it.

Chiara Pasanisi is a Ph.D student in performing arts at University of Rome "La Sapienza" with a research project entitled "Italian actress from 1935 to 1975: stage techniques and gender studies". She has participated in various international conferences and she has recently published the chapter "Le donne e l'esternazione della paura nei *Dialoghi delle carmelitane* di Georges Bernanos" for the volume *Il teatro delle emozioni – La paura* (Padova University Press, 2018). E-mail: chiara.pasanisi@uniroma1.it.

Lilia Pellegrino is a postgraduate in migration studies at the University of Granada. Her field of study focuses on the relationship between schools and immigrant families. E-mail: pellegrino.lilia@alice.it.

Francesco Pira is an aggregate professor of communication and journalism at the Department of Ancient and Modern Civilizations of the University of Messina, where he is Educational Coordinator of the master's in "Social Media Manager". In his researches he paid particular attention to the dynamics of political, public and social communication with a focus on social media and new models of social relations on the web. Component of scientific committees of international series and conferences, he is reviewer of international scientific journals and member of the Research Unit of ICSR Mediterranean Knowledge. He has published over 40 scientific publications and articles. E-mail: fpira@unime.it.

Gabriella Polizzi is associate professor of Sociology of Culture and Communication at Kore University of Enna. She is interested in tourist destination image as well as the prevention of gender violence through communication. On these topics she is co-author of book chapters on "The Image of Cruise Ship Holidays on Italian Television: A Comparative Analysis" (in: R. Dowling & C. Weeden, Eds., 2017, *Cruise Ship Tourism*, Wallingford: CAB International) and "Preventing Male Violence Against Women Through Communication: A Comparative Analysis of the Television Campaigns of the Italian and Spanish Governments" (in press in: S. Marín Conejo, Ed., *El mundo a través de las palabras. Lenguaje, género y comunicación*. Madrid: Dykinson). E-mail: gabriella.polizzi@unikore.it.

Tiziana Ramaci is associate professor of Work and Organizational Psychology at Kore University of Enna. She is member of ICOH (International Commission on Organizational Health), IAC Professional Member (International Association of Counselling) and Associate Editor of Frontiers in Organizational Psychology. Her research interests include topics related to public health education and promotion. Particularly with regard to organizational wellbeing, risk management and job insecurity, vocational guidance and international careers. E-mail: tiziana.ramaci@unikore.it.

Giuseppina Talamo is a researcher in Economics and Aggregate Professor at Kore University of Enna. She obtained her Ph.D in Economics and Development Policies at the University of Naples Federico II and her masters in Development Economics at School of Oriental and African Studies, University of London. Her main research interests are study of corruption, corporate governance, international economics, migration policies, organised crime and vulnerablity. Dr. Talamo's work has been published, among others, in *International Finance Review, Corporate Governance* and *Mediterranean Journal of Human Rights*. E-mail: giuseppina.talamo@unikore.it.

Benedetta Turco is a Ph.D student in Theoretical and applied social reserch in University of *Roma Tre*. She is an expert in the field of *Storia del pensiero sociologico.* She participated in organizational committees of national and international conferences and as a speaker in conferences such as *Mesa Redoda: València-Roma* in University of València (Spain) and IMISCOE Conference 2019 to *International migration, integration and social cohesion* in University of Mälmo (Sweden). She is in the process of publishing about: articles and publication of the acts. She is co-author of *La condizione giovanile in Italia* in Tintori, Cerbara (a cura di) *Giovani alla prova. La condizione giovanile nella Cittàmetropolitana di Roma Capitale*. Aracne editrice, Roma, 2016. E-mail: benedetta.turco@uniroma3.it.

www.ingramcontent.com/pod-product-compliance
Ingram Content Group UK Ltd.
Pitfield, Milton Keynes, MK11 3LW, UK
UKHW041824100926
8556IPUK00002B/10

9 783631 822531